THE PHANTOM TABLE:

Virginia Woolf identified the influence on her work of 'the Cambridge Apostles', the philosophical society which counted G. E. Moore, Bertrand Russell and much of male Bloomsbury among its members, as one more 'capable of description' than 'the influence of my mother'. In this major study of Woolf's relationship to Bloomsbury and the aesthetic and philosophical developments of her time, Ann Banfield subjects that influence to its first full treatment. The theory of knowledge which Moore and Russell formulated, Banfield argues, profoundly affected Woolf's conception of reality, as it did Roger Fry's theory of Post-Impressionism, one source for Woolf's transformations of philosophical principles into aesthetic ones. *The Phantom Table* is a magisterial account of Woolf's engagement with this remarkable trinity of thinkers: Moore, Russell, Fry. It radically revises the epistemology of modernism, reconceiving the relation between realism and formalism to account for Woolf's dual reality of sense impressions and logical forms.

ANN BANFIELD is Professor of English at the University of California, Berkeley. She is the author of *Unspeakable Sentences: Narration and Representation in the Language of Fiction* (1982) which was also published in French in 1995. She is the translator of Jean-Claude Milner's *For the Love of Language* (1990).

THE PHANTOM TABLE

Woolf, Fry, Russell and the Epistemology of Modernism

ANN BANFIELD

CAMBRIDGE
UNIVERSITY PRESS

PUBLISHED BY THE PRESS SYNDICATE OF THE UNIVERSITY OF CAMBRIDGE
The Pitt Building, Trumpington Street, Cambridge, United Kingdom

CAMBRIDGE UNIVERSITY PRESS
The Edinburgh Building, Cambridge CB2 2RU, UK www.cup.cam.ac.uk
40 West 20th Street, New York, NY 10011–4211, USA www.cup.org
10 Stamford Road, Oakleigh, Melbourne 3166, Australia
Ruiz de Alarcón 13, 28014 Madrid, Spain

First published 2000

Printed in the United Kingdom at the University Press, Cambridge

Typeface 11/12.5pt Baskerville [CE]

A catalogue record for this book is available from the British Library

Library of Congress Cataloging-in-Publication Data

Banfield, Ann.
The phantom table: Woolf, Fry, Russell and epistemology of modernism / Ann Banfield.
p. cm.
Includes bibliographical references and index.
ISBN 0 521 77347 4 (hardback)
1. Woolf, Virginia, 1882–1941 – Philosophy.
2. Moore, G. E. (George Edward), 1873–1958 – Influence.
3. Fry, Roger Eliot, 1866–1934 – Influence.
4. Russell, Bertrand, 1872–1970 – Influence.
5. Cambridge Apostles (Society) – History.
6. Modernism (Literature) – Great Britain.
7. Knowledge, Theory of, in literature.
8. Philosophy in literature. 9. Reality in literature.
10. Aesthetics, British. 11. Bloomsbury group. I. Title.
PR6045.072 Z5423 2000
823′.912–dc21 99–051626

ISBN 0 521 77347 4 hardback

To the memory of my father,
Alfred T. Banfield
1913–1999

Contents

List of illustrations *page* viii
Preface ix
List of abbreviations xvii

1 Introduction: table talk 1

PART I: SUBJECT AND OBJECT AND THE NATURE OF REALITY

2 The geometry in the sensible world: Russell's analysis of matter 59

3 The world seen without a self: Woolf's analysis of matter 108

4 Solus ipse, alone in the universe 159

5 The dualism of death 213

PART II: PRINCIPIA AESTHETICA

6 Fry's granite and rainbow: post-impressionism and impressionism 245

7 How describe the world seen without a self? 294

8 The modern elegy 358

Notes 389
Bibliography 415
Index 427

Illustrations

1. Roger Fry, frontispiece to *The Cambridge Fortnightly*, 1888. By permission of the Syndics of Cambridge University Library. *page* 2
2. Nicéphore Nièpce, *La Table Servie*. Courtesy of the Société Française de la Photographie. 57
3. Roger Fry, portrait of Bertrand Russell, 1923. Courtesy of the National Portrait Gallery, London. 61
4. Ernest Mach, "Figure 1," the view from Mach's left eye, *Contributions to the Analysis of Sensations*, 1890. By permission of the Syndics of Cambridge University Library. 161
5. Vanessa Bell, portrait of Virginia Woolf. © Estate of Duncan Grant, courtesy of Henrietta Garnett and Sotheby's, London. 215
6. Paul Cézanne, *Stilleben*, c. 1885. Courtesy of the Neue Pinakothek, Munich. 243
7. Bertrand Russell, map of a five-term complex, *Theory of Knowledge*, 1913 (reproduced upside down). 243
8. Vanessa Bell, Virginia Woolf at Asheham, 1912. © Estate of Vanessa Bell, courtesy of Henrietta Garnett and the National Portrait Gallery, London. 295

Preface

This book came out of the seminar on Virginia Woolf I taught my first year at Berkeley in 1975. One of the series of "senior seminars" on a "major author" in the English department curriculum, it was the first devoted to Woolf because, as a senior member of the department explained, Woolf had not been till then considered a "major author." (At that time, the Penguin edition of her works still identified her as Leslie Stephen's daughter and Leonard Woolf's wife.) In the fall of 1977 I completed a draft of a paper on Woolf and Cambridge theory of knowledge in which G. E. Moore played a large role. By the succeeding draft, Bertrand Russell had supplanted him. I periodically revised the paper between other projects, until it became clear that it was too long to remain an article. The subject's importance began to impress itself on me with increasing force, dictating prolonged research. For underlying Woolf's art was a thought, a philosophical project worthy of new attention. This was the theory of knowledge Russell developed and synthesized between 1912–14, reconnecting in the process with the empiricist tradition Leslie Stephen was instrumental in rediscovering. Inspired by Moore's "Refutation of Idealism" and his sense-data theory, Russell's strange theory of "sensibilia," to which Whitehead made important contributions, emerged in the period of his encounter with Wittgenstein. That encounter took place in the pre-war intellectual ferment out of which Bloomsbury developed. Recent interest in the history of early twentieth-century British philosophy has only begun to reconsider this theory, but there has been little suspicion of its importance not only for Woolf's novels but also for her aesthetic.

Woolf herself, writing about the "influence of my mother" (*MB*, 81), contrasts it with one which "should be more definite" and "capable of description," "for example the influence on me of the Cambridge Apostles" (*MB*, 80), that philosophical society which counted Moore, Russell and much of male Bloomsbury among its members, as well as, in an earlier generation, Woolf's uncle Sir James Stephen. Yet that exemplary influence has yet to find its full description. S. P. Rosenbaum's 1971 ground-breaking essay "Virginia Woolf's Philosophical Realism" makes the first strong case for the importance of Moore's epistemology for Woolf. Jaakko Hintikka's 1979–80 "Virginia Woolf and Our Knowledge of the External World" focuses on Russell, reassuring me that the unexpected predominance I gave Russell was not misperceived. But the work of reconstructing the edifice of a representative achievement of literary modernism so as to discern the "transformations" of thought into art remained to be done. The critical celebration that has changed the perception of Woolf as a "major author" since 1975 continues to ignore a central aspect of her work. The maternal influence has by now been "described" on numerous occasions;[1] it is the "Cambridge Apostolic" (*RF*, 270) influence that, on the paternal side of the inevitable Bloomsbury family tree, has yet to be explored in all its ramifications.

The theory of sense-data and sensibilia is set upon the foundations of a logical philosophy. It has connections to Russell's theory of naming and descriptions,[2] as well as to the whole issue of foundations themselves, of "principles." Not the least of the unexpected discoveries of the Apostolic influence is the importance of the logical framework for what it is legitimate to speak of as Bloomsbury's "Principia Aesthetica." For Woolf, untrained in logic, mathematics and philosophy, it is Roger Fry's theory of Post-Impressionism that provides the crucial link between the logical underpinnings of Cambridge theory of knowledge and her theory of "modern fiction."

The principles of their aesthetic that emerge in the course of this study challenge assumptions in the present reassessment of modernism on issues like its relation to realism, philosophical and otherwise. I have not chosen to engage these assumptions explicitly, however, preferring to let a coherent statement of what amounts to a philosophy of painting, in Fry's case, and of the novel, in Woolf's,

[1] See, to name two, Abel's *Virginia Woolf and the Fictions of Psychoanalysis* and Ellen Rosenman's *The Invisible Presence*.

[2] And to the theory of time and "Cambridge changes" set forth as early as Principles of Mathematics as a response to Bradley's and McTaggart's denial of the reality of time. The extensive material on time in Woolf originally conceived as an integral part of this work had largely to be omitted solely for considerations of length.

stand as alternatives to the current orthodoxy. But the wider implications are there to be explored. William Butler Yeats, in passages cited by Rosenbaum, thought that "[c]ertain typical books – *Ulysses*, Virginia Woolf's *The Waves*, Mr. Ezra Pound's *Draft of XXX Cantos* – suggest a philosophy" like that of sensibilia, with "mental and physical objects alike material"; he invoked, à propos of Joyce, Pound and Proust, "that form of the new realist philosophy which thinks that the secondary and primary qualities alike are independent of consciousness," citing Moore's "The Refutation of Idealism" as its source. The debate about modernism stands in need of a new formulation which takes into account its revolutionary conception of the objects of sensation, at once physical and subjective.

That such a new formulation should call upon analytic philosophy challenges the other assumption of contemporary understanding of modernism – that the only philosophy of relevance to twentieth-century art and literature is continental. This includes the importance accorded Wittgenstein, whom the prevailing opinion, until recently, saw as above all Viennese and largely unmarked by the exchange with Russell. It required a French philosopher with the necessary distance from British philosophy to reinstate Russell as the culmination of one of the two important directions of modern thought. The philosopher was Michel Foucault. He identified "the nineteenth century's double advance, on the one hand towards formalism in thought and on the other towards the discovery of the unconscious – towards Russell and Freud" (*The Order of Things*, 299). There is a relation between the two "advances" suggested in Foucault's speaking of them together. It converges on Bloomsbury, centrally positioned to receive and propagate Russell's logical philosophy and led by a compatible intellectual bent to present to the English-speaking world Freud's psychoanalytic theory. In this light, the present work is a natural complement to Elizabeth's Abel's study of Woolf's response to Freud. But Bloomsbury's espousal of the new French painting turns out to be equally compatible with its philosophical predilections. The otherwise inexplicable fact that "[t]he first extensive and serious analysis of Cézanne's early painting was published by the English critic Roger Fry" (Lewis, *Cézanne's Early Imagery*, 3) could be seen to follow from Fry's encounters with the authors of *Principia Mathematica* as a member of the Apostles; Fry was uniquely situated to recognize and theorize Cézanne's response to the formalism which was beginning to define modern thought.

"Formalism" is the key word in Foucault's statement. While most examinations of the conjunction of "literature and philosophy" have concentrated on themes, it perhaps requires the distance of time as well to recognize how far-reaching have been the advances in modern logic and the foundations of mathematics that characterize one domain of early twentieth-century thought. Foucault's "archeology" of nineteenth-century biology, political economy and linguistics is a major attempt to understand formalism as it expressed itself in three disciplines – unfortunately this aspect of Foucault's work has been largely ignored by his English-speaking readers. It should not be surprising that the major movements in art at the beginning of this century should also have been "formalist," and yet there has been little recent acknowledgement that the formalism of modern art, if not necessarily the result of the influences of formalism in mathematics and logic, was nonetheless a phenomenon in some way possible and explicable only as part of the intellectual history that produced Cantor and Frege, Peano, Whitehead and Russell.[3] The nature of the response to mathematization and logical formalism in modern art is quite varied. But one obvious place to begin exploring the operation of its influences is where it is most documentable, as is the case for the activity of Bloomsbury artists and writers.

The project has even wider implications. The question of how thought informs art and literature and how new ideas are assimilated is more complicated than is frequently assumed. For one thing, to establish that such and such a thinker was a major point of reference in a certain period is not to establish that his or her *thought* is discoverable in the artists and writers who refer to the *thinker*. For anyone who has lived through the period in which linguistics was such a point of reference, it is apparent that many works produced during it are unquestionably marked by the "linguistic turn." But this in no way means that linguistics was universally understood, and indeed many of the works that refer themselves to linguistics have something else as their real source – a way of thinking certainly central in various domains which is nevertheless often a misunderstanding of the linguistic theories it invokes. Intellectual history reveals that the most revolutionary ideas are often the victims of a revisionism which frequently disguises the old thinking under the

[3] James Joyce, for instance, took notes from Russell's *Introduction to Mathematical Philosophy* for *Ulysses* and from the *The ABC of Relativity* for *Finnegan's Wake.* See Joyce, *Joyce's Notes and Early Drafts for Ulysses*, 49–53 and 102–11.

terms for the new. Even though the early stage of "structuralism" in various disciplines arguably did grasp something profound in linguistics, its many misconceptions made way for the revisionism called "post-structuralism." So an intellectual historian would be misled in taking the linguistic theories and the texts which set them forth as reliable guides to the interpretation of every work that seems to acknowledge the existence of linguistics. In the light of this historical example, it would thus seem prudent to approach the influence of Russell on Woolf with skepticism. The conclusion that Woolf's grasp of the whole import of Russell's philosophy was at best vague and at worst wrong is not, however, the conclusion of this study. On the contrary, given the difficulty of the philosophy in question and Woolf's lack of formal training, it is the more striking the way her work and her aesthetic seize the real possibilities of Russell's thought for art which he himself could not see. For the "archeologist" of knowledge, this perhaps points to deeper tendencies and conditions of modern thought from which both Woolf and Russell follow.

The conduit via which Russell's work came to reach a wider audience, it is our argument, is the 1914 theory of knowledge, a kind of incipient philosophy of science. The important link in the philosophical tradition between the logic and the theory of knowledge for Russell is Leibniz, on whom he wrote his dissertation in 1900. Russell's rediscovery of Leibniz was itself perhaps a response to some of the deeper forces invoked above. Marcel Proust, who was under the sway of a philosophy Russell had expressly distanced himself from, that of Bergson, was, as Gilles Deleuze has shown, profoundly marked by Leibniz, a philosopher, Proust tells us, too old-fashioned for the young Marquise de Cambremer, follower of intellectual fashions. When Russell came the closest to suggesting that modern logic might have something to say to someone producing works of the imagination, it was significantly in a Leibnizian language: "logic," he wrote, "instead of being, as formerly, the bar to possibilities, has become the great liberator of the imagination, presenting innumerable alternatives which are closed to unreflective common sense, and leaving to experience thc task of deciding, where decision is possible, between the many worlds which logic offers for our choice" (*PP*, 148). That exercise of the imagination must be preceded by another philosopher's project: "It is necessary to practice methodological doubt, like Descartes, in order to loosen the hold of mental habits; and it is necessary to cultivate logical imagination, in order to have a number of hypotheses at command, and not to be the slave of the one which common sense has rendered easy to imagine. These two processes, of doubting the familiar and imagining the unfamiliar, are correlative" (*OKnExW*, 242). These two processes would not only define the dual stages of Russell's 1914 theory of knowledge but Fry's paired theories of Impressionism and Post-Impressionism. It is as a skeptical attack on common sense and an analysis of the familiar world that Fry conceived the Impressionist project. Out of the idea of possible worlds comes the strange theory of "sensibilia." They become the basis for a "post-impressionist" reconstruction of the external world doubt had analyzed away. From these dual processes Woolf would take the principles of "modern fiction." Creating a formally self-contained world, it did not, however, abjure any relation to "the real world." Instead, it gave its own critique of common-sense realism for which Moore's and Russell's philosophical realism furnishes the abstract scaffolding, the "principles." Hence, this study is also a complement to Alex Zwerdling's *Virginia Woolf and the Real World.*

Woolf's work thus follows a logic. To pursue its logic is our purpose. Its products are novels, each with its characteristic shape, its individual date, in each succeeding one the accent falling differently than of old, multiply reshaping itself. But because the logic knitting together the parts of the vision scattered throughout the works is our goal, any chronologic will be ignored, any differences between individual works. The repetition of themes, of images, makes the oeuvre, in this conception, like the unconscious in its ignorance of time. Such a conception need not be incompatible with a notion of development within it – only it is not our purpose to describe this development but simply the principles generating that constantly shifting yet equilibrious logic of the work as a whole.

The word "logic" permits me to add one final comment on the importance that Russell and, perforce, formalism, has assumed in this work. "Mere formalism" has long been a term of contempt for the left which is perhaps not aware that, currently, it is the one aspect of aesthetic theory and practice which right and left are agreed in dismissing. But, from a distanced perspective, it emerges that – again, this is Foucault speaking – "formalist culture, thought, and art in the first third of the 20th century were generally associated with critical political movements of the Left – and even with revolutionary movements,"[4] their aesthetic precursor or accompaniment, regardless of the political affiliations of individual practictioners, from the Russian Revolution to May 68 and even including the neo-classicism of the French Revolution. Only when such revolutionary moments were over – defeated or distorted – did what is more conventionally thought of as political or social literature appear. It is in this light that the otherwise paradoxical eclipse of Russell and rise of Wittgenstein as the philosopher of engagement can be understood. In Derek Jarman's *Wittgenstein*, only Russell appears throughout in an academic gown, incongruously vested with the symbol of a function – a Cambridge Lectureship – which he did not exercise between 1916, when he was removed because of his active pacifism, and 1944. The film's faulty memory relegates him to the "ivory tower" become now the primary political arena for an academic left whose conception of political practice comes down to interpreting the world. The place of formalism in the life and work of a thinker also interested in changing the world – Russell had approved Marx's conception of the philosopher's dual role – thus needs elucidation. One thing that would have to be made clear is that the acknowledgement of formalism's limits cleared a space – elsewhere – for political activity which was in no way exhausted by the important activities of what Russell called "academic mankind" (*ML*, 77). For there is always another world than the one we occupy where something is happening which may affect our world, whether we are aware of it or not. Precisely because it is not appropriate to discuss that other Russell here, his existence elsewhere, in a separate political sphere, his "world of existence," is the counterweight to any charge of "mere" formalism.

Elizabeth Abel, Ann Smock and Alex Zwerdling all read my original essay. François Rivenc, whom I met on a gravestone in the Cimetière Montparnasse during Simone de Beauvoir's funeral and whose seminar on Russell at the Ecole Normale Supérieure I attended in the spring of 1986, commented on several occasions on my readings of "le Père Russell." Stephen Neale, Martin Jones, Peter Hanks and once, long ago, Pierre Jacob, were also helpful on Russell's logic. Conversations with Joseph Emonds, Jean-Claude Milner, Hans Sluga and Richard Wollheim have, sometimes unbeknownst to them, answered various questions for me. Sean Burke,

[4] Foucault, "How Much Does It Cost for Reason to Tell the Truth," 235.

T. J. Clark, Teri Darmisch, Anne Wagner and Patricia Waugh all made contributions. Zelda Boyd read the longest version of the manuscript, as did Joseph Emonds. Michael Rogin gave its many stages innumerable careful readings. Robert Kawashima was indispensable in the final stages. A University of California President's Fellowship in 1993–4 and a stay as a Scholar-in-Residence at the Villa Serbelloni, Bellagio Study Center as a guest of the Rockefeller Foundation in 1994 allowed me to give uninterrupted attention to Cambridge theories of time. The Collège International de Philosophie gave me the opportunity to present the book's argument in five lectures in Paris in fall, 1993. A generous subvention from the University of California, Berkeley, Committee on Research made it possible for the book to appear in something near its full length. I thank the King's College, Cambridge, Modern Archive Centre, which allowed me to look at early papers of E. M. Forster and John Maynard Keynes, and the Librairie des Lettres of the Ecole Normale Supérieure, rue d'Ulm. Finally, I want to thank Jonathan Miller for his imitation of Lord Russell and Quentin Bell for walking on a stage at Beaubourg in 1983 looking like the ghost of Leslie Stephen. I end by paraphrasing the close of the preface Jaakko Hintikka wrote to his 1998 *The Principles of Mathematics Revisited.* My thanks too "are due to Cambridge University Press" and to two readers and one editor, Ray Ryan, who so well understood the project. For me too it is "a special compliment" for a work treating Cambridge philosophy "to share a publisher with Russell and Whitehead."

Paris/Berkeley, August, 1998

Abbreviations

AAA	Leslie Stephen, *An Agnostic's Apology and Other Essays*
ABCA	Bertrand Russell, *The ABC of Atoms*
ABCR	Bertrand Russell, *The ABC of Relativity*
Aims	Alfred North Whitehead, *The Aims of Education and Other Essays*
AutoBR	Bertrand Russell, *The Autobiography of Bertrand Russell*
BA	Virginia Woolf, *Between the Acts*
BeAg	Leonard Woolf, *Beginning Again*
CE	Virginia Woolf, *Collected Essays*
Cé	Roger Fry, *Cézanne*
CPBR	Bertrand Russell, *The Collected Papers of Bertrand Russell*
CSFVW	Virginia Woolf, *The Complete Shorter Fiction of Virginia Woolf*
CW	Virginia Woolf, *Contemporary Writers*
Diary	Virginia Woolf, *The Diary of Virginia Woolf*
EssaysVW	Virginia Woolf, *The Essays of Virginia Woolf*
HET	Leslie Stephen, *History of English Thought in the Eighteenth Century*
HK	Bertrand Russell, *Human Knowledge*
H-M	Roger Fry, *Henri-Matisse*
HWP	Bertrand Russell, *History of Western Philosophy*
IMP	Bertrand Russell, *Introduction to Mathematical Philosophy*
IMT	Bertrand Russell, *An Inquiry into Meaning and Truth*
JR	Virginia Woolf, *Jacob's Room*
LettersBR	Bertrand Russell, *The Selected Letters of Bertrand Russell*
LettersLW	Leonard Woolf, *The Letters of Leonard Woolf*
LetttersRF	Roger Fry, *The Letters of Roger Fry*
LettersVW	Virginia Woolf, *The Letters of Virginia Woolf*
LK	Bertrand Russell, *Logic and Knowledge*
LL	Roger Fry, *Roger Fry: Last Lectures*
Matter	Bertrand Russell, *The Analysis of Matter*

MB	Virginia Woolf, *Moments of Being*
MBook	Leslie Stephen, *The Mausoleum Book*
Mind	Bertrand Russell, *The Analysis of Mind*
ML	Bertrand Russell, *Mysticism and Logic*
MrsD	Virginia Woolf, *Mrs. Dalloway*
MyPhD	Bertrand Russell, *My Philosophical Development*
ND	Virginia Woolf, *Night and Day*
O	Virginia Woolf, *Orlando: A Biography*
OKnExW	Bertrand Russell, *Our Knowledge of the External World*
OP	Bertrand Russell, *An Outline of Philosophy*
PE	Bertrand Russell, *Philosophical Essays*
"PhilBerg"	Bertrand Russell, *The Philosophy of Bergson*
PM	Bertrand Russell, *Principia Mathematica*
PofM	Bertrand Russell, *Principles of Mathematics*
PP	Bertrand Russell, *The Problems of Philosophy*
PS	G. E. Moore, *Philosophical Studies*
RF	Virginia Woolf, *Roger Fry: A Biography*
Room	Virginia Woolf, *A Room of One's Own*
SMW	Alfred North Whitehead, *Science and the Modern World*
SO	Bertrand Russell, *The Scientific Outlook*
SomeMain	G. E. Moore, *Some Main Problems of Philosophy*
ST	*Scientific Thought*
TFW	Henri Bergson, *Time and Free Will*
TG	Virginia Woolf, *Three Guineas*
TK	Bertrand Russell, *Theory of Knowledge*
TL	Virginia Woolf, *To the Lighthouse*
TR	Roger Fry, *Transformations*
V&D	Roger Fry, *Vision and Design*
VO	Virginia Woolf, *The Voyage Out*
VW	Quentin Bell, *Virginia Woolf*
W	Virginia Woolf, *The Waves*
"WM?"	Leslie Stephen, "What is Materialism?"
Y	Virginia Woolf, *The Years*

CHAPTER I

Introduction: table talk

> He was a curious figure thus sitting often dead silent at the head of the family dinner table. Sometimes he was caustic; sometimes to Thoby especially instructive. He would ask what was the cube root of such and such a number; for he always worked out mathematical problems on railway tickets; or told us how to find the "dominical number" – when Easter falls was it? And mother would protest; no mathematics, she would say, at meals.
>
> (Woolf, *Moments of Being*, 111)

> "Andrew," she said, "hold your plate lower, or I shall spill it." . . . resting her whole weight upon what at the other end of the table her husband was saying about the square root of one thousand two hundred and fifty-three. That was the number, it seemed, on his watch."
>
> (Woolf, *To the Lighthouse*, 158–9)

The universe of Virginia Woolf's novels is a monadology whose plurality of possible worlds includes private points of space and time unobserved, unoccupied by any subject. Its principle of unity is not a pre-established harmony conferred ahead of time by authorial intention. It is constructed *ex post facto* via a style and an art. This art grounds itself on a philosophical system, a theory of knowledge. The theory begins with an analysis of the common-sense world. Objects are reduced to "sense-data" separable from sensations and observing subjects to "perspectives." Atomism multiplies these perspectives. Objects familiar because seen, heard, sensed, observed, tucked cosily into the observer's viewpoint, lose their familiarity once rendered unseen, unheard, unobserved, revealed to have a sensible existence independent of an observer. A perspectivized style records the vision mutely, imparting its strangeness to the vision. The first conclusion of this logic is the idea of death as the separation of subject and object. The second starts from that conclusion, deriving from it an

6d THE · CAMBRIDGE · FORTNIGHTLY · 6d

No 3 Vol. I. CONTENTS· Feb. 21. 1888.

Womens' Degrees.
Notes.
Sir Henry Maine. By Oscar Browning.
A Letter from Davos By Arthur Sidgwick.
This Wicked World. Pt. III. By B.E.O.P.
Poetry.
Lacrosse.
Pot-Luck.

Printed for the Proprietors by F. S. Sheldrick, 11, Bridge Street, Cambridge.

Published by OCTAVUS TOMSON. 16 King's Parade. Cambridge.

Figure 1. Roger Fry, frontispiece to *The Cambridge Fortnightly*, 1888.

elegiac form that is an adequate response to the world revealed by science.

THE LIGHT OF CAMBRIDGE

They say the sky is the same everywhere . . . But above Cambridge . . . there is a difference . . . Is it fanciful to suppose the sky, washed into the crevices of King's College Chapel, lighter, thinner, more sparkling than the sky elsewhere? (Woolf, *Jacob's Room*, 31–2)

The origins of this theory of knowledge were in the pre-war Cambridge of Alfred North Whitehead, G. E. Moore and Bertrand Russell. "The student of British culture, like Virginia Woolf," Irma Rantavaara insists, "cannot escape Cambridge." (*Virginia Woolf and Bloomsbury*, 43). E. M. Forster's *The Longest Journey* (1907) begins abruptly with a dialogue evoking that Cambridge:

"The cow is there," said Ansell . . . There, now. . ."

"I have proved to myself that she isn't," said the voice. "The cow is *not* there." Ansell frowned and lit another match.

"She's not there for me," he declared. "I don't care whether she's there for you or not. Whether I'm in Cambridge or Iceland or dead, the cow will be there."

It was philosophy. They were discussing the existence of objects. Do they exist only when there is some one to look at them? Or have they a real existence of their own? . . . Hence the cow. She seemed to make things easier. She was so familiar, so solid, that surely the truths that she illustrated would in time become familiar and solid also. Is the cow there or not? This was better than deciding between objectivity and subjectivity. So at Oxford, just at the same time, one was asking, "What do our rooms look like in the vac?" (1–2)

Forster's fictional conversation could well be that which takes place in Jacob Flanders' rooms at Cambridge – one never recorded, however, in Woolf's *Jacob's Room*, because the observer-narrator, identified as a woman, is, it is implied, excluded from the conversation.[1] The novel's perspective on Jacob's rooms, "the window being open," is perforce distanced, limited, "legs issuing here," a "pipe was held in the air, then replaced," "lips opened," "a roar of laughter," "only gestures of arms, movements of bodies, could be seen shaping something in the room." So the question "Was it an argument?" (*JR*, 44) cannot be decided. Yet the subject of the debate Forster reproduces – our knowledge of the external world, the nature of perception – does enter Woolf's novels couched in explicit philosophical language. "Subject and object and the nature of reality" is the subject of his father's books, Andrew Ramsay answers Lily Briscoe's inquiry in *To the Lighthouse*, for it is as philosopher obsessed by the problem of knowledge and not as literary critic that Woolf fictionally depicts her own father, who was both. "Think of the kitchen table when you're not there," (38) Andrew adds to illustrate the philosophical realist's position with an example like Forster's cow, "so familiar, so solid," "to make things easier" for the puzzled Lily. In *The Years*, Sara Pargiter is reading a version of the Idealist position:

> "This man," she said, tapping the ugly little brown volume, "says the world's nothing but thought, Maggie" . . .
> "The world's nothing but thought, does he say?" . . .
> "Would there be trees if we didn't see them?" said Maggie.
> "What's 'I'? . . . 'I' . . . [Woolf's ellipses]?" She stopped. She did not know what she meant. She was talking nonsense. (139–40)

With these explicit formulations, Woolf makes evident her familiarity with the terms in which British philosophy presents the problem. They are not incidental, however, as in Forster, but themes. Their full understanding requires an explication provided not simply by the parameters of what is after all an ancient debate – that between Realism and Idealism – but by a particular, historically localizable theory of knowledge. Underlying Woolf's work, albeit not always undisguisedly, it is the key to otherwise unexplained obsessions of the novels which, in isolation, remain puzzling, and it intersects with more familiar ones to make possible new readings.[2]

The Cambridge at the origin of this theory was one won over after 1898 by a new philosophical Realism. This was the "revolt" against Idealism of the young Moore and Russell. Its paradigm of reality in Russell and Whitehead was not first the external world, but mathematical and logical truth. If the conjunction of "some branch of mathematics or philosophy" (*TL*, 15) evokes the names of Russell and Whitehead, it had already marked the intellectual orientation of the philosophers of Woolf's father's generation.[3] "Stephen, Sidgwick, Clifford, Marshall and Venn all came to philosophy through mathematics and gravitated to empiricism . . . It was no accident that whereas Oxford at the end of the century became the home of German Idealism, Cambridge nurtured Bertrand Russell's logic which employed Boolean algebra" (Annan, *Godless Victorian*, 190).[4]

While, later, Oxford would read by the natural light of "ordinary language," the "light of Cambridge" included "the light . . . of symbols and figures" (*JR*, 42). An illustration in Russell's *ABC of Relativity* assigns hypothetical lawyers the view of simultaneity of "a person at rest on the earth" and not "the view of a person traveling in a train" by virtue of their "having been educated at Oxford." Russell dryly comments that "in theoretical physics no such parochial prejudices are permissible" (50).

Theory of knowledge was a further development of the new Realism, the result of the inroads of science at Cambridge at the beginning of the century. Here reality is physical reality. Stages in "the process of understanding" were "philosophy; science" (*W*, 249). The young men Peter Walsh is thinking of in *Mrs. Dalloway* as he passes the British Museum are "reading science, reading philosophy" (76). At "Cambridge . . . Greek burns there; science there; philosophy on the ground floor" (*JR*, 39). Philosophy was then the foundation, strengthened by logic and mathematics. Science's knowledge of the external world was only expressible logically and mathematically. "The thought which science evokes is logical thought," wrote Whitehead (*Aims*, 51).

But the growth and dissemination of theory of knowledge required a wider intellectual setting, a meeting-ground of philosophy not only with science, but, surprisingly, with a burgeoning artistic activity. Such, it is our first hypothesis, was Bloomsbury.

(SOME MAIN) PROBLEMS OF PHILOSOPHY: A BLOOMSBURY EPISTEMOLOGY

[H]ow are we to bridge over the gulf between two contradictories? (Leslie Stephen, *History of English Thought*, 25)

The turn to theory of knowledge coincided with a nascent philosophy of science in the first decades of the century. Its epistemological urgency arose from what Russell called "the gulf between the world of physics and the world of sense" or "the transition from perception to science" (*Matter*, 222). These problems became acute with the breakthroughs of physics in the last decades of the nineteenth century on the kinetic theory of gases and the wave theory of light, Max Planck's discovery of the quantum in 1900, the confirmation and application of Niels Bohr's theory of the atom between

1913 and 1925, Einstein's formulation of the special theory of relativity in 1905 and of the general theory in 1915 and the discoveries of de Broglie, Heisenberg, P. Jordan, Dirac and Schrödinger on wave and particle theories in 1925–6, spanning the years Woolf is writing her first novels. "The new situation in the thought of today arises from the fact that scientific theory is outrunning common sense," wrote Whitehead (*SMW*, 106). The theme prefaces various of Russell's attempts to formulate a theory of knowledge. He elaborated on it in the opening of his 1926 Tarner Lectures on the Philosophy of the Sciences given at Cambridge:

> All empirical evidence consists, in the last analysis, of perceptions, since it is the latter which supplies the evidence of the laws of physics. In the time of Galileo, this fact did not seem to raise any very difficult problems, since the world of physics had not yet become so abstract and remote as subsequent research has made it. But already in the philosophy of Descartes the modern problem is implicit, and with Berkeley it becomes explicit. The problem arises because the world of physics is, prima facie, so different from the world of perception that it is difficult to see how one can afford evidence for the other. (*Matter*, 6)

Russell's conclusion, in the 1914 "The Relation of Sense-Data to Physics," that "it would seem, the correlation with objects of sense, by which physics was to be verified, is itself utterly and for ever unverifiable" (*ML*, 140), echoes Leslie Stephen's conclusion "that matter cannot be brought into relation to spirit, whilst all scientific knowledge rests on their mutual connection" (*HET*, 25–6).

Thus it was a philosophy which addressed the seeming incommensurability of two versions of a knowledge of the external world, one direct apprehension of it through the senses and the other scientific knowledge, chiefly modern physics, that Woolf, with her acknowledged limits in this area, came to know as philosophy. Both versions made empirical claims about the world. All we ever know immediately is not matter, but our own sensations. The object of science is beyond immediate knowledge. But sensation remains the evidence for it. The empirical basis for objective knowledge thus rests on subjective foundations. Yet science means to formulate a knowledge ideally independent of the subject. Hence a solution to the problem of knowledge within the framework of empiricism must be an answer to Idealism, whether Berkeley's or F. H. Bradley's Hegelianism.

Russell's work on the theory of knowledge is concentrated in the period 1910 to 1914. Its history after 1910 – the relevant texts including not only *Our Knowledge of the External World* and "The Relation of Sense-Data to Physics," but the manuscript posthumously published as *Theory of Knowledge*, all of 1914, – has only recently been recounted.[5] Its major influences are the Moore of "The Refutation of Idealism" and *Some Main Problems of Philosophy*, with ever in the background Whitehead's and Russell's monumental work on logic and the foundations of mathematics. Together Moore, Russell and Whitehead define the contours of philosophy as Bloomsbury understood it. Leonard Woolf singles out this triumvirate as the major philosophical influence for his generation:

When I came up to Trinity, [J. McT. E.] McTaggart, though regarded with respect and amused affection as an eccentric, had completely lost his intellectual and philosophical influence. The three other philosophers' reputation was great and growing, and they dominated the younger generation. In 1902 Whitehead was forty-one years old, Russell thirty, and Moore twenty-nine. (*Sowing*, 134)

The years 1911–13 are also those in which the young Wittgenstein entered the English philosophical scene, those of the intense exchange between him and Russell. The profound crisis created for Russell by Wittgenstein's criticisms led to Russell's abandonment of the *Theory of Knowledge* text. Wittgenstein as a philosophical influence sets, according to one dominant assessment of the course of philosophy in the twentieth century, a kind of *terminus ad quem* to the period of the theory of knowledge by making "epistemology. . . peripheral," in the words of Michael Dummett, who "points out," Brian McGuinness writes,

that since the time of Descartes epistemology had been the basic part of philosophy:

"The whole subject had to start from the question, 'What do we know and how?' . . . Descartes's perspective continued to be that which dominated philosophy until this century, when it was overthrown by Wittgenstein, who in the *Tractatus* reinstated philosophical logic as the foundation of philosophy, and relegated epistemology to a peripheral position."

. . . Russell, who came to philosophy before the change signalized by Dummett, perhaps never realized that it had taken place. Despite all his own discoveries in logic and philosophical logic, he tended to think that the Cartesian question was the one with which philosophy began. (*Wittgenstein: A Life*, 83)[6]

The displacement of epistemology marks the break between Russell's dominance and Wittgenstein's.

BLOOMSBURY: THE HOME UNIVERSITY

"Why dont you contribute to the Queen's dolls House, Virginia?" "Is there a W. C. in it, Vita?" "You're a bit hoity toity, Virginia." Well, I was educated in the old Cambridge School. "Ever hear of Moore?" "George Moore the novelist?" "My dear Vita, we start at different ends." (to Clive Bell, *Letters VW,* III, 85–6)

[T]here is still a gulf . . . in which, possibly, literature may crash . . . England has crammed a small aristocratic class with Latin and Greek and logic and metaphysics and mathematics . . . She has left the other class, the immense class to which almost all of us must belong, to pick up what we can in village schools; in factories; in workshops; behind counters; and at home. When one thinks of that criminal injustice one is tempted to say England deserves to have no literature. (*CE* II, 180)

Bloomsbury was both a place and a moment. As a place, it was created by the displacement of two distinct groups from two other places: it was Cambridge and centrally Cambridge philosophy moved to London and it was the private household of the young Stephens moved from Hyde Park Gate to Bloomsbury. "The colour of our minds and thought had been given to us by the climate of Cambridge and Moore's philosophy," Leonard Woolf wrote (*BeAg*, 25). "Bloomsbury grew directly out of Cambridge," he said; it was "intimate friends who had been at Trinity and King's and were now working in London" (*Sowing*, 156). Since the Stephen brothers reached Bloomsbury via Cambridge, the Stephen sisters' arrival defined the specific influence of the Hyde Park Gate contingent: the arts were the sisters' arts; philosophy belonged to the brothers. The Cambridge brothers' philosophy had, moreover, a formal embodiment in that "Fratrum Societati" known as the Cambridge Apostles (Lowe, *Alfred North Whitehead*, I, 120). Although not all of Bloomsbury's nucleus, and notably not the Stephen brothers, were members, its influence was paramount.[7] We can give many names to the conjunction of Cambridge and Hyde Park Gate, but here we will call it the "Home University."

As a moment, Bloomsbury's intellectual history coincides with the work on knowledge. It divides into three sections. The first takes in the formative years 1900 to 1904–5, when Bloomsbury's male members were Cambridge undergraduates. Leonard Woolf pronounced that "1903 was an *annus mirabilis* for Cambridge philosophy, for in that year were published Russell's *Principles of Mathematics* and Moore's *Principia Ethica*" (*Sowing*, 133–4). 1903 also has a landmark in "The Refutation of Idealism," which places sensible and physical reality alongside the mathematical reality of Russell's *Principles*. The second period covers the years 1905 to 1910, those of the first Bloomsbury. The third, from 1910 at least to the outbreak of the War or to Russell's "Logical Atomism" lectures of 1918, includes "the three years 1912 to 1914," when Leonard Woolf remembers "Bloomsbury came into existence," (it for him not having existed during his absence in Ceylon from 1904–11), and when Woolf is writing her first novel, completed in 1913.

Bloomsbury's preoccupation with epistemological questions thus places it squarely within the period of Russell which ends with Wittgenstein's ascendancy. Leonard Woolf, explaining why Virginia had not attended Wittgenstein's lectures, says "nor did I and I don't think many of the older people did" (*LettersLW*, 539). We can thus take the rise of Wittgenstein's influence as a kind of cut-off point for the philosophical background of Bloomsbury. This does not prevent the *Tractatus* from playing a role in our reconstruction of Bloomsbury's intellectual world. It came out of the period of Russell's theory of knowledge, and its conceptions, language and dominant metaphors find their counterparts in Woolf, not because she came under its influence, but because she shared its ways of thinking.

Woolf saw as an inaugural moment for Bloomsbury the turning of the century's first decade. In a famous passage, she wrote that "in or about December 1910 human character changed" (*CE*, I, 320). It marked for her a significant shift in what she calls "atmosphere," Leonard's "climate." We can venture certain hypotheses as to what change Woolf had in mind and what events led her to date it so precisely.

The change was a turn to the "external world"; it was "changing from the general to the particular," as Woolf says of early Bloomsbury conversation (*MB*, 192), echoing the Russellian vocabulary. "The external world" had for Cambridge two embodiments. It was first, we saw, the physical world of science. But the "external world" had a social dimension as well. It was the world outside the narrow circle of Cambridge. For there were other lights than Cambridge. Among the most important was the strong Mediterranean sunlight of a new art, "its light (whether Rossetti's on the wall, or Van Gogh reproduced . . .)" (*JR*, 40–1), to which Cambridge was blind, for "none of that could show clearly through the swaddlings and blanketings of the Cambridge night" (*JR*, 45).[8] Significant for our history, this incompleteness was felt with a new urgency by the philosopher-logician himself. His intensest labor was over, and in the interval which opened up almost as a void, new questions suddenly became visible, new contacts were sought and made. Leslie Stephen, Woolf thought, had remained "ignorant of all depressions and elevations but those that high philosophy bred in him" (*MB*, 37). The philosopher of 1910 turns from "the world of universals" to the world of "particulars," discovering, despite a "temperament" for "the one," "that both have the same claim on our impartial attention" (*PP*, 100).

In December 1910, the first volume of *Principia Mathematica*, which Russell had spent the previous ten years writing with Whitehead, finally appeared. It marks a watershed. The logicist project – the claim that pure mathematics was deducible, via "chains of deductions" (*PofM*, xvi), "from a very small number of fundamental logical principles" (xv) – had arrived at a critical point, both of achievement and exhaustion. The story of Russell's post-*Principia* exhaustion is notorious. He recounted it to many, including Woolf herself.[9] But his personal odyssey is emblematic of Cambridge philosophy's shift in direction at that moment. In 1910, Whitehead moved from Cambridge to London (Lowe, *Alfred North Whitehead*, II, 2), abruptly ending his thirty-year association with Trinity College.[10] In 1911, Russell, finally separated from his first wife, would also take a flat in London, though he was still lecturing at Cambridge. These events mark the end of something. Unlike the parochial Oxford mind of Russell's *The ABC of Relativity*, his Cambridge-educated mind is a mind in motion, with its "view of a person traveling" at high speed, its direction outwards.

1910 also marked new beginnings. From the completion of *Principia Mathematica* can be dated the new interest in the old problem of knowledge that Moore's "The Refutation of Idealism" initiated and Forster already echoed in 1907. In the winter of 1910–11, Moore delivered twenty lectures in London on "the problem of the external world and the problem of general ideas" which became *Some Main Problems of Philosophy* (Wisdom, "Foreword," 5). The revival of interest in knowledge led Russell to extend logic's methods into new terrain, not an imperialist extension but a testimony to the incompleteness of pure logic alone. Logic, redirected to reality, was completed only when its framework was filled in by a reference to the external world. Whatever the reason for the turn to knowledge circa 1910, the fact that the revived interest met a response beyond philosophy is indicative of a climate receptive to it. The turn is philosophy's expression of some more general shift.

One sign is the shift to a new aesthetic, "Post-Impressionism."[11] 1910 was the year that Roger Fry organized the First Post-Impressionist Exhibition; it opened on November 8 and closed on January 15, 1911, partly overlapping with Moore's lectures. This event is the generally accepted explanation for Woolf's locating a change around December, 1910. Fry entered Bloomsbury when he met Vanessa and Clive Bell in January 1910 (Spalding, *Roger Fry*, 123). Woolf makes the year the most natural date for the meeting: "It must have been in 1910 I suppose that Clive one evening rushed upstairs" having "had one of the most interesting conversations in his life." "It was with Roger Fry. They had been discussing the theory of art for hours . . . So Roger appeared" (*MB*, 197). Woolf must have been that "stranger meeting him then for the first time (1910)" which *Roger Fry: A Biography* invokes (149).

It is Fry, elected an Apostle in 1887, one year after McTaggart and two after Whitehead, five years before Russell and seven before Moore, who provides the link between Cambridge philosophy and visual art and aesthetics. Quentin Bell no doubt reflects Bloomsbury's general opinion that "Cambridge at the turn of the century was aesthetically blind" (*VW*, I, 103). Mr. Ramsay's "narrowness, his blindness" (*TL*, 72) is only a special case of "the extraordinary indifference of the English to the visual arts" (*RF*, 52), "the stone-blind eye with which" in general nineteenth-century English writers and thinkers, according to Whitehead, "regarded the importance of aesthetics in a nation's life" (*SMW*, 182). "When abroad," Spalding writes of Leslie Stephen, "he studiously avoided galleries and museums" (*Vanessa Bell*, 18). Woolf sees "the disparity" between her father's "critical and creative powers" in terms of the inability to paint:

> Give him a thought to analyse, the thought of Mill, Bentham, Hobbes; and his is (so Maynard has told me) acute, clear, concise: an admirable model of the Cambridge analy[tical spirit]. But give him a life, a character, and he is so crude, so elementary, so conventional, that a child with a box of coloured chalks is as subtle a portrait painter as he is. (*MB*, 126)

That deficiency of analysis was bound up with the Apostles' "doctrine":

> It is difficult to suppose that Baron Pollock, Lord Derby, Sir James Stephen, Clerk-Maxwell and the Sidgwicks ever discussed . . . the painting of Titian and Velasquez. There is no evidence, apart from MacTaggart's early reference to Rossetti and from one visit in his company to the Royal Academy, that the young men who read so many books and discussed so many problems ever looked at pictures and debated the theory of aesthetics. Politics and philosophy were their chief interests. Art was for them the art of literature; and literature was half prophecy . . . Perhaps then, when Mr Benson talks of the pallor of the Apostles, he hints at something eyeless, abstract and austere in their doctrines. (*RF*, 51–2)

The change Fry introduces opposes itself to the strange word "eyeless," to which we return. Here we only note it as a synonym for Cambridge philosophy's blindness to art. For the shift was more than the replacement of one aesthetic by another; it signalled a new predominance of the visual arts, especially painting. The young Apostles of Woolf's generation were exceptional, in her account, because some among them had a passion for art – Lytton Strachey, for instance, "had French pictures in his rooms" (*MB*, 188).[12] The change in intellectual orientation Strachey represented could not come to fruition in the academic atmosphere of Cambridge, however, but required something cosmopolitan London offered. The fact that the subject of the first Bloomsbury conversation Woolf records was initiated when her sister Vanessa, "having said perhaps that she had been to some picture show, incautiously used the word 'beauty'" (*MB*, 167), thus follows from the hypothesis that Bloomsbury answered a need to supplement the philosophical with the aesthetic. The sequence of key words she then gives – the subject "might be 'beauty,' might be 'good,' might be 'reality'" (*MB*, 167) – places the aesthetic question within the context of philosophy, first ethics and finally theory of knowledge.

The visual in Bloomsbury is synedochic for the sensible, for "those senses which are stimulated so briskly by the moderns; the senses of sight, of sound, of touch" (*CE* II, 158). Fry had supplied the Apostles with the eyes for the philosopher-logicians to discern a sensible reality and complete their picture of the world: "even while they argued his eye was always active" (*RF*, 52). "Art and literature have not merely an indirect effect on the main energies of life," writes Whitehead. "Directly, they give vision" (*Ed*, 58). Like "[t]he geranium in the urn" that "became startlingly visible" to Mr. Ramsay (*TL*, 54), the sensible world suddenly came into focus; the canvases Fry put on display in 1910 presented the look of things at the moment the completion of the logicist project turned the philosopher to the physical world.

But our argument is also that for Woolf Fry showed the importance of the "eyeless" dimension learned from the Apostles' "doctrines" for a "modern" art. At Cambridge, "Fry's mind had opened there; his eyes had opened there" (*RF*, 60) to other objects than those of sense, to universals and logical form. The "perceptual metaphor" Peter Hylton (*Russell*, 232) stresses in Moore and Russell is not simply a metaphor. Russell's first chapter of *The ABC of Relativity*, "Touch and Sight: the Earth and the Heavens," insists that "astronomy differs from terrestrial physics because of its exclusive dependence upon sight" (17). Sight is a safer guide: "As physics has advanced, it has appeared more and more that sight is less misleading than touch as a source of fundamental notions about matter" (12). "Cold grey eyes George Plummer had" in *Jacob's Room*, who might become "Professor of Physics," "but in them was an abstract light" (35). Mr. Ramsay was one of those "thinkers standing with hands to the eyes on some crag above the multitude" (*JR*, 162) gazing at distant things but "blind" to the close, with that "attentiveness, analogous to visual alertness, accompanied by concentrated effort" Elizabeth Ramsden Eames sees in Russell (58). Ultimately, such sight reveals more in the universe than meets the eye.

Cambridge's "abstract light" is roughly defined by Fry's description of Apostles' meetings, which Woolf repeats: "discussing 'things in general'" (*RF*, 51 and 55). Its limitation lay in the fact that it "excluded some things in particular" (*RF*, 51), notably sensible, visible particulars. If the art Fry unveils answers some philosophic need expressed by theory of knowledge, logic provided something Fry required: the invisible aesthetic principles needed to go beyond "the last phase of Impressionism" and complete its vision. The resultant theory is dualistic, relating what Fry labels "vision" and "design," Impressionism and Post-Impressionism. It is the product of a thinking which also gave rise to Moore's, Russell's and Whitehead's persisting dualism, in which "the world of universals" coexists with "the world of existence." There are two realities, one sensible and the other inaccessible to the senses; nonetheless, "both are real, and both are important to the metaphysician" (*PP*, 100). Fry's "vision" complements Moore's and Russell's theory of sense-data which Peter Geach calls "the current Cambridge doctrine" in the period before the war (*Truth, Love and Immortality*, 75) and Russell's theory of sensibilia, central to his full-blown 1914 theory. The knowledge it yields is sensible knowledge, a special case of Russell's "acquaintance." But it is not knowledge in the full sense, nor is Fry's "vision" equivalent to art. His "design," like Russell's logical form, rests upon an "eyeless" knowledge of something unperceivable, in Russell, "knowledge by description."

The "centre," "a nucleus" of "the wider circumference of the moment" (*CE*, II, 294), is December 1910. It represents the encounter between philosophy and art which was Bloomsbury and confirms Allan Janik's and Stephen Toulmin's claim of "a closer connection than books on the history of philosophy sometimes suggest between the intellectual views of Moore and Russell . . . and the radical transformations in practical ethics and aesthetics . . . represented, for example, by Roger Fry's Post-Impressionist Exhibition, the immense success of Diaghilev's Russian Ballet, and the novels of Leonard Woolf's wife, Virginia" (*Wittgenstein's Vienna*, 210–11).

THE OUTSIDE WORLD AND THE OUTSIDERS' SOCIETY

> The excursion to Manchester [to visit an art gallery] was made with friends, but they were not Apostles, a sign that when Roger Fry wished to gratify certain growing curiosities he had to seek company . . . outside the circle of that very select and very famous society (Spalding, *Roger Fry*, 53)

What remains to be explained are the wider forces that brought philosophy and art, Cambridge and Bloomsbury, to their historic rendez-vous in late 1910. This is supplied by the social dimension Woolf explicitly gives to the 1910 change in "human character." It is an alteration in the relation between the classes, sexes and generations: "All human relations have shifted – those between masters and servants, husbands and wives, parents and children" (*CE*, I, 321). The terms of Woolf's "homely illustration" of the "Georgian cook" who no longer inhabits the Victorian cook's "lower depths," but "is a creature of sunshine and fresh air" (*CE*, I, 320) is translatable into the new and old aesthetic oppositions of Fry's exhibition. It resembles the change from "the gloom of a room naturally dark" whose Victorian decor was "much under the influence of Titian" at 22

Hyde Park Gate (*MB*, 164) – what Woolf called "the cage" (*MB*, 116) – to Vanessa Bell's Post-Impressionist inspired Bloomsbury interiors. In Woolf's account of Fry's Exhibition, the link between the social and the aesthetic is made with the same examples: "Everyone argued. Anyone's sensation – his [Fry's] cook's, his housemaid's – was worth having. Learning did not matter; it was the reality that was all-important" (*RF*, 153). Echoing Woolf's description of Fry's ability to bring together Post-Impressionist canvases and "the untutored taste of negresses" (*RF*, 152), both of which, for Fry, gave a better analysis of "the totality of appearances" (Fry, "The Last Phase of Impressionism," 46) than did a blind learning, we can say that "[u]nder his influence," the philosophical, the social and the aesthetic" "all were connected" (*RF*, 152–3). The connector was supplied by the word "reality." What Fry took from the Apostles was a philosophical questioning as to its nature: "Whatever else his new friends had taught him, they had taught him to distinguish between the sham and the reality, 'whatever that reality might be'" (*RF*, 58). Uncovering reality in art itself required a philosophical vision and brought enlightenment. If "[t]he light and the air [of Bloomsbury] after the rich red gloom of Hyde Park Gate were a revelation" (*MB*, 162), "Moore and his book," visual housecleaning of sorts, Leonard Woolf thought, "suddenly removed from our eyes an obscuring accumulation of scales, cobwebs, and curtains, revealing for the first time to us, so it seemed, the nature of truth and reality" via "the fresh air and pure light of plain common sense" (*An Autobiography*, 93). Air and light were at once sensible, aesthetic, intellectual and social.

The social and aesthetic intersect literally as well in Bloomsbury. As a locale on the London map, it provided the neutral meeting ground between two places exclusive of a wider public: Apostolic Cambridge and the society extending from the drawing room of 22 Hyde Park Gate to Mayfair that the Duckworth brothers wanted their half-sisters to inhabit. Sunshine and fresh air are also a new ethos, one which substitutes free exchange for the "prison" – "the cage" – of the old social relations.[13] "Prisons" was the title of a book Russell planned with Ottoline Morrell. One such prison was for Woolf "patriarchy" (*Room*, 33), governed by "the fear that forbids freedom in the private house" (*TG*, 142). Bloomsbury's nucleus was a society of orphans setting up house free of parental authority – the 1910 shift in relations included, for Woolf, those between "parents and children." What better way to inaugurate it than with the death of the father? The society of brothers had already thrown off the yoke of authority in its self-conception. Enlarged to include the sisters in Bloomsbury's "small concentrated world dwelling inside the much larger and looser world of dances and dinners" the Stephen sisters frequented (*MB*, 192), "the free intellectual intercourse, the Athenian liberty of speech and speculation, that was offered by 'the Society' – the Apostles" (Q. Bell, *Bloomsbury*, 24), was extended, as the suffrage would be, here to the unelected. Like the Apostles, it was "the society of equals . . . questioning everything with complete freedom" (*RF*, 51).

One model for Apostolic discussions was Plato's Symposium. That model Woolf explicitly connects to homosexuality – "I had known since I was sixteen or so, all about sodomy, through reading Plato" (*MB*, 104), "I knew there were buggers in Plato's Greece" (*MB*, 172) – but one that makes room for rather than excludes the sisters, allowing us to see Bloomsbury as not only the suspension of parental authority but the neutralization of the sexuality Woolf's Duckworth half-brothers represented, not only in their incestuous attraction to their sisters but also in their goal of marrying them for which their "society" existed. The symposium reinforces the idea of philosophy as the male's exclusive purview, while simultanously opening up the possibility of women joining. In the "society of buggers," Woolf writes, "if you are a woman," "[o]ne fizzes up into some absurd delightful effervescence of soda water or champagne" (*MB*, 172). The neutralization of sexuality as heterosexual courtship rituals was the freedom for nothing but intellectual exchange, desexualizing "male" knowledge. Its phallic character is transformed from tyrannical power to the "support" for imaginative speculation when the father is turned into the brothers. But the brothers must keep a brother's distance, for Woolf's half-brother George Duckworth used the threat of succumbing to unnamed "vices" to force himself sexually on his half-sisters: "I could only conjure up in my virgin consciousness, dimly irradiated by having read the 'Symposium' with Miss Case, horrible visions of the vices to which young men were driven whose sisters did not make them happy at home" (*MB*, 177). It is as if the homosexual observes the incest taboo, not only sexually, as George Duckworth did not, but also politically, by allowing fraternal equality, as the father did not. Bloomsbury permitted the cohabitation of fatherless brothers and sisters and then extended it to the cohabitation of Virginia (Vanessa was by then married) and her brother Adrian with Duncan Grant, Maynard Keynes and Leonard Woolf, an arrangement shocking to George Duckworth (see *VW,* I, 175). Leonard Woolf thus began his relation with Virginia Stephen in the structural position of a good brother, an apostle, while the only proposal of marriage Virginia accepted before Leonard's a little over a year after they became "housemates" was Lytton Strachey's.

The implicit *raison d'être* of Bloomsbury discussions was the extension of knowledge beyond the confines of the university elite.[14] Their wider circumference began with "co-education," itself preceded by various projects for the extension of knowledge. Moore had in 1899 lectured on Kant to the Passmore Edwards Settlement in London (Levy, *G. E. Moore,* 200). Paul Levy recounts the abortive project of Russell and others for publishing "a sort of radical manifesto, with Moore as their acknowledged inspiration" (253). Russell in a 1904 letter to Moore insists that "the scope and purpose of the book is popular, and it is rather important that the first chapter should not be too difficult" and again that "it is quite essential that everything should be intelligible to ordinary educated people, and not only to those who have philosophic capacity" (255). Despite having co-authored one of the most notoriously difficult, specialized books, Russell was concerned with bringing philosophy to the layperson. At Cambridge, Fry had given university extension lectures on art in 1900 (Rosenbaum, *The Bloomsbury Group,* xvii). Woolf herself had felt this educative impulse, alongside the impulse to learn from this milieu: later reading her 1904–5 diary, she records that "I went on to the Waterloo Road and lectured (a class of working men and women) on the Greek Myths." (*MB,* 186). The year 1910 brought together in London many such projects simultaneous with the First Post-Impressionist Exhibition. Whitehead's move to London, for instance, led to a series of addresses on education, starting in 1911 with "The Place of Mathematics in a Liberal Education." (When in *Three Guineas* Woolf says that "[t]he poor college must teach only the arts that can be taught cheaply and practised by poor people," she includes mathematics in her list (34).) Like Woolf's on the Greek myths, Moore's 1910 lectures were given at Morley College, "an evening institute for working men and women . . . set up as an adjunct to the Old Vic" (*VW,* I, 105) like the "poor men's college" where Katherine Hilbery's second cousin "lectures" (*ND,* 120). They were thus destined for a working-class audience. Woolf recalls that "once at least Morgan [Forster] flitted through Bloomsbury lodging for a moment in Fitzroy Square (hence between 1907 and 1911)," talking "of Italy and the Working Men's College" (198). The extension of knowledge was in the air.

One especially indicative educative project was the Home University Library of Modern Knowledge, which began publishing a series of small, inexpensive books written by prominent philosophers, mathematicians, scholars and public figures. Its first titles included Whitehead's 1911 *An Introduction to Mathematics*, Moore's *Ethics*, Lytton Strachey's *Landmarks in French Literature* and, to indicate its scope, J. Ramsay Macdonald's *The Socialist Movement*. The series was from the start bound up with the problem of knowledge: one of its earliest titles was Russell's 1912 *The Problems of Philosophy*, commissioned in the autumn of 1910. Written, Russell says later, as an "escape from the rigours of symbolic deductive reasoning," this book "setting out in popular terms a general outline of my philosophy" (*MyPhD*, 77), his "shilling shocker" detested by Wittgenstein,[15] was just the kind of popular introduction that Mrs. Ambrose, Sara Pargiter, Ottoline Morrell or Virginia Woolf might be supposed to have read, perhaps among the "shilling shockers" Woolf imagined the young men at Cambridge reading in *Jacob's Room* (43). Hylton has hypothesized that the very project of producing what one of the series' editors Gilbert Murray called "a message to the shop-assistants about philosophy"[16] is itself one of the factors explaining "Russell's concern, from 1910 onwards, with the issue of knowledge," so "new in his work" (*Russell*, 361):

> His concern with this question thus represents a shift not in doctrine but in interests; an issue which he had previously neglected came to seem important to him, and came for a time to be a major focus of his work. Why did this occur? The completion of *PM*, in the autumn of 1909, no doubt left Russell looking for a philosophical task of a somewhat different kind. (362)

A factor in Russell's turn, as he states in *The Problems of Philosophy*'s Preface, is the "valuable assistance from unpublished writing of G. E. Moore and J. M. Keynes." Hylton points out that in the Preface to *Some Main Problems of Philosophy*, Moore indicates that "those writings are the first ten of Moore's twenty lectures, which are largely concerned with issues having to do with perception and with knowledge of physical objects" (362). Even if, as Hylton adds, there remains "a question here about the origin of Moore's interest in these issues" which "dates back" to "The Refutation of Idealism" (362), Moore's expansion of the 1903 essay's arguments in the 1910 lectures came at a critical moment of intellectual ferment which had overflowed the boundaries of the university. The problem of knowledge was the philosophical problem through which philosophy was brought to a wider public.

The turn from logic to theory of knowledge was thus bound up with a kind of university extension.[17] But if the audience for the Home University Library was identified as "shop assistants" or "working men," there is evidence it importantly consisted of the women largely excluded from Cambridge.[18] (Woolf does place "a woman" together with "a working-man, a negro" as members of classes who have reason to resent their exclusion (*CE*, II, 144).) The claim has been made that Russell's own turn from the work of *Principia* to epistemology was an attempt to address himself to the woman as lay philosopher, even to plan a collaboration. The woman in question was Ottoline Morrell, but that does not undercut the argument that Russell's epistemology was elaborated in a deliberately widened philosophical arena, in contrast to his logic. This is the point Eames makes in her introduction to the 1914 *Theory of Knowledge* manuscript, explaining that "Russell expressed in letters to Ottoline Morrell a revulsion" against "technical philosophy," the result, he wrote later, of "the long years of concentrated logical work on 'the big book,' *Principia Mathematica*." Instead, he was "rereading philosophers of the past" preparatory "for his next major work at the kind of philosophy which was of interest to Ottoline Morrell":

> Russell attributed to her a broadening of his tastes, interests, and sympathies, and he longed to share his intellectual life with her; at their lovers' meetings they read Plato and Spinoza, and from their discussions a book emerged which they referred to as "Prisons," dealing with the ability of philosophy to free the mind and spirit from the trammels of the here and now. (Eames, intro., Russell, *Theory of Knowledge*, xix)[19]

The book, whose text is lost, "reached the stage of typescript"; its interests, Eames says, "can be seen in the final chapter of *The Problems of Philosophy*" (xix). The "next major work" Russell refers to could also be one of the works contributing to the 1914 theory of knowledge – either *Our Knowledge of the External World*, which, as the Lowell Lectures, Russell called, in a letter to her, his "popular lectures" (McGuinness, *Wittgenstein*, 176), or *Theory of Knowledge.* Hylton, like Eames, speculates that Russell's "affair with Ottoline Morrell, and the desire to read philosophy with her," may have "influenced him. She knew something of philosophy, but nothing of mathematics or (post-Fregean) logic; they could hardly discuss *PM*, but Plato and Descartes and Berkeley might be a different matter" (Hylton, *Russell*, 362). To love can be added the war as an opening to knowledge. McGuinness observes that "Russell himself compared the change between 1910 and 1914 with the life of Faust before and after he met Mephistopheles, a change produced in his case by Ottoline and the war" (*Wittgenstein*, 87).[20] "[T]he world of existence" not only "contains all thoughts and feelings, all the data of sense" but also "everything that can do either good or harm" (*PP*, 100).

Russell deliberately presupposes the intelligent person untrained in philosophy is female (and, of course, that the philosopher is male), and that the layperson-woman's opinion is of importance. "If you say to a person untrained in philosophy . . . he or she will reply," he remarks (*MyPhD*, 101; *IMT*, 140); "If you try to persuade any uneducated person that she cannot call up a visual picture of a friend sitting in a chair, but can only use words describing what such an occurrence would be like, she will conclude that you are mad. (This statement is based upon experiment.)" (*Mind*, 152). Theory of knowledge places on the agenda issues she would know something of.

Russell's attitude, again, comes out of the impulse to share knowledge. The exclusivity of Cambridge was felt by the Cambridge men who opposed it first in the exclusion of women. In 1896–7, a few years before Thoby Stephen and Leonard Woolf arrived in 1899, a great debate, dubbed "The Women's War" by the undergraduates, was carried on at Oxford and Cambridge over the question of whether women should be granted degrees. (Girton and Newnham students "could not put B.A. after their names" (*TG*, 29).) At Cambridge, Whitehead, Henry Sidgwick and F. W. Maitland, all Apostles, had supported the granting of degrees for women, but the Senate voted overwhelmingly against, as had the undergraduates (Lowe, *Alfred North Whitehead*, I, 214–17). A version of the debate had already taken place among the Apostles in early 1894, when Russell advocated in a paper, "Should we like to elect women?" or "Lövberg or Hedda?," that women be elected. Eight of the nine Apostles present, including Moore and Russell, voted Yes. Russell's expectation that, as he then wrote, "it is now merely a question of time, of waiting till enough of the older members have died, and that all the new ones are likely to be in favour of it" (Levy, *G. E. Moore*, 129) proved too optimistic: the Apostles elected the first woman almost a century later in 1970. Russell's raising of the question in 1894, simultaneous with his falling in love with his first wife, Alys Pearsall Smith, testifies to a desire for intellectual exchanges with women; his falling in love with Ottoline in 1911 is then plausibly the impetus behind the desire to direct his philosophy to others than his Cambridge colleagues.

The Apostles of Russell's and Moore's generation and including the older Whitehead thus represented a dissenting sect at Cambridge on the question of "co-education." Victor Lowe holds Cambridge's refusal to change partly responsible for Whitehead's decision to move to London in 1910 and connects it with Cambridge's reception of the Scottish labor leader Keir Hardie:

> London was in the twentieth century, Cambridge was not. Cambridge had shown this in its almost solitary refusal to grant degrees to women and in its shameful treatment of Keir Hardie. The future of England – always something on Whitehead's mind – depended on scrutinizing, then improving, the education of the masses in cities like London . . . In London he would meet the real world. (*Alfred North Whitehead*, I, 317–8)

Bloomsbury then was the place where was accomplished what had been defeated at Cambridge; it connected knowledge to the real world. The presence of two women at 46 Gordon Square for Thoby Stephen's Thursday evenings in 1904 answered some need felt even beyond this group of Cambridge graduates. Far from being an accidental feature of Bloomsbury, it was an essential expression of its ethos.

The impulse to widen the arena in which ideas circulated was not purely philanthropic. It sprung out of a new sense of Cambridge's narrowness and, more generally, of logic's and science's alone. Aesthetics was the sphere in which their limitations were felt most dramatically. Russell himself confessed to Ottoline his sense of incompleteness with respect to the area which was Woolf's more than hers. "I feel myself so rugged & ruthless, & so removed from the whole aesthetic side of life – a sort of logic machine warranted to destroy any ideal that is not very robust," he wrote to her in 1911 (Darroch, *Ottoline*, 90). To Bernard Berenson he wrote, à propos of "A Free Man's Worship," "in my heart, the whole business about Art is external to me – I believe it with my intellect, but in feeling I am a good British Philistine" (*CPBR*, XII, 62). There was not one single response to the question of the "merits [which] belong to science as against literature and art" (*ML*, 38). Moore and Whitehead privileged the aesthetic. Lowe hypothesizes that "Whitehead's emphasis on the aesthetic in his mature philosophy has several sources, of which the chief is his wife Evelyn," adding "it is fair to say at this point that his contact with Roger Fry did something to prepare him for this influence of hers" (*Alfred North Whitehead*, I, 134). Art represents some deficiency of philosophy felt by the philosophers themselves. As the major embodiment of something missing in one way of knowing, it stood for the need to expand knowledge generally. The related turn to theory of knowledge followed.

That the mind can "know" its own private experience is not contestable, but that it can have a knowledge that goes beyond immediate experience, a knowledge of the external world, is subject to doubt. This is the "problem" of knowledge. Leslie Stephen, in a passage we return to shortly, asserts that "we cannot get outside our own consciousness" ("WM?," 135). Russell's whole impulse, at least from the introduction of the notion of "knowledge by description" in 1905 elaborated in *The Problems of Philosophy*, is to deny Stephen's assertion. Such knowledge he insists in 1913 is the "intellectual aim of education, the endeavor to make us see and imagine the world in an objective manner" (*ML*, 37–8). Education "increases through knowledge the wealth and variety of the individual's contacts with the outside world" (*ML*, 37). It produces "citizens of the universe, not only of one walled city at war with all the rest" (*PP*, 161). It propels the individual immured in his private sphere outside its walls to expose him to a world containing other people's experience, ultimately requiring the thought experiment of imagining the world in our absence. "Education" succeeds to the degree that "it gives us a true view of our place in society, of the relation of the whole human society to its non-human environment, and of the nature of the non-human world as it is in itself apart from our desires and interests" (*ML*, 38). The translation of Apostolic discussion from Cambridge to Bloomsbury thus follows the impulse to widen knowledge. It not only educates the outsiders; it transforms the insiders into outsiders, educating the philosopher and not just the person untrained in philosophy. But it aims to educate the latter as well.[21] This is the social aspect of the theory that a knowledge transcending our own experience is possible.

OF MODERN KNOWLEDGE

Her mind was in the state of an intelligent man's in the beginning of the reign of Queen Elizabeth . . . The shape of the earth, the history of the world, how trains worked, or money was invested, what laws were in force, which people wanted what, and why they wanted it, the most elementary idea of a system in modern life – none of this had been imparted to her by any of her professors or mistresses. (Woolf, *The Voyage Out*, 34)

It cannot have been a gain to Plato to have read neither Shakespeare, nor Newton, nor Darwin. (Whitehead, *The Aims of Education*, 47)

The knowledge that sought an audience outside the university was a specifically "modern knowledge," as the Home University Library specified. Indeed, the two concepts, that of a "modern knowledge," "of things that are known and things that are about to be known," as *Jacob's Room*, speaking of Cambridge, puts it (42), and that of a freer, less elitist knowledge, went hand in hand in Bloomsbury's thinking. As an educational project, the Home University Library thus resembled University College, London, where Whitehead came to teach in 1910. In explaining that important move in Whitehead's life, Lowe stresses the interconnection between the fact that, as "the first modern university in Britain," University College "was designed to provide an education in the sciences and modern humane studies, in contrast to the largely classical curricula of Oxford and Cambridge" and its more open admissions – "in 1878 it undertook to grant degrees to women on the same terms as men" (Lowe, *Alfred North Whitehead*, II, 6) and, in general, to "very different" students requiring "a sound education that would fit them for the modern world" (II, 2). It defined "modern knowledge" as centrally mathematical, philosophical and scientific, with an emphasis on physics and astronomy, while "[t]heology had no place in its curriculum" (II, 6).[22] It also included economics, evolution, socialism, history and literature, all aiming at that "enlargement and instruction of men's hearts and minds" Keynes invokes in *The Economic Consequences of the Peace* (297), like Woolf's poor college's "arts" – "medicine, mathematics, music, painting and literature" (*TG*, 34). She approves a Miss Weeton's protest: "'Why are not females permitted to study physics, divinity, astronomy, etc., etc., with their attendants, chemistry, botany, logic, mathematics, &c.?'" (*TG*, 75–6).

Science becomes a paradigm of the Home University Library's "modern knowledge." It conforms to Russell's "ideal" of "an objective view" (*ML*, 38). "The desire for a larger life and wider interests, for an escape from private circumstances . . . is fulfilled by the impersonal cosmic outlook of science as by nothing else" (*ML*, 43). The new logic and mathematics provided a language for science. In his Home University Library *Introduction to Mathematics*, Whitehead had stressed mathematics as "the foundation of exact thought as applied to natural phenomena" (cited in Lowe, *Alfred North Whitehead*, II, 3–4). "He constantly emphasizes the goal of understanding nature," making the book "as much an introduction to mathematical physics as an introduction to mathematics," Lowe writes (II, 4). The modernity of mathematics and logic lies in their ability to make contact with the external world. Logic alone can be self-enclosing, because "it is wholly independent of the accidental facts of the existent world, and can be known, theoretically, without any experience of particular things" (*OKnExW*, 67); logic is unconcerned with facts "about the world in which we happen to find ourselves" (*IMP*, 192).

But logic's generality is also liberating, for the logician can find himself "imprisoned" in the actual empirical world, Russell wrote while himself in prison: "Pure logic, and pure mathematics (which is the same thing) aim at being true, in Leibnizian phraseology, in all possible worlds, not only in this higgledy-piggledy job-lot of a world in which chance has imprisoned us" (*IMP*, 192). Contemplating "the world of being" (*PP*, 100) preserves "a certain lordliness which the logician should preserve" (*IMP*, 192); like "[t]he method" of the "barrister with a philosophic tendency" in *Night and Day* (64), it is "very restful, for it seemed to ignore completely all accidents of human life" (65). Logic's liberating power resides in the very notion of logical possibility. The entertaining of hypotheses is an imaginative act. "By imagining worlds in which" Euclid's axioms "are false, the mathematicians have used logic to loosen the prejudices of common sense" (*PP*, 147). It thus aids in discovering science's counter-intuitive laws. Science is the interface between logic and the world, joining empirical to mathematical reality. Without sense-perception, there is no way out for the logician-philosopher; without logic, there is no knowledge beyond sensation.

Modern knowledge is one which acknowledges the contemporary world. Old William Pepper's learning in *The Voyage Out* almost has the ingredients of modern knowledge: "he knew about a great many things – about mathematics, history, Greek, zoology, economics, and the Icelandic Sagas" (19). But for his knowledge of Greek to be modern it would have to resemble Arthur Verral's (Apostle no. 174), who innovated "the treatment of the classics as literary works of art, rather than texts in a dead language presenting various problems of scholarship" (Levy, *G. E. Moore*, 83). For modernity resided in the notion of the present. "The only use of a knowledge of the past," wrote Whitehead, "is to equip us for the present. No more deadly harm can be done to young minds than by depreciation of the present" (Lowe, *Alfred North Whitehead*, II, 50). Whitehead was dealing "with the fact that an educational revolution was going on," Lowe explains. "Secondary education that is dominated by the classics, as Whitehead's was, is doomed, for classical literature, which he respects, no longer provides a sufficient store of ideas for a liberal education; science has quite altered our world and our ways of thinking." (II, 51). T. S. Eliot's notorious comment that "it is a public misfortune that Mr. Bertrand Russell did not have a classical education" takes sides in a debate about modern knowledge (*Selected Essays*, 486, fn. 1). Russell, defending a scientific education in "The Place of Science in a Liberal Education" (1913), writes: "I have no wish to disparage a classical education. I have not myself enjoyed its benefits, and my knowledge of Greek and Latin authors is derived almost wholly from translations." But "[o]ne defect" he finds "inherent in a wholly classical education – namely, a too exclusive emphasis on the past" (*ML*, 34) – aligns him clearly with Whitehead. *The Voyage Out*'s Mr. Ambrose, classicist, already half philosopher (his "commentary on Aristotle – was it? – appeared at the University Press" [*VO*, 25]), transformed into *To the Lighthouse*'s Mr. Ramsay, philosopher, brings Woolf's university man not only closer to Leslie Stephen but to a thought more in synchrony with the changes occurring in Woolf's intellectual world.

A "classical education," for Russell, was synonymous with "a literary education." It is "generally held indisputable" that "a literary education is superior to one based on science" in "giving that well-informed, impersonal outlook which constitutes culture in the good sense of this much-misused word" (*ML*, 33). This view Russell disputes. But his arguments are all directed to a classical education. We will see later that this is only part of a general tendency of Russell's to counterpose the new philosophy to an art and literature far from new and hence unable to "pierce through everyday surroundings to the essential splendour of contemporary things" (*ML*, 34). Woolf's response will be that a "modern fiction" teaches "the art of understanding other people's lives and minds" (*TG*, 34) as well as their relation to "the non-human environment," making it as enlarging a vision as science. Its modernity requires new aesthetic "principles" on a par with the other *principia*.

These principles owe something to Fry's theory of modern painting. Fry's exhibition likewise exposed to a broader public the new French painting. In its modernist aesthetic, the visual meets the invisible and abstract. Its aim was also educative. What was new in it was understood by those not "wrapt in a cocoon of unreality" (like Woolf's "swaddlings and blanketings of the Cambridge night"): the young and "the uneducated, whose taste had not been perverted by public schools and universities" (*RF*, 164). The "present" is another name for the reality Fry counterposes to academic learning and painting; the young and uneducated are particularly sensitive to it. Contemporary reality will stand for one reality with which we can have acquaintance. Yet there is no contradiction in asserting the "splendour" of the present and making a knowledge which goes beyond the immediately present the ultimate knowledge to which education aspires.

HOURS IN A HOME UNIVERSITY LIBRARY

[H]ow strange it looks, this world of domes and spires, of lecture rooms and laboratories, from our vantage point! (Woolf, *Three Guineas*, 23)

She said that she could never tell which book she wanted to read in bed, poetry, biography, or metaphysics. (Woolf, *Night and Day*, 363)

What external evidence is there that Woolf, daughter of a philosopher, had any exposure to philosophy? What was the extent of her philosophical learning, her understanding of the crucial issues and arguments? For "the daughters of educated men are not members of Cambridge University" (*TG*, 31); they are "restricted to the education of the private house" (*TG*, 37). To answer that question, we begin negatively by recording an obvious fact against which can be weighed more positive evidence: Woolf's lack of any formal philosophical training.[23] This lack might have less significance in a culture in which philosophy were not so contained within a particular program of learning, tied to a class, a sex and its well-defined institutions – the culture of continental Europe, for instance, of

France and Germany, in a tradition where major philosophical works might be addressed to women and connected with literature. In the British tradition and at no time more markedly than in Woolf's formative years, philosophy was a discipline largely confined to those who had passed through either Cambridge or Oxford. "Reading philosophy" in the England of Woolf's period and class was almost nearly synonymous with university study. Philosophy's "academic" nature was reinforced by its growing professionalization: "where Mill, Huxley, and Leslie Stephen had published their articles in the ordinary reviews, Bradley, Moore, and Russell published theirs in the philosophers' professional organ or in the Proceedings of the philosophers' metropolitan forum. This new professional practice of submitting problems and arguments to the expert criticism of fellow craftsmen led to a growing concern with questions of philosophical technique and a growing passion for ratiocinative rigour," Gilbert Ryle writes. "Philosophers had now to be philosophers' philosophers" ("Introduction," 3–4). Moreover, philosophy's dependence on logic and mathematics further determined its confinement to the university.

Woolf's awareness of "her untrained mind" (*TL*, 18), her lack of a university training, indeed, "the fact that I was never at school" (*MB*, 65), is frequently attested to, by herself and others. Lack of a formal education she clearly connects to being a woman and therefore unschooled in mathematics, science and philosophy.[24] She characterizes herself (*Room*, 112) as "[l]ike most uneducated Englishwomen," with both irony and the sense of something missed. Like her writer Bernard in *The Waves*, Woolf might have regretted: "Certain things lie beyond my scope. I shall never understand the harder problems of philosophy" (*W*, 186). Certainly she invoked philosophy cautiously, for "philosophic words, if one has not been educated at a university, are apt to play one false" (*Room*, 113). Perhaps like Mrs. Seal in *Night and Day*, Woolf "lamented her lack of scientific training, and her deficiency in the processes of logic" (263). Perhaps, more disturbing yet, like Lady Bruton in *Mrs. Dalloway*, she felt "[d]ebarred by her sex and some truancy, too, of the logical faculty (she found it impossible to write a letter to the Times)" (275) and heard in her mind the male voice intoning as a general truth Forster's "she had the usual feminine incapacity for grasping philosophy" (*Where Angels Fear to Tread*, 78).[25] At the same time, with the bemused conviction that the reputed feminine weakness in logic touches the sources of fertility of mind, she observes instances of this weakness in herself and others of either sex. It gives rise to the elaborate joke of the sixteen-year-old Virginia Stephen's "Warboys journal," that diary whose "main purpose," according to Quentin Bell, was "to practice the art of writing," on pages she glued to Dr. Isaac Watt's *Logic /or/ the right use of Reason.* "Any other book, almost, would have been too sacred to undergo the desecration that I planned," Bell quotes her as saying (*VW*, I, 65; Rosenbaum, "Philosophical Realism," 354). Yet out of all these admissions of her handicaps in philosophy and her compensatory sense of philosophy's limits, there emerges the acknowledgement on Woolf's part that philosophy also marks a locus of her desire, the longing for some possible world in which she might have gone beyond her limits, that in which her early protagonist Katherine Hilbery studied mathematics and astronomy and in which, if some woman "had left two or three hundred thousand pounds to Fernham, we could have been sitting at our ease tonight and the subject of our talk might have been archaeology, botany, anthropology, physics, the nature of the atom, mathematics, astronomy, relativity, geography" (*Room*, 21).

Woolf's lack of a formal education is not equivalent to ignorance, however, even if her father spent the money he had for university study on Woolf's brothers. "If I said, Look here am I uneducated, because my brothers used all the family funds which is the fact, theyd have said; she has an axe to grind," she writes (*Letters VW*, V, 194–5). It is well known that Leslie Stephen himself provided her with some education. "My father always loved reading aloud," she notes. "When my brothers had gone to school, he still went on reading to my sister and me, but chose more serious books" (*Essays VW*, I, 128). Quentin Bell qualifies Leslie Stephen as "a disastrous teacher of mathematics" to his children, who "made up for it as a teacher of English literature" (*VW*, I, 51), and reports that the "only one of his own children who had aptitude to learn any mathematics from him was Thoby . . . Virginia continued throughout her life to count on her fingers" (I, 26).[26] But the fact that Leslie Stephen attempted to teach his daughter mathematics makes it not implausible that he also instructed her in philosophy. Perhaps, like Clarissa Dalloway, "her favourite reading as a girl was Huxley and Tyndall" (*MrsD*, 117) as Gillian Beer speculates ("The Victorians," 151). Woolf had stayed after his death in Hindhead

House, the home of John Tyndall, scientist and natural philosopher and her father's friend, in 1896 (*Diary*, II, 190), where Russell as a boy had been taken to see Tyndall (*AutoBR*, I, 47).

Woolf's father also gave her access to his own books, so it is not excluded that Woolf "read philosophy" in some other than the technical sense. Allowed to read "any book" in her father's library, "and it was a large library," Woolf wrote (*LettersVW*, V, 91–2), she might have opened at least one book like the "ugly little brown volume" of philosophy she has Sara Pargiter read.[27] We can piece together what precise evidence we have to form a picture of a philosophical learning more extensive and plausible than the sole case of Henri Bergson so often suggested. Writing to Margaret Thwaites, Leonard Woolf asserted of Woolf, with possibly Forster's sense of feminine incapacity for philosophy, "the one type of book she hardly ever read was the philosophical and metaphysical" (*LettersLW*, 486).[28] One wonders if Leonard's attitude to his wife's reading philosophy might not be that of Mr. Ramsay, who "wondered what" his wife "was reading, and exaggerated her ignorance, her simplicity, for he liked to think that she was not clever, not book-learned at all. He wondered if she understood what she was reading" (*TL*, 182).

Hintikka observes that (like her Jacob Flanders) "Young Virginia Woolf spent a great deal of time reading Plato's dialogues. They are as good an introduction to the perenially central problems of philosophy as any. Russell's philosophy is no less a set of footnotes to Plato than ... the rest of Western philosophy is" ("Virginia Woolf," 13).[29] Nor would it be surprising that she should have begun her philosophical education with her father's *History of English Thought in the Eighteenth Century*, which she mentions in her essay "Leslie Stephen."[30] It would have introduced her to Descartes, Locke, Berkeley and Hume. She could have read his *An Agnostic's Apology* as well. She recalls that before her marriage to Leslie Stephen, Julia Stephen had "perhaps read something my father had written. She liked it (he says in the 'Mausoleum Book')" (*MB*, 90), and Woolf imagines her "with a copy of the *Fortnightly*, trying to reason out the case for agnosticism" (*MB*, 91). Or Woolf could have read "his last long book, *The Utilitarians*," with its account of J. S. Mill's philosophy, which she claims Leslie Stephen began on her mother's "assurance" (*MB*, 38). She "read some Berkeley, whom I much admire" (*Diary*, II, 33). "We know that Virginia Woolf read Hume, perhaps not for the first time, in

September 1920," Beer writes ("Hume, Stephen, and Elegy," 80; *Diary*, II, 56). We also know she read in 1908 "several years before her marriage to Leonard Woolf" (Levy, *G. E. Moore*, 274), registering its difficulty and her exhilaration at overcoming it, Moore's *Principia Ethica*.[31] In *Three Guineas*, she cites on several occasions Russell's *The Scientific Outlook*, written for a lay audience (*TG*, 139, 140, 186, fn. 45). She does not say that she "tried Bertie's mathematics," as, she records, Alix Sargant-Florence had (*Diary* I, 152). She nonetheless indicates her cognizance of it. In short, the evidence suggests that whatever philosophical reading Woolf did reflects that "British tradition" David Pears connects Russell to and which, we saw, Leslie Stephen did something to revive.

WITHIN EARSHOT OF A CONVERSATION SOCIETY

I dont get anybody to argue with me now, & I feel the want. I have to delve from books, painfully & all alone, what you get every evening sitting over your fire & smoking your pipe with Strachey, etc. No wonder my knowledge is but scant. There's nothing like talk as an educator I'm sure. (Virginia to Thoby Stephen, May 1903, Q. Bell, *Virginia Woolf*, I, 70)

It is not necessary for Woolf to have "read" philosophy, however, to have early taken from the then current debates something she ultimately found relevant to her purposes. Woolf, we might say, had a knowledge *ex auditu* of philosophy. Such "nonsense" as Forster's undergraduates and Mr. Ramsay talked was part of the intellectual climate in which she developed, that air inhaled in the form of talk: "Talking, talking, talking – as if everything could be talked – the soul itself slipped through the lips in thin silver disks which dissolve in young men's minds like silver, like moonlight." She too "far away" would "remember it," would "come to refresh [herself] again" (*JR*, 40–1).[32] Talk was the form her "university extension" took, the commentary on her interlocutors' reading, just as the "'official' text of *Principia Mathematica* is accompanied by explanatory English, which Whitehead in his letters to Russell calls 'the talk'" (Lowe, *Alfred North Whitehead*, I, 266).

It comes to us, as to the narrator of *Jacob's Room*, as fragments of a conversation historically localizable: it is bounded in time on one end by Woolf's own father's generation and extended beyond the Wittgenstein of the post-war return on the other end, at least to the "good old Cambridge Apostolic discussion" Fry records sometime in the late twenties which Woolf makes representative of many others to "serve to bring back" Fry's "speaking voice" (*RF*, 270–4); it is circumscribed in place by a circle which had at its center some rooms at Cambridge – perhaps off "Neville's Court in Trinity College" which, according to Rantavaara, "came to play an important part as a haven in the mental odyssey" of Cambridge Bloomsbury, "for both Russell and Moore had their rooms on the north side of the court" (*Virginia Woolf and Bloomsbury*, 28), and "Jacob's rooms . . . were in Neville's court" (*JR*, 38). The formal center of that talk was a conversation society, for the Apostles were officially the "Cambridge Conversazione Society." At once the "centre of that centre" of Cambridge education (*RF*, 51), it was also an alternative to it. As Woolf emphasizes of Fry, "it was not the work in lecture-rooms or in laboratories that was most important to him. It was his talk with his friends" (*RF*, 48). Yet "even the talk which had such tremendous results upon the lives and characters of the two Miss Stephens – even talk of this interest and importance is as elusive as smoke" (*MB*, 165). For one thing, the talk of the Apostles, "that very select, very famous and very secret" (*RF*, 50) society, as Woolf never fails to remind us, no matter how free and egalitarian, remained, like Cambridge, exclusive of women. Like the woman narrator outside Jacob's rooms at Cambridge, Woolf could never have been present at a meeting. For the society's "records are private," she observes (*RF*, 51), (and remained so until around 1980); hence an "outsider," *Three Guineas*' name for "woman," can only hope it "permissible . . . to infer" (*RF*, 51) the topics of Apostolic talk.[33] Most of this elusive talk thus either having disappeared unrecorded or been reconstructed on hearsay, our task is to piece together the remnants.

It came first as that "table talk which Virginia Woolf heard all the time she was growing up" which Wittgenstein invokes (Rhees, *Ludwig Wittgenstein*, 207). This is the Cambridge dons' conversation in *The Voyage Out*:

"He left a commentary. Hopeless muddle, I'm told."

"The man had really great abilities," said Ridley.

"His introduction to Jellaby holds its own still," went on Mr. Pepper, "which is surprising, seeing how text-books change."

"There was a theory about the planets, wasn't there?" asked Ridley.

"A screw loose somewhere, no doubt of it," said Mr. Pepper, shaking his head . . .

"There was a book, wasn't there?" Ridley enquired.

"There *was* a book, but there never *will* be a book," said Mr. Pepper with such fierceness that both ladies looked up at him. (*VO*, 15–16)

This talk comes as "[t]he gruff murmur" which assures Mrs. Ramsay, "though she could not hear what was said . . ., that the men were happily talking" (*TL*, 27); as with Charles Tansley's philosophy dissertation, its "subject was now the influence of something upon somebody" (*TL*, 22), or "the influence of somebody upon something" (*TL*, 101–2).[34] Always in the novels' background, some man "went on talking, about settlements, and teaching, and working men, and helping our own class, and lectures" (*TL*, 22), saying, like Charles Tansley to Mr. Ramsay,

who had won this, who had won that, who was a "first-rate man" at Latin verses, who was "brilliant but I think fundamentally unsound," who was undoubtedly the "ablest fellow in Balliol," who had buried his light temporarily at Bristol or Bedford, but was bound to be heard of later when his Prolegomena, of which Mr. Tansley had the first pages in proof with him if Mr. Ramsay would like to see them, to some branch of mathematics or philosophy saw the light of day. That was what they talked about. (*TL*, 15)

That talk in "the ugly academic jargon, that rattled itself off so glibly" (*TL*, 22) made the minds of the women of Woolf's mother's generation wander, the talk at the other end of the table that Mrs. Ramsay listens to absent-mindedly during *To the Lighthouse*'s dinner-party, the talk that Julia Stephen permitted and forbade at the dinner table. For "[e]ach of the ladies, being after the fashion of their sex, highly trained in promoting men's talk without listening to it, could think – about the education of children, about the use of fog sirens in an opera – without betraying herself" (*VO*, 17). But it was picked up and recorded by the daughter, first as the subject of satire. For it was the talk of the old Cambridge, "oblivious of all tumult: they were in Cambridge, and it was probably about the year 1875" (*VO*, 18).

But there was something else in it, something abstract, some mathematical problem that passed, despite the prohibition against mathematics at table, sign of a knowledge of which the daughter was deprived. For abstractness was the positive quality salvaged from academic talk for another, freer, more inclusive, more modern Apostles' talk; "the cause of talk" (*MB*, 189) required debate and logical argument. James Strachey recalled some Apostolic topics; "[w]hen I was a brother," he wrote to Michael Holroyd, "Maynard,

Norton and Hawtrey . . . had constant hard headed arguments about such things as sense-perception or truth or internal relations; and Whitehead, Sanger, Russell and Moore turned up often enough to affect the sort of conversation" (*Lytton Strachey*, 239, fn. 31). It was this abstractness that Virginia Stephen, left behind in the home library, longed for and was jealous of, its content "mostly a matter of guess work" (*JR*, 73). For it forms a hiatus in her aural development between her father's talk and Bloomsbury. Recalling the parties George Duckworth had forced her to attend when still living at home, Woolf remarks: "How strange it was to think that somewhere, there was a world where people did not go to parties – where they perhaps discussed pictures – books – philosophy – But it was not our world" (*MB*, 135). Within the old world, Jack Hills (who married Stella Duckworth, Woolf's half-sister), by contrast, is valued, because: "He read philosophy too; Nettleship, the Oxford philosopher, had been a kind of god to him . . . he tried very laboriously to explain Nettleship's philosophy; he lent us the book; it was at Warboys that I remember him explaining Plato to me and Nessa and Marny Vaughan" (*MB*, 103).

Bloomsbury began, we recall, in Woolf's version, not simply with her and her sister's inclusion in the conversation, but with the pronouncing of an abstract term, a universal: whether the subject was "beauty," "good" or "reality," "it was some abstract question that now drew out all our forces" (*MB*, 189–90; cf. Levy, *G. E. Moore* 115). It developed by logical argumentation: "Never have I listened so intently to each step and half-step in an argument" (*MB*, 189–90). Nor did Woolf merely listen; she participated fully: "Never have I been at such pains to sharpen and launch my own little dart. And then what joy it was when one's own contribution was accepted. No praise has pleased me more than Saxon's saying . . . that he thought I had argued my case very cleverly" (*MB*, 190).[35] Bell, Strachey (Apostle no. 239), Hawtrey (Apostle no. 235) and Sydney-Turner (Apostle no. 240), she adds, "had no 'manners' in the Hyde Park Gate sense. They criticised our arguments as severely as their own" (*MB*, 191). By contrast, with those Adrian Stephen called "Hyde Park Gaters," Woolf says,

we were not asked to use our brains much. Here we used nothing else. And part of the charm of those Thursday evenings was that they were astonishingly abstract. It was not only that Moore's book had set us all discussing philosophy, art, religion; it was that the atmosphere . . . was abstract in the extreme. (*MB*, 168)

Apostolic in form, "the word 'beauty,'" "incautiously" introduced by Vanessa and to which "one of the young men would lift his head slowly and say, 'It depends on what you mean by beauty'" (*MB*, 168), Woolf makes the inaugural word of the Bloomsbury talk, the sisters' contribution subjected to the brothers' logic. In that word, philosophy and art, men and women, meet. But the word "reality," point of reference for Fry more than "beauty," turns out to be no less important. "From such discussions Vanessa and I got probably much the same pleasure that undergraduates get when they meet friends of their own for the first time" (*MB*, 190).

The title "conversation society" also encompassed all the other formal and informal philosophical discussion societies, such as the Aristotelian Society that met in London. If from them ultimately came written works – the amount of published philosophical work originally delivered as public lectures, not just in Cambridge or Oxford, but in London as well, is striking[36] – all of their authors, even the most antisocial, like the Wittgenstein who retreated to a room of his own in Norway (where Moore had to drop in on skis for a bit of talk), participated in that continuous discussion which was a kind of thinking aloud, so that an outsider within its radius need not have read its writings to have picked up bits of the conversation.

Some of her aural knowledge certainly came to Woolf in the guise of formal lectures. Her letters and journals testify that her milieu attended such lectures and that she herself was sometimes present. She writes, "Bertie lectures on Tuesdays" and "I went to one lecture," no doubt Russell on pacifism (*Letters VW*, II, 78).[37] She renounces hearing Russell lecture as part of the series which became *The Analysis of Mind*, asserting "I preferred the songsters of Trafalgar Square" (*Diary*, I, 270). "The touchstone of virtue . . . now is whether you attend Bertie's lectures or not," she comments a week later (*Diary*, I, 273). Whether she attended others in the series she does not say. There is, however, one record – in a February 4, 1913 letter of Lytton Strachey's – of Woolf's presence at a supremely philosophical event in her first year of marriage, when she heard Karin Costelloe, her future sister-in-law Karin Stephen, read a paper to the Aristotelian Society.[38] Through Strachey's account we glimpse Woolf in an audience mixing philosophers and non-philosophers:

There was the strangest collection of people . . . sitting round a long table with Bertie in the middle, presiding, like some Inquisitor, and Moore opposite him, bursting with fat and heat, . . . and Woolf and Virginia crouching, and a strange crew of old cranky Metaphysicians . . . and Karin herself, next to Bertie . . . Bertie, no longer the Grand Inquisitor, but the Joconde, with eyelids a little weary, delivered some pungent criticisms, but the excitement came with Moore, I wish you'd been there . . . the intellectual display [was] terrific . . . Of course it was the very opposite of brilliant – appallingly sensible, and so easy to understand that you wondered why on earth no one else had thought of it. (In Holroyd, *Lytton Strachey*, 523)[39]

The partially unprofessional cast of the audience, which Strachey is at pains to convey, conjures up a philosophical discussion in which the non-philosopher can participate, if only as auditor. The paper was no doubt Karin Costelloe's February 3, 1913 "VI – What Bergson Means by 'Interpenetration,'" a paper marked by Russell's vocabulary. Woolf's Bergson was filtered through Cambridge.

The participants in the endless Bloomsbury talk included the eminent figures of British philosophy; Woolf's friends and acquaintances, she met them as intellectual peers. She published reviews in journals like *The Athenaeum* (cf. June 20, 1919) with Russell, among others. There are numerous records of the presence of Russell and, later, Moore, at intimate gatherings which included Woolf as well. She knew both Whitehead and his wife.[40] She shared a house with Keynes in 1911 while he was finishing *A Treatise on Probability*, mentioned in *The Problems of Philosophy*'s Preface. Philosophical questions were no doubt also discussed in Woolf's brother Adrian's household. His wife Karin was someone Woolf did not simply hear on one formal occasion but saw informally. (Woolf stayed with her, for example, between January 19 and 23, 1911.) Eames calls Karin Stephen Russell's "niece and philosophic protégée." Her letters to Russell furnish one of the "sources for our knowledge" of the development of the 1914 theory (*CPBR* VII, xvii–xviii). The co-editors of *Theory of Knowledge* speculate that the manuscript was perhaps folded to be mailed to Karin (*CPBR* VII, 218). Later, Virginia and Leonard Woolf even had some social encounters with Wittgenstein, though she "did not go to his lectures" (*LettersLW*, 539). References to the two discussions in Woolf's presence of Wittgenstein appear in her letters.[41] Finally, we should not forget that Leonard Woolf was Apostle no. 241.

Mostly we can only guess at what Woolf heard and said. But at times we do hear her conversing, perhaps even daring to disagree, with one of these philosophers. She records an encounter with Russell in 1924 in which he delivers an opinion of Moore "'[w]hen he first came up to Cambridge'" – he "'was the most wonderful creature in the whole world . . . We believed in Berkeley' (perhaps) 'Suddenly, . . . something happened to him and his work. *Principia Ethica* was nothing like so good as his Essay on Judgment (?).'" What she sets down reveals a familiarity with Cambridge philosophy's important titles. Her question mark might record either uncertainty or skepticism; her parenthetical "perhaps" after "Berkeley" suggests her reservations but also her knowledge of the subject (*Diary*, II, 293–4). In her diary, she complains that, not having slept well while awaiting Leonard's return with Moore from the Apostles' annual dinner, "consequently I was too muddled next morning to follow his [Moore's] explanation of Berkeley" (*Diary*, II, 49), revealing that she had heard Moore discuss Berkeley on at least one occasion, while testifying to her sense of her own deficiencies. (Leonard Woolf claimed "that muddle . . . will cause Moore almost physical pain" [*An Autobiography*, 25].) On another occasion, a discussion of Realism and Idealism in Woolf's presence elicits from her the ironic comment: "[Charles] Mauron and Roger [Fry] last night confuted Leonard and Oliver and proved beyond a doubt the non-existence of everything but Idea. So there" (*Letters VW*, IV, 57). Such accounts provide anecdotal evidence that Woolf, as Hintikka puts it, "could easily have acquired through the almost subconscious osmotic processes of conversation and listening" ("Virginia Woolf," 13) the philosophical ideas then current.

THE INFLUENCE OF SOMETHING UPON SOMEBODY

I do not think that Wildon Carr had any influence of importance on anybody . . . I think it probable that Virginia Woolf . . . met Wildon Carr, but I am quite certain he cannot have influenced her since no one in philosophical circles took him seriously. (Letter of Bertrand Russell to Sverre Lyngstad, 1957, *Collected Papers*, VI, 342–3)

How is it that a tacit intellectual co-operation is established between minds placed far apart . . . even when we are unable to point to any direct and overt means of transmission? How far may we believe in the apparent unity of that shifting chaos of speculations of more or less independent thinkers, which forms what we vaguely describe as public opinion, or the spirit of the age? (Stephen, *History of English Thought*, 2)

In "the influence on me of the Cambridge Apostles" (*MB*, 80), the paternal influence neutralized in the brotherhood[42] which, in an earlier generation, had never admitted Leslie Stephen to its ranks (*MB*, 108; *VW*, I, 7; Annan, *Godless Victorian*, 29, 32), was also the modernization of the philosophical patrimony. It is Moore and Russell who will take certain problems Stephen rediscovers in the English tradition and subject them to what Whitehead calls "the genius of the modern world" (*Aims*, 6) in the cause of the new Realism. "It is . . . little short of amazing that study after recent study of Virginia Woolf should fail even to mention Russell and Moore," Hintikka writes ("Virginia Woolf," 5); it is equally amazing that Leslie Stephen as philosopher is so infrequently mentioned.

What was it that Woolf took in of the "Cambridge Apostolic" (*RF*, 270) debates? Andrew Ramsay in *To the Lighthouse* identifies it as the problem of knowledge reintroduced after 1910. Woolf there makes it define the "work" of her father. It is surely plausible she had once asked her brother non-Apostle Thoby, "far more philosophic . . . than Adrian" (*MB*, 126), the same question Lily Briscoe asks Andrew Ramsay (who recalls Thoby) about Mr. Ramsay's "work" (38) and received the same answer. The terms of her familiarity with the problem of knowledge in the British tradition are traceable to the introductory chapter, "The Philosophical Basis," of Leslie Stephen's *History of English Thought* (I, 1–73), "said by some to be his masterpiece," Woolf writes (*CE*, IV, 71). Perhaps it is the model for the book in which William Bankes thinks Ramsay "had made a definite contribution to philosophy" (391); certainly that was Stephen's own assessment of his book. Another source could be the chapter "What Is Materialism?," given to the London Ethical Society in 1886 and printed in *An Agnostic's Apology* in 1893.

Whether or not she actually read these texts, they also "serve to bring back the speaking voice" (*RF*, 274). Introducing "the philosophical basis" of English thought through a historical survey from Descartes to Reid, Hartley and Monboddo, *History of English Thought* explicitly "set out to rescue the English empiricists, Locke, Berkeley and Hume," from being consigned to insignificance, Annan claims (*Godless Victorian*, 223). The same philosophers appear by name in Woolf's work, e.g., "Locke, Hume, Berkeley" are mentioned in *To the Lighthouse* (70). Orlando listens to someone "determined to write philosophy" (*O*, 258) "in an age when words are growing daily so scanty in comparison with ideas," and their interpretation becomes a problem "when one has just read Bishop Berkeley's philosophy for the tenth time" (*O* 258–9).[43]

Stephen presents the problem of knowledge, like Russell, as that of bridging the gap between matter and mind:

> Here then we have our realities. The antithesis between subject and object is represented by the two absolute substances – the soul and matter; . . . How are we to conceive of any reciprocal action between the two or of one upon the other? . . . yet the definitions show that matter cannot be brought into relation to spirit, whilst all scientific knowledge rests on their mutual connection. (*HET*, 25–6)

The formulation is, of course, classic, and can be encountered in any number of sources, just as is Stephen's attachment of it to the problem of perception and the evidence of the senses. But if the classic terms were likely supplied Woolf within the Stephen household, the evidence of the novels points to a more contemporary theoretical framework. Stephen's formulations are necessary, but only the theory of knowledge Moore and Russell developed a generation after is a sufficient source.

From Stephen to Moore and Russell defines the extent of the influence on the basis of the internal evidence. This is exactly what we would predict from the external evidence thus far presented. There is a continuity between Stephen, Moore and Russell that traces British philosophy's line of development from the nineteenth to the twentieth century, one reflected in Ryle's selection of exemplary philosophers to contrast two generations in a passage cited above: "Mill, Huxley, and Leslie Stephen" with "Bradley, Moore, and Russell" ("Introduction," 4). Keynes, writing that "I have been much influenced by W. E. Johnson, G. E. Moore, and Bertrand Russell, that is to say by Cambridge," similarly stresses that it "continues in direct succession the English tradition of Locke, Berkeley and Hume, of Mill and Sidgwick," although Stephen's name is missing. Despite "divergences of doctrine," they "are united" in conceiving "their subject as a branch rather of science than of the creative imagination" (*A Treatise on Probability*, 1). Stephen "is a minor figure in the British empirical school that descends from Locke through Hume and John Stuart Mill to Russell," writes Annan (*His Thought*, vi).

Moore's and Russell's theory of knowledge returns to and "reformulates" this native tradition Stephen revived. Hylton writes that during the first decade of the twentieth century, "Russell's views shift, from a view which has nothing at all in common with the tradition of British Empiricism" – from Hegelian Idealism – "to a view which shares some important elements with that tradition" (*Russell*, 9). Stephen's *History of English Thought*, not "entirely superseded because of its grasp of the broader contexts of thought" (Schneewind, "Leslie Stephen," 14), forms, along with "What Is Materialism?," a strong link between the "British Tradition in Philosophy" and the name of Russell Pears conjoins to it, furnishing examples of the concepts and terms from that "English thought" circulating in Cambridge when Moore and Russell arrive on the scene. The echoes of Stephen's texts in Russell are explicable by their common source in Berkeley, Hume and others, and establish a shared philosophical language, one that is "closer to home" for Woolf herself. This is the weak claim, sufficient for our argument. In Russell's example of "my seeing the sun" versus the sensible data seen (*PP*, 51), we hear Stephen, echoing Hume, on "I see the sun" in contrast to "I have certain sensations of light and heat" (*HET*, 45). In *An Outline of Philosophy*, Russell's "I see a triangle," like Stephen's, is of Berkeley's "abstract idea of a triangle" as "but the idea of a particular triangle regarded as representative" (*HET*, 46). When Russell says "[t]wo objects may be connected in the mental world by the association of ideas, and in the physical world by the law of gravitation" (*TK*, 15) and "[t]he law of gravitation, for example, is a physical law, while the law of association is a psychological law" (*Mind*, 25–6), his analogy resembles Stephen's in his discussion of Hume: "Association is in the mental what gravitation is in the natural world" (*HET*, 44). The point here is not that it is necessarily Stephen's words Russell has in mind, but that Stephen's formulation is representative of a Cambridge thinking from which Russell drew his version of and vocabulary for the history of philosophy.[44]

There is a stronger claim possible – that Stephen's formulation linked Russell's, Moore's and Whitehead's "solution." Stephen stated the problem in such a way that, on more than one occasion, the Russellian solution is traceable in the very text that argued its insolubility. That solution transforms a concept and term from Berkeley which Stephen's reading emphasizes and turns it into the answer to Idealism: the "unperceived perceptions" which for Berkeley (and Stephen) represent a logical contradiction philosophical Realism is unable to surmount are made by Russell into a logical possibility, that of "unperceived perspectives." Registered by such perspectives are the unsensed sensations Russell calls "sensibilia." *Sensibile-ia*, the *OED* (second edition, 1989) states, was a "term popularised by Bertrand Russell." But it occurs in Stephen's entry under "Berkeley" in the *DNB* (vol. II, 354).[45] Moreover, the notion of a sensibile which Russell disengages from that of a sensation will have Moore's notion of a sense-datum as an intermediate stage. The theory of sense-data which Moore presents in 1910 with its examples of patches of blue and yellow, and which is a link to Fry's theory of Impressionist color, is adumbrated in "The Refutation of Idealism" of 1903. Its language has echoes of Stephen's "What is Materialism?," reissued in 1903 with the second edition of *An Agnostic's Apology.* Like Stephen and like Mr. Ramsay, who promised "to talk some nonsense to the young men of Cardiff about Locke, Hume" (*TL*, 70), Russell gave his re-readings of Berkeley, Hume, Locke and Descartes – almost the "five philosophers" Woolf refers to in *The Voyage Out* (208),[46] turning certain of Stephen's emphases into key concepts.

The dominant role of Russell's thought for our reading of Woolf is not in conformity with the standard view, which gives primacy to "[t]he tremendous influence of Moore and his book," *Principia Ethica*, "upon us," i.e., Bloomsbury, as Leonard Woolf put it (*An Autobiography*, 93). But the evidence suggests that Woolf focussed not on Moore on "the Nature of Good" (*VO*, 33), as is commonly asserted, but on Moore on the "Reality of Matter" (*VO*, 33). Both were the subject of the book Mrs. Ambrose reads in *The Voyage Out.* It is clear from her joke to Vanessa that Moore's "followers," to whom she has just been referring, perhaps "no longer exist though" (*Diary*, II, 112), that Woolf associates him first with "The Refutation of Idealism" and the "huge branch of philosophy which is concerned with the different ways in which we know things" and "[h]ow . . . we *know* anything at all" and not with the ethics, which is "quite different" (*SomeMain*, 39–40).

Levy sees the claim of Moore's primacy encapsulated in the idea "that what Moore offered was a set of 'truths' – and, of course, the arguments that validated them." Its "complement" is "that Moore's followers, Leonard and Virginia Woolf, Lytton Strachey, Clive Bell and Keynes himself . . . believed these 'truths' and accepted Moore's arguments for them" (*G. E. Moore*, 6). This view, which Levy contests, assigns the vaguest content to these "truths." We will implicitly address Levy's counter-claim that "Moore's influence," at least upon

Woolf, "was not importantly doctrinal at all, but *personal*" (7) in arguing the relevance of Moore's epistemology for Woolf. The emphasis on the personal is more "orthodox" and less "radical" than Levy makes it seem (8). The precise content of the relevant "truths" is lacking because they are not to be found in "the book" invariably consulted, *Principia Ethica.*

That it should be Russell's thought, stimulated by Moore's treatment of "some main problems of philosophy," which comes to play a role should not be surprising in the light of Russell's incontestable dominance in Cambridge philosophy during Bloomsbury's early years – "Bertie in the middle, presiding," alternatively Inquisitor and sphinx-like Joconde. Quentin Bell comments: "Cambridge at that time had an enormous amount to give; there had, as Leonard Woolf says, been 'an extraordinary outburst of philosophical brilliance.' M'Taggart, Whitehead, Bertrand Russell and G. E. Moore were all Fellows of Trinity; of these, Russell and Moore were immensely important to the young men" (*Bloomsbury,* 24). Russell's contacts with "Bloomsbury" were important enough for him to be considered by some a member. A greater Russellian influence in Bloomsbury is not in contradiction to the testimonies of its various members. Clive Bell, rejecting Moore as "the all-pervading, the binding influence," comments "it must be remembered that Bertrand Russell, though no one has ever called him 'Bloomsbury,' appeared to be a friend and was certainly an influence" (*Old Friends,* 133).[47] "It was only for us, those who were active in 1903, that Moore completely ousted McTaggart, Dickinson, Russell," Keynes wrote in *Two Memoirs* (in Levy, *G. E. Moore,* 240). In his Memoir written before leaving for Spain in 1937, Julian Bell ascribes to the Apostles' meetings of a later generation "an intellectual climate of Bloomsbury *un peu passé* . . . In the background were the two *Principias,*"[48] thus giving equal place, as Leonard Woolf did, to Russell's (and Whitehead's) logic alongside Moore's ethics (*Julian Bell,* 21).[49] Stephen Spender on Bloomsbury likewise lists "Bertrand Russell . . . amongst their friends and colleagues who discussed politics, economics, philosophy, history and literature with them" (*World Within World,* 141). It would not be necessary to insist on Russell's importance if the subsequent course of British philosophy, marked by the influence of the later Wittgenstein and relegating Russell's epistemology to the philosophical past, did not minimize it. It only suffices, however, to read the history of Wittgenstein's early thought to restore Russell's centrality. In the *Tractatus*, "Russell's problems" frequently "were Wittgenstein's starting point" (McGuinness, *Wittgenstein*, 313).[50] It should not be surprising then that, insofar as Virginia Woolf confronts philosophy in her work, she should come up against the thought of Russell, without always recognizing the source. "Russell exerted in many ways a remarkable influence on his friends," Hintikka states ("Virginia Woolf," 5) There is the added evidence of a rivalry between Moore and Russell over their influence with the Apostles (Levy, *G. E. Moore*, 206). The partisans of Moore alleged Russell's jealousy. Wittgenstein's election to the Apostles is the infamous case, with Lytton Strachey making the charges. Recent commentators tend to exonerate Russell. Leonard Woolf, a partisan of Moore, is not unbiased in insisting on his pre-eminence for Woolf.[51] The fact that Fry, we will see, preferred Russell and that, according to Quentin Bell, Woolf suspected Leonard of "a lack of sympathy for Roger" (*VW*, II, 214), might make her skeptical about Leonard's object of reverence.

A greater importance of Russell over Moore in Woolf can be read in the absence of certain of Moore's preoccupations and the presence of recognizably Russellean ones. G. J. Warnock identifies several broad differences in Moore's and Russell's thinking which furnish guidelines. (See also Passmore, *Hundred Years*, 203–41.) For one thing, we put forth the perhaps surprising hypothesis that Moore's preoccupation with meaning (cf. Warnock, *English Philosophy*, 14) finds no really significant echo in Woolf, except as an insistence on clarity and a horror of "muddled thinking" (L. Woolf, *Sowing*, 136). Leonard's claim that she was "deeply affected by the astringent influence of Moore and the purification of that divinely cathartic question which echoed through the Cambridge Courts of my youth . . .: 'What do you mean by that?'" (*BeAg*, 25) finds support in the statement "It depends what you mean by beauty" Woolf makes initiate the Bloomsbury talk (*MB*, 189) and in the question "What is meant by 'reality'?" (*Room*, 113). But the ideal of stylistic purity can as well be traced to Russellian love of logical economy and what Ayer calls the "lucidity of his style" (*Russell and Moore*, 9), the "hard, dry, knobbly, masculine" prose Julian Bell praises in "Bertie Russell" as stylist (*Julian Bell*, 104).[52] We will maintain it is Russell's symbolic logic, so different from ordinary language and able "to span deep abysses with a few simple words" (*ND*, 64), which exerts a key if limited influence on Woolf's thinking about language. This is not to claim that Woolf could use that logical language, but its development will introduce into literature a problem other than that of meaning: the possibility of symbols without meaning.

Although together Moore and Russell represent the turn to Realism, both Warnock and Passmore stress an important division between them: for Moore reality corresponds to what common sense believes and for Russell, to the claims of science, especially physics. "In his *Autobiography*," Passmore writes, "Moore makes a confession which gives us an important clue" about "his influence: 'I do not think,' he writes, 'that the world or the sciences ever suggested to me any philosophical problems.'" What did were "things which other philosophers have said about the world or about natural science" (*Hundred Years*, 203). While "the unshakeable ordinariness of his [Moore's] own assertions makes us most keenly aware of the extreme oddness of the views he objected to," Warnock says (*English Philosophy*, 21), Moore "found the view we all hold, the 'Common Sense view of the world,' to be perfectly unsurprising, undistressing, quite certainly true" (42). By contrast, "Russell's philosophy," Passmore comments, "moves in an atmosphere thick with science" (*Hundred Years*, 204). Holding that "common sense leaves us completely in the dark as to the true intrinsic nature of physical objects," he felt it not justified to reject any opinion "merely because it strikes us as strange." That what a philosopher "offers as the truth is strange ought not to be made a ground of objection to his opinion" (*PP*, 38). Russell concludes *The Problems of Philosophy*'s first chapter by observing that philosophy justifies treating a common object, e.g. a table, with

> the most complete liberty of conjecture. Leibniz tells us that it is a community of souls: Berkeley tells us it is an idea in the mind of God; sober science, scarcely less wonderful, tells us it is a vast collection of electric charges in violent motion.
>
> Among these surprising possibilities, doubt suggests that perhaps there is no table at all. (16)

Warnock finds Russell, "[u]nlike Moore," anxious "to emphasize that his findings would be very curious and surprising." Infinite numbers, which cause Moore uneasiness (*SomeMain*, 217), seem, Russell says, "to contradict logic, but in fact they only contradict confirmed mental habits" (*OKnExW*, 187). He would never have dreamed of defending Common Sense," thinking it "a denial of philosophy." "What philosophy had to reckon with, in Russell's opinion, was not Common Sense, but science." It "must be adequate to the formulation of definite scientific knowledge" but

> need not, and indeed would not, look familiar and ordinary to ordinary men. "The point of philosophy is to start with something so simple as not to seem worth stating, and to end with something so paradoxical that no one will believe it." [*LK*, 193] Mathematics and science after all held plenty of surprises; surely it was proper that philosophy should hold some as well. (Warnock, *English Philosophy*, 27)

Preoccupied with the statement "that's a table" (*TL*, 300), very like Moore's "This is a hand" in his later "Proof of an External World," Woolf was also concerned to reconcile it with another proposition, "It's a miracle," to reconcile Moore with Russell. It is never common sense which for her captures the ultimate truth about the world; if her knowledge of science remained the layperson's, science's mere existence sufficed to alter the landscape for her. "Flying over London," Woolf brings about a Copernican Revolution, dislodging "[h]abit," which had fixed the earth immovably in the centre of the imagination" (*CE*, II, 176). In responding to Russell's reality, she was also responding to Leslie Stephen's, who resembled Russell more than Moore in a persistent reference to science.[53]

Warnock points to the "neutral, disinterested" aspect of Russell's philosophy. "Russell was suspicious," he writes, of the way philosophers "obtained, and some deliberately sought satisfaction from" their theories, something he found "grossly 'unscientific.'" He objected to "the results of philosophical inquiry" being "influenced by the needs and wishes of the inquirer – that for instance McTaggart's 'cheerful' conclusions were esteemed in part at least for the comfort they offered, and not solely because they appeared on investigation to be true" (*Hundred Years*, 26). Berkeley, Warnock's example of a philosopher invested in his opposition to materialism by contrast with Hume, more "neutrally interested" (*English Philosophy*, 29–30), Russell likewise suspects of reducing the world to the reassuring dimensions of human knowledge and desire.[54] The Idealist assumption is that reality is knowable and knowledge modeled on perception. The "matter" of science, essentially unknowable in this sense, is hence unreal (*PP*, 43). Russell's is the "scientific ideal of entirely neutral, disinterested inquiry, altogether unswayed by such irrelevant factors as a desire for consolation, by religious beliefs, or by moral convictions" (Warnock, *English*

Philosophy, 26). Once more, Russell resembles no one more than Leslie Stephen standing over his wife's grave, refusing false consolation. Only when the philosopher has the courage to reject "the consolations of philosophy" posing as a substitute religion will he earn Woolf's admiration. Russell and Woolf alike will choose rather an ethics of the impersonal. This emphasis can be set against *Principia Ethica*'s conclusion "that personal affections and aesthetic enjoyments include all the greatest, and by far the greatest, goods we can imagine" (189) – and the frequent assertion that "what Virginia Woolf symbolized, what she and Bloomsbury derived from Moore was an emphasis upon 'the growth of the private virtues – that is, of personal relations and the creative instincts'" (Annan, in Levy, *G. E. Moore*, 296). The question of the relative influence of Russell and Moore will thus hinge in part on the extent to which an ethic of personal relations coexists in Woolf's thought with an impersonal ideal.

A final question is the relative accessibility of the two philosophers' work to a person untrained in philosophy. The common assumption would decide in favor of the author of *Principia Ethica* over the author of *Principia Mathematica*. But Moore's philosophical exchanges seem to have been confined, until at least late in life, to the narrow circle of Cambridge men, mostly Apostles, in this like Wittgenstein, whose "philosophy," Leonard Woolf wrote, "is so difficult that it would not influence any but the professional philosopher" (*LettersLW*, 539). Although Woolf read *Principia Ethica* in 1908, there is no record that she met Moore until he stayed with the Woolfs in June 1914. Levy observes that Leonard "never commented on what happened at Moore's and Virginia Woolf's infrequent meetings." On the basis of Moore's diary entries for his first visits to the Woolfs, Levy concludes: "If Moore and Mrs Woolf had a great deal to talk about it seems not to have struck Moore as noteworthy enough to record" (*G. E. Moore*, 275).[55] Moore's unintellectual relation to Woolf might be ascribed to an uneasiness with women on the part of a man who did not marry until he was forty-three and to a professionalism which he has been attributed with bringing to philosophy. "Moore," A. J. Ayer comments, "is a philosopher's philosopher" (*Russell and Moore*, 4);[56] he is seconded by Passmore. For all his defense of common sense and "utter clarity and utter simplicity," Passmore writes, "the point and the method of Moore's philosophy are scarcely intelligible to the ordinary educated reader" (*Hundred Years*, 204). Passmore quotes

W. B. Yeats to T. S. Moore: "'I find your brother extraordinarily obscure'" as "the reaction of a literary man, who expects the philosopher to discuss large questions in a large way," adding that "the scientist is likely to be no less disconcerted" (204).

Russell, on the other hand, seems to have had enough interest in Woolf to invite her to visit as early as 1908.[57] She records an encounter with him at a dinner party on December 3, 1921, concluding her account of the conversation "I said that I disagreed with much of this. Yet perhaps I did not expect very much to happen from talking to Bertie. I felt that he had talked to so many people. Thus I did not ask him to come here – I enjoyed it though a good deal" (*Diary*, II, 148). Meeting "the celebrated Mr [Bertrand] Russell" again in 1924 "at Karin [Costelloe Stephens]'s" (*Diary*, II, 293), she concludes,

> One does not like him. Yet he is brilliant of course; perfectly outspoken; familiar; talks of his bowels; likes people; & yet & yet – He disapproves of me perhaps? He has not much body of character. This luminous vigorous mind seems attached to a flimsy little car, like that on a large glinting balloon. His adventures with his wives diminish his importance.[58] . . . Nevertheless, I should like the run of his headpiece. We parted at the corner of the Square; no attempt to meet again. (*Diary*, II, 295)

The series of non-sequiturs resembles in form Lily Briscoe's assessment of Mr. Ramsay. What is important is the fascination with the philosopher and the desire to see the world from his perspective. It mirrors Russell's desire to make philosophy available to the non-philosopher and his interest in philosophical exchanges with women.

Documenting competing claims about philosophical influence I subordinate, however, to demonstrating which philosophical system provides a convincing reading of Woolf's *oeuvre.* The relevance of Russell's 1914 theory of knowledge, itself formed by his intellectual relations with Moore, Whitehead and Wittgenstein, is thus the ultimate evidence offered. But if we cannot be "certain" that Russell's is the most relevant philosophical influence, then we can adopt Apostolic agnosticism and say that the relevant one is a group of philosophic positions rather like Moore's notion of a group whose members show a resemblance consisting not in the possession of any common property but only a disjunctive one, namely that "each *either* is *or* exactly resembles any one of them you like to take" (*SomeMain*, 396). Woolf's philosopher is either Russell or he is

Moore. We can call the group containing members with disjunctive properties "the Apostles." Alternately, we can invoke Russell's well-known facility in absorbing and systematizing other people's ideas and take him finally as the synthesizer of Cambridge-Bloomsbury philosophical thought.[59]

AGNOSTICISM AND KNOWLEDGE

You may either spin formulae out of your brain indefinitely, and be perfectly certain that each is legitimately evolved from its predecessors, but find after all that your whole certainty comes to this, that A is A; or you may give up the attempt at certainty, and obtain any number of propositions which have the merit of being applicable to facts, but the demerit of being radically uncertain. (Stephen, *History of English Thought*, 70)

I came to philosophy through mathematics, or rather through the wish to find some reason to believe in the truth of mathematics. From early youth, I had an ardent desire to believe that there can be such a thing as knowledge, combined with a great difficulty in accepting much that passes as knowledge. (Russell, *Logic and Knowledge*, 323)

Despite the possible borrowing of terms, however, the admission of unperceived perceptions as a logical possibility marks the separation between Stephen's presentation of the classic problem and Moore's and Russell's hypothetical solution. This is because Stephen's *History* is also a kind of agnostic's apology: he repeats "from A to Z" (*TL*, 55) every argument for and against the alternatives, Realism or Idealism, and concludes "no answer can be given." The problem of knowledge resists: "we cannot get outside our own consciousness. We know nothing directly except the modifications of our own consciousness . . . and all statements of knowledge carry with them a reference, explicit or implicit, to the knower. An object without a subject is a meaningless phrase" ("WM?," 135). When we say that "a thing is 'outside' ourselves or outside another thing . . . we are not in this process getting rid of an observer, but only hypothetically extending his powers" ("WM?," 137). Stephen's intellectual effort to escape the prison of solipsism, like Mr. Ramsay's to reach the letter Z, falls short: as for Mr. Ramsay, "R was beyond him" (*TL*, 54), R that we might take to stand for Reality itself.

Against Stephen's suspension of knowledge, Moore will claim a "refutation" of Idealism and Russell to have given, along with Whitehead, "a new turn to the argument about solipsism" (*Matter*,

28). The contested notion of *sensibilia*, which owes much to Moore's "sense-data," is the key. Berkeley is the obvious target. (Among the Woolfs' books was Stephen's copy of Berkeley and Moore's "The Refutation of Idealism." See note 27 above.) Against the "metaphysic" which is "essentially Berkeley's" – "esse est percipi," "whatever is, is perceived" (*Matter*, 213) – Russell, under Moore's influence, was to counterpose one which incorporated that proposition but made it the antidote to Idealism by externalizing perception from the subject. Whatever exists is perceptible, but not necessarily perceived by anyone. This approaches "the abolition of the subject" which Stephen pronounces "[w]e do not get a step nearer" ("WM?," 138).

Some knowledge beyond our own experience – call it "science" in its most sophisticated version – becomes then possible. To arrive at the objects of that knowledge for the Russell of 1914 requires logic, for those objects are not sensible objects, not even unsensed sensible objects, but logical constructions out of them. Russell's "solution" makes rigorous Leslie Stephen's idea of a hypothetical extension of the observer's powers, "'producing' our curves" to "obtain formulae which are independent, in a sense, of our particular position" ("WM?," 137). Russell erects Stephen's non-solution into a solution.

The physical objects Russell constructs out of elements actually and hypothetically observable are themselves unobserved. Hence, his goal is a knowledge which starts out from observation but radically differs from it. From being the focus of a problem, the unobserved becomes a necessary feature of the things knowledge arrives at, the essence of the reality Idealism denies. Russell's Realism denies it is a "self-evident truism" "that whatever can in any way be relevant to our experience must be at least capable of being known by us" or "that if matter were essentially something with which we could not become acquainted, matter would be something which we could not know to exist, and which could have for us no importance whatever" or "that what can have no importance for us cannot be real" (*PP*, 43).

Ultimately, a knowledge of the unobserved is a non-psychological knowledge whose subject matter is irreducible to any subject's mental state. In this sense, a theory of knowledge incorporating the unobserved is another version of epistemological agnosticism.[60] By contrast, "[a] limerick by Ronald Knox, with a reply" from God Russell cites makes Berkeley's a theology of persisting objects:

There was a young man who said, "God
Must think it exceedingly odd
  If he finds that this tree
  Continues to be
When there's no one about in the Quad."

Reply

Dear Sir:
  Your astonishment's odd:
I am always about in the Quad.
  And that's why the tree
  Will continue to be,
Since observed by
  Yours faithfully
    God." (*HWP*, 623)[61]

It is this omniscient, omnipresent observer whose existence is finally in question and not just the object of his observations. Already hovering on the margins of a world whose shape, if it bears the mark of the senses, in no way reveals a person "I am" behind them, the observer disappears into the scene observed.

Yet the vanished observer leaves in his wake not nothing but a world of phantom "solid objects." Hence, because knowledge is not equivalent to perception, the disappearance of the observer does not, in Russell, entail a denial of the possibility of knowledge. In this sense, Russell is not agnostic but a "believer in knowledge" (*TK*, 162). His agnosticism is rather the renunciation of direct perception as the model of all knowledge. Its substitute is knowledge by description. Agnosticism is indeed a tool in the service of knowledge. That tool will have another name: "Occam's Razor" – *Entia non multiplicanda praeter necessitatem.* Its goal is to disburden the theory of knowledge of things whose existence need not be decided upon in order to render defensible a knowledge of those things which can be.

The "kitchen table when you're not there," that "symbol which in her vagueness as to what Mr. Ramsay did think about Andrew had given" to Lily Briscoe (*TL*, 232), identifies Mr. Ramsay's philosophical object with the unobserved. The table is interposed between Woolf's woman-artist and the philosopher, placing the problem of knowledge at the center of Woolf's art. To Lily's consternation, she finds her gaze riveted to the same object the philosopher "Mr. Ramsay kept always his eyes fixed upon" (*TL*, 232). It thrusts itself before her mind's eye, "its four legs in the air" (*TL*, 38), "hung in effigy" (*TL*, 41) upside down. The philosophical problem, whenever explicitly alluded to in the novels, is typically filtered not through the thoughts of a philosopher but through the reactions of a woman – Lily Briscoe, Mrs. Ambrose, Sara Pargiter – perplexed, irritated, at pains to see the point, no doubt because the fictional philosophers are creations of a real woman who, no philosopher herself, hesitates to write their script, recognizing her limits with mingled exasperation, anger and grudging respect for philosophic rigor.

In the table converge two intellectual currents. The philosopher's example – Russell's, for one – , it is also the artist's subject, Cézanne's especially. Of "white deal" (*TL*, 38), the table lacks, however, the color that makes it more naturally the artist's object. For the table Lily imagines, upon which the philosopher grounds his work and which the painter paints, like Mr. Ambrose the classicist's table in *The Voyage Out*, found by his wife, is a "scrubbed kitchen table" seemingly "laid bare by years of muscular integrity," recalling "one of those scrubbed board tables" (*TL*, 38) stripped by the likes of Mrs. McNab. Nonetheless, it is Mr. Ramsay's philosophical investigations which are by implication credited for this integrity in Lily Briscoe's mind.

The intense labor of inquiry reveals the table to be both ordinary and extraordinary: "our familiar table, which has roused but the slightest thoughts in us hitherto, has become a problem full of surprising possibilities" (*PP*, 16). Its reality is dual: it is the visible table, but analysis scours it clean of its appearances to expose an unseen dimension. "The one thing we know about it is that it is not what it seems" (*PP*, 16). The result is "austere," "uncompromisingly plain," "unornamental" (*TL*, 232), like the colorless black and brown books of philosophy themselves, like the "Lighthouse, distant, austere" (*TL*, 23). Its plainness owes something also to its humble, everyday use, and the labor that strips it. It is "this unornamented beauty which so deeply impressed" Lily (*TL*, 232), and Mr. Ramsay's lizard eye which directs her gaze to it. Thus the table is also the "symbol of her profound respect for Mr. Ramsay's mind" (*TL*, 41), for him who she had just decided was "petty, selfish" (*TL*, 40) – and it is as such that it also embodies the respect of artist "Lily's mind" for the philosophic mind, free of the philosopher's foibles, become nothing more than the knowledge it arrives at.

Ultimately, the table itself, washed of all human agency, comes to possess this integrity. The impersonal truth it reveals imparts its austerity to the gazer, as to the scrubbing agent: "But what a face," Lily thinks of Mr. Ramsay, "What had made it like that? Thinking, night after night, she supposed – about the reality of kitchen tables" (*TL*, 232). It imposes on the observer a discipline that lies in its very unobservability – the endurance of philosophic doubt: "He must have had his doubts about that table, she supposed; whether the table was a real table; whether it was worth the time he gave to it; whether he was able after all to find it" (*TL*, 232). The struggle with skepticism historically accompanies the problem of knowledge, as Leslie Stephen presents it. Yet, the "criticism of knowledge," if completely "destructive," yields no knowledge, Russell protests.

> If we adopt the attitude of the complete sceptic, placing ourselves wholly outside all knowledge, and asking, from this outside position, to be compelled to return within the circle of knowledge, we are demanding what is impossible, and our scepticism can never be refuted. For all refutation must begin with some piece of knowledge which the disputants share; from blank doubt, no argument can begin. (*PP*, 150)

That piece of knowledge is provided by the seen table. Nothing can be known with certainty about the unseen one – "there does not exist a method which will safeguard you against the possibility of error. The wish for perfect security is one of those snares we are always falling into, and is just as untenable in the realm of knowledge as in everything else" (*LK*, 181). Agnosticism is the alternative. The unseen table, a logical possibility, leads knowledge outside the comfortable sphere of certainty to another, uncertain knowledge.

THE PHILOSOPHICAL BASIS

> I have, therefore, begun with an account of the contemporary philosophy, . . . repeating a thrice-told tale . . . Further, I have tried to indicate the application of the principles accepted in philosophy . . . and their reflection in the imaginative literature of the time. (Stephen, *History of English Thought*, vi)

A philosophic basis is part of the Bloomsbury ethos. "Philosophy provided the foundation of Keynes' life," Skidelsky writes (*John Maynard Keynes*, 133). Woolf herself tries to demonstrate how art was, for Fry as an Apostle, bound up with intellectual pursuits which included philosophy, quoting a letter of Fry's "dealing with the evils of mysticism" which "breaks off in the middle of a quotation from Alain, from Bertrand Russell, from Flaubert" (*RF*, 234). She also insists "that the art of writing has for backbone some fierce attachment to an idea," via which "the diverse company which includes" Leslie Stephen "reaches the farther shore" (*CE*, II, 50). "Under every poetry . . . there lies a philosophy," wrote Stephen himself in *Hours in a Library.* "The poet and the philosopher . . . are interested in the same truths" (II, 178–9). Stephen's work combined "philosophical speculation and literary criticism" (*VW*, I, 9). "I always read *Hours in a Library* by way of filling out my ideas," Woolf said of her father's criticism (*MB*, 115). "If you would please me," Woolf addresses an audience of potential women writers, "you would write books of travel and adventure, and research and scholarship, and history and biography, and criticism and philosophy and science. By doing so you will certainly profit the art of fiction. For books have a way of influencing each other. Fiction will be much the better for standing cheek by jowl with poetry and philosophy" (*Room*, 113). Woolf identifies as "the contemporary dilemma" of the "art" of writing the "lack of an obstinate conviction" (*CE*, II, 50). Philosophy, then, in the form of speculation on the problem of knowledge, supplies Woolf "that backbone of intellect" (*MB*, 142) she attributes to Leslie Stephen.[62]

Writing's "dilemma" Fry saw as Impressionism's. The impressionism or poetry of the novel's style dissipated into mistiness (*CE*, II, 50) unless sustained by rigorous thought or principles, such as, for Fry, Cézanne's use of geometrical forms. For sensibilia are not the only unobserved things. The truths of logic do not even require that anyone think of them for them to provide support, "upholding the world," so that Mrs. Ramsay need not know what "square roots" are to be able to "lean" on them (*TL*, 159), nor need an artist or a novelist understand them fully for them to provide the framework of his or her Principia Aesthetica. The result in literature is "modern fiction," the Post-Impressionism of writing. Clive Bell, in the book he dedicated to Virginia Woolf and published the same year as *To the Lighthouse*, speaks of "philosophic fiction," a category he places along with "modern poetry and philosophy" itself (*Civilization*, 18). Woolf's fiction is an implicit theory of modern knowledge, divided, just as painting for Fry, into dual realities and dual ways of knowing. Her theory of modern fiction has a visual dimension, taking the visual arts as its model of a modern art. But it has no less "something unvisual beneath" (*W*, 156). The strange notion of unobserved sensibilia we will discover motivates Woolf's equally strange "world seen without a self" (*W*, 287), an unseen vision which reflects the abolition of the subject but not of its object.[63] It presents a reality unaffected by human agency whose literary correlate is the disappearance of the author, even the shadowy, featureless feminine *persona non grata* in the quad in *Jacob's Room*, a disappearance not simply a theme of the novels but a stylistic principle.

The stages of our reading divide, in Part I, into the dualities of matter and mind, of which Russell gave twin analyses. Chapters two and three together provide the "analysis of matter," first Russell's, then Woolf's, sketching the contours of an atomized world with an infinite number of possible perspectives, among which the unobserved object is one possibility – an empiricist monadology. Chapter four, the "analysis of mind," follows the stages of the reduction of the subject to the occupied perspective. Russell's logical atomism is one of mind, too. "The mind receives a myriad impressions" (*CE*, II, 106); there is not just another mind, but other minds. The result of the novels' analysis of matter is the world seen without the self; of the analysis of mind, the self alone without the world. Chapter five ends Part I by drawing a first conclusion from the paired analyses. The selfless world and the worldless self in Woolf yield two versions of one and the same conception of death, that of a world in which "what there is" is not dependent on anyone being there to observe it. Death marks the limits of the self in a world where knowledge is more than acquaintance. In this sense, Woolf's novels are elegiac.

Part II, *Principia Aesthetica*, presents the two versions of modernism: in chapter six, Fry's visual aesthetic of the painting with its blind logical form, and in chapter seven, the stylistic principles of "modern fiction," for which Wittgenstein's picture theory of the proposition and Russell's theory of proper names and descriptions provide surprising commentary. For Post-Impressionism's literary incarnation requires a philosophy of language itself dual, divided between a language of sensation and one of forms. From these principles emerges the new model of the impersonal work, itself dualistic, a logical construction out of reduced sensations which is an implicit theory of knowledge. The concluding chapter eight, complement to Part I's conclusion, returns to the question there raised: the form of a modern elegy adequate to the world scientific knowledge reveals.

Woolf thus places at the center of her novels the encounter between philosopher and artist, philosophy and literature. Of the many such encounters she had with real philosophers, the 1921 one with Russell whose details Woolf records with breathless triumph we take as emblematic of the historically particularized conjunction of literature and philosophy that produces Woolf's art. In it, Woolf embodies the woman as representative layperson, "a woman of sophisticated artistic, intellectual, and political interests, but uneducated in symbolic logic and mathematics," as Eames says of Ottoline, but also the artist – Russell, already in 1921, acknowledged Woolf as a writer. In the absence of Russell's wife and Leonard Woolf (the presence of Leonard, trained in philosophy and convinced it was the one subject his wife did not read, might have been more constraining than an unwitnessed discussion with the philosopher himself),[64] Woolf "got as much out of him as I could carry," in a discussion ranging from poetry to the aesthetics of mathematics in which "we struck out like swimmers who knew their waters" (*Diary*, II, 147).

Woolf's philosophically inflected aesthetic is not one Russsell would have foreseen, however. He defined the limits of philosophy's concerns so as to exclude literature and art. Like her father's creative powers as a "portrait painter," which Woolf had found "crude," "elementary" and "conventional," Russell's conception of art gives no answer to the question the writer Bernard asks in *The Waves*: "how describe the world seen without the self?" Knowing only a Romantic aesthetic, Russell assumes that an art of the unobserved is an oxymoron; art only expresses the personal. Building her novelistic vision on a theory of knowledge that posits unobserved perspectives and not some other philosophy (not Bergson's, for instance), and not finding a preordained place for literature and art within it, Woolf is forced to work out an aesthetic more in conformity with Russell's thought than his outworn romanticism. We return to the details of that meeting in the stages of our reading to decipher the "private code" (*TL*, 10) in which the relation between a thought and an art is spelled out. "Mush," "color," "art," "impersonally," these "words bec[o]me symbols" (*TL*, 219) will become "some of the parts" (*TL*, 222) of our argument. The difference between philosophy and literature will not turn out to lie where Russell assumes it does (*Diary*, II, 148). Although entirely distinct from logical philosophy, literature cannot, any more than philosophy, remain ignorant of the world of science if it aspires to modernity. Here again our argument contests the usual assumption that Woolf's and Bloomsbury's aesthetic was primarily formed by Moore's emphasis on personal relations.[65] It is, rather, an aesthetic of the impersonal. The meeting of philosopher and artist-writer, like that between Lily Briscoe and Mr. Ramsay, is not an "interpersonal" exchange, but mediated by a thing itself "impersonal" – the table, shared object of knowledge. By *To the Lighthouse*'s conclusion, it has become one with the lighthouse, the final object of Mr. Ramsay's quest and Lily's contemplation. "'He must have reached it,' said Lily aloud" (*TL*, 308), surmising he achieved his intellectual goal. For the novel ends with Lily once more thinking of Mr. Ramsay's speculations on the table. But their inner content remains his alone, private, uncommunicated, "now he had nobody to talk to about that table" (*TL*, 233). Any public, shared knowledge is uncertain. "For the Lighthouse had become almost invisible, had melted away into a blue haze, and the effort of looking at it and the effort of thinking of him landing there, which both seemed to be one and the same effort, had stretched her body and mind to the utmost" (*TL*, 308). The philosopher's effort of thought, recalling Russell's overstraining of his mind with *Principia Mathematica*, finds its match in the "painful effort of concentration" with which the artist Lily Briscoe "focussed her mind, not upon the silver-bossed bark of the tree, but . . . upon a phantom kitchen table" (*TL*, 38), not upon the sensible object but upon the unobservable physical object. If Mr. Ramsay's observed table remains private to him, the unobserved one fills in the gap to create continuity between Lily's and his private perspectives. Mr. Ramsay's landing thus coincides with Lily's completion of her painting. A possible contrastive stress on the possessive pronoun in the final sentence "I have had my vision" indicates the complementarity between the philosopher's and the artist's vision.[66] And, like Mr. Ramsay's face, the description each provides – philosophy, on the one hand, fiction, on the other – takes on the impersonal quality of its object, while the persons producing it inevitably disappear. At the center of the vision, unobserved yet fixed, like the light rays, potential sense-data, emanating from a photographic plate, a latent image, the table persists.

PART I

Subject and Object and the Nature of Reality

We could, theoretically, work out the history of mind without ever mentioning matter, and then, at the end, deduce that matter must meanwhile have gone through the corresponding history.

(Russell, *Mysticism and Logic*, 194)

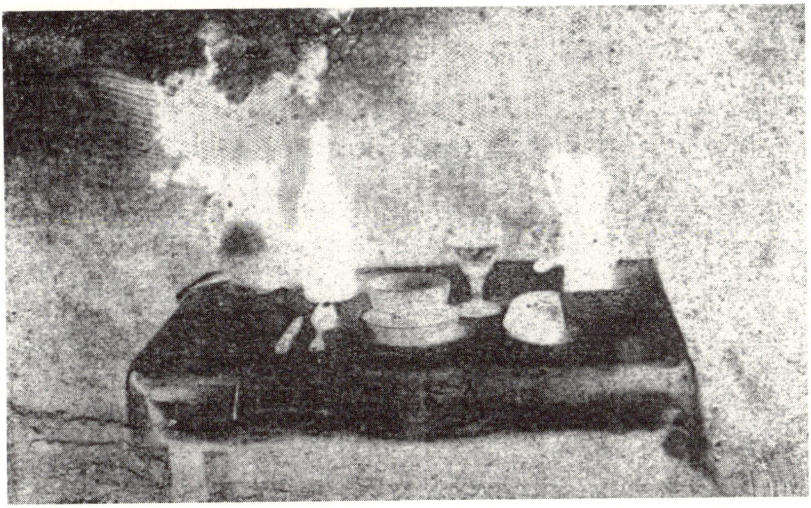

Figure 2. Nicéphore Nièpce. *La Table Servie.*

CHAPTER 2

The geometry in the sensible world: Russell's analysis of matter

> When we consider the world without the knowledge and ignorance that are taught by philosophy, we seem to see that it contains a number of things and persons, and that some of the things are "experienced" by some of the persons . . . Some things, such as the inside of the earth or the other side of the moon, are never experienced by anybody, but are nevertheless believed to exist.
>
> (Russell, *Theory of Knowledge*, 7)

> . . . a consciousness of what I call "reality": a thing I see before me: something abstract; but residing in the downs or sky; beside which nothing matters; in which I shall rest and continue to exist. Reality I call it. And I fancy sometimes this is the most necessary thing to me: that which I seek.
>
> (Woolf, *Diary*, III, 196)

At the center of her concept of the novel Woolf places what she does not hesitate to call "reality." To write is "to live in the presence of reality," she claims in *A Room of One's Own*, a text not only on "women and fiction" (3) but also on fiction, truth and reality (114). Among "philosophic words" Woolf finds "apt to play one false" (*Room*, 113) is the word "reality." "What is meant by 'reality'?" (*Room*, 113), she echoes the beginning of Moore's 1910 lecture "The Meaning of the Real": "What is the meaning of the words 'real,' 'exists,' 'is,' 'is a fact,' 'is true'?" (*SomeMain*, 236). Woolf is fully cognizant of the philosophical problems raised. "I ask myself, what is reality? And who are the judges of reality?" she asks in "Mr Bennett and Mrs Brown," originally read to the Heretics in Cambridge (*CE*, I, 325). The philosophical sense she gives the word "reality" transforms "the question of reality which Mr Bennett raises" from an exhausted "Edwardian" concept of literary realism into one rendered "modern" (*CE*, I, 319).[1]

Reality, however, is ever haunted by its spectral negation, unreality. To write is thus also to "live at enmity with unreality" (*Room*, 114). The exposure to reality is accompanied by a struggle with its opposite. But what constitutes the unreal is no less a problem. The enmity is equally with reality and unreality: "this other thing, this truth, this reality" is also "the presence of this formidable ancient enemy" (*TL*, 236). For the strange truth this intellectual effort reveals is that to bring one possible reality into focus it must be made to seem unreal; "the stillness and the brightness of the day" be made "as strange as the chaos and tumult of night" (*TL*, 203). This is the "sensitiveness to real things" Woolf finds "queer in the sister of George and Gerald" (*MB*, 97). "So," writes Woolf, "coming back from a journey, or after an illness, before habits had spun themselves across the surface, one felt that same unreality, which was so startling; felt something emerge. Life was most vivid then" (*TL*, 285). No sooner is a candidate for the real proffered, than it is transformed by questioning its reality into something strange, unreal, and yet so insistently present one wonders whether its strangeness is its reality.

The doubling of the real by the unreal endows Woolf's vision with a dualism, as Rosenbaum insists ("Philosphical Realism," 321). Orthodox opinion would have it that "psychological reality" is primary for Woolf. But in the novels, it is seized against the backdrop of an absolutely depsychologized reality, what Mrs. Ambrose's "black volume of philosophy" calls in classic terms "the Reality of Matter" (*VO*, 32–3), McTaggart's "truth about the reality of matter and time" (*The Nature of Existence*, II, 26). It aims to "see human beings not always in their relation to each other but in relation to reality" (*Room*, 118). To live exposed to reality so conceived is to "escape a little from the common sitting-room" into the private room (*Room*, 118). Social relations are counterposed to a reality embodied in the view from the room's window. Ultimately even the room is left behind, because knowledge of reality begins by "exposure" to it. Woolf's voyage out follows in this what Pears calls Russell's aim "to achieve the maximum exposure of the ego to the external world" (*BR*, 213), himself following Moore's itinerary after their initial "excursion Into Idealism." Reality for all three is fundamentally external, inhuman – "out of doors, out of the window" (*MrsD*, 45). Just as Woolf's philosopher's gaze is typically directed outside, "the question which primarily interested Russell" in his turn toward knowledge, Ayer asserts, "was not the relation of

Figure 3. Roger Fry, portrait of Bertrand Russell, 1923.

sense-data to the subjects he supposed to be aware of them, but their relation to the physical objects with which they are in some manner associated" (*Bertrand Russell*, 71) – i.e., he was more interested in "the relation of sense-data to physics" than to psychology. The same might be said of the Leslie Stephen of "What Is Materialism?" This is the "prejudice in favour of explanations in terms of physics wherever possible" Russell records (*MyPhD*, 96). For, from the point of view of what there is, "It is not necessary, in an analysis of matter, to decide what 'knowing' is; it is only necessary to decide what is known" (*Matter*, 186). The exposure is not always simply invigorating, as Mrs. Ramsay discovers when she receives a blast of Mr. Ramsay's truth: "she bent her head as if to let the pelt of jagged hail, the drench of dirty water, bespatter her unrebuked" (*TL*, 51). Yet the writer as much as the philosopher must "remove veils from trees" for "to bare reality is to be a poet" (*CE*, II, 302).

The most disturbing aspect of the seeming unreality of the real is raised by the possibility of the unobserved. The disturbance it causes is akin to madness, like that of Septimus Warren Smith, who undertakes the philosopher's thought experiment, testing the persistence of invisible objects by "open[ing] his eyes, to see whether a gramophone was really there" (*MrsD*, 215). For this is the mark of an object's reality: "A thing is real if it persists at times when it is not perceived" (*ML*, 116). Russell's tentative conclusion "that objects of perception do not persist unchanged at times when they are not perceived, although probably objects more or less resembling them do" and "that purely physical laws exist determining the character and duration of objects of perception without any reference to the fact that they are perceived" means to justify a realism "realists" would not necessarily "recognize . . . as realism" (*ML*, 118). It strips away things' ordinary existence and endows them with a fresh and extraordinary reality dispensing with any need for the observer. "But real things – real things were too exciting," Septimus thinks. "He must be cautious. He must not go mad."[2] Septimus goes mad precisely because "all were real," not unreal (*MrsD*, 215).

The possible persistence of objects, an assumption of common sense, becomes itself extraordinary. Raising the table's independent existence, the self discovers not only an unreal real world outside which excludes it but its own ego likewise called into question and, like the table, stripped of its everyday dress, revealing a reduced subject we will examine in chapter four. This subjective reality, without social identity, explains why "[a] character may be real to Mr Bennett and quite unreal to me" (*CE*, II, 325). Table and observer are linked in solitary struggle in a universe cleared of the familiar social relations. "Unreality" names the spectral nature of the reality of one side of the dualism as it appears from the vantage point of the other: the ghostly observer unobserved by the table; the unobserved table "thought of" by the would-be but unobserving observer. The possible unreality of each makes their confirmed reality equally disturbing, as if their vanishing and conjuration by thought, a kind of intellectual sleight-of-hand, the philosopher's fort-da game, demonstrated their independence of thought.

Russell's and Moore's defense of Realism required the combatting of Idealism on two fronts: Berkeley's empiricist version was the ultimate target; the rejection of Bradley's and McTaggart's Hegelianism, the starting point. "I hated the stuffiness involved in supposing that spacc and time were only in my mind . . . and could not bear Kant's view that" the external world "I like best was only a subjective figment," Russell explained later (*MyPhD*, 48). The double objective of a theory of knowledge of the external world which avoids the conclusions of the two versions of Idealism determines two distinct Russellian positions: his "neutral monism" and his "logical atomism."[3] The first, the "new turn to the argument against solipsism" Russell claimed (*Matter*, 28), answers Berkeleyian Idealism. Worked out in the course of 1913–14 with hints already in *The Problems of Philosophy*, it is an extreme version of Moore's position in "The Refutation of Idealism." The second defines itself specifically against English Hegelianism.

Not only is the question of "subject and object and the nature of reality" at stake. Russell includes the idea of "a pluralistic timeless world of Platonic ideas" among those of his and Moore's initial Realism (*Autobiography*, in Passmore, *Hundred Years*, 207). The dualism of particulars as against universals marks another great divide in English philosophy, that between Realism and Nominalism. Mathematics and logic erect an immaterial world which is itself a candidate for an ultimate reality. If "[a] stone, according to common-sense, is a reality; but so undoubtedly is a toothache," according to Leslie Stephen ("WM?," 139), it is no less true that "[a] stone is 'real,' and a thought is 'real'"; "but how the realities are related is a question beyond the ordinary interest" ("WM?," 135). The defender of the different reality of universals and forms inevitably enters the debate with nominalism too, with the theory "which admits only particulars, and dispenses altogether with universals" Russell attributes to "Berkeley and Hume in their polemic against 'abstract ideas'" (*LK*, 111). "A predicate," he writes, "is akin to a scholastic universal, and in maintaining that there are predicates we are classing ourselves with scholastic realists" (*TK*, 92–3).

The reality of thoughts, or rather, propositions, for the early

Russell was a function of their independence of mind, by contrast with thinking, unquestionably mental. It justified avoiding a definition of propositions which "brings in anything mental" (*TK*, 114); i.e., their truth (or falsity) is not dependent on being thought. This is "[t]he metaphysical vision behind" what Hylton calls "Platonic Atomism," in which true and false propositions "are both real and objective" (*Russell*, 27). After 1910 (until 1919), Russell abandoned objective propositions and his "object-based metaphysics" (282), because of the incredibility of objective falsehoods. This did not mean abandoning the idea of an independent reality, however. The role of preserving it, what Hylton calls "guarding against Idealism" (337), was then assigned to "fact." True propositions correspond to facts; false propositions are "unreal" – nothing corresponds to them.

Independence of mind is the cornerstone of Platonic Atomism's rejection of Idealism. Indeed, for Russell, the notion of an independent reality is first in the logic, then becoming a feature of physical matter in the theory of knowledge. The confrontation then is with a reality which presents itself as ruthlessly outside and also "intrinsically different from mind" (*PP*, 36), "this other thing" in Woolf's phrase. "Matter" is one name for external reality; logic and mathematics another. Both bring into play the unobserved, for not only is the question of "The Existence of Matter" presented in terms of whether there is "a table which has a certain intrinsic nature, and continues to exist when I am not looking" (*PP*, 17), but there also exist "logical consequences which perhaps no one perceives" (*TK*, 151). Logic represents a realm whose "truths" ineluctably follow one from the other beyond the range of human interference. Russell's turn to Realism began with an analysis of mathematics and then turned to matter. Physical theories as to its nature, mathematicizing it, make it as abstract as logic, if nonetheless empirical, like the table; "in regard to physical objects . . . the principle that sense-data are signs of physical objects is itself a connexion of universals" (*PP*, 148–9). But eventually Russell and Moore felt the empiricist challenge Leslie Stephen had resurrected. Their "refutation" of Idealism incorporates Berkeley's solipsism, innoculating the result, the theories of sense-data and sensibilia, with the very philosophical position it meant to resist: "solipsism strictly carried out coincides with pure realism" (*Tractatus*, 5.64). Like the argument which uses Berkeley against Idealism, Russell's Realism uses increasingly –

especially "from 1913 or 1914 onwards" (Hylton, *Russell*, 266) – nominalism's method, i.e., Occam's razor, "namely, 'entities are not to be multiplied without necessity'" (*IMP*, 184) or what Hylton calls "analysis as elimination" (*Russell*, 265). Analysis, turned to knowledge, aims at discovering the ultimate reality of the world by a process akin to Descartes' radical doubt whereby the unreal was progressively eliminated or "pruned." The goal is not to dismiss objects or universals as mere "names," but to reduce their number and arrive at "the smallest empirical apparatus – or the smallest apparatus, not necessarily wholly empirical – out of which you can build up" the propositions of science (*LK*, 271). A parsimonious Realism is a more defensible one. Russell's use of Occam's razor stops at the simple and universals are such simple entities; this is the sense in which they are "atoms."[4]

THE TABLE

A table was rooted in the middle. (Woolf, *The Voyage Out*, 18)

In the middle they stood a table. (Woolf, *Between the Acts*, 125)

"Reality – reality," she ejaculated, tapping her finger upon the table as if to emphasize and perhaps explain her isolated utterance of this word (Woolf, *Night and Day*, 472)

A man and a woman are to be sitting at a table talking (Woolf, *A Writer's Diary*, 107)

I have fixed my eyes upon it, I feel I have grasped a plank in the sea . . . Here is something definite, something real. Thus, waking from a midnight dream of horror, one hastily turns on the light and lies quiescent, worshipping the chest of drawers, worshipping solidity, worshipping reality, worshipping the impersonal world which is a proof of some existence other than ours. (Woolf, "The Mark on the Wall," *CSFVW*, 82)

The Problems of Philosophy illustrates McGuinness' claim that for Russell philosophy begins with "the Cartesian question" (*Wittgenstein*, 83), rewriting the *cogito* – "our present experiences" – in the empiricist mode in terms of the existence of the table: "It seems to me that I am now sitting in a chair, at a table of a certain shape, on which I see sheets of paper with writing or print" (*PP*, 7). Russell's skeptic characterizes the person "obsessed by indubitabilities" as one who "thinks he sees tables and chairs" (*TK*, 162).

The table descends from the British philosophical tradition as "the familiar example" of the external object (Ayer, *Bertrand Russell*,

71). Hume uses it to illustrate "the question concerning *external* existence" in a passage perhaps familiar to Woolf through Leslie Stephen (*HET*, 46–7).[5] Hume's table occupies a perceptual space that encompasses all the "ordinary" objects within the thinker-writer's ken: "The paper, on which I write at present, is beyond my hand. The table is beyond the paper. The walls of the chamber beyond the table. And in casting my eye towards the window, I perceive a great extent of fields and buildings beyond my chamber" (*A Treatise*, 190). From the chair and the table, furniture of the material world, the step leads directly to the starry heavens: "By turning my head I see out of the window buildings and clouds and the sun" (*PP*, 7–8). Tables and chairs, things nearest to hand for the sedentary philosopher, who comes to occupy chairs of philosophy, are the furniture of "that room of one's own" from which the real world is observed, the type of what is "beyond" the subject. For Wittgenstein, the propositional sign, "made up of spatial objects (such as tables, chairs, books) instead of written signs," thereby contains the table, etc. (*Tractatus*, 3.1431). Thus, any philosophy addressing our knowledge of the external world first addresses the problem of the table. Moore, accordingly, abandoned Hegelian philosophy because, according to Russell, he found it "inapplicable to chairs and tables."[6]

A table, long the paradigmatic object of knowledge in "the history of English thought," is, then, planted squarely in the center of Woolf's novelistic scenery, standing for "the stuff of the physical world," "the stuff of tables and chairs, sun, moon and stars" (*OP*, 292), for those solid objects "made of wood, separately of great importance, and possessed of shapes like tables and chairs" (*VO*, 124), for "the immense solidity of chairs and tables" (*W*, 183; *Y*, 155), for those "Dear things! . . . Dear chairs and tables!" whose supposed objectivity Mrs. Hilbery's sentimentalizing eye subjectivizes (*ND*, 22). In choosing the table by name – never a "desk," for instance – Woolf explicitly aligns herself with this tradition. From Mr. Ambrose's "kitchen table" in *The Voyage Out* to Katherine Hilbery's table in "her own upper room" (*ND*, 310), to that in Jacob's room (*JR*, 44), to Mr. Ramsay's kitchen table, to the dining table on which Mrs. Ramsay serves the Boeuf en Daube like the "dinner-table" for a "dinner-party" Russell invokes (*PP*, 20; *Matter*, 191–2), that same table of Mrs. Ramsay's which presumably remains in the house in "Time Passes" in her absence, to "the table, the chairs" of the chapter openings of *The Waves* (101), set for no one who ever comes, the table signals the entry of the problem of knowledge into the novels. For, arbitrary as the example is – "consider the table, say" – it is never the bed, that place of sleep, sex and death, not even Clarissa Dalloway's "narrow bed," which excludes the middle term, that comes to the philosopher's mind. Hume's and Russell's writing tables are like Katherine Hilbery's "table that would be cleared for work" on "mathematical problems" (*ND*, 270), supports of places of thought and repast, neutrally outside the mind.[7]

THE SENSIBILIA OF THE TABLE

The metaphysic which we have been developing is essentially Berkeley's: what is, is perceived. But our reasons are somewhat different from his. We do not suggest that there is any impossibility about unperceived existents, but only that no strong ground exists for believing in them. (Russell, *The Analysis of Matter*, 213)

But "it becomes evident that the real table, if there is one, is not the same as what we immediately experience by sight, touch or hearing" (*PP*, 11). Hence, a first distinction is made between the physical table, reality beyond appearances, and "someone perceiving a table" (Ayer, *Bertrand Russell*, 71), the latter analyzed into a group of sensations:

To make our difficulties plain, let us concentrate attention on the table. To the eye it is oblong, brown and shiny, to the touch it is smooth and cool and hard; when I tap it, it gives out a wooden sound . . . Although I believe that the table is really of the same colour all over, the parts that reflect the light look much brighter than the other parts, and some parts look white because of reflected light. I know that, if I move, the parts that reflect the light will be different, so that the apparent distribution of colours on the table will change. It follows that if several people are looking at the table at the same moment, . . . no two can see it from exactly the same point of view. (*PP*, 8–9)

The table is not what it seems. In "the relation of the sense-data to the real table" (*PP*, 12) revealed by the analysis of appearances, the common-sense table is conjured away, opening the gap between physics and sense. For if "perception gives us the most concrete knowledge we possess as to the stuff of the physical world" (*OP*, 292), it does not give us direct knowledge of "'matter,'" which is "a remote supersensuous construction," invisible, imperceptible

(*TK*, 21). Knowledge's empirical foundation is subjective. As Russell puts it, "Physics exhibits sense-data as functions of physical objects, but verification is only possible if physical objects can be exhibited as functions of sense-data" (*ML*, 141).

Thus the real as distinct from the perceived table is not dependent on observation and hence on an observer. Here physics coincides with common sense, which also assumes the persistence of matter in the observer's absence, as Leslie Stephen says à propos of Hume: "it is a plain fact of consciousness that we think of a table or a house as somehow existing independently of our perception of it . . . Why are not the group of sensations which we call table supposed to vanish when they are not felt like the group of sensations which we call toothache?" (*HET*, 46–7). How can the perceived table, if necessarily perceived by someone, then be evidence for the unperceived table? Is there reason to maintain the existence of "a real table at all" (*PP*, 11).

Stephen's presentation of the problem classically distinguishes the physical table from its appearances, equated with an observer's sensations of it. This equation Russell sees as central to Berkeley's argument:

> Other philosophers since Berkeley have also held that, although the table does not depend for its existence upon being seen by me, it does depend upon being seen (or otherwise apprehended in sensation) by *some* mind – not necessarily the mind of God, but more often the whole collective mind of the universe. This they hold, as Berkeley does, chiefly because they think there can be nothing real – or at any rate nothing known to be real – except minds and their thoughts and feelings. (*PP*, 14)

It is this Berkeleyan position which is Russell's target, and it is Berkeley's failure to distinguish the mental act from its object, sensation from the sensed table, which is Russell's point of departure. His argument, building on Moore and Whitehead, proceeds through a series of applications of Occam's razor to the Idealist notion of subjectivity, continually parsing out what is extraneous to sense knowledge alone. The sensed table's externalization from the mind which Russell aims at will allow a separation of the subjective from the mental to turn Berkeley's argument to the service of Realism.[8]

Perhaps something in Berkeley's conceptual schema makes this possible. This Leslie Stephen suggests. "If by perceiving a thing I meant that I perceived that somebody else perceived it, it would follow that my absence would leave it existing in his mind. But this is an impossible meaning," he writes. "Yet his argument seems to imply that a mind is necessary to the existence of an idea, not only, if we may say so, within, but without. We admit that there must be a mind impressed, but why should there be a mind impressing?" Berkeley's "tacitly assuming an idea to be a kind of separable thing which may be taken out of one mind and preserved in another" which he locates as the argument's flaw (*HET*, 41) turns out to be the very notion Moore and Russell's "new turn" adopts. For the first operation in their process of reduction, detaching a thought or sensation from a subject, makes it "a kind of separable thing": "When I look at my table and see a certain brown colour, what is quite certain at once is not '*I* am seeing a brown colour,' but rather, 'a brown colour is being seen'" (*PP*, 19).

We return in chapter four to the discarded subject, focussing here on the core of subjectivity retained: the present act of sensation. Subjecting it to a further reduction, Moore distinguishes *sense-data*, a notion first adumbrated in "The Refutation of Idealism," from sensation: "I propose to call these things, the colour and size and shape, sense-data," distinct both from the physical object and from what "[m]any philosophers have called . . . sensations," which are "my seeing of the colour, not the colour which I now saw" (*SomeMain*, 44).[9] Russell takes up Moore's distinction: "Let us give the name of 'sense-data' to the things that are immediately known in sensation: such things as colours, sounds, smells, hardnesses, roughnesses, and so on" and "the name 'sensation' to the experience of being immediately aware of these things. Thus, whenever we see a colour, we have a sensation of the colour, but the colour itself is a sense-datum, not a sensation" (*PP*, 12).[10] Even if sensation and sense-data were always to co-occur, Moore nevertheless insists that it is "conceivable that the patch of colour which I saw may have continued to exist after I saw it: whereas, of course, when I ceased to see it, my seeing of it ceased to exist" (*SomeMain*, 45). In other words, unperceived appearances are not logically absurd. It is this *logical possibility* of the detachment of sense-data from sensation and, *a fortiori*, from the subject of sensation, which is crucial:

> Logically a sense-datum is an object, a particular of which the subject is aware . . . The existence of the sense-datum is therefore not logically dependent upon that of the subject . . . There is therefore no *a priori* reason why a particular which is a sense-datum should not persist after it has

ceased to be a datum, nor why other similar particulars should not exist without ever being data. (*ML*, 146–7)

The Idealist's seemingly absurd questions "how can that which is sensible be like that which is insensible? Can a real thing in itself *invisible* be like a *color*; or a real thing which is not *audible*, be like a *sound*? In a word, can anything be like a sensation or idea, but another sensation or idea?" (*Three Dialogues*, 41), the "contradiction" to which Berkeley claims to reduce the realist's position – that of maintaining that one can "see a thing which is at the same time unseen," of "conceiving a thing which is unconceived"[11] – Russell finds in no way logically objectionable.

By its possible separability, the sense-datum is an object of the subject's sensation:[12]

The view that sense-data are mental is derived, no doubt, in part from their physiological subjectivity, but in part also from a failure to distinguish between sense-data and "sensations." By a sensation I mean the fact consisting in the subject's awareness of the sense-datum. Thus a sensation is a complex of which the subject is a constituent and which therefore is mental. The sense-datum, on the other hand, stands over against the subject as that external object of which in sensation the subject is aware". (*ML*, 147)

It has the minimal distance from the mind that allows the mind to become acquainted with something distinct from itself.[13]

Russell takes "mental" strictly to mean "in the mind." The deliberate literalism of that locative permits the emergence of a subjectivity external to the mind – "'there' as opposed to 'here'" (*OKnExW*, 80). In "The Relation of Sense-Data to Physics," Russell interprets this to mean that sensibilia are physical, where "physical" designates what is "dealt with" by physics (*ML*, 145). In this extra-mental "subjective" space, the physical and the subjective are conjoined in "physical subjectivity" (*OP*, 282) or "physiological subjectivity" (*ML*, 144, 147), for Berkeley a contradiction but for Russell a logical possibility. But sensibilia need not be positively physical, only crucially non-mental, whether physical or not. Once this minimal subjectivity is externalized from the mind (*PP*, 40–2; *ML*, 123), those features Berkeley attributes to ideas need not be considered mental, even if subjective.

The result is a theory of knowledge with at its center the strange notion of a subjectless subjectivity. Russell calls this seemingly contradictory insensible sensible thing a "sensibile" or "sensibilia." "I shall give the name *sensibilia* to those objects which have the same metaphysical and physical status as sense-data, without necessarily being data to any mind" (*ML*, 143), because "there happen to be no observers to whom they are data" (149). Sensibilia are the sense appearances "not data to anyone" (*ML*, 153): "the 'sensibilia' which would appear from places where there happen to be no minds, and which I suppose to be real although they are no one's data" (*ML*, 152). A sense-datum may in practice always be sensed, but in principle it is independent of the act which seizes it.

Russell distinguishes two questions concerning the nature of sense appearances, the question whether "*sensibilia* which are data at a certain time sometimes continue to exist at times when they are not data" and the question "are sense-data mental or physical?" (*ML*, 146). The question as to the persistence of sense-data in the absence of observers is equivalent to that of their independence from the mind. It is chiefly in the second, physical sense "that Berkeley denies matter," Russell argues – "he does not deny that the sense-data which we commonly take as signs of the existence of the table are really signs of the existence of *something* independent of us," but "does deny" it "is non-mental . . . He admits that there must be something which continues to exist when we go out of the room or shut our eyes" but thinks it "cannot be independent of seeing altogether," only "independent of *our* seeing." Hence, Berkeley's " 'real' table as an idea in the mind of God" – it "has the required permanence and independence of ourselves, without being – as matter would otherwise be – something quite unknowable" (*PP*, 13–14).

Russell's belief in science prevents him, unlike Berkeley, from dismissing the possibility of a matter radically different from its appearances and even the existence of something "inconceivable" by the mind. But his 1914 "solution" makes Berkeley's things "independent of our seeing" yet resembling things seen the link to a matter independent of all seeing. Instead of inferring the thing behind appearances, "the Kantian *Ding an sich*, something wholly remote from the data which nominally support the inference," the abstract world posited by science will be constructed out of appearances with only two inferences allowed: other people's sense-data and *sensibilia* (*ML*, 152).

PRIVATE WORLDS AS OCCUPIED PERSPECTIVES

Leibniz thought that the universe consisted of monads, each of which was a little mind and each of which mirrored the universe . . . There is the space in the private world of each monad, which is the space that the monad can come to know by analysing and arranging data without assuming anything beyond data. (Russell, *My Philosophical Development*, 17–18)

In *The Problems of Philosophy*, Russell had introduced as little more than terminological substitutes for subject and object the terms "private" and "public."[14] By 1913–14, he developed them into new conceptions of subjectivity and objectivity via the "Leibnizian" solution worked out explicitly in the central chapter of *Our Knowledge of the External World*. "Let us imagine that each mind looks out upon the world, as in Leibniz' monadology, from a point of view peculiar to itself" (*OKnExW*, 94; see also *MyPhD*, 17–18), Russell begins, going on to reconceive the monads as structural positions for observation of related collections of sense-data. "The Relation of Sense-Data to Physics" gives another version:

Suppose there are a number of people in a room, all seeing, as they say, the same tables and chairs, walls and pictures, No two of these people have exactly the same sense data, yet there is sufficient similarity among their data to enable them to group together certain of these data as appearances of one "thing" to the several spectators, and others as appearances of another "thing." Besides the appearances which a given thing in the room presents to the actual spectators, there are, we may suppose, other appearances which it would present to other possible spectators. If a man were to sit down between two others, the appearance which the room would present to him would be intermediate between the appearances which it presents to the two others: and although this appearance would not exist as it is without the sense-organs, nerves and brain, of the newly arrived spectator, still it is not unnatural to suppose that, from the position which he now occupies, some appearance of the room existed before his arrival. (*ML*, 149)

In *The Problems of Philosophy*, privacy still is nothing more than the fact that "each person, so far as his sense-data are concerned, lives in a private world" (*ML*, 153). A private world is the point at which sense-data are gathered and given to an observer. By 1914, privacy is no longer defined with respect to the subject but to observation's purely structural position, one already there before an observer arrives. Hence, there is the possibility of an unoccupied privacy. This makes the notion of a "private world" more than a notational variant of the subject. The replacement of the dualism of subject and object, mind and matter, by the public and private does not eliminate dualism, but depsychologizes one side, reducing the distance from one to the other: "the privacy of introspective data" (*Mind*, 230) is built into the structure of the physical world without psychologizing it. The ideal is to "render solipsism scientifically satisfactory" via a strange "solipsism without a subject" (Jager, *Development of Bertrand Russell's Philosophy*, 406), thereby giving "the greatest satisfaction" to one "in whom the human affections are [not] stronger than the desire for logical economy" (*ML*, 152).

UNPERCEIVED PERCEPTIONS, UNOCCUPIED PERSPECTIVES

Unless you can perceive realities as they are not revealed to our perceptive faculties – that is to say, unless you can discover unperceivable perceptions – you are not in the presence of facts, but of phantasms. (Stephen, *History of English Thought*, 29)

The supposed impossibility of combining the different sense-data which are regarded as appearances of the same "thing" to different people has made it seem as though these "sensibilia" must be regarded as mere subjective phantasms. (Russell, *Mysticism and Logic*, 147)

Thus "'sensibilia' are to be recognized as the ultimate constituents of the physical world" (*ML*, 147). They furnish the crucial bridge between Solipsism and Realism, sense perception and physics. For, in between the different private worlds in which sense-data are "given" there are positions unoccupied by any subject which nonetheless record sensibilia, ones "constructed on principles of continuity" (*OKnExW*, 117). Continuity provides the mathematical concept required for assembling and filling in this universe – we return to it in considering time. In Russell's conception, in some sense the private world is already there, like an empty room or chair, to receive the subject and in that sense independent of it, imposing a skeletal framework on his point of view – "if a third man enters and sits between" two others, "a third world, intermediate between the two previous worlds, begins to be perceived" (*OKnExW*, 94). For a private world regardless of whether it contains a subject, Russell adopts the word "perspective" "to obviate the suggestion that a private world is only real when someone views it" (*ML*, 154). "The system consisting of all views of the universe, perceived and unperceived, I shall call the system of 'perspectives'; I shall confine the expression 'private worlds' to such views of the universe as are actually perceived" (*OKnExW*, 95). Continuity both justifies and interrelates the perspectives. What Russell calls "the space of perspectives" is "the space of points of view, since each private world may be regarded as the appearance which the universe presents from a certain point of view" (*ML*, 154). The perspective is a kind of observatory.

The source for the empty perspective should be clear: it is a possible world in a "hypothetical Leibnizian universe." It is "an 'actual' private world when there is an actual spectator to which it appears," and otherwise " 'ideal' " (*OKnExW*, 117) – "we may suppose . . . that each exists entire exactly as it is perceived, and might be exactly as it is even if it were not perceived" (*OKnExW*, 95).[15]

The mere status of unobserved sensibilia as a "hypothetical construction . . . which is logically unobjectionable" (*OKnExW*, 104) is all that is required for Russell's argument contra Berkeley. Berkeley's seeming oxymoron "unperceivable perceptions" is itself three times invoked in *History of English Thought*. Stephen first applies it to "the various assumptions of the Cartesian method" (29). He next agrees that Berkeley "brought out . . . the contradictions inherent in the conception of matter as an unperceivable perception" (39). Again, Stephen adopts Berkeley's language in discussing Hume: "Hence we come to the contradictory conceptions of unperceivable perceptions and inactive activities" (53). Russell thus takes over a term not simply directly from Berkeley but one circulating in Cambridge. Only he transforms it from a problem for Realism to a claimed solution: "If there were, as some have held, a logical impossibility in sense-data persisting after ceasing to be data, that certainly would tend to show that they were mental; but if, as I contend, their non-persistence is merely a probable inference from empirically ascertained causal laws, then it carries no such implication with it, and we are quite free to treat them as part of the subject-matter of physics" (*ML*, 146). Unperceivable perceptions become unperceived perceptions, not impossible but contingently unrealized. "The world we have constructed . . . is therefore a world which may be actual. It fits the facts, and there is no empirical evidence against it; it also is free from logical impossibilities" (*OKnExW*, 101). Thus arises a ghostly virtual reality. Unobserved sensibilia's mere possibility suffices for building up knowledge.

What brings about their actualization is the perspective's occupation by a subject and the corresponding interception of sensibilia by sense-organs located in time and space. Both Moore and Russell, playing on the etymology of "datum," insist on the givenness of sense-data; they are simply presented to someone: "sense-data, things given or presented by the senses" (Moore, 44). The subject is thereby rendered unnecessary to subjectivity by its theoretically possible absence. It does not endow the private world with its privacy. Privacy is a characteristic of both perspectives and private worlds, the latter being only a special case of the former. Only the latter is attached to something "mental." The distinction between a non-mental but nonetheless private perspective and a mental private world accordingly is the counterpart of that between sensibilia and sense-data.

Repeated applications of Occam's razor have thus "pare[d] away what is superfluous in our hypothesis, leaving a residue which may be regarded as an abstract answer to our problem" (*OKnExW*, 94). Subjectivity and the mind are no longer necessarily linked. Their mutual independence means, Russell says, "it is logically possible for one to exist without the other" (*OKnExW*, 81). The unlooked for consequence will be the contingency of the observer to the observed.

THE CENTERED STRUCTURE OF A PERSPECTIVE: PRIVATE TIME AND SPACE

Each group has a centre in the space of percipients; this centre is real if occupied by a percipient, while otherwise it is ideal. (Russell, *The Analysis of Matter*, 211)

From centre to circumference in any case it is a far cry. (Beckett, *The Unnameable*, in *Three Novels*, 295)

Whence comes the perspective's subjectivity if not from the subject? The answer is from its geometry. It is first of all bounded, its limits dividing it absolutely from all others, creating thereby an outside and an inside. Without, its boundaries form a circumference. Within, it encloses a time and space which are "private." Private space has the name "here"; private time "now." "We may define 'here' as the place, in perspective space, which is occupied by our private world" (*OKnExW*, 99). Likewise for "now." "It is not 'here' alone that is private, but also 'now'" (*HK*, 90). The addition of temporality to the spatially conceived perspective is, for Russell, the necessary correction of Leibniz' monadism in the light of modern physics. For "Leibniz did not carry his monadism far enough, since he applied it only spatially. Not only is a man private from other people, but he is also private from his past and future selves" (*HK*, 90).

In this sense, perspectives frame "events," a notion for which Russell acknowledges Whitehead (*MyPhD*, 10).[16] Whitehead's "toning down" of Leibniz' "monads into unified events in space and time" (*SMW*, 68)[17] allows their subjectivity to be defined purely spatially and temporally. Their privacy is their nonanalyzability into smaller spatio-temporal units: "Events may have a structure, but it is convenient to use the word 'event,' in the strict sense, to mean something which, if it has a structure, has no space-time structure, i.e., it does not have parts" (*Matter*, 286). Their temporality is not duration; their spatiality not extension. The perspective structures by conferring what Whitehead calls "a prehensive unity" on groups of events: "This unity of a prehension defines itself as here and now, and the things so gathered into the grasped unity have essential reference to other places and other times" (*SMW*, 68).[18]

Russell's perspective's internal structure is not the same throughout, however. In "the notion of events grouped around a centre, changing partly in accordance with the laws of perspective and partly in ways which are functions of groups with other centres" (*Matter*, 222), the perspective becomes "centered." If "here" names private space in general, in particular it refers to its center. Thus, within private space we feel the objects of the external world, Russell observes, "to be 'there' as opposed to 'here,'" without meaning them to be "spatially external" (*OKnExW*, 80), the locative "here" naming the location of a possible subject in it and "there," the boundaries of the perspective and hence, of the outer reaches of perception. In this way, sense-data can occupy private space and yet partake of that "outness" Berkeley would deny them (*Three Dialogues*, 37; "WM?," 137). The very existence of such pairs of terms suggests perspectives as circles with centers fading into circumferences. Likewise for the temporals "now" and "then." "A sensation fades gradually, passing by continuous gradations to the status of an image" (*Mind*, 174). So also, "in the image which an event leaves behind it, there is a gradual transition," the "resemblance to a sense-datum decays as time goes on, very rapidly at first, then more slowly" (*TK*, 173–4). An event extends out from a center, like the sun, "spreading out from a centre with the velocity of light" (*ML*, 132): "we perceive events, not substances; that is to say, what we perceive occupies a volume of space-time which is small in all four dimensions, not indefinitely extended in one dimension (time)" (*Matter*, 284).

The perspective's center may remain empty without a centered structure thereby lacking. "Perspectives seem to have, built into them, some kind of selectivity," Sainsbury writes (*Russell*, 265). The 1914 theory of knowledge, with its unoccupied perspectives and sensibilia defined by nothing more than a "here" and a "now" and their complements "there" and "then," presents a centeredness grouping events in configurations moving from here to there, now to then, without recourse to a subject, like the covering power of a lens, whose definition falls off toward the edges of the viewing circle. Whitehead's aim to "substitute" "[f]or Berkeley's *mind*, . . . a process of prehensive unification" (*SMW*, 68) makes this explicit. "Modern physics," he says, "reduces matter to a set of events which proceed outward from a centre. If there is something further in the centre itself, we cannot know about it, and it is irrelevant to physics" (*OP*, 163).

But at times Russell counterposes an empty perspective in which all is the same throughout to an occupied one with the characteristic centrally illuminated structure fading off at the edges. The centered structure becomes a factor of awareness, of "the selectiveness of mind" (*TK*, 40; *LK*, 169) – a version of Leslie Stephen's claim that "the power of thus organising impressions implies the existence of an organised mind" (*HET*, 49): "At any moment of my conscious life, there is one object (or at most some very small number of objects) to which I am attending. All knowledge of particulars radiates out from this object. This object is not intrinsically distinguishable from other objects – it just happens," Russell writes, "that I am attending to it" (*LK*, 168; *TK*, 40). As "the last objection" Russell had "urge[d] against neutral monism," he finds missing "that principle of selection which, to a given person at a given moment, makes one object, one subject and one time intimate and near and immediate." For "[i]n a world" without "specifically mental facts," i.e., with only unoccupied perspectives, "there would be a complete impartiality, an evenly diffused light, not the central illumination fading away into outer darkness, which is characteristic of objects in relation to a mind" (*TK*, 40). The unoccupied perspective now becomes the container for a flat, uncentered "here"/"now," lacking any principle for concentrating on some object[s] and not others. It will yield a post-analytic vision, by contrast with the selectiveness of commonsense vision.

NEUTRAL MONISM

The meaning of objective truth is, simply, that which is true both for you and me. When I come to such a neutral "form" as space or time, which is taken to be identical for us all, I can no longer call it either objective or subjective, or I may call it indifferently either. (Stephen, "What Is Materialism?," 149)

The privately localized and temporalized reduced subjectivity receives an objectivity Russell alternately calls *neutral* and *impersonal.* "Neutrality" derives from the "neutral monism" Russell temporarily adopts c. 1919 from William James and Mach. Yet the term *neutral* appears as early as 1912. Russell's "agreement with neutral monism" (*TK*, 22) in 1914, in rejecting that "when an object is known to me, there is in my mind something which may be called an 'idea' of the object," stops at neutral monism's further assumption "that, if anything is immediately present to me, that thing must be part of my mind":

The upholders of "ideas" . . . believe in the duality of the mental and the physical . . . Neutral monists, perceiving (rightly, as I think) that constituents of the physical world can be immediately present to me, infer that the mental and the physical are composed of the same "stuff," and are merely different arrangements of the same elements. (*TK*, 22)

The issue lies not so much in dualism or its rejection but in a different conception of the dualities and, hence, of neutrality. Something present to the mind can without absurdity be independent of it, thereby "neutralized" by its extra-mental location. "Physical subjectivity" entails a modicum of neutrality. The same term "neutrality" is applied to universals. Their neutral status resembles that of sensibilia in that they are "not merely mental. By this is meant that whatever being belongs to them is independent of their being thought of or in any way apprehended by minds" (*PP*, 97). The positive denotation of "neutrality" is not the same in both cases – universals are in no way physical; "relations," for instance, "must be placed in a world which is neither mental nor physical" (*PP*, 90). A relation "is neither in space nor in time, neither material nor mental; yet it is something" (*PP*, 98). Neutrality is merely logical economy in definition: the possession or not of a property remains unspecified (*PP,* 98). The property eliminated in both cases is the mental.

In later texts, Russell treats his and Whitehead's answer to Idealism as a version of neutral monism, claiming it "has led, especially in the works of Dr. Whitehead," "to a new interpretation of physics, which is to make the world of matter less remote from the world of our experience" (*Matter,* 6; cf. *PP,* 258). Instead of "divid[ing] the known world into mind and matter," "[t]he view [of neutral monism] . . . is that both mind and matter are structures composed of a more primitive stuff which is neither mental nor material" (*OP,* 303). Neutrality means that "[t]he datum is a datum equally for physics and for psychology; it is a meeting point of the two. It is neither mental nor physical, . . . but it is part of the raw material of both the mental and the physical worlds" (*OP,* 217). Russell's presentation of neutral monism in this passage is, in fact, very like Leslie Stephen's claim "that spiritual and material do not represent two different categories, either of which can be contemplated alone, but that they correspond to two methods of combining experience, each legitimate in its own sphere" ("WM?," 129).

Russell abandons the briefly espoused neutral monism because of the unavoidability of "a duality . . . essential in any form of knowledge"; there is awareness, "recollection" "of something," "generally, knowing is distinct from that which is known. This duality, after it has been banished from sensation, has to be somehow re-introduced" (*MyPhD,* 104). The perspective itself is "infected" with it, because "every particular of the kind relevant to physics" "is associated with two places; e.g. my sensation of the star is associated with the place where I am and with the place where the star is." Russell's dualism is itself neutrally structural, consisting of "places" or perspectives. "This dualism has nothing to do with any 'mind' that I may be supposed to possess; it exists in exactly the same sense if I am replaced by a photographic plate" (*Mind,* 130). The table is thereby endowed with its own perspective, though in no way with a mind.

THE ATOMISTIC VISION AND PARTICULARS: REALITY IS NOT ONE

[T]here are many things. (Russell, *Mysticism and Logic,* 106)

The ground for our knowledge of the external world is thus reduced to a single perspective, a brief event. But each such perspective is endlessly multiplied. Russell's theory of sensibilia, antidote to Berkeleyan Idealism, is linked to the "absolute pluralism" (*ML*, 106) or "logical atomism" which defines his early "revolt" against the then domininant British Hegelianism. Maintaining the plurality of things,

> it denies that there is a whole composed of those things . . . [P]hilosophical propositions, instead of being concerned with the whole of things collectively, are concerned with all things distributively; and not only must they be concerned with all things, but they must be concerned with such properties of all things as do not depend upon the accidental nature of the things that there happen to be, but are true of any possible world, independently of such facts as can only be discovered by our senses. (*ML*, 106)

This atomism denies "the monism of the idealist" (*TK*, 6, 15 and *LK*, 139), not neutral monism (*LK*, 178, 190). It rejects the belief in unity as oneness Russell labels "mystic": "When I say my logic is atomistic, I mean that I share the common-sense belief that there are many separate things; I do not regard the apparent multiplicity of the world as consisting merely in phases and unreal divisions of a single indivisible Reality" (*LK*, 178). "For some years I was a disciple of Mr. Bradley," Russell explains, "but about 1898 I changed my views, largely as a result of arguments with G. E. Moore . . . I found myself driven to pluralism" (*LK*, 324). In one professing a love for a "clean-shaven picture of reality" (*MyPhD*, 49), this rejection of monism for atomism is motivated by another factor than logic: empirical reality, "the bizarre multiplicity of the world" (*Portraits from Memory*, 38). "The empirical person would naturally say, there are many things. The monistic philosopher attempts to show that there are not. I should propose to refute his *a priori* arguments. I do not consider there is any logical necessity for there to be many things, nor for there not to be many things" (*LK*, 188). "There is no reason why you should not have a universe consisting of one particular and nothing else" – "it is merely an empirical fact that this is not the case" (*LK*, 202). It could always have been otherwise. Empirical reality makes it "essential to the philosophy we are examining," he wrote à propos of Bradley's Idealism, "to deny absolute identity, and retain 'identity in difference.' The apparent multiplicity of the real world is otherwise inexplicable" (*MyPhD*, 47).

In describing his emergence from Idealism – "[i]n the first flush of my belief in separate atoms" (*Portraits from Memory*, 41) – Russell's metaphoric language stresses the liberating power of observation, even for one with the logician's passion: it was "a great liberation, as if I had escaped from a hot-house into a wind-swept headland" (*MyPhD*, 48). What was liberating was the exposure to sense-data in great gusts.[19] As the "furniture" of the world, they should preferably be multiple and outdoors; hence, the table is left behind for the data of physics and astronomy. Russell put it in terms of liking Kant's "starry heavens even better than the moral law" (*MyPhD*, 48). "The world of astronomy dominates my imagination and I am very conscious of the minuteness of our planet in comparison with the systems of galaxies" (*MyPhD*, 96). The move from the table to the heavens with their myriad stars charts the link between perspectivized sense-data and logical atomism via the "Revolt into Pluralism."[20]

Russell replaces the monist's single indivisible Reality with the "monadist"'s "large and varied external world" (*SO*, 80), broken down into "little bits each with its own individuality" (*Matter*, 19) of which the stars are an emblem. "The world consists of a number, perhaps finite, perhaps infinite, of entities" (*LK*, 341). Russell's terms are characteristically plural: relations, sense-data, sensibilia, perspectives, private worlds, events. These "bits" are autonomous and contingent, the existence of one not necessarily dependent on the existence of the others: the proposition "Reality is one" of Bradley's axiom of internal relations is the specific target (*MyPhD*, 43–8), the doctrine that "There can never be two facts concerning the same *thing*" because "a thing is so modified by its relations that it cannot be the same in one relation as in another" (*OKnExW*, 157). Russell's counterposition is that "the world is made up of an immense number of bits, and . . ., so far as logic can show, each bit might be exactly as it is even if other bits did not exist" (*Portraits from Memory*, 42); i.e., the atoms "have various relations to each other" (*LK*, 341). "[T]he reality of relations" (*LK*, 24) for Russell means "external" relations. The method adapted to this atomized world is analysis, which breaks things down, our analyzable table among them, distinguishes one thing from another, establishes relations between them: "all the ordinary objects of daily life are apparently complex entities: such things as tables and chairs, loaves and fishes, persons and principalities and powers" (*LK*, 190). By contrast, "the axiom of internal relations is incompatible with all complexity" and "leads . . . to a rigid monism. There is only one thing, and only one proposition" (*MyPhD*, 47).

The basic empirical units are Russell's "particulars," most typically his sensible monads: "We speak of whatever is given in sensation, or is of the same nature as things given in sensation, as a *particular*" (*PP*, 93). But there are other particulars than sense-data: "A particular with which we are acquainted is either a sense-datum, or a datum of immediate memory, or an image" (*TK*, 173). Particulars are non-repeatable or individual entities or complexes of entities, like the dot Russell makes on the blackboard (*LK*, 178). Each particular is momentary: " 'a particular as a rule is apt to last for a very short time' " (*LK*, 203). Particulars are "terms of relation in atomic facts," i.e., the simplest facts. They have the independence the rejection of internal relations requires: "Particulars have this peculiarity . . . that each of them stands entirely alone and is completely self-subsistent . . . [E]ach particular that there is in the world does not in any way logically depend upon any other particular" (*LK*, 201–2). Particulars are known by direct apprehension or acquaintance. As really occurring entities, they are directly represented by logical terms which Russell calls "logically proper names" (*HK*, 292ff.; *OP*, 177). Woolf uses the term with Russell's sense when she has Neville in *The Waves* say "I gradually lose all knowledge of particulars" and when he speaks of "what particular name" (138).

THE WORLD OF UNIVERSALS

"I hear that Bennett has given up his theory of truth."

Denham . . . proceeded to explain . . . what changes it involved in the philosophy which they both accepted . . . something very obscure about the complex nature of one's apprehension of facts. (Woolf, *Night and Day*, 65)[21]

Modern logic . . . has the effect of enlarging our abstract imagination, and providing an infinite number of possible hypotheses to be applied to the analysis of any complex fact. (Russell, *Our Knowledge of the External World*, 68)

Moore had a nightmare once in which he could not distinguish propositions from tables. But even when he was awake, he could not distinguish love and beauty and truth from the furniture. (Keynes, in Skidelsky, *John Maynard Keynes*, I, 137)

Particulars are not the only entities knowable by acquaintance. So also are universals (known *a priori*). In 1910, Moore had proposed for "general" or "abstract idea" the name, "not so familiar," of "universals" (*SomeMain*, 329), "abstract objects, not perceptible by the senses, having no place in time and space, and neither suffering or producing change," in Sainsbury's paraphrase (*Russell*, 20). The "astonishingly abstract" (*MB*, 190) Bloomsbury talk Woolf took as paradigmatic centered on universals: "beauty," "good," "reality" are her examples (*MB*, 189). Russell's examples are "*whiteness, diversity, brotherhood*" (*PP*, 52). Russell's ontology is marked by "an ultimate dualism between universals and particulars," Ayer says, as is Moore's. This meant "that both particulars and universals were in some sense real, and that neither was reducible to the other" (*Russell and Moore*, 96). In the early Russell, universals constitute, with particulars, the logical terms of propositions, what *Principles of Mathematics* calls "*things* and *concepts*," things including sensible objects and psychological events and concepts, "predicates or class-concepts" and "relations" (*LK*, 109). "Whiteness" is a predicate or quality. Examples of relations are being "earlier" or "later than," "to the left of" something else, "near to" it or "different from" or "identical to" something (*PE*, 157; *SomeMain*, 330). Also "a primitive constituent of our experience" (*TK*, 99) is "logical form," the "new idea" (Hylton, *Russell*, 343) Russell introduces in *Theory of Knowledge*. (The term "logical form" Leslie Stephen had used in "What is Materialism?," 148.)

Universals and forms constitute the "logical foundation" (*AAA*, 86) of knowledge. They preserve Moore's and Russell's early "Platonic atomism," to use Hylton's term, or Realism. Altered between 1910 and 1918, the revisions aimed to preserve "that feeling for reality which ought to be preserved even in the most abstract studies" (*IMP*, 169). Logic is necessary to it, first, because it gives a completer reality: "the outer world – the world, so to speak, which knowledge is aiming at knowing – is not completely described by a lot of 'particulars,'" Russell says (*LK*, 183). Among the atoms, "[s]ome of them will be what I call 'particulars' – such things as little patches of colour or sounds, momentary things – and some of them will be predicates or relations and so on" (*LK*, 179). Logic also provides the means for combining particulars and universals, making possible a knowledge of a reality going beyond Moore's "direct apprehension" (*SomeMain*, 46, 83) or Russell's acquaintance; logical form yields a picture of that reality.

It is "the very peculiar being that belongs to universals" and forms that has led to their being thought "mental" (*PP*, 99). The problem Moore had addressed in "The Nature of Judgement" is how to justify treating them as "real objects" and not "symbolic fictions." In "Being, Fact and Existence," he aims not only "to point out what kind of things 'universals' are" but also "that there are such things – that they are not pure fictions, like chimaeras and griffins" (*SomeMain*, 329). Between *Principles of Mathematics* in 1903 and his works of the twenties, Russell caused the word "reality" to shift from referring to a more to a less inclusive class of objects. Russell's later use of the term "logical fiction" is not meant to concede abstract ideas to either Idealism or nominalism. Moore's "The Refutation of Idealism" and Russell's "On the Nature of Truth and Falsehood," the latter reprinted in *Philosophical Essays* of 1910, both in the Woolfs' library (see chapter 1, n. 27), still defend a theory of truth whose terms – "reality," "truth," "fact" and "fiction" – figure in the opening of *A Room of One's Own*. "Fiction here is likely to contain more truth than fact" (*Room*, 4).

The reality of particulars does not require justification, but that of universals does.[22] Platonic Atomism calls the reality of universals "being," as distinct from the "existence" of particulars. The "fundamental, and all-inclusive, ontological category" of Moore's Realism, according to Hylton, "is being. All things are, or have being. Some things, those which are temporal, also exist" (*Russell*, 130).[23] For Moore "non-existent entities" include "numbers, logical relations, and, paradigmatically, propositions" (132). In *Principles of Mathematics*, the distinct reality claimed for universals and particulars depends on the same distinction between being and existence (Ayer, *Russell and Moore*, 69ff; Hylton, *Russell*, 172ff). "Existence . . . is the prerogative of some only amongst beings" (*PofM*, 449) while being, as in Meinong, "is that which belongs to every conceivable term, to every possible object of thought – in short to everything that can possibly occur in any proposition, true or false, and to all such propositions themselves. Being belongs to whatever can be counted" (*PofM*, 449). While "thoughts and feelings, minds and physical objects *exist*," Russell wrote, "universals do not exist in this sense"; rather, "they *subsist* or *have being*, where 'being' is opposed to 'existence' as being timeless" (*PP*, 100). Hence, this unreal reality of universals is also their atemporality (*LK*, 124). Existence implies temporality. Woolf's combination "moment of being," temporal in one sense, is atemporal in another.

Principles of Mathematics's extreme realism was, Sainsbury remarks, "needlessly ontologically extravagant" (*Russell*, 17), including even entities the Moore of 1910 dismissed as "pure fictions": in the "inventory" of "things" with being Russell lists are "many terms which do not exist, for example, the points in a non-Euclidean space and the pseudo-existents of a novel" (*PofM*, 45), "[n]umbers, the Homeric gods, relations, chimeras and four-dimensional spaces" (*PofM*, 449). This extreme realism proved indefensible and was replaced by a more economical one. "Logic . . . must no more admit a unicorn than zoology can; for logic is concerned with the real world just as truly as zoology, though with its more abstract and general features" (*IMP*, 169). To reduce non-existents with being without eliminating the knowledge they make possible, Russell's solution was to "get down in theory, if not in practice, to ultimate simples, out of which the world is built" (*LK*, 270). The "last residue in analysis" (*LK*, 179) constitutes "the logical atoms." These "simple undefined things" include "particulars and qualities and relations of various orders, a whole hierarchy of different sorts of simples" (*LK*, 270). The reduction distinguishes the simple core of logical atoms sharply from the "complex" entities "built" from it. Complexity provides Russell with an account for non-existent "entities" and ultimately propositions without having to pronounce on their reality. For in cases like "the unicorn," "the distinction between existence and subsistence does not help us" (*LK*, 328). The simple/complex distinction corresponds to two kinds of reality and two forms of knowledge. Each knowledge has its objects, with their peculiar reality. Russell pronounces that "simples have a kind of reality not belonging to anything else" (*LK*, 270), i.e., particulars *and* simple universals. What is knowable by direct apprehension is now simples. Hence the distinction between "knowledge of truths, as opposed to knowledge of objects, which is acquaintance" (*TK*, 155). Knowledge of truths is dependent on another knowledge of objects, "knowledge by description," which, unlike acquaintance, is an "indirect knowledge" (Hylton, *Russell*, 248)[24] – the terms "first-hand, second-hand, direct and indirect knowledge" are Woolf's also (*TG*, 49). Indirect knowledge comes to bear the burden of a move out from privacy.

Acquaintance is a relation to a simple object, a function of its being "given," a "datum." For Russell, there is a special "language" of givenness or "presentation": naming. Naming is simply pointing, as the term "demonstrative" suggests. The only true "logically proper name" is the demonstrative "this" or its like, which for Russell refers to what he calls an "emphatic particular" in 1914 (*TK*) and an "egocentric particular" in 1941 (*IMT*). (I return to this terminology in chapter seven.) A term like "this" refers to an object of acquaintance, particular or universal. It gives no information beyond indicating its presence, pointing to a sense-datum in the same way that the "secondary qualities," according to Leslie Stephen, "point out rather than constitute the object" ("WM?," 130). "Real" and "unreal," "existent" and "nonexistent," normally refer to objects, while truth and falsity apply to propositions. But a sense-datum is either there to be apprehended or not, and no mention can meaningfully be made of its absence. Givenness has no negation: "if 'a' is a name, it *must* name something; what does not name anything is not a name" (*IMT*, 179). There is no "dualism of true and false objects of acquaintance." They raise no doubt. "An object of acquaintance is not true or false, but is simply what it is" (*TK*, 108).

The language of presentation says nothing about things not present, not apprehensible. It does not yield a complete knowledge, since, we saw, the world is more than a collection of particulars. This is the role of knowledge by description, which includes knowledge of non-apprehensible entities, either absent or non-existent. Such "objects" are treated as complex to avoid burdening the theory with non-existent beings à la Meinong. A language for absent objects and for relating particulars is needed: there must be descriptions and propositions. Not namable, physical objects must be "described." But because description's objects are not apprehended, a description might fail to refer. Knowledge of them is not indubitable. "There certainly are objects of perception," Russell comments. If "whether these objects are real is to be a substantial question, there must be in the world two sorts of objects, namely, the real and the unreal, and yet the unreal is supposed to be essentially what there is not" (*ML*, 115). For the reality of objects of perception to be meaningfully raised, they must be able to cease being perceptible. Moreover, some propositions fail to state truths, due to "[t]he fundamental characteristic which distinguishes propositions . . . from objects of acquaintance": the fact that the former only can be true and false (*TK*, 108). Hence, the possibility that there can be sentences with descriptions that are false gives rise to the question of existence or non-existence for unperceived objects. Does the table persist in the absence of an observer? Is there a rhinoceros in the room? For is there not a knowledge which consists in knowing whether an object is real or unreal, existent or non-existent?

So the language which refers to absent objects can also fail to denote any objects at all without being nonsensical, while "this" cannot fail to have a referent. Well-known problems arise in connection with the meaningfulness of statements containing referring expressions without referents. Russell had justified being for unicorns because "if they were not entities of a kind, we could make no propositions about them" (*PofM*, 449). Now he must explain their meaningful appearance in propositions in another fashion. Traditionally, the proposition's complexity of form joins particulars to universals or subjects to predicates. But all subjects cannot name particulars: in "Homer did not exist," "Homer is not the entity which is to be found if our judgment is true, but not if it is false" (*PE*, 152). "The puzzle here is: 'how can a non-entity be the subject of a proposition?,'" Sainsbury comments (*Russell*, 108). Another case is "the present king of France is bald." "By the law of excluded middle, . . . either 'the present King of France is bald' or 'the present King of France is not bald' must be true. Yet if we enumerated the things that are bald, and then the things that are not bald, we should not find the present king of France in either list" (*LK*, 48).[25] Somewhat different is "Scott is the author of Waverly."[26] If George IV wished to know if this proposition were true, he did not wonder whether "Scott is Scott" – "an interest in the law of identity can hardly be attributed to the first gentleman of Europe" (*LK*, 48). (Ordinary proper names Russell will analyze as disguised descriptions although not always consistently so. Some, e.g., "Scott" and "Bismarck," refer; others, e.g., "Hamlet," do not.)

Russell's solution is the Theory of Descriptions, which analyzes the description as a "complex symbol" and assigns it meaning only in the proposition. For "the dualism of true and false among objects," i.e., of "real and unreal objects, or true and fictitious objects," is based upon a failure to distinguish between propositions and presentation (*TK*, 141). "The dualism of true and false . . . presupposes propositions, and does not arise so long as we confine ourselves to acquaintance" (*TK*, 141); only "propositions are the bearers of truth" (Hylton, *Russell*, 280). For Russell, "pairs, such as 'real' and 'unreal,' 'existent' and 'non-existent,' 'valid' and 'invalid,' etc. . . all derived from the one fundamental pair, 'true' and 'false' applicable only . . . to *propositions*" (*ML*, 168). Neither "the author of Waverly" nor "the unicorn" are meaningful in isolation. Russell suspends descriptions' ability to refer until they appear in propositions, treating them as "incomplete symbols." Introduced in "On Denoting" (1905), "incomplete phrases" are those "as only acquire meaning when put into a context which, with them forms a proposition" (*ML*, 168). By contrast, names are "complete," i.e., they refer in isolation but are not "true." "True" and "false" apply only to propositions and derivatively, by their completion in propositions, "to *descriptions*, but not to proper names," not "to data, but only to entities or non-entities described in terms of data" (*ML*, 168–9). Descriptions receive their meaning from propositions also by being analyzed to contain existential propositions, as with that in "the present King of France is bald," which becomes "there is one and only one person who is the present king of France, and that person is bald." "The present king of France is bald" becomes false and meaningful. For, unlike a true name, a description "does not become incapable of occurring signficantly merely on the ground that it describes nothing, the reason being that it is a *complex* symbol, of which the meaning is derived from that of its constituent symbols" (*IMP*, 179). "And so, when we ask whether Homer existed, we are using the word 'Homer' as an abbreviated description: we may replace it by (say) 'the author of the *Iliad* and the *Odyssey*'" (*IMP*, 179). "We may inquire significantly whether Homer existed, which we could not do if 'Homer' were a name" (*IMP*, 178). The "four words together" – "I met a unicorn" – "make a significant proposition, and the word 'unicorn' by itself is significant," but "if we falsely attribute meaning" to "a unicorn," "we find ourselves saddled with 'a unicorn,' and with the problem how there can be such a thing in a world where there are no unicorns" (*IMP*, 170).

Platonic Atomism's over-populated world included not only chimeras but propositions, known also by "direct apprehension" (*SomeMain*, 84). Among Moore's "anti-idealist positions," Hylton writes, is "the objectivity and independence of propositions" (*Russell*, 130). Moore asserts in 1910 "that absolutely all the contents of the Universe, absolutely everything that *is* at all, may be divided into . . . *propositions* . . . and into things which are not propositions . . . There certainly are in the Universe such things as propositions" (*SomeMain*, 71). But false propositions raised a problem, for, Russell observes, "it is very difficult, except under the lash of a tyrannous theory, to admit that *false* propositions are entities" (*TK*, 339). Hence, in the same 1910–11 lecture series in which he had insisted on the reality of propositions, Moore states that "I don't now believe that there are such things as propositions at all" (*SomeMain*, 335). After 1910, Russell also finds "'that propositions are not what you might call 'real.'" In his "inventory of the world, propositions would not come in'" (*LK*, 214; Ayer, *Russell and Moore*, 86, 81–2).

Truth and falsity come to reside in the "belief" or "judgement." How then does Russell avoid suggesting "the mind-dependence of reality" (Hylton, *Russell*, 337)? Via the "fact" which is "independent of the objects of judgement" (338) "The doctrine of facts was very much of a common Cambridge teaching in McTaggart's day," Geach writes. "The young Wittgenstein . . . was solidly persuaded of this ontology of facts" (*Truth, Love, and Immortality*, 39). "The world is the totality of facts, not of things," the *Tractatus* begins (I.I). This "characterization of the universe ('the world') as an aggregate of facts" Black calls "the outstanding innovation of Wittgenstein's ontology" (*Companion*, 27), perhaps one of those "ideas which," as Russell admits, "I learnt from my friend and former pupil Ludwig Wittgenstein" (*LK*, 177). Russell's claim that the world is "not completely described" as an aggregate of particulars (*LK*, 183) Black thinks "probably inspired by the first section of the *Tractatus* (*Companion*, 30). Nonetheless, Moore had already introduced facts in his 1910 lectures. (The importance of the term "fact" in Woolf has been often commented on but never connected to its use in Moore, Russell and Wittgenstein.)[27] In the new theory, "the notion of truth, and of a proposition" are "increasingly" replaced by the "fact" (Hylton, *Russell*, 328). The proposition's objective independence is transferred to it: "the world contains facts"; "these, just as much as particular tables and chairs are part of the real world" (*LK*, 182–3; see Hylton, *Russell*, 337).

The fact's role, we recall, is to preserve the realism of logic. It is the unit of reality to which a logical complex, the proposition (or belief or judgement), now "corresponds." "Reality is compared with propositions," the *Tractatus* says (4.05). In the 1910 Moore, a "correspondance theory of truth" treats facts as "the sorts of entities which *correspond* . . . to true beliefs" (*SomeMain*, 321). So, instead of contrasting propositions and non-propositions, "[w]e may divide all the constituents of the Universe – all the things which are, into two classes," one those only expressible by a clause beginning "the fact that" and "the other all the rest." Russell's new theory of truth also makes "correspondance with fact . . . the *definition* of 'truth', not merely a criterion" (*TK*, 164) and "define[s] falsehood by the absence of a correspondance" (*TK*, 149). The false proposition, eliminated along with "the unicorn," means the true proposition is also eliminated from reality. What remains is the fact.

Facts, by contrast with propositions, Hylton goes on, show "no duality of true and false" (*Russell*, 337). This might suggest that a fact is a simple object of acquaintance, i.e., a particular. But it differs in form from a particular by virtue of its correspondance to propositions, with their true/false duality. The fact is "complex." Hence, naming is not adequate to it. Wittgenstein's ontology of facts also rejects "the traditional conception of the universe as something that can be referred to by a name," Black writes (*Companion*, 28). The particular's simplicity is reflected by the logically proper name, a simple symbol. It stands for a simple knowledge whose structure shows "a dual relation of the mind to a single objective" (*PE*, 157), what Russell calls a "two-term relation in which the object can be *named* but not *asserted*," one "inherently incapable of truth or falsehood" (*ML*, 142). This is the relation of acquaintance.

The proposition or judgement reveals the fact's logical complexity. An "observed complex fact, such as that this patch of red is to the left of that patch of blue," differs radically in "*logical* structure" from "a simple sense-datum," although it is "also to be regarded as a datum" and "epistemologically. . . does not differ greatly from" one (*ML*, 142).[28] To demonstrate this, between the simple name, "this," and the proposition representing the complex fact, e.g. "the knife is to the left of the book," Russell posits the "complex object" of sensation, "knife-to-left-of-book," given and hence certain (*PE*, 157). It seems at once a "single whole," a presentation – "to perceive a complex object, such as 'knife-to-left-of-book,' there must be such an object" (*PE*, 157) – but containing separable elements, Russell's hyphens suggesting separability-in-unity. "If I attend to this complex object and analyse it, I can arrive at the judgement 'the knife is to the left of the book.' Here the knife and the book and their spatial relation are severally before my mind; but in the perception I had the single whole 'knife-to-left-of-book'" (*PE*, 157). Now it "is not a two-term relation, but involves the propositional form," it "gives knowledge of a truth, not mere acquaintance with a particular" (*ML*, 142).

Correspondence with a fact accounts for the true proposition. But how is the false proposition meaningful? Russell's example (*OKnExW*, 68–9; *PE*, 150–1) is the judgement that Charles I died in his bed. Unlike "Charles I died on the scaffold," no fact corresponds to it. "Charles I and death and his bed are objective, but they are not except in my thought, put together as my false belief supposes." Again, the operative notions, as for descriptions without referents, are "complexity" and "incompleteness." What is needed is "some other logical form than a two-term relation" (*OKnExW*, 68): "a multiple relation of the mind to the various terms with which the judgement is concerned" (*PE*, 155).

The "multiple" relation relates a mind not, as in sensation, to one but to two or more objects – e.g., Charles I, death and his bed; the mind brings together these several "fragments of belief, unsoldered and separate, lacking the unity of phrases fashioned by the old believers" (*ND*, 506). Earlier the proposition had done this, but now Russell introduces something new: between belief, judgement and the fact floats "logical form," a kind of phantom proposition. It is the proposition's meaning, independent of its truth or falsity: "what we call believing or understanding is a fact of the same logical form whether the proposition is true or whether it is false"; for belief or understanding, "there is no difference, as regards reality, between true and false propositions" (*TK*, 109). At stake is the proposition's reality. Rather than "admit the reality of false propositions," Russell prefers "a theory which shall regard true and false propositions as alike unreal, i.e. as incomplete symbols" (*TK*, 109), like descriptions and classes, "i.e., some context is necessary before the phrase expressing a proposition acquires a complete meaning" (*TK*, 109) – e.g., "the phrase 'that so and so' has no complete meaning by itself, which would enable it to denote a definite object as (e.g.) the word 'Socrates' does." It is "essentially incomplete, and only acquires full significance when words are added so as to express a judgement, e.g. 'I believe that so and so'" (*PE*, 151). What completes it is the belief or judgement.

The complex objects of the judgement are related by the logical form. In propositions "where all the constituents have been replaced by apparent variables," this "pure form alone remains" (*TK*, 129). "[A]s the type of such propositions" Russell takes "'something is somehow related to something,' i.e. 'there is an x and a y and an R such that x has the relation R to y' or 'xRy is sometimes true'" (*TK*, 129). It is "acquaintance with" the skeletal "'something has some relation to something'"[29] that allows us to understand "'this has this relation to that'" (*TK*, 129), where constants replace the variables. We could think of Leslie Stephen's analysis of "This is a table" as "a general formula with an indefinite term, such that when that term is filled in or defined it indicates the sensations corresponding to any particular case" ("WM?," 138). The difference is the treatment of "this." For Stephen, it is not the name of a particular but, à la Bradley, more like a variable – an indefinite term; for Russell "this" is never general, not a variable term of logical form but a constant introduced into it.

Wishing "to give the name 'form' to genuine objects rather than symbolic fictions" (*TK*, 129), Russell takes what Hylton calls "a strikingly imaginative step." He makes the form "a further entity," a "peculiarly abstract" fact (*Russell*, 346). Given "acquaintance with forms," "then a form must be a genuine object" (346), but "such absolutely general 'facts' as 'something is somehow related to something' have no constituents, are unanalyzable, and must accordingly be called simple. They have therefore all the essential characteristics required of pure forms" (*TK*, 129). This abstract object is the unvarying framework holding together a variety of changing constituents. "The 'form' of a proposition is that, in it, that remains unchanged when every constituent of the proposition is replaced by another" (*IMP*, 199). What was the proposition has now become its after-image, like the Cheshire cat's smile, one of those "pure 'forms' that occur in logic," what "remains" "when all the constituents of a complex have been enumerated" and "which is the way in which the constituents are combined" (*TK*, 98).

It is via the vocabulary of "skeletons" and "scaffolding" that Cambridge philosophy conceptualizes logic's relation to a knowledge of the world. Logic, for Russell, provides a bare structure upon which empirical knowledge is built. "The proposition constructs a world with the help of a logical scaffolding," his "former pupil" writes (Wittgenstein, *Tractatus*, 4.023),[30] or with a "network" (6.35). A "constituentless" fact (i.e. a form) (Hylton, *Russell*, 348) ultimately finds its matching content in another fact whose constituents it unites. "Thus the universe is the incarnation of logic," Leslie Stephen had put it (*HET*, 31). "Through the whole apparatus of logic the physical laws still speak of the objects of the world," the *Tractatus* echoes him (6.3431).

The abstract skeleton, fleshed out, becomes discernible: "one can actually see in the proposition all the logical features possessed by reality if it is true," the *Tractatus* concludes. If it is not, "[o]ne can draw conclusions from false propositions" (4.023). This is Wittgenstein's "picture theory of the (elementary) proposition." "A picture agrees with reality or fails to agree; it is correct or incorrect, true or false" (2.21). In the picture theory, as Russell describes it in his "Introduction" to the *Tractatus*, "the logical proposition is a picture (true or false) of the fact, and has in common with the fact a certain structure" (21). "A proposition can be true or false only in virtue of being a picture of reality" (*Tractatus*, 4.06). Hence, the picture is not of a "nameable entity" but exhibits the proposition's complexity. Black's formulation – "reality must have the character of being what answers to a complete and perfectly faithful chronicle" (the word is not Wittgenstein's), instead of an "all-inclusive catalogue" of things (*Companion*, 30), misleadingly suggests reality's structure is narrative. Woolf's assertion that "history supplies us with the fact" (*TG*, 29) coexists with her sense that narrative is "false" and "unreal" (*Diary*, III, 209–10). We will see in Part II Woolf's conception of logical form, what she calls "pattern," excludes traditional narrative.

Russell's idea of acquaintance with logical form resembles a pictorial view of the proposition. A general shared visual thinking might be traced to that new element of Apostolic thinking Woolf claims Fry introduced which she metaphorizes as eyes bestowed on the blind Apostles; it is a leftover of Platonic Atomism (cf. Hylton). It meets the "abstract," "eyeless" dimension of Apostolic thought she associates with logic. The visual thinking makes the "network" directly apprehensible but also treats it as an "invisible web" (Black, *Companion*, 28) bestowing form, like Tyndall's "Web of relations" (*Lectures on Light*, 31), the metaphor of "an invisible elastic net" Woolf will herself exploit (*TL*, 41). For Wittgenstein, this makes it not representable in any language.[31]

> Propositions can represent the whole of reality, but they cannot represent what they must have in common with reality in order to be able to represent it – the logical form.
>
> To be able to represent the logical form, we should have to be able to put

ourselves with the propositions outside logic, that is outside the world. (*Tractatus*, 4.12)

The form rather "mirrors itself in the propositions" (4.121). For "[t]hat which mirrors itself in language, language cannot represent . . . The propositions *show* the logical form of reality" (4.121). The conclusion – "What can be shown *cannot* be said" (4.121) – thus concerns logical form – it is "capable of being a picture of the fact, but the structure cannot itself be put into words" (21). It is temporary – a scaffolding – to be completed by another reality and then removed. The idea gives rise to the famous conclusion about the *Tractatus*' own propositions: "he who understands me finally recognizes them as senseless" (6.54). Having reached that point, "[h]e must so to speak throw away the ladder, after he has climbed up on it" (6.54). Russell had invoked a similar metaphor for sensibilia in 1914, calling them "a hypothetical scaffolding to be used while the edifice of physics is being raised," to be "removed as soon as the edifice is completed" (*ML*, 152–3).

In this way, extreme realism is abandoned to better defend realism. Russell's nominalist method, as he says of the existence of classes, "abstain[s]" from certain "assumptions" as "an example of Occam's razor." But not "assert[ing] that there are classes" is not "asserting dogmatically that there are none." It is "merely agnostic as regards them: like Laplace, we can say, '*je n'ai pas besoin de cette hypothèse*'" (*IMP*, 184). Not agnosticism but knowledge is, however, the goal of Russell's substitution of complex objects for certain simple objects of knowledge. It complicates knowledge itself. Simples, whether logical or sensible, can be known by direct apprehension; more complex objects require the new emphasis on knowledge by description or knowledge of truths, where what the mind comes to know is in no way observed. Whether that knowledge can sustain the visual analogy is a question we return to.

Truth, although logically constructed, remains nonetheless objective, a discovery, as opposed to a creation, of the mind. In 1903 Russell had written that "all knowledge must be recognition, on pain of being mere delusion; Arithmetic must be discovered in just the same sense in which Columbus discovered the West Indies, and we no more create numbers than he created the Indians" (*PofM*, 451). Mind enters because of the possibility of falsehood, yielding what Russell describes as "the mixture of dependence upon mind and independence of mind" which is "characteristic of truth" (*PE*, 158). "[M]istaken belief," contra William James, cannot be the "cognizing of unreality" (*TK*, 140) because there are no "objective falsehoods" to cognize; "the difference between truth and falsehood" is explained "by reference to *fact*, i.e., to what is actually in the universe whatever we may see fit to believe" (*TK*, 153). While "there could be no falsehood if there were no minds to make mistakes" (*PE*, 152), the conditions for truth exist independent of minds in Mr. Ramsay's "facts uncompromising" (*TL*, 11). It is the case "that there *could* be no true beliefs in the Universe, if there could be no minds in it," Moore says, but "there *could* be truths in the Universe, even if there were no minds in it" (*SomeMain*, 323–4).

Post-1912, logic is increasingly connected to empirical reality. "The sense of reality is vital in logic" – Hamlet's unreality guarantees Napoleon's reality: "If no one thought about Hamlet, there would be nothing left of him; if no one had thought about Napoleon, he would have soon seen to it that some one did" (*IMP*, 169–70). Truths unthought of by anyone can be shown to have instances. Moore had stated that "whenever a man believes in a thing, and his belief is true, what he believes in *is* a fact, even if nobody living could absolutely know it to be so" (*SomeMain*, 325). But there also can be "something which corresponds to a true belief . . . even when no one is believing it" (*SomeMain*, 324). Moreover, as with the discoveries of science, there might be truths still undiscovered, or logical contradictions undetected by the logician. Just as the separation of sense-data from sensation is one step toward sensibilia, so the isolation of the proposition "from its subjective context" raises the possibility of there existing propositions of which no one is aware, even though "we cannot know of the existence of propositions other than those that have been actually thought of" (*TK*, 116). So, when a proposition "aRb" is said to have "meaning," it can't "*mean* that somebody understands it." This is why the definition of "proposition" must allow for "a proposition which has never been understood," for "we cannot know that a proposition of the form *xRy* has ever been understood, if the *R* is one of which there is no instance, and with which consequently no human being is acquainted" (*TK*, 134). Indeed, some "general proposition[s] of which the truth is undeniable," like "the proposition: 'All products of two integers, which never have been and never will be thought of by any human being, are over 100' " are, "from the very nature of the case," such that "we can never give an instance," in this example "because any two numbers we may think of are excluded by the terms of the proposition" (*PP*, 108). The laws of logic are likewise mind-independent: "although belief in the law of contradiction is a thought, the law of contradiction itself is not a thought, but a fact concerning the things in the world" (*PP*, 89). Since truth is not dependent on thinking, "[t]he name 'laws of thought'" for logical truths is "misleading, for what is important is not the fact that we think in accordance with these laws, but the fact that things behave in accordance with them; in other words, the fact that when we think in accordance with them we think truly" (*PP*, 73).

In Woolf's novelistic universe, logic will supply the rigid framework of a cosmic humor, inexorably ruling that this or that statement issuing from a mind is a contradiction, an absurdity, a non-sequitur, whether or not the mind in question is aware of it. The truths of logic, "those abstract ideas – figures, laws, stars, facts" which, for the heroine of *Night and Day*, were all that "remained in whose reality she could believe" (284), are thus at once terrifying and reassuring – terrifying because no sophistry, no thinking, can make them other than they are, reassuring because no thinking is required to make them what they are. Its very independence of the mind explains how "[a] law that might be inscrutable but was certainly omnipotent appealed to her . . . , because she could find nothing like it in possession of human lives" (*ND*, 331). When analysis penetrates the vagueness, "when the mist departed a skeleton world and blankness alone remained – a terrible prospect for the eyes of the living to behold" (*ND*, 412). Those same skeletal forms and inexorable laws will also provide the aesthetic principles for an art equal to this vision, painting and novel-writing doing something comparable to putting incomplete symbols together into propositions.

THE LOGICAL CONSTRUCTION OF PHYSICAL OBJECTS AND BIOGRAPHIES

The meaning of objective truth is, simply, that which is true both for you and me. (Stephen, "What is Materialism?," 149)

What I, for my part, think best in his [Leibniz's] theory of monads is his two kinds of space, one subjective, in the perceptions of each monad, and one objective, consisting of the assemblage of points of view of the various monads . . . still useful in relating perception to physics. (Russell, *A History of Western Philosophy*, 596)

Logical analysis has eliminated physical objects, breaking them down into a plurality of private objects, "helter-skelter sense-data" (*OKnExW*, 112–13). The goal is not, however, to remain immured in privacy but to seek what Leslie Stephen called "a principle of order and unity to bring together the separated fragments" (*HET*, 28). Russell had already eliminated numbers, descriptions and classes as ultimate inferred entities, following his "own version of Ockham's maxim" (Pears, *Bertrand Russell*, 37), what he calls "[t]he supreme maxim in scientific philosophising: *Wherever possible, logical constructions are to be substituted for inferred entities*" (*ML*, 150). For example, "[b]y defining the cardinal number of a given collection as the class of all equally numerous collections," Russell explains, a "metaphysical postulate" becomes unnecessary (*ML*, 151). Treating "[c]lasses or series of particulars" as "logical constructions or symbolic fictions" means they are "collected together" on the basis of "some property which makes it convenient . . . to speak of them as wholes" (*ML*, 124). So also, we saw, "this common element that we call the 'proposition'" (*TK*, 115) is merely "something which a number of mental events have in common" (doubting, desiring, willing, etc.) (*TK*, 114) and which "remains unchanged" (*TK*, 115).

On this model, the physical "thing" is "defined as the class of its appearances" in perspectives (*ML*, 155), the only inferences retained being those to other people's sense-data and sensibilia. The construction is also the class correlating the space of the different senses (*OKnExW*, 118), for "the space of science is neutral as between touch and sight" (*PP*, 29). Things become "assemblages of momentary particulars" (*ML*, 131), e.g., the sun, "a whole assemblage of particulars, existing at different times"; they "will be correlated with each other by a certain continuity and certain intrinsic laws of variation as we pass outward from the centre" (*ML*, 132). This solution is adumbrated in *The Problems of Philosophy*'s example of the dinner table.

One great reason why . . . we must secure a physical object in addition to the sense-data, is that we want the same object for different people. When ten people are sitting round a dinner-table, it seems preposterous to maintain that they are not seeing the same tablecloth, the same knives and forks and spoons and glasses. But sense-data are private to each separate person; what is immediately present to the sight of one is not immediately present to the sight of another: they all see things from slightly different points of view, and therefore see them slightly differently. Thus, if there are to be public neutral objects, which can be in some sense known to many different people, there must be something over and above the private and particular sense-data which appear to various people. (*PP*, 20–1)

The shared, "neutral" domain between the multiplicity of private points of view is Russell's "public" sphere. The public object is constructed via a Russellian monadology that puts together the different perspectives on the table, "ordered in one space," "the space of points of view" (*ML*, 154). This space "might seem at first sight . . . packed much fuller than it could possibly hold. At every place between us and the sun there are particulars" (*ML*, 132). But this one "space of the real world is a space of six dimensions" in which "there is plenty of room for all the particulars for which we want to find positions," by contrast with the three-dimensional space of one man's sensible objects. "There are therefore a multitude of three-dimensional spaces in the world: there are all those perceived by observers, and presumably all those which are not perceived, merely because no observer is suitably situated for perceiving them" (*ML*, 133). Places in them, none of which are in common, are "correlated" in a "three-dimensional order" into "members (or aspects) of one physical thing" (*ML*, 133–4), "correlation" being the way to make "the transition from perception to physics" (*Matter*, 333).[32] And just as a man may "sit down between two others," actualizing appearances "intermediate" between those of the other two men, so sensibilia function to fill the interstices "on principles of continuity" between two occupied perspectives much as Berkeley, according to Leslie Stephen, meant mind rather than matter to provide the "substratum . . . necessary to preserve the continuity of the external world" (*HET*, 41), formulae "so constructed that when the necessary data are filled in they give the experience corresponding to that position" ("WM?," 137). "No logically cogent argument proves that anything unperceived exists; we assume this, first instinctively, then for the sake of continuity, because a merely sensational world would be intolerably jagged," Russell explains (*CPBR*, IX, 264). In this way the appearances of, e.g., a penny are collected together, all of those in which it appears circular, for instance, placed "on one straight line," ordered "in a series by the variations in the apparent size of the penny," and then all those in which it "appears as a straight line" and so on (*ML*, 155).

The construction assembled by correlating similar but different sensibilia contrasts with Leibniz' monadology, where "since each monad mirrored the whole universe, there was in each perspective a 'sensibile' which was an appearance of each thing." "In our system of perspectives," Russell explains, "we made no such assumption of completeness. A given thing will have appearances in some perspectives, but not in certain others" (*ML*, 155). Each spatial unit contributes to the construction of "the one all-embracing space of physics" (*ML*, 156); in the resultant "public space, each monad occupies a point or, at any rate, a very small region" (*MyPhD*, 24). This yields a world – that of perception – which is "fragmentary, absurd, lawless, but not self-contradictory" (*Matter*, 199). Not governed by any "pre-established harmony," it is only subject to the Law of Non-Contradiction.

The physical object as construction might be seen in embryo in Leslie Stephen's conception that "[w]e know all that can be known" about the material object "when we have combined all that our senses can tell us" ("WM?," 130).[33] "What, then, are we doing when we raise this vast structure of physical science, composed essentially of time and space formulae?" Stephen asks ("WM?," 134):

> We are filling up the gaps in our immediate perceptions. Each man's is fragmentary, discontinuous, and narrow . . . We extend the range and supply the intervals of our knowledge . . . I shut my eyes for an instant, and believe that my pen and paper are still there. I believe that I should see them if my eyes were open, and that other persons may see them still. If I look back to the past, or, forward to the future, or away to furthest abysses of space, I am carrying on the same construction . . . I form, then, a kind of hypothetical consciousness, of which my own is an essential part, but which extends indefinitely beyond it. By this artifice (if it may be called so) I state a general truth without explicit reference to my own perceptions. I do so when upon seeing a man first at one window and then at another I supply the intermediate positions and infer his relations to other objects by correcting my own perspective. Kepler constructed the solar system in the same way. He observed a planet in certain positions; he supplied the intermediate positions by discovering the curve which passed through all the observed positions. ("WM?," 135–6)

The term "construction" has only to be made rigorous in order to "arrive at assemblages of 'sensibilia' which are found to obey certain simple laws, namely those of dynamics" (*ML*, 165).

Not only "things" but persons are also logical constructions, what Russell calls "biographies." Counterpart to the spatially constructed object, the biography is a temporal construct, constituted by a "direct time-relation of before and after" between "two perspectives which both belong to one person's experience"; it is "everything that is (directly) earlier or later than, or simultaneous with, a given sensibile" (*ML*, 161). The times in the different biographies are then correlated to yield a public series which is "the history of the world . . . divided into a number of mutually exclusive biographies" (*ML*, 162). The biography's units avoid "introducing experience or anything mental" (*ML*, 161). This is how the permanent person is constructed. "'I think first this and then that'" should not "mean that there is a single entity 'I' which 'has' two successive thoughts" but "that there are two successive thoughts" with "causal relations" such that we "call them parts of one biography" (*OP*, 171; see also *Portraits from Memory*, 149). "The real man . . .," Russell writes, "however the police may swear to his identity, is really a series of momentary men, each different from the other, and bound together, not by a numerical identity, but by continuity" (*ML*, 124). Presumably the public table itself would have a biography, since it persists over time, just as the person, Scott or Bismarck, would be a "public neutral object" with spatial continuity, known by description: "what applies to men applies equally to tables and chairs, the sun, moon and stars. Each of these is to be regarded, not as one single persistent entity, but as a series of entities succeeding each other in time, each lasting for a very brief period" (*ML*, 124). "Any series of sensations [or rather, sense-data] in the same place in perspective space would constitute a biography," Sainsbury explains, "even if all the sensations were unsensed" (*Russell*, 267). For, "just as a perspective need not be actually perceived by any one, so a biography need not be actually lived by any one" (*ML*, 136). Treating "both a mind and a piece of matter as logical constructions formed out of materials not differing vitally," a neutral sensation "grouped" with "other occurrences by a memory chain . . . becomes part of a mind"; "grouped with its causal antecedents," it "appears as part of the physical world" (*MyPhD*, 103). This is another sense in which Russell's perspective space is a monadology: as in Leibniz, levels of monads reflect the universe more or less distinctly, some simples and others aggregates, some possessed of perception and others only of a dimmer "apperception" (See note 18). The group of temporally and spatially ordered sense-data called "table" is a monad like the group of sense-data and sensations we call "person"; it simply reflects the universe less distinctly than the person.

"Descartes believed in 'substance', both in the mental and in the material world" (*OP*, 171). The logical construction eliminates both. As Pears comments, "The wafer is made out of things . . . in themselves neither mental nor physical, but neutral between two categories. Cut one way, the wafer yields the psychological histories of people. Cut another way, it yields the physical histories of objects" (*Bertrand Russell*, 42, fn. 29). The construction makes " 'matter' merely a name for certain strings of sets of events," there not being "a definite entity, a piece of matter, which is now in one place and now in another" (*OP*, 171). The result is not so much a loss of reality, but a redefinition of it that only increases the conviction of its mind-independence. Hintikka can thus conclude that "the Russellian resolution of physical objects into complexes of actual and potential sense-data was not intended as a proof of their irreality" but its "impact" for "the happy few who understood it was to alienate them from subjectivism and psychologism in the philosophy of mathematics" ("Virginia Woolf," 11–12).

As an aspect of their independence, logical constructions are as a whole technically unobserved, i.e., not objects of acquaintance, even if they are made up of observable entities – sense-data. Russell rejects the unity he qualifies as "mystic" in his attack on that other form of Idealism – Hegelianism. A person's "reflection" of the universe is a knowledge all of which is not at any given moment conscious but possessed as a series of judgements. Russell's reconstruction of the external world thus makes no recourse either to Descartes', Leibniz' or Berkeley's God, building the object on some other model than that of a single omniscient mind or pre-established harmony. This is the sense in which real knowledge is "by description," i.e., a construction grounded in acquaintance. "Art," understood as such a construction connected by what is common to different perspectives, is "the most universal and the most permanent of all forms of religious expression," Clive Bell writes, "because the significance of formal combinations can be appreciated by one race and one age as another, and because that significance is as independent as mathematical truth of human vicissitudes" (*Art*, 278).

THE GEOMETRY OF TIME AND SPACE

If we pronounce time and space to be merely subjective, we take leave of all relation to fact, and verbally construct the universe out of bare logic, or we create a mystical theory from emotions cast into some show of logical form. (Stephen, "What is Materialism?," 148)

A donnish joke . . . has it that while time was created to keep everything from happening at once, space was created to keep everything from happening in Cambridge. (Skidelsky, *John Maynard Keynes*, II, in C. Lehmann-Haupt, *New York Times*, 14/2/94)

The sensible table appears in the private "here" and "now." The physical table is constructed in "public" space and time. Its temporal as well as spatial dimension gives further prominence to an aspect of the theory of sensibilia: the continuity of an object with discontinuous parts. Bergson thought continuity is "destroyed when" space and time "are resolved into points and instants" by mathematicians, Russell paraphrases him (*OKnExW*, 135); time was thereby "spatialized." Bergson calls experienced time "duration," which is "not a succession of moments" but "flows in an indivisible continuity," Passmore writes (*Hundred Years*, 106). This is "What Bergson Means by 'Interpenetration,'" to invoke Karin Stephen's Aristotelian Society title. For Russell, the experience of continuity is "easier to feel than to define" (*OKnExW*, 135); there is little reason "to believe the world of sense continuous" (*OKnExW*, 154). When analyzed, "the experience of time" turns out to consist of a succession of discrete moments, like the series of the penny's appearances; they are correlated with the series of positions showing the relations of earlier and later that form public time.

Bergson's objections that physical, spatialized time fails to explain how time passes, Russell argues, show a misunderstanding of the theory of continuity (*OKnExW*, 135). Mathematical continuity is a property of "*series* of terms," i.e., "terms arranged in an order, so that . . . of any two . . . one comes *before* the other" (*OKnExW*, 137). The continuity relevant to time is its "compactness": "A series is called 'compact' when no two terms are consecutive, but between any two there are others" (*OKnExW*, 138). Russell "imagine[s] a tiny speck of light moving along a scale" (*OKnExW*, 139). Because "we agreed that the continuity of motion excludes the possibility of sudden jumps," "the speck will not jump suddenly from the one to the other, but will pass through an infinite number of other positions on the way" (*OKnExW*, 140). The analogy with "unperceived particulars," assumed "for the sake of continuity" and the avoidance of jaggedness (*CPBR*, IX, 263), is apparent; "a gradual transition" is posited, as in "a coloured surface whose colour changes gradually" (*OKnExW*, 155). In both cases, the transition moves "through an infinite number of intermediaries" (*OKnExW*, 142). Moreover, to avoid certain paradoxes, "we must reject the hypothesis . . . that there are consecutive points and instants. Hence the continuity of motion must not be supposed to consist in a body's occupying consecutive positions at consecutive times" (*OKnExW*, 140–1). "In a continuous motion," Russell explains,

> at any given instant the moving body occupies a certain position, and at other instants it occupies other positions; the interval between any two instants and between any two positions is always finite, but the continuity of the motion is shown in the fact that, however near together we take the two positions and the two instants, there are an infinite number of positions still nearer together. (*OKnExW*, 142)

Both the theory of continuous motion and "Bergson's position" revisit "Zeno's argument of the arrow" (*HWP*, 804). At stake is the notion of change and motion. "By bisection of [the] view . . . that there are *things* which *change*, philosophers have developed two paradoxes." "Heraclitus and Bergson said that there were changes but no things," "a flight but no arrow" ("PhilBerg," 339; *HWP*, 805). Zeno and, more recently, McTaggart claim "that there were things but no changes," "an arrow but no flight" ("PhilBerg," 339; *HWP*, 805). In rejecting clock time, Bergson clearly invests the clock's hands with the arrow's motionlessness:

> When I follow with my eyes on the dial of a clock the movement of the hand which corresponds to the oscillation of the pendulum, I do not measure duration, as seems to thought; I merely count simultaneities . . . Outside me, in space, there is never more than a single position of the hand and the pendulum, for nothing is left of the past positions . . . and hence no duration. (*TFW*, 107–8)

Russell takes the "middle" position "that there is both the arrow and its flight," claiming to be "pierced, like St. Sebastian, by the arrow from one side and by its flight from the other" ("PhilBerg," 340; *HWP*, 805). As early as *Principles of Mathematics*, he found "so monstrous a paradox" that "the arrow in its flight is immovable" in fact "a very plain statement of a very elementary fact" (350). One must only distinguish the moving point's being always in the instant and its being at rest: "At a given instant, it is where it is, like Zeno's arrow; but we cannot say that it is at rest at the instant" because "[r]est consists in being in the same position at all the instants throughout a certain finite period, however short" (*OKnExW*, 142).

The "solution" of Zeno's paradox "lies in the theory of continuous series: we find it hard to avoid supposing that, when the arrow is in flight, there is a *next* position occupied at the *next* moment; but in fact there is no next position and no next moment" (*OKnExW*, 179–80). A hypothetical perspective on "a period consisting of a thousand instants" in which "the arrow is in flight throughout" would see at each instant "the arrow is where it is, though at the very next instant it is somewhere else. It is never moving, but in some miraculous way the change of position has to occur *between* the instants, that is to say, not at any time whatever" (*OKnExW*, 179). Each new position is an "upheaval," yet in place. Russell accepts "what M. Bergson" dismisses as "the cinematographic representation of reality" (*OKnExW*, 179), where there is "an infinite number of pictures," but "never a *next* picture" (*HWP*, 805). If it is an accurate picture of motion, "there will be nothing empirically discoverable to show that objects of sense are not continuous," Russell explains (*OKnExW*, 154–5). But sense, properly analyzed, must be discontinuous, and continuity, unobservable in sense, occur in the intervals between positions. The notion of interval also functions in the theory of relativity. Time and space are subjective. "The interval between two events" is one "not dependent upon the particular circumstances of the observer" (*ABCR*, 58). "What is objective is a kind of mixture of the two called "space-time" (*ABCR*, 33), "a physical fact which can be inferred from the distance in time together with the distance in space. This is what is called the 'interval' in space-time" (*ABCR*, 56). These "intervals are discrete" (*Matter*, 372). The intervals, like sensibilia, contribute to form the scaffolding for constructing the world.

Moreover, the positions are logically related, being either earlier or later than or simultaneous with other positions. Their order is defined independent of the experience of time, even though they can be "correlated" with the experienced series "past, present, future." Each present "now" is fixed forever in the temporal series. This is "a theory of change which may be called *static*, since it allows the justice of Zeno's remark" (*PofM*, 350). Russell admits, then, to a certain timelessness in his theory of time. "'If,'" he says, citing Aristotle, "'what is moving is always in the *now*, then the moving arrow is motionless'" (*OKnExW*, 179). Such a conception of change conjugates the "discontinuous and immobile" (*HWP*, 794):

> Weierstrass . . . has at last shown that we live in an unchanging world, and that the arrow in its flight is truly at rest. Zeno's only error lay in inferring (if he did infer) that, because there is no such thing as change, therefore the world is in the same state at any one time as at any other. (*ML*, 76)

Experienced discontinuity – whether Whitehead's "doctrine of the atomicity of time" (Lowe, *Alfred North Whitehead*, II, 171), Moore's enumeration of "the seconds, minutes, hours and days of which we talk in ordinary life" which he "emphasize[s] is what I mean by Time" (*SomeMain*, 208), Russell's "succession of different immobilities" (*OKnExW*, 136) or Broad's "fresh slices of existence" – is then the first thing Woolf derives from Cambridge thinking on time. "Instead of something steady and continuous, such as the percept seems to be," Russell writes, "the process in the gas is supposed to be a large number of separated sudden discrete upheavals" (*Matter*, 339). The consequence will be Woolf's notion of "the moment," itself discontinuous and immobile. But Russell's successive instants, felt to "give a jerky motion," and "not the smooth transitions with which the senses have made us familiar" (*OKnExW*, 136), once their mathematical continuity is demonstrated, must be not just "abstractly" (*OKnExW*, 136) but "imaginatively realized" (*OKnExW*, 179–80). Hence, continuity as a formal property of Woolf's and Fry's aesthetic, one which unites apparent discontinuities, will be a second consequence of the influence of Cambridge time-thinking. Forster pronounces the novelist cannot ignore the "narrative of events arranged in their time sequence," represented by "Tuesday after Monday, decay after death" (*Aspects of the Novel*, 27), the shorthand Woolf also uses for the time-sequence (*W*, 262; 283). Its geometry achieves an unchanging order: "Now one thought of it," Mrs. Ramsay reflects on "this night," "cleared of chatter and emotion, it seemed always to have been, only was shown now and so being shown, struck everything into stability" (*TL*, 170).

Real time thus includes an unobserved but not necessarily unknown time as well as space: "That space, for instance, that there is at this moment between here and Charing Cross, and which we believe really does exist at this moment, even though nobody is directly apprehending any part of it; and the Time, for instance, which has elapsed between now and the Battle of Waterloo"

(*SomeMain*, 209). The compact series of "instants of time" means we "either bring in events wholly outside our experience or assume that experienced events have parts which we do not experience, or postulate that we can experience an infinite number of events at once" (*OKnExW*, 126). Knowledge of the unobserved is also of past and future. "Prediction" is one name for knowledge of the future. But science also makes predictions about the unexperienced past, prehistory, that covered by Mrs. Swithin's Outline of History, or the past of the solar system, arrived at as for predictions of eclipses. In these cases, it awaits confirmation in the form of future evidence from the past, just as it does from the future.

THE UNOBSERVED

"To what dark antre of the unvisited earth, or wind-brushed forest, shall we go now?" (Woolf, *Between the Acts*, 51)

Thus at the heart of Russell's theory of knowledge is the old problem of unobserved objects, of the cow, the table, the room during those times when you're not there, ultimately to be resolved in the seeming paradox of unoccupied perspectives and unsensed sensibilia. Their status as mere logical possibilities make the "'sensibilia' which would appear from places where there happen to be no minds" what Stephen had called "phantasms." Russell is careful to surround them with caveats: "It may be thought monstrous to maintain that a thing can present any appearance at all in a place where no sense-organs and nervous structure exist," although "I do not myself feel the monstrosity." Still, he treats "these supposed appearances" as only "a hypothetical scaffolding," "an illustrative hypothesis," "an aid in preliminary statement" and not physical dogma "in its final form" (*ML*, 152–3), "a model hypothesis as a help for the imagination" (*OKnExW*, 94). If, of the two inferred entities "which are unavoidable," the one which "will probably be allowed to pass unchallenged" – other people's sense-data – is the one that would give Russell "the greatest satisfaction to be able to dispense with" (*ML*, 152), the sense-data, "not data to anyone," despite the objections he anticipates, seem indispensable to his argument; their admission would in no way disturb this solipsistic basis, except to render it selfless. Nevertheless, he concludes his essay by hoping "that, with further elaboration, the part played by unperceived 'sensibilia' could be indefinitely diminished, probably by invoking the history of a 'thing' to eke out the inferences derivable from its momentary appearance" (*ML*, 173).

Ghostly sensibilia form the "framework of construction" (Eames, *Bertrand Russell's Theory of Knowledge*, 82) for building no less ghostly logical constructions. They "build a logical bridge from such [sense] data to the abstract and imperceptible objects of our mathematical formulae" (*CPBR*, IX, 263). Via this scaffolding, we ascend from the reality of particulars, private objects of acquaintance, themselves made to seem "unreal" when subjected to analysis, to the reality of public objects, scaling the edifice of knowledge to break free of the prison of privacy. The voyage out only requires that we leave behind, without a backward glance, the direct knowledge whose model is sensation.

CHAPTER 3

The world seen without a self: Woolf's analysis of matter

[W]e creep . . . out into a wider world

(Woolf, *The Waves*, 271)

Some such trajectory as Russell's voyage out into "the vast external world" (*ND*, 331) can then be traced in the novels. Woolf endows the heroine of her early *Night and Day* with a need to be "surrounded by the spaces of the night and the open air" (192) and with an imagination, like Russell's, dominated by astronomy and mathematics, one counterposed to her mother's vague poetry. Woolf herself never masters that knowledge, but this does not prevent her from acknowledging as the "intellectual scaffolding" upon which she hangs her vision something like Moore's and Russell's analysis of matter. Like Russell's "hypothetical scaffolding" and Wittgenstein's ladder, it is to be removed "as soon as the edifice is completed." Our own analysis of the philosophical underpinning should be so treated, as a necessary but temporary preparation to the appreciation of the completed vision.

THE SHOWER OF INNUMERABLE ATOMS

There are many rooms – many Bernards. (Woolf, *The Waves*, 260)

. . . lost in the crowd of worlds. (Berkeley, *Three Dialogues Between Hylas and Philonous*, 46)

The route out leads from the reality of the unobserved table to its multiple and fragmentary nature, to "the multiplicity of things" (*TL*, 65), "all those innumerable things" (*TL*, 303), "perhaps the atoms themselves," as Woolf quotes Fry as saying (*RF*, 278). The world the novel must find a form and a language for is not an unbroken whole. The table is not one table, but many; the furniture of the world presents "an incessant shower of innumerable atoms" (*CE*, II, 106), "a million atoms of soft blue" (*W*, 5), "atoms of grey-blue" (*W*, 149). Myriad points of space and time, of "night and day," events, sense-data, crowd the atomist's vision, all characteristically plural; "the observer is choked with observations" (*JR*, 68).[1] The first injunction is "to record the atoms" (*CE*, II, 107). The result is the characteristic features of Woolf's universe. Constructed, like London at night, out of a multitude of rooms and houses, it is punctuated by points of light, private worlds: "The light burns behind yellow blinds and pink blinds, and above fanlights, and down in basement windows" (*JR*, 97); "burning lights from the window-panes flash" (*W*, 10); "here – in Lombard Street and Fetter Lane and Bedford Square – each insect carries a globe of the world in his head" (*JR*, 163). These circles and squares of lighted windows reflect the night skies: "Infinite millions of miles away powdered stars twinkled" (*JR*, 52). "'There are millions of stars,' said Charlotte with conviction" (*JR*, 59). The skies "hold aloft clear planets, plates of brightness" (*TL*, 192), signs of the infinite number of possible perspectives, mirrored in turn in Mrs. Ramsay's public dinner table, with "all the plates making white circles on it" (*TL*, 125). "Now there are rounds of white china, and silver streaks beside each plate" (*W*, 11).

In this atomized universe, the lights of human habitations, like that of the old lady in *Mrs. Dalloway* (283), indicate here and there occupied perspectives: "high among the bare trees are hung oblong frames of reddish yellow light – windows; there are points of brilliance burning steadily like low stars – lamps; this empty ground . . . set about by offices and houses where at this hour fierce lights burn over maps, over documents, over desks where clerks sit . . . or more suffusedly the firelight wavers and the lamplight falls upon the privacy of some drawing room, its easy chairs, its papers, its china, its inlaid table and the figure of a woman" (*CE*, IV, 156–7). "Now little sparks, which are not steady, but fitful as if somebody were doubtful, come across the field . . . The lamp sinks down; then it burns up . . . [T]he moment is laced about with . . . lamp lightings" (*CE*, II, 293–4). "A window tinged yellow about two feet across alone combatted the white fields and the black trees" (*JR*, 98); "a star here and there makes a point of light" (*CE*, II, 293), reflecting the "lamps of London" (*JR*, 97).

For this atomized universe is also a monadology in which each atom is a perspective. The "blocks of matter" and "patches of light" (*VO*, 292) – "patch" the word favored by Moore and Russell for primitive units of color – into which the world is analyzed, constitute so many faceted refracting and reflecting monads. And each perspective, like Leibniz' "garden full of plants" and "pond full of fishes," in which "each branch of every plant" and "each drop of its liquid parts is also some such garden or pond" (*Monadology*, 67, 256), further contains a multiplicity of events (*JR*, 110). This property of perspectives is figured in two ways: as a surface whose borders separate a portion from the surrounding space, its surface a mirror, or, alternatively, as a container enclosing an interior perceptible only from within, but invisible from without – a kind of "black box." These two models of the perspective will take various forms in the novels: windows, mirrors, ponds, islands, rooms, books, minds. Each window-room, each mirror-pool, for Woolf, either frames within its boundaries a sense-datum or collection of sense-data or interiorizes them in its depths. The multiplicity of things is grouped around a visible center or contracts and retreats to depths imperceptible from without. In each case, a momentary order is imposed on the unordered units.

PRIVATE WORLDS AND PRIVATE ROOMS

Even his [Leibniz] monads can still be useful as suggesting possible ways of viewing perception, though they cannot be regarded as windowless." Russell (*A History of Western Philosophy*, 596)[2]

The division was on the question, "Study or marketplace?" Whitehead's vote was sensible . . . "Study," he wrote, "with windows"; and he drew this little sketch: ⊞ (Lowe, on an Apostle's meeting, *Alfred North Whitehead*, I, 144)

Suppose, for instance, that I am in my room. I exist, and my room exists, but does "in" exist? Yet obviously the word "in" has a meaning; it denotes a relation which holds between me and my room. (Russell, *The Problems of Philosophy*, 90)

Within this conceptualization, the room as symbol finds its precise philosophical gloss in Woolf's work, as the "here" and "now" from which or upon which a perspective is perceived. Mrs. Ramsay looks out from her room at the lighthouse in the house all of whose rooms she had "made full of life – the drawing-room; and behind the drawing-room the kitchen; above the kitchen the bedrooms; and beyond them the nurseries; they must be furnished" (*TL*, 59), and Lily can only guess what she sees. "Each of us is an absolute unit, cut off by an impassable abyss from a direct knowledge of other consciousness" is Leslie Stephen's formulation ("WM?," 148). For the rooms of the house are "the chambers of the mind and heart" (*TL*, 79), "bedrooms . . . sealed like ovens" (*TL*, 44) containing things unseen by those outside. "Her mind was like her room . . . she was full of locked drawers, stuffed with letters" (*CSFVW*, 219). Mrs. Dalloway retreats to her attic room with its single bed. Each monad, rooted in one perspective, has "a room of its own," "some duskier chamber of the being" (*CE*, IV, 157), beginning with the space occupied by its body. "Outside the undifferentiated forces roar; inside we are very private, very explicit, have a sense indeed, that it is here, in this little room, that we make whatever day of the week it may be" (*W*, 255). "I believe," as Moore voices common sense, "that my acts of consciousness are taking place now in this room, where my body is. At the present moment I am hearing and seeing and thinking here, in this room" (*SomeMain*, 7).

The room is both the perspective and what houses it, dividing it from other perspectives and giving what is shapeless a form, like a mollusk shell enclosing "something alive in the centre" (*Y*, 125). "A shell forms upon the soft soul, nacreous, shiny upon which sensations tap their beaks in vain" (*W*, 255). The body is such a protection against the entry of sensations. Instead of "the body [being] a sheet of plain glass through which the soul looks straight and clear . . . the very opposite is true . . . All day, all night the body intervenes" (*CE*, IV, 193).

But unlike Leibniz' monads, Woolf's rooms have windows for contact. "The creature within can only gaze through the pane – smudged or rosy; it cannot separate off from the body like the sheath of a knife or the pod of a pea for a single instant" (*CE*, IV, 193). This is Russell's empiricist addition to Leibniz. The window gives the first third of *To the Lighthouse* its title, frames Mrs. Ramsay's field of perception, while for Lily Briscoe, she is framed by it. Mrs. Dalloway, solitary in her room, looks at the old lady "in the room opposite," "crossing the room, coming to the window" and wonders "Could she see her?" (*MrsD*, 283). The tightly-shut shell is not impregnable: birds, "dry-beaked, ruthless, abrupt . . . tapped furiously, methodically, until the shell broke and something slimy oozed from the crack" (*W*, 109).

From without, the view is partial. Fragments of arms and legs can be seen, as in Jacob's rooms. "Here and there one could see brown panelling inside the hall door" (*JR*, 95). The private room is impenetrable to an observer, demonstrating "[t]hat windows should be open, and doors shut" (*TL*, 44). "One room it seemed was always shut, was always disturbed now and then, by some groan or outburst," remembers Woolf of her father's room (*MB*, 40). Nonetheless, the mind keeps vigils "beneath the windows of others," of the "young man" Jacob. "As for following him back to his rooms, no" (*JR*, 95); instead, "[s]tanding out in the street, one may build up all the chambers of an imaginary house and furnish them at one's will with sofa, table, carpet" (*CE*, IV, 160). Each object reads as a sign of the occupant: "Under the stress of thinking about Isabella, her room became more shadowy and symbolic; the corners seemed darker, the legs of chairs and tables more spindly and hieroglyphic" (*CSFVW*, 217). Novel-writing becomes the imaginative construction and furnishing of private rooms.

For rooms are furnished, invariably with chairs and tables. A room may be occupied or empty, however, its furniture observed or unobserved: "the empty sitting-room and the sitting-room with fifty people in it are liable at any moment to blow music into the air" (*JR*, 112). Its occupation is only contingent, passing; ultimately, it empties out. "[I]f no human being ever came" to the Pointz Hall empty library, "the books would be mouldy, the fire out" (*BA*, 17). "Listless is the air in an empty room, just swelling the curtain; the flowers in the jar shift. One fibre in the wicker arm-chair creaks, though no one sits there" (*JR*, 39). The writer's goal is to "light a torch in that vast chamber where nobody has yet been" (*Room*, 88).

THE CIRCLES OF LIGHT

[E]ach particular that there is in the world does not in any way logically depend upon any other particular. Each one might happen to be the whole universe. (Russell, *Logic and Knowledge*, 202)

I don't think one realises how very discrete (in the mathematical sense) one's existence is. My doings at school don't seem to have the remotest connection with my doings up here: nor my life in one term with my life in any other. (Keynes to A. L. Hobhouse, in Skidelsky, *John Maynard Keynes*, I, 129)

How vast and dark it must be to-night, . . . and in all this great space it was curious to think how few the towns were, and how like little rings of light they were, scattered here and there among the swelling uncultivated folds of the world. And in those towns were little men and women, tiny men and women. (Woolf, *The Voyage Out*, 345)

The perspectives are discrete circles of light, enclosed, cut off and cast into relief by zones of darkness. This structure of their privacy endows them with "the mystery that encircled them" (*MB*, 34). Light and dark alternate: "One view of the world plunged in darkness" (*ND*, 265), another of the sun "risen to its full height" (*W*, 148). The world of sense-data is created by an initial separation of light from darkness "to create an abyss between oneself and others" (*VO*, 36): "In the failing light they all looked sharp-edged," "divided by great distances" (*TL*, 111); "solidity suddenly vanished, and such vast spaces lay between them" (*TL*, 147). Atomism is the result. "Spaces of complete immobility separated each of these movements" (*JR*, 99), "space-like intervals" and "time-like intervals" (*Matter*, 370), dividing night from day as the horizon divides "the sea from the sky" (*W*, 5) or miles divide both night from day and Cambridge from Turkey, where always someone "at this very moment, was seated in a minute speck of light somewhere to the east of her" (*ND*, 106), where "there are other centres of consciousness besides my own" ("WM?," 149):[3]

A step or two beyond the window there was nothing at all, except the enclosing buildings – chimneys upright, roofs horizontal; too much brick and building for a May night, perhaps. And then before one's eyes would come the bare hills of Turkey . . . women, standing naked-legged in the stream to beat linen on the stones. (*JR*, 44–5; cf also *O*, 326.)

The division is also between possible worlds, "the dark, the slumbrous shapes in her mind, shapes of a world not realised but turning in their darkness" (*TL*, 281), worlds that can be realized, illuminated, by the novel: drops from a fountain "catching here and there, a spark of light: Greece, Rome, Constantinople" (*TL*, 281). Their imaginative realization makes the thinker's own world contract: "Athough in its private world there is a private space which from its private point of view is immense, the whole of this immensity shrinks into a tiny pin-point when the monad is placed among other monads" (*MyPhD*, 18); "the earth, after the voyage, still seemed an island to him" (*MrsD*, 77). Each such island takes its place among others: "Small as it was . . . , it had, she supposed, a place in the universe – even that little island?" (*TL*, 281).

This division between light and darkness is absolute. It marks the topography of "a London street. . . , with its islands of light and its long groves of darkness" (*CE*, IV, 156) and gives to "hidden compartments of different colours" their "boundaries" (*CE*, II, 294), creating those rectangles of darkness, "this empty ground, which holds the country in it and its peace" that indicate "only a London square" (*CE*, IV, 156). It shapes Woolf's conception of each successive work: "islands of light – islands in the stream that I am trying to convey," she says of what will be *The Waves* (*Diary*, III, 229). The darkness outside converts the light into an interior, like the walls of the child's bucket in which a crab "slowly circled round the bottom" (*JR*, 14) or "[a]s the sides of a lantern protect the flame so that it burns steady even in the wildest night – burns gravely and illumines the tree-trunks – so inside the Chapel all was orderly" (*JR*, 32). To pass from outside within is to cross an absolute frontier. This boundary, the perspective's "threshhold," sets limits to it, and what is known as "shift in point of view" will be negotiated via it.

If the line between outside and inside is sharp, not everywhere is the same within. This is the consequence of the perspective's structure – at least the occupied one's. The light emanates from its center, enclosing its privacy in a characteristic configuration. This can be demonstrated by an experiment: "If you stand a lantern under a tree every insect in the forest creeps up to it – a curious assembly," which "knock their heads against the glass" (*JR*, 32). By the very placing of the lamp everything within the circle of light's circumference tends toward the lamp, a fact of perception giving order to the random atoms circling it, "like a stone fallen into a pond round which minnows swarm" (*W*, 136).

> When a fly touches the surface of a stagnant pool, it causes ripples which move outward in widening circles. The center of the circle at any moment is the point of the pool touched by the fly. If the fly moves about over the surface of the pool, it does not remain at the center of the ripples. (*ABCR*, 42)

Any event can act as the center, like Lily Briscoe's "nick[ing] the catch of her paint-box to": "the nick seemed to surround in a circle forever the paint-box, the lawn, Mr. Bankes" (*TL*, 83). The observer's "march" beneath the windows of others, like the moth's circling of the flame, has "for center, for magnet, a young man alone in a room" (*JR*, 95). "Every moment is the centre and meeting-place of an extraordinary number of perceptions" (*CE*, II, 229).

The light itself then creates the space of perception, that "region" which for Russell was "specially warm and intimate and bright, surrounded in all directions by gradually growing darkness" (*IMT*, 102), endowing objects with "intimacy and nearness" (*TK*, 40). "Animals," Russell writes, "including human beings, view the world from a center consisting of the here and the now. Our senses, like a candle in the night, spread a gradually diminishing illumination upon objects as they become more distant" (*Portraits from Memory*, 178). Russell's metaphor privileges sight and the visual, standing in for all sense perception. Sounds within the region of sensation analogously die in intensity to near inaudibility at its far rim. "The sound we heard a few seconds ago, but are not hearing now, may still be an object of acquaintance" ("On the Experience of Time," 225). Just as the pool of light is surrounded by darkness, the sound room is encircled by silence. Within, things can be closer or farther from the center, the light, in Russell's conception, falling off, like "those sandhills dwindling away into darkness" (*TL*, 104): outside "the wider circumference of the moment," within, "[h]ere in the centre is a knot of consciousness; a nucleus divided up into four heads, eight legs, eight arms, and four separate bodies" (*CE*, II, 294). The result is a characteristic order: "the warmth of sensation gradually dies out of receding objects, as if we saw them under a fading light" ("On the Experience of Time," 225).

Woolf's perspective is similarly configured. It is "the warm corner of the mind's inglenook" (*CE*, IV, 162), "my own snug home" (*W*, 266), "the flame of the spirit become[] a visible hearth" (*CE*, IV, 51), "this warm place, this pocket of still air, which one comes on at the edge of a wood sometimes in the evening, when, because of a fall in the ground, or some arrangement of the trees (one must be above all, scientific), warmth lingers," warmth in which Septimus too lingers before leaping into the exposed spaces beyond (*MrsD*, 218). At Mrs. Ramsay's dinner party, when "all the candles were lit up, and the faces on both sides of the table were brought nearer by the candle light," they were "composed, as they had not been in the twilight, into a party round a table" (*TL*, 146), the table forming the lighted center. Light creates the very "intimacy" "the room was full of" (*JR*, 46). Its cosiness can make privacy a refuge, familiar and reassuring, because outside "[i]t was not easy or snug this world" (*TL*, 197). Childhood in Woolf's memory was such an enclosure: "Many bright colours; many distinct sounds; some human beings, caricatures; comic; several violent moments of being, always including a circle of the scene which they cut out: and all surrounded by a vast space – that is a rough visual description of childhood" (*MB*, 79).[4] Woolf's "first impression" at St. Ives is centered in an "intensity" at the heart of a womb-like nursery – "the feeling . . . of lying in a grape and seeing through a film of semi-transparent yellow" (*MB*, 65). This feeling Woolf ascribes "partly" to the distances in time and space traversed between perspectives – the "change of nursery" being "a great change" – between winter and summer, London and St. Ives: "there was the long train journey . . . the dark; the lights; the stir of the going up to bed" (*MB*, 65). Distance is thus the equivalent of darkness. The private world must be left behind, its occupant become an exile exposed to the rain of sensation. But the private world is also a prison; its warmth makes it, in Russell's metaphor, "a hothouse." The movement out is then also a longed-for escape, like Russell's from Idealism or the young Stephens' from Hyde Park Gate's cloying atmosphere.

Whether the centered structure created by light fading into darkness is due to an observer-occupant or to the center alone, even unoccupied, is, we saw, unclear. The light can stand for consciousness and knowledge. One can "talk of a light, of Cambridge burning" (*JR*, 46), of "the lamp of learning" there (*JR*, 39) or Mr. Ramsay's "own little light" of knowledge (*TL*, 56). In any case, the distance to the outer limits isolates any observer at the center. Beyond "the little island" of light, "half swallowed up in the sea" is "the land dwindling away" (*TL*, 106); the "tide of darkness breaks . . . We are out of doors" (*W*, 177).

THE MOMENT

The things that are really real last a very short time. (Russell, *Logic and Knowledge*, 274)

Now had become eternal as he sat talking to his friends in a Cambridge room. (Spalding, *Roger Fry*, 60)

June, July, August! Each still remained almost whole, and, as if to catch the falling drop, Clarissa (crossing to the dressing-table) plunged into the very heart of the moment there. (Woolf, *Mrs. Dalloway*, 54)

The perspective is also a temporal unit, Woolf's "moment," which excludes interpenetration and places change, contra Bergson, outside experience. It resembles Whitehead's event, as Hintikka has suggested,[5] like it with "finite extension and duration" (*OKnExW*, 154). Its nucleus Woolf specifies as "the present moment."[6] In the essay "The Moment," "the present moment" "is largely composed of visual and of sense impressions" (*CE*, II, 293). At its center is "the table in the garden" growing "whiter and whiter" (*CE*, II, 293), like Russsell's table, parts of which "look white because of reflected light" (*PP*, 8). Sense knowledge is thus its foundation: "Let me touch the table – so – and thus recover my sense of the moment" (*W*, 267). The moment shows the sensible object's randomness. Hence, "The Moment" begins with an unordered list of simultaneous sounds, sights and feelings: "An owl . . . crossed the fading sky with a black spot between its claws. The trees murmured. An aeroplane hummed like a piece of plucked wire. There was also, on the roads, the distant explosion of a motor cycle, shooting further and further away down the road" (*CE*, II, 293). This randomness means that, within, the moment has no temporal order. "Past and present became jumbled together" in it, as it does in Kitty Lasswade's sleep (*Y*, 271). Its sensible content, "embedded in a kind of nondescript cotton wool" (*MB*, 70), stands out sharply against it, with the perspective's sharp resolution, each detail simultaneously present. The Impressionist eye for Fry will see as through a transparent lens with a distinctness missing in ordinary seeing, its present as yet unclouded by past or future. Its vision, unformed by habit, has a child's "curious focus," seeing "with extreme distinctness," as Woolf writes. "If you are young, the future lies upon the present, like a piece of glass, making it tremble and quiver. If you are old, the past lies upon the present, like a thick glass, making it waver, distorting it" (*CE*, II, 293). The metaphor is echoed in *Jacob's Room*: "We start transparent, and then the cloud thickens. All history backs our pane of glass" (49). Lily's "white" (*TL*, 234) canvas is such a *tabula rasa*; her blank look before it, like "the blankness of her mind" upon awakening (*TL*, 217), is the child's.

The moment is random also in being one of an infinite number of possible moments. Separated by moments of non-being, like the darkness-encircled lights, "these points are enclosed in vast empty spaces" (*MB*, 78). They are collections of sound surrounded by silence: "Silence will close behind us . . . silence closes over our transient passage. This I say is the present moment" (*W*, 65). They are "floating incidents" (*MB*, 77), undatable, unconnected to before and after: "like a bee laden with the moment. But what room? What moment?" (*MrsD*, 74–5). Within each moment, time remains suspended, "the moment, transfixed" (*MrsD*, 54), as is Zeno's arrow, at "the still space that lies about the heart of things, where one could move or rest" (*TL*, 158). The moment in this sense resembles Leonard Woolf's characterization of Moore's "states of mind"[7] as "consist[ing] in timeless, passionate states of contemplation and communion, largely unattached to 'before' and 'after'" (*Sowing*, 146).

The window which gives the title to part one of *To the Lighthouse* represents one moment's frame. It opens on the *plein air*, and yields that "vivid enjoyment of immediate sense-data" when, according to Whitehead, "[t]he present moment is then all in all" (*Symbolism*, 42). Knowledge must continuously return to this source, for "everybody believes that the present is something" (*CE*, II, 293), even if, as Broad thinks, the future is "simply nothing." The present is sole object of acquaintance. "'After Vic.,'" i.e., the Victorian period, Miss La Trobe writes into her script on "a June day in 1939" (*BA*, 179), "'try ten mins. of present time. Swallows, cows, etc.,'" in order to reconnect with that reality (*BA*, 179). The experiment is repeated at the end of *Orlando*. "The little platform of present time on which I stand" (*MB*, 85), not duration, provides the pre-temporal foundation for any notion of time. "The moment at least seemed extraordinarily fertile" (*TL*, 256).

A window opening on the present, the moment is also, however, a door opened, then closed, between moment and moment. For the moment becomes part of a series. Poised between past and future, like Mrs. Ramsay on the dining room threshold after the dinner-party, waiting "a moment longer in a scene which was vanishing even as she looked" (*TL*, 167), or like Lady Bruton "as she stood hesitating one moment on the threshold of her drawing-room" (*MrsD*, 44), it is the entrance into time, as "the threshold of the private house" is "the bridge which connects the private house with the world of public life" (*TG*, 18). Hence, Mrs. Dalloway's entrance into the room is signalled by St. Margaret's striking. Time passes through the series of discrete, arrested moments. For Woolf's moment is ultimately not simply equivalent to the present. Some moments only constitute what Woolf calls "moments of being": "These separate moments of being were however embedded in many more moments of non-being" (*MB*, 70). The word qualifying them suggests Russell's "being" as opposed to "existence." Certain moments cease being present and become endowed with the permanence of the world of being, only showing their contingent origin via their relations: no longer "present," they are either earlier, later or simultaneous with other moments. Time's passing is fixed in a still sequence of timeless positions – "the absurd proposition that motion is made up of immobilities" that is "Bergson's objection" (*OKnExW*, 162).

PUBLIC CONSTRUCTIONS: THE HOUSE, THE HIVE AND THE DINNER TABLE

"The roar of London," said Louis, "is round us. Motor-cars, vans, omnibuses pass and repass continuously. All are merged in one turning wheel of single sound. All separate sounds – wheels, bells, the cries of drunkards, of merrymakers – all churned into one sound, steel blue, circular." (Woolf, *The Waves*, 135)

The points of light combat the chaos of darkness. Against it, here and there the private worlds are grouped together into public units – rooms into houses, "[f]actories, cathedrals, glass domes, institutions and theatres" into cities, into "many-pointed and many-domed London" (*W*, 111). "Out at sea a great city will cast a brightness into the night" (*JR*, 31); "at night, far out at sea over the tumbling waves, one saw a haze on the waters, a city illuminated, a whiteness even in the sky" (*JR*, 42). Each self has "his own cell in the enormous honeycomb" (*Room*, 33), in "the hives with their murmurs and their stirrings; the hives, which were people" (*TL*, 80); each student a room of his own at Trinity. The bees come and go, in and out, from the hive, "in and out of rooms, in and out of peoples' minds" (*VO*, 259): "upstairs they went and down they went, . . . the hive full of bees, the bees home thick with gold, drowsy, humming, suddenly vocal" (*JR*, 42–3). Augustus Carmichael, feasting his eyes on the plate of fruit in *To the Lighthouse*, "plunged in, broke off a bloom there, a tassel here, and returned, after feasting, to his hive" (146), as the guests at the Ramsays' dinner table come from their rooms and return to them, "the young man – back to his rooms" (*JR*, 46). Or the public sphere is the Opera House, where chairs are filled nightly, all, like Russell's men in a room, with different perspectives on the same object and "two thousand hearts in the semi-darkness remembered, anticipated, travelled dark labyrinths" (*JR*, 68). For "to prevent us from being submerged by chaos, nature and society between them have arranged a system of classification which is simplicity itself; stalls, boxes, amphitheatre, gallery" (*JR*, 68–9). The scattered occupants of the house in *To the Lighthouse* finally form "a party round a table" (146). (When the lights are all put out in "Time Passes," like "the electric light [that] suddenly goes out" in Russell's "dinner-party" example, it remains to be seen if "no one doubts that his neighbors and the dinner-table . . . still exist, although at the moment they are unperceived" [*Matter*, 191–2].) Thus it is that the private, unobserved table of Mr. Ramsay's philosophy is transformed, by Mrs. Ramsay, into the public table – "an infinitely long table and plates and knives" (*TL*, 125). In this way, as around a table in *The Waves*, many perspectives

> come together . . . to make one thing, not enduring – for what endures? – but seen by many eyes simultaneously. There is a red carnation in that vase. A single flower as we sat here waiting, but now a seven-sided flower, many-petalled, red, puce, purple-shaded, stiff with silver-tinted leaves – a whole flower to which every eye brings its contribution. (*W*, 127)

What is created is a logical construction, public, neutral object or person.

THE FURNITURE OF THE WORLD: TABLES, CHAIRS, SUN, MOON AND STARS

> How vivid and radiant is the luster of the fixed stars! How magnificent and rich that negligent profusion, with which they appear to be scattered throughout the whole azure vault! Yet if you take the telescope, it brings into your sight a new host of stars that escape the naked eye. Here they seem contiguous and minute, but to a nearer view immense orbs of light at various distances, far sunk in the abyss of space. Now you must call imagination to your aid. The feeble narrow sense cannot descry innumerable worlds revolving round the central fires; and in those worlds the energy of an all-perfect mind displayed in endless forms. But neither sense nor imagination are big enough to comprehend the boundless extent with all its glittering furniture. (Berkeley, *Three Dialogues Between Hylas and Philonous*, 45–6)

Hence the "innumerable glitter" (*W*, 148) of the furniture of the novels, the list of images which, unlike Forster's cow, proliferate in Woolf's descriptions. The world of the novels consists of many things, many perspectives – my sense-data of the table today and yesterday and other people's of it. Among them are the hypothetical sensibilia of a tabular appearance given to no observer, endowed with a disturbing life of its own. "We naturally believe," writes

Russell, "that tables and chairs, trees and mountains, are still there when we turn our backs upon them . . . As soon as the question is seriously raised whether, because we have seen them, we have a right to suppose that they are there still, we feel that some kind of argument must be produced" (*OKnExW*, 77). Then "I begin to doubt the fixity of tables, the reality of here and now, to tap my knuckles smartly upon the edges of apparently solid objects and say, 'Are you hard?'" (*W*, 288). Hence the strangeness.

Woolfian description displays other objects suggestive of the unobserved besides the table and the "sheeted chairs" of "Time Passes" (195). Forms of nature in an empty landscape, "the reality; the moors and Byron; the sea and the lighthouse; the sheep's jaw with the yellow teeth in it" (*JR*, 36) function as recurrent reminders of the externality of "that unfeeling universe that sleeps when we are at our quickest and burns red when we lie asleep" (*W*, 280). "The very trees and the green merging into the blue distance became symbols of the vast external world which recks so little of the happiness, of the marriages or deaths of individuals" (*ND*, 331). Such landscapes present familiar illustrations borrowed, like the table, from the philosopher's list of external objects: "A terrifying volley of pistol-shots rings out . . . a tree has fallen, a sort of death in the forest" (*JR*, 32). "The cat marches across the hearth-rug. No one observes her" (*JR*, 50). "The stream crept along by the road unseen by any one" (*JR*, 98).

But especially sun, moon and stars, often perceptible only by instruments, from being so long the objects of the physicist's and astronomer's calculations, evoke that world of physics unapprehendable directly that Katherine Hilbery wishes to know. Even more urgently than with the table, science has required "the inference that the sun and moon and planets exist when no one is observing them" (*Matter*, 176). That idea "that the sun and stars would exist if no one was aware of them" was one of those liberating consequences of Russell's escape from Idealism (*Autobiography*, in Passmore, *Hundred Years*, 207). Already emblematic of the plurality of things, the starry heavens become that of the inhuman perspective as well. "A thousand stars were flashing across the blue wastes of the sky. One seemed alone with an inscrutable society. All human beings were laid asleep – prone, horizontal, dumb" (*Room*, 24). For if the heavens are structured like the social world – the house, the city, with their rooms and windows – multiplying the possible perspectives, they only coldly and distantly return the glow of the cozy, warmly-lit spaces of occupied privacy. Their distance is temporal as well, shadowed by their eventual extinction – "the waste of the years and the perishing of stars" (*TL*, 56). Their effect is like the war at the end of *Between the Acts*, exposing the briefness of human light. "The stars did their usual work upon the mind, froze to cinders the whole of our short human history and reduced the human body to an ape-like, furry form, crouching amid the brushwood of a barbarous clod of mud. This stage was soon succeeded by another, in which there was nothing in the universe save stars and the light of stars; as she looked up the pupils of her eyes so dilated with starlight that the whole of her seemed dissolved in silver and spilt over the ledges of the stars for ever and ever indefinitely through space" (*ND*, 196–7). The perspective of the stars is that of physics or God. But this God is not a personal one, only a hypothetical unoccupied perspective representing "a hard reality, remote as the stars" (*ND*, 270) from the tiny specks of human light. The gazer is thinned to the point of being nothing but a blank reflector or transmitter of light. "For if exaltation lasted we should be blown like foam in the air. The stars would shine through us. We should go down the gale in salt drops" (*JR*, 120).

Standing for pure externality, for mindlessness, for what Berkeley calls "unthinking things," as Leslie Stephen reminds us, the *res cogitans*'s contrary, the stars, the sky, the uninhabited wastes of forest and seashore, all mark the edges over which the mind may peer. Stephen had pointed the outward direction of investigation: "we have to pass beyond all possible limits of observation, and to postulate atoms which, by their nature, are imperceptible" ("WM?," 131). Unthinking things lead the thinking thing inevitably beyond the occupied perspectives to the world's strand, like Mr. Ramsay, whose "fate" it was "to come out thus on a spit of land . . . to stand . . . facing the dark of human ignorance" (*TL*, 68). This is also Russell's itinerary from the table to the stars, "from a hot-house into a wind-swept headland," from private worlds to unoccupied perspectives, from the island's center to land's end.

THE WAVES OF LIGHT AND SOUND

When it became established that light consists of waves, this velocity was that of propagation of waves in the ether – at least they used to be in the ether, but now the ether has been given up, though the waves remain. (Russell, *The ABC of Relativity*, 35)

[M]y first memory, . . . the most important of all my memories . . . is of hearing the waves breaking, one, two, one, two (Woolf, *Moments of Being*, 64–5)

Could one not get the waves to be heard all through? (Woolf, *Diary*, III, 236)

There, at the insular world's edge, at perception's limits, beat the waves; like the steamers in *Jacob's Room*, "resounding like gigantic tuning-forks, [they] state the old old fact – how there is a sea coldly, greenly, swaying outside" (162). The novels' world, like England itself, is never so far from the sea that it is cut off from sense-contact with the waves, "so restless the English are, with the waves at their very door" (*CE*, IV, 162): "They were so far from the sea. A hundred miles away, Mrs. Swithin said; no, perhaps a hundred and fifty. 'But they do say,' she continued, 'one can hear the waves on a still night. After a storm, they say, you can hear a wave break'" (*BA*, 28). So, among the sleepers in "Time Passes," "Lily Briscoe laid her head on the pillow in the clean room and heard the sea" (*TL*, 213).

The waves' ubiquitousness in the Woolfian universe is an allusion to physical theory.[8] For if the stars reflect the ultimately empty perspective, "above all, the white sand bays with the waves breaking unseen by any one" (*JR*, 49) stand for the unsensed matter of science, those "waves that I see dashing themselves to pieces on the Cornish coast" that "may have come all the way from Brazil" Russell invokes for a substance's impermanence (*OP*, 290). The waves at Land's End in *Jacob's Room* or those in *To the Lighthouse* may have travelled all the way from the fictional South American shores of *The Voyage Out*, like the light of distant stars. As does the darkness between lights, they endow perspectives with their island-like self-containment: "The sigh of all the seas breaking in measure round the isles soothed them; the night wrapped them" (*TL*, 214); "they were all conscious of making a party in a hollow, on an island; had their common cause against that fluidity out there" (*TL*, 147). The waves' property of encircling and delineating[9] leads Woolf to transfer the real summer house of her childhood from the Cornish peninsula to the Hebrides of *To the Lighthouse*.

The waves differentiate by being both the absense of sensibilia and their unsensed physical causes, the waves of light and sound continuously bombarding any sense organ or instrument in its vicinity. What is known, according to the "causal theory of perception" – "What I see" – is "causally dependent upon the light waves that reach my eye" (*Matter*, 181) which give the sensible world its color, as the sun does in *The Waves*, which "is nothing but waves of probability" (*SO*, 95). Woolf could have read in Tyndall's *Lectures on Light* about waves of light and color theory and their analogues in sound. "Through all the flowers the same wave of light passed in a sudden flaunt and flash as if a fin cut the green glass of a lake" (*W*, 182). "So the landscape returned to me; so I saw fields rolling in waves of colour" (*W*, 286). "[T]he generally assumed physical causation of perceptions – e.g., by light-waves or sound-waves" (*Matter*, 8) – also explains the "chime of bells" (*PP*, 102) tolling public time. "The frail waves of sound broke among the stiff gorse and the hawthorn twigs as the church clock divided time into quarters" (*JR*, 133); there is "the ring after ring of sound" as St. Margaret's strikes (*MrsD*, 56); "all sorts of little things came flooding and lapping and dancing in on the wake of that solemn stroke which lay flat like a bar of gold on the sea" (*MrsD*, 141); the sound of the late clock "seemed to break like the spray on an exhausted wave" (*MrsD*, 142). "The clock was striking. The leaden circles dissolved in the air" (*MrsD*, 206). "Drop upon drop," said Bernard, "silence falls . . . hear silence fall and sweep its rings to the farthest edges" (*W*, 224).

The clock's strokes find their counterpart "[w]hen darkness fell" in "the stroke of the Lighthouse" (*TL*, 199). For the stars are not the only beacons suggesting unseen physical causes. Other lights shine in the atomized night, star-like in their exclusion of the observer. "Rotating lighthouses at night send out beams which can be seen travelling with great rapidity," Russell writes (*Matter*, 164). It is first as the source of waves of light that the lighthouse functions in Woolf's universe; in both *Jacob's Room* and *To the Lighthouse* it is the counterpart of *Mrs. Dalloway*'s clocks: "The beam from the lighthouse strode rapidly across the water . . . the waves slapped the boat, and crashed . . . against the rocks" (*JR*, 52).

Yet the waves are not simply the empty spaces between perspectives; they emanate themselves from other centers, the "ripples" which "spread" from the fallen tree (*JR*, 32), the rings from striking clocks, the spokes from rotating lighthouses, like the widening ripples of Russell's fly touching the pool (*ABCR*, 42). "[T]he waves isuing from uncounted centres cross, coincide, oppose, and pass through each other, without confusion or ultimate extinction . . . every star is seen across the entanglement of wave motions produced by all other stars" (Tyndall, *On Radiation*, 11). For, "if a light signal is sent out from a body, that body will remain at the center of the waves as they travel outward, no matter how it may be moving – at least that will be the view of observers moving with the body" (*ABCR*, 39). It is as waves that light or sound endows the perspectives with their characteristic concentric shapes: "Each spreads the same ripple. The being grows rings, like a tree" (*W*, 283). Each island is surrounded by such waves spreading in circles, which at their outer rim, diminishing, meet those from other centers.

Some of these light and sound waves reach human sense organs: "The sound of Big Ben flooded Clarissa's drawing-room" (*MrsD*, 130); "into his brain waves of sound . . ., concussing, broke" (*MrsD*, 32). Some go unobserved: "Motionless and broad-baked the moors received the statement 'It is fifteen minutes past the hour,' but made no answer, unless a bramble stirred" (*JR*, 133). "Only the Lighthouse beam entered the rooms for a moment, sent its sudden stare over the bed and wall in the darkness of winter, looked with equanimity at the thistle and the swallow, the rat and the straw" (*TL*, 207–8). "Slowly wheeling, like the rays of a searchlight, the days, the weeks, the years passed one after another across the sky" (*Y*, 6). "Erratically rays of light flashed and wandered, like signals from sunken islands" (*W*, 207).

Waves and particles, then, constitute that hypothetical matter we seek to know. This is the significance of the waves' omnipresence, of "the elastic air with its particles" (*JR*, 36). In alternative theories, one or the other are the ultimate constituents of those objects of which the table is the paradigm. Waves or particles of light and sound are radiated by these objects. They fall upon the various perspectives – an eye, an ear, a window, little mirrors intermittently emitting flashes of reflected light, echoes of sound. Their persistence is the table's in the observer's absence: "We think of matter as having existed long before there were any minds" (*PP*, 37). Lighthouse and clock, on the horizon of perception, send out these waves. The voyage "to the lighthouse" necessarily lies then over the waves. For the traveller, their reality, beyond observation, takes on the quality of unreality. "The unreal world must be round all this – the phantom waves," Woolf writes of the projected novel *The Moths*, to become *The Waves* (*Diary*, III, 236).

The waves trace the boundaries of the perspectives, "burning on the rim of the dark" (*CE*, I, 48), but in the inter-perspectival region of blackness and silence lapping round the murmuring islands of light, Leslie Stephen's Idealist's "unknowable, which lies beyond" ("WM?," 144), Whitehead's "vague world which lies beyond [our bodily organs]" (*Symbolism*, 43), the conditions under which appearances may be registered are removed, distinctions blurred and washed away. "[T]he waves shape themselves symmetrically from the cliff top, but to the swimmer among them are divided by steep gulfs, and foaming crests" (*TL*, 235). That negation of appearances is the reduction to their physical causes of all perceivable differences. Appearances reduce, however, not to the monist's oneness of all things, but to an atomism of waves or particles by definition invisible, inaudible, imperceptible, indistinguishable except as a countable series. Wave after wave arrives, in "thick strokes moving, one after another, beneath the surface, following each other, pursuing each other, perpetually" (*W*, 5). Night after night is dealt "equally, evenly, with indefatigable fingers" (*TL*, 192), with no allowance for individual differences. The "night flowing down" (*TL*, 213), like the moor, "accepted everything" indistinguishably (*JR*, 134). For the "downpouring of immense darkness" (*TL*, 189) has a water-like power to wash away all perceptible differences. Each perspective faces "the fluidity of life" (*TL*, 237), "the flowing, the fleeting, the spectral" (*TL*, 158), "the showery darkness" (*W*, 237). "Nothing, it seemed, could survive the flood, the profusion of darkness" (*TL*, 191). It "swallowed up here a jug and basin, there a bowl of red and yellow dahlias, there the sharp edges and firm bulk of a chest of drawers." It wipes out the "thisness" of the particular: "Not only was furniture confounded; there was scarcely anything left of body or mind by which one could say, 'This is he' or 'This is she'" (*TL*, 190).

In one such interval of night *The Waves* begins, when as yet "[t]he sea was indistinguishable from the sky" (*W*, 7). It ends when once more "[s]ky and sea were indistinguishable" (*W*, 236). They merge to become that "vast space" (*TL*, 111) which separates and marks off all things from one another and yet in which eventually every distinction fades, "as perhaps at midnight, when all boundaries are lost, the country reverts to its ancient shape, as the Romans saw it, lying cloudy" (*MrsD*, 35). The succession of nights and days alternates the "chaos" in the night's blurring of distinctions with the clarity of day's lighted perspective. A "veil" of silence (*TL*, 196) similarly muffles sound: "like a mist rising, quiet rose" (*TL*, 213); "silence laps smooth over sound" (*JR*, 32); "the sands" are "of oblivion" (*TL*, 209); "the curtains" are "of dark" (*TL*, 214). Fluidity blurs "mass and edge," engulfs the solidity of things, which become "dim and unsubstantial" (*W*, 8).

The waves of light and sound which are the causes of sensibilia alternate then with "waves of darkness" (*W*, 237) and silence. "Now and again some level and masterly blast blew the multitudinous leaves up and down and then, as the wind flagged, each blade regained its identity" (*W*, 182). The perspective's brief clarity stands poised between the acts of nature's pageant: "the mouldy little room was saved from the salt breeze only by the depth of a brick" (*JR*, 54). "Above, the air rushed; beneath was water. She stood between two fluidities" (*BA*, 204). In time's passing, night encroaches on day, "the sea eats away the land we stand on" (*TL*, 68–9), "month and year, month and day, ran shapelessly together" (*TL*, 203), "the monotonous fall of the waves on the beach . . . remorselessly beat the measure of life, made one think of the destruction of the island and its engulfment in the sea" (*TL*, 27–8). The house "deserted" (*TL*, 206), "gone to rack and ruin" (*TL*, 207), threatens to be engulfed by "briars and hemlocks" which would have "blotted out the path, step, and window" (*TL*, 208). The tiny spot of light circled by darkness, of intimacy by the fertility of nature (the very fertility multiplying the worlds and hence diminishing any single one) – stars, pools, houses, rooms, red-hot pokers in the nettles, boots in the sand, figures on the horizon – that bright spot may suddenly be snuffed out. "Mr. Pearce had extinguished the lamp. The garden went out" (*JR*, 17). So, in "Time Passes," "One by one the lamps were all extinguished" (*TL*, 189), until Mr. Carmichael "blew out his candle" and the Virgil he was reading went out too (*TL*, 192).

The alternation of fluid and solid gives the world its shape. The fluidities which sandwich the little strip between them confer on sea, sky and the dunes of the beaches their special symbolism. Formless themselves, they meet at the horizon to outline the perspectives in a rigid framework: "It was the earth; the world against the sky; the horizon of how many glances" (*JR*, 17). Difference exists only within the perspectives; in between, it is wiped out. "They say the sky is the same everywhere. Travellers, the shipwrecked, exiles, and the dying draw comfort from the thought, and no doubt if you are of a mystical tendency, consolation, and even explanation, shower down from the unbroken surface" (*JR*, 31). The perspectives are particulars; the zone in between is the reign of universals, showing the "lack of colour and definite outline" (*BA*, 20) of the "vast clouds of an indifferent world" (*MrsD*, 73).

This omnipresent, eternal element surrounding all things is at once destructive and constructive, for, as "Time Passes" demonstrates, "[t]ables and chairs lose their legs, stones are split by frost, and mountains cleft by earthquakes and eruptions" (*OKnExW*, 82), things "furred, tarnished, cracked" (*TL*, 194) by the vaporous airs. Yet dividing one perspective from another and linking each to each, it invisibly imparts form, constructing the "scaffolding" to give rigidity and permanence to the fleeting event. The surrounding element is also the "logical space," to use the *Tractatus*' term, in which the relations between facts are drawn. "The logical scaffolding round the picture determines the logical space" (Wittgenstein, *Tractatus*, 3.42). This form-giving surrounding space not only maps the geography of Woolf's universe but also of an aesthetics where art holds together an otherwise fluid experience. So, only when "the night was now shut off by panes of glass, which, far from giving any accurate view of the outside world, rippled it so strangely," making "there, outside, a reflection in which things wavered and vanished, waterily," can "here, inside the room," there "seem[] to be order and dry land" (*TL*, 146–7). Fluidity without creates Mrs. Ramsay's interiority within round a table, poised precariously, like the lighthouse, on the edge of "Time Passes." The "reflection" makes of the window a mirror, "backs" the pane to cloud transparency and dissolve the view outside, rendering all clear within. What lacks form is what creates form.

ON THE EDGES OF THE PRIVATE WORLD: DISTANT SIGHTS AND SOUNDS AND THE UNOBSERVED

The *matter* of a given thing is the limit of its appearances as their distance from the thing diminishes. (Russell, *Mysticism and Logic*, 159)

[T]he barking of the dogs, at night . . . at the limit of earshot . . . the brief scattered lights . . . They were the things that scarcely were, on the confines of silence and dark, and soon ceased. (Beckett, *Three Novels*, 206)

The world the novels imaginatively build up like the chambers of a house is thus first that of sense experience; the language which provides the medium is descriptive. As in Russell's Cartesian method, the knowledge so constructed is grounded on a privacy multiplied and extended to take in unoccupied perspectives. The latter fill the gaps for the continuity of a public world. The aim is never the "expression" of my known world, but the projection of knowledge into other unknown worlds, "the whole problem of how knowledge can transcend personal experience" (*TK*, 10). The attempt to extend the boundaries of the bright circle of certainty into the surrounding darkness is a straining to catch "the external signs" (*JR*, 49) of other worlds. For, no matter how irrevocably far from any self-occupied center sense-data remain, no private world in Woolf is so sealed as to be untouched at its outer limits by the downpour of atoms, movement of waves, arriving to the perceptive apparatus from some outside source. Such is the Russellian "causal theory of perception."

The relation between objective source and subjective registering of its sense-data is that of Russell's "two places," "the active and passive places" (*Mind*, 130), two centers, one emitting the waves or particles – a rotating lighthouse sending out radiating beams – and the other receiving them – a mirror or window. The passive place may be nothing more than the reception of the data, regardless of whether or not an observer receives them. The internal structure of the perspective, proceeding from a center out through a range of decreasing sharpness, gives a kind of varying depth of field. Sensation itself falls off at the edges: "Sensations do not decay suddenly, but fade gradually, though very quickly" (*Matter*, 254). A varying distance is created then between a self occupying a center and its sense-data. Hence, in Woolf most sensations are visual or audial as opposed to tactile.

There is an "inference from near to distant appearances" (*Matter*, 220) and from distant to unsensed appearances. Distant sense-data offer evidence for the unobserved which motivates the seemingly random consistency of Woolf's descriptions and the otherwise unexplained recurrence of images of distant sights and sounds in them. They present "cases of 'vagueness,' in a certain precise sense." "Sounds may be stopped by obstacles, and die away completely in a sufficient distance from their sources." "When we see a man a hundred yards away, we cannot tell whether he is handsome or plain. When we can only just distinguish a person's voice, we cannot tell what is being said" (*Matter*, 220).

"[F]aint and peripheral sensations" (*LK*, 131) have another related significance. Raising the question "[a]re faint and peripheral sensations included in 'experience'?" (*TK*, 8), Russell answers that

> we can, by an effort of will, attend to what is in the margin. It is obvious that, when we do so, what we attend to is indubitably experienced. Thus the question we have to consider is whether attention constitutes experience, or whether things not attended to are also experienced. It seems we must admit things to which we do not attend, for attention is a selection among objects that are "before the mind," and therefore presupposes a larger field. (*TK*, 8–9)

The distinction here between "attention" and "experience" allows unattended sense-data to be caught on the periphery of a perspective, as if the sense-organs don't always require a mind – "the fringe of my intelligence floating unattached caught those distant sensations which after a time the mind draws in and works upon; the chime of bells; general murmurs" (*W*, 249). Hence, faint sensations provide grounds for supposing unsensed sensations. As against it seeming "as though the experience of each moment must be a prison for the knowledge of that moment, and as though its boundaries must be the boundaries of our present world," the private world is now revealed to contain within its boundaries things in some sense unknown to us, to show "that we can know what we do not know" (*TK*, 10).[10]

The look of Woolf's world is thus marked by things barely made out, "Constantinople seen through a mist" (*TL*, 112), or vanishing on the horizon: "All looked distant and peaceful and strange. The shore seemed far away, unreal" (*TL*, 188). A distantly remembered person takes on Mrs. Ramsay's "remoteness" (*TL*, 75), "like a figure standing at the cross roads at dusk, which grows more and more remote as the dog-cart spins away . . . , though her arms are outstretched, and as she sees the figure dwindle and disappear, still she cries out how she would do anything in the world, anything, anything, anything" (*MrsD*, 240); "my friends pass dark across the horizon, . . . stepping off the rim of the world into the ship which waits to take them into storm or serenity" (*CSFVW*, 104). Reality "seems to dwell in shapes too far away for us to discern what their nature is" (*Room*, 114). The stars are perforce all distant.[11]

Distant, disembodied sounds likewise recur in recognizable categories in Woolf's descriptions, little clusters of sense-data fading into sensibilia far from any center of consciousness lodged in a character. There are everywhere on the edge of awareness "odd irrelevant noises" (*Diary*, III, 236), dogs barking, sheep and cattle grazing and coughing, everywhere. "A dog barked, barked, barked down in the hollow" (*JR*, 118). "Here perhaps in some southern wood an old man lit dry ferns and the birds were startled. The sheep coughed; one flower bent slightly towards another" (*JR*, 160). "The barking of a thousand dogs sounded in her ears. Carriage wheels rushed ceaselessly in a circle. Leaves sighed overhead" (*O*, 285). "There was no sound of cropping" (*W*, 156); "she heard a bough creaking in the garden, a sheep coughing in the park, a swift screaming past the window" (*O*, 320); one was "hearing nothing but the sheep cropping the grass close to the roots" (*ND*, 48); "wild dogs bark far away" (*W*, 17) for "[d]ogs will bark" (*Room*, 53). "Looking up, backwards, he saw the legs of children deep in the grass, and the legs of cows. Munch, munch, he heard" (*JR*, 37). There are distant voices, murmuring, shouting. Cut off from the speakers who emit them, they are not the means of contact between subjects. "The voices came to her very strangely, as if they were voices at a service in a cathedral, for she did not listen to the words" (*TL*, 27); "[t]he words . . . sounded as if they were floating like flowers on water out there, cut off from all" (*TL*, 166). Everywhere "[s]houts came from a world far away" (*TL*, 255), "like a faint scent, or a violin next door (so strange is the power of sounds at certain moments)" (*MrsD*, 47); "voices crinkled" the veil, like sights the surface of water (*TL*, 276). Emanating from other worlds, the voices of unseen speakers, the music of unseen musicians – "someone was practicing scales" (*BA*, 83–4) – penetrate my world from time to time, faintly, briefly, like "the cry which in London when I thrust the window open someone cries" (*BA*, 110) and which exists for me only when the window is opened; "the fringe of my intelligence floating unattached caught those distant sensations which after a time the mind draws in" (*W*, 249). Or a meteor-like flare of sound may seemingly only graze the perspective's edge: "some insect dashed at her, boomed in her ear, and was gone" (*JR*, 19); "[n]ow and then as if a door opened and shut or the veil parted and closed, the roar boomed and faded" (*Y*, 243); " '[s]uddenly a bee booms in my ear . . . It is here; it is past' " (*W*, 11); "snow flopped from a branch, otherwise all was silent, save when a sheep coughed" (*Y*, 243). Briefly a door opens and light and sound rush in to reveal the existence of a world perhaps not destroyed by its closing although once more unapprehensible.

Beside the "space-like intervals" separating a sense organ from a sense-datum, there are also "time-like intervals" (*Matter*, 370). Typically a time-like interval is a temporary loss of consciousness, the interval of sleep, of inattention, of distractedness. Each perspective in time holds a set of sense-data – "there rose that half-heard melody, that intermittent music which the ear half catches but lets fall; a bark, a bleat; irregular, intermittent, yet somehow related; the hum of an insect, the tremor of cut grass, dissevered yet somehow belonging; the jar of a doorbeetle, the squeak of a wheel, loud, low, but mysteriously related; which the ear strains to bring together and is always on the verge of harmonizing, but they are never quite heard, never fully harmonized," so that they eventually fade into night, when "at last, in the evening, one after another the sounds die out, and the harmony falters, and silence falls" (*TL*, 212). That is the form that "Time Passes" repeats: for the sleepers in the house, its night begins with the muffling of the sense-organs, "as the curtains of dark wrapped themselves over the house, over Mrs. Beckwith, Mr. Carmichael, and Lily Briscoe so that they lay with several folds of blackness on their eyes." It ends with the return of sight and sound: "nothing broke their sleep, until, the birds beginning and the dawn weaving their thin voices in to its whiteness, a cart grinding, a dog somewhere barking" (*TL*, 214); "I hear . . . far off, far away, faint and far, the chorus beginning; wheels; dogs; men shouting; church bells; the chorus beginning" (*W*, 27); "the darkness dims so soon, and so soon a bird sings, a cock crows, or a faint green quickens, like a turning leaf, in the hollow of a wave" (*TL*, 192). The boundaries of a day likewise frame *The Waves*' chapter openings, beginning at dawn and ending in nightfall. In between are other self-enclosed days – "these October days are to me a little strained and surrounded with silence," Woolf records in her diary (*Diary*, III, 259). Each "short space" of a day bounded by darkness contains a collection of sensibilia, "the long summer days, when the empty rooms seemed to murmur with the echoes of the fields and the hum of flies" (*TL*, 200). Each is set apart, like a vignette – something "had parted the curtain and displayed behind it, single, distinct, the hare erect; the wave falling; the boat rocking" (*TL*, 192), a collection of events.

Not mere realistic details, Woolf's images of the far reaches of perception, that point of falling off of audibility and visibility that Russell calls "fading (akoluthic) sensation" (*Mind*, 175), suggest a world whose distance from the observer becomes a sign of his or her contingency. In "far away sounds, [is] the suggestion they brought in of other worlds, indifferent to this world" (*Y*, 388). They are also signs of the interval: it is "doubtful whether we ever directly apprehend" the passage of time, Moore says, but within the moments between intervals "a light growing brighter, a colour changing, or a sound growing louder" is recorded, all that is ever "directly apprehended" (*SomeMain*, 206). Intervals of no sound or sight enclose sensibilia, "the swaying mantle of silence . . . wove into itself the falling cries of birds, ships hooting, the drone and hum of the fields, a dog's bark, a man's shout, and folded them round the house in silence" (*TL*, 195). The far sound trails off into the absence of sound: "Then there was a silence, and a cow coughed" (*BA*, 7). "The Moonlight Sonata tinkled away" in *Jacob's Room* (43), enclosed somewhere inside rooms at Cambridge; "then there broke out laughter" as the narrator stands in the dark outside. "The laughter died in the air. The sound of it could scarcely have reached any one standing by the Chapel . . . A step or two beyond the window there was nothing at all" (*JR*, 44).

Nothing beyond the window invokes a Cambridge immured in Idealism. But the text does not stop at Cambridge's limits. Beyond the window, on the other side of the zone of silence and darkness, there exists a world unknown to Cambridge where women wash clothes in a stream beneath the sun. Faint sounds or sights are perhaps loud and clear in some other perspective, close to a center off-center. If the listening ear or watching eye intercepts them, might not another full world exist beyond the ken of the organ? For "the senses," Leslie Stephen writes, "indicate the varying relations of bodies, and, through them, of other conscious beings." Via the spatial-temporal framework organizing "all the shifting scenery of consciousness . . . signals are thrown out to us from other centres," like the sudden beams from a lighthouse ("WM?," 148).

The images of sights blurring on the horizon and sounds increasingly inaudible convey the sensible world's now familiar geography, with discrete perspectives characteristically fading from a center of great clarity to a vaguer rim. Hence, voice is divided from ear, which remains outside the world of aural sense-data coming to it at great removes. Its position is the eye's in Wittgenstein's *Tractatus*, which "does not belong to the world" but is its "limit" (5.632; 5.64). "So much depends then, thought Lily Briscoe, . . . upon distance:

whether people are near us or far from us; for her feeling for Mr. Ramsay changed as he sailed further and further across the bay. It seemed to be elongated, stretched out; he seemed to become more and more remote. He and his children seemed to be swallowed up in that blue, that distance" (*TL*, 284). And always at the very farthest reaches marked by the lighthouse[12] there were the waves: "There was a sound like the breaking of waves on a shore far away" (*Y*, 293).

BEYOND THE PRIVATE WORLD: LOST OBJECTS AND MEMORIES

> To show how very little control of our possessions we have – what an accidental affair this living is after all our civilization – let me just count over a few of the things lost in one lifetime . . . there were the bird cages, the iron hoops, the steel skates, the Queen Anne coal-scuttle, the bagatelle board, the hand organ – all gone, and jewels too. Opals and emeralds, they lie about the roots of turnips . . . The wonder is that I've any clothes on my back, that I sit surrounded by solid furniture at this moment. Why, if one wants to compare life to anything, one must liken it to being blown through the Tube at fifty miles an hour – landing at the other end without a single hairpin in one's hair! Shot out at the feet of God entirely naked! Tumbling head over heels in the asphodel meadows like brown paper parcels pitched down a shoot in the post office! (Woolf, "The Mark on the Wall," *CSFVW*, 78)

Out of sight and beyond earshot lie then, perhaps, sights and sounds unseen and unheard. For out of sight is not necessarily out of mind nor existence. The sound or sight, "come to an end of the period of fading" (*Mind*, 175), joins the distant past and the imperceptible distances beyond privacy. Unretrievable, it is lost. Precisely because Woolf's universe is a plurality of occupied and unoccupied perspectives, the objects which fill it are always unobserved by someone. This is the meaning of another set of recurring images in the novels: that of lost objects. Separated from their owners in time and space, lost objects do not necessarily cease thereby to exist. Their possible persistence suggests that they are somewhere to be found – or why should so much time be wasted looking for them? Why "be drowned looking for a pearl brooch" (*TL*, 261), Minta's brooch, "half-hidden by some stone" (*TL*, 153), an indefinite stone only inferred, or her book, "for she had left the third volume of *Middlemarch* in the train and she never knew what happened in the end" (*TL*, 148). Lost or misplaced things obsess Woolf's characters and clutter the novels' empty spaces. "I've left my bag somewhere – where?" a character exclaims, and she retraces her steps, "in the preoccupied manner of people who have to think about something that is lost" (*ND*, 332–3), with the distractedness that distances the searcher from present surroundings.

On the seashore the sun glitters on the waves' debris, "showed the rusty cartwheel, the white bone, or the boot without laces stuck, black as iron, in the sand" (*W*, 148). Perhaps "among the pebbles" is one of the "thousands" of spectacle cases Mrs. Ramsay had lost (*TL*, 293). In the tidepool, "some fish, stranded, lashed its tail as the wave drew back" (*W*, 166), but no one witnesses its agony; on the tool-house wall, "the adder's skin hung from the nail empty" (*W*, 236); left outside Jacob's room, "the child's bucket was half-full of rainwater" (*JR*, 14); "the empty snail shells" lay beneath "the solitary thorn tree" (*W*, 237). In "Time Passes"'s abandoned house, there are "only hangings that flapped, wood that creaked, the bare legs of tables, saucepans and china . . . What people had shed and left – a pair of shoes, a shooting cap, some faded skirts and coats in wardrobes – those alone kept the human shape and in the emptiness indicated how once they were filled and animated" (*TL*, 194). There in the musty rooms are "the torn letters in the wastepaper basket, the flowers, the books" (*TL*, 190), among them "old Sir Walter's" (*TL*, 176) "Waverley novels" whose survival had troubled Mr. Ramsay and which, along with a tea-set, Mrs. McNab "fetched up from oblivion . . . one morning" (*TL*, 209). "There were boots and shoes; and a brush and comb left on the dressing-table, for all the world as if she expected to come back tomorrow" (*TL*, 204) and "the old grey cloak" which Mrs. Ramsay wore gardening" (*TL*, 205). And there is the pig's skull in the children's bedroom with the shawl Mrs. Ramsay had hung on it to assuage Cam's fears and "the picture on the easel" that Lily Briscoe left unfinished (*TL*, 191). In the garden, flowers volunteer among weeds: "Poppies sowed themselves among the dahlias; the lawn waved with long grass; giant artichokes towered among roses; a fringed carnation flowered among the cabbages . . . until some trespasser, losing his way, could have told only by a red-hot poker among the nettles, or a scrap of china in the hemlock, that here once some one had lived; there had been a house" (*TL*, 207–9). "Here," in the empty house, "are chairs turned but nobody sits on them. Here are empty tables and nobody any more coming to dine at them tonight" (*W*, 294). The novels' lost objects argue the persistence of things unperceived, like Martin Pargiter's walrus: "It's awfully queer, she thought, touching the ink-corroded patch of bristles on the back of Martin's walrus with the point of her pen, that *that* should have gone on all these years. That solid object might survive them all. If she threw it away it could still exist somewhere or other" (*Y*, 91).

Both space-like and time-like intervals separate a lost object from its bereft possessor. A former object of immediate knowledge, its present whereabouts are somewhere unknown. It belongs now to the owner's inaccessible past, no longer perceptible at will. Yet, some trace of it lingers for a time via the "memory-image" of the "immediate past" (*Mind*, 174). "Immediate memory is important both because it provides experience of succession, and because it bridges the gulf between sensations and the images which are their copies" (*Mind*, 175). Immediate memory thus makes lost objects resemble sensations falling off at the edges: "we think our knowledge of the past decays gradually" whereas "really acquaintance with an image [is] growing progressively less like the past" (*TK*, 173–4). For in its original attachment "memory resembles the knowledge derived from the senses": the memory-image is an object of acquaintance. "It is immediate, not inferred, not abstract; it differs from perception mainly by being referred to the past" (*Mind*, 173).

Recently lost objects thus exist somewhere in the vicinity of their bereft owners' perspectives, like fading sensations, still attached via a relation of memory spanning an interval of time. "A thread united them – visible, invisible, like those threads, now seen, now not, that unite trembling grass blades in autumn before the sun rises" (*BA*, 56). Like that "spider's thread of attachment" (*MrsD*, 173), that "thin thread" attaching Lady Bruton to Richard Dalloway and Hugh Whitbread, with whom she has just lunched and who are moving ever farther from her, immediate memory will "stretch and stretch, get thinner and thinner" (*MrsD*, 170), like the "ball of memories" which Mrs. McNab "unwound" (*TL*, 211). It will become the line of life itself, binding together the perspectives into a biography via the "experience of succession."

The immediate memory-image lingers only so long, however. "Time-relations to the subject seem to be twofold: there is pastness in general, and there are definite temporal distances," Russell states (*TK*, 170); "beyond the immediate past, events remembered are simply past, and their greater or less distance from the present is a matter of inference" (*TK*, 171). In other words, like Russell's example of Bismarck (*PP*, 54ff.), "[t]he object believed to be in the remote past may not be given in acquaintance, but only known by description" (*TK*, 172). There are thus two kinds of memory, one a form of acquaintance whose object is the memory and not the past itself. Uncharacteristically acknowledging Bergson, Russell distinguishes the immediate from true memory: "True memory, as opposed to 'immediate memory,' applies only to events sufficiently distant to have come to an end of the period of fading" (*Mind*, 175).

The space separating memories from their possessor is that of a forgetting: "Between acquaintance-memory and descriptive memory there is, as a matter of logical form, an absolute gulf, with no possibility of gradual transition" (*TK*, 173). The condition for descriptive memory, which requires a reconstruction or inference, is the disappearance of immediate memory. In that sense, "[o]ne of the obvious empirical refutations" of our not knowing anything beyond present sensible experience is "derived from the knowledge that we have forgotten something. When, for example, we try to recall a person's name, we may be perfectly certain that the name came into our experience in the past, but for all our efforts it will not come into our present experience" (*TK*, 11). Lost objects furnish another example. The name, which has dropped somewhere in the mind inaccessible to consciousness is like the brooch fallen somewhere unseen by its owner. Lost objects pass, like sound, once faded, into the world beyond the observer's ken; their sense-data become sensibilia. So Lily Briscoe's mind, in part three of *To the Lighthouse*, "throws up from its depths, scenes, and names, and sayings, and memories and ideas" (238), forgotten left-overs from the day of part one, like debris from the waves, and the solution for finishing her painting as well "had been knocking about in her mind all these years" unbeknownst to her (220).

Past experiences might themselves hypothetically continue to exist somewhere inaccessible to us, like lost objects, somewhere observable. There is no way to reenter or reobserve them save in mind, as Mrs. Ramsay returns in memory to a drawing room of the past: "it fascinated her, as if, while she had changed, that particular day, now become very still and beautiful, had remained there, all these years" (*TL*, 132). Woolf treats certain memories, Proust-like and Freud-like in their seeming independence of the will, in such a hypothetical fashion:

> At times I can go back to St Ives more completely than I can this morning. I can reach a state where I seem to be watching things happen as if I were there . . . my memory supplies what I had forgotten, so that it seems as if it were happening independently, though I am really making it happen . . . Now if this is so, is it not possible – I often wonder – that things we have felt with great intensity have an existence independent of our minds; are in fact still in existence? (*MB*, 67)

The empty spaces lost objects give off their appearances in are thus those of the past, for the perceptible is present in both space and time. The past, like the world's wastes, is a repository of objects either not presently or never observed. The former, like Russell's forgotten name, provide evidence for the latter. Like unoccupied perspectives in Russell's construction of the public world, they furnish the continuity required to reconstruct the distant past.

For the thread of memory attaching image to sensation may be completely severed, as "Millicent Bruton, lying on the sofa, let the thread snap; snored" (*MrsD*, 170). Lost possessions come to reside in those terrifying spaces outside the mind where cows cough unheard and trees fall unbeknownst to man, "at midnight when no one speaks or gallops" (*JR*, 134). They accumulate in the vast corridors of the past, in the Roman camps and the museum at Scarborough with its "[c]annon-balls; arrow-heads; Roman glass and a forceps green with verdegris" (*JR*, 19), once an instrument of birth for the now dead. At the Roman camp at Scarborough, "[a] garnet brooch has dropped into its grass" (*JR*, 133) – Betty Flander's brooch. "How many needles Betty Flanders had lost there! and her garnet brooch" (*JR*, 132).

> Was Mrs. Flanders' two-penny-halfpenny brooch forever part of the rich accumulation? . . . The moor accepted everything. Tom Gage cries aloud so long as his tombstone endures. The Roman skeletons are in safe keeping. Betty Flanders' darning needles are safe too and her garnet brooch. And sometimes at midday, in the sunshine, the moor seems to hoard these little treasures, like a nurse. (*JR*, 132–4)

Eventually, lost objects drop out of perspectives into the darkness and silence of the eternal waves. The questions foolish to ask are the old philosophical questions raised by the problem of the persistence of objects in the absence of the observer: "The church clock struck ten. Did the strokes reach the furze bush, or did the thorn tree hear them?" (*JR*, 131). The philosopher searching for an answer resembles "a person who has dropped some grain of pearl or diamond into the grass and parts the tall blades very carefully" (*MrsD*, 182).

THE IMPERSONAL LANDSCAPE AND THE UNREMEMBERED PAST

Our historical knowledge tells us of ages in the past when, so far as we can see, no living being existed on earth. . . of countless star-systems, whose detailed history remains beyond our ken . . . Our perceptions lead us to infer that there is something happening in the stars, something happening within the earth, and something happening on the far side of the moon. Also they tell us that in remote ages there were things happening. (Whitehead, *Science and the Modern World*, 85)

There is thus an unoccupied landscape, with its own contours, which is also the landscape of the past; stars light years away seen by no living person. It is recognizable by its multiplicity of things and its absence of one thing, by its atomism and emptiness. Its emptiness, its aridity, contains without contradiction an uncontrolled fertility, the desert and the jungle are equally full of many things, equally empty: "the empty moor" (*W*, 65) with its rich accumulation of arrows and needles, "the sandhills with their innumerable glitter . . . the arid waste of the desert . . . sprinkled with stunted dark-green jungle-trees" (*W*, 148).

What is this fertile emptiness? If what man has observed and discarded remains, what makes a landscape littered with the flotsam and jetsam of time, drenched with the shower of atoms, filled with the harvest of randomly sowed seeds as in the garden of "Time Passes," nonetheless empty? The absence is that of the human observer: "there is no life anywhere in the abysses of space" (*W*, 225). Nature is ultimately "some moon country, uninhabited of men" (*TL*, 23), "a blazing island on which no foot could rest" (*W*, 165). In it, "[o]ne could walk all day without meeting a soul" (*TL*, 105).

If the distance travelled is far enough, man's absence is complete: far from any occupied center one reaches the "dark antre of the unvisited earth, or wind brushed forest" the chorus in *Between the Acts* (40) invokes, a past so distant that it is not only forgotten but never lived, "the unexperienced past" (*IMT*, 123) containing "empirical impersonal knowledge" (*IMT*, 126), the "little sandy beaches where no one had been since the beginning of time" (*TL*, 105). Separated from the present by great passages of space and time, this is outer space or prehistory – Mrs. Swithin's Outline of History with its "rhododendron forests in Piccadilly," "when the entire continent, not then, she understood, divided by a channel, was all one; populated, she understood, by elephant-bodied, seal-necked, heaving, surging, slowly writhing, and she supposed, barking monsters; the iguanodon, the mammoth, and the mastodon; from whom presumably she thought, jerking the window open, we descend" (*BA*, 10). There was a time "[b]efore there was a channel, when the earth, upon which the Windsor chair was planted, was a riot of rhododendrons," as Mrs. Swithin "had read that morning in her Outline of History" (*BA*, 108). All this presuming and supposing is because the bark heard by no human ears is reconstructed by description. There can be no acquaintance with prehistory, synonymous with the pre-human, but only with fossils, long lost objects: "when the whole earth is sheeted and slippery, some undulation, some irregularity of surface will mark the boundary of an ancient garden" (*CE*, IV, 198); "beneath these pavements are shells, bones and silence" (*W*, 97). Even the remembered past becomes, by its very pastness, as inaccessible as prehistory: "The autumn trees, ravaged as they are, take on the flash of tattered flags kindling in the gloom of cool cathedral caves where gold letters on marble pages describe death in battle and how bones bleach and burn far away in Indian sands" (*TL*, 193). Mrs. Swithin looks to Ida "as if she had been a dinosaur or a very diminutive mammoth. Extinct she must be, since she had lived in the reign of Queen Victoria" (*BA*, 174). The one night of "Time Passes" becomes equivalent to "ten million years" (*MrsD*, 124) because it is separated by an infinitely divisible interval from the morrow in which the sleepers awake.

The future is equally unobservable; "what we should see if we could live a thousand years hence or had lived a thousand years ago," in Leslie Stephen's words ("WM?," 137), are alternative versions of knowledge by description. The constructed future is the time "when Torrington Square is a reef of coral perhaps and the fishes shoot in and out where your bedroom window used to be; or perhaps the forest will have reclaimed those pavements and the wombat and the ratel will be shuffling on uncertain feet among the green undergrowth that will then tangle the area railings" (*CE*, IV, 59–60) Woolf's examples, recalling Mrs. Swithin's pre-historic London, emphasize the future's ressemblance to the distant past.

In the emptiness of this landscape lies the external world's very externality, the realm of "solid bodies" (*OKnExW*, 82), its lack of consciousness. "If there is one thing that may be said, in the popular estimation, to characterize mind," Russell explains, "that one thing is 'consciousness.' . . . tables and chairs are not 'conscious.' We think that when we sit in a chair, we are aware of sitting in it, but it is not aware of being sat in . . . there is some difference between us and the chair in this respect" (*Mind*, 11). Chairs and tables, we recall, are Berkeley's "unthinking things."

The landscape is empty, then, because it is mindless, as the pig's skull is emptied of brain. But if this is its reality, then the observer, should there be one, is purely contingent. The unoccupied landscape is that before man's arrival, whether his imminent arrival – the table in *The Waves* is set for absent guests – or his appearance in history. The description of the empty beach at *The Waves*' opening not accidentally recalls *Genesis* before man's creation: "The sun had not yet risen . . . Gradually as the sky whitened a dark line lay on the horizon dividing the sea from the sky" (*W*, 5). What the landscape can be said to be unconscious of is the observer. Like the fields in "Time Passes," it is "entirely careless of what was done or thought by the beholders" (*TL*, 198). So also the sky is indifferent. Its "blue that had never filtered down; that had escaped registration," that "never fell as sun, shadow, or rain upon the world," coldly "disregarded the little coloured ball of earth entirely. No flower felt it; no field; no garden" (*BA*, 22–3).

If the landscape mindlessly collects the traces the observer leaves behind, they stand merely as signs of the transitoriness and contingence of his or her passing amid the persistence of things. " 'That's what makes a view so sad,' said Mrs. Swithin . . . 'And so beautiful. It'll be there,' she nodded at . . . the distant fields, 'when we're not' " (*BA*, 53). For those infinite stretches of space and time which the body cannot live the mind can think of. So William Bankes and Lily Briscoe "looked at the dunes far away, and instead of merriment felt come over them some sadness . . . because distant views seem to outlast by a million years (Lily thought) the gazer and to be communing already with a sky which beholds an earth entirely at rest" (*TL*, 34). That this "sorrow" is "brewed by the earth itself" is proffered as an "interpretation of Jacob's gloom" at sea beyond Land's End, that perspective's edge (*JR*, 49). The empty landscape reduces the individual – "a little strip of time presented itself to her eyes: her fifty years" (*TL*, 91), those "brief years" Russell evokes (*ML*, 46) – amidst "the world moving through the abysses of infinite space. It roars; the lighted strip of history is past and our Kings and Queens; we are gone; our civilization; the Nile; and all life. Our separate drops are dissolved; we are extinct, lost in the abysses of time, in the darkness" (*W*, 225). Such meditations lead inexorably to the conclusion that "there was a time when none of this had any existence" (*JR*, 19) or will. The little, contentless word "this," Russell's "logically proper name," bears the weight of contingence. "This" is always "pathetically small," Mr. Ramsay's "[p]oor little place" (*TL*, 106). It is "this" which disappears, one instant in the vast landscape of time past.

PUBLIC TIME, CLOCK TIME

> [B]y pronouncing time and space to be independent realities, we get a solid mathematical universe of indestructible matter. (Stephen, "What Is Materialism?," 147)

> [G]iving herself the little shake that one gives a watch that has stopped, the old familiar pulse began beating, as the watch begins ticking – one, two, three, one, two, three. And so on and so on, she repeated, listening to it, sheltering and fostering the still feeble pulse. (Woolf, *To the Lighthouse*, 126)

Between "The Window" and "The Lighthouse," the room and the clock, in the world's unobserved regions, lies then the gap between the realms of sense and physics which logical relations are meant to bridge via unoccupied perspectives; in that gap time simply passes, laying down layer upon layer of moments, some once occupied, others not, but all finally emptied of consciousness. The clocks' striking and the lighthouses' rotation regularly divides time's passing, for, just as we live "in the light of this great clock, yellow-faced" (*W*, 20), the lighthouse is a kind of light-clock punctuating the darkness at regular intervals.[13] "Here was a Thursday morning in the process of manufacture; each second was minted fresh by the clock upon the mantelpiece" (*ND*, 113). This is the theme concentrated in "Time Passes," which links two days separated by a night but between which yet other nights succeed nights, and days, days. The same theme is sounded in the chapter openings of *The Waves* and *The Years*.

In *The ABC of Relativity* Russell raises the question: "what really is measured by a clock?," given that "[t]he universal cosmic time which used to be taken for granted is . . . no longer admissable": in the post-Einstein universe, "[f]or each body, there is a definite time order for the events in its neighborhood; this may be called the 'proper' time for that body" (50). In the theory of relativity, he points out, "anything which goes through some regular periodic performance" is a clock. "The earth is a clock, because it rotates once every twenty-three hours and fifty-six minutes. An atom is a clock, because the electrons go round the nucleus a certain number of times in a second; its properties as a clock are exhibited to us in its spectrum, which is due to light waves of various frequencies" (*ABCR*, 50–1). In this sense, *The Waves*' chapter openings, structured by one rotation of the earth, correspond to *Mrs. Dalloway*'s composition, in which "clocks made by human hands" (*ABCR*, 50) measure one day.[14] And at "half-past eleven" when "the sound of St. Margaret's glides into the recesses of the heart" (*MrsD*, 74), making Peter Walsh wonder why he had "been so profoundly happy when the clock was striking" (*MrsD*, 75), his sudden remembrance "as the sound of St. Margaret's languished" that Clarissa had been ill – "It was her heart," and "the sudden loudness of the final stroke tolled for death" (*MrsD*, 75) – brings home the fact that the heart too is a clock, like the "clock . . . striking – one, two, three" after the death of Septimus (*MrsD*, 227).

"If cosmic time is abandoned, what is really measured by a clock in the wide sense that we have just given to the term?" The answer is that "[e]ach clock gives a correct measure of its own 'proper' time" (*ABCR*, 51). For this reason, "[y]ou cannot say that one is right and the other wrong, any more than you could if one used a clock showing Greenwich time and another a clock showing New York time" (*ABCR*, 39). Where time is measured by observers in motion, discrepancies exist; yet it cannot be said that any one observer is mistaken: "each is equally justified and is only wrong to ascribe an objective validity to subjective measures" (*ABCR*, 56). Any "discrepancy is owing to the fact that the two watches do not keep perfect time, in spite of the fact that each is accurate from its owner's point of view." (*ABCR*, 41–2). Thus, "the two clocks, which strike at the same moment because each keeps perfect time" with which Leibniz illustrates "the pre-established harmony" (*HWP*, 584; Russell, *A Critical Exposition*, 136), receive their post-relativity reformulation. The harmony of Woolf's monadology of the novel is similarly adjusted. In *Night and Day*, "the clocks had come into their reign, the grandfather's clock in the hall ticking in competition with the small clock on the landing" (108), and there is "the slowness of the kitchen clock" (122). In *Mrs. Dalloway*, "clock time" is measured both by Big Ben, "indifferent, inconsiderate" (71), giving "the hour, irrevocable" (170) and St. Margaret's, "the other clock, the clock which always struck two minutes after Big Ben, . . . shuffling in with its lap full of odds and ends, which it dumped down as if Big Ben were all very well with his majesty . . . , but she must remember all sorts of little things besides" (193): "the late clock sounded, coming in on the wake of Big Ben . . . like the spray of an exhausted wave" (194), "like a hostess who comes into her drawing-room on the very stroke of the hour and finds her guests there already. I am not late. No, it is precisely half-past eleven, she says. Yet, though she is perfectly right, her voice . . . is reluctant to inflict its individuality" (74). In the same London, "[i]t was precisely twelve o'clock; twelve by Big Ben; whose stroke was wafted over the northern part of London; blent with that of other clocks" (*MrsD*, 142), but by the other clock, it is two minutes to twelve. Both are accurate from their own point of view. In this London with at least two clocks, the inhabitants are "solitary travellers," "sets of observers in rapid motion relatively to each other" (*ABCR*, 45). Some, like Hugh Whitbread, are "subconsciously . . . grateful to Rigby and Lowndes for giving one time ratified by Greenwich" (*MrsD*, 155), for one clock pronounces, by another law than Einstein's, only itself accurate; but, even on this map, there is more than one "observatory," "say Greenwich Observatory and Kew Observatory" (*ABCR*, 44). Hugh Whitbread and Richard Dalloway are both bodies in the "neighborhood" of Greenwich time; Hugh arrived at "half-past one" (*MrsD*, 155) at Lady Bruton's doorstep; Richard "arrived at the next moment" (*MrsD*, 157). By contrast, Clarissa, associated with St. Margaret's time, is seldom in Lady Bruton's neighborhood; hence they "seldom met" (*MrsD*, 161). So also, in *To the Lighthouse*, there are two lighthouses and "the other was also the Lighthouse . . . The other Lighthouse was true too" (*TL*, 277).

The frequent assumption that Woolf rejects logical realism, as a version of Bradley's Hegelianism and his avowed position that, as Russell puts it, "all truth is self-contradictory" (*Matter*, 386–7) or of her sister-in-law Karin Stephen's later Bergson-inspired anti-logic, is thus a misreading. In Hussey's version, with the two lighthouses Woolf rejects Moore's epigraph to *Principia Ethica*, "Everything is what it is, and not another thing." True, the fact that there are many clocks yields a universe in which "undeniable, everlasting, contradictory things" (*TL*, 40) might be neither true nor false, but as with the question whether "there is progress in the universe," where "optimism and pessimism are neither true nor false," it "depend[s] upon the choice of clocks" (*ABCR*, 225). This is not equivalent to the view that "everything in the physical world is relative to an observer" however (*ABCR*, 14). In the world of physics a clock is an observer just as much as a mind (*ABCR*, 219), and the theory of relativity "is wholly concerned to exclude what is relative and arrive at a statement of physical laws that shall in no way depend upon the circumstances of the observer" (*ABCR*, 14). Within this world, there is no one cosmic time, but there is public time. Public time is real time. In Woolf, time really passes. Hence the clocktower extends its dominion not just over the city but over unpeopled nature as well; it strikes over the moors, as the lighthouse combs the sea.

Lily "with the Ramsays" is "made to feel violently two opposite things at the same time; that's what you feel, was one; that's what I feel, was the other, and then they fought together" in the mind (TL, 154). Woolf marks their incompatibility by making one male and the other female. Both cannot be true without violating the principle of non-contradiction. But the voice Lily Briscoe hears "saying . . . contradictory things" (*TL*, 40), like "[t]he relationship between your grandfather and mother" Woolf describes to her nephew Julian Bell, "the flute voices of two birds in tune, . . . only reached by rich, rapid scales of discord, and incongruity" (*MB*, 37), does not establish "the identity of opposites" (*ML*, 3), because its statements concern events in time, like, centrally, the Ramsays' disagreement about the morrow's weather. There is no "simultaneous assertion of contradictory propositions" (*ML*, 9). The contradictions are resolved in real time. "Every year they said, would it be wet or fine; and every year it was – one or the other" (*BA*, 22). " 'And even if it isn't fine tomorrow,' said Mrs. Ramsay . . . 'it will be another day' " (*TL*, 42). For the weather is "variable" over time. In the continuous tidal expansion and retraction, the thinning and thickening – "Tick, tick, tick, went the machine in the bushes" (*BA*, 174) – is created the "gigantic pattern," "half remembered, half foreseen" (*Y*, 369).

Time's inexorable passing, forever ticking the minutes and striking the hours, producing what Whitehead calls "the settled actuality of the universe in which is the source of all conditions" (*Symbolism*, 39), introduces the idea of death. At the same time, it gives a compensatory vision of something which persists in the random absence of some observer, like the table – "here she's been sitting all the time

I've been in India; mending her dress," Peter Walsh thinks (*MrsD*, 61). "The clock began striking. The young man had killed himself; but she did not pity him; with the clock striking the hour, one, two, three, she did not pity him, with all this going on" (*MrsD*, 283). In the unreality imparted to one from the distanced perspective of the other arises the haunting beauty of each. Art discloses this beauty in conferring a timeless form on time's passing: "The word 'time' split its husk; poured its riches" in "an immortal ode to Time" (*MrsD*, 105). The novel will ultimately perform an elegiac function.

BETWEEN THE PRIVATE WORLDS: THE INTERLUDES WITHOUT A SELF

[T]he arrow . . . is never moving, but in some miraculous way the change of position has to occur *between* the instants. (Russell, *Our Knowledge of the External World*, 179)

[S]he attained a dancing rhythmical movement, as if the pauses were one part of the rhythm and the strokes another and all were related. (Woolf, *To the Lighthouse*, 236)

The voyage out reaches unpeopled space and prehistoric time "at the limits of analysis" (*LK*, 337). There lies the darkness delineating the lighted window, the silence wrapping round the cries of birds. For "between things, beyond things" (*TL*, 285), it is plausible, Moore says, that "there is an infinite extent of absolutely empty space – space in which there is nothing whatever" (*SomeMain*, 195).

Yet if the interval is in one sense empty, in another, due to "the nature of compact series," "[e]mpty it was not, but full to the brim" (*TL*, 285). To construct a public world out of the private, there must be continuity between perspectives; "there is not a beginning and end of the instant with an interval between them" (*OKnExW*, 142). Between each day lies a series of days – "day after day, light turned" (*TL*, 194) – for "between any two [terms] there are others" (*OKnExW*, 138). "But what after all is one night? . . . Night, however, succeeds to night . . . They lengthen; they darken" (*TL*, 192). So also, the reason for positing sensibilia was "on grounds of continuity and resemblance": to "include among appearances not only . . . actual sense-data, but also those 'sensibilia,' . . . belonging to the same system of appearances" (*ML*, 148–9).

Just as for Russell and Leslie Stephen "continuity" was created by filling in the "intervals," so Woolf created textual continuity by what she called "the interludes." The description of unoccupied places and times – the moors, the snowfield, the sea and the dunes of the seashore, the forest, the sky with its distant stars – is a constant feature of the novels' scenery, filling the interstices between characters' points of view. In *Jacob's Room*, they are interspersed throughout, sometimes separating the occupied worlds, sometimes marking a chapter end. With *To the Lighthouse*, "the images & symbols" of the unoccupied are given a formal place: "The lyric portions of *To the Lighthouse* are collected in the 10-year lapse" of part two "and don't interfere with the text so much as usual," Woolf writes (*Diary*, III, 106–7). Presenting "an empty house, no people's characters, the passage of time" (*Diary*, III, 76), "Time Passes" bridges the occupied worlds of parts one and three. "I hope to have kept the sound of the sea & the birds, dawn & garden subconsciously present, doing their work under ground" (*Diary*, IV, 11). This is "that intermittent music" (*TL*, 212) heard at part two's end, as the sleepers awaken. *The Waves* Woolf called at one point "a litter of fragments" (*Diary*, III, 285, 287), "a book so full of holes and patches; that will need re-building" (*Diary*, III, 302). This is because it removes all structure but the "series of dramatic soliloquies," clusters of sensations, memories, thoughts in perspectives. In-between, the sequence of days and seasons form the "interludes," which Woolf pronounces "essential; so as to bridge and also to give a background – the sea; insensitive nature – I dont know" (*Diary*, III, 285). In *The Years*, Woolf returned to these chapter openings of *The Waves*. The concept of a theatrical interlude operates in *Between the Acts* to contribute a title as well as a unifying device, Mrs. Swithin's empty Outline of History punctuating the pageant-play of human history.

The interludes, then, collect the thematically exploited images of sensibilia and erect them into an explicit formal expression of the geometry in the external world. They constitute the novels' "logical bridge" (*CPBR*, IX, 263), in the sense in which for Russell an "absolute gulf" can become a logical relation creating logical form. Significantly, the interlude in *To the Lighthouse* in which the novel's cast of consciousnesses sleep, absent themselves and, in some cases, die, is called "Time Passes." Woolf called it "this impersonal thing, which I'm dared to do by my friends, the flight of time, & the consequent break of unity in my design. That passage (I conceive the book in 3 parts: 1. at the drawing room window; 2. seven years passed; 3. the voyage:)," she adds, "interests me very much. A new problem like that breaks fresh ground in ones mind; prevents the regular ruts" (*Diary*, III, 36). The space in the text in which "time passes" between "The Window," summarized by Woolf as "father & mother & child in the garden," and "The Lighthouse," "the sail to the lighthouse," will also be "the death" (*Diary*, III, 36). It is the passage between childhood and adulthood, between the Victorian period – Woolf wished in "The Window" to "extract a section of Victorian life, like one of those cases with glass covers in which one is shown ants or bees going about their affairs" (*MB*, 127) – and the "modern," Post-War epoque, a winter between two summers, a night between two days, but it stretches to include that dark night of time, that "deep pool of past time" (*ND*, 113). The novels' interludes have their counterparts in Woolf's own experience: she describes illness, including her periods of madness, as "these curious intervals in life," of which she "had many" (*Diary*, III, 254, *TL*, 73). A logical "fiction," made up of private elements but creating a public whole that escapes their limits, is constructed by the formlessness surrounding its units. Like the "one interval of space-time, which replaces the two intervals of space and time of the older physics" (*ABCR*, 60) in post-Einsteinian physics, the interludes represent an "objective residue," for "the spatial and temporal properties of physical occurrences are found to be in large part dependent upon the observer; only a residue can be attributed to the occurrences in themselves" (*ABCR*, 32).

GRANITE AND RAINBOW

[W]e are *within* a world of colours, sounds, and other sense-objects, related in space and time to enduring objects such as stones, trees, and human bodies. (Whitehead, *Science and the Modern World*, 85)

These thoughts I am now working on are as hard as granite. (Wittgenstein to Drury, *Recollections*, 159, in Monk, *Wittgenstein*, 514, 537)

To give a sense of matter, need one make so much use of words like "solid" and "block" . . . But the style, the general form, . . . seem to be an immense improvement on all your other descriptive writing . . . your power . . . of lifting the veil and showing inanimate things in the mystery and beauty of their reality. (Clive Bell to Virginia Stephen on *The Voyage Out*, in Quentin Bell, *Virginia Woolf*, I, 208)

A dualism divides Woolf's external world, like Moore's and Russell's, "between concepts which can exist in parts of time and concepts which seem to be cut off from existence altogether" (Moore, *The Early Essays*, 74), between "[t]he world of existence . . . fleeting, vague, without sharp boundaries" and "[t]he world of being . . . unchangeable, rigid, exact" (*PP*, 100). These "antinomies which bother the metaphysician" ("WM?," 135) Woolf calls "granite and rainbow."

Granite stands for the primary qualities of matter, those "stripped of all sensible properties," as Berkeley puts it (*Three Dialogues*, 28): "extension, figure, solidity, gravity" (23). Its tangibility is purely figurative: physical matter cannot strictly speaking be touched. Yet "[w]e all feel that touch gives more evidence of 'reality' than sight; ghosts and rainbows can be seen but not touched," Russell says (*OP*, 162). Hence, the tangible condenses all the range of tactile sensations – the smooth, the rough, the sharp, the wet, the dry, the soft, the viscous – to the sole property of hardness. It is "something hard" (*CE*, II, 220), "the reality of sticks and stones" ("WM?," 134) – i.e., granite represents not a sensation but a support, what gives shape and rigidity. Describing a crisis in childhood, "when for no reason I could discover, everything suddenly became unreal," Woolf associates the feeling of unreality with needing "to touch something" (*MB*, 78), i.e., to lean on something. Without a support, "the whole world became unreal" (*MB*, 78). Yet physics' "hard facts" (*AAA*, 6) depend on its increasing reliance on sight over "misleading conceptions derived from the sense of touch" (*ABCR*, 18; see also *OP*, 162). The result Leslie Stephen had already described:

> To common-sense, nothing can be more real than the stone which Johnson kicked to confute Berkeley. Strip it of the secondary qualities which are obviously dependent upon the observing eye, and the residuum is a block of solidified space: matter resisting and embodying geometrical relations, and nothing else. Out of such blocks . . . the whole material universe is constructed for the mathematician. ("WM?," 133–4)

The "solid mathematical universe" ("WM?," 147) supplies an abstract, intangible support, one ultimately also invisible in its "rigid formalism" (*ML*, 90). It imparts "the same definition of outline, the same stable, solid, objective qualities" Keynes claimed that both universals like love, truth and beauty and the furniture "took on" for Moore (Skidelsky, *John Maynard Keynes*, I, 137). This is the solidity of "chimneys upright, roofs horizontal; too much brick and building" of the Cambridge night as well as that of "the bare hills of Turkey," with their "dry earth" (*JR*, 44). Solid objects are also those which persist unobserved: "as Mr. Micawber would say, the physical world of physics is solid but not indubitable, while the physical world of daily experience is indubitable but not solid," Russell writes. "In this statement I am using the word 'solid' to mean 'existing independently of my mental life'" (*Portraits from Memory*, 152). Things with rock-like solidity are endowed with the timelessness "of indestructible matter" ("WM?," 147). In the English landscape as in physics, these properties strangely meet and mix in the fluid waves at the land's edges, "the stormy Atlantic beat[ing] upon the granite shores of Cornwall" (*SO*, 266).

Against granite is set the insubstantiality of rainbow, of the secondary qualities. Rainbow belongs with things with "almost no permanence or rigidity" (*OKnExW*, 82), everything fleeting, "ephemeral as a rainbow" (*TL*, 28), "intangible to touch or taste" (*TL*, 80). This follows from the momentariness of sense-data, their shifting through all the colors of the spectrum; the mantle sways. The "stuff," "fabric" or "cotton wool" is a metaphor for sensation, "weaving this marvellous web of the outward world," as Stephen puts it ("WM?," 139). So Tyndall could characterize the "sky-particles" as "like a delicate gauze" and the "quench[ing]" of their glare as "ressembling exactly the withdrawal of a veil" (*Essays*, 37). The veil is stirred by "the little airs" that invade the house, also without rigidity. But they confer, like the waves, the rigid permanence and inviolability of physical laws. Chairs and tables may decay, but physical matter, the atoms and waves beyond perspectives, outlast the rainbow, the fabric. The little airs in "Time Passes" "scarcely disturbed the peace, the indifference, the air of pure integrity" in which "loveliness and stillness clasped hands . . . among the shrouded jars and sheeted chairs" by "reiterating their questions – 'Will you fade? Will you perish?'"; they "scarcely needed" to "answer: we remain" (*TL*, 195). The shawl, precariously veiling the bare bones, is subject to the little airs, which change it with time. Eventually the shawl falls to granite, both of nature and man (the repeated shocks are shelling from a ship): "once in the middle of the night with a roar, with a rupture, as after centuries of quiescence, a rock rends itself from the mountain and hurtles crashing into the valley, one fold of the shawl loosened and swung to and fro" (*TL*, 195–6). The skull beneath remains.

The two contrasted worlds are, however, bridged by relations.

The "so-called secondary qualities" are "in some way dependent upon the geometrical properties" ("WM?," 130), on the "iron girders spanning the swaying fabric" (*TL*, 159).[15] Granite furnishes the "something solid to cling to," like the "sheet of hard dates to take home with them" Woolf "provided" her Morley College students to counterbalance "the vagueness of my speech" (*VW*, I, 203) or the "hard separate facts" (*CSFVW*, 79) titling the chapters in *The Years.* The "Stephenesque" quality Leonard Woolf saw in the Stephens' opinions he had defined as "something marmoreal or lapidary"; if it reminded him of "the Ten Commandments," it was because they were "engraved upon the tables of stone" (*Sowing*, 184). Rainbow is "spread like a veil upon a rock," like Septimus's body (*MrsD*, 103). It covers with flesh the spare frame, lays "coloured flowers, and colour on the shoulders of the women" and the bare hills of sunlit Turkey (*JR*, 44). Stella Duckworth's "ripple of sweetness and laughter" plays "over a shape, dimly discerned, as of statuesque marble," "Greek" (*MB*, 42), like Mrs. Ramsay's beauty, "very clearly Greek, straight" (*TL*, 47), formal. Mrs. Ramsay's "reddish-brown" wool is knitted "in the round" (because it is a stocking) on a "frame" of three "steel needles," as "the green shawl," first hung over the edge of "the gilt frame" which "outlined" her head and "the authenticated masterpiece by Michael Angelo" (*TL*, 48) by Mrs. Ramsay and then removed from the frame (*TL*, 100) and pulled around herself (*TL*, 100, 141), is later hung on the boar's skull nailed up in the children's room. Structuring the formless granite gives permanence to the evanescent, transfixes an arrow in time's flight, anchors color in weight. The circles of the striking clock are "leaden" (*MrsD*, 206), the "very distant" cloud in *Between the Acts* "had hardened to golden alabaster; was made of immortal marble" (23). It achieves the rigid immobility of Greek sculpture. So, when "the shock of the event" of the dinner party gives Mrs Ramsay "a sense of movement," she "used the branches of the elm trees outside to help her to stabilize her position. Her world was changing: they were still" (*TL*, 169).

The draped skull marks at *To the Lighthouse*'s center the uneasy union of the two principles, the one's solidity, the other's fragility, like the marriage of Mr. and Mrs. Ramsay. The tissue of appearances is upheld by granite supports; it masks them while revealing its own truth. The veil is torn by the force of the Lighthouse itself from the other truth. From it – i.e., the fact that "Time Passes" confirms his weather prediction – Mr. Ramsay borrows his authority. But it is not in his power to make it rain; he only correctly forecasts it.

For what upholds the fabric is not ultimately an intelligence, a mind; it is fact, the totality of things that are. Mathematical truths or the facts of history, "Timothy Durrant's notebook of scientific observations" (*JR*, 49), can provide support like propositions true although never thought of or understood, as Mrs. Ramsay can let her mind wander while square roots are discussed and come back to it "still being fabricated" (*TL*, 159). Something persists, but not the rainbow nor the flesh covering the skeleton, only the waves, the atoms, or Leslie Stephen's sole "residuum," not consciousness but the formula's mathematical underpinning: "Nothing seems to be left but purely intellectual perception, an eternal consciousness that two and two make four" ("WM?," 152). This residue is as indifferent as the night air and silent as the mantle, its truth meaningless, fabricated without a thought of human desire. For to have meaning is to be seen from the human perspective, from the window on the "world of existence."

The language of the veil and the shape behind it, "this reality" which "emerged stark at the back of appearances" (*TL*, 236), shows traces of Bradleyian Idealism which, Hylton argues, left a lasting impression on Moore's and Russell's philosophies. Stephen had himself spoken of "weav[ing] the whole universe out of the senses," calling "[t]ime and space" "the warp and woof upon which is embroidered all the shifting scenery of consciousness" ("WM?," 148). Idealism had infected the materialist with Bradley's nostalgia for one of the two worlds from the perspective of the other. But science, too, had gone "behind the drop-scene of the senses," as Tyndall wrote (*Essays*, 15). Logic propels the thinker beyond his own private fireside, creating a homesickness for the cozy circle of light, the need to recreate it at another level. Bradley finds the intellectual scaffolding "as cold and ghost-like as the dreariest materialism":

> That the glory of this world in the end is appearance leaves the world more glorious, if we feel it is a show of some fuller splendour; but the sensuous curtain is a deception and a cheat, if it hides some colourless movement of atoms, some spectral woof of impalpable abstractions. (*Principles of Logic*, 591)

"What is Materialism?" is plausibly in dialogue with this 1883 text of Bradley's, published three years before Stephen's paper was first given to the London Ethical Society. We can, writes Stephen, either

> verbally construct the universe out of bare logic, or we create a mystical theory from emotions cast into some show of logical form. But such constructions . . . end in presenting a shifting phantasmagoria of vision, coloured, as dreams are coloured, by the predilections of each dreamer. We have to hold fast to the realities. We must recognise the truth which is distorted by the materialist conclusion. Emotions and feelings, I have said, are as "real" as stocks and stones. ("WM?," 148)

Stephen's vacillation between being or existence, granite or rainbow, his wistful sense of loss in having to choose one, becomes the apology for agnosticism, transforming vacillation into a justifiable philosophical position. "The true line, according to the Agnostic, is . . . to get rid of the recriminations as to the reality of one world or the other" ("WM?," 165). The resolution permits realities on both sides. The "mathematical world, which threatened to be not only real but the sole reality" ("WM?," 134) is an "oppressive reality" ("WM?," 134) he pronounces "rigorously unthinkable" ("WM?," 151), not because unreal, but because it is not alone real. "Can we assert that there is anything knowable or conceivable which has not a material aspect?" ("WM?," 151), Stephen asks, where "material" means "sensible." The empiricist answers the Idealist: "The curtain is the reality. The effort to look behind it . . . only plunges us into the transcendental region of antinomies and cobwebs of the brain" ("WM?," 144). Stephen rejects Idealism's belief "that the world which we perceive is an illusion, – a mere screen of transitory appearances which hides the permanent realities behind; and you must retire to the world of transcendental reality, where, indeed, it is possible to obtain absolute truth, but truths which cannot by any ingenuity be brought into contact with the facts of perception" (*HET*, 70).

Moore's and Russell's revolt against Idealism was then preceded by Stephen's. They allow the possibility that there is an unknowable truth as a remnant of an earlier Bradleyianism, denying, we saw, the Berkeleyan proposition "nothing can be true without being known," as Russell says in *The Philosophy of Leibniz* (182). But they never make it the ultimate Reality, like Stephen "always keeping in mind the limitations of knowledge" ("WM?," 147), and like him refusing to erect the unknowable into "hyperboles about the Absolute and the

Infinite" ("WM?," 166). But, whereas Stephen's native agnosticism often stalled at choosing between competing hypotheses, being "modest enough to confess himself a provisional Agnostic" ("WM?," 133), Russell's was, we saw, Occam's method in Laplace's version (*IMP*, 184).

THE HAUNTED HOUSE, THE PHANTOM TABLE

I have talked so far about the unreality of the things we think real. I want to speak with equal emphasis about the reality of things we think unreal, such as phantoms and hallucinations . . . , among the ultimate constituents of the world. (Russell, *Logic and Knowledge*, 274)

The respectable particulars in the world are all of them linked up with other particulars in respectable, conventional ways. Then sometimes you get a wild particular, like a merely visual chair that you cannot sit on, and say it is a phantom, a hallucination, you exhaust all the vocabulary of abuse upon it. That is what one means by calling it unreal." (*Ibid.*, 275–6)

With Bradley's words "spectral" and "ghost-like," a vocabulary British Realism takes from British Idealism, we return to our chapter's opening theme of a reality shadowed by a pale unreality, the contrast of two competing realities, subjected alternately to Stephen's "point of view of the physical inquirer" ("WM?," 129) and his "mathematical point of view" ("WM?," 134). "The one we do not prefer will probably seem to us a pale shadow of the one we prefer," Russell writes. Yet "both are real" (*PP*, 100). Philosophy, as a consequence, like the motherless Stephen children, is "haunted by great ghosts" (*MB*, 53). The metaphor, which Woolf continuously returns to, is that of Realism's refutation of Idealism.

Ghostliness is first attributable to rainbow appearances, starting with their weightlessness. A phantom is "apart from all embodiment" ("WM?," 150), it is "all spirit, disembodied, ghostly" (*MrsD*, 42). To be bodiless is to be visible but intangible, "[f]aint and unreal," like "this smoke; this fine early morning air" (*TL*, 241). "Breath, smoke, clouds" are "seen but not touched," Russell observes, adding "the usual mark of a ghost is that it can be seen but not touched" (*OKnExW*, 82).[16] In this sense, "the heavenly bodies," because they "cannot be touched, heard, smelled, or tasted" (*ABCR*, 15), are themselves ghostly. Phantom appearances are also flitting, wavering, changing. The "life" which "Modern Fiction" aims to capture is an elusive "unknown and uncircumscribed spirit" (*CE*, II,

105). It moves "aimlessly" (*TL*, 203), "casually," like "some random light" (*TL*, 191), unmoored, a "gigantic chaos" (*TL*, 202). "Idly, aimlessly, the swaying shawl swung to and fro" (*TL*, 207).

What is without permanence is the shape of appearances. As the sheet of flesh over the skeleton, shape comes to it from the world of permanent forms. Woolf's *res extensa* is the body as skeleton, an invisible, rigid frame to which the "bodiless" sensations, the body as sense-organ, are fixed. Its "life" is "a halo, a semi-transparent envelope surrounding us from the beginning of consciousness to the end" (*CE*, II, 106).[17] Liberated from that skeletal structure, they become protean, "amorphous" (*TL*, 202). Their formlessness manifests itself through changes in color or shape. Without attachments to the unchanging world of matter, the sensible ephemerids are released into a vague, random wandering, like Lily Briscoe's dancing gnats.

It is light which dissolves forms, as the "failing light," we saw, renders "ethereal" (*TL*, 111), or turns objects into so many moons, "ghastly beautiful with light from the sunken day" (*MrsD*, 62). Light, in the intervals of *The Waves*, imparts to the table its ever-changing color in an ever shifting series of perspectives; it "whitens" and sets free appearances from the structure beneath, like a spirit freed from the body, to be captured in the glass which mirrors only the look of things: "light bent to its own image in adoration on the bedroom wall" (*TL*, 196). In the "the rising sun," "[t]he looking-glass whitened its pool upon the wall. The real flower on the window-sill was attended by the phantom flower. Yet the phantom was part of the flower for when a bud broke free, the paler flower in the glass opened a bud too" (*W*, 75). The eerie light endows Stella Duckworth with "her phantom loveliness" – "the pale luminous complexion, the changing light in the eyes, the movement and ripple of the whole" (*MB*, 42). Death is the final separation of appearances from permanent forms, flesh from bones. The freed appearances may return like lost souls to haunt those once acquainted with them, as "the ghosts flocked thick and shoulders with Mrs. Flanders in the circle" (*JR*, 132), reacquainting them with their memory: "How many people are there still able to think about Stella on the 20th June 1939?" (*MB*, 95). This is Cam's vision from the boat of "the shore, wrapped in its mantle of peace; as if the people there were fallen asleep, she thought; were free like smoke, were free to come and go like ghosts" (*TL*, 253). Hence also the haunting effect of those "solid objects" which dissolve under analysis that Woolf made the theme of an early story: "Looked at again and again half consciously by a mind thinking of something else, any object mixes itself so profoundly with the stuff of thought that it loses its actual form and recomposes itself a little differently in an ideal shape which haunts the brain when we least expect it" (*CSFVW*, 216). They become obsessions of the thinker like the novels' recurrent images.

Stripped of the living's aura, the skeleton becomes stone, a statue, like the man and woman who meet at the end of *The Years*. But the solid object of common sense which seemed most real, Johnson's stone, is also conjured away, replaced by a structure composed of just those ghostly sensibilia to which it had been counterposed:

> Instead of supposing that matter is what is "really real" in the physical world and that the immediate objects of sense are mere phantasms, we must regard matter as a logical construction, of which the constituents will be just such evanescent particulars as may, when an observer happens to be present, become data of sense to that observer. (*ML*, 131–2)

These evanescent building blocks, until activated by an observer, are the " 'sensibilia' " which seem "subjective phantasms" (*ML*, 147). But "[t]he things that we call real, like tables and chairs, are systems, series of classes of particulars, and the particulars are the real things, . . . being sense-data when they happen to be given to you" (*LK*, 274). The ultimate furniture of the world, "crazy ghosts of chairs and tables" (*TL*, 43), shimmering unseen, haunts "the empty house" (*TL*, 202) and "empty rooms" (*TL*, 200) of "Time Passes" and *The Waves*' interludes. "Already the room, with its swing-doors, its tables heaped with fruit, with cold joints, wears the wavering, unreal appearance of a place where one waits expecting something to happen. Things quiver as if not yet in being" (*W*, 118). Poised between the two worlds, the neutral sensibilia fill with color if given to an observer or disintegrate into the colorless physical atoms; the "leaden circles" are "dissolved in the air" (*MrsD*, 54, 206). "I insubstantise, wilfully to some extent, distrusting reality – its cheapness," Woolf writes. "Have I the power of conveying the true reality? . . . To get to the bones" (*Diary*, II, 248). The absence of the very properties which render appearances ghost-like makes what underlies them equally phantasmatic. The ghostliness of matter's primary properties lies in their invisibility, a reduction of the visible, of sunset colors to a plain table (*TL*, 38, 28). The unobservable waves posited by physics are likewise "phantom waves" (*Diary*, III, 236), pounding in the background "like a ghostly roll of drums" (*TL*, 27–8). So also Bradley's "colourless movement of atoms" is an "unearthly ballet of bloodless categories" (*Principles of Logic*, 591). "[T]he solar system was once a 'cosmic mist,' a whirl of incoherent atoms," Leslie Stephen had said ("WM?," 143), "the mysterious dance of a whirlwind of infinitesimal particles of dust" ("WM?," 132), "the dust dance," Woolf echoes (*W*, 284 and 285), the ever-shifting "clouds and phantoms made of dust too, of dust that changed" (*W*, 285). "Physics and physiology between them assure me that what is there independently of my seeing, is something very unlike a visual experience, namely, a mad dance of billions of electrons" (*Portraits from Memory*, 151), Russell writes. Composed of such, the table of Mr. Ramsay's speculations melts into "a phantom kitchen table" (*TL*, 38). So in "Time Passes" it is not only sensibilia which haunt the empty house, but also "those fumbling airs" which represent the encroachment of matter and time on the living; they hover "ghostlily" over "the shut eyes" of the sleepers behind "bedroom doors" with sense-organs closed to the sensibilia given to no one (*TL*, 191). The physical world's colorlessness takes on the "eyelessness" Woolf attributes to the Apostles' doctrines.

Yet something permanent persists which Woolf names the "pattern." The circles of light of the atomized night, so many *feux follets* of the world of existence, fade into mathematical points: "The lights of the town and of the harbour and of the boats seemed like a phantom net floating there to mark something that had sunk" (*TL*, 104). Whatever had weight "sunk," leaving the trace of a logical form. It gathers the sparkling appearances into a construction: "the skeleton only is picked out in fairy lamps" (*CSFVW*, 286). The eyeless vision penetrates to forms without which the colors of existence dissolve. For, ultimately, neither world can stand without the other. Form gives structure and permanence to the colors of the sensible world; color endows the lifeless forms of being with vivacity.

Language also is at a ghostly remove from some reality: "proper names, as ordinarily understood, are ghosts of substances" (*HK*, 73), like "the smoke words languishing and melting in the sky" left by the airplane's vapor in *Mrs. Dalloway* (31). In "Mr Bennett and Mrs Brown," the name "Brown" is a "will-o'-the-wisp," "the phantom" which says to the novelist "Come and catch me if you can" (*CE*, I, 319). Such names reduce to even more ghostly descriptions.

Words thus pale before a disappearing reality: "How describe or say anything in articulate words again? – save that it fades," Woolf asks. "Blindness returns . . . Loveliness returns as one looks with all its train of phantom phrases" (*W*, 287). Modern fiction's goal, we will see in Part II, is to find a language to relate the two realities, endowing both with a new reality.

For ghostliness, whether of sense-data or logical form, sustains reality. For one thing, "it is far harder to kill a phantom than a reality," Woolf observes (*CE*, II, 286). "Ghost, air, nothingness, a thing you could play with safely," like a philosophical problem, Lily Briscoe thinks, only to discover, when "[s]uddenly the window at which she was looking was whitened by some light stuff behind it" (*TL*, 299) – "[s]ome wave of white went over the window pane" (*TL*, 300) – that this ghost organized a perspective around her emptiness (*TL*, 266). Its "shadow" materializes as the dead Mrs. Ramsay, who "sat there quite simply, in the chair," and "cast her shadow on the step. There she sat" (*TL*, 300).[18] The return of Mrs. Ramsay's shade, fixing an instant the canvas' "greens and blues" (*TL*, 309), makes the painting's completion possible, just as the "mathematical fiction" of points "can lead to important physical results" (*ML*, 112).

The haunting light of the empty perspective blazes an instant, then goes out. It has carried us to "the outskirts of the world" (*CE*, I, 48) beyond the mind, the end of our analysis of matter. "[W]e are outsiders, condemned for ever to haunt the borders and margins" (*CE*, II, 236); "we have reached the edge" (*CE*, II, 243). Outside the flowing and fleeting is also "the spectral" (*TL*, 158), raising the question: "If matter, instead of the consciousness, is to be the mere phantom, does not the whole world become a dream, an unreal web spun by the dreamer – a 'subjective' construction which has no longer any safe anchorage in fact?" ("WM?," 134). Like the solitary traveller, "haunter of lanes" (*MrsD*, 85), Leslie Stephen's "unwary wanderer" ("WM?," 135), having encountered "one of those spectral presences which rise in twilight in woods" (*MrsD*, 85), we pass with Mr. Ramsay's "vigilance which spared no phantom and luxuriated in no vision" (*TL*, 69), across the threshold separating self from world, returning inward, to the room. The self occupying it, discernable in the unnatural light, "'attentuates itself to a thoroughly ghostly condition,'" as Russell quotes William James (*Mind*, 22). We turn now to this ghost of the former self.

CHAPTER 4

Solus ipse, alone in the universe

> Belief in the unreality of the world of sense arises with irresistible force in certain moods . . . The conviction born of these moods is the source of most mysticism and of most metaphysics.
>
> (Russell, *Our Knowledge of the External World*, 55)

> I cannot recover, save by fits and starts, the focus, the proportions of the external world.
>
> (Woolf, *Moments of Being*, 78)

One more ghost hovers round the worlds of existence and being: the occupant of the private world. It gazes on the objects discerned by philosophy with a sense of its own unreality, "incompletely . . . merged" with them. "On the outskirts of every agony sits some observant fellow who points" (*W*, 248). Materialism sees "the mind as a phantom looking on (if a phantom can look on) at the mysterious dance . . . of dust" ("WM?," 132). Stephen's argument explicitly "condemns" the position "that 'matter' is an ultimate reality, and that thoughts and emotions are mere nothings or phantasms" ("WM?," 143). Yet the Agnostic's observer himself dissolves: "The *animula vagula blandula* is a flitting phantom which cannot hold its own in this solid world" ("WM?," 152–3). The philosopher's language conjures up Clarissa Dalloway's "strange transcendental theory" (*MrsD*, 231) that because "our apparitions, the part of us which appears, . . . are so momentary compared with the other, the unseen part of us," there is "(for all her scepticism)" the possibility of "the unseen . . . haunting certain places after death" (*MrsD*, 232). Thinking returns to haunt the world persisting in its absence and pre-existing its arrival.

Distanced from any idea of immortality and subjected to Peter Walsh's skepticism, this strange theory centers on "the ghost of the subject" (*Mind*, 18). The mind's flight, projecting itself into other minds and into the unobserved, is a kind of haunting. "One becomes aware that we are spectators and also passive participants in a pageant. And as nothing can interfere with the order, we have nothing to do but accept, and watch" (*CE*, II, 293). The watching is both weightless and invisible. Mrs. Ramsay's musing over the past has her "gliding like a ghost among the chairs and tables of that drawing-room on the banks of the Thames where she had been" years before (*TL*, 132). The dinner party ended, "[w]ith her foot on the threshold she waited a moment longer," already haunting the edge of the dining room while the scene itself "was vanishing even as she looked" (*TL*, 167). By the end of "Time Passes," Mrs. Ramsay, one of the sleepers in the ghostly bedrooms, has vanished into the intangible emptiness Mr. Ramsay embraces one night, like the "unlovable phantom" that the Stephen family's grief had substituted "for the shape of a most true and vivid mother" (*MB*, 45). Herself become a spectre, "faint and flickering, like a yellow beam or the circle at the end of a telescope, . . . wandering over the bedroom wall" (*TL*, 205), just as the "[l]ighthouse beam sent its sudden stare over the bed and wall" (*TL*, 208), she is conjured up in the empty house by Mrs. McNab, "seeing in imagination what we should see through a telescope" ("WM?," 137). Ultimately this ghost-like invisibility will be the condition of the writer, of Bernard at the end of *The Waves*, who "saw fields rolling in waves of colour beneath me, but now with this difference; I saw but was not seen. I walked unshadowed; I came unheralded . . . Thin, as a ghost, leaving no trace where I trod, perceiving merely, I walked alone in a new world, never trodden" (286–7). The exercise is alternately to make reality a ghost of itself or to make oneself, as observer, a ghost amidst real things, to entertain "this feeling of being something not herself, and that every one was unreal in one way, much more real in another" (*MrsD*, 259), like Cam's "eyeless" realization in the boat at the end of *To the Lighthouse*:

> Cam could see nothing. She was thinking how all those paths and the lawn, thick and knotted with the lives they had lived there, were gone: were rubbed out; were past; were unreal, and now this was real; the boat and the sail with its patch; Macalister with his earrings; the noise of the waves – all this was real. (248–9)

The alternation of real and unreal is incorporated in the logically proper name: "that," "those," on the edge of the perspective, become unreal; "this" remains real.

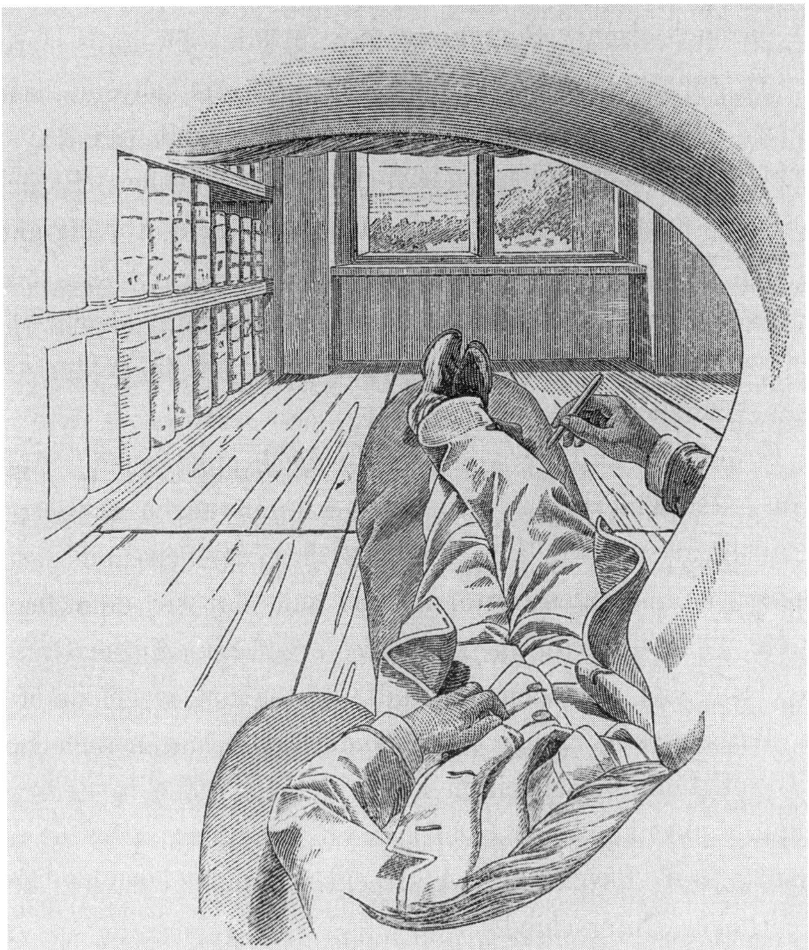

Figure 4. Ernst Mach, "Figure 1," the view from Mach's left eye, *Contributions to the Analysis of Sensations*, 1890.

An "independent world which thought apprehends but does not create" (*PP*, 98) is then a logical possibility. Its strange corollary is the mind contemplating its own absence. Where then, what then, is the self without the world in which the table continues to exist when it is not there? Does it so much as cast a shadow on the table or does it merely disappear into the table's sense-data?

RUSSELL'S PARING DOWN OF THE I

Descartes . . . says "I think, therefore I am," and he goes on . . . to assert "I am a thing that thinks." It would be difficult to pack so large a number of errors into so few words. To begin with "I think," the word "I" is thrust in to conform with grammar, and grammar embodies the metaphysic of our original Indo-European ancestors . . . We must, therefore, cut out the word "I." (Russell, *Portraits from Memory*, 147)

Legs, body, hands, the whole of her must be laid out passively to take part in this universal process of thinking which the man said was the world living. She stretched herself out. Where did thought begin?

In the feet? she asked . . . They seemed separated, very far away. She closed her eyes . . . She became something; a root; lying sunk in the earth. (Woolf, *The Years*, 133)

Every power poured its treasures on his head, and his hands lay there on the back of the sofa, as he had seen his hand lie when he was bathing, floating, on the top of the waves, while far away on shore he heard dogs barking and barking far away. (Woolf, *Mrs. Dalloway*, 211)

These questions raise the problem of the subject in Cambridge philosophy. Empirically, the sense-datum the self is acquainted with is certain; the self, however, falls to doubt: "the real Self is as hard to arrive at as the real table, and does not seem to have that absolute, convincing certainty that belongs to particular experiences," Russell observes. My seeing a brown table "involves something (or somebody) which (or who) sees the brown colour" but not "that more or less permanent person whom we call 'I.' So far as immediate certainty goes, it might be that the something which sees the brown colour is quite momentary, and not the same as the something which has some different experience the next moment" (*PP*, 19). "[A] sense-datum," Russell says, "does not contain the subject as a part, as . . . beliefs and volitions do" (*ML*, 146).

Even where the subject is "tentatively" retained, as with the notions of acquaintance and of occupied perspectives (*TK*, 36, fn. 1), its role is as supernumerary in a theory which nonetheless remains Cartesian in its aim to "establish physics upon a solipsistic basis" (*ML*, 152). Not simply the subject of sensation is eliminated but that of the *cogito*: "the grammatical forms 'I think,' 'you think,' and 'Mr. Jones thinks,' are misleading" as "an analysis of a single thought. It would be better to say 'it thinks in me,' like 'it rains here'; or better still, 'there is a thought in me'" (*Mind*, 18). Russell elaborates elsewhere: "'I think, therefore I am' is what he [Descartes] says, but this won't do as it stands. What . . . he should profess to know is not 'I think,' but 'there is thinking.' He finds doubt going on" but "[to] translate this into 'I think' is to assume . . . that thoughts imply a thinker. But why should they?" (*OP*, 171).

What is *de trop* in Russell's economical universe involves the first person: "'*I* think, therefore *I* am' says rather more than is strictly certain" (*PP*, 19). Descartes' doubt ceases before "a certain occurrence" which "'I think'" is to designate. "But the words were not quite an accurate representation of the occurrence"; despite his being "justified in feeling" it to have occurred, "he was not justified in bringing in the word 'I' in describing this occurrence" (*OP*, 172). Yet Descartes' argument depends on the occurrence being one "concerning which doubt was impossible" (*OP*, 172). This indubitability is its privacy, which *I* is meant to represent. If eliminated from *cogito*, some residue must provide subjective certainty. The project thus entails an analysis of *I* which identifies the subjective core sufficient to guarantee indubitability.

This project does not originate with Russell. It can be traced to the German physicist Georg Lichtenberg, and to those philosophers from Vienna to Cambridge who invoked Lichtenberg's critique of Descartes. Moore records that Wittgenstein "said that '. . . no Ego is involved in thinking in having toothache'; and he quoted, with apparent approval, Lichtenberg's saying 'Instead of "I think" we ought to say "It thinks"' ('it' being used, as he said, as 'Es' is used in 'Es blitzet')" (*Philosophical Papers*, 309). Moore places the reference to Lichtenberg in the period 1930–3, but the passage from *The Problems of Philosophy* above suggests Russell had Lichtenberg in mind as early as 1911, perhaps in reading Mach and Meinong. The conviction that something the first person represents is eliminable from the *cogito* is then contemporaneous with Russell's attempt to rescue the patch of color from Berkeleyan Idealism, predating his adoption of Mach's and James' "neutral monism." A consistent neutralization of *I* thus subtends the various changes in Russell's epistemology from 1912 to 1921.

That neutralization begins with "the meaning of the word 'I'" which "must not be confused with the meaning of 'the ego,'" whose meaning "is universal," i.e., "that general characteristic, whatever it is, which makes each one of us call himself 'I' . . . But 'I' itself is not a universal" (*TK*, 36). Not a universal, "I" names a particular: "on each occasion of its use, there is only one person who is I, though this person differs according to the speaker." It is like "[t]he word 'this,'" which is "always a proper name" in that "it applies directly to" – i.e., it does not "describe" – "just one object" (*TK*, 39). Russell's position on the demonstratives differs from the Hegelian one British Idealism adopted. His is the "traditional view" in which demonstratives are, in Wollheim's words, "verbal equivalences of pointing at a particular thing or place," which "Bradley rejects," holding that "'This,' 'now,' and 'mine' are all universals" (*F. H. Bradley*, 55).

Russell is not entirely satisfied with so treating *I* as a "logically proper name," because it designates something more than words like *this*. Over and above the particular who is speaking, *I* first implies a "permanent person" (*PP*, 19) – this is the concept of the "person" or of identity. Since in a "cogito"-like statement such as "I see a triangle" the goal is "to arrive at the contribution to your knowledge which is made by seeing the triangle at the moment" and "the word 'I' takes you beyond this contribution, we must cut it out" (*OP*, 215) or "pare away from 'I' . . . the past and future," which do "not belong to the subject of the present experience" (*TK*, 36). What is essential in "I" is momentary. For this Russell reserves the term "subject"; the persisting thing he calls the "person" or "mind": "we do not identify a mind with a subject. A mind . . . persists through a certain period of time, but it must not be assumed that . . . the subject of one experience is the same as the subject of another" (*TK*, 35). Momentariness is built into the demonstrative *this*, but not into the grammar of *I*. *I* "take[s] us beyond what the momentary event reveals," denoting "the person who had certain remembered experiences and is expected to have certain future experiences" (*OP*, 215). *I* thus includes things uncertain.

Secondly, *I* implies consciousness, "that which is aware of things" (*PP*, 51), where "awareness" Russell makes synonymous with "acquaintance" (*TK*, 35). The "'subject'" is defined "as any entity which is acquainted with something" (*TK*, 35). It has "acquaintance in sensation with the data of the outer senses," in "introspection" with that of the inner sense – thoughts, feelings, desires, in memory with their past objects (*PP*, 51). But is *I* not just subject but also object of acquaintance? Russell, like Hume, thinks "acquaintance with the contents of our minds," if "self-consciousness," is not "consciousness of our self: it is consciousness of particular thoughts and feelings." There is no certainty "we are also acquainted with our bare selves." "When we try to look into ourselves we always seem to come upon some particular thought and feeling, and not upon the 'I' which has the thought or feeling." But Russell concedes "some reasons for thinking that we are acquainted with the 'I,'" Since "we know the truth 'I am acquainted with this sense-datum,'" i.e, the sun, it seems plausible we are "acquainted with something which we call 'I,'" not necessarily the "more or less permanent person, the same to-day as yesterday" but "that thing, whatever its nature, which sees the sun and has acquaintance with sense-data" (*PP*, 50–1). By the time of *Theory of Knowledge*, Russell questions "whether 'I' . . . is something with which we are acquainted" (*TK*, 36). We can "become aware of our own experiences, but never . . . of the subject itself" (*TK*, 36). This is the "elusiveness of the subject in introspection" (*TK*, 36). "I am hardly aware of myself, but only of the sensation," Woolf writes of two early memories. "I am only the container of the feeling of ecstasy, of the feeling of rapture" (*MB*, 67). That minimal container Russell calls "[t]he bare subject which thinks and is aware of objects" (*OKnExW*, 81; *TK*, 37). Unfortunately for accuracy, the bare "subject attending to 'this'" is normally "called 'I'" (*LK*, 168; *TK*, 40).

What less misleading formulation for the bare subject in the *cogito* is there? Russell's "it thinks in me" or "there is a thought in me," aims to de-emphasize *I*. But the permanent *I* remains. The impersonal constructions "it thinks" or "there is thinking" with expletive *it* or *there*, on the other hand, retain no subjective term guaranteeing indubitability. Is there some demonstrative other than *I* to capture the subject's momentariness? Russell in 1940 would speak of the "I-now" (*IMT*, 102).

Even the bare subject, briefly maintained, is ultimately abandoned and, with it, the sensation/sense-data distinction, which, Russell argues, entails the subject. Sense-data and sensation become indistinguishably non-mental sensation, for, as Russell pointed out, "the emphatic part" of the distinction "was the assertion that the colour is physical, not psychical" (*Mind*, 142–3). So, analogously, thinking and thought become indistinguishable. "Thinking" seems "the act of a person," but "Meinong's 'act' is the ghost of the subject." We suppose "that thoughts cannot just come and go, but need a person to think them." But "the person is not an ingredient in the single thought," even if "thoughts can be collected into bundles, so that one bundle is my thoughts, another is your thoughts, and a third is the thoughts of Mr. Jones" (*Mind*, 18).

Certainty now resides not in the subject but in thoughts, beliefs and memories, like sensations, detached from the subject. But again, its Lichtenbergian representations, e.g., "there is thinking," which "leave the word 'think,' but without a subject" (Russell, *Portraits from Memory*, 147), fail to reintroduce a subjective term which renders the statement indubitable. Some demonstrative is wanted, such as "here is thinking" or "this is a triangle." We postpone a discussion of the solution the novel provides Woolf until chapter seven.

There is now no way to call some thoughts "mine" – they are indistinct from reduced subjectivity. Not objects of acquaintance, the person and the self are replaced, like the table, by a logical construction, the "biography," which gathers thoughts and sensations into bundles. There are no primitive "mental *entities*" but only "mental *facts*" which contain "acquaintance or some relation presupposing acquaintance as a component" (*TK*, 35). The subject becomes knowable only by description: "both a mind and a piece of matter" become "logical constructions formed out of materials not differing vitally" (*MyPhD*, 10). *I* is analyzable not as a demonstrative but as a description, like the name "Scott."

There are problems with this account. Onc McTaggart had raised. "McTaggart cannot accept this Humean view because he can discover no relation between mental states which could determine the bundle to which they belong other than one through the self," Vesey writes, quoting McTaggart that it would "be a vicious circle if I described 'I' as being that bundle of states of which my use of the word is a member, and then distinguished that bundle from other groups by describing it as that group of mental states which are states of 'I'"" ("Self-Acquaintance," 340–1). The problem Russell himself recognized: "We might regard the mind as an assemblage of particulars" he suggests, but if "the quality designated by the word 'mental'" is simply "[t]he common quality of all states of mind," we still have no way to attach some mental states to one person – "we should have to suppose that each separate person's states of mind have some common characteristic distinguishing them from the states of mind of other people" (ML, 126). Russell's solution is that "the sensations be connected by mnemic relations" (Sainsbury,

Russell, 267; *Mind*, 129). "We may define a 'mind' as a collection of events connected with each other by memory chains backwards and forwards," Russell explains (*MyPhD*, 26). Thus, "a sensation may be grouped with a number of other occurrences by a memory-chain, in which case it becomes part of a mind; or it may be grouped with its causal antecedents, in which case it appears as part of the physical world" (*MyPhD*, 10). It is "mnemic phenomena which constitute the unity of one 'experience' " (*Mind*, 129). Sainsbury argues the unsatisfactoriness of this solution (*Russell*, 267). The same problem is posed for the bundle of sense-data constituting a single object, where mnemic relations cannot be invoked. A related problem is how to transform a biography into a self as opposed to a table. For the self is constructed now out of the same subjective yet impersonal material the public table is. Its correlate is the extinction of consciousness: the self becomes as unconscious as the table. Mnemic relations are again invoked; they "transform a biography (in our technical sense) into a life" and "give the continuity of a 'person' or a 'mind' " (*Mind*, 129). This is again where Russell found lacking a "principle of selection" (*TK*, 40; *LK*, 169) usually supplied by consciousness or mind. Surprisingly, what are problems for Russell's account will turn out to provide artist and novelist principles for an aesthetic experiment.

The excision of the *I* is now complete. Russell, like William James, concludes "that the supposed subject is 'the name of a nonentity' " (*MyPhD*, 100). It is the passive register of "presence" to which the object presents itself. Via the Russellian logic, the subject is led to posit its own expendibility, becoming a stranger who comes and goes within its own private world, a brief flare of consciousness without identity. The thinning of what Clive Bell, in a familiar Bloomsbury mode, called "thick little egos"[1] ends in the conscious subject's disappearing in its sensation or thought, the eye in the window. The observer, Pears says, has "vanished into the glass" (*Bertrand Russell*, 41–2).

The windowpane in which the subject disappears is an unoccupied perspective. Some perspectives are occupied, however. Their occupant transforms them into "private worlds" by entering "into the relation of acquaintance" with a particular, as the bachelor becomes the husband by the arrival of an object which brings him "into the relation of marriage" in Russell's analogy (*ML*, 143). What does this transient occupant's presence add? "What the mind adds to sensibilia . . . is merely awareness" (*ML*, 145), Russell answers.

Awareness includes thoughts, beliefs, desires and volitions, emotions and memories in *The Analysis of Mind.* The sense-datum "does not contain the subject as a part," Russell states, but "beliefs and volitions do" (*ML*, 146), just as the sensation, "complex of which the subject is a constituent," is "therefore mental" (*ML*, 147). Yet even thoughts separate from their thinker. The subject divides into the neutral screen projecting data, perhaps overlaid with intervening media, and its excluded observer: "I am not part of the street – no, I observe the street. One splits off, therefore" (*W*, 115).

Leslie Stephen had already conjured up free-floating mental states released by the Humean dissolution of the self. "Can we form any picture of thoughts and emotions going about bodiless and bare, with no link between them and ourselves? Are they not superfluous, if not rigorously unthinkable?," he asks ("WM?," 151). Stephen's "flitting phantom" ("WM?," 152), reasoned away by thought, is not completely exorcized. Loosed from its moorings in its private world, with no permanent identity or fixed abode, the thinking, feeling, perceiving becomes detached, a by-product of analysis. The unnamed ghost banished from the perspective drifts in the no-man's land outside, puts an eye to its world, peers through the window, as it had looked out from behind it, like Henry James' Maisie, who "could only get at experience by flattening her nose against a pane of glass" (*What Maisie Knew*, 101).

WOOLF'S SHADOW OF THE I, THE SHADOW OF A SELF

Everything falls in a tremendous shower, dissolving me. (Woolf, *The Waves*, 206)

Woolf's self also rids itself of something intolerable in the first person pronoun which, in *A Room of One's Own*, cuts a page of novel writing with a dark diagonal: "a shadow seemed to lie across the page. It was a straight dark bar, a shadow shaped something like the letter 'I' " (*Room*, 103). What in "I" has this effect on the novelist? Woolf's answer adds something unmentioned in Russell: a specifically sexual identity. The key is an association between *I* and a "Manx cat" (*Room*, 104)[2] which crosses the path of the essay's arbitrarily named first persona – "Here was I (call me Mary Beton, Mary Seton, Mary Carmichael or by any name you please)" (5) – on her visit to Oxbridge:

if things had been a little different from what they were, one would not have seen, presumably, a cat without a tail. The sight of that abrupt and truncated animal padding softly across the quadrangle changed by some fluke of the subconscious intelligence the emotional light for me. It was as if some one had let fall a shade . . . something seemed lacking. (*Room*, 11; see *TL*, 11)

"It is strange what a difference a tail makes," the narrator comments (*Room*, 13).

By a chain of "subconscious" associations, the Manx cat's shadow, suggestive of its missing tail, recalls that cast by the *I*; and the absent ego-tail, the phallus that the narrator lacks. Her sex is the reason she is forbidden to cross the quad that the animal transects. The association between the letter *I* and the phallus is clear – the writer, for one, that the narrator is reading when the shadow falls is a male novelist, "Mr. A" (*Room*, 103),[3] just as in *The Years* it is a male writer who imposes himself as *I* when the woman's "attention wandered": "I, I, I – he went on. It was like a vulture's beak pecking, or a vacuum-cleaner sucking, or a telephone bell ringing." Yet "[t]he fire went out of his face when she said 'I' . . . He can't be 'you' – he must be 'I' " (*Y*, 361).[4]

Elsewhere, Woolf made the analogy between phallus and *I* explicit: "reading consists in the complete elimination of the ego; and it's the ego that erects itself like another part of the body I dont dare to name" (*Letters VW*, V, 319). A passage excised from a draft of *Three Guineas* uses the metaphor of an erection to suggest that the phallus-ego is engorged: "He has become an egomaniac; always writing about I . . . What is that but the cry of a goose's swollen liver? the demand of the inflamed 'I' for pity, sympathy in its sufferings caused by a red and swollen egotism?"[5] Mr. Ramsay's "egotism" is a phallic "beak of brass" (*TL*, 58).

Thus, Woolf's use of Occam's razor invokes "castration" because *I*'s gender, despite grammar, is masculine. Like the phantom table, the phantom self, a shadow of its former self, is shrunk to the perspective's truncated *cogito*. Or castration is the removal of a hard covering, "the outer crust of the self, one's personality" (*MB*), to bare a ganglion of sensitivity, "some nervous fibre or fan like membrane" (*Diary*, III, 191); "the shell-like covering which our souls have excreted to house themselves, to make for themselves a shape distinct from others, is broken" (*CE*, IV, 156).[6] The neutralized physical sensibility is an exposed nerve: "her mind was like a wound exposed to dry in the air" (*VO*, 13), and Septimus' body was "macerated until only the nerve fibres were left" (*MrsD*, 102–3). Exposure to the outside world means penetration by "arrows of sensation striking strangely through the envelope of personality, which shelters us conveniently from our fellows" (*ND*, 271) Underneath is what "there is left of all these wrinkles and roughnesses a central oyster of perceptiveness, an enormous eye" (*CE*, IV, 156). The raw mollusk-eye is sexed, or rather, unsexed. The incarnation of Russell's neutral or neutered subjectivity is a female sexual organ.

The need to say "I" is thus for Woolf male. But not every man and some women feel it. "William Bankes . . . was entirely free from all such vanity." Mr. Ramsay "had the other temperament, which must have praise, which must have encouragement" (*TL*, 161); he is "vain, egotistical" (*TL*, 40), "absorbed in himself" (*TL*, 72). The need to say "I" arises from a consciousness of disability, for instance, of social disadvantage. Charles Tansley "was thinking of himself and the impression he was making, as she could tell by the sound of his voice, and his emphasis" (*TL*, 160) because "his grandfather was a fisherman; his father a chemist" (*TL*, 138). Hence, he "wanted to assert himself, and so it would always be with him till he got his Professorship or married his wife, and so need not be always saying, 'I – I – I'" (*TL*, 160).

The *I* is an engorged phallus. The woman's function is first to increase its enlargement by "these lies, these exaggerations" (*TL*, 63): "Women have served all these centuries as a looking-glass possessing the magic and delicious power of reflecting the figure of man at twice its natural size" (*Room*, 35). The woman disburdens the man: "she was friendly to him now – he was relieved of his egotism" (*TL*, 139). The consequence of "the egotistical man'"s demands is, however, that "there was scarcely a shell of herself left for her to know herself by" (*TL*, 60). The deflated ego has become the woman's depleted self, the magnifying glass enlarges by diminishing, effacing, itself. In the confrontation of the sexes, one ego disappears in the other.

This devouring egoism Woolf conceives as the opposite of procreative. "[T]he fatal sterility of the male plunged itself, like a beak of brass, barren and bare" (TL, 58). The father's "arid scimitar" (TL, 60) blights by "the dominance of the letter 'I' . . . the aridity, which, like the giant beech tree, it casts within its shade. Nothing will grow there" (Room, 104). Indeed, the scimitar *is* the blade; it elicits

James' counter-urge to resort to the axe (*TL*, 10), the jousting of "I" against "I," a kind of fruitless phallic logic-chopping. Against it Mrs. Ramsay, as James "stood stiff between her knees" (*TL*, 60), returns a "rain of energy, a column of spray" (*TL*, 58). The strange metaphor associates woman with ejaculation. The erect phallus is sterile; egoism, typically if not exclusively male – "What an egoist, how aloof she was!," a character thinks (*ND*, 271); "I talked, egotistically, excitedly, about my own affairs no doubt," Woolf recalls (*MB*, 173). But the seminal fluid has only beneficial associations. This is the conclusion to be drawn from Woolf's account of the scene in which, while Virginia chattered "egotistically" and "Vanessa sat silent and did something mysterious with her needle or her scissors" – the couple the sisters formed recalling Mr. and Mrs. Ramsay, the latter who, in her meditation, "accomplished here something dexterous with her needles" (*TL*, 96) – "[s]uddenly the door opened and the long and sinister figure of Mr. Lytton Strachey stood on the threshold. He pointed his finger at a stain on Vanessa's white dress."

"Semen," he said.

Can one really say it? I thought and we burst out laughing. With that one word all barriers of reticence and reserve went down. A flood of the sacred fluid seemed to overwhelm us. Sex permeated our conversation. (*MB*, 173–4)

Lytton's elongated form and pointing finger breaks the barriers between private worlds. Tumescent egoism is a necessary prelude to creation brought to term. This is why Woolf's aesthetic will require art to have a phallic stiffening, some "background rods" (*MB*, 73) or the "iron girders" of "the masculine intelligence," as "the long reddish-brown stocking dangling" (*TL*, 99) needs the steel frame.[7] Woolf read her father "to fill out; to correct; to stiffen my fluid vision" (in Rosenbaum, *Victorian Bloomsbury*, 48). But egoism releases something antithetical to the stiff phallus. This fluid, abundant energy is expressed in the verb "squirt," which recurs in Woolf, alternating with "spurt." It begins as an almost aggressive thrust: in D. H. Lawrence's style, "up spurt the sentences as round, as hard, as direct as water thrown out in all directions by the impact of a stone" (*CE*, I, 355); Lily Briscoe's mind before her canvas is "like a fountain spurting" (*TL*, 238); for Cam "there spurted up a fountain of joy" (*TL*, 280). Its association with blood connects sexual energy with the wound to the ego of a castration-birth: "'Now the cock crows like a spurt of hard, red water in the white tide,' said Bernard" (*W*, 10). Writing the "mad part" of *Mrs. Dalloway*, Woolf says, "makes my mind squirt so badly" (*A Writer's Diary*, 56; *Diary*, II, 248, reads it "squints"). Ejaculation becomes the accomplishment of castration; the "I'"s reduction is a detumescence. It displaces both ejaculation and the depletion subsequent to erection onto the woman. Fertilization has as its *terminus ad quem* and its *sine qua non* the loss of self. Mrs. Ramsay is emptied – "all was so lavished and spent" (*TL*, 60). She demands Lily Briscoe conform to the same "code of behavior . . . whose seventh article" commands "the woman . . . go to the help of the young man opposite [in this case, Charles Tansley] so that he may expose and relieve . . . his urgent desire to assert himself" (*TL*, 137). But disliking his saying "Women can't write, women can't paint," she thinks "why should I help him to relieve himself?" (*TL*, 137). Only when she "say[s] something nice" to him (*TL*, 138) and later, "remembering how he sneered at women, 'can't paint, can't write,'" she lops off the grammatical subject – either "women" or "I" – and repeats the words "without being aware any longer who originally spoke them" (*TL*, 237), can she begin again the uncompleted painting, grammatical castration triggering creative ejaculation: "as if some juice necessary for the lubrication of her faculties were spontaneously squirted, she began precariously dipping among the blues and umbers". (*TL*, 237). She is also disburdened of the need for self-assertion. Mrs. Ramsay dead, Lily, after initially resisting, gives in to Mr. Ramsay's "demand that she should surrender herself up to him entirely" (*TL*, 226) – "the war had drawn the sting of her femininity" (*TL*, 238). "Femininity" has its phallus.

Ejaculation in the story of Vanessa's stain is only the utterance of a word, the fierce violation of a taboo. The famous Bloomsbury talk is thus a form of sexual intercourse, "the society of buggers'" symposium (see Chapter 1, pp. 16–17) with the "the sacred fluid" flowing freely, regardless of sex. Indiscriminate talk has replaced the heterosexual couple, one talking egotistically, the other silently knitting, of the older generation.

For the *I* is specifically an impediment for the writer: "some impediment of Mr. A's mind" associated with "the dominance of the letter 'I'" "blocked the fountain of creative energy" (*Room*, 104). Its shadow falls always across a page. "A shadow was on the page" as Augustus Carmichael shuffles past even for Mrs. Ramsay, reading the tale of the Fisherman's Wife and thinking that "her husband's last book was not quite his best book" (*TL*, 62). Mr. Carmichael has this effect not because he represents male egotism, but because he stands in Mrs. Ramsay's eyes for an unspoken criticism of her. The wife allows the male's demands to mar his writing. Mr. Ramsay's mind as well casts the pall of a judgement on Mrs. Ramsay: "through the crepuscular walls of their intimacy, . . . she could feel his mind like a raised hand shadowing her mind" (*TL*, 184). Ultimately, the *I*'s shadow bars the woman writer's page. In order "to review books I should need to do battle with a certain phantom. And the phantom was a woman," the one called "The Angel in the House" (*CE*, II, 285). Like Luther against the tempter, "whenever I felt the shadow of her wing or the radiance of her halo upon my page, I took up the inkpot and flung it at her" (*CE*, II, 286). What one expects the woman writer to defend is the right to say "I." But this is not Woolf's conclusion. The danger she sees is that male egotism may provoke the woman's counter-assertion of self. "[T]he novels of women" then show "another characteristic which may be traced to the writer's sex": as "[i]n *Middlemarch* and in *Jane Eyre*," we become aware "of a woman's presence – of someone resenting the treatment of her sex and pleading for its rights. This brings into women's writing an element which is entirely absent from a man's, unless, indeed, he happens to be a working-man, a negro, or one who for some other reason is conscious of disability." Jane Austen's and Emily Brontë's "genius" is to be "unperturbed by scorn or censure" (*CE*, II, 144). By turn, the women's movement provokes the reactive anger of men: "virility has now become self-conscious – men, that is to say, are now writing only with the male side of their brains" (*Room*, 105). The result is that "[t]he ridicule, the censure, the assurance of inferiority in one form or another which were lavished upon women who practised an art," as well as some men, make their "vision" "too masculine" or "too feminine," depriving it of "its most essential quality as a work of art" (*CE*, II, 144–5).[8] Only out of mutual release from the "I" flows artistic creativity.

The temptation for the artist is to not accept that "'I' is only a convenient term for somebody who has no real being" (*Room*, 4). The sex of this nonentity is woman, i.e., the non-sex. "The Angel was dead; what then remained? . . . now that she had rid herself of falsehood, that young woman had only to be herself. Ah, but what is 'herself'? I mean, what is a woman? I assure you, I do not know"

(*CE*, II, 286). The question "'What am I?'" is matched by the one about the object: "'What is this?'" (*TL*, 198). The nonentity's appropriate name is "Anon" – "no name." (Anonymity we will discover is a literary directive.) "Castration" is the loss of "personality." One motivation for Russell's replacing the term "subjective" with "private" was to avoid any suggestion of the personal. Woolf's terms are to be glossed by Russell's. Woolf's "real Self" is "impersonal," Russell's synonym for "neutral."

Loss of personality is finally the condition of knowledge; *I*, an impediment to it. It blocks observation of the world: "One began dodging this way and that to catch a glimpse of the landscape behind it . . . Back one was always hailed to the letter 'I'" (*Room*, 103). The "I" renders the view as murky as those regions that lie between the sharply focussed perspectives: "But . . . the worst of it is that in the shadow of the letter 'I' all is shapeless as mist. Is that a tree? No, it is a woman" (*Room*, 104). As long as Lily Briscoe and Charles Tansley feel the need to assert themselves, "She would never know him. He would never know her" (*TL*, 139). The reduced self is free to pursue knowledge unimpeded, first as the perspective neutrally registering the world's data and then as the flight of the mind toward the public sphere.

THE ESCAPE FROM THE PRIVATE ROOM: FROM ACQUAINTANCE TO PUBLIC KNOWLEDGE

Let us chase our imaginations to the heavens, or to the utmost limits of the universe; we never can really advance a step beyond ourselves, nor can conceive any kind of existence but those perceptions which have appeared in that narrow compass. (Stephen, *History of English Thought*, 46)

Now, logic presents many kinds of space as possible apart from experience. (Russell, *The Problems of Philosophy*, 148)

All acquisition of knowledge is an enlargement of the Self . . . we start from the not-Self, and through its greatness the boundaries of Self are enlarged. (*Ibid.*, 158–9)

"The effort to look behind" the "curtain" is the "effort to get out of ourselves," in Leslie Stephen's phrase. Stephen's history of English thought, in which Locke, "like Descartes, is trying to get outside himself" (*HET*, 37) reaches with Hume an impasse: "the method by which alone, as dogmatists and skeptics agreed, truth could be discoverable, led to the hopeless attempt of getting outside ourselves and seeing things as we do not see them" (*HET*, 55). With Kant, the attempt "is abandoned" (*HET*, 55). By contrast with the skepticism of "English Thought," Russell proclaims himself one of the "advocates of knowledge" (*TK*, 163) of "the outer world – the world, so to speak, which knowledge is aiming at knowing" (*LK*, 183). It is reached by a two-tiered ascent which begins, Cartesian-fashion, with private, limited knowledge. The dualism of knowledge underscores the inadequacy of acquaintance. Acquaintance with sense-data, for Russell, cannot "properly be described as a case of 'knowledge.' It gives rise to knowledge," yet "in itself it is not knowledge" (*OP*, 217). "Perceptions" are "simply natural events with no more knowledge status than (say) a shower" (*Mind*, 143), also Woolf's metaphor for sensation. "We cannot know, from perception alone, anything about other times or about the perceptions of others or about bodies understood in an impersonal sense" (*OP*, 139). From "the momentary object of perception," which is "the least questionable thing in our experience" (*PP*, 151), one must cross, by a leap, over the gap between sense-data and physics. For all real knowledge lies on the other side. "The distinction between knowledge by acquaintance and knowledge by description is introduced to allow for the possibility of my having knowledge about an object with which I am not acquainted," Hylton writes (*Russell*, 245–6). Such knowledge is the aim. Stephen had himself recognized this: "The basis of the knowledge of every individual is his own current of consciousness, which is transformed into knowledge by reflection" ("WM?," 135).

Acquaintance itself is already a step outside, consisting "in a relation between the mind and something other than the mind; it is this that constitutes the mind's power of knowing things. If we say that the things known must be in the mind, we are either unduly limiting the mind's power of knowing, or we are uttering a mere tautology" (*PP*, 42). The object's exteriority suggests that "the experience of one mind may overlap that of another." This, Russell says, applies "to all experiencing of universals and abstracts" in fact and "as a theoretic possibility, to the things of sense" (*TK*, 34). Hence the importance of making sense-data independent of the mind. "It is true that the sense-datum is in many cases in the subject's body, but the subject's body is as distinct from the subject as tables and chairs are" (*ML*, 147). Acquaintance, albeit private, is thus the prelude to knowledge by description, which continues the movement out. Woolf gives in similar terms her reasons for reading Freud – it aims "to enlarge the circumference. [sic] to give my brain a wider scope: to make it objective; to get outside" (*Diary*, V, 248). History, geology, astronomy figure importantly in her novels as knowledge of remote worlds: the "horizon seemed to her limitless. There were all the places she had not seen; the Indian plains" (*TL*, 96). Remoteness applies equally to interior worlds, to "an experiencing," which is "only capable of being experienced by one person" (*TK*, 34). Biography for Woolf represents such knowledge of other minds: "There is thus no longer any reason to be confined to the minute span of actual experience which is still, for us, so narrow, so circumscribed. We can supplement it by looking at the picture of the lives of others" (*TG*, 7). The single private world is enlarged by constructing a public one it cannot know directly. The construction presupposes the preliminary reduction: stripping the self of its common-sense world and exposing it to the strange uninterpreted world of sense-data.

Woolf's private monad-rooms, like Russell's contra Leibniz, are not completely world-tight, doorless and windowless, nor privacy inviolate. Contact is made at two openings, window and door. The window allows observation: "the open staircase window . . . let in blinds flapping, dogs barking, let in . . . the grinding, blowing, flowering of the day." The reduced self, its back to the familiar interior reality, is already leaving it behind, Clarissa looking out, already "out of doors, out of the window, out of her body and brain which now failed" (*MrsD*, 45).[9] Stepping "outdoors" permits complete escape, collisions with sense-data, interruptions. The shower of sense-data bombards the perspective; the moment is "interrupted, torn, pricked and plucked at by sensations, spontaneous and irrelevant" (*W*, 114), like that through which, sign of the haphazard, "that wild villain, Cam," dashes (*TL*, 83), giving experience piecemeal. The door also permits social interaction: "gossip," "chatter," "traffic." The novels' characters must step out into "the sociability of the streets" (*CE*, IV, 156). A "fish-like self" inhabits watery depths, then "suddenly she shoots to the surface and sports on the wind-wrinkled waves; that is, has a positive need to brush, scrape, kindle herself, gossiping" (*MrsD*, 244). The role of the novels' hostesses is to create the conditions for "acquaintance." Mrs. Ramsay succeeds in making her party against the "rippled" windows (*TL*, 146–7) while Mrs. Dalloway "lacked . . . something warm which broke up surfaces and rippled the cold contact of man and woman, of women together" (*MrsD*, 46). Removing the barriers to intimacy, Mrs. Ramsay is the principle of interruption itself, victim and agent, even self-inflicting, "interrupting what she was saying to Mr. Bankes to speak to the maid" (*TL*, 131).[10] "They came to her, naturally, since she was a woman, all day long; one wanting this, another that" (*TL*, 51); "the atoms of my attention dispersed, swarmed round the interruption" (*W*, 261). The ego's defense against interruption is a refusal of knowledge. One must be drenched by the rain of data. Charles Tansley resents the chatter at Mrs. Ramsay's dinner table. "If only he could be in his room working," he thinks (*TL*, 131). Instead "silly women" "did nothing but talk, talk, talk, eat, eat, eat" (*TL*, 129). Mr. Ramsay's "child-like resentment of interruption" (*TL*, 41), "some curious gathering together of his person, as if he wrapped himself about and needed privacy" (*TL*, 49), closes off the world; "he . . . slammed his private door on them" (*TL*, 42); the others had "encroached upon a privacy" (*TL*, 31). "Don't interrupt me," he seemed to be saying (*TL*, 179).[11] So, "safe," "restored to his privacy," he "looked once at his wife and son in the window, and as one raises one's eyes from a page in an express train and sees a farm, a tree, a cluster of cottages as an illustration, a confirmation of something on the printed page to which one returns, fortified, and satisfied," scarcely allowing the evidence of the senses to penetrate: "so without his distinguishing either his son or his wife, the sight of them . . . consecrated his effort" (*TL*, 53).

"All those interruptions annoyed" William Bankes as well (*TL*, 133). "How trifling it all is, how boring it all is, he thought, compared with the other thing – work . . . He wished only to be alone and to take up that book" (*TL*, 134). But Bankes' desire for uninterrupted work is sacrificed; the exception, we saw, – "if it had not been for Mr. Bankes" (*TL*, 139) – to male egotism. "[R]est[ing] in contemplation of" mother and child, subject of Lily's painting, he "felt, as he felt when he had proved something absolute about the digestive system of plants, that barbarity was tamed, the reign of chaos subdued" (*TL*, 74). They "had upon him precisely the same effect as the solution of a scientific problem" (*TL*, 73–4). His was the selfless "love that never attempted to clutch its object; but, like the love which mathematicians bear their symbols, or poets their phrases, was meant to be spread over the world" (*TL*, 74). Mr. Ramsay's demands for self-confirmation interrupt others.

"Ramsay bore down on" Lily (*TL*, 31) as she paints, "almost knock[ing] her easel over" (*TL*, 29). Bankes' disinterested detachment – "[n]othing could be cooler and quieter" (*TL*, 81) – has not the paralyzing effect of Tansley's taunt, "women can't paint": "Mr. Bankes was less alarming" (*TL*, 80). Taking "scientifically in complete good faith" Lily's explanation of her painting's non-representationality ("the picture was not of them" [*TL*, 81]), he tries to rise above "his prejudices," which "were on the other side" (*TL*, 82), again the mirror of Lily, "subduing all her impressions as a woman" (*TL*, 82). By contrast, Ramsay, uncertain whether "the progress of civilization depend[ed] on great men" (*TL*, 67), needs to denigrate art: "he would find some way of snubbing the predominance of the arts. He would argue that the world exists for the average human being; that the arts are merely a decoration imposed on the top of human life" (*TL*, 67). Not Mr. Ramsay's philosophy falls short of the ideal of impersonal knowledge, but Mr. Ramsay, egoist. ("Bertie is a fervid egoist," Woolf observes about Russell [*Diary*, II, 147].) Bankes' "impersonality, and the white scientific coat which seemed to clothe him" (*TL*, 73) make science's detachment the model of knowledge transcending privacy. "I respect you (she [Lily] addressed him silently in person) in every atom; you are not vain; you are entirely impersonal; you are finer than Mr. Ramsay. . . you live for science" (*TL*, 39). Ramsay the metaphysician has not Bankes the botanist's[12] egoless openness to the world. Scientist and artist, mathematician and poet, alike aim for this impersonality. Mr. Bankes' stance, "with his glasses raised to the scientific examination of her canvas" (*TL*, 82), mirrors Lily's "painting position with" its "absent-minded manner" (*TL*, 82) and Mrs. Ramsay's absent-mindedness (*TL*, 121), her "remoteness" (*TL*, 98), cause of Mr. Ramsay's feeling that he "could not interrupt her" (*TL*, 100). Mrs. Ramsay too has an intellectual project to carry her beyond the confines of the private house, for she "wrote down in columns carefully ruled for the purpose wages and spendings, employment and unemployment, in the hope that thus she would cease to be a private woman." If it was to "become what with her untrained mind she greatly admired, an investigator, elucidating the social problem" (*TL*, 18), the social was to be approached via an impersonal intellectual effort.

For interruptions finally violate some inner sanctuary; they distract from another reality the sensible world only points to. Again, its structure is continuity. Since imagination "suggests an independent existence of our perceptions" and reason refuses "to recognise an unperceived perception as possible," Leslie Stephen observes, "philosophers have hit upon the expedient of attributing interruption to our perceptions and independent continuity to 'objects'" (*HET*, 47). The sensible world presents a broken surface. Contact, so essential initially, blocks access to its geometry. To reach it one must leave behind the dinner table and the streets, "escape . . . from the common sitting-room" (*Room*, 118). Clarissa Dalloway's impulse to privacy, feeling it "outrageous to be interrupted at eleven o'clock," follows her immersion in the streets. She "began to go slowly upstairs . . . as if she had left a party, . . . shut the door and gone out and stood alone, a single figure against the appalling night" (*MrsD*, 45). Privacy must be alternately relinquished and protected, the thinker passing via expansion and contraction in and out of frames. Only after an exposure can one withdraw into a region where "[a]ll the being and doing, expansive, glittering, vocal, evaporated" (*TL*, 95). The two kinds of knowledge are two stages whose order is crucial. Each aspirant to knowledge must shed the "I," opening to the world, then return to privacy.

Mrs. Ramsay also stands on the threshold, privacy's protector. She "opened bedroom windows. She shut doors" (*TL*, 76). Charles Tansley "heard her come out; shut a door; say they must keep the windows open and the doors shut" (*TL*, 24). The theme is reiterated:

> Still, if every door in a house is left open, things must spoil. Every door was left open; it sounded as if the bedroom doors were open; and certainly the window on the landing was open, for that she had opened herself. That windows should be open, and doors shut – simple as it was, could none of them remember it? (*TL*, 44)

Closing doors against the annihilating effects of the salt air, Mrs. Ramsay's predictions, like Mr. Ramsay's weather forecast, prove true. In "Time Passes," the "stray airs" invade the house, despite its "doors locked" (*TL*, 194), "blustered in, brushed bare boards, nibbled and fanned, met nothing in bedroom and drawing-room that wholly resisted them" (*TL*, 194). Doors are also closed against intrusions from others. To that end Mrs. Ramsay regulates the comings and goings of the house's occupants. Each, like the books in the British Museum, is "bade" to "go in and out" (*TL*, 59), to be continuously "restored each to his own cell in the enormous honeycomb" (*Room*, 33).

A core of impenetrable privacy is ultimately reached, "cleared of chatter" (*TL*, 170), inaccessible to any intruder. Mrs. Ramsay "lived away in another division of the world" (*TL*, 123–4); "the eight sons and daughters of Mr. and Mrs. Ramsay sought their bedrooms, their fastnesses in a house where there was no other privacy" (*TL*, 16); "Nancy made off, after lunch, to her attic, to escape the horror of family life" (*TL*, 112) or "waded out to her own rocks and searched her own pools" (*TL*, 114); Charles Tansley "had gone upstairs to work" (*TL*, 174). Mr. and Mrs. Ramsay retire to a room to read, both immured in their privacy. She "saw that he did not want to be interrupted" (*TL*, 176). "Their eyes met for a second; but they did not want to speak to each other" (*TL*, 179). The return to a privacy deep in the perspective's center, far from its outer fringes where contact occurs, paradoxically exits into pure exteriority, "drifting into that strange no-man's land where to follow people is impossible" (*TL*, 127). One penetrates to "something real, something private, which she shared neither with her children nor with her husband" (*TL*, 91–2). After her dinner party, Mrs. Ramsay "felt rather inclined . . . to stand still after all that chatter, and pick out one particular thing; the thing that mattered; to detach it; separate it off; clean it of all the emotions and odds and ends of things" (*TL*, 169). "For now she need not think about anybody. She could be herself, by herself" (*TL*, 95). Lily Briscoe also "liked to be alone; she liked to be herself" (*TL*, 77). Alone "to think; well, not even to think," one "shrunk . . . to being oneself" (*TL*, 95). But the essential self is not that of "our apparitions, the things you know us by" (*TL*, 96); it requires losing oneself: "Not as oneself did one find rest ever, in her experience . . . but as a wedge of darkness. Losing personality, one lost the fret, the hurry, the stir" (*TL*, 96). Clarissa, "like a virgin protecting chastity, respecting privacy" (*MrsD*, 59), retreats to the private room both as a chosen cloister – "[l]ike a nun withdrawing, . . . she went upstairs, paused at the window" (*MrsD*, 45) – and an inevitable tomb – "[t]he sheets were clean, tight stretched in a broad white band from side to side. Narrower and narrower would her bed be" (*MrsD*, 45–6). For "[t]here was an emptiness at the heart of life; an attic room" (*MrsD*, 45). Lily Briscoe is also "drawn out of gossip, out of living, out of community with people" (*TL*, 236) into a privacy in which "she lost consciousness of outer things, and her name and her personality and her appearance, and whether Mr. Carmichael was there or not" (*TL*, 238).

The point is that the voyage out beyond the social must be preceded by a voyage in. That escape to an essential privacy is also from the little circle of experience rooted in the sense organs. The mind "does not occupy a certain region in space" (*ML*, 126). The shrunken self, an acute awareness, takes off from its object, as Mr. Bentley from "his strip of turf at Greenwich," for whom the skywriting airplane is a symbol of man's determination "to get outside his body, beyond his house, by means of thought, Einstein, speculation, mathematics, the Mendelian theory" (*MrsD*, 41). The metaphor of flight Russell counterposes to the mental prison. "The old logic put thought in fetters, while the new logic gives it wings" (*OKnExW*, 68). "[T]he flight of the mind" (in *VW*, I, 138) sometimes achieves a direct apprehension of the distant: "unmoored as I am from a private being," I "embrace these engrossed flocks" (*W*, 114). More often, however, it makes no contact; vast spaces separate thought from its object. Intimacy is only a remembered directness for which a longing remains, as if sense perception were a paradise lost. Direct apprehension must be left behind. Then "this self having shed its attachments was free for the strangest adventures. When life sank down for a moment, the range of experience seemed limitless" (*TL*, 95–6). Woolf's reduced self discovers its essential state, incognito, in a self-imposed exile outside its private world: "This core of darkness could go anywhere, for no one saw it" (*TL*, 96). It is her solitary traveller, her street haunter, her feminine "self, who fish-like inhabits deep seas and plies among obscurities threading her way . . . over sun-flickered spaces and on and on into gloom, cold, deep, inscrutable" (*MrsD*, 244). Its state is star-like because it occupies the timeless intervals between perspectives; fish-like because they consist of waves. It soars above its perspective to take in others with a "complete emancipation from her present surrounding" (*ND*, 45). "Only like a bee, drawn by some sweetness or sharpness in the air intangible to touch or taste, one haunted the dome-shaped hive, ranged the wastes of the air over the countries of the world alone" (*TL*, 79–80).

THE MIND WANDERS

The mind is certainly a very mysterious organ . . . there are severances and oppositions in the mind . . . What does one mean by "the unity of the mind," I pondered, for clearly the mind has so great a power of concentrating at any point at any moment that it seems to have no single state of being. It can separate itself from the people in the street, for example, and think of itself as apart from them, at an upper window looking down on them. Or it can think with other people spontaneously, as, for instance, in a crowd waiting to hear some piece of news read out . . . Again if one is a woman one is often surprised by a sudden splitting off of consciousness, say in walking down Whitehall, when from being the natural inheritor of that civilization, she becomes, on the contrary, outside of it, alien and critical. (Woolf, *A Room of One's Own*, 101)

Once Leslie Stephen's "ordinary mind, to which common-sense supplies the pole-star" ("WM?," 134), once "a healthy, out of door, moor striding mind" (*MB*, 115) leaves its room and opens itself to distraction, it becomes Woolf's "ordinary mind on an ordinary day" (*CE*, II, 106), sensitized to the atomization of the world, led by the dancing atoms in random directions. Stephen's "mind is conscious of a series of sensations of colour, form, and so forth" (*HET*, 46–7); Woolf's "receives a myriad impressions – trivial, fantastic, evanescent, or engraved with the sharpness of steel" (*CE*, II, 106), like Katherine Mansfield's "mind – a terribly sensitive mind – . . . registering one after another such diverse impressions" (*CE*, I, 356). Stephen's "whirl of incoherent atoms, which has gradually shaken down into such order as we see around us" ("WM?," 143), is Woolf's "incessant shower of innumerable atoms" which "as they fall, . . . shape themselves" (*CE*, II, 106).

For the ordinary mind wanders; it overleaps the limits of direct perception in its vagaries. This is the proposition everywhere demonstrated, not without a certain humor, as if the novels' universe was filled with stray thoughts circulating, like shooting stars or skywriting airplanes or bees suddenly zooming past: "Kitty's mind wandered" (*Y*, 280); "Eleanor's attention wandered" (*Y*, 162); "Mr. Streatfield had lost the thread of his discourse" (*BA*, 134); "she lost the thread of her discourse" (*ND*, 264); "Dear, how my mind wanders" (*BA*, 174); "his mind then began to wander" (*ND*, 28); "her attention seemed to wander" (*ND*, 371); "rambling over an infinite variety of thoughts . . . [h]er mind made excursions into the dark of the air, or settled upon the surface of the sea . . . or with equal unreason it returned to its couch of bracken beneath the stars of midnight, and visited the snow valleys of the moon" (*ND*, 434); "[h]er mind skimmed leagues where Mrs. Pascoe's mind adhered to its solitary patch" (*JR*, 56); "[s]he found her mind uncomfortably full of different trains of thought" (*ND*, 171); "Mary immediately let her attention wander" (*ND*, 131); "as a single spider's thread after wavering here and there attaches itself to the point of a leaf, so Richards's mind . . . set now on his wife" (*MrsD*, 173). Woolf's characters are typically caught at chance moments in attitudes of vacancy. They are "absent-minded" (*ND*, 137, 270, 333, 460), "[s]targazing" (*MrsD*, 53) or, like Mrs. Ramsay with "her knitting" (*TL*, 48), "[o]nly wool-gathering" (*TL*, 104). Even Leslie Stephen admitted he was "apt also to be a little absent in mind" (*MBook*, 89).

Stated as a general truth – "Surely, if the mind wanders (and Jacob looked extraordinarily vacant, his head thrown back, his hymnbook open at the wrong place)" – its source is located in the multifarious interruptions of sense-data: "if the mind wanders it is because several hat shops and cupboards upon cupboards of coloured dresses are displayed upon rush-bottomed chairs" (*JR*, 33). Woolf presents various ways in which this happens. The sense organs may receive impressions without immediately processing them. The object is present as to an unoccupied perspective, Russell's "physical subjectivity," from which the mind is momentarily absent. This phenomenon Russell calls "inattentive acquaintance," "the experience constantly of becoming attentive to an object which we know was already given in sense before we became attentive to it" (*TK*, 125–6). "Kitty's eyes alone registered what she saw . . . She could add nothing to what she saw" (*Y*, 217). "Her mind was a perfect blank for a moment" (*Y*, 242). It simply "record[s] the atoms . . . in the order in which they fall" (*CE*, II, 107); the mind "made no pattern out of the sights he saw" (*ND*, 157).

Or there may be a delay between sensation and reflection, factor of the sensation's gradual fading: "we can attend to an experience which is in the immediate past" (*TK*, 126), the phenomenon "intermediate between sensation and image" already considered that Russell calls " 'immediate memory,' " where a just sensed datum differs from a present sensation and its "memory-image" days or weeks hence, "the experience of noticing (say) that the clock *has been* striking" but not "while it was striking" or "hear[ing] a remark spoken" and being "conscious of the earlier words while the later ones are being uttered" (*Mind*, 174). The passage of time becomes apprehensible. Clarissa Dalloway's words "Remember my party" fade in Peter Walsh's mind as he hears "the last tremors of the great booming voice" of Big Ben striking half-past eleven (*MrsD*, 72–3). Mrs. Ramsay belatedly interprets the sentence "Someone had blundered": "Starting from her musing she gave meaning to words which she had held meaningless in her mind for a long time" (*TL*, 36).

The mind can register sense-data in "the distracted way of someone who with their surface senses watches what is being done, but at the same time thinks of something else" (*Y*, 316). This "discrepancy – that was what she was thinking, this was what she was doing – " (*TL*, 126) Mrs. Ramsay notes. Such distractedness endows Mrs. Swithin, having "spent the hours between three and five thinking of rhododendron forests in Piccadilly" (*BA*, 8), with "the divided glance": "It took her five seconds in actual time, in mind time ever so much longer, to separate Grace herself, with blue china on a tray, from the leather-covered grunting monster who was about, as the door opened, to demolish a whole tree in the steaming undergrowth of the primeval forest. Naturally she jumped, as Grace put the tray down." " 'Batty,' " Grace pronounces her, "as she felt on her face the divided glance that was half meant for a beast in the swamp, half for a maid in a print frock and white apron" (*BA*, 9). Mrs. Swithin in her flightiness acts "as if she were of two minds, and they fluttered to right and to left" (*BA*, 74). The mind's divisions also consist of simultaneously held contradictions, like Lily Briscoe's opinions of Mr. Ramsay.

The mind's vagaries constitute a series of non-sequiturs coming out in "talk," which is "naturally led" from subject to subject (*CE*, II, 233). No logical sequence orders Betty Flanders' thoughts: " 'Dear Mr. Floyd,' she wrote. – 'Did I forget about the cheese?' she wondered, laying down her pen. No, she had told Rebecca that the cheese was in the hall. 'I am much surprised . . .' she wrote" (*JR*, 21). Or those of Miss Marchmont, trying "to explain her philosophy. The rhythm of the soul depends upon it – ('how rude the little boys are!' she would say), and Mr. Asquith's Irish policy, and Shakespeare comes in, 'and Queen Alexandra most graciously once acknowledged a copy of my pamphlet,' she would say" (*JR*, 105–6). Lucy Swithin's conversation is similarly jumbled. She tries to recall what she was saying: " 'How did we begin this talk?' She counted on her fingers. 'The Pharaohs. Dentists. Fish . . . [Woolf's ellipses] Oh yes, you were saying, Isa, you ordered fish; and you were afraid it wouldn't be fresh. And I said, "That's the problem" ' " (*BA*, 31). No logic governs hers and Mrs. Sands' musings, Lucy's skipping "side-long, from yeast to alcohol; so to fermentation; so to inebriation; so to Bacchus; and lay under purple lamps in a vineyard in Italy . . . while Sands heard the clock tick; saw the cat; noted a fly buzz; and registered, as her lips showed, a grudge she mustn't speak against people making work in the kitchen while they had a high old time hanging paper roses in the Barn" (*BA*, 34). Mrs. Ramsay's thinking lacks logical connections: "She supposed it was all right leaving him to his own devices, Mrs. Ramsay said, wondering whether it was any use sending down bulbs; did they want them?" (*TL*, 101); "There was always a woman dying of cancer even here. And yet she had said to all these children, you shall go through with it. To eight people she had said relentlessly that (and the bill for the greenhouse would be fifty pounds)" (*TL*, 93); or "'And now,' she said, thinking that Lily's charm was her Chinese eyes . . . but it would take a clever man to see it, 'and now stand up, and let me measure your leg,' for they might go to the Lighthouse after all, and she must see if the stocking did not need to be an inch or two longer in the leg" (*TL*, 42). Everywhere the non-sequitur is the mark of her mind:

> But then, Mrs. Ramsay, though instantly taking his side against all the silly Giddingses in the world, then, she thought, intimating by a little pressure on his arm that he walked uphill too fast for her, and she must stop a moment to see whether those were fresh mole-hills on the bank, then, she thought, stooping down to look, a great mind like his must be different in every way from ours. All the great men she had ever known, she thought, deciding that a rabbit must have got in, were like that, and it was good for young men (though the atmosphere of lecture rooms was stuffy and depressing to her beyond endurance almost) simply to hear him, simply to look at him. But without shooting rabbits, how was one to keep them down? she wondered. It might be a rabbit; it might be a mole. Some creature anyhow was ruining her Evening Primroses. And looking up, she saw above the thin trees the first pulse of the full-throbbing star, and wanted to make her husband look at it; for the sight gave her such keen pleasure. But she stopped herself. He never looked at things. (*TL*, 107–8)

Absence of logic achieves logic's freedom. Thought becomes flight into an element offering no checks, the realm of logical possibility; it floats "without a self, weightless and visionless, through a world weightless, without illusion" (*W*, 285). Images of flight represent the mind: a bird (a hawk [*TL*, 158]), an owl in "The Moment" [*CE*, II, 293], swallows and rooks), a fish, a bee, an airplane, a flag, the balloon to which Woolf likens Russell's head. "Could we not fly too, with broad wings . . . be all one wing; all embracing, all gathering, and these boundaries, these pryings over hedge into hidden compartments of different colours be all swept into one colour by the brush of the wing; and so visit in splendour, augustly, peaks; and there lie exposed, bare, on the spine, high up, to the cold light of the moon rising" (*CE*, II, 297)? Thought is "the power of the mind to quit the body" (*JR*, 92), to imagine other worlds: "without their bodies their thoughts wandered in and out freely, friendly and communicative, in the common pool" (*CSFVW*, 220).

THE ORDINARY MIND WOOL-GATHERING

> McTaggart used often to use the word "woolly" as a name for a characteristic of some philosophers to which he particularly objected. "Wooliness" was, of course, incompatible with the kind of clarity at which he aimed; . . . a philosopher might, of course, be obscure without being "woolly." (Moore, "An Autobiography," 18–19)[13]

The ordinary mind is both "vague and wandering" (*ND*, 385). The adjective *vague* is one of the erring descendents of the same Indo-European root as the verb *wander.* "The subject of vagueness is of some importance," Russell writes (*TK*, 175) and undertakes "the logical analysis of 'vagueness'" (*TK*, 176). Russell attributes it to "the vagueness of the representative character of images" (*TK*, 175) of remembered sensations. "I find my imagination haunted by a scene which has the dimness and vagueness commonly characteristic of imagination," he writes (*TK*, 172). Such "descriptive" memories have "a certain vagueness" because of an imprecision in "the relation of 'representing,' which holds between images and sense-data" (*TK*, 174). So in Woolf's first memories, "[e]verything would be large and dim; and what was seen would at the same time be heard" (*MB*, 66).

Vagueness is a lack of clarity, the blurring of outlines, confused perception, as when "Mrs. Ramsay did not quite catch the meaning" of Charles Tansley's conversation, but "only the words, here and there . . . dissertation . . . fellowship . . . readership . . . lectureship" (*TL*, 22). "The gruff murmur" she half-hears of the men's philosophic talk takes "its place soothingly in the scale of sounds pressing on top of her, such as the tap of balls upon bats, the sharp sudden bark now and then, 'How's that? How's that?' of the children playing cricket," partially blotting out "the monotonous fall of the waves" (*TL*, 27), one sound muffling another. Or a filter, like Russell's blue spectacles (*OKnExW*, 85ff.), intervenes. Vague and wavy is the world's blur seen through women's tears. Through those of Betty Flanders, the "bay quivered" and "the lighthouse wobbled." "Tears made all the dahlias in her garden undulate in red waves and flashed the glass house in her eyes, and spangled the kitchen with bright knives" (*JR*, 7), "like Jacob in the blur of her outline" (*JR*, 91). When Fanny Elmer looks in the mapseller's window, "The equator swam behind tears" (*JR*, 171). In "the bright yet vague glance of the young" woman "who walks fast, and yet anything distracts her," things go in and out of focus: "Now she seems to see, and now to notice nothing" (*JR*, 113). "The eyes of all the nurses, mothers, and wandering women are a little glazed, absorbed" (*JR*, 118). It might be the very look of the world, as when "[w]ith the sunset sharpness was lost" (*TL*, 212) or, in the night of "Time Passes," "a drench of hail" covers things "and so breaks them, so confuses them" (*TL*, 193).

Vagueness is the inability to distinguish one thing from another. It characterizes Miss Marchmont's research, "seeking through millions of pages" for "[s]ometimes one thing, sometimes another, to confirm her philosophy that colour was sound – or, perhaps, it has something to do with music. She could never quite say, though it was not for lack of trying" (*JR*, 105). So in Woolf's first impressions, "sounds would come through this petal or leaf – sounds indistinguishable from sights" (*MB*, 66). Vagueness explains Mrs. Dalloway's confusion of "the Albanians, or was it the Armenians?" (*MrsD*, 182). For Miss Marchmont, Fanny Elmer and Clarissa Dalloway belong, like the six-year-old James Ramsay, "to that great clan which cannot keep this feeling separate from that" (*TL*, 9). Vagueness is the merging of what is distinct.

Vagueness is "the absence of *attention* to the form in ordinary thinking" (*TK*, 129); analysis is the discipline of the ordinary mind, fixing attention and discerning objects in the mist of ordinary thinking: "We may say broadly that it is easier to attend to particulars than to universals, and to universals than to logical forms" (*TK*, 129).

> We thus arrive at a hierarchy of cognitive relations, according to the "abstractness" of the most abstract of the objects involved. If this most abstract object is a particular, we have sensation, imagination, or memory; if a universal, we have conception and complex perception; if a logical form, i.e. a fact containing no constants, we have understanding, belief, disbelief, doubt, and probably many other relations; if the logical form is

molecular, we have also inference and the knowledge of the propositions of logic and their instances. (*TK*, 131–2)

Philosophical ideas, in fact, are "essentially infected with vagueness" (*LK*, 341). Vagueness is the "obstacle" to the "creation of a correct logical language" (*LK*, 338). Analysis is thus a corrective not just for the ordinary mind but for philosophy, a method for avoiding detours from the straight path to truth, for focussing the diffuse and making the vague "precise, clear, definite":

I think vagueness is very much more important in a theory of knowledge than you would judge it to be from the writings of most people. Everything is vague to a degree you do not realize till you have tried to make it precise. (*LK*, 179–80)

The goal of Russell's logic is to bring out the outline in the blur, in Woolf's "cotton wool of daily life" (*MB*, 72). "Vagueness, no doubt, is omnipresent and unavoidable; but it is only in proportion as we overcome it that exact science becomes possible. And we overcome it most by analysis and concentration, not by a diffused ecstatic mystical vision" (*Matter*, 200).

THE ANALYTIC MIND

The most analytic mind has some spark of creative power, and the great creators are capable of deliberate dissection. (Stephen, *Hours in a Library*, III, 5)

For, if the mind wanders partly because of some vagueness in the world, fortunately there exists a mind extraordinary in its clarity and directness. This is "the Cambridge analy[tical spirit]" (*MB*, 126), formed by that university education Woolf lacked. She rarely attempted the likes of Russell's "luminous vigorous mind" (*Diary*, II, 295). Perhaps Woolf, who skipped "Bertie's lectures" (*Diary*, I, 273) on *The Analysis of Mind*, feared infection by her female characters' "truancy . . . of the logical faculty" (*MrsD*, 275) and felt inadequate to the task. Her single extended portrait of the philosopher is a kind of parody: Mr. Ramsay is no less ridiculous than formidable; humor justified the distance and sketchiness.

Although modelled on Woolf's father, Mr. Ramsay stands for the Cambridge philosopher. It would be surprising if Woolf, writing over twenty years after her father's death, did not include aspects of philosophers of her acquaintance.[14] Like Leslie Stephen, speaking, according to his daughter, "between the puffs of his pipe" (*CE*, IV, 77), but like Russell and Moore as well, and Mr. Ambrose the classicist (*VO*, 170), Mr. Ramsay "stopped to light his pipe" as a preliminary to "his effort to arrive at a perfectly clear understanding of the problem which now engaged the energies of his splendid mind" (*TL*, 39). (We hear an echo of Tyndall's "endeavor to obtain a perfectly clear understanding of the problem now before us" [*On Radiation*, 13].) For his was a philosophy "irregularly broken by the taking out of pipes and the putting in of pipes" (*TL*, 27), the thought of men.[15] Like Stephen, who wrote that "[o]rdinary men believe in the reality of the external world" (*HET*, 62), Mr. Ramsay "would argue that the world existed for the average human being" (*TL*, 67).

More significantly, however, like Russell, who observed to Woolf "my mind is absolutely relevant. I cant ramble. I stick to facts" (*Diary*, II, 294), Mr. Ramsay's mind never wanders. He is "a steady goer," "plodding and perservering" onward in a straight line, the leader of a polar expedition (*TL*, 55, 231), the "express train" itself (*TL*, 52). Mr. Ramsay, "fixed upon" the table, he "never allowed himself to be distracted" (*TL*, 232), just as Ralph Denham "seemed to look straightly and keenly at one object" (*ND*, 29). Theirs were "those clear-cut trenchant intellects, immovably encased in a hard shell of abstractions" Whitehead invokes (*SMW*, 58). This single-mindedness is expressed in a logical sequence of discrete units:

> For if thought is like the keyboard of a piano, divided into so many notes, or like the alphabet is ranged into twenty-six letters all in order, then his splendid mind had no sort of difficulty in running over those letters one by one, firmly and accurately, until it had reached, say, the letter Q. He reached Q . . . After Q there are a number of letters the last of which is scarcely visible to mortal eyes, but glimmers red in the distance. Z is only reached by one man in a generation. Still, if he could reach R it would be something. Here at least was Q. He dug his heels in at Q. Q he was sure of. Q he could demonstrate. If Q then is Q – R – Here he knocked his pipe out, with two or three resonant taps . . . , and proceeded. "Then R . . ." (*TL*, 53–4)

Mr. Ramsay, working through the alphabet, has been identified as Leslie Stephen editing *The Dictionary of National Biography* (Bazin, *Virginia Woolf*, 13–14), "drafting sentiments in alphabetical order" (*MrsD*, 167), like Hugh Whitbread, "reduc[ing] Lady Bruton's tangles to sense, to grammar such as the editor of the Times, Lady Bruton felt . . . must respect" (*MrsD*, 166), like the British Museum's catalogue under "woman" before which *A Room of One's Own*'s woman narrator, "unfortunately" with "no training in a university" (*Room*, 28), admits "[m]y mind wandered" (*Room*, 27) or like the male reader's notes, "headed often with an A or a B or a C," at which she is "glancing with envy" (*Room*, 30). But the letters are also logical symbols, tools of analysis for breaking things down into ever simpler parts, "netting and separating one thing from another" (*TL*, 161). They are arbitrarily chosen ("say, the letter Q"), yet recognizable to anyone who had looked at "books of algebraic symbols" filled with "pages all speckled with dots and dashes and twisted bars" (*ND*, 300), "pages of neatly written mathematical signs" (*ND*, 216) – the first pages of *Principia Mathematica* would suffice. In its notation, "small letters of the ordinary alphabet," "*p*, *q*, *r* will be called *propositional letters*" (*PM*, 5), part of "an alphabetical list of propositions"; the elementary proposition is also indicated in the *Tractatus* "by the letters *p*, *q*, *r*" (4.24). Its units are not "unreal divisions" (*LK*, 178). Mr. Ramsay's letter *R* hence not only suggests his name; it stands also for the Reality blocked by the letter "I," one "not made into a reality by its capital letter" like the Idealist's ("WM?," 144) but denoting the reality of external relations: the relation R of the proposition xRy representing logical form.

The mind which thinks through logical symbolism is identified as "masculine." Its strength, that "of young men," was "their love of abstract principles" (*MrsD*, 75), of mathematical symbols (*TL*, 74):

> What did it all mean? To this day she had no notion. A square root? What was that? Her sons knew. She leant on them; on cubes and square roots; that was what they were talking about now . . . she let it uphold her and sustain her, this admirable fabric of the masculine intelligence, which ran up and down, crossing this and that, like iron girders spanning the swaying fabric, upholding the world, so that she could trust herself to it utterly, even shut her eyes, or flicker them for a moment. (*TL*, 159)

The extraordinary mind has its limits, however. Not discussed at the Ramsay's dinner table is painting, although one guest is a painter. Mr. Ramsay's limits are the failure of a vision; something escapes in an eyeblink: "A shutter like the leathern eyelid of a lizard, flickered over the intensity of his gaze and obscured the letter R. In that flash of darkness he heard people saying – he was a failure" (*TL*, 54). The male intelligence's girders are also "the thigh bones, the ribs, of his vanity" (*TL*, 137). For there is another way to knowledge than the analytic method:

he could see, without wishing it, that old, that obvious distinction between two classes of men; on the one hand the steady goers of superhuman strength who, plodding and perservering, repeat the whole alphabet in order, twenty-six letters in all, from start to finish; on the other hand the gifted, the inspired who, miraculously, lump all the letters together in one flash – the way of genius. He had not genius; he laid no claim to that: but he had, or might have had, the power to repeat every letter of the alphabet from A to Z accurately in order. Meanwhile he stuck at Q. On, then, on to R. (*TL*, 55)

Ramsay, "one of those men who do their best work before they are forty" (*TL*, 39), recalls Leslie Stephen's "failure as a philosopher, as a writer" (*MB*, 125) – if "the history of English thought in the nineteenth century should ever be written, my name will only be mentioned in small type and footnotes" (*MBook*, 93). Ramsay, who "should have been a great philosopher" (*TL*, 19), but, after "one little book" written "when he was only five and twenty," his work "was more or less amplification, repetition" (*TL*, 39), might even recall Moore, who only published collections of essays after *Principia Ethica*.

Failure is measured against "the way of genius" Russell attributed to Wittgenstein as to Moore.[16] Her father's "frustrated desire to be a man of genius" led, Woolf writes, to his "self-centredness" (*MB*, 110). But what is this other "way"? Is it not the wandering the analytic method aims to contain? Its practicioners are for the most part women, for "the ordinary mind" is paradigmatically feminine. Woolf perversely makes not Mr. Ramsay's "splendid mind" (*TL*, 53) but Mrs. Ramsay's wandering mind the unmarked case of the "neutral" or neuter mind. Far from being a merely passive receptacle of "myriad impressions," it is the female mind which leaps and lumps. In Mr. Ramsay's "distinction between two classes of men" (cf. *LK*, 181) is the amusing conceit that one of them is women.

MYSTICISM AND LOGIC, RAINBOW AND GRANITE, VISION AND FACT

Circumstances had long forced her, as they force most women . . . , to consider . . . that part of life which is conspicuously without order; . . . she had been forced to deny herself any contemplation of that other part of life. (*Night and Day*, 331)

It seems that a profound, impartial, and absolutely just opinion of our fellow-creatures is utterly unknown. Either we are men, or we are women. Either we are cold, or we are sentimental. Either we are young, or growing old. (Woolf, *Jacob's Room*, 71–2)

The ordinary and the analytic mind are the negation one of the other. One is rambling, vague, illogical, opens itself indiscriminately to the unpredictableness of sense-data but ultimately detaches itself from the immediate; it demonstrates "blankness of mind, . . . combined with profusion, mother wit, old wives' tales, haphazard ways, moments of astonishing daring, humour and sentimentality" (*JR*, 11). The other is sterile, precise, rigorous, formal, breaks things down into discrete units and orders them. The two classes of mind are so mutually exclusive that they illustrate Moore's theory of the group whose members possess a disjunctive property "in common." His example is a characteristically Bloomsbury one – the group that contains the two sexes:

It is as if we should say: The only property which belongs to every member of the human race and to nothing else is the disjunctive one of being *either* a man or a woman. All the men are men, and all the women are women: and nothing else in the Universe is *either* a man *or* a woman. So that each member of the human race, whether a man or a woman, does possess the disjunctive property of being *either* a man *or* a woman: *but* there is no other property which is both common and peculiar to them all. (*SomeMain*, 394–5)

Everywhere in Woolf the disjunctiveness of minds is asserted; everywhere she translates it in terms of the sexes: "'This is he' or 'This is she'" (TL, 190). "Wherever one looked men thought about women and thought differently" (*Room*, 30). "What she saw he didn't; what he saw she didn't" (*BA*, 26); "she belonged to the unifiers; he to the separatists" (*BA*, 118).

The two minds are a source of mutual annoyance and puzzlement; two gazes, one divided and the other intense, are repeatedly crossing blindly; "neither can experience the other's experiencing" (*TK*, 35), "two different notes, one high, one low, struck together" (*TL*, 61), sounds in counterpoint in their disagreement over the morrow's weather. Woolf presents their rivalry as the comic failure of two private worlds to find a public language. When Mr. and Mrs. Ramsay clash over the weather, Mr. Ramsay is irritated: "The extraordinary irrationality . . . , the folly of women's minds enraged him" (*TL*, 50). Later, seeing Lily Briscoe "gazing with her vague, now rather frightened eyes fixed where no house was," he "thought, women are always like that; the vagueness of their minds is hopeless . . . It had been so with her – his wife. They could not keep anything clearly fixed in their minds" (*TL*, 249). Similarly, "Fraser, the atheist," sitting opposite Miss Marchmont's falling pile of books in the British Museum, "abhorred vagueness" (*JR*, 105). Woman in "male society, cloistered rooms" (*JR*, 82) threatens to disturb the "exclusively masculine" (*ND*, 140) intellect, a cloistered room itself, with the mind's waywardness. Jacob's distractions in chapel are caused by feminine hats. Like the dog who "wanders down an aisle," women "destroy[] the service completely" (*JR*, 33). Florinda produces his "reversion" towards masculine society. "The problem is insoluble. The body is harnessed to a brain. Beauty goes hand in hand with stupidity" (*JR*, 81–2).

The irritation is reciprocated. Mrs. Ramsay "could not follow the ugly academic jargon, that rattled itself off so glibly" (*TL*, 22). Woolf's philosopher becomes subject, like the fat Hume sunk in a bog and forced by an old woman to recite the creed – a story recounted in Lytton Strachey and Leslie Stephen over which Mr. Ramsay chuckles (*TL*, 98, 111)[17] – to a chorus of female intelligences. They demonstrate "the crippling effect of Cambridge; and its one-sided education" (*MB*, 126), Mr. Ramsay's, as Leslie Stephen's, "dependence on women. . . to sympathize, to flatter, to console" (*MB*, 125).

Two warring principles, embodying, for all its social comedy, what Cambridge saw as two divisions of thought itself, rival "ways of knowing" (*ML*, 10), are seated symbolically at either end of the tabular object of knowledge: "there they were, he at one end of the table, she at the other, as usual" (*TL*, 297). These "two very different human impulses" Russell designates by the words "mysticism" and "logic," whose respective objects are the world of existence, "vague, without sharp boundaries," attracting the wooly mind, and that of universals, "delightful to the mathematician, the logician, the builder of metaphysical systems" (*PP*, 100). The lighthouse has a masculine and feminine version: it is a "silvery, misty-looking tower with a yellow eye" but also "the tower, stark and straight; . . . barred with black and white" (*TL*, 276–7). But Mrs. Ramsay also "was stern, she was searching, she was beautiful like that light" (*TL*, 97). Two lighthouses impose time's law, two clocks, Big Ben and St. Margaret's in *Mrs. Dalloway*, the first "laying down the law"

(*MrsD*, 193), presiding over the Houses of Parliament, the male domain of "Proportion," what *Three Guineas* labels "public"; the second presiding, like the hostess, over the social, also public. "According to our temperaments," Russell observes, "we shall prefer the contemplation of the one or of the other" (*PP*, 100).

Mysticism's first characteristic is "its belief in unity, and its refusal to admit opposition or division anywhere" (*ML*, 9). Thus Miss Marchmont's "philosophy – that colour is sound" presents a version of mysticism's proposition that all is one – "It all came into her philosophy" (*JR*, 108). Logic's atomism "denies" any "whole composed of" its atoms (*ML*, 106). "The essence of philosophy as thus conceived is analysis, not synthesis" (*ML*, 108). Its object is broken down into primitive elements, just as "the physicists cut up matter" (*ML*, 121). "Divide and conquer" is analysis' motto (*ML*, 108). Mysticism builds up "systems of the world, like Heine's German professor who knit together fragments of life and made an intelligible system"; logic aims at "the division of traditional problems into a number of separate and less baffling questions" (*ML*, 108).

A second characteristic of mysticism is "the belief in insight as against discursive analytic knowledge" (*ML*, 8). The lumping of "all the letters together in one flash" is such a "moment of insight" (*ML*, 8, 11). Science, by contrast, relies on "sense, reason, and analysis," regarded by mysticism "as blind guides leading to the morass of illusion" (*ML*, 9), on "the slower and more groping methods of the intellect" (*ML*, 15), "cautious and patient investigation" (*ML*, 11). Connected with mysticism's belief in "revelation or insight" (*ML*, 9) is "the conception of a Reality behind the world of appearance and utterly different from it" (*ML*, 9). The belief in unity, indeed, follows from "the mystic illumination," which is "the apparent revelation of the oneness of all things" (*ML*, 17). "[T]he moment of illumination" (*ML*, 9) is an experience of unity, like Mrs. Ramsay's at the dinner table (*ML*, 108).

The dichotomy between logic and mysticism is Woolf's "granite and rainbow," which also divides minds. "On the one hand there is truth" – "of granite-like solidity" – "on the other there is personality" – "of rainbow-like intangibility" (*CE*, IV, 229). Woolf's impersonal truth, like Russell's, is "cold and colourless" (*CE*, IV, 230). "Personality" is "coloured," as Leslie Stephen puts it, "by the predilections of each dreamer" ("WM?," 148). Leslie Stephen was "the very type . . . of so many Cambridge intellectuals," Woolf writes, "like a steel engraving, without colour, or warmth or body; but with an infinity of precise clear lines"; "other types," measured with "my Cambridge intellectual yard measure . . . fall short," yet "give me colour" (*MB*, 109). "I was afraid there would be a softness, & a fear of hard sharp outlines in your intellect," Russell writes Ottoline Morrell (Darroch, *Ottoline*, 106). For, "[l]ike the philosophers of ancient Greece," Russell said, "I prefer sharp outlines and definite separations" (*Portraits from Memory*, 38).

They are two kinds of vision. Vague seeing is suffused with color, veiled. Mr. Ramsay's blindness "to the ordinary" is compensated by his eagle-eye "to the extraordinary." It abstracts by turning off the organs of sense. "But did he notice the flowers? No. Did he notice the view? No" (*TL*, 107). He apprehends the logical scaffolding. "Naturally, if one's days were passed in this seeing of angular essences . . . (and it was a mark of the finest minds so to do), naturally one could not be judged like an ordinary person" (*TL*, 38). Yet the "eyeless" vision Woolf qualifies as also "mystic." Tyndall pronounces "the speculative faculty . . . will nevertheless wander into regions where the hope of certainty would seem to be entirely shut out" (*Essays*, 41). To reach his omega, the logician needs illumination: "attention wanders to such unimportant objects" as pure forms, Russell writes (*TK*, 133), themselves "fugitive to attention" (*TK*, 132). The "mystical way of feeling" is "the inspirer of what is best in Man" (*ML*, 11). What Woolf suggests, with hesitation and humor, as if it might not be the ultimate joke on Mr. Ramsay and Charles Tansley, is that in the search for truth, the philosophic mind also wanders. Does not the failure to differentiate underlie Russell's attempt to reduce images to sensations? Miss Marchmont's reduction of color to sound applies the principle of parsimony; after all, Tyndall "likened [daylight] to a noise" which "quenches the stars," whose "radiance" is "a whisper" (*Essays*, 37). For "what pitch is to the ear, colour is to the eye" (*Lectures on Light*, 54). Generalization uses vagueness, Russell suggests: a word is "vague" "when it is in fact applicable to a number of different objects because, in virtue of some common property, they have not appeared, to the person using the word, to be distinct" (*Mind*, 184).

Yet the mind's flight is not guaranteed to arrive at truth. Septimus too soars. Mrs. Ramsay's promise of the trip to the lighthouse is, at least temporarily, unfounded. At the same time, Mr. Ramsay's and Charles Tansley's meteoric predictions, although borne out by events, are uttered with a disregard for the limits of science's predictive power: "There wasn't the slightest possible chance that they would go to the Lighthouse tomorrow" (*TL*, 50). The humor directed at mystical thought divorced from reality in Woolf's ironic treatment of Cobden-Sanderson's "unity of the whole," whereby "Englishmen and Germans blowing each other's heads off in the trenches were . . . conspiring to 'create the great emotions which in turn create the greater emotions which in turn create the greater creation,'" is scarcely different from Russell's attitude:[18]

> Instead of becoming clearer, therefore, the vision, iterated and reiterated, becomes more and more nebulous, until after two volumes of explanation we are left asking, with Sister Edith: "But, Mr. Sanderson, how does one 'fly to the great Rhythm'? . . . What, in short, does the word Cosmos mean?' . . . by degrees the ideal got the upper hand. The sense of reality grew fainter. (*CE*, IV, 94–5)

There is a vagueness to be avoided, a flight that reaches no impersonal perspective, a logic which leads to absurdity, an Idealism that drowns out the world.

Via which method will knowledge be arrived at then? Cloistered Cambridge cannot alone attain full knowledge, reach the lighthouse. Is the shutting out of the world's interruptions "that receptivity to fact which is the essence of the scientific attitude towards the world" (*ML*, 103)? Is the glance bestowed from the express train without distinguishing son or wife (*TL*, 51–2) the triumph over vagueness? Mysticism's danger, Russell insists, is "the self-assertion of a confident reliance upon intuition" and not "that largeness of contemplation, that impersonal disinterestedness" (*ML*, 17) science aspires to – the impediment of the letter "I," not among the logician's symbols. Doubt having relieved the self of the egoism which blocks out the world, mysticism and logic can meet in both "union and conflict" (*ML*, 1).

FLIGHT AND RETURN: THE ANDROGYNOUS MIND

> This . . . was in fact the natural diffidence with which a person who acts from instinct regards the person who acts by logic – or professes to be so guided. You, it seems to such a one, have a theory and a rule and therefore you must have higher principles than I . . . Her [Julia Stephen's] instincts were far more to be trusted than my ratiocinations. (Stephen, *The Mausoleum Book*, 95)

Ever since I was engaged on *Principia Mathematica*, I have had a certain method of which at first I was scarcely conscious, but which has gradually become more explicit in my thinking. The method consists in an attempt to build a bridge between the world of sense and the world of science. I accept both as, in broad outline, not to be questioned. As in making a tunnel through an Alpine mountain, work must proceed from both ends in the hope that at last the labour will be crowned by a meeting in the middle. (Russell, *My Philosophical Development*, 151)

The old problem: how to keep the flight of the mind, yet be exact. (Woolf, *Diary*, V, 298)

The same differences that irritate also elicit that "pleasure" of the pre-war relations between the sexes regretted in *A Room of One's Own* and enjoyed in Woolf's 1921 encounter with Russell. Their dialogue is the sparring of rivals with mutual respect. The ideal is collaborative union. Leslie Stephen, in a characteristic Victorian vocabulary, wrote that "every man ought to be feminine, i.e. to have quick and delicate feelings; but no man ought to be effeminate, i.e. to let his feelings get the better of his intellect" (Annan, *Godless Victorian*, 304). Woolf parodies a similar passage from her father – "'exquisite sensibility . . . thoroughly masculine . . . feminine delicacy'" – to show his "very simply constructed view of the world" (*MB*, 115). Yet she retains the metaphor of an "alliance" in which each sex receives "something that their own sex was unable to supply . . . some stimulus, some renewal of creative power which is in the gift only of the opposite sex to bestow" (*Room*, 90). Woolf's metaphor of granite and rainbow makes "the aim . . . to weld these two into one seamless whole," yet "the problem is a stiff one" (*CE*, 229). The deficiency of the self alone which Leslie Stephen suggests could be corrected "if we could see the back of our heads as well as what lies in front of us" ("WM?," 137) Woolf formulates as a deficiency of one sex alone. "It is one of the good offices that sex can discharge for sex – to describe that spot the size of a shilling at the back of the head which one can never see for oneself" (*Room*, 94), that "dark place at the back of the head" of women men have been pointing out for centuries. "Think how much women have profited by the comments of Juvenal; by the criticism of Strindberg" (*Room*, 94), Woolf dryly observes. The comparable spot on men's heads women must point out.

Sexual union stands for the fruitful combination of two intellectual impulses. Russell speaks of a "marriage" of the mystic impulse wed to the empirical: "It is only in marriage with the world that our ideals can bear fruit: divorced from it, they remain barren. But marriage with the world is not to be achieved by an ideal which shrinks from fact, or demands in advance that the world shall conform to its desires" (*ML*, 7). For "the highest eminence, as I think, that it is possible to achieve in the world of thought," asserts the Russell of the liaison with Ottoline Morrell, is "the true union of the mystic and the man of science" (*ML*, 3). Biography, Woolf says, must have an "art subtle and bold enough to present that queer amalgamation of dream and reality, that perpetual marriage of granite and rainbow" (*CE*, IV, 235). Mrs. Ramsay tries to arrange a marriage of science and art in William Bankes, " 'the first scientist of his age, my husband says' " and Lily Briscoe, painter with "a scientific mind; . . . she was so exact" (*TL*, 261).

This intellectual union takes the form of two successive stages, at both of which mysticism is subjected to logic. The impulse is first liberated from " 'imprisonment in egotism,' " in the phrase of Fry's Woolf quotes (*RF*, 295), which exposes it to the world, as with Russell's escape from Idealism, for "insight, untested and unsupported, is an insufficient guarantee of truth, in spite of the fact that much of the most important truth is first suggested by its means" (*ML*, 11). The pure recording of data then undergoes logic's corrective analysis. The particulars the eye isolates are composed in a network of relations, erected into Russell's "fact," the eye's vision supplemented with an eyeless one. The "mush" Woolf indicates to Russell, with a wave of the hand around the dinner table, she says he "can . . . see through" (*Diary*, II, 146–7). Yet logical form is sterile without renewed contact with sense-data; the granite-like principle, "the strength of a man," stands in need of "a woman's grace" (*O*, 138). "Look," Rezia implores Septimus, for Dr. Holmes wanted him to "take an interest in things outside himself" (*MrsD*, 31). Logic requires what Woolf calls "the sense of reality" (*CSFVW*, 82). Woolf, Russell says, wants colors for her writing. We recall that facts preserve the realism of logic. As Russell explains, "the facts of science" must feed "the flame of the soul" (*ML*, 7). The inability to take in data renders Septimus' flights madness: "he could not taste, he could not feel . . . He could reason, . . . he could add up his bill; his brain was perfect; it must be the fault of the world then" (*MrsD*, 132–3). Led to leap from the private world, he nonetheless cannot escape the reality which is the ground of all truth; he returns to the earth which persists in his absence. (Ironically, once he does so,

Cobden-Sanderson's mystic belief that he was more related to the hills and the streams turns out to be flatly true; he becomes one with the shells and bones under the London streets Mrs. Dalloway thinks of.) Septimus' state is like Woolf's periods of madness, "illnesses" which she believes "are in my case – how shall I express it? – partly mystical. Something happens in my mind. It refuses to go on registering impressions. It shuts itself up. It becomes chrysalis. I lie quite torpid . . . Then suddenly something springs" (*Diary*, III, 287). Woolf pronounces them "the most fruitful artistically – one becomes fertilised" (*Diary*, III, 254).

Here the alliance must be precisely calibrated to achieve "the connection between her madness and her writing" Leonard calls "close and complicated" (*BeAg*, 81). The moth must emerge before the chrysalis smashes to earth. Its mad flight has the erratic pattern of the non-sequitur. Far from being that "passive place,"[19] as Russell terms it, the mind is in perception, and which "can be replaced by a photographic plate" (*Mind*, 130), the wandering mind provides the richness of hypothesis science requires. Its role is "to indulge impossible desires to embrace the whole world with the arms of understanding" (*W*, 114). "The essential, practical function of 'consciousness' and 'thought' is that they enable us to act with reference to what is distant in time and space, even though it is not at present stimulating our senses" (*Mind*, 292). Mrs. Ramsay's absent-mindedness, disengaging "while they were all talking about boots," "hover[ing] like a hawk suspended; like a flag float[ing] in an element of joy" (*TL*, 157), shows the mind's ability to absent itself from its immediate surroundings. Her musings about "a coherence in things," their being "immune from change" (*TL*, 158), have the features Russell ascribes to mysticism: the "belief in unity" (*ML*, 9), "the denial of division" and "the reality of time" (*ML*, 10). For "the whole effort of merging and flowing and creating rested on her. Again, she felt, as a fact without hostility, the sterility of men" (*TL*, 126). Her mystical flight is not allowed to lose contact with the world, however. Her openness to interruption obeys the principle of acquaintance. Unlike Septimus, her wool-gathering never cuts the thread attached to the world. Thought finds "anchorage in these thwarting currents of being" (*CE*, IV, 161). Russell, asserting that "the opposition of instinct and reason is mainly illusory," similarly makes logic the merely sterile corrective of mysticism: "Instinct, intuition, or insight is what first leads to the beliefs which subsequent reason confirms or confutes . . . Reason is a harmonising, controlling force rather than a creative one" (*ML*, 12). Condemned to come after insight; it lacks ideas of its own. "Even in the most purely logical realm," Russell writes, "it is insight that first arrives at what is new" (*ML*, 12). Analysis, beginning with that of sense-data, disciplines Russell's and Moore's original Hegelianism. So Mrs. Ramsay, filling the house via nature's fertility, needed, like George Eliot in Woolf's account of her, a steady arm to lean on while she muses, Lily accepts Mr. Bankes' scientific reaction to her painting, and the women in King's College Chapel are "vouched for by the theology, mathematics, Latin, and Greek of their husbands" (*JR*, 33).

The writer, the artist, who presents this dichotomy – between Mr. and Mrs. Ramsay, logician and mystic – does not ultimately choose between the two. Lily Briscoe, first painting Mrs. Ramsay, must finally confront Mr. Ramsay – the order is crucial. "One says, Anyhow Mrs Bell is a woman;" Woolf writes, "and then half way round the room one says, But she may be a man" (Antor, *The Bloomsbury Group*, 171). Despite "the unwomanly nature of the science" as "opposed to literature" (*ND*, 46) and art, neither way alone suffices to reach knowledge: "the greatest men who have been philosophers have felt the need both of science and of mysticism." It is "the attempt to harmonize the two" that "make[s] philosophy, to some minds, a greater thing than either science or religion" (*ML*, 1). This harmony is what Woolf illustrates with Coleridge's statement that great minds are androgynous. For the union of mysticism and logic is an incessant movement back and forth between the two modes.[20]

THE TRUE SELF

Our thoughts and fancies change and flicker, rise and vanish, while our bodies remain permanent objects of consciousness. (Stephen, "What is Materialism?," 153)

One's always first cousin to oneself, but the relationship is not much nearer. (J. M. Keynes to A. L. Hobhouse, in Skidelsky, *John Maynard Keynes*, I, 129)

He had no centre. (Woolf, *Roger Fry*, 295)

The mind's power to wander disconnects it from its own biography. The androgynous self floats free of its identity. "We are no longer quite ourselves" (*CE*, IV, 155). From the paring down of the "I" emerges what Russell and Woolf call "the real Self" (*PP*, 19) or "the true self," uncertain, by definition wandering. What is the nature of this separable thing exiled from its perspective home?

Woolf's fullest answers occur in *Orlando* and in "Street Haunting," where city walking becomes a metaphor for the self's activity.[21] In January the ghost-self imagines it is a June night;[22] in the street it imagines itself on a balcony:

> it is a winter's evening; we are walking to the Strand to buy a pencil. How, then, are we also on a balcony, wearing pearls in June? What could be more absurd? Yet it is nature's folly, not ours. When she set about her chief masterpiece, the making of man, she should have thought of one thing only. Instead, turning her head, looking over her shoulder, into each one of us she let creep instincts and desires which are utterly at variance with his main being, so that we are streaked, variegated, all of a mixture; the colours have run. Is the true self this which stands on the pavement in January, or that which bends over the balcony in June? Am I here or am I there? Or is the true self neither this nor that, neither here nor there, but something so varied and wandering that it is only when we give rein to its wishes and let it take its way unimpeded that we are indeed ourselves? (*CE*, IV, 160–1)

The passage is inspired by Shakespeare's Sonnet XX, addressed by the poet-speaker to the "master-mistress of [his] passion." Androgyny is its extended trope. Woolf's chameleon-like, rainbow self, wandering amid the city's "vast flocks of variegated feather," suggests Shakespeare's "man in hue, all hues in his controlling" (line 7); it too, like the young man of the sonnet, is "acquainted with shifting change, as is false women's fashion." The spectrum represents the range of its metamorphoses and explains why in the society of homosexuals one sees "the world tinged with all the colours of the rainbow" (*MB*, 172). Ultimately, rainbow is sexuality of any shade; granite, a sexless truth. The mixture of sexes in Shakespeare's young man is ascribed to the "addition" of "one thing to my purpose nothing" (line 12), what "prick'd" him "out for women's pleasure" (line 13). Thus Woolf's echoes of Sonnet XX attach her speculations on the self once more to the phallus, something both superfluous and counterposed to infinite variety: "one thing only" – i.e., that unchanging identity called "I." For Woolf blames nature for the mixing of sexes and the running of all colors into one, as does the sonnet: "And for a woman wert thou first created; / Till Nature, as she wrought thee fell a-doting" (lines 9–10). This doting nature is a woman endowed with Miss Marchmont's propensity to lump all together; instead of thinking "of one thing only," her mind wandered. Nature has the chameleon eye, like the young man's in the sonnet, "bright," "gilding the object whereupon it gazeth." But it is also like those insects who are "all eye," "drinking crimson until they became crimson; then flitting on to violet; then to a vivid green, and becoming for the moment the thing they saw" (*CE*, II, 234); like the "white wax" of children, it becomes "streaked and stained" (*W*, 241). The artist-maker of man, Nature, flitting from color to color, imparts, through her waywardness of thought, a wanderlust to her "masterpiece." "The march that the mind keeps beneath the windows of others is queer enough. Now distracted by brown panelling; now by a fern in a pot; here improvising a few phrases to dance with the barrel-organ; again snatching a detached gaiety from a drunken man; then altogether absorbed by words the poor shout across the street at each other" (*JR*, 95). Essentially changing, a shifting point of observation, this ghost-self's characteristic activity is "street haunting"; its prerequisite, the abandonment of privacy for the sequential occupation of different perspectives: "As we step out of the house on a fine evening between four and six, we shed the self our friends know us by and become part of that vast republican army of anonymous troupers, whose society is so agreeable after the solitude of one's own room" (*CE*, IV, 155).

In *Orlando*, this wanderer becomes a plurality of selves, conceived, Proust-like, as occupying different moments:[23]

For if there are (at a venture) seventy-six different times all ticking in the mind at once, how many different people are there not – Heaven help us – all having lodgement at one time or another in the human spirit? . . . these selves of which we are built up, one on top of another, as plates are piled on a waiter's hand, have attachments elsewhere, sympathies, little constitutions and rights of their own. (*O*, 308)

Or plurality is contradictory beliefs warring within a single individual. The "true self" has no singleness of purpose; "we come up differently, for ever and ever" (*W*, 114). For, Mrs. Ramsay repeats, "all the lives we ever lived / And all the lives to be, / Are full of trees and changing leaves" (*TL*, 178). They contain the world's mutabililty. *Orlando* is a Russellian biography. Its androgynous persona is "built up" of selves (*O*, 308).

Against this protean self Woolf sets "the Captain self, the Key self" (*O*, 310), "my central stability, otherwise so monstrously absurd as I breast the stream of this crowded thoroughfare, making always a passage for myself" (*W*, 114–15); it is "the conscious self, which is the uppermost, and has the power to desire, wishes to be nothing but one self" (*O*, 310):[24]

> That was her self – pointed; dartlike; definite. That was her self when some effort, some call on her to be her self, drew the parts together, she alone knew how different, how incompatible and composed so for the world only into one centre, one diamond, one woman who sat in her drawing-room and made a meeting-point, a radiancy. (*MrsD*, 55)

To the Captain Self falls reponsibility for "assembling that diamond shape, that single person" (*MrsD*, 56). For the series of selves is multi-faceted, the eye/lens's various surfaces assembling perspectives. Only in the moment are they fused into a whole. It perhaps supplies that "principle of selection" Russell was looking for. Perhaps also to it is attached name and identity. But Woolf imagines a "central stability": without either, in which "I do not remember my special gifts, or idiosyncrasy, or the marks I bear on my person, eyes, nose or mouth. I am not, at this moment, myself" (*W*, 114–15). Moreover, the Captain Self's power to unite has its limits. Death will be one such. "'I' shall not, if wishing can alter it, usurp Heaven too, and condemn us, who have played our parts here as William or Alice, to remain William or Alice forever" (*CE*, IV, 199).

THE SOLITARY TRAVELLER'S WANDERING AT THE END OF THE WORLD

> Window with falling snow is arrayed
> Long tolls the vesper bell,
> The house is provided well,
> The table is for many laid.
> Wandering ones, more than a few,
> Come to the door on darksome courses.
> (G. Trakl, cited in M. Heidegger, "Language," 210)

> Those "wayfarers" must first wander their way to house and table through the darkness of their courses; they must do . . . for the many, because the many think that if they only install themselves in houses and sit at tables, they are already bethinged, conditioned, by things and have arrived at dwelling. (Heidegger, "Language," 200)

> [H]ere is a chair, a table, glasses, knives, and thus we are boxed in and housed. (Woolf, *Collected Essays*, II, 297)

The subject's reduction has led it to that same vague fluidity at the perspective's edge that the pursuit of the table reached. Colorless, silent, odorless, untouchable, the phantom reality arrived at is drained of acquaintance's properties; it cannot be embraced, tasted, heard, seen. Russell's Realism built on solipsism propels the self into unfamiliar territory more effectively than Idealism. The intellectual exercise of imagining the unobserved table brings that sudden sense of isolation which comes to all thinkers. One finds oneself beyond the traffic, far from the mundane, alone thinking, "a soul reft of body" (*TL*, 237). At such moments, "belief in the unreality of the world of sense arises with irresistible force" (*OKnExW*, 55), and skepticism suggests "that the whole outer world is nothing but a dream, and that we alone exist" (*PP*, 17). The emancipation from present surroundings Mrs. Ramsay feels equally reveals a desert in which, Woolf writes, "anxiety & nothingness surround me with a vacuum" (*Diary*, V, 63). The flesh-and-blood wanderer evaporates, "a ghost among the chairs and tables," themselves ghostly (*TL*, 132). Not being able "to resist the extraordinary stimulus to range hither and thither in search of some absolute good, . . . remote from the known pleasures and familiar virtues, something alien to the processes of domestic life" (*TL*, 199), the philosophic mind finds itself "at sea," cut adrift from normal contact with chairs and tables.

This then is homeless thought's itinerary. The novels' landscape is criss-crossed with the tracks of lone figures: Rachel Vinrace on the Euphrosyne, "an inhabitant of the great world, which has so few inhabitants, travelling all day across an empty universe, with veils drawn before her and behind . . . more lonely than the caravan crossing the desert" (*VO*, 32); "the little company setting sail" in *To the Lighthouse* (241), one boat "rather apart from the others" (*TL*, 242), "the brown speck of Mr. Ramsay's sailing boat" (*TL*, 286); the street haunter; the sleepless, "the wakeful, the hopeful, walking the beach" in the night of "Time Passes" (*TL*, 198), who are also "[t]he mystic, the visionary" (*TL*, 197), connected by a thread to "the sleepers (the house was full again)" (*TL*, 213), as Peter Walsh's nap in Regent's Park is to the journey of "the solitary traveller" (*MrsD*, 85). In "Street Haunting" and in *Mrs. Dalloway*'s little "traveller's story brought from the heart of deep forests" (*ND*, 216), Woolf assigns these lone figures their full philosophical dimensions, tempered by a flickering humor at its exaggeration. Ultimately, the philosopher's "solitary wandering" (*ND*, 435) turns out to be the artist's, the novelist's also: "an odd road to be walking, this of painting. Out and out one went" (*TL*, 256).

The solitary traveller's journey occupies a time and place independent of *Mrs. Dalloway*'s sequence of hours, a nowhere in the interstices of Peter Walsh's two wakeful moments, presided over by the nurse knitting. It charts allegorically the dissociation from the moment. The traveller is, like Leslie Stephen, a great walker, like Russell and Moore, a pipe-smoker – may I "never knock out my pipe," he thinks (*MrsD*, 86) – and like Charles Tansley, Mr. Ramsay, Russell and even Mrs. Dalloway, "by conviction an atheist" (*MrsD*, 85). Like Peter Walsh, Clarissa Dalloway and Mrs. Ramsay, "he is elderly, past fifty now" (*MrsD*, 86). His is "the keen intellect, always voyaging . . . in ice-bound seas" in "the agony and loneliness of thought" (*MB*, 37).

The journey's trajectory shifts back and forth between two versions of reality and unreality, from the familiar "lamplight" and "sitting-room" with its chairs and tables (*MrsD*, 86), out to the world of ghostly objects and spectral presences, just as street haunting leaves behind in the room the objects "which express the oddity of our own temperaments and enforce the memories of our own experience" (*CE*, IV, 155). The route is the philosopher's, pondering, alternately, the existence and non-existence of the world outside the mind, for if existence is to be meaningfully asserted, its negation must be conceivable: "Nothing exists outside us except a state of mind, he thinks . . . But if he can conceive of her, then in some sort she exists, he thinks" (*MrsD*, 85). She exists, she does not exist – the world is taken from and restored to the thinker by a reasoning akin to the game of peek-a-boo we invoked in the beginning. This is the alternation between "separate moments of being" and of "non-being" (*MB*, 70), immediate experience and dissociation from it – "the thought of her being surrounded by the spaces of the night" while he is "constraining himself . . . to limit his thoughts to this one room" (*ND*, 192). It gives the abrupt shifts in perspective of the mind's flight, as in the movement to and fro in "The Lighthouse" from the boat, from which "Cam could see nothing," to the house: "She was thinking how all those paths and the lawn, thick and knotted with the lives they had lived there, were gone: were rubbed out; were past; were unreal, and now this was real; the boat and the sail . . . , the noise of the waves – all this was real" (*TL*, 248–9). From the perspective of "this," the invisible house is only restored "by description" – Mr. Ramsay has to correct Cam on its location with the compass.

The pattern has the voyage out into public spaces followed by a return to acquaintance's cozy solipsism; skepticism, provisional, relapses into belief. At Cambridge, once more "[a]ll the lights were coming out round the courts . . . The young men were now back in their rooms" (*JR*, 42). But there is always a risk of the journey being only one-way, of the vision in the dusk at journey's end "overpowering the solitary traveller and taking away from him the sense of the earth, the wish to return" (*MrsD*, 86). He only regains it within "the outer wall of security" Woolf complained the war had taken away (*Diary*, V, 299), "indoors among ordinary things" (*MrsD*, 87), the kitchen table there, "here the chair turned as we left it" (*CE*, IV, 166); the street haunter comes back to her "own doorstep again": "it is comforting to feel the old possessions, the old prejudices, fold us round; and the self, which has been blown about at so many street corners, which has battered like a moth at the flame of so many inaccessible lanterns, sheltered and enclosed" (*CE*, IV, 166). When the traveller's landlady "takes the marmelade" and "shuts it in the cupboard," she asks: "There is nothing more tonight, sir?" and the passage ends with the philosophical problem with which it began: "But to whom does the solitary traveller make reply?" (*MrsD*, 87–8). For what the lone thinker "exalted on a peak" (*CE*, IV, 195) above the world discovers is the world's disinterestedness, nature's impersonality. "There he stood their representative spokesman; their symbol; themselves; a butt, a clod, laughed at by looking-glasses; ignored by the cows, condemned by the clouds which continued their majestic rearrangement of the celestial landscape; an irrelevant forked stake in the flow and majesty of the summer silent world" (*BA*, 190–1). The private world is that stake in the midst of the waves.

Hence the solitary traveller's atheism, Mr. Ramsay's in the bow of the boat, "as if he were saying, 'There is no God,' . . . as if he were leaping into space" (*TL*, 236), like Leslie Stephen hanging over a ledge in "A Bad Five Minutes in the Alps," thinking of dinner, and presumably the dinner table, going on without him. Suicide – or any death confronted and accepted – is conceived as a solitary flight into nothingness, like Septimus' leap, or the young Virginia Stephen's. "Human beings do not go hand in hand the whole stretch of the way" (*CE*, IV, 196). The last stretch they must travel alone. The sick ask for sympathy, "But sympathy we cannot have" (*CE*, IV, 195). "We perished, each alone," Mr. Ramsay shouts, expressing "that loneliness which was" for James and him, "the truth about things" (*TL*, 301). The words "Perished" and "Alone" Lily hears mixed with "Going to the Lighthouse" (*TL*, 219–20): someone perishes alone going to the lighthouse. "*Dispersed are we*," the chorus echoes in *Between the Acts* (95). The mind in the healthy body wanders fearlessly because it can return, like the traveller to the house with the table laid, to common-sense belief. But, ultimately, it knows, there is no return.

THE SNOWFIELD OF THE MIND AND THE WORLD'S ANNIHILATION IN SNOW

> The environment may be a field of snow, an Alpine slope . . . It represents pure exteriority, radical spatiality; its undifferentiation, its monotony, and its whiteness manifest this absolute nudity of substance. (Sartre, *Being and Nothingness*, 742–3)

> [I]f we cannot be sure of the independent existence of objects, we shall be left alone in a desert. (Russell, *The Problems of Philosophy*, 17)

In "On Being Ill," Woolf takes the mind in the sick body, wrapt in the narcissism of its own pain, impervious to sense-data, as emblematic of the self's isolation. The metaphor Woolf there uses is that of someone moving "across leagues of snow and desert" (*CE*, IV, 194). The landscape traversed is the analogue of the subject's isolation. The snowfall represents the world obliterated, perhaps still there but no longer accessible to the senses. It presents a trackless whiteness, a muffled silence. It is "that snowfield of the mind, where man has not trodden" (*CE*, IV, 198). "In the solitude of the bedrooms" (*CE*, IV, 194), the sick are alone, "solitary amid nothing," in Whitehead's phrase (*SMW*, 86). The lone explorer penetrates "the blankness in the heart of his vision" (*ND*, 423). The world has become "a skeleton world and blankness alone remained" (*ND*, 412); "the things that existed were so immense and desolate" (*VO*, 125); "silence closes over our transient passage" (*W*, 55). "The snow, which had been falling all night" in *Jacob's Room* creates a stark relief: "Uncompromising was the severity of the country" (98).

This blank severity is recognizable as the world of physics – the snowfield is only an alternate for the unbroken expanse of the sea whose waves represent the ultimate reduction of matter. "[V]ery few people thought about the sea" – "[f]or all they imagined, the ships when they vanished on the sky-line dissolved, like snow in water" (*VO*, 31–2). Snow is the absence of color and sound. And the "desolate expedition across the icy solitudes of the Polar region" (*TL*, 54), like those of the Alpinist Tyndall investigating the glaciers, figures the philosophical quest. Mr. Ramsay pushing on to R is this expedition's "leader, the guide" (*TL*, 54) who, "now that the snow has begun to fall and the mountain top is covered in mist, knows that he must lay himself down and die before morning comes" (*TL*, 55); "his mind was scaling the highest pinnacles of his alps, where there was only starlight and untrodden snow" (*ND*, 69, 260) just as "her mind made excursions into the dark of the air, or settled upon the surface of the sea, which could be discovered over there, or with equal unreason it returned to its couch of bracken beneath the stars of midnight, and visited the snow valleys of the moon" (*ND*, 434).

Thought leads to uncharted territory within as well as without, to the discovery of "the dark, the slumberous shapes in her mind" (*ND*, 214). "There is a virgin forest in each; a snowfield where even the print of birds' feet is unknown" (*CE*, IV, 196). Its deep interior is untouched, not yet penetrated, virginal like Mrs. Dalloway's bed, like Lily Briscoe's canvas, "stark and uncompromising" (*TL*, 234). Interior emptiness only reflects the world without *I* at its center, as when Lily Briscoe "looked blankly at the canvas" and it returns "its uncompromising white stare" (*TL*, 234), with "[t]he blankness of the white table-cloth" that "glares" (*W*, 118). Or Mr. Ramsay's intellectual quest's alpine topography ends up "paling the colour of his eyes, giving him . . . the bleached look of withered old age" (*TL*, 55). These pale eyes, "fixed on the storm" and trying "to pierce the darkness," are directed to the letters P, Q, R, those stark symbols of a truth drained of the sensible world's reassuring features. His eyes only reflect their colorlessness, like that of the unpainted deal table, which he looks at "until his face . . . partook of this unornamented beauty" (*TL*, 232).

"No echo comes back," Woolf wrote during the war. "I have no surroundings. I have so little sense of a public . . . Those familiar circumvolutions – those standards – which have for so many years given back an echo & so thickened my identity are all wide & wild as the desert now" (*Diary*, V, 299). This thinning of self Mr. Ramsay achieves on his way at last to the lighthouse, undergoing the inevitable paring away, "whether he wished it or not" able "suddenly to shed all superfluities, to shrink and diminish so that he looked barer and felt sparer, even physically, yet lost none of his intensity of mind" (*TL*, 68). He had, in that "final phase," "shed the hope of sympathy and the desire for praise, had entered some other region . . . at the head of that little procession out of one's range" (*TL*, 233). Lily Briscoe reaches the same selfless state, "losing consciousness of outer things . . . and her name and her personality and her appearance" while "her mind kept throwing up from its depths, scenes, and names, and sayings, and memories and ideas . . . over that glaring, hideously difficult white space" of her painting (*TL*, 238). The voyage out enters "the sunless territory of non-identity. . . beyond this circle of bright light" (*W*, 116).

THE FACELESS FACE

Down there my eyes are the lidless eyes of a stone figure in a desert by the Nile. (Woolf, *The Waves*, 12)

The annihilated world casts its lunar light on its observer's face, and the face returns the blank look. The white and frozen world's mirror is the faceless face. It masks the city's "anonymous trampers": "Blank expectant faces stare at us as we rattle and flash through stations" (*W*, 111). "The roar of the traffic, the passage of undifferentiated faces, this way and that way, . . . rubs the features from faces" (*W*, 113). The face become featureless loses exactly those sense organs which maintain contact with the world, faces of sleepers with "shut eyes" (*TL*, 191) and babies asleep: "the perfectly smooth eyelids fitted over their eyes as if they sealed them completely" (*Y*, 196). "He looked at the sleeping baby with its eyes sealed and its thumb in its mouth" (*Y*, 198). The infant face has its counterpart in age: "How terrible old age was, she thought, shearing off one's faculties, one by one" (*Y*, 125). The old woman selling violets in *The Years* is such an image of living death, with the knowledge of accumulated experience at the quick, but no way to receive new impressions: "She wore a hat over her face . . . She had no nose; her face was seamed with white patches; there were red rims for nostrils. She had no nose – she had pulled her hat down to hide the fact" (*Y*, 190). Mrs. McNab too had her faculties "sheared off": she "leered (for her eyes fell on nothing directly . . .)"; she was "toothless" (*TL*, 196). This vague contact with sense-data is the philosopher Ramsay's, "born blind, deaf and dumb, to the ordinary things" (*TL*, 107).

The faceless face is also robbed of those identifying "features," "marks I bear on my person, eyes, nose or mouth" (*W*, 115). "I am nobody" because "I have no face" (*W*, 197). The old woman's is "the voice of no age or sex"; a woman – "for she wore a skirt" – but otherwise unidentifiable as such (*MrsD*, 122). Memory, identity are erased: "I cannot remember my past, my nose, or the colour of my eyes" (*W*, 113). Facelessness becomes the androgynous "true self"'s very lack of identity. "Hume's inability to perceive himself was not peculiar, and I think most unprejudiced observers would agree with him. Even if by great exertion some rare person could catch a glimpse of himself, this would not suffice," Russell observes (*TK*, 36). "We cannot see our face (except the nose, by squinting) or our head or our back," he writes (*Matter*, 201). Russell is no doubt thinking of Mach's drawing of the subject, nothing more than the unrecognizable bridge of a nose "seen without a head" (*Contributions*, 16, Fig. 1, see Fig. 4), or rather what "I" sees if it closes its right eye: "[I]n a frame formed by the ridge of my eyebrow, by my nose, and by my moustache, appears a part of my body, so far as is visible, with its environment" (Mach, *Contributions*, 15). There is, Russell writes, a "distinction between things of which I am aware – for instance, between the things I see before my eyes and the things behind my back" (*TK*, 31). Among the latter is the back of my own head, that epitome of an unobserved space within the self for Leslie Stephen and Woolf. Strangely, however, apart from mirrored images, one's own face is equally invisible to oneself as the back of one's head.

The unidentifiable face, like those "pale faces" which "rise to the surface" out of the ghostly waves in the solitary traveller's vision (*MrsD*, 86), is the source of terror but also of a strange beauty, the Greek beauty of classical statues with "blank eyes" (*W*, 171), like Jacob Flanders', "statuesque, noble, and eyeless" (*JR*, 170). It is abstract, universal and unchanging, a symbol. "Let these odd men and women . . . be symbols, – featureless but dignified, symbols of age, of youth, of motherhood, of learning" (*VO*, 37). Such are the anonymous lovers glimpsed at *The Years*' beginning and end, first by Delia (17), then by Eleanor (348), or the couple which disappears in a London taxi at *A Room of One's Own*'s conclusion, symbol of the writer's mind, which must "celebrate its nuptials in darkness" (108). The couple from which springs the multiplicity of life has the same severe, classical beauty with "the undifferentiated features" of De Quincy's portraits (*CE*, IV, 5) whose "power lay in suggesting . . .

faces without features" (*CE*, IV, 3). This deliberate omission of features marks a series of portraits Vanessa Bell did of Woolf in 1914 (see figures 5 and 8).[25] The classical face is also timeless. Seeing "two people without faces, leaning like statues against the sky" induces Rhoda's vision of a sphere which "partook of eternity" (*W*, 249): "I find faces rid of features, robed in beauty . . . There is then a world immune from change" (*W*, 249). This immobile monumentality is that of the dead, of Woolf's mother long dead; living, "[s]he was not so rubbed out and featureless, not so dominated by the beauty of her face" (*MB*, 85).

Facelessness becomes a link to the inhuman world. The colorlessness of the waves surrounding the pinpoints of privacy washes away their particularity at the margins, the biographies' beginnings and the terminations: "All faces – Greek, Levantine, Turkish, English – would have looked much the same in that darkness" (*JR*, 162) surrounded by "the faces of the tall blind houses" (*JR*, 163); "large faces and lean ones, the powdered and the hairy, all alike were red in the sunset" (*JR*, 174). The "old blind woman" (*JR*, 67) and the old woman with "a mouth" only "a mere hole" (*MrsD*, 123) blend with the unoccupied past: an "ancient song" "issued" from it (*MrsD*, 122). An unconscious nature speaks through the empty face, unseeing mirror of "Time Passes"'s "fields wide-eyed and watchful" but unseeing (*TL*, 198), with their "flowers . . . looking before them, looking up, yet beholding nothing, eyeless, and so terrible" (*TL*, 203). This blind world the thinker-wanderer traverses: "'Where do I wander?' she mused. 'Down what draughty tunnels? Where the eyeless wind blows? And there grows nothing for the eye.' All has been levelled by thought. 'All's equal there'" (*BA*, 154–5).

Consciousness, contracted to a vacant eye, surrounded by the absence of all sense-data, fails to receive the echo which "thickens" the ego. "As silence falls I am dissolved utterly and become featureless and scarcely to be distinguished from another" (*W*, 224–5). But the shearing of faculties "leav[es] something alive in the centre" (*Y*, 125), a conscious core wrapt within cotton wool like "the swathed figure in the hairdresser's shop" (*W*, 284). In a world "with all the lamps put out," as in "Time Passes" (*TL*, 189), insomniac consciousness lies wide awake, like "lidless eyes"; or muffled sounds reach the ear which can never close of the sleeper who can neither see, speak, move nor act upon the world. This state is the terrifying side of the rapture of dissociation from the moment. "I've had no ears, eyes, or nose," Woolf describes an impending mental breakdown (*Diary*, V, 22). Above all, it is expressed in the "eyeless . . . face" (*W*, 131). Sight concentrating all senses, eyelessness becomes the essence of facelessness, detaching the self within from the world outside, making it the nexus of a quivering life without identity, a point of naked awareness. In the empty eyes of the faceless the beholder catches the flicker of unextinguished consciousness, something vestigial within, sealed off entry, Leslie Stephen's Cartesian "soul looking on from a pineal gland or elsewhere" ("WM?," 147), "shrink[ing] to an extensionless point" like the subject of the *Tractatus* (5.64). The eyeless face is the mirror of sensibilia given to no one, like pupils glassily, thoughtlessly, reflecting, like those of Mr. Ramsay, looking up from his book – "it was not to see anything" (*TL*, 283). Applied by Woolf to the Apostles' "doctrines" (*RA*, 52), eyelessness is linked to abstractness, to the unobserved, to Tyndall's "obscure map" (*On Radiation*, 13) and "non-visual waves" (*Lectures on Light*, 128), to what does not need the human to persist in existing.

Finally, in the loss of contact with external reality, subjectivity sees itself become "part of nature, a thing" (*ML*, 41), transformed into a skeletal physical object, a skull with empty sockets, its terror frozen and silent, "that blank and brutal face" of the dead Percy, "abstract, facing me eyeless at the end of the avenue" (*W*, 154), terrifying like the figure embodying the solitary traveller's destination. For we have arrived at "the margin of [the] mind" where Miss LaTrobe notes: "This is death" (*BA*, 180), its logic's ultimate conclusion.

CHAPTER 5

The dualism of death

> [I]f my body could remain in exactly the same state in which it is, although my mind had ceased to exist, precisely that object which I now see . . . would exist, although of course I should not see it, since my seeing is mental.
>
> (Russell, *Mysticism and Logic*, 125)

> But I now made the contribution of maturity to childhood's intuitions – satiety and doom; the sense of what is inescapable in our lot; death; the knowledge of limitations; how life is more obdurate than one had thought it.
>
> (Woolf, *The Waves*, 268–9)

> . . . as if the sun were sinking. Often that image comes to me with some sense of my physical state being colder now, the sun just off one; the old disc of one's being growing cooler – but it is only just beginning: & one will turn cold & silver like the moon.
>
> (Woolf, *Diary* III, 196)

Philosophical speculation has brought the thinker to the edge of the private world where the prospect, like Andrew's, peering into the future of "Time Passes," is "almost too dark to see" (*TL*, 189). The goal is now to leave one's perspective and imaginatively project oneself into other perspectives, even the *possible* ones inhumanly unoccupied, to experience the world as it would be without the thinker.

Via such reasoning, Woolf is led to the idea of death. This conclusion takes her thinking beyond Cambridge philosophy to that omega Mr. Ramsay's reasonings never reach, "the end of the corridor of years" (*TL*, 260), the "long corridor of sleep" (*RF*). Death, pronounced by Wittgenstein "not an event in life" (*Tractatus*, 6.4311, 72), almost the last word of *The Waves*, is the ultimate name for those future perspectives the self will not occupy. There are "under D, [many] ways of naming death" (*W*, 291) – as physical suffering, as violence and bloodshed, as emotional loss, as chance, as fate. Woolf's characteristic conception of death is the separation of subject and object, the possibility of one observing nothing and the other existing unobserved. Death is one name for their independence.

Death and the unobserved became associated at an early moment in Woolf's psychic history. She recounts a childhood memory in which "I overheard my father or my mother say that Mr Valpy had killed himself":

> The next thing I remember is being in the garden at night and walking on the path by the apple tree. It seemed to me that the apple tree was connected with the horror of Mr Valpy's suicide. I could not pass it. I stood there looking at the grey-green creases of the bark – it was a moonlit night – in a trance of horror. I seemed to be dragged down, hopelessly, into some pit of absolute despair from which I could not escape. (*MB*, 71)

The tree's grey-green creased bark identifies it with the pear tree in which Lily Briscoe sees the phantom table upside down like an inverted negative image. So the unobserved table, the empty perspective, is linked to death. Science's vision, along with a social vision that emerges from the war, answers a need of the personal history – Lily Briscoe, seeing Mrs. Ramsay "putting her wreath to her forehead," "sought something to base her vision on" (*TL*, 270). That something – table or dead mother – is an absence that escapes all intimate acquaintance. Bernard sees Percival's death as creating an empty center: "About him my feeling was: he was there at the centre. Now I go to that spot no longer. The place is empty" (*W*, 153). Such is the empty house which survives the deaths – Mrs. Ramsay's, Prue Ramsay's in childbirth, Andrew Ramsay's in the war – in "Time Passes"; such the drawing room steps on which Mrs. Ramsay's absence makes "a centre of complete emptiness" (*TL*, 265); such, the empty rooms through which the light passes in *The Waves*, with their vestiges of human habitation, in which "the blind stirred slightly" in "the bedroom window" in the morning, the table is set at midday and in the evening, but no one comes; such, Jacob's empty room at the end of the novel: "He left everything just as it was . . . What did he expect? Did he think he would come back? . . . Listless is the air in an empty room, just swelling the curtains; the flowers in the jar shifts. One fibre in the wicker armchair creaks, though no one sits there" (*JR*, 176). Only the unconscious furniture persists.

Figure 5. Vanessa Bell, portrait of Virginia Woolf.

Death, marked by the dualism of subject and object, becomes the ultimate argument against Idealism, demonstrating the "egoism" of its doctrine of internal relations, "that illusion of a world so shaped that it echoes every groan, of human beings so tied together by common needs and fears that a twist at one wrist jerks another, where however far you travel in your own mind someone has been there before you" (*CE*, IV, 196), Mr. Ramsay's illusion, "thinking that if his little finger ached the whole world must come to an end" (*TL*, 54), that his pain reverberates throughout the world. But each particular, we remember, "stands entirely alone." Idealism maintains a perfect coincidence between self and world. Mortality enters under the guise of a lag between the two: one might cease short of the other. The mind is not all-encompassing: there exists a mindless world in which something survives. Death is in this sense the end of illusion Miss La Trobe leads her audience to in *Between the Acts*: her empty stage is the world seen without the self. If death is the separation of subject and object, experience's very privacy is a kind of death, for "wherever I seat myself I die in exile" (*JR*, 69). "Whether I'm in Cambridge or Iceland or dead, the cow will be there" (Forster, *The Longest Journey*, 1). The skull is the death's head, the reality under the veil. The "skeleton is wrapped in flesh" (*JR*, 162); its truth eventually will out. Despite the shawl, Mrs. Ramsay succumbs to "the perfectly indifferent chill night air" (*TL*, 173). Septimus' ravings come true: "Scientifically speaking, the flesh was melted off the world" (*MrsD*, 102). As reality, the deaths that shaped Woolf's biography were also the sign for her of life's authenticity:

> I would reason, or fancy, that if life were thus made to rear and kick, it was at any rate, the real thing. Nobody could say that I had been fobbed off with an unmeaning slip of the precious matter. So I came to think of life as something of extreme reality. And this, of course, increased my feeling of my own importance. Not in relation to human beings: in relation to the force which had respected me sufficiently to make me feel what was real. (*MB*, 118)

In the debate between Realism and Idealism it is not Berkeley who disturbs a reassuring universe; it is the possibility of things or persons outlasting the subject. "For it was extraordinary to think that they had been capable of going on living all these years when she had not thought of them more than once all that time" (*TL*, 132). Alternatively, the subject may remain a node of awareness after the world has ceased to be, in the form of a longing, a "want" Woolf calls "the old horror" (*TL*, 300). Death means either the absence of the living subject in an enduring world where it is decreed "There Self must die," as Russell writes (*ML*, 50), or it is the condemnation of thought to a ghost-like wandering above the world's wastes, freed from its sense-data, from the body, from life, for "Here we go alone, and like it better so" (*CE*, IV, 196). Death is both the death of the self and the annihilation of the world. By this logic, the mind is led via the twin analyses of matter and mind to contemplate the two faces of death, from the blankness of the eyeless gaze to the blankness of world. The road to knowledge passes "through the valley of death" (*TL*, 49).

CROSSING THE THRESHOLD

Life is as I've said since I was 10, awfully interesting – if anything, quicker, keener at 44 than 24 – more desperate I suppose, as the river shoots to Niagara – my new vision of death; active, positive, like all the rest, exciting; & of great importance – as an experience. (Woolf, *Diary*, III, 117)

[T]here is a cavern of darkness to be traversed. (Russell, *Mysticism and Logic*, 50)

Death as a destination of knowledge is an object of acquaintance or description. It is the experience of dying that acquaintance makes its object. Death is the type of the private event "the experience" of which "cannot be imparted" (*CE*, IV, 195). Death is the irreducibly strange experience – "one could not get over the strangeness of it" (*CE*, I, 360), "how unbelievable death was!" (*MrsD*, 135). The "other people" who have had it are no longer "people" who can impart it – "if they knew, could they tell one what they knew?" (*TL*, 78). "The insignificant little creature now knew death," the "I" of "The Death of the Moth" comments of a presumed knowledge she does not share, "moved . . . strangely" by the struggle of "an insignificant little moth . . . to retain what no one else valued or desired to keep" (*CE*, I, 361). It knows death by acquaintance, aware of crossing a threshold without return, "cross[ing] the river of death this way and that incessantly" (*JR*, 109), grasping at the transition between present and past, like Mrs. Ramsay pausing as "she passed through the door" Augustus Carmichael held open for her. The intervals between perspectives disconnecting subject and object are so many little deaths. One plunges into the "abyss between oneself and others" (*VO*, 36). It is in this space of dissolution that the self, already thinned to a shadow, tries to grasp its final experience, applying to it the demonstrative that indicates an object of acquaintance: "A blank intervened; her thoughts became spaced; . . . This is sleep, she said to herself, half opening her eyes" (*Y*, 271). "This is death, death, death, she noted in the margin of her mind" (*BA*, 180). "Oh! thought Clarissa, in the middle of my party, here's death . . . Always her body went through it first, when she was told, suddenly, of an accident; her dress flamed, her body burnt" (*MrsD*, 279–80). But the threshold experience both wished for and feared eludes the spectre self; a blank in the text intervenes, that break between chapters XVII and XVIII in "The Window," for instance, or the one at the Solitary Traveller's return, when Peter Walsh "woke with extreme suddenness, repeating to himself a phrase out of the past, 'The death of the soul' " (*MrsD*, 88), unable to bring back an account from sleep. No subject who encounters death has the opportunity to translate its privacy into knowledge by description. " 'The one experience I shall never describe' I said to Vita yesterday," Woolf writes (*Diary*, III, 117). For the living, like pre-history, it is like glimpsing time as it passes, the movement of the arrow between "The Window," occupied by Mrs. Ramsay, and "The Lighthouse" she never reaches. For between perspectives there is no experience, only the waves' nothingness.

"The co-operative imagination of mankind" (*CE*, IV, 198) can only imagine a heavenly utopia peopled by ordinary things, only "adumbrate little interviews with celebrated people on the tufts of thyme" and "speculate thus carnally" (*CE*, IV, 199). Imagining death is a solitary exercise, the thought experiment philosophy has made us familiar with it: thinking of the kitchen table when you're not there. Mrs. Dalloway's reflections in the crowded London streets practice it: "did it matter that she should cease completely; all this must go on without her" (*MrsD*, 12). "What would the world be . . . without 'I' in it?" Martin wonders in *The Years* (242). This also is the theme of Bernard's thoughts on Percival's death:

> This then is the world that Percival sees no longer. Let me look. The butcher delivers meat next door; two old men stumble along the pavement; sparrows alight. The machine then works; I note the rhythm, the throb, but as a thing in which I have no part, since he sees it no longer. (*W*, 153)

In this sense, Woolf's novels set up a series of imaginary approximations of the fact that "I" must die, peering across that Acheron where subjectivity is shed. Quentin Bell writes that Woolf felt it "odd to be living in a world that did not contain" her brother (*VW*, I, 112). This very oddness Woolf's art aims to capture through the representation of certain mental states ressembling dying in all but its permanence. The process of falling asleep, illness, philosophical analysis itself, approximate the awareness of the passage from one state to another. Only in that "forlorn solitude" in which one is placed by philosophy, by illness, by hanging over a ledge or nodding to sleep over a book or on a park bench, by the passing of funerals in crowded streets, "to which men, thus suddenly reminded of the passing of their own bodies, lifted their hats" (*Room*, 100), do these intimations come.

FALLING ASLEEP

When my perceptions are removed for any time, as by sound sleep; so long am I insensible of myself, and may truly be said not to exist. And were all my perceptions remov'd by death, and cou'd I neither think, nor feel, nor see . . . , I shou'd be entirely annihilated, . . . a perfect non-entity. (Hume, *A Treatise of Human Nature*, Bk. I, iv, Sect. 6, 252)

Strange spectacles meet us everywhere in a period of speculative fermentation, when men's thoughts are heaving and working they know not why, and their minds, like those half-aroused sleepers, are unable to distinguish between dreams and perceived realities. (Stephen, *An Agnostic's Apology*, 86)

[T]imes when we are sleeping pass almost as if they did not exist. (Russell, *The Problems of Philosophy*, 32)

We begin with that state in which "I" am "dead to the world." Sleep is unconsciousness; Jacob "fast asleep" is "profoundly unconscious" (*JR*, 14). Indeed, Russell makes sleep the paradigm case of unconsciousness: "What is the relation we call being 'conscious of' something? Take the difference between a person awake and a person asleep. The former reacts to all kinds of stimuli to which the latter does not react; we therefore say that the latter is not 'conscious of' what is happening in his neighborhood" (*OP*, 219). So, in sleep, the sleeper becomes an object, like the table, looks to observers "far from them, rapt in the calm that sometimes gives the sleeper the look of the dead" (*Y*, 379).

The process of falling asleep allows the one soon to be unconscious a glimpse of him or herself become an object: "Being tired, her mind still rising and falling with the sea, the taste and smell that places have after long absence possessing her, the candles wavering in her eyes, . . .[Lily Briscoe] had lost herself and gone under" (*TL*, 222). In the process of falling asleep contact with the world of sense diminishes and the distance between subject and object widens. It is therefore akin to the perception of distant or receding objects and the phenomenon of "immediate memory." Before consciousness is completely extinguished, the world of the awake continues distantly present to the mind loosening its hold on it, the distance between self and world becomes perceptible. The drowsy, dozing consciousness is dimly aware of sight and sound. Typically such passages present the familiar collection of sense-data becoming sensibilia. Then the lids droop, the ears hear muffled sounds, until the world is eclipsed.

Such is Lady Lasswade's falling asleep in *The Years*, which coincides with the movement of the train she is on. What her eyes perceive just before dropping off are receding sense-data; seemingly cut off from her as observer, they are converted into sensibilia: "Then she saw the tea-urn sliding past" (*Y*, 269). Their appearance of moving gives to the objects receding from consciousness an independent existence. The structural division in *The Years* between the shifting points of view within chapters – "other people's sense data" – and the impersonal descriptions of the chapter openings – sensibilia – (similar to *The Waves*' interludes) underscores this. For in a chapter opening's unoccupied perspective, the generalized description of "[t]ravellers" in the railroad stations shows us the tea-urn sliding by with no onlooker: "Now the guard standing with his hand raised dropped his flag and the tea-urn slid past" (*Y*, 192–3). The landscape, repository of sensibilia, rushing by the sleeper's window, assumes the alien quality it has in the interludes: "Elongated lights slid past; lights in factories and warehouses; lights in obscure back streets" (*Y*, 270). It recedes, and in the brief transition the world without the sleeper is glimpsed, like "a pool at evening, far distant, seen from a train window, vanishing so quickly that" it "is scarcely robbed of its solitude, though once seen" (*TL*, 195). Then the annihilation of consciousness is complete, if not permanent, while time and sensibilia continue rushing past the window. "We were extinguished for a moment" (*W*, 27).

The intervening interval occupied by Kitty Lasswade's sleep is represented by a blank in the text, as if the fictional world had also ceased to exist. This is how it seems to the sleeper, but not what the whole novel suggests. Elsewhere in Woolf, a character's falling asleep is the occasion for describing the world without the sleeping self. So "Lady Bruton went ponderously, majestically, up to her room, lay one arm extended, on the sofa. She sighed, she snored, not that she was asleep, only drowsy and heavy, like a field of clover in the sunshine this hot June day," thinking of "[t]hose kind fellows, Richard Dalloway, Hugh Whitbread," with whom she has just lunched, and who "had gone this hot day through the streets whose growl came up to her lying on the sofa" (*MrsD*, 168–9). She dozes, while the text presents to us their simultaneous existence far from her, never threatened by her temporary extinction in a snore.

> And they went farther and farther from her, being attached to her by a thin thread (since they had lunched with her) which would stretch and stretch, get thinner and thinner as they walked across London; as if one's friends were attached to one's body, after lunching with them, by a thin thread, which (as she dozed there) became hazy with the sound of bells, striking the hour or ringing service, as a single spider's thread is blotted with raindrops, and, burdened, sags down. So she slept.
>
> And Richard Dalloway and Hugh Whitbread hesitated on the corner of Conduit Street at the very moment that Millicent Bruton, lying on a sofa, let the thread snap; snored. (*MrsD*, 170)

The "thread of vital light" (*CE*, I, 360) is consciousness itself, attached by immediate memory to the receding lunch guests, by sensation to the sounds of afternoon; its stretching and unwinding measures the increasing distance of sleeper from world. The sagging filament stands between acquaintance and total annihilation.

Peter Walsh's nap in Regent's Park is a similar severance from a world which continues around his inert body. The tablet of his mind, receiver of sense impressions, is erased by sleep. In the moment of erasure, the collection of sense-data flashes by: "A great brush swept smooth across his mind, sweeping across it moving branches, children's voices, the shuffle of feet, and people passing, and humming traffic, rising and falling traffic. Down, down he sank into the plumes and feathers of sleep, sank, and was muffled over" (*MrsD*, 84–5). The text moves outside his obliterated thoughts to the nurse, "the champion of the rights of sleepers," beside him, who "resumed her knitting, as Peter Walsh, in the hot seat beside her, began snoring" (*MrsD*, 85). Time continues to pass, but the thread of life connecting sleeper to world, like "that sound, that string" – "[g]igantic" – which, "when Big Ben struck," jerked the old lady at the window (*MrsD*, 192), is finally cut. Clarissa Dalloway, Peter Walsh, Lady Bruton, all subside at midday, amidst sense-data, Peter Walsh reduced to an object on a park bench, while the solitary traveller is released.

The process of awakening is the mirror image of falling asleep. It is felt as the return of sense-data, first of sound (for the ears have remained open): "before waking, the voices of birds and the sound of wheels chime and chatter in a queer harmony, grow louder and louder, and the sleeper feels himself drawing to the shores of life, the sun growing hotter, cries sounding louder" (*MrsD*, 104). So the world returns to the sleepers at the end of "Time Passes"'s long night: "Gently the waves would break (Lily heard them in her sleep); tenderly the light fell (it seemed to come through her eyelids)" (*TL*, 214). Then the series of sounds penetrates: "the sun lifted the curtains, broke the veil on their eyes, and Lily Briscoe stirring in her sleep" (*TL*, 214).[1] Color, the paradigmatic sense-datum, loud and life-giving, even prevents sleep. Blue flames into red and keeps the sleeper from "visiting the blind land"; sight becomes a birth: "Blue, like a match struck right in the ball of the innermost eye, he flies, burns, bursts the seal of sleep; the kingfisher; so that now floods back refluent like a tide, the red, thick stream of life again; bubbling, dripping; and we rise, and our eyes . . . fall on – " (*O*, 295). Yet, despite the sensible world's gradual return at sleep's edge, a chasm must be traversed between sleep and waking, with always the danger that the sleeper, like Leslie Stephen in "A Bad Five Minutes in the Alps," will fall in the space between and never return: "She clutched at her blankets as a faller clutches at the turf on the edge of a cliff. Her eyes opened wide. Here she was again, she thought, sitting bolt upright in bed. Awake" (*TL*, 214). The alternation between sleep and wakening follows the perspectives' geography, passing from spaces filled with sense-data through intervals of nothingness; McTaggart speaks of "the oscillation over the whole content of the self . . . shown whenever a man first concentrates his attention, and then relaxes it again, and when a man gradually becomes drowsy and then again wakeful" (*The Nature of Existence*, II, 234).

The temporary transformation of subject to object in sleep has its amusing side: the substitution of a gaping mouth for open eyes and of a snore for human speech. But there is a terror in an elderly woman's doze: "Eleanor snored. She was nodding off, shamelessly, helplessly. There was an obscenity in unconsciousness, he thought. Her mouth was open; her head was on one side" (*Y*, 378). Her observing nephew North, in turn, feels the same unconsciousness engulf him: "But now it was his turn. Silence gaped. One has to egg it on, he thought; somebody has to say something, . . . to feed the immense vacancy of that primeval maw" (*Y*, 378). For "the chopping up small of body and mind which precedes unconsciousness and perhaps death itself" (*O*, 307) accomplishes the paring down of the self. The vague sense-data the dozer receives, like those on the perspective's edge, have lost the organizing principle consciousness provides. They fly apart, their disintegration the self's as well.

Sleep, then, prophesies the ultimate absence of self from world, "sleep, sleep, so deep that all shapes are ground to dust of infinite softness, water of dimness inscrutable, and there, folded, shrouded, like a mummy, like a moth, prone let us lie on the sand at the bottom of sleep" (*O*, 295). That is why the house in "Time Passes" is at once empty and populated by sleepers; in it, nothing persists but unconscious things, shrouded furniture.

THE DISCOVERY OF THE RECUMBENT: THE DEATH OF THE SELF AND THE PERSISTENCE OF THE WORLD

And life, what was that? It was only a light passing over the surface and vanishing, as in time she would vanish, though the furniture in the room would remain. (Woolf, *The Voyage Out*, 125)

Here are chairs turned but nobody sits on them. Here are empty tables and nobody any more coming to dine at them tonight. (Woolf, *The Waves*, 294)

Sleep's drowsy glimpse of the world in which I no longer exist is also given to the sick. In "On Being Ill," the healthy, "the army of the upright," enter the march of events "with the heroism of the ant and bee": "Mrs. Jones catches her train. Mr. Smith mends his motor. The cows are driven home to be milked. Men thatch the roof. The dogs bark . . . The wave of life flings itself out indefatigably" (*CE*, IV, 198). "Thin, as a ghost, leaving no trace" (*W*, 286), the ill self, its body-room's window-senses clouded, discovers, as in philosophic speculation, the distance between listening mind and barking dog. The knowledge that outside the sickroom "the whole landscape of life lies remote and fair, like the shore seen from a ship far at sea"

(*CE*, IV, 195), is a reminder of "how 'you' and 'I' and 'she' pass and vanish; nothing stays!" (*TL*, 204), that "by death, by illness," among other realities, is learned "that the world was not made for us," as Russell puts it (*ML*, 49). This Woolf's sick learn, "[n]ow lying recumbent, staring straight up" in the position of the dead: "the sky [is] discovered to be something so different from" "the background for man" they thought it in health (*CE*, IV, 197). The discovery is the burden of "Time Passes." "This then has been going on all the time without our knowledge! . . . left to work its will year in year out . . . this gigantic cinema play[ed] perpetually to an empty house" (*CE*, IV, 197). "It is only the recumbent who know what, after all, Nature is at no pains to conceal – that she in the end will conquer; heat will leave the world; stiff with frost we shall cease to drag ourselves about the fields; ice will lie thick upon factory and engine; the sun will go out" (*CE*, IV, 198). As her allusions reveal, the author herself profits from readings like Mrs. Swithin's Outline of History or the assertions of Russell's "A Free Man's Worship" "that no fire, no heroism, no intensity of thought and feeling, can preserve an individual life beyond the grave," "that all the labours of the ages, . . . are destined to extinction in the vast death of the solar system," that "Man's achievement must inevitably be buried beneath the débris of a universe in ruins" (*ML*, 45).

THE SELF BEREFT OF THE WORLD

The kitchen door slams. Wild dogs bark far away. Look, the loop of the figure is beginning to fill with time; it holds the world in it. I begin to draw a figure and the world is looped in it, and I myself am outside the loop; which I now join – so – and seal up, and make entire. The world is entire, and I am outside of it, crying, "Oh, save me, from being blown for ever outside the loop of time!" (Woolf, *The Waves*, 21–2)

Imagining a world without self, the self may awaken suddenly in a world empty of all but itself, the last residue of Cartesian doubt. Such awakenings reveal the other side of death's faceless face. The perspective's occupant discovers at its wave-beaten shore "the huge blackness of what is outside us, of what we are not" (*W*, 277). Death is not just the sensibilia-filled unoccupied perspective; it is also sensual deprivation in the world of being.

Falling asleep, the mind continues for a few minutes cut off from its receding sense-data. Eyes closed to the world, the sleeper hears from a great distance the train "raking through her mind, rolling out her thought" (*Y*, 271). All data may be wiped out without the mind ceasing: losing the thread of the conversation, Patrick's "eyes became mild and vacant as if the engine were cut off, and his mind glided on silently" (*Y*, 402); after staying up reading Plato, "for five minutes Jacob's mind continues alone, onwards, into the darkness" (*JR*, 110). It travels like his brother Archer's voice calling "Ja–cob! Ja–cob!," with the unreciprocated ache of solipsism itself, "going out into the world, solitary, unanswered" (*JR*, 9). With no anchor weighing it down to sensible reality, the mind, incommunicado, discovers "the horror and the terror of being alone" (*BA*, 211).

> This self now as I leant over the gate looking down over fields rolling in waves of colour beneath me made no answer . . . I waited. I listened. Nothing came, nothing. I cried then with a sudden conviction of complete desertion. Now there is nothing. No fin breaks the waste of this immeasurable sea. Life has destroyed me. No echo comes back when I speak, no varied words. (*W*, 284)

Death is the wandering self's insomnia in the dark as well as the sleeping self's unawareness of the light. Its ghostly isolation is an invisibility; it traverses shadowless landscapes thought allows it to imagine. "I saw but was not seen" (*W*, 286); "she wished that no one in the whole world would think of her" (*ND*, 197). "La Trobe was invisible" (*BA*, 191). The faceless self, still feeling the tremor of unextinguished consciousness, persists as the very terror of its eventual engulfment in snow – "Even the recumbent spring up at the mere imagination of frost about the toes" (*CE*, IV, 198). "This is more truly Death than the death of friends, than the death of youth" (*W*, 284).

THE EMBRACE OF DEATH

> He was a creator whose philosophy served him to keep ever in the forefront of his mind that critical spirit, that respect for truth, which alone, it seems, can preserve a creator from nauseous egotism or sprawling optimism . . . that may have been because a philosopher was ever at hand to remind him, that the one wholly good gift the gods have given man is death. (Clive Bell, *Proust*, 104)

The impossible experience of death, source of its terror, is also source of a longing. Object of knowledge becomes object of desire. Death exerts an attraction, causing "moments of extraordinary exaltation," those which take the solitary traveller "by surprise" (*MrsD*, 85) or the "sudden exhilaration" of the Ramsay dinner party (*TL*, 147). For the ill, for Woolf herself during her mental breakdowns, death beckons, offering comfort, an end to solitary awareness. The sleeper from whom the world recedes grasps its fading as the living subject reaches for its dead. The embrace is a plunge into the world of objects and facts.

The will-'o-the-wisp which beckons from the other side of the threshold is invariably a female figure. The grammatical gender assigned the object of the philosophic traveller's speculations – it is "she" – is the sign of its desirability: "advancing down the path with his eyes upon sky and branches he rapidly endows them with womanhood" (*MrsD*, 85). Its womanliness assumes the proportions of the maternal figure, becoming "the giant figure at the end of the ride" whose "spectral" presence (*MrsD*, 85) frightens the traveller and the child at bedtime by the very gesture affording protection.

Nurse, fate and siren mingle in this mother. The comfort she offers is twisted with that of the fates whose role is never to drop a stitch: Mrs. Ramsay "flicked her needles to and fro, knitted her reddish-brown stocking," ceaslessly, inexorably counting her stiches throughout part one, continuing even in Lily's memory as "part of her perfect goodness" (*TL*, 300); the grey nurse "resumed her knitting" (*MrsD*, 85) over Peter Walsh, just as Clarissa seemed to him to have been "sitting all the time" he was "in India; mending her dress" (*MrsD*, 61). "I see her knitting on the hall step while we play cricket," Woolf writes of her mother (*MB*, 84); "she seemed to watch, like some wise Fate, the birth, growth, flower and death of innumerable lives all round her" (*MB*, 34). She who knits also cuts: "Change had to come . . . or there'd have been yards and yards of Papa's beard, of Mama's knitting" (*BA*, 174). Symbols of endless becoming, they meet a Greek fate, "[s]hredding and slicing, dividing and subdividing," like "the clocks of Harley Street" (*MrsD*, 154–5). For maternal comfort, the lighthouse's feminine caress, is as lethal as "the fertility, the insensibility of nature" (*TL*, 207), connected to Mrs. Ramsay's "fountain and spray of life" (*TL*, 58), like "those fumbling airs that breathe and bend over the bed itself" (*TL*, 191), like "the love of man for woman, . . . bearing in its bosom the seeds of death" (*TL*, 151), like "the long steady stroke" of the lighthouse Mrs. Ramsay watches, which "was her stroke" (*TL*, 99) – "she looked at the steady light, the pitiless, the remorseless, which was so much her, yet so little her." Its ministering posture over the bed of mother and father is that of one covering sleeping children or shrouding the faces of the dead: "she woke in the night and saw it bent across their bed, stroking the floor" (*TL*, 99); the skull hangs in the nursery. Enforcing what first appears as the father's law – the negation of "if it's fine tomorrow" (*TL*, 9) – it only accomplishes the law of nature, man's "unthinking Mother," as Russell says, "Death, the mark and seal of the parental control" (*ML*, 46) that the father is as powerless to alter as the mother. (So also the war, a man-made phenomenon, becomes a law unto itself that escapes the law-making fathers who initiated it.) Mrs. Ramsay's rainbow shawl, ephemeral victim of time's passing, is also its handmaiden. In covering the skull's naked truth, it calms Cam's bedtime fears with "all the lovely things I could imagine. Rainbows and bells" that Woolf's mother used to put her to sleep as a child (*MB*, 82), as it protects Mrs. Ramsay against the night airs – "and what else? oh, yes, it might be cold: a shawl" (*TL*, 123). It hides the granite-hard "thing that lies beneath the semblance of the thing" (*W*, 163), making "these lovers" "people entering into illusion" (*TL*, 151); it softens but does not stay the lighthouse's eventual triumph:

> the stroke of the Lighthouse, which had laid itself with such authority upon the carpet in the darkness, tracing its pattern, came now in the softer light of spring mixed with moonlight gliding gently as if it laid its caress and lingered stealthily and looked and came lovingly again. But in the very lull of this loving caress, as the long stroke leant upon the bed, the rock was rent asunder; another fold of the shawl loosened; there it hung, and swayed. (*TL*, 199–200)

The sudden stroke of light is the flash of a blade nonetheless, the "scimitar of his father" (*TL*, 60) works behind the veiling mother. The united parental figures emerge as impersonal forces: "All was dim, yet intense too, as if the scarf which the dusk had flung over the garden were torn asunder by star or sword – the flash of some terrible reality leaping, as its way was, out of the heart of the spring" (*Room*, 17).

The other-worldly mother's attraction is thus siren-like. Just as Mrs. Ramsay lures the lovers Minta and Paul into marriage, the solitary traveller's visions endowed with womanhood are "like sirens lolloping away on the green sea waves," like "pale faces which fishermen flounder through floods to embrace" (*MrsD*, 86). The embrace of the faceless, giant mother ends in a struggle, that one which Lily Briscoe has with "that other thing," the reality behind appearances. The "struggle," that of the moth with death (*CE*, I, 361), is Virginia Stephen's with her series of deaths: "I would typify a contest between myself and 'them' – some invisible giant" (*MB*, 118).

Yet if "death" is "when illusion fails" (*BA*, 180), the attraction of death is no less an illusion. The annihilation the solitary traveller yearns for interprets the world with mysticism's monism:

> Such are the visions which ceaselessly float up, pace beside, put their faces in front of, the actual thing; often overpowering the solitary traveller and taking away from him . . . the wish to return, and giving him for substitute a general peace, as if . . . all this fever of living were simplicity itself; and myriads of things merged in one thing; and this figure, made of sky and branches as it is, had risen from the troubled sea (he is elderly, past fifty now) as a shape might be sucked up out of the waves to shower down from her magnificent hands compassion, comprehension, absolution. So, he thinks, may I never go back to the lamplight; to the sitting-room; never finish my book; never knock out my pipe; never ring for Mrs. Turner to clear away; rather let me walk straight on to this great figure, who will, with a toss of her head, mount me on her streamers and let me blow to nothingness with the rest. (*MrsD*, 86–7)

For reality is also the life death lures him from. The mystic promises acquaintance with death's reality. "Death was defiance," Clarissa Dalloway thinks of Septimus' suicide. "Death was an attempt to communicate; people feeling the impossibility of reaching the centre which, mystically, evaded them; closeness drew apart; rapture faded; one was alone. There was an embrace in death" (*MrsD*, 280–1). It grasps for a knowledge whose name is "intimacy," Lily Briscoe's wish to enter Mrs. Ramsay's private world as into a tomb:

> in the chambers of the mind and heart of the woman who was, physically, touching her, were stood, like the treasures in the tombs of kings, tablets bearing sacred inscriptions, which if one could spell them out, would teach one everything, but they would never be offered openly, never made public . . . for it was not knowledge but unity that she desired, not inscriptions on tablets, nothing that could be written in any language known to men, but intimacy itself, which is knowledge. (*TL*, 79)

The impulse makes Lily "feel[] the old horror come back – to want and want and not to have" (*TL*, 300). But, instead of the mystic's refusal of any knowledge less than acquaintance for what is only knowable by description, she renounces knowledge as never achieved intimacy and returns to the struggle "alone in the presence of her old antagonist, life" (*TL*, 120).

The embrace of death is thus a version of the mystic's illusion, promising the "great revelation" whereas one must resign oneself to "little daily miracles, illuminations, matches struck unexpectedly in the dark" (*TL*, 240). So, until the final moment of no return, the solitary traveller's biography consists in the alternation of moments, of "getting up and going to bed again" (*TL*, 197), of voyages out and returns, all presided over by the maternal figure, alternately fate and nurse, both beckoning at the ends of the world and awaiting the return to life. As fate, it is stripped to the stark dimensions of physical reality itself; as nurse, it is clothed in the familiar habits of the everyday, the grey-uniformed, grey-haired nurse, the aproned old woman, Mrs. Pascoe in "a blue print dress and a white apron . . . shading her eyes and looking out to sea" (*JR*, 53), a tiny figure, one of the "miserable pigmies" (*MrsD*, 85) the traveller had left behind:[2]

> The solitary traveller is soon beyond the wood; and there, coming to the door with shaded eyes, possibly to look for his return, with hands raised, with white apron blowing, is an elderly woman who seems (so powerful is this infirmity) to seek, over a desert, a lost son; to search for a rider destroyed; to be the figure of the mother whose sons have been killed in the battles of the world. So, as the solitary traveller advances down the village street where the women stand knitting and the men dig in the garden, the evening seems ominous; the figures still; as if some august fate, known to them, awaited without fear, were about to sweep them into complete annihilation. (*MrsD*, 87)

The living mother, the one left and returned to, is small, vulnerable, old; the dead one, the one taken from us, assumes Death's unchanging Greek proportions, "a power of such magnitude" against which the "insignificant little moth" (*CE*, I, 361) is "a tiny bead of pure life" (*CE*, I, 360). Her Alice-in-Wonderlandesque alternation in proportions, like "the two senses of that vastness and this tininess" of Nancy's god-like expansion of pool into ocean and its shrinkage into pool again (*TL*, 115), is the difference in perspective between the landlocked "grown-up view," "not much clearer than the view of the little creatures in bathing drawers" on ships at sea and "[t]he people in ships," who took a "singular view of England":

> Not only did it appear to them to be an island, and a very small island, but it was a shrinking island in which people were imprisoned . . . The disease attacked other parts of the earth; Europe shrank, Asia shrank, Africa and America shrank, until it seemed doubtful whether the ship would ever run

against any of those winkled little rocks again. But, on the other hand, an immense dignity had descended upon her; she was an inhabitant of the great world. (*VO*, 32)

So the giant mother diminishes, as "[t]he hand dwindles in his hand" (*TL*, 193), into the tiny old woman, as the child expands, a process of the years themselves. From a vantage point on the world's edge, beyond its battles, the traveller has the perspective on the little world of village and childhood that Mr. Ramsay has, from Q (which "[v]ery few people in the whole of England ever reach"), on his wife and son, "now far, far away, . . . occupied with little trifles at their feet and somehow defenceless against a doom which he perceived" (*TL*, 53). The irony does not entirely call the vision into question. True, Mr. Ramsay depends on the illusion of the figures' tininess and their needing "his protection" (*TL*, 53) to sustain him, whereas it is Mrs. Ramsay who brings him "within the circle of life" (*TL*, 59). "Yet the power was there all the same, massed outside, indifferent, impersonal, not attending to anything in particular" (*CE*, I, 361). Ultimately, their tininess is not the illusion but his power to protect. For Mrs. Ramsay's vision is not so different from her philosopher-husband's: "With her mind she had always seized the fact that there is no reason, order, justice: but suffering, death, the poor . . . No happiness lasted; she knew that" (*TL*, 98).

"Just as life had been strange a few minutes before, so death was now as strange" (*CE*, I, 361). The alternating magnification and telescoping results from the shift in perspective from a death whose simplicity the traveller longs to lose himself in to a life whose myriad trivialities he clutches at, for "one helped oneself out of solitude reluctantly by laying hold of some little odd or end, some sound, some sight" (*TL*, 99). So too, Mrs. McNab, by "get[ting] this done; . . . that done," rescues the house from "the sands of oblivion" (*TL*, 209) at that crucial moment of "hesitation when dawn trembles and night pauses" between perspectives (*TL*, 208). All depends on the diminutive figures, the Mrs. McNabs, capable, like the moth, of "gigantic effort" (*CE*, I, 361); there are no giant figures except in visions. "Who could tell what was going to last in literature or indeed anything else?" (*TL*, 204). All Mr. Ramsay's worries about Scott are proved true, for in the end his great works must be disinterred and rescued from oblivion by a charwoman. From the insignificant comes "that sudden revivification" which rouses Mr. Ramsay "(when she praised his boots), that sudden recovery of vitality and interest in ordinary human things, which too passed and changed (for he was always changing . . .)" (*TL*, 233). But until the trivial sense-datum is within sight or hearing, the traveller must pause on the limits of a scene in which he has no part, the things seen "become unreal" (*TL*, 285). From life's perspective, death assumes the overpowering proportions of the father's truths, arrested in the mother's severe beauty, in the Greek symbolism of universals; from death's perspective, life has the pathos of the infinitely small, of the moment from the perspective of eternity: "she could not shake herself free from the sense that everything this morning was happening for the first time, perhaps for the last time, as a traveller, even though he is half asleep, knows, looking out of the train window, that he must look now, for he will never see that town, or that mule-cart, or that woman at work in the fields, again" (*TL*, 288). Death's attraction and repulsion is itself part of the alternation. What must be practiced is a kind of rhythmic restraint. Led out "on a narrow plank, perfectly alone, over the sea" (*TL*, 256), to feel "again her own headlong desire to throw herself off the cliff and be drowned looking for a pearl brooch on a beach" (*TL*, 261), the trick is to come so far, yet refrain from the impulse to jump.

For life returns. Death's embrace is matched by the traveller's impulse to hug the landlady, become the "adorable emblem which only the recollection of cold human contacts forbids us to embrace" (*MrsD*, 87). So Leslie Stephen, returning from philosophy's heights, would "recognize instantly the real presence" Julia Stephen represented (*MB*, 37). The clutching of the ordinary is also an embrace. It is that perpetual curiosity and "power of recovery" that Woolf discovers in herself: "Great excitability & search after something. Great content – almost always enjoying what I'm at, but with constant change of mood. I don't think I'm ever bored . . . I enjoy epicurean ways of society; sipping & then shutting my eyes to taste. I enjoy almost everything. Yet I have some restless searcher in me" (*Diary*, III, 62). It is the "faith in life" that makes Fry conclude: "I must hurry on with this business of living which lasts as long as life lasts" (*RF*, 278).

The embrace of life will be the Impressionist plunge into the bath of sense-data. It is the first impulse to knowledge, that desire of direct apprehension. Russell describes the early scientists as "in love with the world" (*SO*, 262). His lovers of the world discover, however, the skeleton under appearances, as Septimus thinks Rezia will when he gives her his arm – "a piece of bone" (*MrsD*, 23). That discovery is of death as an object of knowledge which escapes acquaintance:

> The lover of nature has been baffled . . . As physics has developed, it has deprived us step by step of what we thought we knew concerning the intimate nature of the physical world. Colour and sound, light and shade, form and texture, belong no longer to that external nature that the Ionians sought as the bride of their devotion. All these things have been transferred from the beloved to the lover, and the beloved has become a skeleton of rattling bones, cold and dreadful, but perhaps a mere phantom. The poor physicists, appalled at the desert that their formulae have revealed, call upon God to give them comfort, but God must share the ghostliness of His creation. (*SO*, 263)

Mr. Ramsay's encounter with death, like the scientist's with physical reality, is with a ghost: "one dark morning" he stretched his arms out" for dead Mrs. Ramsay, but they "remained empty" (*TL*, 194).[3] Once Mrs. Ramsay quits the window, there remains only the lighthouse's empty perspective, the shawled skull in the house whence all the living have departed. "Strip off all the web of sense-given fact which runs through and supports our whole conceptions of the world," writes Leslie Stephen, "and the residuum is painfully like nothing" ("WM?," 151).

Magnifying and telescoping explain the swings in the observer's mood from exhilaration, and the English weather's from radiance, to gloom. The distance traversed is infinitesimal yet absolute. "For the philosopher is right who says that nothing thicker than a knife's blade separates happiness from melancholy" (*O*, 45). Indeed, the love of the world is up to a point indistinguishable from the death wish. Orlando's exaltation in sense-data places him on the blade's very edge: "Sights disturbed him, like that of his mother . . .; sights exalted him . . . made him in love with death – all these sights, and the garden sounds too, the hammer beating, the wood chopping, began that riot and confusion of the passions and emotions" (*O*, 16).

Terror and ecstasy mingle then on that precarious threshold between life and death on which the house is poised a hairsbreadth from oblivion, it "make[s] one remember the overpowering sorrow" (*JR*, 49) but also reveals "the overmastering beauty of human existence" (*ML*, 52), the contrast like that Woolf makes between her dead mother, laid out, and the setting sun on Paddington Station

(*MB*, 93). It was Woolf, like the old lady deliberately putting out her light or Augustus Carmichael blowing out his candle (*TL*, 192), who took the advice of Hume's posthumously published essay on suicide ("Hume," *DNB*, 225) not to make death part of "the common life of day by day" (*ML*, 52), as Hume is said to have done in his own dying, but to retain all of its strangeness. It was she who stepped into the void, like Mr. Ramsay stepping from the boat in pursuit of his alphabet's final symbol, while "surrounding the narrow raft illumined by the flickering light" is "the dark ocean on whose rolling waves we toss for a brief hour" Russell invokes (*ML*, 52).

The knowledge philosophy pursues must encompass the fact of death without either diminishing or inflating it. Mr. Ramsay's impulse is "[t]o pursue truth with such astonishing lack of consideration for other people's feelings, to rend the thin veils of civilization" (*TL*, 51), to point to the boar's skull. James, who hated this in his father, nevertheless, unlike Cam, who wishes it veiled, wants assurance it "was still there under the shawl" (*TL*, 173), like his father, "the image of stark and uncompromising severity" (*TL*, 10). Not understanding his impulse, Mrs. Bast and Mrs. McNab, seeing it years after, can only muse, "Whatever did they want to hang a beast's skull there?" (*TL*, 211). The problem then is not with the father's philosophy but that "so brave a man in thought should be so timid in life" (*TL*, 70). Mr. Ramsay's reaction to truth is exaggerated, his mode of reaction not adjusted to the reality; it blocks the view. "He said the most melancholy things, but she noticed that directly he had said them he always seemed more cheerful than usual. All this phrase-making was a game, she thought, for if she had said half what he said, she would have blown her brains out by now" (*TL*, 106). For tragedy is not the final truth, but only that from the individual observer's perspective. While Mr. Ramsay casts "a veil of crape" (*TL*, 227), Mrs. Ramsay's own tendency is to diminish, to cover the skeleton: "she was relieved to find that the ruin was veiled; domesticity triumphed; custom crooned its soothing rhythm" (*TL*, 49). Not betraying to her son her anxiety, she ends her story of the fisherman and his wife: "there they are living still at this very time" (*TL*, 94). As the veiler of truth, "who shall deny that in these respects every woman is nicer than any man?" (*JR*, 11). Yet in veiling the skull, Mrs. Ramsay only does what nature does, and, in asserting of what "Cam thought . . . a horrid thing, branching at her all over the room" – "it's only an old pig" (*TL*, 172) – she does what logic does: she neutralizes its meaning for human life, in both cases "refusing to admit mere empty phrases as solutions" ("WM?," 147). For if the truth is that the skull is the death's head, it is no less true that it is only an old pig. The two realities continue to exert an equal force, each simply what they are. The tragic mode must neither veil nor unveil, but let the awful shape, the "failures and disenchantments of the world of fact" (*ML*, 50), show austerely through the beauty of appearances, as Mrs. Ramsay "so stiffened and composed her face in a habit of sternness" (*TL*, 98) that it took on the hardness of granite. When Mr. Ramsay, passing, notes "the sternness at the heart of her beauty," like the skull under the shawl, he recognizes the appropriateness of her posture: "her remoteness pained him, and he felt, as he passed, that he could not protect her . . . He could do nothing to help her. He must stand by and watch her" (*TL*, 98–9), a painful awareness "free" only, as Russell says, "to examine, to criticise, to know, and in imagination to create" (*ML*, 46). The embrace of the world as the impulse to knowledge, when it closes on skeletal nothingness, brings home the observer's powerlessness to intervene "in the spectacle of Death"; "as by some strange marriage of pain, the sufferer is bound to the world by bonds of sorrow" (*ML*, 51). The pain lies in the fact that "Nature," no more considerate of people's feelings than the philosopher, is "omnipotent but blind" while her "child" is "subject still to her power, but gifted with sight" (*ML*, 46); its eyes reflect the eyeless world. This helplessness is what Lily Briscoe and Augustus Carmichael feel watching Mr. Ramsay's tiny boat reach the Lighthouse. "'He has landed,' she said aloud. 'It is finished'" (*TL*, 309). This "consummatum est" pronounced, like that at the end of "The Death of the Moth," they stand, the image of the mothers of the world looking out to the sea over which the guns of August are earlier heard ("there came later in the summer ominous sounds like the measured blows of hammers dulled on felt" (*TL*, 200), Mr. Carmichael "shading his eyes with his hand": "He stood there as if he were spreading his hands over all the weakness and suffering of mankind." The gesture Lily imagines – "as if she had seen him let fall from his great height a wreath of violets and asphodels . . . upon the earth" (*TL*, 309) – like Rhoda's "throw[ing] my violets, my offering to Percival" "into the wave" (*W*, 164), is a valedictory one, casting flowers on Mr. Ramsay's funeral barge.

ART: ELEGY AND EPITAPH FOR THE SEPARATION OF SELF AND WORLD

In all the multiform facts of the world – in the visual shapes of trees and mountains and clouds, in the events of the life of man, even in the very omnipotence of Death – the insight of creative idealism can find the reflection of a beauty which its own thoughts first made. In this way mind asserts its subtle mastery over the thoughtless forces of Nature. (Russell, *Mysticism and Logic*, 51)

She kept herself marvellously alive to all the changes that went on round her, as though she heard perpetually the ticking of a vast clock and could never forget that some day it would cease for all of us . . . living thus at high pressure she contrived to invest the whole scene with an inimitable bravery as though she saw it properly composed, of fools, clowns and splendid Queens, a vast procession on the march towards death. (Woolf, *Moments of Being*, 35–6)

But enough of death – its life that matters. (Woolf, *Diary*, II, 301)

The impulse to intervene is also the writer's. Watching the death of the moth, she "stretched out a pencil, meaning to right him" but learns her powerlessness as well, so "laid the pencil down again" (*CE*, I, 360), then "lifted the pencil again, useless though I knew it to be" (*CE*, I, 361). Instead, Woolf wrote her novels to memorialize the dead. In "On Being Ill," she observes that no one writes "epic poems to typhoid" (*CE*, IV, 193), but Leon Edel thinks *Jacob's Room* "an elegy for her brother Thoby" (*Bloomsbury*, 66), dead of typhus. So also is *The Waves*. Bell explains in his biography of Woolf: "Thoby's death was a disaster from which Virginia could not easily recover" (*VW*, I, 112). "It was always 'my brother . . . my brother' who rose from the depths of her lily pool" (*BA*, 206). Bell continues: "Twice she returns to a kind of bittersweet speculation concerning the vanished being whom we reconstruct in our mind's eye – *ex pede Herculem* – deducing Jacob from his room, Percival from" his friends (*VW*, I, 112). The importance of Thoby's death for *The Waves* is apparent from Woolf's diary entry the day she completed it: "I must record, heaven be praised, the end of The Waves. I wrote the words O Death fifteen minutes ago . . . Anyhow, it is done; & I have been sitting here these fifteen minutes in a state of glory, & calm, & some tears, thinking of Thoby & if I could write Julian Thoby Stephen 1881–1906 on the first page" (*Diary*, IV, 10). While "making up *To the Lighthouse*," Woolf writes, "I have an idea that I will invent a new name for my books to supplant 'novel.' A new – by Virginia Woolf. But what? Elegy?" (*Diary*, III, 34). It is an elegy for the pre-war Victorian past, childhood, the war dead, her parents, above all, her mother. John Mepham writes in "Mourning and Modernism": "If *To the Lighthouse* is fiction as elegy, *Jacob's Room* is fiction as epitaph, for [Woolf's] brother Thoby. As for *The Waves*, it can be seen as a kind of shrine to Thoby's memory" (142). All Woolf's dead gather in her novels like the ghosts in the Roman encampment at Scarborough in *Jacob's Room*. *Mrs. Dalloway* and *To the Lighthouse* memorialize the war dead along with her personal dead: Mrs. Ramsay is "a shade across the fields" in a landscape in which "[a]ll had been part of the fields of death" (*TL*, 270). The elegy is also an Apostolic form, from Apostle no. 70 Tennyson's *In Memoriam*, dedicated to Apostle no. 68 Arthur Hallam, to Apostle no. 252 Wittgenstein's *Tractatus*, "Dedicated to the Memory of My Friend David H. Pinsent," as in *Lycidas* it was already a Cambridge form.

Woolf's elegiac form is not poetry, however, but a prose fiction she qualifies as "modern." Its modernity partly lies in its not flinching before the reality of death in all its starkness, a literary embodiment of that unadorned grief for the death of his first wife Leslie Stephen professed:

> Standing by an open grave, . . . we all, I think . . . must feel that the Psalmist takes his sorrow like a man, and as we, with whatever difference of dialect, should wish to take our own sorrows; while the Apostle is desperately trying to shirk the inevitable, and at best resembles the weak comforters who try to cover up the terrible reality under a veil of well-meant fiction. I would rather face the inevitable with open eyes. (*AAA*, 91–2)

The modern prose elegy is harsher than Milton's "melodious tear." But recording "how it is certain we must die" (*MrsD*, 267) unflinchingly instead of veiling the skull with fiction is not sufficient to be modern. Death must also be stripped of its heavy Victorian drapery of mourning. It is well-known how Leslie Stephen took "his sorrow like a man" – as Spinoza's "man of sad passions," in this a representative Victorian confronting the modern world.[4] Woolf did not find her father's grief the "dialect" appropriate to the bare reality. For to death as simply a limit the response cannot be a limitless grief. Literature must find the language for death as fact, what Roland Barthes calls "flat death," ordinary as the kitchen table. It does not suffice for the modern elegy to set down the brutal reality, it must also end mourning. The call to weep must become that to "weep no more." This Woolf recognizes in pronouncing of her parents' deaths that whereas she "used to think of him & mother daily," "writing The Lighthouse, laid them in my mind" (*Diary*, III, 208). The image is clearly one of laying them to rest. Elsewhere, pronouncing that "I ceased to be obsessed by mother" in writing that novel, she adds "I suppose that I did for myself what psychoanalysts do for their patients. I expressed some very long felt and deeply felt emotion . . . and then laid it to rest" (*MB*, 81). So to end mourning she identifies as a Freudian project: it is the *Trauerarbeit* or "work of mourning."

The modern elegiac form for Woolf will be the "unnamed variety of the novel" (*CE*, II, 228) which combines "the exaltation of poetry" with "the ordinariness of prose" (*CE*, II, 224). Poetry is necessary to meet its first requirement, to reach the level of the reality's out-of-ordinariness: "Can it chant the elegy . . . ?" Woolf asks of prose, and answers "I think not" (*CE*, II, 226). It must be like Augustus Carmichael's war poetry, "extremely impersonal; it said something about death; it said very little about love. There was an impersonality about him" (*TL*, 290). It thus refuses Leslie Stephen's exaggerated grief as egoism. For death only becomes all-consuming within the private world. Although "when he had heard of Andrew Ramsay's death (he was killed in a second by a shell; he should have been a great mathematician) Mr. Carmichael had 'lost all interest in life'" (*TL*, 289), his poetry mourning Andrew's "death in battle" does not express personal loss. For the reality of death lies in its impersonality. The role of prose, by contrast to poetry, is to contain the response to death, not just "face" but accept "the inevitable with open eyes": "did she resent it; or did it not become consoling to believe that death ended absolutely?" (*MrsD*, 12). The poetic and the prosaic set the parameters of two stylistic registers adequate to two realities, what Woolf will refer to as the "extraordinary" and the "ordinary." Death makes the world extraordinary, calling forth a poetic response, like Lily Briscoe's to the loss of Mrs. Ramsay: "Her heart leapt at her and seized her and tortured her. 'Mrs. Ramsay! Mrs. Ramsay!' she cried." But the vocative must be checked and the extraordinary brought back so "then, quietly, as if she refrained, that too became part of ordinary experience, was on a level with the chair, with the table" (*TL*, 300). *The Voyage Out* does not yet successfully contain the terror in the everyday, the novel's ending in death is too dramatic; *Jacob's Room* already relativizes it in Jacob's room abandoned amidst a city of occupied ones. The other novels include death, but do not end with it because death is never the end outside the private world. Mrs. Dalloway from her bedroom window saying "There! the old lady had put out her light!" (*MrsD*, 206) and thinking of Septimus' suicide before returning to her party, flatly records the event. *To the Lighthouse* and *The Waves* instead place death at the center, a position which will have an aesthetic function as well. Death, at every point the conclusion of a certain logic, is in no way the final word; the world does not vanish with the perspective but persists elsewhere, "where thought constructs a destiny which is independent of human beings" (*ND*, 331). If the writer-"I" of *The Waves* ends by defying "Death . . . the enemy" with the poetry "Against you I will fling myself, unvanquished and unyielding, O Death!" (*W*, 297), the novel concludes with the prose statement "*The waves broke on the shore*" (*W*, 297).

The classical elegy had ended mourning by "apotheosis," the "well-meant fiction" of transforming the dead into immortals. The novel replaces the elegy's apotheosis, in this world without gods, by the imaginative occupation of emptied perspectives. "The elegiac triumph of the novel is to sustain entity. People survive when you are not there, when they are not there," Beer writes ("Hume, Stephen, and Elegy," 93). But the inclusion of unoccupied perspectives among those the novel imaginatively creates records as firmly the persistence of the table and the disappearance, and not the survival, of the human observer. Beer is right to assert that "the Ramsays . . . are there when we are not" (90). But their persistence at a given unobserved moment is not equivalent to their persistence at all moments. The novel must show how death frames in darkness and silence a sudden, random illumination of sense-data, life in its privacy, preserved "like the body of a young man laid up in peat for a century, with the red fresh on his lips" (*TL*, 35; see also *TL*, 36). But it must also look beyond death, flattening it along with other events. The restraint Leslie Stephen lacks is the inability to return to life. This is the burden of the passage read from Spinoza at McTaggart's funeral which leads Fry to comment "So for once the right thing was said" (*RF*, 278) and which Russell cites (*HWP*, 574) and Woolf ends her biography of Fry with: "A free man thinks of death least of all things; and his wisdom is a meditation not of death but of life" (*RF*, 298). The reality at the back of appearances is no more death than life. Death is outside life, giving it what attaches us to it: its momentariness.

The novel's "work of mourning" ends it by incessantly returning to life after confronting death. The problem, for the novelist as for the philosopher, is to find a form for the rhythmic movement from the ordinary to the extraordinary and back, a new aesthetic to insure the elegy's modernity. Our analysis suggests this aesthetic will begin with a silent observation in which the lamentations of the grieving "I" are not heard. That observation resembles the looking without past Proust associates, in a passage Clive Bell cites, with a mirror into which the gazer has not recently looked or a photograph, an observation in which the "I" briefly enjoys "la faculté d'assister brusquement à notre propre absence" by being reduced only to "le témoin, l'observateur, . . . l'étranger qui n'est pas de la maison, le photographe qui vient prendre un cliché des lieux qu'on ne reverra plus" (*Proust*, 76). This "I"-less looking's sudden glimpse of the world without the self Proust contrasts with necromancy, the art of conjuring up the dead (*Proust*, 77) with "notre oeil," "chargé de pensée," thereby clothing death with familiar traits. Necromancy is as false as habitual memory in recapturing the dead; Proust's novel emulates the mirror or photograph's stark reflection. Woolf's new elegiac aesthetic will likewise incorporate the model of the mirroring lens-like eye. Grief, Woolf herself claims, has a power akin to a lens, one that magnifies, to make us see with an unaccustomed eye: "when you examine feelings with the intense microscope that sorrow lends, it is amazing how they stretch, like the finest goldbeater's skin, over immense tracts of substance. And we, poor children that we were, conceived it to be our duty evermore to go searching for these atoms, wherever they might lie sprinkled about the surface, the great mountains and oceans, of the world" (*MB*, 59). In Woolf's personal history, the mirror has an originary association with the first death in a series. "At any rate I remember the long looking-glass; . . . and the great bed on which my mother lay," she recalls (*MB*, 91–2). But it will be not through Proust but through Roger Fry's theory of Impressionism that the eye disburdened of thought enters Woolf's aesthetic. His theory of Post-Impressionism will give it an eyeless dimension. Proust's thoughtless photograph-mirror will become the work of art as a mirror-instrument of knowledge. The meeting of Fry's aesthetic with Cambridge theory of knowledge transforms that particular reflection of death into the mirror of art become empty perspective, in which, as in a photograph, an impression is fixed with "the irrevocableness of a vanished past" (*ML*, 51). For "Death was the glass; death was between us; coming to the woman first, hundreds of years ago, leaving the house, sealing all the windows; the rooms were darkened" (*CSFVW*, 116). In this blank look of things, in the flowers "eyeless, and so terrible" (*TL*, 203), by an unexpected logic, the end of mourning is reached. "[H]owever indifferent the sky or disdainful the flowers" (*CE*, IV, 198), in things with their "self-possession," Woolf discovers, we "find sympathy" (*CE*, IV, 197); flowers "lie . . . upon the pillows of the dead," unseeing. "It is in their indifference that they are comforting . . . as, in another sphere, it is the great artists, the Miltons and the Popes, who console not by their thought of us but by their forgetfulness" (*CE*, IV, 198). Art itself incorporates this forgetfulness. "Mercifully" its mindless vision can "lay to rest the incessant activity" of Bernard's consciousness, mourning for Percival (*W*, 156). The old woman singing that "death's enormous sickle had swept those tremendous hills" in *Mrs. Dalloway*, "when at last she laid her hoary and immensely aged head on the earth, now become a mere cinder of ice, she implored the Gods to lay by her side a bunch of purple heather, there on her high burial place which the last rays of the last sun caressed; for then the pageant of the universe would be over" (*MrsD*, 123).

The new art will also instrumentalize a process, that of the passing of time, the process of life as well of death. The mechanism Woolf imagines can be linked to the one invoked in Fry's remarks on McTaggart's funeral:

> And while the Bach Chorale was being played the coffin moved by hidden mechanism through the doors into? – How odd that this up to date, hygienic, scientific machine-made and machine-worked disposal of the body is ten times more impressive, more really symbolic than that age-long consecrated business of earth-to-earth – with the ugliness of the big hole – so unsuggestive of the infinities which surround us. . . Whereas this with its slow silent movement through doors into the unknown is really dramatic and a perfect symbol of the inevitable mechanism of things and the futility of our protests against its irresistible force . . . [Woolf's ellipses] (*RF*, 278)

The reality of Stephen's "open grave," Fry's "big hole," is itself inadequate to "the terrible reality." Woolf's own equivalent of "the inevitable mechanism of things" is a style through which the temporal series ordered by the logical relations of earlier and later, symbolized by mechanisms like the clock or the "reel" on which "Time has whizzed back an inch or two" (*W*, 113) or the kaleidoscope, is correlated with the immobilized series of "moments." Via the mechanism, death places the mourned particular within the series. Of Stella Duckworth's death, Woolf recalled, "sometimes it appeared almost in the light of a work of art; more often it revealed a shapeless catastrophe" (*MB*, 55). The elegiac novel both records the chaos and gives it retrospective order. That order remains without meaning, however. Like Mrs. Ramsay's shawl, which first wraps a living woman, then is the winding sheet for a skeleton, it must clothe in beauty a reality it also shows: "she quickly took her own shawl off and wound it round the skull, . . . and then she came back to Cam and laid her head almost flat on the pillow beside Cam's and said how lovely it looked now" (*TL*, 172).

PART II

Principia Aesthetica

Ainsi s'efface le conflit qui a parfois opposé au logicien et au physicien le philosophe, défenseur des réalités de la vie et de l'art.

(Nicod, *La Géométrie dans le Monde Sensible*, 48)

Figure 6. Paul Cézanne, *Stilleben*, c. 1885.

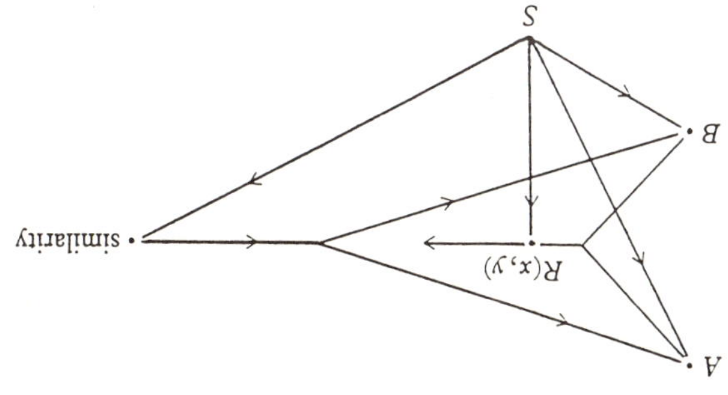

Figure 7. Bertrand Russell, map of a five-term complex, *Theory of Knowledge*, 1913 (reproduced upside down)

CHAPTER 6

Fry's granite and rainbow: post-impressionism and impressionism

> The two characteristic instincts of the philosopher are the desire for certainty and the desire for harmony . . . In some minds the desire for unity of system is the more strongly developed; in others the desire for conformity to facts . . . a definitive philosophy will give full satisfaction to both instincts.
>
> (Stephen, *History of English Thought*, 5–6)

> Metaphysics, or the attempt to conceive the world as whole by means of thought, has been developed, from the first, by the union and conflict of two very different human impulses, the one urging men towards mysticism, the other urging them towards science.
>
> (Russell, *Mysticism and Logic*, 1)

> While he [Fry] was arguing about the theory of art in the abstract his eye was ranging over the picture . . . Then there was a moment of fusion, of comprehension . . . how was it done? By the union, it seemed to me, of two different qualities, his reason and his sensibility.
>
> (Woolf, *Collected Essays*, IV, 89)

In pursuit of knowledge, philosophy has revealed a world whose reality seems unreal. This is the world remade by science. "The extraordinary unreality was frightening; but it was also exciting" (*TL*, 220). "The natural escape of the English mind," Leslie Stephen wrote, "was to some form of what was called common sense" whose "aim was to obtain a doctrine sufficiently plausible to give some kind of unity" (*HET*, 71). But scientific analysis had broken the "one seamless whole" (*CE*, IV, 229) of common-sense whereby, in Stephen's account, "I conceive of the world as something different from a series of sensations" and "interpret the stream of feelings of which consciousness is composed as implying an organised system of real existences" and "believe in a set of permanent relations independent of our individual consciousness" (*HET,* 45). The result, heritage of Hume's empiricism, is that "[t]he old bonds which held things together have been completely dissolved" (*HET,* 44).

The particular crisis of "English thought" was thus a problem of unity, Stephen reiterates as a major theme: "What are the elements of which the universe is composed, and how are they woven into a continuous whole? 'I see the sun.' How does that statement differ from the statement, 'I have certain sensations of light and heat?' " (*HET,* 45). The dissolution is that of both physical object and subject traced in Part I: "The soul is dissolved by the analysis which has been fatal to its antithesis" (*HET,* 44). Common-sense is the unity consciousness confers on experience. Atomism and the reduction of the ego together destroy it: "the objective and the subjective links disappear together, and we are forced to admit that 'the uniting principle amongst our internal perceptions is as unintelligible as that among external objects,' " Stephen quotes Hume (*HET,* 51). The disintegration begins with the analysis of appearances and the attack on causal connections. "Destroy the conception of cause and [Berkeley's] philosophy crumbles to atoms. Nothing is left but a series of sensations, strictly made up of atomic units" (*HET,* 43). "The world, given in sense-presentations, is not the aboriginal experience of the lower organisms, later to be sophisticated by the inference to causal efficacy," Whitehead writes. "The contrary is the case. First the causal side of experience is dominating, then the sense-presentation gains in subtlety" (*Symbolism*, 49).

Yet the "ultimate end of philosophy" remains, Stephen asserts, "to detect the permanent order which underlies the infinite variety of the universe as revealed to our perception" (*HET,* 69–70). That end must not subvert philosophy's other goal, the pursuit of truth. Philosophy must thus resolve the "conflict" (*ML*, 1) of two distinct goals. "The love of abstract truth, the love of consistency" that Stephen invokes (*HET,* 10) or Russell's "two very different human impulses" directed "towards mysticism" or "towards science," are not easily reconcilable. Logic and science begin by taking the world apart. Hume, in whom, according to Russell, "the scientific impulse reigns unchecked" (*ML*, 1), thus shatters the world. If not irrevocably fragmented, some new notion of unity must join together what analysis has put asunder. But it must represent some real order in things. The impossible marriage of two contradictory impulses Bloomsbury consummated in its common effort. Logic and mathematics, via "the understanding of general forms" (*ML*, 108) and "the logic of relations" (*LK*, 325), "reduc[es] the haphazard untidy world of immediate sensation to the smooth orderly world of geometry and kinematics."[1] The importance of the theory of continuity is apparent.

The literature acknowledging the reality which analysis reveals consequently confronts philosophy's methodological problems. Hence the need for a new aesthetic, already felt in the attempt to describe the unobserved world, is also a problem of unity. The old ontology of the novel's literary realism is rendered outmoded, for it holds to unanalyzed common-sense reality. For Woolf's "modern" fiction, "the word realism seems as impertinent as idealism would be in reference to such a creation." It adopts the new philosophical realism inoculated with Berkeley's Idealism. It atomizes the novelistic world, thereby creating the problem of "how the whole is held together" (*TL*, 160) which traditional narrative form is inadequate to solve. The solution is initially worked out, however, in the theory of the visual arts – the art that is inadequately described as either "realist" or "idealist" is Cézanne's and the commentator Roger Fry (*Cé*, 69). Through the intermediary of Fry's "rare mixture of logic and sympathy" (*CE*, IV, 90), philosophy developed eyes, and art, including that of the novel, gained eyeless principles.

EYELESS IN CAMBRIDGE: THE REALISMS OF THE VISIBLE AND THE INVISIBLE

"I suppose we're all deficient somewhere," said Bertie. (Lawrence, "The Blind Man," 361)[2]

[W]hile not without aptitude for pure mathematics, I was completely destitute of the concrete kinds of skill . . . necessary in science. Moreover, within mathematics it was the most abstract parts which I understood best: I . . . could never succeed in mastering optics. (Russell, *Selected Papers of Bertrand Russell*, ix–x)

[T]he eye gives no help to the imagination. (Russell, *Principia Mathematica*, 2)

Woolf's aesthetic was not then articulated in theoretical isolation but in Apostolic Bloomsbury, in which Fry's position was so pivotal that Woolf "wish[ed]" she "dedicated" *To the Lighthouse* to Fry (*Letters VW*, III, 385), recognizing "his aesthetic guidance" (*VW*, II, 129), and came to write his biography after his death. The connection between

Woolf's thinking about art and Fry's is by now well-established (Roberts, "Vision and Design," 843). What is not is the extent to which Fry's aesthetic derives from analytic philosophy. Fittingly, the chance meeting introducing into Bloomsbury the person who would move between art and philosophy, Bloomsbury and Cambridge, took place "while waiting on Cambridge station for the arrival of the London train" (Spalding, *Roger Fry*, 123).

With Fry's arrival, the "abstract" doctrines Vanessa and Virginia Stephen and the young Apostles debated, in encountering Impressionism, rediscovered empiricism. "The old skeleton arguments of primitive Bloomsbury about art and beauty put on flesh and blood" (*MB*, 175). "[T]he English unaesthetic eye" (*CE*, II, 268) Woolf attributes to the Apostles, Mr. Ramsay's failure to notice view or flowers (*TL*, 107), had excluded the visual. Not only were the blind now given eyes; in Woolf's metaphor, the bare bones' flesh and blood was color: "The Post-Impressionist movement had cast – not its shadow – but its bunch of variegated lights upon us" (*MB*, 178). Visual art replaced the prophetic literature Woolf saw as Stephen's generation's paradigm of art. It furnishes the model for "modern" fiction.[3] "Though they must part in the end," Woolf wrote, "painting and writing have much to tell each other" (*CE*, II, 241).

Seeing was bound up with "[t]he pervasiveness of perceptual language in Moore's talk of abstract knowledge" Hylton pronounces "striking"; it "seems quite literally meant" (*Russell*, 127–8). Knowledge was the seeing of reality itself visual. Desmond MacCarthy in a 1900 Apostle's paper said of his generation, "we who do analyse more also trust our eyes more," by contrast with the previous, which "did not analyse so much" and "trusted their eyes less" (Skidelsky, *John Maynard Keynes*, I, 135). Russell sees the dominance of the visual in "the substitution of sight for touch as the source of physical ideas" in physics (*ABCR*, 197). Russell's view of philosophy's goal as "the endeavor to see clearly, and to make others see clearly" (Hylton, *Russell*, 232) will find its echo in Woolf on literature: "The novelist after all wants to make us see" (*CE*, II, 241), as Lytton Strachey, according to Woolf, "had to open our eyes before he made us see" (*CE*, I, 335).

Cambridge philosophy's eyelessness did not disappear, however. It lingered in realism's logical framework, "unseen"[4] laws contributed to Stephen's "knowledge of the visible universe" (*HET*, 54). It informs Fry's Post-Impressionism. Through the latter's intermediary, it will provide other than a "baby language" (*CE*, II, 124) for "the criticism of fiction," for discussing form and the "laws of fiction" (*CE*, II, 53). "This word 'form,' of course," Woolf comments, "comes from the visual arts" (*CE*, II, 124). Of Fry Woolf claims, with some caveats, that "many of his theories held good for both arts. Design, rhythm, texture – there they were again – in Flaubert as well as Cézanne. And he would hold up a book to the light as if it were a picture and show where in his view – it was a painter's of course – it fell short" (*RF*, 241).

Fry combined the eye and eyelessness, color and skeletal form. According to Woolf, "there were two Roger Frys; one who had been trained at Cambridge to reason and hold his own in argument with McTaggart and Lowes Dickinson, and another who was . . . very diffident in the presence of painters, and who felt vaguely that if he could paint he would paint differently from the artists of his own generation" (*RF*, 85–6). The first Fry was a friend from boyhood of McTaggart (though he never became an Idealist) and an actively argumentative Apostle. This Fry wonders, in a letter Woolf quotes, "if there's any truth in the ordinary idea about me that I am purely 'intellectual' in art" (*RF*, 273). She presents him at the Post-Impressionist Exhibition displaying his Apostolic training: "He demonstrated; he persuaded; he argued. The argument rose and soared. It vanished into the clouds. Then it swooped back into the picture" (*RF*, 152). To "serve for the skeleton of many such talks, and to give the skeleton flesh and blood" (*RF*, 270), Woolf gives "extracts" from letters. One, she tells us, "galloped across philosophy, religion, science, and art" (*RF*, 271) and also includes "mysticism," "painting," "literature." "Science interested him profoundly," Woolf writes. "As a young man he had been trained as a scientist" (*CE*, IV, 90)[5] – as a botanist, like William Bankes. "Thanks to his scientific mind he understood – a proof of disinterested intelligence which had pleased her," Lily Briscoe thinks of Bankes (*TL*, 262–3). The second Fry allowed other "curiosities" to intervene: "as the years at Cambridge went on, art was more and more frequently interrupting science" (*RF*, 52). But if he abandoned a scientific career, he never rid himself of his scientific bent: "The result was a compromise and a strange one," Woolf observes, "the first time his dissertation was purely scientific" while "the second time he tried to combine science and art – his dissertation was 'On the Laws of Phenomenology and their application to Greek painting'" (*RF*, 60).

Fry's personal biography anticipated the Apostles' development into Bloomsbury.

If the negotiator of the compromise was philosophy, it was not the Cambridge philosophy most commentators mention – not Moore's ethics but Moore's and Russell's epistemology and the other *Principia*, Russell's and Whitehead's. Clive Bell, arguing Russell's "influence" and Fry's "authority" within Bloomsbury, writes that "Roger Fry . . . was definitely anti-Moorist" (*Old Friends*, 133). It is telling that Fry painted two portraits of Russell but none of Moore.[6] Unlike T. S. Eliot, Fry found "Bertie's article [*A Free Man's Worship*] . . . very fine indeed" (*RF*, 118). Fry wrote to Marie Mauron to suggest she "learn English so as to" translate Russell "into French":

> Just now I am reading Bertrand Russell's books. He is one of the men of genius of our time. With help from others he is starting a real metaphysic based on fundamental ideas about mathematics – a humble, unpretentious metaphysic with the same solidity as other sciences. They have definitely resolved some of Zeno's paradoxes (Achilles and the Tortoise (?)) [sic] which have tortured the human mind for two thousand years . . . it puts all the pretentions, systems and tendencies of the great philosophers in their place; such systems are entirely anthropocentric, full of human desires and prejudices. (*LettersRF*, II, 485)

"Mathematics," "solidity," "sciences," anti-"ethical bias" – all go into Fry's aesthetic thinking.

The importance of science and logic for Fry's aesthetic explains his penchant for Russell over Moore: the artist rejects common sense. Both Fry and Woolf felt the imaginative power of the "scientific outlook," just as had the Leslie Stephen who wrote "Make philosophy one of the physical sciences" (*HET*, 66). Woolf quotes a letter in which Fry describes "a good old Cambridge Apostolic discussion about existence, whether good was absolute or not" with "Charles [Mauron] and I representing modern science" (*RF*, 270) and arguing "that Oliver [Strachey] and Leonard [Woolf] were mystics. They could not accept the complete relativity of everything to human nature and the impossibility of talking at all about things in themselves" (*RF*, 270). Fry wished to align art with science, and not, as we shall see Russell does, make it a form of mysticism. But analysis alone was inadequate for artistic creation. "I suppose you feel . . .", Fry wrote Woolf, "that I will go on analysing when you want to make a certain whole and look without pulling it apart'" (*RF*, 284). For, she says, "if Roger Fry received the impulse to create from the work of art rather than from the thing itself, it was because a work of art posed an intellectual problem and thus gratified that intense intellectual curiosity, the desire 'to pull apart and to analyse,' which . . . was either too active, or too separate, to let him submit, as perhaps an artist must submit, completely and unconsciously to the experience itself" (*RF*, 284). But Fry's aesthetic acknowledges the limits of the analysis of experience, which was only preliminary, and seeks in logic the principles to complete it.

As in Russell, the artist's reconstruction of the external world makes its foundation "fundamental ideas about mathematics," proceeding via a dual seeing. First the look of the world is registered; then its non-visual structure brought to light. In Moore's and Russell's early Platonism, the objects of sight are dual. There are sense-data seen with the body's eyes. There are also directly apprehended abstract objects: universals, propositions, logical forms – "perceptions of relations" (*PE*, 76). As Hylton puts it, "truths are perceived with the eye of the mind rather than with the eyes of the body" (*Russell*, 197). For, in the search for knowledge, it is not enough to scrutinize appearances. One must penetrate to the forms beneath. These are revealed in stark outline to Mr. Ramsay's "fiery unworldliness; he knows nothing about trifles" (*TL*, 40). The condition of seeing them is the dimming of sensible vision, Mr. Ramsay's blindness to "ordinary things" (*TL*, 107), for they are hidden by appearances. Only certain categories of "gazers" – for Woolf the insomniac, the restless wanderer, the philosopher – can see otherwise than with the senses: "But who, save the nerve-worn and sleepless, or thinkers standing with hands to the eyes on some crag above the multitude, see things thus in skeleton outline, bare of flesh?" (*JR*, 154). Their refrain is "Damn your eyes, damn your eyes" (*TL*, 113). The statue's stone face with its "fixed marble eyes" (*JR*, 172), Mr. Ramsay's "lizard's eye" (*TL*, 54), his "eye like an eagle's" (*TL*, 107), can "pierce the darkness" (*TL*, 55), "the eyeless dark" (*CE*, II, 296), discerning "extraordinary things" (*TL*, 107) like logical symbols: "After Q there are a number of letters the last of which is scarcely visible to mortal eyes" (*TL*, 53).

The extent to which visualizability could be maintained for the objects of logic depended on the status of logical form. It was a lingering influence of Bradleyian Idealism in Russell's realism; its visibility is momentary and skeletal, like Tyndall's demonstrations, when "the design instantly flashes forth" (*Lectures on Light*, 130), eventually to disappear into the "theory . . . apprehended logically" (*OKnExW*, 136). Clive Bell's "'significant form' was form behind which we catch a sense of ultimate reality . . . revealing itself through pure form" (*Art*, 54). Whitehead tentatively dismisses the possibility that "relationships are unperceivable" (*Symbolism*, 43). A bare core of the invisible, logical form, is discernible. "The structure is now visible; what is inchoate is here stated; . . . we have made oblongs and stood them upon squares" (*W*, 163) It wavers on the edge of a ghostly apprehendability, difficult to seize: "the isolated understanding of a pure form is more difficult than the understanding of an instance" because "pure forms are fugitive to attention"; even if "simpler," they are "not necessarily, or even usually, easier than what is more complex" (*TK*, 132). "'[T]he book, the thing'" the novelist "'made, lies imprisoned in the volume, and our glimpse of it was too fleeting . . . to leave us with a lasting knowledge of its form,'" Woolf quotes Percy Lubbock. Yet something like a directly apprehended logical form, "a gigantic pattern, momentarily perceptible" (*Y*, 369), also "fixes and makes permanent," as Woolf says of reality itself, and thus prevents "whatever it touches" (*Room*, 114), like a photographic image, from otherwise fading in the light of time. Yet it may remain vague, as in Woolf's preconception of the unwritten "Time Passes" – "I cannot make it out"; it is "abstract," "all eyeless and featureless" (*Diary*, III, 76). The tangible, representing, we saw, not the sensible but form, will mark the limits of form's visualizability in Fry's "plastic color," in which vision admits the "control of non-visual – specifically of tactile – experiences" (*H-M*, 11). Woolf likewise conceives the novelist's form as impossible to visualize; it must be "felt," albeit more abstractly: the novelist, "under the power of that vision which she had seen clearly once and must now grope for" (*TL*, 82), emulates science, which "felt not quite blindly for the law that ruled" the "endless variations" of nature (*ND*, 331). Lubbock's form is "interposed between us and the book," "an alien substance which requires to be visualized" (*CE*, II, 126), whereas we may not be "in a position to perceive the form itself" (*CE*, II, 124), we must be "free from images," because Lubbock's "'book itself' is not form which you see, but emotion which you feel." Starting from impressions and emotions, form is "feeling their right relations." Once the relations are established, "with our eyes we see nothing at all" (*CE*, II, 126).

Russell's logical economy aims to make perceptible what is not by compressing and streamlining: "We naturally interpret the world pictorially – that is to say, we imagine that what goes on is more or less like what we see. But in fact this likeness can only extend to certain formal logical properties expressing structure" (*ABCR*, 227). The "terseness" of logical symbolism, *Principia Mathematica*'s Introduction explains, is what "enables a whole proposition to be represented to the eyesight as one whole, or at most in two or three parts divided where the natural breaks, represented in the symbolism, occur" (2). It condenses "trains of reasoning" to show what is normally discoverable by a process not akin to sight. This is why "in a logically correct symbolism there will always be a fundamental identity of structure between a fact and the symbol for it" (*LK*, 197). The idea of a "pictorial" logical structure revealed by the symbolism returns us to the *Tractatus*' picture theory; "we perceive a proposition," Wittgenstein states in 4.012, "as a picture." Russell's "illustration" in *The ABC of Relativity* no doubt alludes to the *Tractatus*' "picture theory of propositions." "Between a piece of orchestral music as played, and the same piece of music as printed in the score, there is a certain resemblance, which may be described as a resemblance in structure," he writes (*ABCR*, 227). In *Tractatus* 4.014, Wittgenstein states that "[t]he gramophone record, the musical thought, the score, the waves of sound, all stand to one another in that pictorial internal relation, which holds between language and the world. To all of them the logical structure is common."[7] From his examples, Anthony Kenny comments, Wittgenstein clearly "would count as pictures not only paintings, drawings, photographs and other obviously pictorial representations in two dimensions, but also maps, sculptures, three-dimensional models, and even such things as musical scores and gramophone records" ("Bradley," 54). "Photographs," Woolf herself says, "are not arguments addressed to the reason; they are simply statements of fact addressed to the eye" (*TG*, 10). This "very simplicity" allows the photograph to function as a kind of "atomic" proposition representing an "atomic fact." The proposition as a form picturing reality thus permits a picture to be a proposition.

The visual metaphor means "acquaintance remains the paradigm of knowledge," as Hylton says (*Russell*, 376). "All knowledge" for Moore, Hylton claims, "ultimately has the characteristics of directness and immediacy which are, arguably, possessed by the perception of simple sensory qualities" (127–8). "In the first exuberance of liberation, I became a naïve realist," Russell would say later (*MyPhD*, 48). Knowledge by description, subsequently introduced, is in a stronger sense eyeless, less naïve. What is knowable only by description cannot be visualized. Here is perhaps a difference between Wittgenstein and Russell attributable to the "disconcerting role of visual imagery" in the *Tractatus* which Black pronounces "disturbing" (*Companion*, 17). Russell's growing emphasis after 1905 and especially after 1912 on description accompanies the theory of knowledge itself. To know becomes no longer simply to see. Acquaintance is not fully knowledge: "A patch of colour is certainly not knowledge, and therefore we cannot say that pure sensation is cognitive" (*Mind*). Then, the perceptual metaphor was too close for Russell to the mystical belief in insight alone (*ML*, 8–9). "Science," Tyndall writes, "is only in part a thing of the senses" (*Lectures on Light*, 4). Science requires another kind of knowledge. Russell had characterized science's necessary abstractness, as had Tyndall, precisely as representing what cannot be visualized, where logical representation is an alternative to picturing:

men cannot frame sufficiently abstract hypotheses; imagination is always intruding upon logic, and causing men to make pictures of occurrences which are essentially incapable of being visualized . . . The world that we can picture is the world that we see; but the world of physics is an abstract world that cannot be seen. (*SO*, 67)

Explaining relativity, at one point Russell remarks parenthetically: "I advise the reader not to try to picture this, because it is impossible" (*ABCR*, 129). The "logical imagination" he prescribes for understanding mathematical continuity he counterposes to "visualizing." Bergson's "failure to realize imaginatively, as well as abstractly, the nature of continuous series as they appear in mathematics" (*OKnExW*, 136) Russell attributes to the fact that "Bergson is a strong visualizer, whose thought is always conducted by means of visual images." He "always exalts the sense of sight at the expense of the other senses, and his views on space would seem to be largely determined by this fact" ("PhilBerg," 330). This explains his attack on mathematical continuity: "Bergson's views depend upon the predominance of the sense of sight in him. There is no logical necessity to range the strokes of a clock in an imaginary space" ("PhilBerg," 336). Continuity requires a non-visual model:

When a theory has been apprehended logically, there is often a long and serious labour still required in order to *feel* it: it is necessary to . . . acquire the kind of intimacy which, in the case of a foreign language, would enable us to think and dream in it, not merely to construct laborious sentences by the help of grammar and dictionary" (*OKnExW*, 136)

The counter-intuitive effort involved means the apprehension of form is not full knowledge.

Can the mind become as it were "acquainted" with a knowledge by description? The analogy with language learning, the work of time, suggests that certain truths are grasped not "together in one flash," but serially, as Mr. Ramsay does (*TL*, 55). In fact, although Wittgenstein's idea of the form being "shown" (or "mirrored") but not "said" might lead one, Black says, to "think that what is shown must somehow be 'seen' in some single non-discursive act: just as we see the visual pattern of some design 'in a flash'," this is a mistake, Black argues: "Wittgenstein's conception does not require us to apprehend logical form in a single act of insight" (*Companion*, 192). Russell criticizes Berkeley for assuming that anything "cannot be radically different in nature from what we see" (*PP*, 13–14). The logical construction builds pieces of visuality into the "physical object" we cannot directly see; precisely the whole is not grasped visually, however, but only knowable "by description." A chain of "sense, reason, and analysis, which are regarded as blind guides" by mysticism (*ML*, 9), distances the knower from the known, just as, for Wittgenstein, "[l]ogical form is discovered by calculation with signs – not by intuition"; it is "revealed discursively" (Black, *Companion*, 192). Nicod's "preuve géométrique," "une chaîne de raisonnements formels," in a certain sense "aveugles" (*La Géométrie*, 8), allows one to proceed "ainsi les yeux fermés" (9). Hence, another justification Russell gives for logical symbolism is that it "aids the intuition in regions too abstract for the imagination readily to present to the mind the true relation between the ideas employed." Here it does not make visible but reveals that the eye deceives. For instance, where similarity of grammatical structure misrepresents differences of logical relations, symbolism reveals the true dissimilarity: "'a whale is big' and 'one is a number' both look alike" (*PM*, 2). Science is indeed the knowledge of the blind. "It is sometimes said that 'light *is* a form of wave-motion,'" Russell writes, but "the light which we immediately see" is "quite different – something which we all know if we are not blind, though we cannot describe it" whereas

> [a] wave-motion, on the contrary, could quite well be described to a blind man, since he can acquire a knowledge of space by the sense of touch; and he can experience a wave-motion by a sea voyage . . . But this, which a blind man can understand, is not what we mean by *light*: we mean by *light* just that which a blind man can never understand, and which we can never describe to him.
>
> Now this something, which all of us who are not blind know, is not, according to science, really to be found in the outer world: it is something caused by the action of certain waves upon the eyes and nerves and brain of the person who sees the light. When it is said that light *is* waves, what is really meant is that waves are the physical cause of our sensations of light. But light itself, the thing which seeing people experience and blind people do not, is not supposed by science to form any part of the world that is independent of us and our senses. (*PP*, 28–9)

The blind can have an eyeless knowledge of light, but they cannot "visualize" it. Mauron, blind, seeks aesthetic principles "[e]n tâtonnant" (*Introduction à la psychanalyse de Mallarmé*, 213). They are not revealed "at once."[8]

An eyeless logical form completes Fry's visual aesthetic: art is more than a picture of appearances. First, it is a directly apprehendable pattern or "scale" (Wittgenstein, *Tractatus* 2.1512). "[T]he generalising intellect" for Fry finds its "analogue, in art," where "the recognition of relations is immediate and sensational" (*V&D*, 81); in art "fundamental relationships are recognized by a kind of sensual logic" (*LettersRF*, II, 497). Form crystallizes the geometry in the sensible world. For Fry, the innovation of Cézanne is to show it through welding it to color and not through outlining. The dual aims of representing appearances and revealing their underlying order motivate Fry's theory of the relation between Impressionism and Post-Impressionism. The first of the two great modern movements in painting takes an important preliminary step beyond common sense, a refinement of "Descartes's method," which "is on the whole a sound one for the starting-point" (*LK*, 181). In Fry's version of the history of painting, Impressionism exhausted the project of art as solely "the representation of the totality of appearance" (*V&D*, 11), failing to present anything more than the look of things. Its impasse was the crisis of unity – in painting, the crisis of design. Impressionism's equation of art with the exact reproduction of appearances had destroyed coherent design.

Post-Impressionism, akin to logical philosophy, goes beyond recording the data of experience, taking them as "a sign of some 'reality' behind" (PP, 16). It organizes vision – color – via geometry, mathematics and logic, revealing "the scattered beauty which needs only to be combined by artists in order to become visible to all" (*TG*, 114). Cézanne, "among those great imaginative artists to whom some actual vision is necessary as a point of departure" (*Cé*, 82), combines "radical analysis and reconstruction" (*ML*, 130). "Of these two processes," Woolf writes, "the first – to receive impressions – is undoubtedly the easier, the simpler, and the pleasanter" (*CE*, II, 132). The second is to construct out of these impressions something hard and enduring. In Clive Bell's slightly different version, "a great emotional renaissance must be preceded by an intellectual, destructive movement" (*Art*, 205). Fry's well-known formalism is thus linked to Russellian formalization. Lily Briscoe paints "with the dim eyes" to "subdue her impressions . . . to something much more general" (*TL*, 82). The distancing from the Impressionist canvas famously required for optimal viewing – "Lily stepped back to get her canvas – so – into perspective" (*TL*, 256) – is already a step toward Post-Impressionism. The artist wishes, like the old nurse in *The Waves*, "who turns the pages of the picture-book," to say " 'Look. This is the truth' " (287). The novel must first be a "picture-book," an art of the eye, then an "abstract mystical eyeless book" (*Diary*, III, 203).

Ultimately, art is concerned with knowledge, like philosophy itself. Impressionism is a form of acquaintance; Post-Impressionism, a knowledge by description. Speaking of Fry's painting, Woolf asks "is it a good thing that an artist should also be a critic, or does it inhibit his creative power?" (*CE*, IV, 92). Her answer espouses an intellectual art which does "research," makes "discoveries," with experiments and rigor, and aims for a "solution of the artistic problem" (*Cé*, 53) that goes beyond vision: "Is it necessary that an artist, in order to use his genius fully, should live half submerged in the dim world of ignorance, or . . . does knowledge and the consciousness that comes with it lead him to be more daring and more drastic in his researches and discoveries" (*CE*, IV, 92)? As with Henry James, " '[t]he only real *scholar* in the art' beats the amateurs" (*CE*, II, 128).

Both stages of this dual aesthetic derive from science's method of making the familiar strange; both depart from common sense. "Obviousness is the enemy of correctness," Russell asserts. "Hence we invent some new and difficult symbolism, in which nothing seems obvious" (*ML*, 73). Fry also "looked at the carpet from the wrong side" Woolf writes, "but he made it for that very reason display unexpected patterns" (*RF*, 241; also *RF*, 259). Impressionism makes "our familiar table" (*PP*, 16) unfamiliar by seeing it "of different colours from different points of view" (*PP*, 9), as Lily upends the table in her mind's eye. Fry's artist, too, must show the extraordinary in "ordinary experience" – "a chair," "a table" (*TL*, 300).

It is for its ordinariness that in his 1927 *Cézanne*, contemporary with *To the Lighthouse*, Fry takes as Cézanne's "point of departure" the "kitchen table" (*Cé*, 49). Fry had already made that point in 1924: "no one who has a real understanding of the art of painting attaches any importance to what we call the subject of a picture," he wrote, adding that Cézanne "expressed some of his grandest conceptions in pictures of fruit and crockery on a common kitchen table" (*The Artist and Psychoanalysis*, 16).[9] The philosophical tradition from Hume through Leslie Stephen and Russell gave Woolf the table; Cézanne through Fry made philosophy's and art's common object a kitchen table. Together their analyses render it "startlingly visible" (*TL*, 54). Cézanne's genius was to create a single vision out of two realities, to unite the visible to the eyeless.

RAINBOW AND GRANITE/VISION AND DESIGN

Vision is the necessary antecedent to control and to direction. (Whitehead, "Technical Education and its Relation to Science and Literature," *The Aims of Education and Other Essays*, 58)

The dualism Russell sees marking reality itself justifies the method which moves from experience to what is outside it, attempting "the correlation" of physics "with objects of sense" (*ML*, 140). Dividing the reality art represents too, Woolf's granite and rainbow translates into Fry's "dual nature of painting" (*TR*, 154), his "vision and design." Fry's visual and unvisual are specifically color and the colorless, "shape and weight, something unvisual beneath" (*W*, 156). Rainbow, standing synecdochically for all sensible qualities, is first the spectrum of colors. Appearances are saturated with color, while granite, a matter without sensible qualities itself, is essentially drained of color, leaving a rigid form.

This reduction of the primary qualities to the absence of color or sound is a commonplace of Cambridge realism. The "immediate data of sense" are "certain patches of colour, sounds, tastes, smells, etc., with certain spatio-temporal relations." Matter, by contrast, consists of colorless atoms or soundless waves, for "molecules have no colour, atoms make no noise, electrons have no taste, and corpuscles do not even smell" (*ML*, 140). "Nature is a dull affair," Whitehead writes, "soundless, scentless, colourless; merely the hurrying of material, endlessly, meaninglessly" (*SMW*, 55); "colours and sounds," Russells echoes him, "are absent from the scientific world of matter," as likewise "*space* as we get it through sight or touch" (*PP*, 29). "Roughly speaking," Wittgenstein states, "objects are colourless" (*Tractatus*, 2.0232). Russell would describe his escape from Idealism in terms of the substitution of color for its lack: "With a sense of escaping from prison, we allowed ourselves to think that grass is green," Russell wrote. "The world, which had been thin and logical, suddenly became rich and varied and solid" (Passmore, *Hundred Years*, 207). Sense appearances "paint" an otherwise colorless matter. Yet "Russell's own world . . . was to become progressively 'thin and logical,'" Passmore comments (207), as Mr. Ramsay's "gaze seemed to fall dolefully over the sunny grass and discolour it" (*TL*, 227). The thing seen bleaches the vision too, "gently putting out with a damp sponge the colour in one's own eyes" (*CE*, II, 293). His "seeing of angular essences" consisted of the "reducing of lovely evenings, with all their flamingo clouds and blue and silver to a white deal four-legged table," i.e, an unpainted, mathematicized one (*TL*, 38). Beyond the rainbow clouds was "blue, pure blue, black blue," the ultimate colorlessness of matter (*BA*, 23). In the analytic gaze, some things disappear, like the "trees and colours" about which Sara Pargiter wonders: "Would they be there if we didn't see them?" (*Y*, 140). Yet other things come into sight in it. Mrs. Ramsay too has a revelation through such a reduction: "as if a shade had fallen, . . . robbed of colour, she saw things truly" (*TL*, 126). In the blackness of night, things lose color but gain weight:

> dark descends, pours over the outlines of houses and towers; bleak hillsides soften and fall in. But though they are gone, the night is full of them; robbed of colour, blank of windows, they exist more ponderously, . . . huddled together in the darkness; reft of the relief which dawn brings, when, washing the walls white and grey, spotting each window-pane, lifting the mist from the fields, showing the red-brown cows peacefully grazing, all is once more decked out to the eye; exists again. (*MrsD*, 34–5)

What persists in the colorless dark are the slumbering forms of things, like the white sheeted furniture in "Time Passes." The table's "'real' shape is not what we see," Russell tells us (*PP*, 11). Unobserved sensibilia crystallize in the logical skeleton. The table's pallor, a result of x-ray vision, is its ghostly image, repeated in "the hoary lighthouse" (*TL*, 23), qualified as "stone-white" (*MrsD*, 247).[10] The contrast of visible and invisible is seconded by that of audible and inaudible, apparent in Woolf's imagery. "The wheelbarrow, the lawnmower, the sound of poplar trees, leaves whitening before rain, rooks cawing, brooms knocking, dresses rustling" – the familiar list of sensibilia – "all these . . . so coloured and distinguished in his mind" against "the image of stark and uncompromising severity" (*TL*, 10) of "blocks" of matter.

The relation between colorful sense-data and colorless matter establishes the philosophical framework for an aesthetic, one worked out paradigmatically for the visual arts in the theories of Fry and Clive Bell, and for literature by Mauron and Woolf herself. In Fry, it borrowed its oppositions from an ancient quarrel in the history of painting, that between the "colorists" – a word which Fry uses fluently – and the proponents of drawing or design.[11] "Insistence on design is perhaps the most obvious characteristic of the movement," Clive Bell comments (*Art*, 235). Echoes of the quarrel are heard in Woolf. "All great writers are great colourists," she writes (*CE*, II, 241). "Pope has no great range of colours; he is more draughtsman than colourist" (*CE*, II, 242). The two terms Fry's aesthetic sought to reconcile are reframed within the theory of knowledge. The "problem of colour," as Fry called it (*Cé*, 57), was resolved by forms conferring unity. Because truth was the aim, that unity, like science's hypotheses, had to conform to the shape of what there is.

Color and design also oppose beauty and life. Life, like sense-data, is particular, atomized, accidental, formless. "Appearance and movement are the lures" of life (*CE*, II, 135); "the swarm and confusion of life" (*CE*, II, 135) are a function of its atomism:

> So when the wind roams through a forest innumerable twigs stir; hives are brushed; insects sway on grass blades; the spider runs rapidly up a crease in the bark; and the whole air is tremulous with breathing; elastic with filaments . . . the stir in the air is the indescribable agitation of life. (*JR*, 163)

Color in Woolf is lifeblood, a liquid that throbs through veins – of plants, of living flesh: "colour returns; runs up the stalks of grass; blows out into tulips and crocuses; . . . fills the gauze of the air"; it "paints the lustrous bellying crimson curtains" (*JR*, 163); it is "the pulse of colour" (*TL*, 33), "the fluidity of life" (*TL*, 237).[12] Its liquidity can burst into flame, so alive is it: "It was strange that the earth, with all those flowers incandescent – the lilies, the roses, and clumps of white flowers and bushes of burning green – should still be hard. From the earth green waters seemed to rise over her" (*BA*, 210–11). Life is what *Ulysses* captures. "If we want life itself, here surely we have it," Woolf asserts (*CE*, II, 107).

Against life is set a beauty of form which must first be separated from aestheticism, from "'Beautiful pictures. Beautiful phrases'" (*TL*, 287) that elicit a Bloomsbury suspicion of beauty.[13] This is accomplished in two stages: "pure vision abstracted from necessity" (*V&D*, 25) first strips life of beauty "to reveal the flickerings of that innermost flame which flashes its messages through the brain" (*CE*, II, 107). For beauty, like reality, is dual. There is an

> apparent contradiction between two distinct uses of the word beauty, one for that which has sensuous charm, and one for the aesthetic approval of works of imaginative art where the objects presented to us are often of extreme ugliness. Beauty in the former sense belongs to works of art where only the perceptual aspect of the imaginative life is exercised" (*V&D*, 30–1).

Clive Bell similarly "distinguish[es] between the beauty of a work of art and the beauty of a flower," concluding, "Is it not simpler to use different words?" (Art, 191). One beauty is the eye's: "For the eye has this strange property: it rests only on beauty; like a butterfly it seeks colour and basks in warmth" (*CE*, IV, 157). The Impressionist eye substitutes dispassionate, indiscriminate observation. Fry's insistence on the ordinariness of the artist's subject was one aspect of this anti-aestheticism.[14] The artist's "vision" was not a sensitivity to beauty; beauty, like common sense, is an impediment to vision. "The artist is of all men the most constantly observant of his surroundings, and the least affected by their intrinsic aesthetic value," he wrote (*V&D*, 54). Art may require "the sacrifice of sensual beauty" indispensible in an object: "there is no excuse for a china pot being ugly, there is every reason why Rembrandt's and Degas' pictures should be, from the purely sensual point of view, supremely and magnificently ugly" (*V&D*, 30). "Beauty is part ugliness" in the modern world is Woolf's version; its art cannot be purely aesthetic:

> For example: It is a spring night, the moon is up, the nightingale singing, the willows bending over the river. Yes, but at the same time a diseased old woman is picking over her greasy rags on a hideous iron bench. She and the spring enter his [the modern writer's] mind together. (*CE*, II, 222–3)[15]

The beauty art requires is purely formal, i.e., eyeless: "beauty in the second sense becomes as it were supersensual" (*V&D*, 31). Its properties are those of the physical table: abstractness, austerity, stonelike rigidity. Such beauty Russell attributes to mathematics:

Mathematics, rightly viewed, possesses not only truth, but supreme beauty – a beauty cold and austere, like that of sculpture, . . . without the gorgeous trappings of a painting or music, yet sublimely pure, and capable of a stern perfection such as only the greatest art can show. (*ML*, 57)

The analogy with sculpture emphasizes colorlessness and the tangibility that stands for form. Russell introduces this abstract aesthetic in his 1921 encounter with Woolf. She records his saying:

God does mathematics. That's my feeling. It is the most exalted form of art.
Art? I said.
Well, theres style in mathematics as there is in writing, he said. I get the keenest aesthetic pleasure from reading well written mathematics. (*Diary*, II, 147)

Woolf "said that I disagreed with much of this." Yet Fry agrees when he considers the aesthetic emotions "like a mathematician's recognition of the validity of an equation" (*RF*, 273). Fry may have eventually led Woolf to Russell's position, for she later writes that the novelist can lead us to take a pleasure in the mind's "power to make patterns . . . to bring out relations . . . akin, perhaps, to the pleasure of mathematics" in "the impersonality of numbers" (*CE*, II, 82).

Fry's formal aesthetics is thus not aestheticism. The colored and the colorless, the quivering and the still, observe Russell's division between existence and being. The first contains "everything that makes any difference to the value of life"; the second appeals to "all who love perfection more than life" (*PP*, 100). This is exactly Fry's opposition between the mechanistic and the vital, where "mechanistic" is purely descriptive and not perjorative:

the conscious mind tends to a mechanistic view of things, a view amenable to mathematical statement: the unconscious brings in the vital element which eludes mathematical statement. The intellect finds its satisfaction in mathematical uniformity . . . it finds in the inorganic world of the crystal a perfect mathematical arrangement. The order it seeks for, and partially establishes, is one of absolute uniformity – all circles are identical statements of a proposition – all ellipses which correspond to a given formula are identical. But the distinguishing characteristic of living things is precisely that each one is unique. (*LL*, 28)

The balance between vision and design was thus that fine balance between life and a form which held "life itself" still without destroying it so "life becomes . . . able to stand by itself – a sort of impersonal miracle" (*CE*, II, 135). From the point of view of one the other is only a "pale shadow." Russell's Platonic language evokes those ghosts of objects and persons that haunt Woolf's fiction. But "no sooner have we distinguished the two worlds than it becomes necessary to consider their relations" (*PP*, 100). The logical "relation of sense-data to physics" is not only Russell's solution to the problem of knowledge but for Fry Post-Impressionism's solution to Impressionism's "problem of colour." Beauty of eye, analyzed away, is replaced by a formal, unaestheticized beauty. The "pulse of colour that flooded the bay with blue" is, like the sense-datum in a perspective, "only the next instant to be checked and chilled by the prickly blackness on the ruffled waves" (*TL*, 33). "Life is subjected to a thousand disciplines and exercises" so that it is "stiffened" as bone corrects posture. "There emerges from the mist something stark, something formidable and enduring, the bone and substance upon which our rush of indiscriminating emotion was founded" (*CE*, II, 131–2), "a pinnacle, a dome, prominent things, without names" (*TL*, 112–13). Yet "beauty was not everything" (*TL*, 264). Life is what escapes its mathematical perfection. "Whether we call it life or spirit, truth or reality," it names "this, the essential thing" whose allusiveness art must capture in order to give "the solidity, the likeness to life" (*CE*, II, 105). In painting Mrs. Ramsay, it cannot be "her beauty merely that one thought of, one must remember the quivering thing, the living thing," then "work it into the picture" (*TL*, 47).

IMPRESSIONIST COLOR: PAINTING WITH LIGHT

[N]ature has given heightened perceptions to animals, from the care she has taken to provide them with organs, which collect numerous rays of light, or numerous undulations of the air. (Leibniz, *The Monadology* 25, 231)

Were we once insects . . . ; all eye? Do we still preserve the capacity for drinking, eating, indeed becoming colour furled up in us . . . ? On first entering a picture gallery, whose stillness, warmth and seclusion from the perils of the street reproduce the conditions of the primeval forest, it often seems as if we reverted to the insect stage of our long life . . . became completely and solely an insect, all eye. (Woolf, *Collected Essays*, II, 234–5)

Painting begins then with seeing appearances of which color is the primary example. This means the painter learns, contra naturam, to not see what common sense sees. To break the habit of ordinary seeing "is why, in the search for data," Russell concludes, "we are driven to analysis" (139). The problem is that "the thing seen" (*TR*, 194) disappears when seeing endows it with meaning, for, "when seven or eight people dined together," they agreed that "in the eyes of a motorist red is not a colour but simply a danger signal. We shall very soon lose our sense of colour" in "the change wrought upon our senses by modern conditions" (*CE*, II, 233). "[T]he talk turned" then "to colour":

> how different people see colour differently; how painters are affected by their place of birth, whether in the blue South or the grey North; how colour blazes, unrelated to any object, in the eyes of children; how politicians and business men are blind, days spent in an office leading to atrophy of the eye; and so, by contrast, to those insects, said still to be found in the primeval forests of South America, in whom the eye is so developed that they are all eye, the body a tuft of leather, serving merely to connect the two great chambers of vision. (*CE*, II, 234)

Seeing color requires the faculty Fry calls "sensibility," which responds to life and "corresponds to our desire for variety, multiplicity, chance, the unforeseeable" (*LL*, 28). Fry's "sensibility" is equivalent to Russell's "sensitivity" to sense-data. As "the creative vision," it becomes "the furthest perversion of the gifts of nature" (*V&D*, 51) by "removing the automatism of perception" (*V&D*, 16). It requires a pure, sensuous eye severed from a mind, not "the incessant activity of the mind's eye" (*W*, 156). In creative vision, "[t]he eye . . . , the brain sleeps perhaps as it looks" (*CE*, IV, 156). "Eye and brain are torn asunder ruthlessly," Woolf writes (*CE*, II, 269); "our conscious mind must be all body, and then the unconscious mind leaps to the top and strips off veils" (*CE*, II, 302); "the brain, agreeably titillated, settles down to watch things happening without bestirring itself to think" (*CE*, II, 268). The philosophers of Fry's acquaintance, commenting on common-sense vision, explicitly contrast it with the artist's. The artist, both Russell and Whitehead say and perhaps came to realize from some unrecorded conversation with their "friend the artist" Fry, must "unlearn the habit of thinking that things seem to have the colour which common sense says they 'really' have, and to learn the habit of seeing things as they appear" (*PP*, 9). Whitehead insists, like Fry, on the unnaturalness of the artist's vision:

> We look up and see a coloured shape in front of us, and we say, – there is a chair. But what we have seen is the mere coloured shape. Perhaps an artist might not have jumped to the notion of a chair. He might have stopped at the mere contemplation of a beautiful colour and a beautiful shape. But those of us who are not artists are very prone, especially if we are tired, to pass straight from the perception of a coloured shape to the enjoyment of the chair . . . my friend the artist, who kept himself to the contemplation of colour, shape and position, was a very highly trained man, and had acquired this facility of ignoring the chair at the cost of great labour . . . if we had been accompanied by a puppy dog, in addition to the artist, the dog would have acted immediately on the hypothesis of a chair and would have jumped onto it by way of using it as such. Again, if the dog had refrained from such action, it would have been because it was a well-trained dog . . . we – men and puppy dogs – require careful training if we are to refrain from acting upon it [the hypothesis]. (Whitehead, *Symbolism*, 3–4)

Pure seeing is detached from use; common-sense vision, Whitehead implies, is essentially utilitarian. "The artists who called themselves impressionists" for Fry also saw without practical purpose, maintaining "the complete detachment of the artistic vision from the values imposed on vision by everyday life" (*V&D*, 10): "Biologically speaking, art is a blasphemy. We were given our eyes to see things, not to look at them . . . differences of appearance that have a utility value still continue to be appreciated, while large and unimportant visual characters, provided they are useless for life, will pass unnoticed" (*V&D*, 47). "It is only when an object exists in our lives for no other purpose than to be seen that we really look at it" (*V&D*, 25). Russell extends this even to seeing logical form:

> Attention, as a psychical occurrence, is governed by biological considerations: particulars may be good to eat or likely to kill us, and therefore it is useful to pay attention to them; but logical forms are not edible or hostile, and attention to them is not a cause of longevity. This sufficiently explains why it is only a few eccentric persons, unusually relieved from the struggle for existence, whose attention wanders to such unimportant objects. (*TK*, 132–3)

Russell too contrasts the painter with "the practical man" (*PP*, 9).

Pure seeing, like scientific observation, is indiscriminate seeing, so different, Russell says, from "the selectiveness of our perceptual apparatus" (*ABCR*, 185). By qualifying "particulars" as "emphatic" (*TK*, 40) as opposed to the later "ego-centric" (*IMT*, 102), Russell implied the perspective's "selectiveness" was built-in, function of its centered structure. But we saw that he does not exclude the suspension of selectiveness in "inattentive acquaintance" (*TK*, 125). The principle of selection is indeed what philosopher, scientist and Impressionist alike have to unlearn. The scientific instrument's sensitivity becomes the idealization of unselective observation. "All primitive consciousness is selective; the 'sensible continuum,' which rejects nothing, is the product of the psychologist's scientific impartiality"; to it, "all selection is abhorrent" (*TK*, 124). Instead of highlighting, the instrument-eye must shed an even light. The Lighthouse's "stare" shows such unselectiveness; it "looked with equanimity" at all things (*TL*, 208). Such impartiality involves "great difficulties in the analysis of sense-data," the beginning of "the labour of thought required to discover the more abstract constituents of quite easily apprehended facts" (*TK*, 120). Only by a comparable labor, according to Fry, do artists "become true spectators, not selecting what we will see, but seeing everything equally, and thereby we come to notice a number of appearances and relations of appearances, which would have escaped our notice before, owing to that perpetual economising by selection of what impressions we assimilate, which in life we perform by unconscious processes" (*V&D*, 20). Via the equalizing vision, a portrait is flattened into a still-life, as with Cézanne's self-portrait, where the object blends with its surroundings:

> the bony structure of the skull reveals itself through subtle variations of the contour, and how much more objectively he gazes on himself. He poses to himself as he wished his sitters to pose, "as an apple," and he looks at his own head with precisely the same regard as he turned on an apple on the kitchen table. (*Cé*, 56)

Common-sense vision is selective; Fry's non-representational formalism refuses to privilege any subject matter, giving even the minutest constituents equal value. Its impartiality is science's, in Russell's conception: "After Socrates has explained that there is an idea of the good, but not of such things as hair and mud and dirt, Parmenides advises him 'not to despise even the meanest things,' and this advice shows the genuine scientific temper" (*ML*, 7). The scientific temper applied in art becomes "entirely absorbed in apprehending the relation of forms and colour to one another, as they cohere within the object" (*V&D*, 49). The artist looks at "objects from which both the aesthetic and even the curious vision would turn away instinctively, or which they may never notice" (*V&D*, 53) to ensure that the canvas' unity is not the imposition of habitual seeing, elevating some patches of color to prominence and overlooking others. "In such circumstances the greatest object of art becomes of no more significance than any casual piece of matter; a man's head is no more and no less important than a pumpkin" (*V&D*, 52). The exercise is necessary because otherwise the artist "may be tempted to relapse into an aesthetic vision, and so see them as unities apart from their surroundings." Aesthetic vision, like egotism, has the emphasis of selection. To avoid it, the artist "turns to objects which make no strong aesthetic appeal in themselves" (*V&D*, 52–3). In this sense, aesthetic vision duplicates common sense, and Fry's "anti-aesthetic" defamiliarizes. "Aesthetic" has various synonyms: "dramatic," "rhetorical," "representational," "poetic," "literary."[16] All highlight the familiar object. The dissolving of its contours in the equalization of sense-data is, by contrast, "undramatic." Cézanne "accepts the most ordinary situations, the arrangements of objects which result from everyday life" without "dramatic purpose." There is no "drama of his fruit dishes, his baskets of vegetables, his apples spilt upon the kitchen table"; yet they are "grave events" achieved by "a process of elimination and concentration" (*Cé*, 42).

Alone among tables, the kitchen table has the requisite flatness, lacks "'poetisation', making things out more interesting than they really are" (*RF*, 241). The scenes it provides the stage for are nothing but Whitehead's events brought out in an even, prehensive relief, "dramas deprived of all dramatic incident" (*Cé*, 42). The "refusal of the assistance which romantic interpretations offer" (*Cé*, 73) marks Cézanne's style. Matisse's art achieves a similar levelling; in it "a familiar scene of every-day life takes on an air of almost monumental grandeur without any sense of rhetorical falsification" (*H-M*, 25). "Rhetorical" designates the false power to heighten. "The shock of the word rhetorical in relation to Matisse proves, by the by, the fundamental simplicity and sincerity of his attitude to life" (*H-M*, 25). Cézanne too is anti-rhetorical: "He alone was sincere enough to rely on his sensations and abandon all efforts at eloquence or emphasis" (*Cé*, 72). When only appearances are noticed, the result is a riot of color. The elimination of "what common sense regards as persistent things" (*ML*, 165) and the suppression of any principle of selection allow appearances to float free in a disordered chaos of colliding atoms. Non-emphasis randomly gives new emphases. In Woolf's image for Tchekov's art, a new room is entered:

> The emphasis is laid upon such unexpected places that at first it seems as if there were no emphasis at all; and then, as the eyes accustom themselves to twilight and discern the shapes of things in a room we see how complete the story is, how profound, and how truly in obedience to his vision Tchekov has chosen this, that, and the other, and placed them together to compose something new. (*CE*, II, 108–9)

As the atom-shower settles, "the accent falls differently from of old; the moment of importance came not here but there" (*CE*, II, 106), just as when Mrs. Ramsay leaves the room, it "shaped itself differently" (*TL*, 168).

Looking thus becomes a reduction of seeing, matching the self's reduction. In penetrating, the "arrows of sensation" open the child's sensitive body to the world (*W*, 239), exposing the "central oyster of perceptiveness, an enormous eye" (*CE*, IV, 156). The self become female organ is a sense organ, a sensitive instrument, recording what is "so vivid to my eyes" and "also to some nervous fibre" (*Diary*, III, 191). The sense-data it absorbs are fluid: "the eye licks it all up instantaneously" (*CE*, II, 268). "I am a porous vessel afloat on a sensation; a sensitive plate exposed to invisible rays" (*MB*, 133). The mollusk-organ is both eye and tongue. This absorptive eye is for Fry the experiment that defined Impressionism. Monet was "only an eye but what an eye" (*Cé*, 57).

Fry's reduction returns to the empiricist tradition's conception of the child's blankness of mind: "in Impressionism the eye, by an act of supreme renunciation, succeeds in purifying itself of all those inductions from the visual image which the whole business of life requires us to make before we leave our cradles. In Impressionism the artist's eye deliberately recovers the long lost naïveté of the new born baby's" (*H-M*, 12).

That naïveté knows nothing of the common-sense world. Woolf's "baby, who can just distinguish a great blot of blue and purple on a black background" (*MB*, 79), is an Impressionist. Fry opposes this childlike "looking" to "seeing": "Even the grown man keeps something of his unbiological, disinterested vision with regard to a few things" (*V&D*, 48) – except Woolf's "blind" "politicians and business men" (*CE*, II, 234). Fry's grown man, uniting the botanist William

Bankes' scientific curiosity with the artist's, unlike Mr. Ramsay, "still looks at flowers, and does not merely see them" (*V&D*, 48).

The child's eye means for Fry primarily a sensitivity to color, "the childish delight in pure ultramarines and vermilions," Fra Angelico's "almost childish delight in pure primary colours" (TR, 214), Cézanne's "chromatic sensibility" (*Cé*, 17). Likewise, "Van Gogh was in a sense a colourist," in that he "had a special sensitiveness to colour," an "intoxication" with it. "His reaction to colour" was "elementary and childlike" (*TR*, 183). "Colour is with him an almost physiological excitement rather than as with Cézanne an aspect of formal design. He values certain colours almost in and by themselves, as children do when they talk of their favorite colour," Fry writes elsewhere ("The Courtauld Fund," in McLaurin, *Virginia Woolf*, 73). Woolf echoes Fry in asserting that "[n]obody who can walk down Bond Street in the year 1933 without exciting suspicion in the heart of the policeman, can simplify sufficiently to see colour only. One must be a fly in order to die in aromatic pain" (*CE*, II, 235). We saw her claiming that it "blazes" in children's eyes (*CE*, II, 234), the verb the same which elsewhere represents the baby's sensation: "The flower blazed between the angles of the roots" (*BA*, 11).

Pure color, the "distinct idea" contributed by the Impressionists, was "the quasi-scientific description of new effects of atmospheric colour and atmospheric perspective, thereby endowing painting with . . . harmonies which had not been cultivated by European painters for many hundreds of years" (*V&D*, 10). "Atmospheric" covers those differences in the way the table looks from different points of view that Russell pronounces "unimportant" "[f]or most practical purposes" but "to the painter . . . all-important" (*PP*, 10). Differences in point of view are differences in color and shape. For, "as we all have to learn if we try to draw, a given thing looks different in shape from every different point of view" (*PP*, 10). Pure color is without purpose or meaning, lacks order and form. Like Seurat's "myriads of minute dots of colour" (*TR*, 190), it consists of what Herbert Feigl, in commenting on Russell, calls "'pointillistic' sense-data" ("Russell and Schlick," 323), the "logical atoms" like "patches of colour and sounds" that are the "last residue in analysis" (*LK*, 179). Thus, Impressionism begins, like *The Problems of Philosophy*, with an analysis of "Appearance and Reality," of light, as Newton, in Tyndall's words, "unravelled the texture of solar light" (*On Radiation*, 6). Both combine analysis with seeing. *The Compotier* of Cézanne, according to

Fry, is "the careful analysis of coloured surfaces" (*Cé*, 42). Art too grounds itself on the certainty of sense-data: "real artistes, even if they are destined to paint highly imaginative works . . . like Van Gogh, generally begin by making an elaborate study of an old pair of boots or something of that kind" (Fry, *The Artist and Psychoanalysis*, 15). Cézanne's object of analysis Fry identifies in *Le Compotier* as "the kitchen table" (*Cé*, 49); on *Still-Life with a Ginger Jar*'s table, "the oranges, greens and reds of the fruit tell with glowing intensity and freshness." In *Still-life with a Soup-tureen and Bottle*, "[t]he tablecloth is of a dark, rich vermilion, modified by bluish inflections where the light falls on it from the window. The citron yellows of the apples and the vivid black of the bottle stand out forcibly on the roses and pale greens which compose the background" (*Cé*, 52).

The artist's color-sensitivity arouses Woolf the novelist's jealousy: "The Grafton [Post-Impressionist Exhibition], thank God, is over; artists are an abominable race. The furious excitement of these people over their pieces of canvas coloured green and blue, is odious. Roger is now turning them upon chairs and tables," she ends, referring to the Omega Workshops (*Letters VW*, II, 15). Woolf's description attempts to render "the colours, salts, tones of existence" (*MrsD*, 45) in a very literal sense. "But what a little I can get down with my pen of what is so vivid to my eyes," she laments (*Diary*, III, 191). Her oft-noted impressionism of style deliberately imitates the Monet-like analysis of appearances, recording the way color changes under "the mysterious play of light upon matter" (*TR*, 40), like "the colour thinning and thickening from blue to the green of a hollow wave" (*MrsD*, 32). "By artificial light the green shone" in Clarissa Dalloway's dress, which has the green of the waves, "but lost its colour now in the sun" (*MrsD*, 45).

Pure color is thematized in *The Waves*. In the interludes, the light plays over objects, the "[r]ivers became blue" (*W*, 108) as, finally at its height, the sun "gave to everything its exact measure of colour . . . , to the wild grasses their glancing green" (*W*, 148). The table itself becomes a focus of the sun's unprejudiced eye, giving the objects of daily life unfamiliar colors and shapes. The table is alternately "filmed with red, orange, purple like the bloom on the skin of ripe fruit" (*W*, 110) and "inlaid . . . with lozenges of brown and yellow" (*W*, 208), its "white table-cloths" "stitched . . . with fine gold wires" (*W*, 29). For "colour is not something which is inherent in the table, but something depending upon the table and the spectator and the way the light falls on the table" (*PP*, 9). Just as "[w]ith the naked eye one can see the grain" of Russell's table (*PP*, 10), so in *The Waves* "the grain of the wood" with the sun's course "became more and more finely engraved" (*W*, 110). Just as "the pale sun" in *A Passage to India* "pencilled shadows down" the "creases" of the hills, the sun in *The Waves* applies the "brush stroke," now "precise," now "swollen and lopsided" (*W*, 236). In some lights, shading is applied; in others, "[e]verything was without shadow" (*W*, 110).

The sunlight itself does the pure, mindless eye's work of analysis, expunging the shapes common sense imposes and presenting a series of changes, now only shapeless color, now new shapes. Its light breaks things down, a kind of analysis of matter into ultimate simples, removing the world's familiar structure: "the air seemed to become fibrous and to tear away from the green surface flickering and flaming in red and yellow fibres like the smoky fire that roars from a bonfire. Gradually the fibres of the burning bonfire were fused into one haze, one incandescence which lifted the weight of the woolen grey sky on top of it and turned it to a million atoms of soft blue" (*W*, 7). Sunlight on dew "made the garden like a mosaic of single sparks not yet formed into one whole" (*W*, 29). It dissolves the units common sense calls "things": "though each was separate they seemed inextricably involved" (*W*, 75). "Everything became softly amorphous, as if the china of the plate flowed and the steel of the knife were liquid" (*W*, 29).[17] For the sun, like a sense organ, records an indubitable knowledge: it "burnt uncompromising, undeniable" (*W*, 148).

TRANSFORMATIONS: BEYOND IMPRESSIONISM

This table, these chairs, this metal vase with its three red flowers are about to undergo an extraordinary transformation. (Woolf, *The Waves*, 118)

The process of sound philosophizing, to my mind, consists mainly in passing from those obvious, vague, ambiguous things, that we feel quite sure of, to something precise, clear, definite, which by reflection and analysis we find is involved in the vague thing that we start from, and is, so to speak, the real truth of which that vague thing is a sort of shadow. (Russell, *Logic and Knowledge*, 179–80)

Although a necessary preamble to any reconstruction of "the visible world" (*H-M*, 24), Impressionism's analytic eye cannot remake the atomized world; its skeptical reduction of things to their appearances "could not altogether satisfy such a nature as Cézanne's" (*Cé*, 40). For Impressionism had created a problem for art, as Berkeley and Hume had for philosophy; in destroying the common-sense organization of experience, it "destroyed the surface organization of the picture more completely than . . . hitherto" (*TR*, 218).

As against these great advantages which art owes to impressionism we must set the fact that the pseudo-scientific and analytic method of these painters forced artists to accept pictures which lacked design and formal coordination to a degree which had never before been permitted. They, or rather some of them, reduced the artistic vision to a continuous patchwork or mosaic of coloured patches without architectural framework or structural coherence. (*V&D*, 11)

Clive Bell also complains of "the bad science of Claude Monet" (*Art*, 208); "some of the Impressionists," he says, "were content to cover their canvases with charming forms and colours, not caring overmuch whether or how they were co-ordinated. Certainly this was a weakness in Impressionism," he concludes (*Art*, 229). Impressionism thought to "represent things as they are – scientifically," e.g., light, to "paint what we see, not the intellectual superstructure that we build over our sensations" (*Art*, 186–7). It confused science with empiricism.

Pure color is formless, meriting the epithet "vague." For "colours . . . in nature have almost always a certain vagueness and elusiveness" (*V&D*, 51), precisely "the vagueness of sense-data" (Whitehead, *Symbolism*, 40), of the world of existence, "vague," "without any clear plan or arrangement" (*PP*, 100). It quickly burns itself out: "Colours went spirally through my body lighting a flare as if a rocket fell through the night and lit up greens and browns, grass and trees . . . Colour warmed, thrilled, chafed, burnt, soothed, fed and finally exhausted me. For though the life of colour is a glorious life it is a short one. Soon the eye can hold no more; it shuts itself in sleep" (*CE*, II, 235). Vagueness is the danger of Impressionism, parodied in *To the Lighthouse* through the painter Paunceforte, representative of the St. Ives group of painters,[18] "dipping; imbuing the tip of his brush in some soft mound of green or pink" (24); "the colour . . . thinned and faded; the shapes etherealised; that was how Paunceforte would have seen it" (75). "Putty" is Clive Bell's word (*Art*, 230); Woolf's, "cotton wool." Charles Tansley, with the Cambridge ignorance of painting, takes from Mrs. Ramsay's criticism of Paunceforte Fry's of Impressionism (*V&D*, 225): "So Mr. Tansley supposed she meant him to see that that man's picture was skimpy, was that what one said? The colours weren't solid?" (TL, 24). Impressionism's deficiencies followed from an art of pure sensibilia: their fleetingness and impalpability – Whitehead's "immediacy of the show of things" (*Symbolism*, 44) – were only sufficient to represent the world of sense, which, "for all its decorative sense-experience, is barren. It displays a world concealed under an adventitious show, a show of our own bodily production" (*Symbolism*, 43–4). The lack of permanent form affects color; it becomes thin when formless. Thus, Woolf's "first impressions" as a child are Paunceforte-like: "pale yellow, silver, green" (*MB*, 66).

For Fry, Impressionism was the ultimate outcome of artistic representation as "verisimilitude," i.e., the imitation of surface appearances, a realism of sense-data:

> In this, impressionism marked the climax of a movement which had been going on more or less steadily from the thirteenth century – the tendency to approximate the forms of art more and more exactly to the representation of the totality of appearance. When once representation had been pushed to this point where further development was impossible, it was inevitable that artists should turn round and question the validity of the fundamental assumption that art aimed at representation; and the moment the question was fairly posed it became clear that the pseudo-scientific assumption that fidelity to appearance was the measure of art had no logical foundation. (*V&D*, 18–19)

Clive Bell likewise finds "[t]he French Impressionists profess to do no more than push the accepted theory of representation to its logical conclusion" (*Art*, 182). The result was "dead matter – literal transcriptions from nature, intellectual machinery" (*Art*, 230). Impressionism's inadequacy was that of a realism limited to knowledge by acquaintance of objects discernable by eyesight; "[w]e are in danger of digging deeper than the eye approves . . . Let us dally a little longer, be content still with surfaces only" (*CE*, IV, 157). The point of saturation had been reached:

> it became evident that art had arrived at a critical point, and that the greatest revolution in art that had taken place since Graeco-Roman impressionism became converted into Byzantine formalism was inevitable. It was this revolution that Cézanne inaugurated and that Gauguin and Van Gogh continued . . . the re-establishment of purely aesthetic criteria in

place of the criterion of conformity to appearance – the rediscovery of the principles of structural design and harmony. (*V&D*, 19)

Impressionism is all eye. "The eye," Woolf says, brings back "trophies," "breaks off little lumps of emerald and coral . . . The thing it cannot do . . . is to compose these trophies"; it only gives "beauty pure and uncomposed" (*CE*, IV, 157). Post-Impressionism must reach the unseen world of persisting objects, of enduring forms, to complete Impressionism's Cartesian project with design. "There is no shape for these apparitions," Woolf, discussing failed novels, echoes Fry (*CE*, II, 133). The design which gathers together vision's shimmering particles "transforms" them, "pass[ing] from the vague to the precise by the method of analysis and reflection" (*LK*, 180). So Cézanne realizes "a picture which owes nothing to the data of any actual vision" (*Cé*, 77), "an art based on passionate study of actual life, but ending in a complete transformation of its data" (*Cé*, 87). Such is the meaning of Fry's title "Transformations."

The discovery of intellectual form in chaotic sense-data is then Fry's understanding of Post-Impressionism's accomplishment. Impressionism is pure empiricism; Post-Impressionism transforms its data as scientific theory does. Albeit beginning with "his visual sensations" (*Cé*, 53), "Cézanne respects far less obediently the data of the actual sensation" (*Cé*, 77). Seurat also takes only as his point of departure "the large body of new data which Impressionism supplied" (*TR*, 196), new because the analytic eye is investigative. "Appearance as revealed by Impressionist researches is nothing to him [Seurat] but the raw material out of which he builds" (*TR*, 196). He penetrates to another reality beyond surfaces:

his building is so purely logical and architectural, so precisely balanced and so nicely proportioned that the final result is utterly remote from appearance. The question of verisimilitude hardly occurs to one, so little can we refer his pictures to anything outside themselves, so completely does the created reality hold us by the laws of its self-contained system. (*TR*, 196)

Seurat's "Jeune Femme se poudrant," "[f]or all its decorative flatness, for all its theoretical and abstract colouring, . . . is intensely real, but for all its reality nothing of the original theme, of the thing seen, remains untransformed, all has been assimilated and remade by the idea. . . . as a picture attains to this independent reality and inherent significance the element of illustration drops out" (*TR*, 195). The transformation is abstract – a "complete transmutation of the theme by the idea" (*TR*, 195). Likewise Matisse's method disintegrates and then intellectually reconstructs the visual world: "By the magic of an intensely coherent style our familiar every day world . . . has been broken to pieces . . . and then put together again into a far more coherent unity in which all the visual values are mysteriously changed – in which plastic forms can be read as pattern" (*H-M*, 21). In Matisse, the dissatisfaction with the representation of appearances amounts to a "horror of verisimilitude" (*H-M*, 14):

> he pushed the systematic understanding of plastic form, as ascertained by unaided vision, to lengths that perhaps Rembrandt alone had attained, . . . his record of this analysis was so pure, so little encumbered with the apparatus of mere verisimilitude that the total result, for all its intense reality, appears strangely unlike the texture of actual appearance, becomes indeed intensely anti-photographic. (*H-M*, 14–15)

Van Gogh, on the other hand, "was incapable of seizing the complex interrelations and correspondences of such profoundly meditated colour structures as Cézanne built up with a kind of intellectual sensibility" (*TR*, 183). His achievement shows deficiencies not unlike Impressionism's:

> How utterly different is Van Gogh's reading of Provençal nature from Cézanne's contemplative and reflective penetration of its luminous structure! Here all is stated with the crudity of first impressions . . . of a nature that vibrated instantly and completely to certain dramatic appeals in the appearances of nature. In striking contrast to Cézanne, too, is Van Gogh's indifference to the plastic structure of his terrain. (*TR*, 184)[19]

The "dramatic" appeals in nature are akin to the beauty the artist must learn not to see. It will be equivalently rejected by a "modern" fiction.

The respective limitations of the colored and the colorless defined, in their 1921 encounter, the difference between Russell's and Woolf's position.[20] Woolf, in waving her hand at the dinner table – like one that she would depict – had pronounced "this is mush" but that Russell, with "a telescope to [his] eye," could "see through" it. His reaction was " 'If you had my brain you would find the world a thin, colourless place,' " Woolf replied, "But my colours are so foolish," and Russell answered, "You want them for your writing" (*Diary*, II, 146–7).

"Mush" recalls the "cotton wool" Woolf equates with "non-being" (*MB*, 71). Its formlessness is sense-data's deficiency; its colorlessness that of mathematicized matter. All impressions are then perforce "first"; design comes after, "post"-dates them, at a remove from their immediacy and primacy. Post-Impressionism's building blocks are Impressionism's analyzed colors; like Miss La Trobe, it "makes rise from its amorphous mass a re-created world" (*BA*, 153). "Transformations" represent "the process of art as a logic of sensations" – the phrase Fry finds in Cézanne – in which "we must remember that the premises are sensations" leading to conclusions beyond them (*V&D*, 82).

POST-IMPRESSIONISM: THE GEOMETRY IN THE COLORED WORLD

[L]a logique . . . ignore les couleurs et n'en préfère aucune. (Nicod, *La Géométrie dans le Monde Sensible*, 43)

The essence of a propositional sign is very clearly seen if we imagine one composed of spatial objects (such as tables, chairs, and books) instead of written signs.

The mutual spatial arrangement of these things then expresses the sense of the proposition. (Wittgenstein, *Tractatus*, 3.1431)

Space, time and colour (colouredness) are forms of objects . . . But the network is *purely* geometrical. (*Ibid.*, 2.0251, 6.35)

"Transformations" in the visual arts are solutions to a problem, that of unorganized color, "Cézanne's solution of the problem of colour" (*Cé*, 57). "Each canvas had to be a new investigation and a new solution" (*Cé*, 57). Fry baptized "plastic colour" the resolution of the ancient debate between colorists and draughtsmen, art's androgyny, its neutral monism, the "combination of lines and colours," as Bell puts it (*Art*, 281), in a "significant form" (*Art*, 229), "a balance between the emotions and the intellect, between Vision and Design" (*RF*, 245), "that razor edge of balance between two opposite forces" Lily's painting will "achieve" (*TL*, 287). The Post-Impressionists "design in colour, that is in coloured shapes" (*Art*, 236). For Fry, the Post-Impressionist project requires "[t]he transposition of all the data of nature into values of plastic colour" (*Cé*, 69);[21] Leslie Stephen's "transformed sensations" – "mental forms somehow imposed upon chaotic sense materials" ("WM?," 135) – Wittgenstein's "logical form of colour" (Black, *Companion*, 104) – are then versions of plastic color.[22]

The plastic dimension added to color is the form to sustain it, solving Lily Briscoe's "problem about a foreground of a picture" (*TL*, 220), the "problem" Woolf saw in a Vanessa Bell painting – the need "to buttress up this lyricism with solidity,"[23] Woolf's problem in writing *The Waves* "that the interesting things aren't firmly based," that "there's no quite solid table on which to put it" (*Diary*, III, 264). The analyzed fragments of sense-data must be held together by a "bare abstraction" (*SO*, 127). We re-encounter the vocabulary of "scaffoldings" and "skeletons." "The highly abstract scheme of physics gives," in Russell's metaphor, "the causal skeleton of the world, while leaving out all the colour and variety and individuality of the things that compose the world" (*SO*, 127). Sensibilia, as "a hypothetical scaffolding" (*ML*, 152–3), permit the object's construction by filling in the discontinuities between perspectives. Wittgenstein's logical space is similarly conceptualized. "The geometrical and the logical place agree," he writes (*Tractatus* 3.411), then adds "[t]he logical scaffolding round the picture determines the logical space" (3.42). Mauron also equates architectural scaffolding with logic or geometry: "It will be made of syllogisms if it is a question of geometry, of beams if it is a question of architecture" (*The Nature of Beauty in Art and Literature*, 81).

Logical philosophy thus furnishes the vocabulary for Bloomsbury formalism. "Critics of the Impressionist age," Clive Bell writes, "are vexed by the naked bones and muscles of Post-Impressionist pictures" (*Art*, 237). Nakedness is colorlessness. "Bones" always "bleach" (*TL*, 192), i.e., lose the "colours, sounds, smells," the "so-called secondary qualities," which "point out rather than constitute the object," Leslie Stephen explains, and are treated "as in some way dependent upon the geometrical properties" ("WM?," 130). Cézanne's and Seurat's "design" is thus a logical framework which, via the principle of acquaintance, supports and unites the patches of color "as a vision of an ideated space" (*H-M*, 22). Fry's Platonic Atomism is apparent in the repeated word "ideated" (*H-M*, 11). The same terms appear in the text of Mauron's which Fry translated and the Woolfs published the year of *To the Lighthouse*. "Every reality," writes Mauron, "of whatever order it is, has always a scaffolding." Mauron goes on to assert that as "a poem is a reality it must have a framework" (*The Nature of Beauty in Art and Literature*, 81). Like Woolf, he figures this undergirding as a bone structure. Literature's goal is, in Woolf's language, "[t]o get to the bones" (*Diary*, II, 248). "Now the Moths will I think fill out the skeleton which I dashed in here,"

Woolf writes of her outline for *The Waves* (*Diary*, III, 139). "What is more essential, more fundamental in a man than this skeleton, in a work than its construction?" Mauron asks (*The Nature of Beauty in Art and Literature*, 81).

But form's invisibility means that it requires color to show, to point it out, to use Stephen's words. Fry's version of the history of painting traces "a gradual tendency towards a view of colour as an inherent part of the expressive quality of form, a tendency to recombine into a single indissoluble whole all the aspects of form instead of proceeding by the schematic division into line, shade and colour" (*TR*, 214). Canvases of colorist tendency had a scaffolding, but one added independently of color application, which thus remained a surface decorative element: "The tendency of art of the last few centuries has been to regard contrasts of tone as the essential plastic scaffolding which bore and held up the coloured surface. Colour thereby became an addition to light and shade, and had the separate *rôle* of a kind of musical accompaniment" (*TR*, 220).[24] This combination of drawing and color Bell sees as an outlining, "those circumambient blacklines that are intended to give definition to forms and to reveal the construction of the picture." Bell contrasts this " 'imposed design' " to " 'architectural design' " via a comparison between Cézanne and Whistler (*Art*, 235). Structural design draws with color.

Impressionism effaced the outlines of things. Yet although "the discoveries of the Impressionists increased in some directions the plastic expressiveness of colour," they "tended to destroy any clear and logical articulation of volumes within the picture space." Because "[t]he artists yielded to . . . a simple physiological delight in brilliance and purity of colour," they were blind to form. "It was here that Cézanne intervened," Fry wrote; "with Cézanne colour has ceased to play any separate *rôle* from drawing" (*TR*, 218). Cézanne represents a break with Impressionism and a return to the project of painting begun in the Renaissance: "the whole of modern art is coloured in some way by the impulse of Cézanne" (*TR*, 219); what "he had to 'realize,' according to his own favorite expression" (*Cé*, 38) was plastic color. "Realizing, for him, did not mean verisimilitude," Fry wrote, "but the discovery in appearances of some underlying structural unity."[25] The eyeless truth must be made "visible." Form is not imposed; it is seen *in* color. Cézanne "gave himself up entirely to his own desperate search for the reality hidden beneath the veil of appearance, this reality which he had to draw forth and render apparent" (*Cé*, 38). The discovery "was the construction of clearly articulated plastic wholes by means of the interplay of coloured planes – planes defined rather by their colour relations than by their relations in light and dark" (*TR*, 220). So also in Matisse, "apparently flat patterns are read as diversely inclined planes" (*H-M*, 21). They are no longer defined by contrasts of tone. Cézanne prefers "colour transitions over transitions of light and dark in contradistinction to Rembrandt" (*TR*, 218). His colors, following a Cartesian method, lose the "vagueness" Fry attributed to color "in nature," "become so definite and clear to him, owing to their now necessary relation to other colours" (*V&D*, 51).

The notion of "realizing" allowed Fry to bring together two concepts of form's role: that of the "discovery" of form beneath color, as the truths of mathematics or science are for Russell discovered, and that of form as a "definite and coherent plastic construction" (*Cé*, 80) of color elements as Russell constructed the object from the sense-data of different perspectives. Although hesitant to decide "[w]hether Cézanne regarded this as a discovery of objective truth, as something like a law of nature," Fry found "[i]ts real meaning" was that in Cézanne's "endeavour to handle the infinite diversity of nature he found these forms convenient as a kind of intellectual scaffolding to which the actual form could be related and referred" (*Cé*, 52–3).

Artistic form, at any rate, is subject to logic, like scientific laws: "In this abstract world these elements are perfectly co-ordinated and organized by the artist's sensual intelligence, they attain logical consistency" (*Cé*, 58). The logical form discovered has the status of a scientific law which approximates to some fact. Art thus became an inquiry into the nature of reality akin to physics. It is not simple empirical observation: the surface of things is the data for hypotheses instead of *the* reality it aims faithfully to record. Nor is it pure design, counterpoint to "[p]ure mathematics," which, Russell writes, "depends at no point upon observation" and "can be studied without the help of experiment" (*SO*, 111–12). The Post-Impressionist is like "[t]he physicist," who "asserts that the mathematical symbols which he is employing can be used for the interpretation, colligation, and prediction of sense impressions. However abstract his work may become, it never loses its relation to experience." Plastic color, like "mathematical formulae," can "express certain laws governing the world that we observe," to apply Russell's words to Cézanne (*SO*, 112). Fry's language of scaffolding and the veil of appearances retains the lingering Kantian or Bradleyan overtones we earlier noted in Apostolic Bloomsbury talk. Form is a "reality" beneath appearances, beneath color; "beneath the colour there was the shape," Lily Briscoe thinks (*TL*, 32). But Fry never endows the invisible reality with mystical unknowability.

Plasticity gives to the picture surface weight, building out of visual and tactile data "the luminous atmosphere with which our actual three dimensional space is filled" (*H-M*, 11). "By experience of the correlation of touch and sight sensations, we become able to associate a certain place in touch-space with a certain corresponding place in sight-space" (*OKnExW*, 88; also *ML*, 153). This weight stands for something not literally tactile, a logical form whose apprehensibility does not necessarily yield a gestalt. Impressionism's two-dimensional surface takes on volume: "the artist," after seeing appearances as a "mosaic of flat patches of colour, finds, when he records this vision on his canvas, that the flat surface takes on the whole curvature of the visual hemisphere and objects spring into clear relief" (*H-M*, 12). Form lends to ethereal color the weight of the colorless, for, we recall, "robbed of their colour," things "exist more ponderously" (*MrsD*, 34–5). Color achieves a stone-like denseness in Woolf's descriptions, emulating Post-Impressionism's heavy color: "Lined with shadows their weight seemed more ponderous as if colour, tilted, had run to one side" (*W*, 208). So convinced is Woolf of Fry's plastic color that in her descriptions the more color deepens to Cézannesque intensity, the heavier and more structured it becomes: "The earth absorbs colour like a sponge, slowly drinking water. It puts on weight; rounds itself; hangs pendant; settles and swings beneath our feet" (*W*, 286). Cézanne's colors are "solid," by contrast with Paunceforte's. Impressionism gave Cézanne pure color – "emerald green and cobalts, . . . cadmium greens and a whole series of oranges passing from ochre almost to vermilion" (*Cé*, 77), an "intensity of the colour, the flash of oranges and reds against pure greens, violets and cobalts". (*Cé*, 80) "To say that the artists of the movement insist on design is not to deny that some of them are exceptionally fine colourists," Clive Bell writes, "Cézanne is one of the greatest colourists that ever lived; Henri-Matisse is a great colourist. Yet all, or nearly all, use colour as a mode of form" (*Art*, 236).

For "the interplay of coloured planes" is constituted of logical relations. Van Gogh's limitation was his failure to value colors "as part of a necessary system of relations" ("The Courtauld Fund," 614). Cézanne sought, in his use of color, "never the *effect* but the harmonic sequences of planes" (*TR*, 218). These planes function like the relations of Russell's observed complex fact "the knife is to the left of the book": "all the main directions given by the rectilinear lines of the napkin and the knife . . . make us feel so vividly this horizontal extension" (*Cé*, 47). By supplying the logical form relating the logical simples, Cézanne makes his pictures propositions.

Matisse too had an Impressionist's response to pure color: "in the clear light of his atelier at Nice . . . he developed richer more alluring arabesques of gay and sonorous[26] colour than ever before" (*H-M*, 24). His sensitivity to color and its "etherialized expression" (*H-M*, 24) were joined, however, to Matisse's "other" genius for "formal system" (Fry's *The Artist and Psychoanalysis*, 7), once more for Fry expressed in the relations of color planes, "one in which plastic evocations play a larger part, one in which, though he never loses sight of surface organization, this is effected by the relation of large geometrical units, which attain a more architectural, more monumental unity" (*H-M*, 25). Seurat was the third great Post-Impressionist to discover a geometry of color, although his "supreme merits as a designer . . . were hidden from" Fry at first by the "transparent veil of pointillism – a pseudo-scientific system of atmospheric colour notation" (*V&D*, 288). Seurat's "building" was, we saw, "purely logical and architectural" (*TR*, 196).

The deficiencies Woolf attributes to the pure eye are now apparent: it cannot "compose" so "as to bring out the more obscure angles and relationships" (*CE*, IV, 157). "Obscure angles" echoes "oblique angles," as "this angular shape in my mind" which leads Woolf to anticipate *The Waves* "will be very sharply cornered" (*Diary*, III, 219). The term implies a geometry of painting. "Relationships" are logical. "It's curious how difficult it is to root out that mediaeval habit of thinking of 'substances' of things existing apart from all relations,'" Woolf quotes Fry (*RF*, 270) evoking a position Russell attacks in his *Leibniz* (14–15). Impressionism lacks the doctrine of external relations.

A painting's logical relations create its aesthetic qualities, the "pleasure in the recognition of order, of inevitability in relations" which "come very near to the pleasure derived from the contemplation of intellectual constructions united by logical inevitability" (Fry, *The Artist and Psychoanalysis*, 19). Fry's "intellectualism" he himself called "a sort of excited recognition of the aptness of formal relations" (*RF*, 273). For the basic aesthetic response is "a reaction to a relation and not to sensations or objects or person or events" (*TR*, 3). In that the scaffolding was architectural, it resembled those "iron girders" (*TL*, 122) which evoked, we saw, the nineteenth century's reinforced "crystal palaces." "The engineers, who have at least a scientific problem to solve, create, in factories and railway-bridges, our most creditable monuments. They at least are not ashamed of their construction" nor "smother it in beauty," Clive Bell argues (*Art*, 221). In that it was mathematical, Woolf equates its "girders" with "square roots"; it has the "crystalline architecture" science discovered in the visible world (Tyndall, *Lectures on Light*, 76).

The bare scaffolding's schematic nature applies logical economy: "Cézanne's method of interpreting form" is "to seize on a few clearly related, almost geometrical elements" (*Cé*, 75). The "infinite complexity of experience" (*Cé*, 70), vague and chaotic, is thereby translated into "the most simple and logical relations" (*Cé*, 47). It is a reduction not to but of appearances. Fry invokes the statement attributed to Cézanne that "natural forms all tend to the sphere, the cone, and the cylinder" (*Cé*, 52)[27] to insist that the observable forms are reducible to a few. The consequence is a thinning of physical reality, like the "minimum definition of matter" Russell compares to "Isabella's gruel in Jane Austen [sic], 'thin, but not too thin'" (*ABCR*, 229), eliminating the detail which Clive Bell calls "the fatty degeneration of art" (*Art*, 222). The result is radically eyeless, correcting the vision which extends out from our earthly perspective and misleads us as to the world's structure:

> what is seen does not belong solely to the physical process observed, but also to the standpoint of the observer. Measurements of distances and times do not directly reveal properties of the things measured, but relations of the things to the measurer. What observation can tell us about the physical world is therefore more abstract than we have hitherto believed . . . only our obstinately earthbound imagination . . . makes us suppose a geometry separate from physics to be possible. (*ABCR*, 118–19)

"Simplification is the conversion of irrelevant detail into significant form," Clive Bell explains (*Art*, 185); "Simplification and Design" is one of the chapter titles of *Art*. "The tendency of the [contemporary] movement" in art, according to Bell, "is to simplify away all this mess of detail which painters have introduced into pictures" (*Art*, 222). A parsimony of style belongs also to

> a Matisse who responded to a quite different kind of appeal from the visible world. A Matisse who felt the appeal of a stark, structural architecture, who loved above all a bare economy, who would, for the austerer delights of such forms willingly sacrifice the intricate charm of his dancing arabesque. (*H-M*, 24–5)

The "transformation" of experience *is* the process of simplification, like that accomplished by scientific language: "Ordinary language is totally unsuited for expressing what physics really asserts, since the words of everyday life are not sufficiently abstract. Only mathematics and mathematical logic can say as little as the physicist means to say." Not holding that "all reality is concrete," they cannot hold that "abstraction is falsification" (*SO*, 82). Only with the "formulae expressible solely in terms of space and time" which Leslie Stephen treats as transformations of sense-data ("WM?," 135) can the invisible logical form be apprehended, in "the outline, not the detail" (*TL*, 289).

Simplification does not sacrifice empirical complexity, however. The model is rather a mathematicized, empirical science than logic alone, wherein "geometry, as taught in schools since Greek times, ceases to exist as a separate science, and becomes merged in physics," Russell argues (*ABCR*, 118). The reverse is true as well: "Just as geometry has become physics, so, in a sense, physics has become geometry" (*ABCR*, 129). Plastic color is a comparable merger in art. Cézanne "it was who first . . . conceived this method of organizing the infinite complexity of appearance by referring it to a geometrical scaffolding," achieving "[t]he concordance . . . between an intellect rigorous, abstract and exacting to a degree, and a sensibility of extreme delicacy and quickness of response" (*Cé*, 70). This makes it possible "on top of this clearly held framework, to give to every part of the contour the utmost subtlety of variation which his visual sensibility could discover and his nervous drawing record" (*Cé*, 75). The framework contains and organizes a visual data collected and recorded, fitting it, as Fry says about Seurat's "La Grande Jatte," into a "preconceived geometric scheme" and "closely knit system" (*TR*, 192). The commitment to the formal explains why, "though the desire to remain absolutely loyal to" actual visual sensations "was an obsession with Cézanne," his realism is no simple verisimilitude (*Cé*, 69). Plastic color thus also joins "life" – the element of chance, interruption, Woolf's "jar upon the nerves," her "nervous tremor which distinguishes the hand-made pot from the machine-made" (*RF*, 242) – to beauty; it retains the contingency of detail within form's elegance: "as though this elementary approach to the subject might, by its too primitive, too hieratic simplicity, check the impression of the accident of life, Cézanne has instinctively corrected this in his detailed treatment" (*Cé*, 68):

> At first sight the volumes and contours declare themselves boldly to the eye. They are of a surprising simplicity, and are clearly apprehended. But the more one looks the more . . . [t]he apparent continuity of the contour is illusory . . . There is no uniformity in the tracing of the smallest curve . . . We then get at once the notion of extreme simplicity in the general result and of infinite variety in every part. It is this infinitely changing quality of the very stuff of the painting which communicates so vivid a sense of life. In spite of the austerity of the forms, all is vibration and movement. Nothing is less schematic than these works, even when, as here, the general forms have an almost geometrical appearance. (*Cé*, 51)

The word "stuff" uses the metaphor of the woven fabric stretched upon the frame, the veil of appearances; "the true Impressionists" – Guillaumin and Pissaro – "sought to weave across their canvas the unbroken weft of colour which their eyes had learned to perceive in nature" (*Cé*, 39–40). The thin gruel is a reduction like the Boeuf en Daube – provençal like Cézanne; Mrs. Ramsay saw "its confusion of savoury brown and yellow meats and its bay leaves and its wine, and thought" (*TL*, 151).[28]

The insistence is on abstract continuity and particularized discontinuity. Post-Impressionist form also imaginatively realizes the ghostly mathematical continuity in space which, as with Russell's account of change, coexists with Impressionism's atomized appearances. Cézanne's formalism holds a quivering, myriad life still; it thus introduces a timeless element. The unchanging form imparted to fleeting appearances is plastic color in the temporal order. Its material is the granite of monuments, designed to outlast the living and contain the dispersal of rainbow appearances. Its "monumentality" also gives grandeur to the small, the particular.

> This architectural rigour and this primitive simplicity in the angle of approach, reveals the essence of Cézanne's conception. Everything here reinforces the idea of gravity, density and resistance. In relation to this may

be considered the phrase, reported by M. Joachim Gasquet: "Everything we see is dispersed and disappears. Nature is always the same, but nothing remains of it, nothing of what we see. Our art should give to nature the thrill of continuance with the appearance of all its changes. It should enable us to feel nature as eternal." (*Cé*, 54)

Life is captured in an enduring form, but not eliminated. "The feeling of life is no less intense than that of eternal stillness and repose" (*Cé*, 73). Cézanne "can give the feeling of living reality by a still more generalized interpretation of the actual vision" (*Cé*, 76). So also, Matisse's monumentality does not crush life: "It would be wrong to suppose that there is anything morose or oppressive about this aspect of Matisse's personality, for he is . . . always responsive to sensual delights" (*H-M*, 25). Seurat achieves a similar balance between life and form, even though the "Grande Jatte" "presents a world from which life and movement are banished, and all is fixed for ever in the rigid frame of its geometry" (*TR*, 192). "Jeune Femme Se Poudrant" carries its subject "into a region of abstract beauty" (*TR*, 194), and the "mood" evoked by the "almost inhuman detachment" of "The Bathers" (*TR*, 190), "like that which comes to us from some of Piero della Francesca's monumental and motionless groups," withdraws "into a region of pure and almost abstract harmony":

For that, indeed, is the secret of this great composition, the compelling harmony of all these forms . . . Boots and trousers lose their everyday banality when they are implicated in so close-woven a texture of formal harmony, however relentlessly their shapes are defined. One is forced even to rejoice that boots have tabs, so evidently do they here become the key to a whole sequence of rhythmic phrasing. And no less does the beauty and charm of the summer sunshine sink into the background of consciousness and become only another part of the colour organisation. (*TR*, 191)

Woolf applies these same criteria to Fry's own *oeuvre*: "Cézanne stands out among Roger Fry's books like Mont Sainte-Victoire, solid in structure and bathed in light" (*RF*, 286).

Seurat's boots with tabs are like Mrs. Ramsay's "deer-stalker's hat" and her "goloshes," "something incongruous to be worked into the harmony of her face," "into the picture" of her (*TL*, 47). In the still form, experience is emptied of its aestheticized "beauty"; beauty becomes abstract, like that of mathematics. The balance between life and formal beauty is that of the dual systems of time, correlating a private fleeting "now" to a public series in which what is before is always before and what after always after. The result is something like Woolf's "moment of being":

> in spite of the exactitude and rigour of its harmony, this picture retains also something of its quality of immediacy, of a thing that was actually seen and seized on by the imagination in a single ecstatic moment. It is just that quality that Seurat's passionate research for abstract principles and scientific method might, one guesses, endanger. (*TR*, 191)

Mrs. Ramsay achieves a similar balance. Leaning on "the masculine intelligence," she had "leant . . . on cubes and squares roots" (*TL*, 159). Her dinner-party is thus a Post-Impressionist creation.

The same mathematical knowledge which sustains Mrs. Ramsay undergirds Lily's painting, whose "pauses" and "strokes" formed a "rhythmical movement": "all were related"; "she scored her canvas with brown running nervous lines which had no sooner settled there than they enclosed . . . a space" (*TL*, 236). The painting discloses Mrs. Ramsay's core: "A mother and child might be reduced to a shadow without irreverence" (*TL*, 81–2). It is a "triangular shadow" (*TL*, 299), but also a "triangular purple shape" (*TL*, 81), thus an example of "plastic color," as is Rose's fruitbowl, in which Mrs. Ramsay's eyes put "a yellow against a purple, a curved shape against a round shape" (*TL*, 163). Via "the relations of those lines cutting across, slicing down, and in the mass of the hedge with its green cave of blues and browns" (*TL*, 235), worked out earlier by the salt cellar's relation to a leaf pattern in the tablecloth (*TL*, 128, 140, 154), Lily solves her "problem." "It was a question, she remembered, how to connect this mass on the right hand with that on the left" (*TL*, 82–3). The solution – "something to the right, something to the left; and the whole is held together" (*TL*, 160) – again resembles Russell's "observed complex fact," where "this patch of red is to the left of that patch of blue" (*ML*, 142); close to "a simple sense-datum," it transforms "its *logical* structure" into a proposition. (*ML*, 142).

Lily's solution is found when she "drew a line there, in the centre" (*TL*, 310). Thomas Matro calls it "a literal version of the 'central line' that Fry uses in *Vision and Design* to explain his aesthetic" ("Only Relations," 213).[29] Matro quotes Woolf's response to Fry, who wondered if the arrival at the lighthouse had symbolic meaning: "I meant *nothing* by *The Lighthouse*. One has to have a central line down the middle of the book to hold the design together" (in *VW*, II, 129).

This aesthetic of the centrally divided canvas Fry argues is Post-Impressionist, finding it in Cézanne's "Maisons au bord de la Marne": "a tree trunk divides the composition in half with the rigid vertical of its trunk, above which its foliage forms an almost symmetrical pyramid" (*Cé*, 61). Fry attributes it to Poussin: "Poussin pushed his intense feeling for balance so far that he habitually divided his compositions by a marked central line or gap – as it were a cesura in the line" (*Cé*, 53–4). He finds it in Seurat's "Poseuses": "The picture is thus divided exactly into two equal halves, a bold application of Poussin's favourite practice. One half is occupied by the 'Grande Jatte,' the other by the nearly blank wall at right angles to it" (*TR*, 193).

For Fry, "unity is due to a balancing of the attractions of the eye about the central line of the picture" so "the eye rests willingly within the bounds of the picture" (*V&D*, 31). It parallels the fact that, as Russell says, in "the field of vision," "if we are attending to anything seen, it is to what is in the centre of the field" (*LK*, 131–2). The centrally divided composition is a geometrically arranged one – Fry describes the resultant shape as a "pyramid." He even finds Poussin's composition in a painting in which Cézanne "arranges the table exactly in the middle" (*Cé*, 54). "Reason held the centre of the stage alone," in *Between the Acts*. "In the middle there stood a table" (*BA*, 125).

The centrally divided canvas becomes the very picture of the "logical form" of the proposition "'something has some relation to something'" (*TK*, 134). Two complexes will "'have the same form,'" Russell explains, "whenever there is some one symbol composed wholly of variables, such as 'xRy' for instance, from which both can be derived by giving values to the variables" (*TK*, 113). This is the same "logical structure" (*Tractatus*, 4.014) of the "proposition of the form *aRb*" Wittgenstein claims "we perceive" (*Tractatus*, 4.012). The position in the center configures objects in facts, as "Mrs. Ramsay in the midst of this hubbub" prevents "disintegration" (*TL*, 168) and Fry himself, as Woolf presents him, was a cohesive force: "His presence seemed to increase the sensation of everything in the room. But at the centre of that vibration was a gravity and stillness" (*RF*, 297). Lily's "picture" of Mrs. Ramsay is of a fact. Mrs. Ramsay had already undergone the reduction of self by "sitting and looking, until she became the thing she looked at – that light, for example" (*TL*, 97), "shrunk" to "a wedge-shaped core of darkness, something invisible to others," colorless, geometrical (*TL*, 95), one of Tyndall's "wedge-shaped crystal[s]" (*Lectures on Light*, 109). A perspective on the lighthouse's shafted beam, Mrs. Ramsay "has the same form" as it, its dark after-image; as a picture of her, Lily's painting will also. The painting "corresponds" to the fact and so represents a truth. Likewise in *The Waves*, the sun "began to bring out circles and lines" (75), its light revealing geometrical structure beneath appearances; "[s]unlight . . . vanquished chaos" (*JR*, 163). As at *The Waves*' opening, the genesis of the geometry in the sensible world is in the elemental gesture dividing light from darkness.

Thus, when Lily Briscoe builds her "frail shape . . . upon the table" (*TL*, 220), it is upon that of Mr. Ramsay's philosophy, "bare, hard, not ornamental . . . all edges and angles," with "no colour to it" (*TL*, 232). The artist too practices a reduction of the sensible world to reconstruct what analysis has deconstructed. For "no abundance of sensation or fineness of perception would avail unless she would build up out of the fleeting and the personal the lasting edifice," Woolf says of the woman writer (*Room*, 96–7). The table's solid architecture supports Lily's colors, just as Proust's novels are both "evanescent as a butterfly's bloom" and "as tough as catgut" (*CE*, II, 7) and the table simultaneously "visionary, austere" (*TL*, 232). Lily "saw the colour burning on a framework of steel; the light of a butterfly's wing lying upon the arches of a cathedral" (*TL*, 75):

> Beautiful and bright it should be on the surface, feathery and evanescent, one colour melting into another like the colours on a butterfly's wing; but beneath the fabric must be clamped together with bolts of iron. It was to be a thing you could ruffle with your breath; and a thing you could not dislodge with a team of horses. (*TL*, 255)

Form intensifies color – Cézanne's and Matisse's vibrant purple, orange, cobalt blue and above all deep green colors Woolf prefers to Paunceforte's "pale, elegant, semitransparent" pink (*TL*, 23–4). Plasticity and color were to meet in Lily Briscoe's canvas, as in Cézanne's.

Lily begins in the Impressionist manner Mrs. Ramsay's portrait from life, first painting *en plein air* what she directly apprehends. But a problem of design arises whose solution, sketched in part one, is "to put the tree further in the middle" (*TL*, 128), "to move the tree to the middle" (*TL*, 130). It is ultimately supplied by a ghost-like apparition – "somebody had come into the drawing-room; somebody was sitting in the chair," we never know who it is – like the table of physics behind the sensed table, apparent only in part three when Mrs. Ramsay has ceased being the object of Lily's direct observation. Hers becomes a "portrait from memory." Lily's solution is the "discovery" in the accidental arrangement a form – "whoever it was stayed still inside; had settled by some stroke of luck so as to throw an odd-shaped triangular shadow over the step. It altered the composition of the picture a little" (*TL*, 299). The window discloses, in Fry's words on Seurat, "a pyramid into which the seated figure is almost forcibly fitted" (*TR*, 193). "She had built up a whole structure of imagination" (*TL*, 258) out of a geometric figure. Lily's completed painting is a Post-Impressionist one.

So Mr. Ramsay's logical philosophy, found wanting in "The Window," becomes the philosophical "backbone" of Woolf's artist's art. "If I were painting myself I should have to find some – rod, shall I say – something that would stand for the conception," Woolf writes; "one is living all the time in relation to certain background rods or conceptions" (*MB*, 73), she continues. Lily's painting, unable to bring back the living Mrs. Ramsay, attempts no "pale reflex"; it "transforms" the vision of which she was part, uniting lighthouse and window by applying, as critics have observed (see Matro, "Only Relations," 212), the aesthetic of the central division to *To the Lighthouse*'s own composition. Lily renders her impressions of Mrs. Ramsay in part one and completes the portrait in part three; in between occurs time's passing, what Woolf called "the consequent break of unity in my design" (*Diary*, III, 36), the relation R uniting life and logic. That central section also places the "Lighthouse . . . in the midst" of "the great plateful of blue water" Mrs. Ramsay sees before her (*TL*, 23).

Likewise, the history of painting traced in *The Waves*, following the sun's path across the sky, places a Post-Impressionist light and color at the novel's literal center, when the sun was at its zenith "in the middle of the sky" (151), surrounded by morning and evening's vague Impressionism.[30] For "[w]ith the sunset, sharpness was lost" (*TL*, 212), the sinking sun "robbed of light" the waves (*W*, 207) and "[a]ll the colours in the room had overflown their banks" (*W*, 236), as the waves of darkness washed over them. By contrast, "uncompromising, undeniable" (*W*, 148), like Mr. Ramsay's philosophy itself, the noontide light reveals "[s]harp-edged wedges of light" (*W*, 150).

"The sun sharpened the walls of the house" (*W*, 8). "It sharpened the edges of chairs and tables" (*W*, 29). "Then shapes took on mass and edge. Here was the boss of a chair; here the bulk of a cupboard" (*W*, 110). "The veins on the glaze of the china, . . . the fibres of the matting became more and more finely engraved" (*W*, 110). Day's irreal clarity is increasingly focussed as the zenith is approached: "Gradually the dark bar on the horizon became clear as if the sediment in an old wine-bottle had sunk and left the glass green. Behind it, too, the sky cleared as if the white sediment there had sunk" (*W*, 7). In the morning light, the birds "sang as if the edge of being were sharpened and must cut, must split the softness of the blue-green light, the dampness of the wet earth; the fumes and steams of the greasy kitchen vapour; the hot breath of mutton and beef" (*W*, 109). The birdsongs are so clear-cut that they give to blurred sensibilia a definition tantamount to creation out of ill-defined, decaying matter. They function as sunlight at the perspective's center, drawing out the unobserved furniture of the world from the surrounding fluidity:

The sun fell in sharp wedges inside the room. Whatever the light touched became dowered with a fanatical existence. A plate was like a white lake. A knife looked like a dagger of ice. Suddenly tumblers revealed themselves upheld by streaks of light. Tables and chairs rose to the surface as if they had been sunk under water and rose, filmed with red, orange, purple like the bloom on the skin of ripe fruit. (*W*, 109–10)

Under such "vision," a complex object of sense is analyzed into a complex fact: "Here the scents, the sounds among the dry heather-roots, the grassblades pressed upon the palm of her hand, were all so perceptible that she could experience each one separately" (*ND*, 434). Fry's art history, in which Cézanne's and Matisse's "Mediterranean" paintings post-dated the northern Impressionists, lent itself fittingly to the Cambridge mathematicians. "It was Whitehead who was the serpent in this paradise of Mediterranean clarity," Russell recounts:[31]

He said to me once: "You think the world is what it looks like in fine weather at noon day; I think it is what it seems like in the early morning when one first wakes from deep sleep." At last he showed me how to apply the technique of mathematical logic to his vague and higgledy-piggedly world . . . This technique which I learned from him delighted me, and I no longer demanded that the naked truth should be as good as the truth in its mathematical Sunday best. (*Portraits from Memory*, 39–40)

The idea that clarity is meridional explains Woolf's "logical as the sun" (*Room*, 104). A vague "first" Impressionism of early morning gives us the world of sense, to be clarified by the mathematician's world of being.

THE EMPTY PLACES

[T]he electrons and protons in the neighborhood of your feet exert a repulsion on your feet which is just enough to overcome the earth's gravitation. This is what prevents you from falling through the earth, which, solid as it looks, is mostly empty space. (Russell, *The ABC of Relativity*, not in 1925 edn., but in the Mentor edn., 127)

For how could one express in words . . . that emptiness there? (She was looking at the drawing room steps; they looked extraordinarily empty.) . . . Suddenly, the empty drawing-room steps, the frill of the chair inside, the puppy tumbling on the terrace, the whole wave and whisper of the garden became like curves and arabesques flourishing round a centre of complete emptiness. (Woolf, *To the Lighthouse*, 265)

The central divide of the picture space, variously described by Fry as a "gap" and a "cesura," opens out onto a strange, final property of Post-Impressionism implicit in Fry's account but whose philosophical implications Woolf's art will make explicit. In itself, the divide contains nothing, being simply the formal relation between other spaces. But in his commentary on Seurat, Fry allows us to glimpse vistas suggested by this nothingness, without linking it to the aesthetic of the centrally divided canvas. "Who before Seurat ever conceived exactly the pictorial possibilities of empty space?" he asks:

Whoever before conceived that such vast areas of flat, unbroken surfaces as we see in his "Gravelines" could become the elements of a plastic design? And yet nothing less "empty," pictorially speaking, can be imagined . . . the effort of the imagination in cutting away so much material [is] proportional to the vastness and emptiness of the space thus excavated. (*TR*, 189)[32]

This "hollowing out" (Seurat's term), Fry's account suggests, forms a center by the absence of any observer amidst the glare of appearances. From it stretch the unpeopled spaces of Post-Impressionism. Whence the importance, in Cézanne especially, of landscapes and still lifes on kitchen tables.[33] In them lie what Fry calls "solid objects." Having been dissolved by analysis into "a mosaic of visual patches" (*V&D*, 52), their solidity must be reconstituted. "'The art of painting,'" Fry quotes an unnamed painter "'is the art of imitating solid objects upon a flat surface by means of pigments" (*V&D*, 16). The shimmer of their evanescent colors, made to adhere to the atemporality of universals, is given that balance of contradictories: a "still life." "All were still," like Septimus' "real things," his gramophone's "green trumpet": "None of these things moved" (*MrsD*, 215).[34] For "the still space that lies about the heart of things" (*TL*, 158) has been reached. Cézanne's achievement is "of something that has found its centre and can never be moved" (*Cé*, 72).

"The Post-Impressionist movement . . . was by no means confined to painting. He [Fry] read books by the light of it too," Woolf comments (*RF*, 172). The centered composition of *To the Lighthouse* also opens out onto empty spaces like the one Lily Briscoe is "looking at" at the end, with "the sea which had scarcely a stain on it, which was so soft that the sails and the clouds seemed set in its blue" (*TL*, 284). The scene could be that of Seurat's "Port in Bessin" with its lighthouse and boat (Pl. XXX.B, *TR*, 195), "where the shadows of still clouds hanging over the sunlit sea make an exquisite arabesque" and "the planes stretch to infinite distances" (*TL*, 195). The novel's middle section is strewn about with "solid furniture" (*CSFVW*, 78), arranged as still lifes, at once still – dead – and alive, in an empty landscape. "Solid Objects" is the title of an early story by Woolf (*CSFVW*, 96–101), just as she calls the walrus paperweight in *The Years* a "solid object" (74). With the properties of granite, "so hard, so concentrated, so definite an object compared with the vague sea and the hazy shore" (*CSFVW*, 97), the solid object belongs to the world of physics, "so cold and heavy . . . alien to the earth" and with an "origin in one of the dead stars" (*CSFVW*, 100). *The Waves*' interludes also present a series of still lifes, almost identifiable Cézannes, in which pass across the table both solid objects and objects dissolved by the light: "as if the china of the plate flowed and the steel of the knife were liquid" (*W*, 29), knives and forks "lengthened" (*W*, 208), tumblers "[s]uddenly . . . revealed themselves upheld by streaks of light," and "[a] jar was so green that the eye seemed sucked up through a funnel by its intensity," while "as the light increased, flocks of shadow . . . hung in many-pleated folds in the background" (*W*, 110). They present a series of tables or of perspectives on the table, for "any change in the point of view makes some change in the way the light is reflected" (*PP*, 9) and in no two will there be "exactly the same distribution of colours," Russell says of the table (*PP*, 8).

The successive still lifes form part of the series of landscapes,[35] presenting "[t]he entire gamut of the view's changes" (*JR*, 17) through the unoccupied perspectives of the interludes with their collections of sensibilia. "Think of things in themselves," Woolf counsels the woman writer (*Room*, 115), of "the sky, too, and the trees or whatever it may be in themselves . . . for no human being should shut out the view" (*Room*, 118). The emergence of the empty spaces at the center of the Post-Impressionist canvas is not, however, simply a theme the novelist must include. It defines the aesthetic theory which, discovered by Fry in Cézanne, Woolf then reaches as that solid "something to base her vision on" (*TL*, 270). Its principles, the reduction of the ego to the perspective, of sensation to sensiblia and the logical possibility of unoccupied perspectives, become in "modern fiction" linguistic ones, the elimination of the first person and the representation of a third person privacy. It is the Interludes themselves, format for the empty places, which provide the necessary scaffolding to correlate the third person perspectives via an impersonal style for the description of sensibilia.

CHAPTER 7

How describe the world seen without a self?

> Last night Mark Gertler dined here and denounced . . . the inferiority of what he called "literature"; compared with the integrity of painting. "For it always deals with Mr. and Mrs. Brown," – he said – with the personal, the trivial, that is; a criticism which has its sting . . . Yet if one could give a sense of my mother's personality one would have to be an artist. It would be as difficult to do that . . . as to paint a Cézanne.
>
> (Woolf, *Moments of Being*, 85)

Impressionism is where Woolf begins. "One of her first pieces, Kew Gardens, prompted Arnold Bennett to question 'the possibility that some writers might do in words what the Neo-Impressionists have done in paint'," Torgovnick writes. "Woolf replied in a way that suggests that she did, indeed, conceive of her work in this way" (*The Visual Arts*, 63–4). The novelist must first "record the atoms as they fall upon the mind" (*CE*, II, 107), as the painter begins with the analysis of sense-data. Planning *Jacob's Room*, Woolf conceives of "a new form for a new novel . . . no scaffolding; scarcely a brick to be seen" (*Diary*, II, 13). This initial approach coincides with the child Virginia Stephen's "first impressions." Hintikka, asking "How can a mere mark on the wall, a mere sense-datum, be the focal point of a story by Virginia Woolf the philosophical realist?" ("Virginia Woolf," 11), connects this impressionism to Russell's epistemology. It is the Cartesian foundation she "reaches": "If I were a painter I should paint these first impressions . . . I should make a picture" without "giving a clear outline," she tells us:

> Sound and sight seem to make equal parts of these first impressions . . . I also hear the caw of rooks falling from a great height. The sound seems to fall through an elastic, gummy air; which holds it up; which prevents it from being sharp and distinct . . . the rooks cawing is part of the waves breaking – one, two, one, two – and the splash as the wave drew back and

Figure 8. Vanessa Bell, Virginia Woolf at Asheham, 1912.

then it gathered again, and I lay there half awake, half asleep, drawing in such ecstasy as I cannot describe.

The next memory . . . The gardens gave off a murmur of bees; the apples were red and gold; there were also pink flowers; and grey and silver leaves. The buzz, the croon, the smell, all seemed to press voluptuously against some membrane; not to burst it" (*MB*, 66–7)

We recognize the recurrent list of sense-data, for "all these colour-and-sound memories hang together at St Ives," with "all making a whole" (*MB*, 66–7). But Woolf is not a painter. She stresses "the medium in which a novelist works," criticizing *Aspects of the Novel* because "a wise and brilliant book like Mr. Forster's can be written about fiction" in which "[a]lmost nothing is said about words" (*CE*, II, 110). Woolf's project is thus to find a language with the powers of Cézanne's painting, equivalent of Russell's project of a logical language in whose "new and difficult symbolism" nothing will seem "obvious" (*LK*, 180), one "designed to correct the misleading logic suggested by common speech" (*TK*, 93) by stripping away common-sense assumptions inherent in grammar. Ordinary language familiarizes; logical language makes strange by making the vague precise, since "everything precise is so remote from everything that we normally think" (*LK*, 180). The goal of "strict symbolic form" (*ML*, 76) is to awaken from "'dogmatic slumbers,'" justifying "that love of formalism which appears, to those who are ignorant of its motive, to be mere outrageous pedantry" (*ML*, 90–1).

Russell's "logical atomism" reduces "things, regarded as logical constructions, to the most basic things, the nameable particulars" and "all propositions to atomic, or basic, propositions," e.g., "This is white," which must contain some particular (Urmson, *Philosophical Analysis*, 54). The elementary atoms, "'particulars'" like momentary "patches of colour" and "predicates or relations" (*LK*, 179), we have encountered already. Particulars or logically proper names include demonstrative "words like 'this' or 'that'" (*LK*, 201) and "pronouns." "Pronouns stand for particulars," Russell says (*PP*, 93). "The word 'now' stands for a particular, namely the present moment" (*PP*, 93). Particulars mark "the sharp point, in language, of the essential privacy of each individual's experience" (*HK*, 90):

> We say "This is white." If you agree that "this is white," meaning the "this" that you see, you are using "this" as a proper name. But if you try to apprehend the proposition that I am expressing when I say "This is white," you cannot do it. If you mean this piece of chalk as a physical object, then you are not using a proper name. (*LK*, 201)

This private language is not language in the full sense: "No words exist for describing the actual occurrence in all its particularity; all words, even [ordinary] proper names, are general, with the possible exception of 'this.'" To "translate the occurrence into words" is to "mak[e] generalizations and inferences," as "when you say 'there is a chair.'" Privacy means that "what is really a datum is unutterable" (*OP*, 12). Traditional logic's mistake was "in assimilating propositions of the form 'The so and so is *B*' (such as 'The carpet in the hall is red') to propositions of the form 'This is *B*' (such as 'This is red')." The first is a general, the second is a singular proposition, "unintelligible if there is nothing that 'this' can refer to" (Urmson, *Philosophical Analysis*, 23).

Particulars furnish a language of sense-data and atomic propositions, "the starting-point," "the premiss for theory of knowledge." They are not "anything objective," but what "will vary from man to man" (*LK*, 180). Russell's notion of a private language of sensation became the target of the later Wittgenstein's "private language argument."[1] Woolf's aesthetic is similarly acquaintance-based. She accepts the idea of a "private code" (*TL*, 10), a "secret code" (*JR*, 69) or "secret language" (*TL*, 10) recording sensations, close to painting's mute disclosure of the world. In "The Cinema," she asks whether film's "picture-making power" to render what is not "accessible to words and to words alone" is "some secret language which we feel and see, but never speak, and if so, could this be made visible to the eye" and "without the help of words?" (*CE*, II, 270–1). This is the project of a language of sensibilia invoked at the end of *The Waves*: "how describe the world seen without a self?" (287). The past participle "seen" calls for commentary. Omitted in the title of Naremore's *The World Without a Self*, it has generally gone unnoticed. Glossed by Russell's theory of knowledge, it receives its meaning, for "seen" places unobserved sensibilia at the center of Woolf's aesthetic as well as vision.

The Russellian theory of naming and description, we saw, shows the dualism of private and public. Definite descriptions like "the kitchen table" denote physical objects unknowable by acquaintance. The problem is to move from private statements to public. For "we can never know any proposition of the form 'this is a physical object', where 'this' is something immediately known" for "all our knowledge of physical objects is such that no actual instance can be given" as it can for "the associated sense-data" (*PP*, 108). Leslie Stephen's analyzes "This is a table" to mean not just "I see a table," but also "that you have an analogous set of impressions, and that if we changed places we should also change sensations. It is a compact formula," indicating "the sensations of an observer at a particular time and place, but also" those "of every other observer as those which would be perceived by the same observer at other times and places." It is, "as it were, postulating an omnipresent consciousness, which may be for the moment focussed at any particular point, and the one phrase defines what will be its perceptions at that point" ("WM?," 137–8).

We earlier compared Stephen's "compact formula" to Russell's logical form "something is somehow related to something," Stephen interpreting "this" as a variable and making the formula contain any number of atomic propositions of the form "this has this relation to that." At any rate, Stephen makes "This is a table" the point where privacy becomes the beginning, not the end, of knowledge. While not using logical language, Woolf understood that for "modern fiction" to paint "something seen with precision," "thus compelling words to its shape" (*CE*, II, 50), to "supply rigor" to the "vagueness of the finest prose" (*ND*, 46), the novelist must first undo ordinary language and register sense-data in a defamiliarizing language of appearances, one multi-perspectival and atomized, with, among the seen atoms, selfless unseen ones. The novel will strip ordinary language of the "I," thereby completing the Lichtenbergian project. But modern fiction ultimately aims to describe a reality beyond privacy and erect into an aesthetic "really the most essential function of words, namely that, originally through their connection with images, they bring us into touch with what is remote in time and space" (*Mind*, 203). For that, the neutral language of sensibilia supplies the bridge.

THE DEMONSTRATIVE LANGUAGE OF SENSE-DATA

I could describe every chair, table, luncher here copiously, freely. (Woolf, *The Waves*, 117)

The look of things has a great power over me. Even now, I have to watch the rooks beating up against the wind . . . I say to myself instinctively "What's the phrase for that?" & try to make more & more vivid the roughness of the air current & the tremor of the rooks wing . . . But what a little I can get down into my pen of what is so vivid to my eyes. (Woolf, *Diary*, III, 191)

The language of Impressionism Woolf calls "a little language" (*W*, 238). Its smallness first consists in a return to a prior state. Seeing Vanessa, "I go back to words of one syllable," Woolf wrote (*Diary*, III, 186). The prior state is childhood; the language a nursery language registering the child's pure looking, with the "primitive," "hieratic simplicity" Fry finds in Cézanne (*Cé*, 68). It consists of "simple" symbols "whose parts are not symbols" (*LK*, 194). Instead of describing, words like "this" "name" or point. Color words are also simple symbols.[2] Moore's "The Refutation of Idealism" had argued that "language offers us no means of referring to such objects as 'blue' and 'green' and 'sweet,' except by calling them sensations; it is an obvious violation of language to call them 'things' or 'objects' or 'terms.'" But Moore thought it "hardly likely that if philosophers had clearly distinguished in the past between a sensation or idea and . . . its object, there should have been no separate name for the latter," instead of "the same name for these two different 'things'" (*PS*, 19). Russell makes "red" one of Moore's missing names, a predicate dependent "upon direct acquaintance with the objects which are the meanings of certain simple symbols" (*LK*, 194). "Red" is as mutely attached to sensible reality as "this": "'red' could not be understood except by seeing red things. You might object to that on the ground that you can define red for example, as 'The colour with the greatest wave-length'" (*LK*, 194). But "This is red" yields "a different proposition altogether" from "This has the colour with the greatest wave-length." Someone "who knows nothing of the physical theory of colour can understand" the former without knowing "that 'This has the colour which has the greatest wave-length,'" while someone "who could not see red, but who understood the physical theory of colour" could understand the latter without understanding the former (*LK*, 194). We recognize the argument from the blind person with respect to light here directed to certain simple terms.

Thus in Woolf's Impressionist vocabulary, like paint to the artist, will be color words, "words, like little shaded lights, one red, one blue, one yellow" (*TL*, 179), "all the reds and blues and lights and shades of the scene" (*CE*, II, 131). Their usage, "this ladling out of sentences which have the dripping brilliance of words that live upon real lips," is for "the methods of life" (*CE*, II, 134). The writer using them, like Walter Pater, is "the writer who from words made blue and gold and green; marble, brick, the wax petals of flowers; warmth too and scents; all things that the hand delighted to touch and the nostrils to smell" (*Books and Portraits*, 15). De Quincey's failure was "'to observe too little'"; its result, a "vision" diffused "to a general vagueness," "a colourless monotony" (*CE*, IV, 5).

Atomic propositions result from the analysis of "atomic facts." The simplest "consist in the possession of a quality by some particular thing, such facts, say, as 'This is white'" (*LK*, 199). The next simplest resemble the familiar "the knife is to the left of the book," result of analyzing "complex objects" like "knife-to-left-of-book" into terms and relations (*PE*, 157). A proposition like "This is a table" is atomic where "table" stands for a complex object of sense. This is the burden of Leslie Stephen's calling it "a phrase which in the first place asserts that I have a certain set of organized sense-impressions" ("WM?," 137). Woolf's language abounds in names and statements of atomic facts, like the demonstrative "all this" accompanied by her wave of the hand in the dinner table encounter with Russell or the color words which "lit up in the dark of her [Mrs. Ramsay's] mind" (*TL*, 178), flashing "this is white, or this is red" (*TL*, 179). They point to the simple objects of the child's Impressionist eye the blind cannot be acquainted with. Atomic propositions, obeying "the voice that says as I stroll past, 'Look! Take note of that!'" (*W*, 115), formalize the nursery language of *The Waves*' opening chapter, evoked retrospectively near the novel's end: "let us turn over these scenes as children turn over the pages of a picture-book and the nurse says, pointing: 'That's a cow. That's a boat'" (*W*, 239). Woolf's use of them is deliberate: "The rain pelts – look at it (as the people in The Waves are always saying) now" (*Diary*, III, 311). So Lily Briscoe "keeps on looking" (*TL*, 299) and wields "her brush deliberately" to paint the same atomic fact: "simply that's a chair, that's a table" (*TL*, 300). Russell's question "How are you to express in words an atomic proposition?" acknowledges that because "[a]n atomic proposition is one which does mention actual particulars, not merely describe them but actually name them" (*LK*, 200), it is scarcely more than such a mute pointing. The answer to Woolf's question "how describe the world seen without the self?" is in this way Russellian: "There are no words. Blue, red – even they . . . hide with thickness instead of letting the light through" (*W*, 287). The function of demonstrative language is ostension, Russell's "presentation": silently to show the sensible world. The Impressionist aesthetic begins by "signalling . . . [n]ot indeed in actual words; that is, he could not read the language yet; . . . this exquisite beauty" but in "smoke words languishing and melting in the sky" (*MrsD*, 31).

THE MEANINGLESSNESS OF A PURELY DEMONSTRATIVE LANGUAGE

[B]ooks of algebraic symbols, pages all speckled with dots and dashes and twisted bars, came before her eyes. (Woolf, *Night and Day*, 300)

The "little language" is then not fully language but only "inarticulate words" (*W*, 238). One consequence is that naming confers no meaning. Of course, as Russell observes, "meaning" denotes "different things" (*LK*, 186) with "different kinds of relations between symbol and what is symbolized" (*LK*, 185). "*Words* all have meaning," simply as "symbols which stand for something other than themselves." Meaning in the full sense he reserves first for descriptions, "such concepts as *a man*," which are "symbolic in their own logical nature," having "the property which I call *denoting*," and secondly propositions. "[A] proposition . . . does not itself contain words" but "the entities" they indicate (*PofM*, 47), i.e., "when *a man* occurs in a proposition (*e.g.* 'I met a man in the street'), the proposition is not about the concept *a man*, but . . . some actual biped denoted by the concept." The actual man means by being assigned to "systems of classes or series" (*LK*, 201), defined by properties.

Meaning "thus understood" as definition does not apply to the name (*PofM*, 47), "whose meaning is a particular" (*LK*, 201), i.e., is its object. It is incapable of definition, definition transforming it into a description: "if you define 'red' as 'The colour with the greatest wave-length,' you are not giving the actual meaning of the word" but only "a true description," "actual meaning" being distinct from meaning as definition. "In that sense the word 'red' cannot be defined, though in the sense in which a correct description constitutes a definition it can be defined" (*LK*, 194–5). So for "this": "it would be an error to suppose that 'this' means 'the object to which I am now attending'"; it "is not waiting to be defined by the property of being given; first it is actually given, and then reflection shows that it is 'that which is given'" (*TK*, 40).[3] Names are thus prior to meaning: "'This' is the point from which the whole process starts, and 'this' itself is not defined, but simply given" (*TK*, 40); "in the case of many object-words, it must be strictly impossible to *say* what they mean, except by a tautology, for it is with them that language begins" (*IMT*, 24). Again, they are not fully linguistic, since "the whole function of language is to have meaning," Russell writes ("Introduction," *Tractatus*, 8). Russell's position derives from his Idealist legacy: "It is customary to regard all propositions as having a subject and a predicate, *i.e.* as having an immediate *this*, and a general concept attached to it by way of description," he writes. "This doctrine develops . . . into the theory of Mr. Bradley's Logic, that all words stand for ideas having what he calls *meaning*, and that in every judgment there is a something . . . not an idea and which does not have meaning" (*PofM*, 47). In Russell, however, this becomes the form of only certain, "atomic" propositions.

Denoting is to description what truth and falsity is to the proposition. Meaning is thus bound up with the dualism of true and false. Russell concurs with Wittgenstein that "*propositions are not names for facts*" because "there are *two* propositions corresponding to each fact," one true, the other false, "whereas in the case of a name, there is only one relation that it can have to what it names" (*LK*, 187). Hence the importance of a description's possible failure of reference by contrast with the name, which will only "do while we are all here and can see" the object named (*LK*, 200); "we can never point to an object and say: 'This lies outside my present experience'" (*TK*, 10). In a proposition, "the kitchen table" means because it need not be present to be denoted.

Thus atomic propositions like "'This is here,'" "'This is now'" (*W*, 23) or "'this is what I see'" (*TL*, 32) also do not mean in the full sense, by their correspondence to atomic facts, which, we saw, lack the "duality of true and false." They are "rough and vague and have that sort of obviousness that belongs to things of which you never know what they mean." The simplest merely say "here is a thing" (*LK*, 189). In an atomic proposition, there is no assertion that the thing named exists. Hence its logical representation is actually "This white," for "'is' was superfluous," as Urmson explains (*Philosophical Analysis*, 18–19). Russell had argued that the "conception of existence is the result of a confusion between descriptions and true proper names. Of an actually given *this*, an object of acquaintance, it is meaningless to say that it 'exists.'" Otherwise "this" must be interpreted "as a description," e.g., "meaning 'the object of my present attention exists,' or 'the object I am pointing to exists'" (*TK*, 138).

The atomic proposition provides the solipsistic grounding to which all propositions are ultimately brought into contact. Via names like "this," they anchor language to bits of sensible reality and would "be unintelligible if there is nothing that 'this' can refer to" (Urmson, *Philosophical Analysis*, 23). Likewise for "the immediate objects in illusions, hallucinations, and dreams, it is meaningless to ask whether they 'exist' or are 'real.' There they are, and that ends the matter" (*ML*, 170). "But we may legitimately inquire as to the existence or reality of 'things' or other 'sensibilia' inferred from such objects," Russell adds (*ML*, 170). The goal is "'knowledge' in the strict sense" (*Mind*, 13), i.e., of "what is remote" (*Mind*, 203) and uncertain, not present and certain. In "here is a thing" there is "a truth buried" which must be "extracted" so we "can say, now that is true" (*LK*, 189). "Visual impressions often communicate . . . briefly statements we shall in time come to uncover and coax into words" (*W*, 18). The statement is not "the same as the thing we started from" but something "much more analytic and precise" (*LK*, 189). But moving "from the vague to the precise" means that "you always run a certain risk of error" (*LK*, 180). To say "that is true" means it could be false. All Russell's theory of knowledge bears witness to the "singular fact" that "everything you are really sure of, right off is something that you do not know the meaning of, and the moment you get a precise statement you will not be sure whether it is true or false, at least right off" (*LK*, 179).

The artist too begins with a "bare visual impression . . . unattached to any line of reason" (*W*, 189), "discordant, and so meaningless" (*Y*, 345), like voices "crying out the Latin words of a service in some Roman Catholic Cathedral" (*TL*, 166). Woolf's "little" language of atomic propositions is prior to meaning: knowing "only this is white, or this is red," one "did not know at first what the words meant at all" (*TL*, 179). It parallels Fry's painter's unlearning of habitual seeing, a process of stripping away "the meaning-for-life of appearances" (*V&D*, 47). "Colours are used . . . as signals now"; they "suggest action merely," Woolf echoes him (*CE*, II, 233). By contrast, the creative vision "demands the most complete detachment from any of the meanings and implications of appearances" (*V&D*, 51);[4] it sees "a meaningless mosaic" (*H-M*, 12), "the thing itself before it has been made anything" (*TL*, 287).

The Bloomsbury aesthetic thus rethinks meaning in the light of a theory of symbolism whose symbols are in some sense meaningless. Art – the sentiment is Mauron's – should not be "propaganda, orienting the viewer toward future action" (Hutcheon, *Formalism*, 58, on Mauron *c.* 1925, 18); "propaganda . . . shuts off the contemplative penetration of life," Woolf quotes Fry as saying. If he also thought "[w]riters . . . were propagandists," "[a]s a critic of literature, then, he was not what is called a safe guide" (*RF*, 240). For there is a literature which, like visual art, rejects a utilitarian approach to language. Words, Woolf says, "hate being useful; they hate making money" (*CE*, II, 250). Modern fiction does not require its readers "do something – . . . join a society, . . . write a cheque" (*CE*, I, 326). "Sterne and Jane Austen were interested in things in themselves; in character, in itself; in the book in itself" (*CE*, I, 327). Cézanne's "whole series of still-lifes . . . devoted to studies of skulls" are exercises in which "a skull was merely a complicated variation upon the sphere." The skull functions like a logical symbol, form "its pure essence and without reference to associated ideas" (*Cé*, 53). Cézanne's disinterested interest in it shows "the love which mathematicians bear their symbols" (*TL*, 73–4). We might compare these studies to Woolf's use of the skull in *To the Lighthouse.* It is the presentation of a meaningless solid object, even its association with death emptied of meaning.

AN ATOMIZED LANGUAGE

[I]n his mind a sentence. And he wanted to make other sentences . . . provided only with broken sentences, single words. (Woolf, *The Years*, 330)

Descriptions are incomplete symbols, with no meaning independent of context. The sentence fragments Lily Briscoe hears the morning after the night of "Time Passes" are such incomplete symbols: "('Alone' she heard him say, 'Perished' she heard him say) and like everything else this strange morning the words became symbols, wrote themselves all over the grey-green walls" (*TL*, 219). The morning's "extraordinary unreality" comes from them: "Going to the Lighthouse. But what does one send to the Lighthouse? Perished. Alone. The grey-green light on the wall opposite. The empty places" (*TL*, 220). "His first words (the breeze had risen; the leaves were rustling) were lost. Then he was heard saying: 'What.' To that word he added another 'Message'; and at last a whole sentence emerged; not comprehensible; say rather audible. 'What message,' it seemed he was asking, 'was our pageant meant to convey?'" (*BA*, 191). "They were singing, but not a word reached the audience" (*BA*, 78).

"They were singing; but only a word or two was audible '. . . *wore ruts in the grass . . . built the house in the lane*' . . .The wind blew away the connecting words of their chant" (*BA*, 80). "*The Queen of this great land* . . . those were the first words that could be heard" (*BA*, 83–4); "all they heard was . . . *reason holds sway*" (*BA*, 123). "The words died away. Only a few great names – Babylon, Nineveh, Clytemnestra, Agamemnon, Troy – floated across the open space. The wind rose, and in the rustle of the leaves even the great words became inaudible; . . . mouths opened, but no sound came out" (*BA*, 140). The elimination of connectives leaves logical atoms. It is a "little language such as lovers use, broken words" (*W*, 238), "half-sentences . . . like flags" (*JR*, 50), "scrap[s] of conversation" (*JR*, 127), "sentences that came now here, now there" (*JR*, 57), like Jacob's "half a sentence" – "It follows . . .," or the words "'Objective something,' said Bonamy; and 'common ground' and something else – all very long words," which Mrs. Papworth "noted," eavesdropping on Jacob's and Bonamy's conversation (*JR*, 102), or like the skywriting spelling out: "But what letters? A C was it? an E, then an L? Only for a moment did they lie still; then they moved and melted and were rubbed out . . . and the aeroplane . . . began writing a K, an E, a Y perhaps" (*MrsD*, 29). The snippets of experience in the Old Kent Road includes bits of lettering on banners "upon which was written 'Ra - Un,' but what else? Meat was very red . . . 'Amor Vin – that was over a porch . . . Applejohn and Applebed, Undert – '" (*O*, 307).

This atomization is a function of the aim "to record the atoms as they fall" (*CE*, II, 107) without comment, "a refusal to accept the unity of each object" in an "abstract system of plastic rhythms," where "the disintegration is pushed to such a point, the volumes are so decomposed into small indications of movement scattered over the surface, that at first sight we get the impression of some vaguely patterned carpet or embroidery" (*Cé*, 78–9). For "[n]othing could be seen whole or read from start to finish. What was seen begun . . . was never seen ended. After twenty minutes the body and mind were like scraps of torn paper tumbling from a sack" (*O*, 216–7). What is set down are merely discrete events ununified by a mind. Woolf's ellipses indicate the "[s]paces" that "separated" the "movements" (*JR*, 99):

At six o'clock a man's figure carrying a lantern crossed the field. . . A raft of twig stayed upon a stone, suddenly detached itself, and floated towards the culvert. . . A load of snow slipped and fell from a fir branch. . . Later there was a mournful cry . . . A motor car came along the road shoving the dark before it . . . The dark shut down behind it . . ." (*JR*, 98–9)

The "parts" dismantled by analysis include the relation "opposite" and the color-word "grey-green." The novels' very titles, from *To the Lighthouse* and *Between the Acts* to proper names like *Mrs. Dalloway*, present incomplete symbols. Isolated, they have no meaning. "Such were some of the parts," Lily Briscoe thinks (*TL*, 220). "If only she could put them together, she felt, write them out in some sentence, then she would have got at the truth of things" (*TL*, 219). Woolf's artist's goal is to "read in the littered pieces the clear words of truth" (*TL*, 193), possible when the parts form something like a proposition.

To "bring them together" (*TL*, 220) requires a logical form, itself incomplete and meaningless: "The natural way to symbolize a form is to take some phrase in which actual entities are put together in that form, and replace all these entities by 'variables,' i.e. by letters having no meaning" (*TK*, 98). Only when particulars or denoting words are inserted into the positions of variables can the whole take on meaning:

And suddenly the meaning which, for no reason at all . . . descends on people, making them symbolical, making them representative, came upon them, and made them in the dusk standing, looking, the symbols of marriage, husband and wife. Then, after an instant, the symbolical outline which transcended the real figures sank down again, and they became, as they met them, Mr. and Mrs. Ramsay watching the children throwing catches. (*TL*, 110–11)

Just as in "this is a man," "a concept is in some sense attached to what is not a concept" (*PofM*, 47), so Mr. and Mrs. Ramsay, inserted within a logical framework, become "a husband and a wife." The fragments function as symbols only within the logical form, which uses the colorless language of universals, "general particulars" Russell called them in one place (*LK*, 201), "hard, white, imperishable words" (*MrsD*, 105). In the "lapse from the particular to the general" (*CE*, I, 5), Mr. and Mrs. Ramsay assume the dimensions of universals. This represents "one way of knowing people," i.e., "to know the outline, not the detail" (*TL*, 289), "the stable, the permanent, the original human being" (*CE*, I, 4). Giving, "as poetry does, the outline rather than the detail" (*CE*, II, 224–5), the new novel will borrow its starkness from mathematics also, associated by

Woolf with poetry. The universal dimension endows it with a Greek form, a mediterranean clarity.

THE WHEEL OF SENSATION AND THE LANGUAGE OF SHIFTING REFERENCE

Clearly the mind is always altering its focus, and bringing the world into different perspectives. (Woolf, *A Room of One's Own*, 101)

Sense-data are momentary. Each patch and arrangement of color represents what Woolf calls "any turn in the wheel of sensation" (*TL*, 9); the wandering mind "is like a kaleidoscope" (*CE*, I, 179). The metaphor is borrowed from Fry, who speaks of "[a]lmost any turn of the kaleidoscope of nature," the telescope-like instrument meant to embody the artist's "detached and impassioned vision" by giving "the (aesthetically) chaotic and accidental conjunction of forms and colours" (*V&D*, 51). Reflector of changes of color and form between two mirrors, it combines the lens with the series of frames, capturing perspectives but also randomly shifting them. Matisse's "design is built on the strangest, most unfamiliar appositions, the oddest turns of nature's kaleidoscope" (*H-M*, 23). As mirror, it incarnates Impressionist vision. As a mechanism for shifting frames, it recalls Bergson's cinematograph that Russell makes the model of change minus the gradual rearrangement of elements creating continuity. In fact, Bergson uses the kaleidoscope for "la méthode cinématographe": the perception of movement "va d'un arrangement à un réarrangement, imprimant chaque fois au kaléïdoscope, sans une nouvelle secousse, mais ne s'intéressant pas à la secousse et ne voyant que la nouvelle figure" (*Oeuvres*, 754). Fry's mechanism is also a kind of roving camera, incorporating "the rhythm that obsesses the artist" (*V&D*, 52). "The little apparatus of observation is unhinged" (*W*, 243). It holds the chaotic shimmer of sensible reality in the instant of each turn within a circle of light. Its "power," in Woolf's echo of Fry, is to "transfix the moment upon which its gloom or radiance rests" (*TL*, 9). Each turn arrests a temporal unit: "gloom or radiance," night or day, rain or shine. "Time has given the arrangement another shake" (*W*, 271).

The language of sensation is likewise shifting. "Russell introduced us to the idea that demonstrative identification is . . . quite unlike descriptive identification," Gareth Evans observes (*The Varieties of Reference*, 143). With each use, "this," "there" or "here" points to something different: "the designatum of 'this' is continually changing" (*IMT*, 103). "[O]n different occasions" it "applies to different objects" (*TK*, 39), as in Mrs. Ramsay's "this, and this, and this" (*TL*, 40). Russell calls this "ambiguity" (*PP*, 93). "Now" also "stands for an ambiguous particular, because the present is always changing" (*PP*, 93). Thus, in "now a bird was dashed against the pane, and now there was a clap of thunder" (*O*, 184), the two "nows" are not coreferential; likewise in "*Now*, she murmured, shutting her eyes, we are passing the white house on the hill; *now* we are going through the tunnel; *now* we are crossing the bridge over the river" (*Y*, 271; Woolf's italics). Woolf uses this property of particulars to temporally and spatially perspectivize her language, as with the series of "theres," and "heres" below:

> There is the very powerful, bottle-green engine . . . we start forward . . . There is a bristling of chimneys and towers. There is a white church; there a mast among the spires. There a canal. Now there are open spaces . . . There is a hill striped with red houses. (*W*, 31)

> Here was a market. Here a funeral. Here a procession with banners. (*O*, 306–7)

> Here are pictures. Here are cold madonnas among their pillars . . . Here are gardens; and Venus among her flowers; here are saints and blue madonnas. Mercifully these pictures make no reference; they do not nudge; they do not point. (*W*, 156)

Rather, they point to nothing but themselves. Logically proper names or demonstratives indicate an ever-changing series of sense-data, in contrast with descriptions, which continue to denote the same objects over different uses. Their difference corresponds to the difference in their objects. Sense-data named by particulars are momentary whereas the physical objects denoted by descriptions are "more or less permanent."[5]

This changeableness Woolf values in words themselves: "they hate anything that stamps them with one meaning or confines them to one attitude, for it is their nature to change." This is "because the truth they try to catch is many-sided, flashing this way, then that . . . We pin them down to one meaning, their useful meaning" (*CE*, II, 251). The particular's shifting – "this way, then that" – is thus the ability to capture a perspectival, momentary reality Woolf is looking for in language. Via series of demonstratives, the novels create series of perspectives. *The Waves*' structure most programatically follows this model, alternating unoccupied perspectives in the "interludes" with occupied ones in the dialogues. The sun rises over the unoccupied landscape, light makes perception possible and a series of atomic propositions succeed one another:

"I see a ring," said Bernard, "hanging above me. It quivers and hangs in a loop of light."

"I see a slab of pale yellow," said Susan, "spreading away until it meets a purple stripe."

"I hear a sound," said Rhoda, "cheep, chirp; cheep, chirp; going up and down."

"I see a globe," said Neville, "hanging down in a drop against the enormous flank of some hill." (*W*, 9)

The "I see" construction of the empiricist "cogito" alternates with the nursery-book "Look!": "'Look at the spider's web on the corner of the balcony,' said Bernard. 'Look at the house,' said Jinny, 'with all its windows white with blinds.'" Each dialogue presents a turn in the wheel, a kaleidoscopic shift. Sight predominates, but other sensations occur: "'Stones are cold to my feet,' said Neville. 'I feel each one, round or pointed, separately.'" "'The back of my hand burns,' said Jinny, 'but the palm is clammy and damp with dew.'" Each turn presents a private world – the images of circles, rings, globes, curls, "[i]slands of light," "birds' eyes . . . bright in the tunnels," "drops of water," "[a] caterpillar . . . curled in a green ring," "[t]he grey-shelled snail" (*W*, 9–10), all underscore their self-enclosed quality, just as the passage is circular and repetitive. It captures "[t]he illusion" of the demonstrative "that something adheres for a moment, has roundness, weight, depth, is completed" (*W*, 238). Each perspective's autonomy is spatial and temporal, the chapters dividing perspectives spatially and the series of chapters dividing them temporally.

The shift's newness is underscored by making the speakers children. Their bodies are "embryo lives" (*CE*, IV, 199), sense-data-sensitive plates or *tabulae rasae* receiving the shower of atoms:[6]

In the beginning, there was the nursery, with windows opening on to a garden, and beyond that the sea. I saw something brighten – no doubt the brass handle of a cupboard. Then Mrs. Constable raised the sponge above her head, squeezed it, and out shot, right, left, all down the spine, arrows of sensation. And so, as long as we draw breath, for the rest of time, if we knock against a chair, a table, or a woman, we are pierced with arrows of sensation . . . Sometimes, indeed, when I pass a cottage with a light in the window where a child has been born, I could implore them not to squeeze the sponge over that new body. (*W*, 239)

So "the mackerel in the bowl" over which Rhoda sees "'[c]old water begin[] to run from the scullery tap'" is in the child's neutral position between subject and object.

Woolf visualized the novel's opening with the speakers seated round the table: "it [the Moths] will begin like this: dawn; the shells on a beach; I dont know – voices of cock & nightingale; & then all the children at a long table . . . Then the person who is at the table can call out any one of them at any moment" (*Diary*, III, 236). The children's impressions are like Woolf's own "first impressions" (*MB*, 66), like the June morning of *Mrs. Dalloway*'s opening (3), "fresh as if issued to children on a beach"; their perspectives reduced egos whose directness of vision is uncolored by personality or habitual perception accumulated over time.[7]

Yet the atomic statements in dialogue retain the first person Russell objected to in "cogito." In calling particulars "ego-centric" Russell seems to make "I" the reference point of the particulars: they are words "of which the denotation is relative to the speaker" (*IMT*, 102). But he also claims that "[a]ll egocentric words can be defined in terms of 'this,'" whereas it is not "equally feasible to take some other egocentric word as fundamental, and define 'this' in terms of it" (*IMT*, 102). Elsewhere he pronounced "'here-now' . . . fundamental to our present problem" (*HK*, 90). "I" turns out the least fundamental particular, for the very reason Russell eliminates it from "cogito": even if "I" is "an ambiguous proper name" (*TK*, 36) because its bearer shifts with each new speaker, nonetheless "it applies to something that persists throughout a certain period of time" (*OP*, 215).

"I"'s persistence turns out to be a linguistic property which separates it from the other shifting terms, one Russell discovers in the example "I see a triangle now and I saw a square a moment ago." The "word 'I' has exactly the same meaning in its two occurrences in this sentence," he comments (*OP*, 215). *I*'s permanence is built in, its behavior contrasting with that of the other particulars. "I," unlike "this," is not "applied to different objects on every two occasions when it is used" (*IMT*, 103). "I" is thus not strictly a logically proper name, but, like an ordinary proper name, reducible to a description. This is the source of the objections to the "cogito." The surprising consequence is that ordinary language has no true name for the subject, which cannot by definition be denoted by a description. Hence the later neologism "I-now" (*IMT*, 107), a combination Woolf also uses (*MB*, 75). Particulars are "centered" but not "egocentric."

Yet "I," like "this," is "not like the name 'Smith,' which applies to many objects, but to each always" (*IMT*, 103). "I" shifts, but not with each use, but only when a new speaker is introduced, as in direct speech. *The Waves*' dialogue form is thus dictated by grammar. It permits the shifting and so multiplication of first-person perspectives. *The Waves*' form is, however, unique among Woolf's novels. The other novels shift perspectives not by dialogue but by a sentence belonging uniquely to the novel's style which eliminates "I" yet retains a subjective third-person pronoun. Escaping speech's egocenteredness, it creates a language of multiple perspectives without multiplying speaking I's, representing both classes of inferred entities which for the 1914 Russell remained "unavoidable" – "the sense-data of other people" and "sensibilia" (*ML*, 152). The elimination of "I" met the demands of the earliest impulses of Woolf's art. These philosophical reflections had defined with a hard precision a problem in want of a solution: that of point of view. Its solution yields what Auerbach called Woolf's "multipersonal method" with its "multiplicity of persons" (*Mimesis*, 536), each "separate, self-absorbed, on business of their own" (*Room*, 100). It will use the language of sensation to construct character as Cézanne used color to build geometrical planes.

POINT OF VIEW AND PRIVATE LANGUAGE

[T]he physical world itself, as known, is infected through and through with subjectivity . . . [A]s the theory of relativity suggests, the physical universe contains the diversity of points of view which we . . . regard as distinctively psychological. (Russell, *The Analysis Mind*, 230)

One wanted fifty pairs of eyes to see with, she reflected . . . some secret sense, fine as air, with which to steal through keyholes and surround her where she sat knitting, talking, sitting silent in the window alone" (Woolf, *To the Lighthouse*, 294)

But is there no absolute point of view? (Woolf, *Three Guineas*, 9)

"Ever since I was a child," Woolf wrote, "I've had the habit of getting full of some biography, & wanting to build up my imaginary figure of the person" (*Diary*, I, 180). The novel's language provided the means to "build up by that person the mood" (*Diary*, III, 236) and thereby escape privacy. It was the project of getting beyond the impasse her father, who spoke of "the hopeless attempt of getting outside ourselves" (*HET*, 55) and "had no idea what other people felt" (*MB*, 126), had posed, both as personality and intellectual.[8] The solution was what, according to Stephen himself, Kepler had done to "construct" the solar system, namely, "to place himself in imagination at a different point of view from which the relations asserted to exist might be matters of direct observation":

> seeing in imagination what we should see through a telescope or a microscope, or should see if we moved to Sirius, or could touch a ray of light; what we should see if we could live a thousand years hence or had lived a thousand years ago: or if we could see the back of our heads as well as what lies in front of us. We are still only doing what we are doing when we shut our eyes or imagine the chair behind us. ("WM?," 136–7)

The novel had to cultivate "the habit of considering everything from many different points of view" (*ND*, 29) by occupying other places and times imaginatively, like Mrs. Ramsay, who "felt herself pushing aside the thick leather curtain of a church in Rome" (*TL*, 96). That exercise was, according to Annan, Julia Stephen's, who "responded to other people's feelings instinctively; she could . . . read thoughts before they were uttered" (*His Thought*, 101). What Michael Holroyd saw as a "peculiarly bloodless and trivial" curiosity in Woolf "about all human activity," had really the form of a philosophical thought experiment:

> In place of direct personal involvement, she continued with unanswerable childlike persistence to pose strings of improbable questions. What must it feel like to be a king? A newly-married bride? A bus conductor? Craving to be set free from her egomania by something or someone stronger and altogether dissimilar to herself, she speculated endlessly upon the unknown. (*Lytton Strachey and the Bloomsbury Group*, 26)[9]

In philosophy as well, "we need observation from different points of view, and throughout a certain period of time" (*Matter*, 225). For "[e]ach of course saw something different" (*BA*, 213).

The method of multiple perspectives is the novelist's route to wider knowledge. Shakespeare's sister will become a writer by "drawing her life from the lives of the unknown who were her forerunners, as her brother did before her" (*Room*, 172). Woolf treats biography and autobiography as "supplements" to a circumscribed experience (*TG*, 34). In "The Lady in the Looking-Glass: A Reflection," the goal was to "prize her open with the first tool that came to hand – the imagination," she who "concealed so much and knew so much" (*CSFVW*, 217) – "as if she were as oyster" (*CSFVW*, 219). "One must put oneself in her shoes" (*CSFVW*, 218). In "Street Haunting," the question is " 'What, then, is it like to be a dwarf?' " (*CE*, IV, 157). For Lily Briscoe, painting Mrs. Ramsay, it is: "What did the hedge mean to her, what did the garden mean to her, what did it mean to her when a wave broke?" (*TL*, 294). In *Jacob's Room*, the question "What do we seek through millions of pages?" is answered with "oh, here is Jacob's room" (*JR*, 97). We are "surprised in the window corner by the sudden vision that the young man in the chair is of all things in the world the most real, the most solid, the best known to us" yet "the moment after we know nothing about him. Such is the manner of our seeing. Such the conditions of our love" (*JR*, 72). Jacob can be revealed like the table at high noon: "The light drenched Jacob from head to toe. You could see the pattern on his trousers; the old thorns on his stick; his shoe laces [like Seurat's boot tabs]; bare hands; and face." But Impressionism only sees the surface. "Whether we know what was in his mind is another question" (*JR*, 94). To be "real," Woolf says, a character must have "the power to make you think not merely of itself, but of all sorts of things through its eyes" (*CE*, I, 325). One plunges hypothetically into another privacy, "in and out of rooms, in and out of peoples' minds" (*VO*, 259):

> Into each of these lives one could penetrate a little . . . to give oneself the illusion that one is not tethered to a single mind, but can put on briefly for a few moments the bodies and minds of others. One could become a washerwoman, a publican, a street singer. And what greater delight and wonder can there be than to leave the straight lines of personality and deviate into those footpaths . . . into the heart of the forest where live those wild beasts, our fellow men? (*CE*, IV, 165)

As a child, Woolf had written a story about "souls flying round and choosing bodies to be born into" (*MB*, 95). Of Russell she had expressed the desire to have "the run of his headpiece" (*Diary*, II, 295). The theater-goer's urge to "doff" hers for another is that of occupying more than one of the hierarchical seats in a tiered theatre simultaneously and not sequentially:

> The moulds are filled nightly . . . But the difficulty remains – one has to choose. For though I have no wish to be Queen of England – or only for a

moment – I would willingly sit beside her; I would hear the Prime Minister's gossip; the countess whisper, and share her memories of halls and gardens; the massive fronts of the respectable conceal after all their secret code; or why so impermeable? And then, doffing one's own headpiece, how strange to assume for a moment some one's – any one's – to be a man of valour who has ruled the Empire; to refer while Brangaena sings to the fragments of Sophocles, or see in a flash, as the shepherd sings his tune, bridges and aqueducts. But no – we must choose. Never was there a harsher necessity! . . . for wherever I seat myself, I die in exile: Whittaker in his lodging-house; Lady Charles at the Manor. (*JR*, 68–9)[10]

The urge Holroyd found morbid is the impulse to knowledge: "this making up of scenes about them is what we call 'knowing' people, 'thinking' of them . . . ! Not a word of it was true; she had made it up; but it was what she knew them by all the same" (*TL*, 258). The Impressionist eye, recording momentary particulars, must itself multiply, faceted into as many eyes as moments seen.

The novel gives form to the imaginative adoption of multiple perspectives through a style unique to it which Woolf erects into a structural and thematic principle, her fiction's branching scaffolding. Her "manner" she had herself called "oratio obliqua," Latin grammar's term for indirect discourse, contrasting it to her "few direct sentences" (*Diary*, III, 106). By "oratio obliqua" she means not indirect speech as traditionally designated, but what Clive Bell means by it, namely the translation of Proust's term "style indirect" ("A Propos du 'Style,'" 590).

Discussing Proust's "illuminating notes on Flaubert's use of the imperfect," Bell connects the style to the "suppression of inverted commas" – Proust had talked of Flaubert's resolution "d'user le moins possible des guillemets" (590). Having read Proust and no doubt familiar with his essay via Bell's commentary, Woolf would have recognized that the style meant was what in 1912 Charles Bally called "style indirect libre," suggesting it combined direct and indirect discourse, "libre" designating syntactic non-subordination. No established English term then existed for the style, but in 1924 Jespersen used "represented speech," which I revised as "represented speech and thought" since both thought *and* speech are "represented" in it.[11]

Proust found the style comparable to philosophy, specifically theory of knowledge – with it, Flaubert "a renouvelé presque autant notre vision des choses que Kant, avec ses Catégories, les théories de la Connaissance et de la Réalité du monde extérieur" ("A Propos du 'Style'," 586). Bell cited and pronounced "perfect" a metaphor of Proust's for the style's manipulation of perspectives: "'donc, cet imparfait, si nouveau dans la littérature, change entièrement l'aspect des choses et des êtres, comme fait une lampe qu'on a déplacée'" (*Proust*, 32). The image recalls the "series of gig lamps" of "Modern Fiction" (*CE*, II, 106) or the "lamp . . . in the centre" of the yet unwritten *The Waves* (*Diary*, III, 229). For represented thought builds in language the perspective's centrally illuminated structure and permits shifts of perspective.

Proust singled out Flaubert's "l'usage entièrement nouveau" of the pronouns and tenses in defining the style. In the English-speaking world, Joyce described it by these very grammatical features: "a short sentence about himself containing a subject in the third person and a predicate in the past tense" (*Dubliners*, 108). What Joyce calls "odd" is the use of the third instead of the first person to refer to the sentence's "point of view" and of a past tense (in French, the *imparfait*) peculiar in its cotemporality with particulars like "now" in speech only cooccurring with the present. "But whose foot was he thinking of and in what garden did all this happen?" James reflects in *To the Lighthouse* (275), and the reader attributes the question to him and interprets "this" as pointing to something in his imaginary perspective. Such grammatically subjective terms and constructions like them are referred to the third person and represent its perspective. This is possible because there is no "I," for when an "I" is added, e.g. "in what garden of mine did this all happen?," it is no longer possible to interpret the sentence as his question.[12] This novelistic third person becomes the name for the momentary subject, a reduced *cogito*: "*(s)he* was thinking."

The "(s)he was thinking" itself is not required, as Russell argues for the "cogito," eliminating both "I" and the verb "see" in "I see a triangle." But what remains must be minimally private to be indubitable. By the presence of demonstratives, direct questions, exclamations, and other subjective constructions, with a past cotemporal with "now" but lacking an overt third-person pronoun, sentences presenting typical cases of represented thought show the necessary grammatical privacy – e.g., in "Here he sat drumming his fingers on the table-cloth when he might have been – he took a flashing bird's-eye view of his work. What a waste of time it all was to be sure!" (*TL*, 134). The final sentence, with no "he," but exclamatory and, thus, grammatically subjective, is interpreted as "his" point of view.[13]

The third person of represented thought behaves, moreover, as a genuine logically proper name in that it may (though need not) shift reference from sentence to sentence, as do the third person feminine pronouns in the following sequence:

Why hadn't she stayed at home? she cried, twisting the knob of the iron railing.

That girl, thought Mrs. Dempster . . . don't know a thing yet; and really it seemed to her better to be a little stout. (*MrsD*, 39)

Thus built into this shifting language is the possibility of multiple perspectives. Each sentence of represented thought linguistically represents a subject's occupied perspective. Shifting from perspective to perspective, the novel's language constructs a public world which "enables us to pass beyond the limits of our private experience" (*PP*, 59). As with Russell's logical constructions, the novel's perspectival language must contain representations of unoccupied perspectives for the sake of continuity.

THE LANGUAGE OF THE UNOBSERVED

Here are empty coffee-cups . . . How much better is silence; the coffee-cup, the table . . . Let me sit here with bare things, this coffee-cup, this knife, this fork, things in themselves, myself being myself. (Woolf, *The Waves*, 295)

The thing itself went on whatever happened to the artist – in books, in pictures, in buildings and pots and chairs and tables. (Woolf, *Roger Fry*, 242)

Without a parenthetical "(s)he thought" or its equivalent, the represented thought or sensation is potentially separable from a mind, "not *logically* dependent" on a subject. It contracts to an unoccupied perspective, becomes a statement about sensibilia. We recall that the various translations of "cogitatur" use impersonal constructions – "it thinks" or "there is thinking." But they eliminate too much, as Russell acknowledges in noting the difference "between the propositions 'There is a triangle' and 'I see a triangle' " (*OP*, 214). The first "makes inferences to something public" and "has passed far beyond the region of immediate certainty" (*OP*, 215). But Russell's analysis then uncovers an ambiguity in English "there is," one translatable by " 'voilà' or 'da ist' " and the other by " 'il y a' or 'es giebt' " (*OP*, 216). "Il y a" contains the impersonal "il" of "il pleut." "Voilà" functions as a demonstrative by virtue of the element "là." In the existential statement "there is a table in the room," the table referred to is a physical object while in "this [here] is the table,"[14] it is a sensed table. Russell had a "voilà"-like substitute for "cogitatur" in "it rains here" (*Mind*, 18) or better "it is raining here." Although he never adopts it in his search for "a correct verbal expression for what is added to our knowledge by seeing the triangle" (*OP*, 215), it allows the conclusion Russell reserves for "A visual triangle is occurring," namely, that with it "we have arrived at what is indubitable" (*OP*, 216).

It is striking that, alongside the sentences representing subjects, the novels show sentences like "it was raining here," differing only in the past tense cotemporal with "now" that signals represented thought. They realize, like Seurat's canvases, the "possibilities of empty space."[15] Scattered throughout, they especially congregate in the "interludes," in "Time Passes" in *To the Lighthouse* and the chapter openings or "lyrical portions" of *The Waves* and *The Years*. These Woolf conceived of as difficult experiments. "Time Passes" was "the most difficult piece of abstract writing" (*Diary*, III, 76). "The interludes [of *The Waves*] are very difficult" (*Diary*, III, 285). These sentences representing sensibilia are atomic sentences. The "simples" they contain are particulars such as "here" and "now," centered but neither "egocentric" nor "subject-centered" because occurring in contexts with no first- or third-person pronouns to attribute them to. They point to empty landscapes. Adverbs like "now" are particularly important; their cotemporality with the past tense makes them indistinguishable in isolation from sentences of represented thought, save that they contain no exclamations and other such subject-centered elements. "We cannot define a perspective as all the data of one percipient at one time," Russell explains,

> because we wish to allow the possibility of perspectives which are not perceived by any one. There will be need, therefore, in defining a perspective, of some principle derived neither from psychology nor from space.
>
> Such a principle may be obtained from the consideration of *time*. (*ML*, 135)

The "here/now" in the past is thus crucial in creating perspectives whose language is subjective without being psychological:

> And *now*, curving up and up, straight up, like something mounting in

ecstasy, in pure delight, out from behind poured white smoke looping, writing a T, an O, an F. (*MrsD*, 42; my italics)

[I]t fell upon the arid waste of the desert, *here* wind-scourged into furrows, *here* sprinkled with stunted dark-green jungle-trees. (*W*, 148; my italics)

Passages without particulars like "here/now" can also represent sensibilia:

It was the middle of February. The roofs of Hampstead Garden Suburb lay in a tremulous haze. It was too hot to walk. A dog barked, barked, barked down in the hollow. (*JR*, 118)

The unobserved thus finds in the novel a "neutral monist" language. The dualism of sensible and physical dividing the grammar of referring expressions divides Russell's two propositions, "I see a triangle" and "There is a triangle"; in between falls the neutral "Here was now a triangle," which "has no duality," representing "a datum . . . neither mental nor physical" (*OP*, 217). The novels contain both "l'aspect des choses et des êtres" Proust invokes and Bell quotes, both still lifes of objects and portraits of character. Once "I" ceases to block the view, not only can other points of view be adopted, but an unobserved "reality" can be seen. Such is the conclusion of *A Room of One's Own*, Woolf's long essay on "women and fiction." A new fiction can, like Katherine Hilbery's mathematics, "work out something in figures – something that hasn't got to do with human beings" (*ND*, 195). It can "face the fact . . . that our relation is to the world of reality and not only to the world of men and women" (*Room*, 118). The novel presents the "[s]tark nakedness" Woolf finds in Vanessa Bell's painting: "One says, She is interested in children; one has to add, But she is equally interested in rocks" (Rosenbaum, *The Bloomsbury Group*, 171). For among the "parts" Lily Briscoe's art must "write out," there are not just her sense-data – "[t]he grey-green light – but also sensibilia, "[t]he empty places" (*TL*, 220).

THE GEOMETRY OF PERSPECTIVES:[16] SENSE-DATA INTO OBJECTS AND PERSPECTIVES INTO CHARACTER-BIOGRAPHIES

If this description holds good . . . and is not, as it may well be, entirely dependent upon our position at the table. (Woolf, *Collected Essays*, II, 239)

The parts are recorded. Woolf's problem remains "how to pull it together, how to compost it – press it into one" (*Diary*, III, 285), as for Woolf's artist, Lily Briscoe: "how bring them together?" Fearing "interruption," Lily then "turned her back to the window" (*TL*, 220). The sense-data entering through the window that "should be open" (*TL*, 44) now distract. The door must next be shut, the "material" furnished by impressions taken "into solitude" (*CE*, II, 132). The language of the Interludes is the first step of that retreat from the world. The Impressionist phase has exhausted itself. "Modern fiction" must unify, not just compositionally, as in *To the Lighthouse* and *The Waves*. It must find a linguistic counterpart for "plastic color." Like Julia Stephen, the novelist must be "no aesthetic spectator, collecting impressions for her own amusement" (*MB*, 35),[17] but instead must recognize "how our lives are pieces in a pattern and to judge one truly you must consider how this side is squeezed and that indented and a third expanded and none are really isolated" (*MB*, 30). Having recorded the atoms, she must go on to "trace the pattern" (*CE*, II, 107). The solution must be more than "an incongruous mixture of soft and hard, transient and enduring" (*CE*, II, 132); a transformation must weld the atoms to the pattern.

How then can the collections of sense-data set adrift by analysis be tied down and bound together? How can a home be found for what Feigl calls "the 'homeless qualities'" of "a purely physical (physicalist) world description" ("Russell and Schlick," 337), an owner for thoughts, beliefs, volitions, memories and even sensations, now that neither person nor subject is given? Finally, how can the disparate points of view be assembled into a novel? The problem of the table's persistence in the observer's absence is thus, for the novelist, not unlike the problem of character, "the pseudo-existents of a novel," in Russell's phrase (*PM*, 45). If "modern fiction" initially records the atoms "all in oratio obliqua," an "Impressionist" language, how are they "transformed," in Fry's sense, into something public, permanent, Post-Impressionist? The problem is "not to go making 'reality' this and that, whereas it is one thing" (*Diary*, III, 196), i.e., "how does one add up this and that?" (*TL*, 40). "Now perhaps this is my gift," Woolf says (*Diary*, III, 196).

A literary equivalent to plastic color was discussed within Bloomsbury. One version offered is Mauron's concept of "psychological volume." "In a picture," he explains in a work Hogarth published the same year as *To the Lighthouse*, "colour is added to the volume" (*The Nature of Beauty*, 65). "Volume" is Mauron's term for a painting's design. "What analogue in literature shall we give to volume?" he asks. For "in both domains our aesthetic sensibility rejects realities that are too simple, geometric volumes in one and pure ideas in the other." In the "spatial world there remains the vast crowd of complex volumes"; in that of ideas, "there remain the everyday realities of our soul, all the forms of our inner life." So, "'[a]s the painter creates a spatial being, the writer creates a psychological being'" (66–7).

Mauron's terms echo Bloomsbury's vocabulary. "The psychological reality" or "complex" is conceptualized as a hollowed out perspective, like "Seurat's own definition of the art of painting as 'the art of hollowing out a canvas'" (*TR*, 189).[18] Woolf conceptualizes character-creation in such terms: "I dig out beautiful caves behind my characters" to achieve "depth" (*Diary*, II, 263). "Instead of enumerating details," the writer of modern fiction "will mould blocks" (*CE*, II, 228). Woolf's perspective is the flat surface of a mirror, screen or pool reflecting sense-data like an Impressionist canvas becoming transparent to reveal hidden depths; the atoms become, in Stephen's phrase, "internal atoms" (*HET*, 68). The "obscure angles and relationships" (*CE*, IV, 157) Woolf found the Impressionist eye incapable of "compos[ing]" which we interpreted as a geometry are also angles of vision, equated with one of the interiors into which the street haunter withdraws, one of the thoughts the novel's language represents. The eye alone cannot build character – this marks the difference between film and the novel: "The eye says, 'Here is Anna Karenina.' . . . But the brain says,'" No. "For the brain knows Anna most entirely by the inside of her mind" (*CE*, II, 269–70).

Something is still missing to transform the novel's perspectival language into an architectonics. The multiplication of perspectives, possibility of represented thought, supplies the framework to connect them. The psychological volumes collect around multiple centers "a myriad impressions," like "these moments of being of mine," and assemble them into "scaffolding in the background," both "invisible and silent" (*MB*, 73). In approving Mauron's suggestion "that just as the artist models visual volumes, the writer models 'psychological volumes,'" Fry insists on "the successive états d'âme of which our psychological existence consists" as "the stuff in which the literary artist works." "These may be so small as, in the case of a short lyric, to consist of a single état d'âme, but generally – as in a novel – the volumes the writer builds for us are extremely complex and intricate, implying innumerable états d'âme" (*LettersRF*, I, 75).[19] As with what Seurat calls "ma méthode" (*TR*, 191), Woolf's also emphasizes the interlinking of many volumes, "[t]he idea . . . that the caves shall connect, & each comes to daylight at the present moment" (*Diary*, II, 263). Their randomness, logical independence and self-subsistence (*LK*, 202) enter a system of relations; "the writer of this exacting book," the poetic novel, must "bring to bear upon his tumultuous and contradictory emotions the generalizing and simplifying power of a strict and logical imagination . . . everything in a work of art should be mastered and ordered" (*CE*, II, 228). So, like Vanessa Bell's paintings, novels "yield their full meaning only to those who can tunnel their way behind the canvas into masses and passages and relations and values of which we know nothing," Woolf writes.[20] Their geometry is in time as well as space, a single individual's as well as different individuals' "successive" states of mind. That is why Lily Briscoe "went tunnelling her way into her picture, into the past" (*TL*, 258).

Russell's Leibniz-inspired logical construction gathers together the otherwise disconnected spatially and temporally contiguous sense-data belonging to different private worlds, reassembling the physical table out of the series of private tables and the identifiable person out of momentary selves. The aim is twofold: "to construct enduring things, selves or physical objects, out of transitory things" and "to construct the mental and physical out of some entities which are neither mental nor physical" (Sainsbury, *Russell*, 261). In the first case, all constructions are "biographies." In the second, the person resembles chairs and tables, which, Russell is fond of recalling, are not conscious, even if the atoms composing it are in some sense.[21]

THE CONFERRING OF IDENTITY

Tuesday follows Monday; then comes Wednesday. The mind grows rings; the identity becomes robust. (Woolf, *The Waves*, 257)

Each sensation expressed between quotation marks at *The Waves*' opening shows nothing yet to identify its subject – Rhoda describes the same sound of birds chirping as Susan. Hence the reader's difficulty in keeping the characters distinct, one some criticism tries to overcome by reinterpreting it as a traditional novel.[22] Immediate experience always begins when the adult's "envelope of personality"

(*ND*, 271) is "pierced" (*W*, 239) through to the impressionable child, exposing the oyster-eye. For the child is a minimal core of pure difference, unidentifiable, " 'a new and nameless experience' " (*RF*, 265) – "we were all different" – "stained" by each event "differently. We suffered terribly as we became separate bodies" (*W*, 241).

Identity requires minimally two terms. The self is not acquainted with its own identity, because there is nothing to be identical to in the moment. "Who knows what we are, what we feel? Who knows even at the moment of intimacy, This is knowledge?" (*TL*, 256). Woolf questions "the unity of the mind" (*Room*, 100), substituting a series of states, only one knowable by acquaintance at a time: "the two people, I now, I then, come out in contrast" (*MB*, 75), separated from what comes before and after. Recognizing "how, life being made of little separate incidents which one lived one by one, became curled and whole like a wave" (*TL*, 73) is a discovery occurring in time. The "transparent" recording screen accumulates layers of screens, "leaf upon leaf," we will see (*TL*, 251–2); "our pane of glass" becomes coated (*JR*, 49):

> Oak apples, ferns with little clusters of seeds on their backs, the Regatta, Charlie Pearce, the click of the garden gate, the ants swarming on the step, buying tintacks, sailing, the smell of Halestown bog, splits for tea in the farmhouse at Trevail, the floor of the sea changing. Mr. Wolstenholme in his beehive chair, the spotted elm leaves on the lawn, the rooks cawing as they flew over the house in the morning, the escallonia leaves changing from green to grey, the arc in the air when the powder magazine exploded at Hayle, the boom of the buoy; these are for some reason uppermost in my mind, thinking of St Ives. (*MB*, 135)

The "incongruous miscellaneous catalogue" becomes "little corks that mark a sunken net" (*MB*, 135).

The biography is the net connecting disparate moments fished out; it is only knowable by description. From the fact that "a biography is a set of sensations that are earlier or later than or simultaneous with a given sensation" (Sainsbury, *Russell*, 266), it receives two distinct conceptualizations, expressed in two metaphors. Part of the Bloomsbury vocabulary, the two suggest difference of opinion about how identity is constructed. In one, random elements cohere simultaneously in a recognizable whole by the imposition of form – the mirror is framed, the face, symbol of identity, or the pool is outlined or encircled: "Among all these liquid thoughts some seemed to stick together and to form recognisable people – just for a moment. And one saw a whiskered red face formed in the pool leaning low over it, drinking it" (*CSFVW*, 220).[23] The screen-face absorbs data, coalescing into a complex object. But it exists only at a single moment. The second metaphor's unity is the ordered series of earlier and later, "[t]he happy concatenation of one event following another in our lives" like "the knocking of railway trucks in a siding" (*W*, 234). The series is also like a string of beads, "a pretty image" Clive Bell "propose[s] to borrow" from "my friend, Leonard Woolf" "[t]o illustrate this theory of personality": "Personality he likens to a thread from which depend beads, which beads are our various selves" (*Proust*, 63). Woolf uses the same image of "beads . . . run together on the string" (*JR*, 65) or "strung upon a string" (*BA*, 128). The structure is linear. So the "load of her accumulated impressions" (*TL*, 28), thc "cold stream of visual impressions" (*MrsD*, 182), develop into the "little strip of time . . . , her fifty years" (*TL*, 69), add up cumulatively to a "biography."

The question Clive Bell raises about the series is whether "there must be some permanent tube," "some permanent experiencer," connecting the units or beads. "Grant that we run through a score of *egos* in a week, there is always one which we believe at any rate more real than the rest," he writes (*Proust*, 60), clearly answering some unnamed opponent who denies the permanent entity:

> That we have an illusion – if illusion it be – of continuous experience does seem to imply some permanent experiencer. At times, I agree, the continuity wears thin. When I am talking . . . with old friends about some event in Cambridge days, I can think of, and visualise, myself almost as if the undergraduate, Clive Bell, were another of those old friends, were some one other than my present self. (*Proust*, 62)

The permanent experiencer is considered in *The Waves* via Bell's metaphor. If such a person exists, discontinuous moments reconnect in a single continuous experience: "if the train were to cut me in two, I should come together on the further side, being one, being indivisible" (*W*, 234). The train, like the underground, runs through a permanent tube. Throughout its metamorphoses, the self feels: "it returns. One cannot extinguish that persistent smell. It steals in through some crack in the structure – one's identity" (*W*, 115). It is not necessarily personal – only some fingerprint permitting two thoughts to be traced to the same thinker. But elsewhere Woolf seems to reject this idea. Reflecting on "why it is so difficult to give any account of the person to whom things happen," she observes that when "people write what they call 'lives' of other people," what they do is "collect a number of events, and leave the person to whom it happened unknown" (*MB*, 69). The permanent experiencer is only the sum of its parts, a Russellian class, defined as a "group of particulars." The person is a history, "a thing that happened," composed of many events, as Woolf says her mother was (*MB*, 39). The novels' fictional persons are "more than individuals"; they are "made up of many different things in cohesion." To unite them one must "piece together in a laborious and elementary fashion fragments of belief, unsoldered and separate, lacking the unity" of common sense but with an experimental unity (*ND*, 506). A certain arbitrariness is built into the person-biography.

Modern fiction is charged with finding a more accurate representation of the bearer of the proper name "Mrs. Brown" than do Arnold Bennett's novels. Rejecting Bennett's focus on external facts in favor of the injunction of "Look within" (*CE*, II, 106), Woolf begins with represented thought's disposible *he* and *she*. But its unanchored interiority must be attached to external form. To Bennett's claim that the novel's survival is dependent on its characters being real, Woolf responds, but "what is reality?" (*CE*, I, 325). The novel's realism must relate two competing realities, the private world and the public persona. Lytton Strachey's assessment of *Mrs. Dalloway*, in Woolf's report – even though "it is a whole," "the book does not ring solid" due to "some discrepancy" in the central character – assumes, in now familiar terms, "your method" to reconcile Impressionism and formalism. To Strachey's suggestion to be "wilder & more fantastic," Woolf responds "then I should lose touch with emotions," to which "he agreed, there must be reality for you to start from" (*Diary*, III, 32). Bennett has only descriptions but no direct acquaintance. The sentence of represented thought, containing particulars, puts the novel in touch with one reality, "life," but its "primitives" must be connected to more permanent forms.

The process has its linguistic counterpart. To fix a momentary "he," "she" or "this," the logically proper name designating the momentary subject or experience, to a permanent and identifiable person, requires an ordinary proper name or description coreferential with the pronoun, perhaps the subject of the parenthetical's verb, e.g., "Mrs. Ramsay supposed." *The Waves*' opening arbitrarily attaches collections of sense-data presented in direct speech to such narrative parentheticals ("said Bernard," "said Susan") whose grammatical subjects are proper names (here only the child's given name) – the novels' six characters. "'Hullo,' one says, 'there's Jinny. That's Neville. That's Louis in grey flannel with a snake belt. That's Rhoda.'" Identities emerge from the accumulation of experiences: "It was Susan who cried, that day when I was in the tool-house with Neville; and I felt my indifference melt. Neville did not melt. 'Therefore,' I said, 'I am myself, not Neville,' a wonderful discovery" (*W*, 240). Arrested in a moment, the experience is coupled with a before and after: "All these things happen in one second and last for ever" (*W*, 240). By "listening to" the demonstrative voice "striking off these observations spontaneously I elaborate myself; differentiate myself" (*W*, 115).

Character is thus constructed by uniting the series of particulars via the ordinary proper noun and the description. On its opening pages, Jacob's brother Archer calls out "'Ja–cob!'" at intervals. The novel sends out the proper name in search of "the object to which the name applies" (*PP*, 54), the biography labelled "Jacob Flanders," just as Mr. Streatfield, uttering "the gifted lady," looks round "for an object corresponding to this description" without success, the referent wishing "to remain anonymous" (*BA*, 194). When "in came" Peter Walsh, "for a single second" Clarissa "could not remember what he was called (*MrsO*, 59), for there is a lag between name and object of acquaintance. Orlando or any person calls "directly they are alone, Orlando? (if that is one's name) meaning by that Come, come! I'm sick to death of this particular self. I want another" (*O*, 308). *Mrs. Dalloway* begins with the proper name: "Mrs. Dalloway said she would buy the flowers herself"; the novel then enters her perspective: "And then, thought Clarissa Dalloway, what a morning" (3). In "Mr. Bennett and Mrs. Brown," Woolf, asserting that "all novels begin with an old lady in the corner opposite" (*CE*, I, 324), starts with the description, "[t]he elderly lady," which then receives a name: "whom I will call Mrs. Brown." It is the sentence of represented thought "She would not let Smith touch it" (*CE*, I, 324) which gives "the elderly lady" Mrs. Brown psychological volume or "life," briefly lighting her interior, just as Lily Briscoe brings Mrs. Ramsay to life novelistically by the imaginative recreation of an "old-fashioned scene" (*TL*, 295) in which Mrs. Ramsay accepts Mr. Ramsay's marriage-proposal in represented thought: "Mrs. Ramsay had thought (Lily supposed) the time has come now.

Yes, she would say it now. Yes, she would marry him" (*TL*, 295). Woolf's novels are filled with individualizing proper names (given and surname), often denoting characters with autonomy whose brief appearances, brief flares of consciousness, suggest possibilities never actualized, like those through which the mysterious motor car and the skywriting airplane are presented in *Mrs. Dalloway*: Miss Pym, Edgar J. Watkiss, Sir John Buckhurst, Moll Pratt, Sarah Bletchley, Emily Coates, Mr. Bowley, Carrie Dempster, Mr. Bentley and an unnamed "seedy-looking nondescript man carrying a leather bag" (*MrsD*, 41), along with Clarissa Dalloway, Hugh Whitbread, Septimus and Lucrezia Warren Smith. As in the necklace metaphor, a character's "own past," a private world, "a book known only to him," is linked to the name or "title, James Spalding" and to the description "a man with a red moustache":

> At Mudie's corner in Oxford Street all the red and blue beads had run together on the string. The motor omnibuses were locked. Mr. Spalding going to the city looked at Mr. Charles Budgeon bound for Shepherd's Bush. The proximity of the omnibuses gave the outside passengers an opportunity to stare into each other's faces. Yet few took advantage of it. Each had his own business to think of. Each had his past shut in him like the leaves of a book known to him by heart; and his friends could only read the title, James Spalding, or Charles Budgeon, and the passengers going the opposite way could read nothing at all – save "a man with a red moustache," "a young man in grey smoking a pipe." (*JR*, 6)

This coreference of private pronoun with public description ties the series of selves to the permanent name, e.g., "Orlando." So when "[t]hey went and published things he [Augustus Carmichael] had written forty years ago" (*TL*, 288), it could then be said: "There was a famous man now called Carmichael" (*TL*, 288–9), demonstrating "how many shapes one person might wear, how he was that in the newspapers, but here the same as he had always been" (*TL*, 289).

The operation assembling the represented moments into a "public" self is thus akin to memory. Woolf's past is related to the present, in Proustian fashion, via the sense-data preserved in self-enclosed past moments, like the "squeak of the hinges" at Bourton Mrs. Dalloway "could hear now" (*MrsD*, 3) or the cold of the drawing-room Mrs. Ramsay had felt twenty years before (*TL*, 132). Woolf is aware of the importance of sensations in Proust – viz. her remark, à propos of D. H. Lawrence, that sensations "are not there – as in Proust – for themselves," (*CE*, I, 353). Hence the significance she attaches to the early memory of the "'large red oriental poppies'" in his "'private and particular garden'" with which Fry begins his "fragment of autobiography" and she her biography of him (*RF*, 11). Hence also her own "first memory" of "A Sketch of the Past" – "of red and purple flowers on a black ground – my mother's dress" (*MB*, 64). James, in *To the Lighthouse*'s part three, suddenly recalls a moment from part one, attached, in his memory, to a patch of color:

There was a flash of blue, he remembered, and then somebody sitting with him laughed, surrendered, and he was very angry. It must have been his mother, he thought, . . . with his father standing over her. He began to search among the infinite series of impressions which time had laid down, leaf upon leaf, fold upon fold softly, incessantly upon his brain; among scents, sounds; voices, harsh, hollow, sweet; and lights passing, and brooms tapping; and the wash and hush of the sea, how a man had marched up and down and stopped dead, upright, over them. (*TL*, 251–2)

That blue lies buried, like Betty Flanders' garnet ring among the Roman relics, along with the familiar collection of sights and sounds marking the perspective's edge, as inaccessible to consciousness as any lost object. Woolf's conceptualization of unconscious memory, in this portrait of her psychoanalyst brother, is as a perspective no longer occupied by the subject. Its language is the represented murmur of "Time Passes," connecting to pre-history's unremembered past.

THE EXPERIMENTAL UNITY OF THE CONSTRUCTION

Fry explained Mallarmé's poems by reference to Cubism: in both the subject or theme is broken to pieces, analysed and reconstructed "not according to the relations of experience but of pure poetical necessity." (Spalding, *Roger Fry*, 272)

[I]t is an open question in what sense Orlando can be said to have existed at the present moment. Indeed we should have given her over for a person entirely disassembled. (Woolf, *Orlando*, 307)

The Russellian biography is not a notational variant of the commonsense persisting object or person; it predicts all but not only these. Sainsbury identifies this as the unsolved problem in "Russell's construction of a person" via "the notion of a biography" (*Russell*, 266) "to which Russell gives rather scant attention: how are we to gather sensibilia or appearances into the appropriate classes without specifying the class of appearances of a given thing?" (243). Russell insists that the class is redundant once the appearances are specified:

> even if we assume a "real" table, the particulars which are its aspects have to be collected together by their relations to each other, not to it, since it is merely inferred from them. We have only, therefore, to notice how they are collected together, and we can then keep the collection without assuming any "real" table as distinct from the collection. (*Mind*, 98–9)

But what is to prevent particulars being collected into persons not corresponding to plausible individuals, Sainsbury objects, if "a perspective is a set of 'simultaneous' sensations, where 'simultaneous' means in effect able to be co-experienced"?:

> It is, then, merely contingent that two people do not have the same biography, and in virtue of the way in which the notion of a biography is elaborated to yield, supposedly, the notion of a person, it follows that it is merely contingent that two people are not one. Plainly, something has gone wrong. (*Russell*, 266)

"A precisely analogous criticism applies to Russell's construction of the self," Sainsbury adds (*Russell*, 266). This is the same McTaggart had raised for Russell's Humean self (see chapter 4). The same problem affects the object as construction: what prevents sensibilia of the table and the chair being combined into a single object? These were Russell's very objections to neutral monism: it made "the group of my present experiences" indistinguishable "from other things." For "at any given moment, some of the things in the world, but not all, are somehow collected together into a bundle consisting of what now lies within my immediate experience." Neutral monism lacks "a tenable account of the bond which unites the parts of this bundle, and the difference which marks them out from the rest of the things in the world" (*TK*, 28–9).

Insofar as it gathers in a plurality of data and not just the single datum, the perspective shows structural resemblances with the construction of simultaneous sense-data. Its possible neutralization of emphasis is crucial. Common sense emphasizes separate objects. "Chairs and tables," Russell says, "originally form part of one visual continuum"; we "become aware of them as separate objects" by narrowing attention, without this concentration being analysis. To realize "the relation of the new partial objects to the old total one" that "analysis requires" (*TK*, 123), selection must be suspended. We recall Russell's objection that neutral monism provides no "principle of selection" for "such 'emphatic particulars' as 'this' and 'I' and 'now'" which "involve a selectiveness not possible in a purely material world" (*TK*, 100). The flat perspective that we treated as post-analytic lacks built-in selectivity, sweeping all indiscriminately within its frame.

The logical construction's introduction of a blind selection parallels Impressionism's suppression of selection. Whatever the validity of objections like Sainsbury's to the Russellian logical construction's too great power, Fry's Post-Impressionism and Woolf's modern fiction contain precisely the entities the construction predicts, namely objects corresponding to no common-sense object or person alongside those with such correspondences. The transformations of vision into design experimentally apply the principle of the construction to a random selection of sense-data, actualizing possible objects and biographies on canvas or within the novel. A painting may group fragments of different common-sense objects:

> In such a creative vision the objects as such tend to disappear, to lose their separate unities, and to take their places as so many bits in the whole mosaic of vision. The texture of the whole field of vision becomes so close that the coherence of the separate patches of tone and colour within each object is no stronger than the coherence with every other tone and colour throughout the field. (*V&D*, 51–2)

The frame confers the unity on the painting's patches of color. "The frame of the mirror," Fry writes, functions by "not selecting what we will see, but seeing everything equally"; it thereby "makes its surface into a very rudimentary work of art, since it helps us to attain to the artistic vision" (*V&D*, 20). The arbitrariness becomes apparent: framing converts any random collection, what Gilles Deleuze calls "any-instant-whatever" (*Cinema*, I, 4), into a single perspective. The confines of the pool on "Time Passes"'s beach and the frame of the mirror hanging in its empty rooms gather in random sensibilia. The frame imposes the order: "the square draws its lines round us, and here is a chair, a table, glasses, knives" (*CE*, II, 297); a flower becomes a whole when "a ring enclosed what was the flower" (*MB*, 71). Even in rendering a common-sense object, framing it removes it from use, blocking the principle of selection which prevents its being seen. "Every solid object" which "is subject to the play of light and shade . . . becomes a mosaic of visual patches." Having undergone Impressionist analysis, it falls unselectively into a flat formal pattern: each visual patch "for the artist is related to other visual patches in the surroundings" (*V&D*, 52). Lines begin to "stand out so clearly from the rest"; the kaleidoscopic jumble "begins to crystallise into a harmony" (*V&D*, 51). This Mrs. Ramsay accomplishes, to whom "[t]hey came . . . with this and that" (*TL*, 28); "she brought together this and that and then this" (*TL*, 239–40): "They would, she thought, going on again, however long they lived, come back to this night; this moon; this wind; this house: and to her too . . . and this, and this, and this, she thought . . . it was all one stream, and chairs, tables, maps, were hers, were theirs" (*TL*, 170). The framing process does "not seek to give what can, after all, be but a pale reflex of actual appearance, but to arouse the conviction of a new and definite reality." The aim is not "to imitate form, but to create form, not to imitate life, but to find an equivalent for life." The new images are generated "by the clearness of their logical structure, and by their closely-knit unity of texture" so as to "appear to our disinterested and contemplative imagination with something of the same vividness as the things of actual life," aiming "not at illusion but at reality" (*RF*, 164).

New "objects" are created from the sense-data the painting's frame gathers into "complex systems bound together" by "that sort of unity that leads to the bestowal of a single appellation" (*LK*, 190). It thus attaches a name to them – "Le Compotier" or "Jeune Femme se Poudrant," like Russell's example "Twelfth Night" (*LK*, 190), or the framed configuration can be called "the Cézanne" or "a Seurat" without implying a person – for "those things we think of as single objects are those we can name, and we are thus brought to the issue of naming and Russell's theory of proper names," writes Moore. The things named are not the common-sense objects of Fry's "practical vision" or "specialization of vision" that sees "just enough to recognise and identify each object or person; that done, they go into an entry in our mental catalogue and are no more really seen" (*V&D*, 24–5), have "no more concern after we have read the label on the object" (*V&D*, 48). Instead, the things named are Post-Impressionist constructions.

Just as for Fry the painting's frame assembles patches of color into hitherto unknown "objects," with no name but the painting's title, so the novel creates "characters" out of bundles of more than one person's experiences, forming biographies in which "it is merely contingent that two people are not one." This is radically the case in *Jacob's Room*.[24] But not just the series of private worlds – Jacob's rooms – must be caught by the name. When Russell argues that proper names are analyzable as descriptions, he is claiming that the name's bearer escapes self-acquaintance, consisting also of other people's knowledge:

Suppose some statement about Bismarck. Assuming that there is such a thing as direct acquaintance with oneself, Bismarck himself might have used his name directly to designate the particular person with whom he was acquainted . . . Here the proper name has the direct use which it always wishes to have, as simply standing for a certain object, and not for a description of the object. But if a person who knew Bismarck made a judgement about him, the case is different. What this person was acquainted with were certain sense-data which he connected . . . with Bismarck's body. His body, as a physical object, and still more his mind, were only known as the body and the mind connected with these sense-data. That is, they were known by description. (*PP*, 54–5)

Jacob's room is thus less seen from within by Jacob than from without – by the novel's narrator-"observer of external sights down below" (*JR*, 50), the only of Woolf's novels to have one, or by other characters. The novel contains only one unambiguous representation of Jacob's consciousness[25] – most often he appears as "profoundly unconscious" (*JR*, 14) or "absolutely indifferent" (*JR*, 31). Like the "sensation of the star" associated with the star's and the star's observer's place" (*Mind*, 130), represented thought can give the perspective on one character's private world from that of others, some created for the nonce simply to catch him within the circle of their observation:[26] Mrs. Flanders' perspective on Jacob, Bonamy's, Clara Durrant's, Florinda's, Mrs. Papworth's, Sandra Wentworth Williams', Fanny Elmer's, who, like the novel's narrator, "passed right beneath Jacob's window" (*JR*, 114), Julia Hedge the feminist's, who like *A Room of One's Own*'s narrator observes the young man next to her in the British Museum and "disliked him naturally enough" (*JR*, 107): "That young man for example. What had he got to do except copy out poetry? And she must study statistics" (*JR*, 106). For Mrs. Papworth, who washed up for Bonamy, Jacob is "Mr. Sanders," a "young gentleman":

Mr. Sanders was there again; Flanders she meant; and where an inquisitive old woman gets a name wrong, what chance is there that she will faithfully report an argument? . . . she listened: heard Sanders speaking in a loud rather overbearing tone of voice: "good," he said, and "absolute" and "justice" and "punishment," and "the will of the majority." Then her gentleman piped up; she backed him for arguments against Sanders. Yet Sanders was a fine young fellow . . . "Women" – she thought, and wondered what Sanders and her gentleman did in that line . . . she heard Sanders at it again ("He don't give Bonamy a chance," she thought). (*JR*, 102)

She half-hears Bonamy's words, registering only "Objective something," just as Mrs. Ramsay hears Charles Tansley say "something upon somebody" (*TL*, 22) The text's knowledge of the words is limited to Mrs. Papworth's – he and Jacob "never noticed her" (*JR*, 102) – and to Mrs. Ramsay's. Their subjective thoughts acquaint us with the listeners, but render their objects – Jacob and Tansley – by description.

When Jacob goes up to Cambridge in October, 1906, he shares a train compartment with Mrs. Norman, who sizes him up like a table-turning Mrs. Brown, observing instead of being observed. "Nobody sees any one as he is, let alone an elderly lady sitting opposite a strange young man in a railway carriage. They see a whole – they see all sorts of things – they see themselves" (*JR*, 30–1). Yet her thoughts go into the bundle constructing Jacob:

Taking note of socks (loose), of tie (shabby), she once more reached his face. She dwelt upon his mouth. The lips were shut. The eyes bent down, since he was reading. All was firm, yet youthful, indifferent, unconscious – as for knocking one down! No, no, no! She looked out of the window, smiling slightly now, and then came back again, for he didn't notice her. Grave, unconscious . . . [Woolf's ellipses] now he looked up, past her . . .

But since, even at her age, she noted his indifference, presumably he was in some way or other – to her at least – nice, handsome, interesting, distinguished, well built, like her own boy? One must do the best one can with her report. Anyhow, this was Jacob Flanders, aged nineteen. It is no use trying to sum people up. One must follow hints, not exactly what was said, not yet entirely what was done. (*JR*, 30–1)

Jacob, then, consists of Mrs. Papworth's Sanders and Mrs. Norman's young man in the carriage as much as of his private experience. "Hence events in different people would be collected into a single Russellian 'self'" (Sainsbury, *Russell*, 267). The knowledge of Jacob by description makes him only the list of his properties; he could not have been other than he is. In this sense, the novel's ending both mourns Jacob's death and questions whether he would have accomplished anything if he had lived, at once the sister's elegy and the feminist's tract.

The artist Lily Briscoe confronts the problem for knowledge Mr.

and Mrs. Ramsay present. Trying to reconcile conflicting "impressions" that "poured in upon her of those two men" Ramsay and William Bankes, she wonders "How then did it work out, all this? How did one judge people, think of them?" (*TL*, 40). Ramsay and Bankes are built up of Lily's and the different characters' conflicting opinions. So Woolf can say of "the character of Mrs Dalloway": "I can bring innumerable other characters to her support" (*Diary*, II, 272). Because the enduring person, distinct from the subject, can be constructed as a whole "without introducing . . . any thing mental" (*ML*, 161), it can include other people's sense-data. In this sense, it might be possible that pieces of a biography occur after the person's death – as Percy's is reconstructed "from the sensations of his circumambient friends," in Quentin Bell's phrase (*VW*, I, 112). Or there might not even be a name to attach to the collections of experience, as the list of characters reacting to the motor car and its occupant – the Queen?, the Prince of Wales?, the "Proime Minister"? (*MrsD*, 20, 25) or only "a disk inscribed with a name" never read (*MrsD*, 24) by any of the observers finally adds up simply to an event-thing. Everybody thought, "Nobody knew" (*MrsD*, 20), for knowledge is not thought but a construct of thoughts. "The face itself had been seen only once by three people for a few seconds. Even the sex was now in dispute" (*MrsD*, 23). Or thoughts belonging to different names add up to the fragmentary words the plane is writing – " 'Glaxo,' said Mrs. Coates," " 'Kreemo,' murmured Mrs. Bletchley" (*MrsD*, 29), "the letters E, G, or L" (*MrsD*, 30) – add up to "life; London; this moment of June" (*MrsD*, 5), a construct of many experiences.

Across these mental screens briefly pass other characters, the mad Septimus, for instance, seen by Maisie Johnson, who "positively felt she must cry Oh! (for that young man on the seat had given her quite a turn)" (*MrsD*, 39). Hence Bernard can conclude: "when I meet an unknown person, and try to break off, here at this table, what I call 'my life,' it is not one life that I look back upon; I am not one person; I am many people; I do not altogether know who I am – Jinny, Susan, Neville, Rhoda, or Louis: or how to distinguish my life from theirs" (*W*, 276). "There are many rooms – many Bernards" (*W*, 260), just as Jacob has many rooms. "I sought my oldest friend, who had known me when I was Byron; when I was Meredith's young man,[27] and also that hero in a book by Dostoevsky whose name I have forgotten" (*W*, 272). Or his mind, "shut in him like the leaves of a book" (*JR*, 65), may contain Shakespeare:[28] "there is a vast accumulation of unrecorded matter in my head. Now and then I break off a lump, Shakespeare it may be, it may be some old woman called Peck" (*W*, 272–3), just as, after reading the *Phaedrus* in the British Museum (Julia Hedge did not know it was philosophy not poetry) (*JR*, 106), Jacob becomes "momentarily part of this rolling, imperturbable energy, which has driven darkness before it" and "Plato's argument is stowed away in Jacob's mind" (*JR*, 110), as it is also in the "enormous mind" (*JR*, 108), the "vast mind . . . sheeted with stone" (*JR*, 109) of the museum dome-head:

> Stone lies solid over the British Museum, as bone lies cool over the visions and heat of the brain. Only here the brain is Plato's brain and Shakespeare's; the brain has made pots and statues, great bulls and little jewels . . . Meanwhile, Plato continues his dialogue; in spite of the rain; in spite of the cab whistles. (*JR*, 109)

The *Phaedrus* persists even when not read, like the copy of Spinoza in Jacob's room (*JR*, 39), an unconscious part of that giant psychological volume which is the museum itself.

Biographies are, then, "transformations" of the raw data in which contiguous atoms of analysis are recombined arbitrarily. Painting and novel-writing, applying the principle experimentally, level everything to the status of a possible object, "the object *ex hypothesi*" (*V&D*, 48). Each canvas or novel is one application of the principle, a study: "in writing I seem to be discovering what belongs to what; making a scene come right; making a character come together" (*MB*, 72). If painting is more properly concerned with constructing public neutral objects out of spatially contiguous sensibilia, the novel builds up temporal structures, "forms . . . presented to us in such a sequence that each successive element is felt to have a fundamental and harmonious relation with that which preceded it" (*V&D*, 33).

The biography-construction for Woolf, as for Fry, is contrasted with false forms of unity supplied by common sense and the ego. "Cézanne and Picasso had shown the way; writers should fling representation to the winds and follow suit," Woolf represents Fry's opinion (*RF*, 172). What Woolf dismisses as "narrative" is the story's false cohesiveness – not to be confused with "successive unity." So Leslie Stephen distinguishes "dropping into narrative" from "a different order" (*MBook*, 66). Woolf's suspicion of narrative is shared with the Bloomsbury artists. Vanessa Bell, for instance, "as Roger had done, distrusted its [surrealism's] return to story-telling" (*VB*, 285). "No stories are told" in Bell's painting (Rosenbaum, *The Bloomsbury Group*, 171). Fry himself "detested the storytelling spirit which has clouded our painting and confused our criticism" (*CE*, IV, 90–1).

Narrative suggests traditional biography, those "'lives' of other people" (*MB*, 69). The Russellian "biography" is its alternative. Woolf, daughter of the editor of *The Dictionary of National Biography* and author herself of *Roger Fry: A Biography* and the canine life *Flush*, rethought biography as the construction of the person.[29] *Orlando: A Biography* erects the Russellian biography into a genre and parodies biography as the story of a life. "Once I had a biographer," Bernard says. "That is the biographic style, and it does to tack together torn bits of stuff, stuff with raw edges" (*W*, 259). It is false when it pretends to be complete. For, given the number of "selves of which we are built up" (*O*, 308), the "biographer" so frequently invoked in *Orlando* "has far more than we have been able to find room for, since a biography is considered complete if it merely accounts for six or seven selves, whereas a person may well have as many thousand" (*O*, 309). The old biography has the "I"'s false completeness. To the question "how did they compose what people called a life?," the answer "[p]erhaps there's 'I' at the middle of it, . . . a knot; a centre" is unsatisfactory: "she saw herself sitting at her table drawing on the blotting-paper, digging little holes from which spokes radiated" (*Y*, 367).

In insisting in *Aspects of the Novel* that in the novel the story "runs like a backbone – or may I say a tapeworm, for its beginning and end are arbitrary" (26), Forster seems to take exception to Bloomsbury's hostility to narrative. "Yes – oh, dear, yes, – the novel tells a story. That is the fundamental aspect without which it could not exist . . . I wish it was not so, that it could be something different – melody, or perception of the truth, not this low atavistic form" (26). Woolf, by contrast, associates narrative – "stories of childhood, stories of school, love, marriage, death, and so on" – with the false and unreal: "none of them are true" she concludes (*W*, 238). "[T]he real novelist"'s storytelling imposes a false order and a completeness, like the selectiveness of common sense, "this appalling narrative business of the realist: getting on from lunch to dinner: it is false, unreal, merely conventional" (*Diary*, III, 209–10).

Absence of narrative and drama is the corollary of Woolf's

reliance on represented thought. *To the Lighthouse* is "hopelessly undramatic" because "all in oratio obliqua." No narrator's commentary links private worlds. Only parentheticals like "Mrs. Ramsay wondered" connect named self to denoted person. Otherwise, almost all sentences represent perspectives either occupied by a "she" or "he" or empty. The non-narrative series of represented thoughts presents random fragments; it follows "my tunnelling process, by which I tell the past by instalments, as I have need of it" (*Diary*, II, 272). Its "representative" moments of being are not those common sense selects to get from lunch to dinner; they are unselective moments whose representativeness comes strangely from their randomness. Like a physics built on solipsism, the novel begins with the hollowed out interior and then attaches it to an exterior. "[W]riting exteriorly" Woolf counterposes to when "I dig." Pronouncing "even externality is good," she aims at "some combination of them" (*Diary*, III, 209).

THE INVISIBLE NETWORK OF FORMAL RELATIONS

To the eye or to the touch, ordinary matter appears to be continuous; our dinner-table, or the chairs on which we sit, seem to present an unbroken surface. We think that if there were too many holes the chairs would not be safe to sit on. Science, however, compels us to accept a quite different conception of what we are pleased to call "solid" matter; it is, in fact, something much more like the Irishman's definition of a net, "a number of holes tied together with pieces of string." Only it would be necessary to imagine the strings cut away until only the knots were left. (Russell, *The ABC of Atoms*, 7)

[T]hey groped in this difficult region, where the unfinished, the unfulfilled, the unwritten, the unreturned, came together in their ghostly way and wore the semblance of the complete and the satisfactory. (Woolf, *Night and Day*, 506).

[I]t gives me . . . a great delight to put the severed parts together. (Woolf, *Moments of Being*, 72)

The constructions bundling together the "data" of the novels gather fragments into a scaffolding, the pattern produced by the wheel of sensation's arbitrary turnings in which the fragments are still visible. Woolf's recurrent figure for this Post-Impressionist design is the net flung over the chaotic, ever-moving shower of atoms.[30] It imposes form, as the passing clouds "caught a whole village in the fling of their net" (*W*, 183), as a flock of rooks "looked as if a vast net with thousands of black knots in it has been cast up into the air" (*CE*, I, 359): "All this danced up and down, like a company of gnats, each separate, but all marvellously controlled in an invisible elastic net" (*TL*, 40–1). So also "people [are] related to each other by a net of sensations" (*CE*, I, 353). In literature, it is "words like nets" (*O*, 313) which give the disparate form. "The trees, scattered, put on order . . . I netted them under with a sudden phrase. I retrieved them from formlessness with words" (*W*, 270). The separate impressions are "little corks that mark a sunken net" (*MB*, 135); the form is the net of relations. It remains "invisible," "a phantom net" (*TL*, 104), until an eyeless vision seizes the collection's logical relatedness: "changes, unseen in the day, coming in succession seem to make an order evident" (*CE*, II, 293). So "ordinary pebbles" will, "if you look at them steadily," reveal "multiplicity becomes unity" (*JR*, 131), and Impressionist data assume geometrical patterns in Cézanne:

> The more one looks the more do these dispersed indications begin to play together, to compose rhythmic phrases which articulate the apparent confusion, till at last all seems to come together to the eye into an austere and impressive architectural construction, which is all the more moving in that it emerges from this apparent chaos. (*Cé*, 79)

We already met the network-metaphor in the *Tractatus*. Wittgenstein's use is not unlike Woolf's; it occurs "[a]mong the most important of these metaphors" Black identifies: "the *mosaic*, the *chain*, the *logical network*, the *picture*, and the *mirror*," which with "pervasive notions" like "*logical form*" compose the "list of Wittgenstein's chief leitmotifs":

> The baldest summary of Wittgenstein's conception might run as follows: Reality ("the world") is a *mosaic* of independent items – the "atomic facts"; each of these is like a *chain* in which "objects" (logical simples) "hang in one another"; the objects are connected in a *network* of logical possibilities ("logical space"); the simplest elementary propositions are *pictures* of atomic facts, themselves facts in which names are concatenated, and all other propositions are truth-functions of the elementary ones; language is the great *mirror* in which the logical network is reflected, "shown," manifested. (*Companion*, 3)

Black's paraphrase of Wittgenstein evokes Fry's discriptions of Post-Impressionism: "logical space is one and indivisible," Black writes, "the atoms of the great contingent mosaic are connected by the invisible web of formal connexions" (28).

Woolf's netted collection or class is repeatedly a flock of birds or cloud of gnats, a "gabble of rooks and doves" (*W*, 268). Everywhere "[b]irds swooped and circled . . . as if there were one body cut into a thousand shreds. Birds fell like a net descending on the tree-tops" (*W*, 182). "The sparrows fluttering, rising, and falling in jagged fountains were part of the pattern; white and blue, barred with black branches" (*MrsD*, 32–3). The single bird or gnat is a monad in motion; the flock or cloud, a monadology.[31] The dancing atoms coalesce only momentarily: as sensation's wheel turns, what falls together within the kaleidoscope's frame falls back into chaos or another configuration, "so that the vision must be perpetually remade" (*TL*, 270). "The rooks, rising in a net," then "fall in a net upon the elm trees" (*CE*, IV, 198). "The rooks settled; the rooks rose . . . Up went the rooks and down again, rising in lesser numbers each time." Even after "settling down for sleep," any new interruption of data – "far off, a familiar sound," "the dinner bell at the house" – suffices to "scare[ ] sleepy wings into the air again" (*JR*, 56–7). So also the philosopher continually revises his hypotheses, as Russell did. The theory holds provisionally.

"[T]he absorbing pursuit" of the pattern in chaos, "the shattering and piecing together," is never completed: "it is the perpetual warfare," "the daily battle, defeat or victory" (*W*, 269–70). The rhythm of chaos and order is the waves' ebb and flow. "Yes, yes, yes, the tide rushed out embracing. No, no, no, it contracted" (*BA*, 215). Every proposition has its contradictory.[32] Juggling its data like a pile of note cards, the ordinary mind weighs the alternatives, but the question "flies like a flock hither and thither, helter-skelter" (*Room*, 28). "[T]he scattered parts of the vision within," once "assemble[d] outwardly" (*TL*, 198), fly apart again; the pool grows still, then its mirror-surface is broken. A biography consists of such alternations. Hence, any series can end in either unity or disunity. If an instant before *To the Lighthouse* ends, Lily Briscoe finds her canvas "blurred" (310), immediately after "she saw it clear for a second" and, laying down her brush, the novel closes. But *The Waves* ends with night and the waves breaking on the shore, the nineteenth century in *Orlando* ends when "the words went dashing and circling like wild hawks together among the belfries and higher and higher . . . till they crashed and fell in a shower of fragments" (262) and *Between the Acts* ends in the darkness of war, on a note of disharmony – "[a] kind of growl between the cuckoos and t'other birds" (*Diary*,

V, 293). Its final dissonance explains why the flock-image, usually visual, has become aural. In it, the flocking birds are rooks or starlings, the familiar English gregarious birds – "the starling (who is a more sociable bird than the lark)" (*O*, 270), the "Four and twenty blackbirds, strung upon a string" (*BA*, 178) that become the means to "hustle us and shuffle us, and bid us, like the starlings and rooks, come together, crowd together" with "many-tongued much syllabling" (*BA*, 120). They are contrasted to the similarly non-solitary martins and "swallows swooping, swerving, flinging themselves in and out, round and round, yet always with perfect control as if elastics held them; and the flies rising and falling" (*MrsD*, 104), whistling and moving in harmony. Rooks are abrupt, disruptive, yet still flocking. As a collection of sounds, they are cacophonous; like the "magpie & . . . first spring birds" Woolf heard at Rodmell, they are "sharp egotistical" (*Diary*, IV, 7), violently agressive:

> Then suddenly the starlings attacked the tree . . . In one flock they pelted it like so many winged stones. The whole tree hummed with the whizz they made, as if each bird plucked a wire. A whizz, a buzz rose from the bird-buzzing, bird-vibrant, bird-blackened tree. The tree became a rhapsody, a quivering cacophony, a whizz and vibrant rapture, branches, leaves, birds syllabling discordantly life, life, life, without measure, without stop devouring the tree. Then up! Then off!
>
> What interrupted? (*BA*, 209)

The birds' discordance is echoed throughout *Between the Acts* by clusters of jarring, monosyllabic words, often verbs, frequently denoting harsh sounds or abrupt movements:[33] "coughed" (3); "whizzed, whirred, buzzed" (15); "flapped" (17); "jerked," "glared," "yielded, pitched, plunged, then pulled" (66); "snored" (68); "brayed and blared," "cracked" (79); "bawled," "mooed," "twittered" (84); "gashed," "brewed," "spilt" (94); "blared," "chanted," "moaned," "lamented" (95); "flopped," "sucked" (116); "crunched," "chattered," "scattered, shattered" (119); "trilled and tinkled" (157); "rattled and sniggered; chattered and jibbered." They constitute so many "[s]craps, orts and fragments!" (192).

The rooks' and starlings' discordance is an anti-symphony; their separateness held in by the chorus of notes. In this they are connected to the jazz rhythm the novel invokes:

> The tune changed; snapped; broke; jagged. Foxtrot, was it? Jazz? . . . the rhythm kicked, reared, snapped short. What a jingle and a jangle! . . . What a cackle and a cacophony! Nothing ended. So abrupt. And corrupt

> . . . To disrupt? Jog and trot? Jerk and smirk? . . . Squint and pry? Peak and spy? . . . The young, who can't make, but only break; shiver into splinters the old vision; smash to atoms what was whole. What a cackle, what a rattle, what a yaffle – as they call the woodpecker, the laughing bird that flits from tree to tree. (*BA*, 183)

The rooks' visual aspect is the accompaniment to their sound: characteristically caught at the moment of dispersion, they "pelt" the tree, "winged stones" linked to the image of "Prehistoric man," who "roused himself from his semi-crouching position and raised great stones" (*BA*, 218), an allusion to armed conflict. Rooks, rocks, stones, starlings, the very alliteration and rhyme repeats the paired staccato and pizzicato sounds.

Such disruptiveness is not simply a threat to art's precarious harmony. "Miss La Trobe rais[ing] herself from her stooping position" (*BA*, 208) assumes the pre-historic posture. Her stone words, part of the history of violence, are also the "hard . . . words" that "flew to attach themselves to their places" in Septimus' ode (*MrsD*, 105), granite-like yet alive, with the energy belonging to "the young" and their new jazz and to Septimus' as to Woolf's madness. The starlings' attack makes the tree "vibrant," their cacophony is "quivering," their song is "life," as also in *Orlando* (270), that cry of rooks Woolf had associated with her earliest memory. The struggle between harmony and chaos is that between "Beautiful pictures," "Beautiful phrases" and "that very jar on the nerves" Lily "wished to get hold of" (*TL*, 287), what interrupted the birds – "life," reality uninterpreted, meaningless, shapeless. "Beauty had this penalty – it came too readily, came too completely. It stilled life – froze it. One forgot the little agitations; the flush, the pallor, some queer distortion, some light or shadow, which made the face unrecognisable for a moment and yet added a quality one saw forever after" (*TL*, 264). To make life the sole goal is to stop where Impressionism does; to make beauty "everything" is to lose contact with life. The goal is to balance "Mrs. Ramsay and the picture" (*TL*, 287), to catch her momentarily unrecognizable look, like "La Grande Jatte," forever in the freeze-frame of a network.

Reality, then, is a shock, arresting the observer, whose sensitivity intensifies into acute pain. The pure eye is a raw nerve. But exposure may reveal order, as when the child Virginia, "looking at the flower bed by the front door," says "'That is the whole'" (*MB*, 71). Some shocks fail to yield a pattern, Woolf explains, bringing "a peculiar horror and a physical collapse; they seemed dominant; myself passive" (*MB*, 72). In others, an initial Impressionism is subjected to logic, the child to the adult: "in the case of the flower I found a reason" to help "deal with the sensation . . . conscious – if only at a distance – that I should in time explain it" (*MB*, 72). For "as one gets older one has a greater power through reason to provide an explanation" which "blunts the sledge-hammer force of the blow." The shock is "followed by the desire to explain it." It "is not, as I thought as a child, simply a blow from an enemy hidden behind" ordinary experience but "a revelation of some order," the "token of some real thing behind appearances; and I make it real by putting it into words" (*MB*, 72). The order follows Russell's method, rejecting the "tendency" to discount anything "the product of previous thought and analysis and reflection on your part," to cling to vagueness instead of attempting to clarify. "You do not want to go back to the vagueness of the child," Russell insists. "It is quite clear that a highly educated person sees, hears, feels, does everything in a very different way from a young child or animal, and that this whole manner of experiencing the world and of thinking about the world is very much more analytic than that of a more primitive experience" (*LK*, 181). The child's shock is Impressionism's encounter with sense-data; the pattern's disclosure, Post-Impressionism's logical explanation.

The pattern is discovered, part of its reality – "it seems given to me, not made by me" (*MB*, 72). In Cézanne's words, art "realizes" (*Cé*, 38) some possibility in reality, some shape lurking behind the shimmering veil of appearances. "A scene always comes to the top; arranged; representative" (*MB*, 142). This Woolf says is "what I might call a philosophy; at any rate it is a constant idea of mine; that behind the cotton wool is hidden a pattern . . . that the whole world is a work of art; that we are parts of the work. And I see this when I have a shock" (*MB*, 72).

For the artist, the process is also a reduction of the ego. The impurities and irrelevancies "fired out of" Shakespeare "and consumed" include "hardship and grievance" (*Room*, 58), all expressions of ego; similarly, Fry "the critic's own identity has been consumed" in his criticism (*RF*, 285). That is why, "though we say that we know nothing about Shakespeare's state of mind, even as we say that, we are saying something about Shakespeare's state of mind" (*Room*, 58). Ultimately, the disappearance of the authorial voice reposes the question of unity, for the novel can then no longer take the linguistic shape of an identifiable speaker's voice.

ANON: THE PROBLEM OF THE NARRATOR

I become anonymous, a person who writes for the love of it . . . without any praise I should be content to go on. This is what Duncan said of his painting the other night. (Woolf, *Diary*, II, 248)

[E]ven if he had to hire a room to house his canvases, and the canvases themselves must be rolled up, he painted. (Woolf, *Roger Fry*, 238)

The words . . . sounded . . . as if no one had said them, but they had come into existence of themselves. (Woolf, *To the Lighthouse*, 166)

To hypothesize that "[t]he world held . . . other people, and each other person possessed . . . some fragment of what privately she called 'reality'" (*ND*, 345) is "the first step in that mysterious process in which Jane Austen was so great an adept." For "[t]o believe that your impressions hold good for others is to be released from the cramp and confinement of personality" (*CE*, II, 159). The next step is to construct a public world from these hypothetical perspectives. "The little grain of experience once selected," Woolf says of Austen, once "set outside herself, could be put precisely in its place," to be made "into that complete statement which is literature" (*CE*, II, 159).

The failure to achieve the second step Woolf makes the justification for her reservations about Joyce's *Ulysses*. Joyce had, like Impressionism, captured "life itself." The "reason a work of such originality yet fails" is because it remains immured in privacy, "because of the comparative poverty of the writer's mind"; it gives a "sense of being in a bright yet narrow room, confined and shut in, rather than enlarged and set free" (*CE*, II, 108). We recognize the figure of the private world. So crucial for the writer, the room is also an impediment: "the danger is the damned egotistical self; which ruins Joyce & [Dorothy] Richardson to my mind: is one pliant and rich enough to provide a wall for the book from oneself without its becoming, as in Joyce & Richardson, narrowing and restricting?" (*Diary*, II, 14). (The problem Woolf links to the question "What the unity shall be" of the "unwritten" novel to become *Jacob's Room*.) Is it due to "some limitation imposed by the method as well as by the mind" that one feels "centred in a self which, in spite of its tremor of susceptibility, never embraces or creates what is outside itself and beyond? Does the emphasis laid, perhaps didactically, upon indecency, contribute to the effect of something angular and isolated?" (*CE*, II, 107–8). The alternative is the flight from privacy. The method needs logic, by means of which, Russell explains, "[i]nstead of being shut in within narrow walls, of which every nook and cranny could be explored, we find ourselves in an open world of free possibilities, where much remains unknown because there is so much to know" (*PP*, 148). The room's inhabitant must become the street haunter who imaginatively occupies many perspectives in sequence: "when the door shuts on us, all that vanishes" (*CE*, IV, 156), Woolf writes of "the solitude of one's own room" (*CE*, IV, 155).

By what "method" does the novelist achieve this multiplication and assemblage of perspectives? The answer is the author's disappearance in the work. Its model is the hidden observation of "one of those naturalists who, covered with grass and leaves, lie watching the shyest animals" while "themselves unseen," watching "things that never happen, so it seems, if someone is looking" (*CSFVW*, 215). Its practitioner, like Orlando, "made a point sometimes of passing beneath the windows of a coffee house, where she could see the wits without being seen" (*O*, 222), adopting the vantage point of the street haunting Katharine Hilbery, who "stood unobserved and absorbed" (*ND*, 439), or the narrator's outside Jacob's rooms. Without Berkeley's "God in the quad"'s omnipresence, she is excluded, we recall, from some places in the universe by virtue of her sex. Such is the condition of all seeing, to have a partial view. The woman-narrator makes her invisibility and expendability a way to overcome her partiality. The vantage-point becomes unoccupied: after *Jacob's Room*, this shadowy narrator vanishes.

The novel's suppression of "I" is the literary registration of the reduced self. The phenomenon Woolf connects to death: "the writing 'I,' has vanished. No audience. No echo. Thats part of one's death" (*Diary*, V, 293). While the passage applies exclusively to her writing of *Between the Acts*, amidst the war and on the verge of suicide, the "I"'s disappearance is not a late theme. Elsewhere she associates it with Flaubert, placing Fry's "humble" artist among "that confraternity to whom 'Cézanne and Flaubert have become in a sort the patron saints'" (*RF*, 242). The novelist, Woolf writes, "can put himself at any point of view" or "combine several points of view. He can appear in person, like Thackery; or disappear (never perhaps completely), like Flaubert" (*CE*, II, 127). The writer's disappearance yields a self-generated language beyond a speaker's control, like the voice Lily Briscoe hears "which speaks too quickly to be taken down" (*TL*, 40), like the words of Septimus' ode, which "from his lips fell . . . without his making them" (*MrsD*, 105), like Woolf's evocation of writing *To the Lighthouse*: "Blowing bubbles out of a pipe gives the feeling of the rapid crowd of ideas and scenes which blew out of my mind, so that my lips seemed syllabling of their own accord as I walked. What blew the bubbles? Why then?" (*MB*, 81). Musing about the shape *The Waves* would take – "I am not trying to tell a story. Yet perhaps it might be done in that way. A mind thinking" (*Diary*, III, 229) – Woolf raises the question "Who thinks it? And am I outside the thinker?" (*Diary*, III, 257). This question she connects to the question "is there a pattern; a theme, recurring, like music; half remembered, half foreseen?" (*Y*, 369), for if "there was a pattern," then "who makes it? Who thinks it?" (*Y*, 369).

Woolf's answer is a literary version of Bloomsbury agnosticism, rejecting the theological vocabulary of an omnipresent, onmiscient "narrator" as the text's hidden God.[34] Such an invisible presence is merely a hypothesis to hold the fragmentary world together, a personification of the pattern, much like the god of Descartes, Leibniz and Berkeley. Omniscience is attributed to this god because knowledge is assumed to imply a knower. Descartes "would say that thoughts imply a thinker." "But why should they?," Russell had voiced the Lichtenbergian position (*OP*, 171). The knowledge to which Woolf's "modern fiction" aspires surpasses the finite individual's acquaintance, but to equate it with divine omniscience would be to ignore Woolf's own rejection of the analogy.[35] Her "philosophy" that "Hamlet or a Beethoven quartet is the truth about this vast mass that we call the world" (*MB*, 72) unambiguously denies an author in this creation: "there is no Shakespeare, there is no Beethoven; certainly and emphatically there is no God" (*MB*, 72). Hence the novelist must "look past Milton's bogey" (*Room*, 118). Literary creation is like the universe's formation, a play which "unfolded itself," as Russell calls it (*ML*, 44). The play is Greek in its fatefulness: "Tragedy begins with a dance of Anons," F. L. Lucas comments (*Tragedy*, 60). Hence Woolf's refusal "to talk about an artist," as Corner claims ("Mysticism and Atheism," 411), follows logically from Bloomsbury agnosticism, displaying Mrs. Ramsay's skepticism – "How could any Lord have made this world?" (*TL*, 98). An author is no lord of creation.

The artist's disappearance in the work is a Bloomsbury theme. Forster's attempt "to explain *his* ideas and *his* emotions" in *A Passage to India* Fry thought "misses the great thing." Woolf calls "that imposition of the writer's personality for which there is no exact critical term" a "sin" Fry "discovered" (*RF*, 241). For Fry this is the failure of literature by contrast to painting. Forster, on the other hand, saw the disappearance of the author as literature's achievement. Hogarth published his tract *Anonymity: An Enquiry* in 1925, the year of *Mrs. Dalloway*. It opens with the question "Do you know who a book's by?," pronouncing it "more profound and even more literary than may appear." "Books are composed of words," which "have two functions": "to give information or . . . create an atmosphere" (8). From this Forster concludes "that what is information ought to be signed" but "what is not information need not be signed" (13). We remember the poet "before we begin the poem and after we finish it, but during the poem nothing exists but the poem" (14). "The poet wrote the poem no doubt, but he forgot himself while he wrote it, and we forget him while we read" (16–17). For the author's elimination is not an ideal art aspires to but a fact the writer encounters. It is not that writers should not impose their personality but that, finally, they cannot: "it was not the speaker who was in the beginning but the Word" (17). "A letter comes off the surface: it is naturally signed. Literature tries to be unsigned" (18). The prohibition is really a law of nature that places the work in the world of the unobserved, maintained in existence by no deity but simply part of what there is:

> all literature tends towards a condition of anonymity, and . . . so far as words are creative, a signature merely distracts us from their true significance. I do not say literature "ought" not to be signed, because literature is alive, and consequently "ought" is the wrong word to use. It wants not to be signed . . . saying in effect: "I, not my author, exist really." So do the trees, flowers and human beings say "I really exist, not God," and continue to say so despite the admonitions to the contrary addressed to them by clergymen and scientists. To forget the Creator is one of the functions of a Creation. (15)

Each painting, each book, whether in the British Museum, the book store in "Street Haunting" or the library of Pointz Hall, encloses an unobserved world.

Woolf's model of a creation in which the creator is absent is an ancient oral literature, the ballad. Forster had seen the "demand that literature should express personality" (18) and the idea "that we are right in asking for his name" because "[i]t is his property – he ought to have the credit" as a modern one, "for in the past neither writers nor readers attached the high importance to personality that we do today" (15). His anonymous writers par excellence were "the mediaeval balladists, who, like the Cathedral builders, left their works unsigned" (16).[36] It is the ballad writer/singer who also for Woolf is "Anon." Invariably a woman, "anon" stands for the myriad obscure voices whose only traces are the unattributed songs which the theory of "unmoved mover" and "first cause" requires have a composer. "I would venture to guess that Anon, who wrote so many poems without signing them, was often a woman" (*Room*, 51). For a woman's "life has an anonymous character" (*CE*, II, 146). "Anonymity runs in their blood," she says of women. "The desire to be veiled still possesses them," being unconcerned about "their fame as men are," they "will pass a tombstone or a signpost without feeling an irresistible desire to cut their names on it, as Alf, Bert or Chas. must do" (*Room*, 52). Considering the conditional "if a woman in Shakespeare's day had had Shakespeare's genius" (*Room*, 50), Woolf concludes that "her work would have gone unsigned." Miss LaTrobe, or rather "Misswhatshername" (*BA*, 184 and 196), "wish[ing] it seems to remain anonymous" (*BA*, 194) and not to be seen in her work – "LaTrobe was invisible" (*BA*, 191) – writes a kind of medieval pageant-play. Currer Bell, George Eliot and George Sand, seeking "to veil themselves by using the name of a man," thus observed the convention "that publicity in woman is detestable" (*Room*, 52). So Lily is finally indifferent to the possibility her canvas "would be rolled up and stuffed under a sofa" (*TL*, 237) or "hung in the attics," that "it would be destroyed," as Fry resolves to " 'never show again' " but " 'go on painting, and when the canvases are dry, . . . roll them up' " (*RF*, 236).[37] Fry's artist "leads his laborious life 'indifferent to the world's praise or blame' " (*RF*, 262). With "what did that matter?" (*TL*, 309–10), Lily acknowledges that the work is finally independent of its creator, coming to occupy those unobserved spaces where lay the Waverly novels, Mrs. Ramsay's shawl, Minta's brooch, her copy of *Middlemarch* and the pig's skull.

The novels' obscure representatives of the ballad tradition demonstrate how the writer's namelessness[38] is conjugated with the song's independence. "Mrs. McNab, tearing the veil of silence," is one such singer: "As she lurched" and "rolled from room to room, she sang"

(*TL*, 196). Like the "old blind woman . . . singing out loud, not for coppers, no, from the depths of her gay wild heart" (*JR*, 67), the song is not consciously shaped to her intentions; it rises involuntarily: "Rubbing the glass of the long looking-glass and leering sideways at her swinging figure a sound issued from her lips" (*TL*, 196). Its unintentionality reduces the author to something less than human – literally to a source:

> A sound interrupted him; a frail quivering sound, a voice bubbling up without direction, vigour, beginning or end, running weakly and shrilly and with an absence of all human meaning into
>
> e um fah um so
> foo swee too eem oo –
>
> the voice of no age or sex, the voice of an ancient spring sprouting from the earth; which issued, just opposite Regent's Park Tube Station, from a tall quivering shape, like a funnel, like a rusty pump. (*MrsD*, 123)

Anonymity strips the song's author of identity. She becomes sexless, ageless, faceless, like the "little figure – a woman, veiled; or a man?" in the school of Canaletto painting in *Between the Acts* (214), like the faceless old woman selling violets in *The Years* and Mrs. McNab, whose femininity shows only in that "she wore a skirt" (*MrsD*, 122), like Clarissa "feeling herself suddenly shrivelled, aged, breastless" (*MrsD*, 45). The old woman is the reduced self, a singer "sheared" of her faculties, her sense organs, her wits, reduced to a mouth, impersonal conduit or spring of song:

> As the ancient song bubbled up opposite Regent's Park Tube Station, still the earth seemed green and flowery; still, though it issued from so rude a mouth, a mere hole in the earth, muddy too, matted with root-fibres and tangled grasses, still the old bubbling burbling song, soaking through the knotted roots of infinite age, and skeletons and treasure, streamed away in rivulets over the pavement and all along the Marylebone Road, and down towards Euston, fertilizing, leaving a damp stain. (*MrsD*, 123)

This song-producing "hole" suggests the female organ, the oyster-self. Reduced to a mere instrument or principle of song – funnel or pump – it externalizes the song from its author, like sense-data from the mind. In that sense, the song, like semen both produced and received by its source, is neutral: "My body is a stalk. I press the stalk. A drop oozes from the hole at the mouth and slowly, thickly, grows larger and larger. Now something pink passes through the eyehole. Now an eyebeam is slid through the chink. Its beam strikes me" (*W*, 12–13). The "final question" about Woolf's narrative "voice" – "What is the sex" of the voice? "Is the style of *To the Lighthouse* feminine? masculine? androgynous?"[39] – thus receives its answer: like the old woman's song, it truly enjoys "the immunity of all biographers and historians from any sex whatever" (*O*, 220) that Woolf attributes ironically to works displaying male prejudices. If "anon" invariably turns out to be a woman, it is only because Woolf's woman is a kind of "zero degree" of humankind, rid of "that one thing" of Shakespeare's Sonnet XX Woolf interprets as the ego. Anonymity reveals the structure of Woolf's androgyny.[40] Not the merging of two points of view, its colorless neutrality consists of bundles of colored perspectives whose separateness is maintained. There is no merging except momentarily, because no single narrating "I" 's authority exists to unite them.

The song reflects the singer's absence of mind; it was "something that had been gay twenty years before on the stage perhaps, had been hummed and danced to, but now, coming from the toothless, bonneted, care-taking woman, was robbed of meaning, was like the voice of witlessness, humour, persistency itself, trodden down but springing up again" (*TL*, 196–7). Persistence is a property of those objects which, like chairs, tables and songs, like lost objects, "skeletons and treasure," knotted in the roots of song, have no consciousness. Mrs. MacNab "was witless, she knew it" (*TL*, 196). For there is "a force working, something not highly conscious" (*TL*, 209); the ancient, empty hole gives birth to nature's evergreen profusion; reproduction reproduces unconsciously. Like Forster's creation, it "comes from the depths." "While the author wrote, he forgot his name; while we read him we forget both his name and our own" (*Anonymity*, 22). The song contains, like the moor, the ocean's floor, the British Museum or that in Scarborough, a history no one need be thinking of for it to be forever what happened:

> Through all the ages – when the pavement was grass, when it was swamp, through the age of tusk and mammoth, through the age of silent sunrise – the battered woman – for she wore a skirt – . . . stood singing of love – love which has lasted a million years, she sang, love which prevails, and millions of years ago her lover, who had been dead these centuries, had walked, she crooned, with her in May; but in the course of ages, long as summer days, and flaming, she remembered, with nothing but red asters, he had gone. (*MrsD*, 122–3)

Unconsciousness does not prevent truth's recording. The song thus resembles the proposition no one ever thinks about which nonetheless corresponds to a fact. It works as Mrs. McNab does to sustain the world in the observer's absence.

The ballad's "I" is anonymous, but the novel alone has developed a language in which the "I" disappears. "Language can never be anything but anthropocentric," Beer claims ("Hume, Stephen, and Elegy," 87). "It is impossible to think of the kitchen table when you are not there," J. Hillis Miller asserts, in the manner of Leslie Stephen invoking "the hopeless attempt to get outside ourselves" (*HET*, 55), because "language itself forbids" it ("Mr. Carmichael," 181). "Language always reimports some 'you,' some 'I,' some 'he,' or 'she'" (182). But in stating that "no egocentric particulars occur in the language of physics," Russell has the position that there exists language unmarked by the speaker's presence: "A physicist will not say 'I saw a table,' but like Neurath or Julius Caesar, 'Otto saw a table'" (*IMT*, 102). It has the anonymity Forster reserves for literature:

> "Literature wants not to be signed" I suggested. Whether those words are signed or unsigned becomes, as soon as the imagination redeems us, a matter of no importance, because we have approximated to the state in which they were written, and there are no names down there, no personality as we understand personality. (*Anonymity*, 23)

The language of universals is likewise egoless. "Anonymous statements have," Forster writes, "a universal air about them. Absolute truth, the collected wisdom of the universe, seems to be speaking, not the feeble voice of a man" (23). That "two and two are four" is in no way dependent on the speaker.

The novel's speakerless sentences are not subjectless, however; they contain subjective "hes" and "shes." The locative metaphor of the narrator entering a character's mind only approximates to how the novelist represents subjectivity. For neither characters' minds nor a narrator to enter them exist. Rather, the writer writes sentences which, because "unspoken" by one named "I," permit the linguistic representation of an imagined perspective. The principle of parsimony eliminates the invisible, "omniscient" "third-person narrator" from the theory of the novel as an unjustified metaphysical entity. The consequence of the narrating "I"'s disappearance is the novel's collection of shifting points-of-view. This is because the "I" alone guarantees the permanence of perspective from sentence to sentence. Grammatically then, the novel's style permits us "to live[]

out those embryo lives which . . . 'I' suppressed" (*CE*, IV, 199). The shifting of perspectives, like the shuttle of a loom, creates the network of logical relations, the fabric of a world. Sentences representing unoccupied perspectives become crucial. They fill in the interstices, creating "the continued uninterrupted existence" of objects of perception "annihilated by our absence" (Hume, *A Treatise*, 207) by a hypothetical "continuity," Hume's "fiction of the imagination." Having "handle[d] nature's continuity," à la Cézanne, by conceiving it "as discontinuous" (*Cé*, 40), "the effect of plastic continuity" (*Cé*, 77) is restored.

The narrator's disappearance in the novel's multi-consciousness style is attached to the theme of impersonality associated with Flaubert and "the impersonal conventions of storytelling."[41] Without the personal authority of the first person, all but local representations of subjectivity are eliminated. The result is an impersonal style with little stretches of the personal. The novels' language, like the song, detached from all human agency, thus expresses the universe one of whose possibilities is the unobserved. It plays itself, like the gramophone music in Miss La Trobe's play: "Every sound in nature was painfully audible; the swish of the trees; the gulp of a cow; even the skim of the swallows over the grass could be heard. But no one spoke. Whom could they make responsible? Whom could they thank for their entertainment? Was there no one?" (*BA*, 135). There was no one. "For the stage was empty" (*BA*, 98). Of Dante and Shakespeare Forster writes, "We are conscious only of the world they have created, and we are in a sense co-partners in it" (*Anonymity*, 18).[42] The disembodied voice is like that which Jacob's brother Archer sends in search of Jacob: "The voice had an extraordinary sadness. Pure from all body, pure from all passion, going out into the world, solitary, unanswered, breaking against rocks – so it sounded" (*JR*, 8–9). Only an impersonal style, it bespeaks nature's indifference, like the waves, like Betty Flander's brooch, once connected to human life but now, "unanswered," only part of Mrs. Swithin's The Outline of History. But its world-creating ability permits "transformations" of the empty center at its origin. Its sadness becomes gay: "Cheerfully, almost gaily, the invincible thread of sound wound up into the air like the smoke from a cottage chimney . . . 'And if some one should see, what matter they?'" (*MrsD*, 125). It is the very persistence which objects have in the observer's absence that turns Mrs. McNab's song's sorrow into hope:

How long, she asked, creaking and groaning on her knees under the bed, dusting the boards, how long shall it endure? . . . as if, after all, she had her consolations, as if indeed there twined about her dirge some incorrigible hope . . . Some cleavage of the dark there must have been, some channel in the depths of obscurity through which light enough issued to twist her face grinning in the glass and make her, turning to her job again, mumble out the old music hall song. (*TL*, 196–7)

The light issuing like song strikes the mirror in which this nonentity is reflected sideways and, mysteriously, the sleepless, stirring the pool in the night of time passes and raising philosophical questions, receive suddenly an answer.

Hence, Mr. Ramsay's final indifference to Scott's and his own survival – "not only fame but even his own name was forgotten by him" (*TL*, 68–9) – matched by Lily's "what did that matter?" à propos of her canvas forgotten in the attic, like *Principia Mathematica*, which notoriously "[a]lmost no one could be expected to read . . . other than a few logicians, Russell told Ottoline" (Hampshire, "Russell's Paradox," 8), is not, as Corner sees it, a moral achievement, substituting selfless atheism for atheism as "a form of egoistic lament" (418). Mr. Ramsay sheds ego because it is stripped from him; he learns not a moral lesson but a law of time, the self's inevitable end amidst the indifference of things. The world teaches it, beginning with Mrs. Ramsay's death, which delivers a blow to the demand for sympathy. "Il faut que l'on se résigne à ne pas croire même dans sa propre personnalité," Fry explains. "La vie n'est qu'une longue apprentissage dans l'art de se ficher complètement de son égo" (*RF*, 252). This is the apprenticeship for an art bent on showing reality. Hence, as in "the earlier modes of criticism where a poem was not an expression but a discovery, . . . shown to the poet by God" that Forster invokes (*Anonymity*, 18), *To the Lighthouse* ends with a vision, not a lesson.

A STYLE TO TRACE THE MIND'S WANDERINGS

[T]he reader next door . . . was making the neatest of abstracts, . . . while my own notebook rioted with the wildest scribble of contradictory jottings. (Woolf, *A Room of One's Own*, 30)

Finally, there should grow the most austere of all mental qualities; I mean the sense for style. It is an aesthetic sense, based on admiration for the direct attainment of a foreseen end, simply and without waste. Style in art, style in literature, style in science, style in logic, style in practical execution have fundamentally the same aesthetic qualities, namely, attainment and restraint. The love of a subject in itself and for itself . . . is the love of style as manifested in that study. (Whitehead, *The Aims of Education and Other Essays*, 12)

Woolf's style twists Impressionist vagueness into form. Its first inspiration is the famous Bloomsbury talk, its origins a conversation society whose typical member "wanders Apostolically around the edges of his subject" (Levy, *G. E. Moore*, 207). Woolf hears its convolutions with horror and humor, for "talk has a way of turning" (*CE*, II, 234), of free associating. This becomes apparent if it is written down: "those who try to record it are aware that it runs hither and thither, seldom sticks to the point, abounds in exaggeration and inaccuracy" (*CE*, II, 233). Erratic movement marks it, figured by the walker's pursuit of "the flow of faces streaming" (*ND*, 269), "the jolting of a stage coach" (*CE*, I, 179) or the stirrings of the "little airs." "Street Haunting," extended metaphor of novel writing, wanders, like the other essays, from one subject to another, yet its "ramblings" return to where they begin: the pretext for walking across London – the purchase of a pencil, "the only spoil we have retrieved from all the treasures of the city" (*CE*, IV, 166). The passion (*CE*, IV, 155), reverence and tenderness (*CE*, IV, 166) bestowed on this instrument disclose that the street haunter is the writer. To follow Woolf's sentences' wandering itinerary, their sequential adoption of points of view, as "to follow her thought," "was like following a voice which speaks too quickly to be taken down by one's pencil" (*TL*, 40) – here the pencil pursues the streets' selves. The street haunter-novelist becomes a shifting observation-point, like the "captain's mind" in "The Captain's Deathbed":

He hops from thing to thing. Now he rattles off the history of Liège; next moment he discourses upon reason and instinct; then he considers what degree of pain is inflicted upon fish by taking them with the hook; and then, taking a walk through the streets, it strikes him how very seldom you now meet with a name beginning with X. (*CE*, I, 179)

To write, then, is "to stumble after my own voice, or almost, after some sort of speaker (as when I was mad) I was almost afraid, remembering the voices that used to fly ahead" (*Diary*, IV, 10), to pursue "stray voices, voices without bodies, symbolical voices" (*BA*, 151), "wandering bodies and floating voices" (*BA*, 153).

The world's fragmentary nature, "the vast extent of London and the impossibility of finding any single figure that wandered off this way and that way, turned to the right and to the left" (*ND*, 441), impose this disruptive sentence. For "reality"

> would seem to be something very erratic, very undependable – now to be found in a dusty road, now in a scrap of newspaper in the street, now in a daffodil in the sun. It lights up a group in a room and stamps some casual saying. It overwhelms one walking home beneath the stars and makes the silent world more real than the world of speech – and then there it is again in an omnibus in the uproar of Piccadilly. Sometimes, too, it seems to dwell in shapes too far away for us to discern what their nature is. (*Room*, 114)

Movement also characterizes the mind pursuing this reality: "no, the wheels of a carriage may rest, even the body for a time may rest, but the mind will not" (*CE*, I, 179). The novel's sentence must catch "life itself," "the sneer, the contrast, the question, the closeness and complexity of life" (*CE*, II, 226). It must be open to sense-data. Its erratic and jerky rhythm must "trace the pattern, however disconnected and incoherent in appearance, which each sight and incident scores upon the consciousness" (*CE*, II, 107). The distance travelled leaves in its wake a description which maps the geography of the spaces traversed.

Out of it is molded "the democratic art of prose," with "its freedom, its fearlessness, its flexibility" (*CE*, II, 226):

> For prose is so humble that it can go anywhere; no place is too low, too sordid, or too mean for it . . . It can lick up with its long glutinous tongue the most minute fragments of fact and mass them into the most subtle labyrinths, and listen silently at doors behind which only a murmur, only a whisper, is to be heard. With all the suppleness of a tool which is in constant use it can follow the windings and record the changes which are typical of the modern mind. (*CE*, II, 226)

The wandering sentence expresses thought unfettered by logic. Hence, its characteristic features: the non-sequitur and the contradiction. In the first, one proposition fails to follow from another; thought does not proceed directly to its point but veers continuously in unpredictable directions, like Mrs. McNab "aimlessly . . . taking up mats, putting down china," "bringing things out and putting them away again" (*TL*, 197) or Mrs. Swithin, saying "'This daily round; this going up and down stairs'; this saying 'What am I going for? My specs? I have 'em on my nose'" (*BA*, 152). And just as the paradigmatic ordinary mind is typically a woman's, so it is some scatter-brained woman's sentence which for Woolf had the prototypical structure of "ordinary thinking" with its "divided glance." Its exaggeration and its "random ways" (*CE*, IV, 74) are those of Woolf's aunt Anny Thackery, Lady Ritchie, who "lost trains, mixed names, confused numbers" (*CE*, IV, 74). Her style, to which Woolf devoted an essay, resembles Mrs. Flanders' epistolary style, as in general that of "the unpublished works of women, written by the fireside in pale profusion" (*JR*, 91), marked by faulty logic, perhaps "the hand itself rambling" (*JR*, 94):

> "Do you remember old Miss Wargreave, who used to be so kind when you had the whooping-cough?" she wrote; "she's dead at last, poor thing. They would like it if you wrote. Ellen came over and we spent a nice day shopping. Old Mouse gets very stiff, and we have to walk him up the smallest hill. Rebecca, at last, after I don't know how long, went into Mr. Adamson's. Three teeth, he says must come out. Such mild weather for the time of year, the little buds actually on the pear trees. And Mrs. Jarvis tells me – ." (*JR*, 90–1)

In Betty Flanders' tear-stained manner, Woolf's own long and winding sentence, with shifts of direction, "dissolved the full stop" (*JR*, 7). Interruptions or distractions intervene, signalled by commas, dashes, parentheses, to break the syntax. Within one line of thought another erupts, like Mrs. Ramsay's non-sequitur on the bill for the greenhouse roof. "Could I do it in a parenthesis? so that one had the sense of reading the two things at the same time?," Woolf wonders about Lily's final look at her painting (*Diary*, III, 106). It is also the world's intrusion: within parentheses in "Time Passes" Mrs. Ramsay's death disrupts Mr. Ramsay's night walking.

The sentence Annie Thackery's style exemplifies also states " 'that everybody is right and nobody knows anything' " (*CE*, IV, 73). "Her most typical, and, indeed, inimitable sentences rope together a handful of swiftly gathered opposites," Woolf wrote. "To embrace oddities and produce a charming, laughing harmony from incongruities was her genius" (*CE*, IV, 73–4). Such a sentence takes "the mold of that queer conglomeration of incongruous things – the modern mind" (*CE*, II, 226). Like *Jacob's Room*'s contrast between men in the Cambridge night and women in the Mediterranean sunlight, things in it are "incongruously coupled" in androgynous union; "they blend but do not mix" (*CE*, II, 223).

Writing begins in path-breaking meanderings. But the novels' violations of the principle of non-Contradiction are resolved. A subsequent logic post-dates a preliminary freedom, like the translation of "It is now raining" to "It rained on such and such a day."[43]

It works like Leslie Stephen, with his admitted "pedantic mania for correcting [Anny Thackery's] flights of imagination." "Sometimes with one word . . . he would dispose of the tissue of exaggerations which his own sobriety seemed to provoke. 'There are 40,000,000 unmarried women in London alone!' Lady Ritchie once informed him. 'Oh, Annie, Annie!' my father exclaimed" (*CE*, IV, 77).[44] Only it should be self-administered. So Margaret of Newcastle "should have been taught to . . . reason scientifically." But "[n]o one checked her" (*Room*, 65).

Street haunting is the metaphor for the preliminary empirical "process," literature's *Ecole de Plein Air*; withdrawing into a room is for the post-wandering logic. "[T]o retire to one's study in fear of life is equally fatal," Woolf writes; the novelist must remain "terribly exposed to life" (*CE*, II, 131). "But at a certain moment he must leave the company and withdraw, alone, to that mysterious room where his body is hardened and fashioned into permanence by processes" like crystallization (*CE*, II, 136) and shut out the sense-data of the streets. The itinerant observer's data are submitted *a posteriori* to logic's transformations: in "some solitary room" novelists "like Flaubert" "have mastered their perceptions, hardened them" (*CE*, II, 131). "So drastic is the process of selection that in its final state we can often find no trace of the actual scene upon which the chapter was based. For in that solitary room, whose door the critics are for ever trying to unlock, processes of the strangest kind are gone through" (*CE*, II, 132). These processes emulate empirical science, making the vague precise, formulating arguments, testing hypotheses. In explaining that he had never been "a pure Impressionist" but "always had some kind of aesthetic," Fry explains that "scientific curiosity" had "impelled" him "to make generalizations, to attempt some kind of logical coordination of my impressions." But he had "never worked out for myself a complete system such as the metaphysicians deduce from a priori principles":

> My aesthetic has been a purely practical one, a tentative expedient, an attempt to reduce to some kind of order my aesthetic impressions . . . until such time as fresh experiences might confirm or modify it. Moreover, I have always looked on my system with a certain suspicion. I have recognized that if it ever formed too solid a crust it might stop the inlets of fresh experience. (*V&D*, 285)

Its logic is not Karin Stephen's "a priori form imposed by intellectual activity upon" an object (*The Misuse of Mind*, 54) – "not by way of a willed and a priori invention, but through the acceptance and final assimilation of appearance" is Post-Impressionism "achieved" (*Cé*, 77). It erects the empirical into something like the "causal skeleton" of physics. Like Cézanne's method, "at once thinking in terms of extremely simplified geometrical forms, and allowing those to be infinitely and infinitesimally modified at each point by his visual sensations" (*Cé*, 53), it is neither "hampered by the exigency of . . . data" (*Cé*, 86) nor unexposed to it. As in Seurat, "the harmony has been arrived at almost by trial and error, by a perpetual adjustment and readjustment," not as "the result of any merely intellectual calculation" (*TR*, 192).

For what is surprising is that wandering ultimately constructs the relations between the unrelated moments, creating through its syntax unexpected correlations between the worlds of sense and logic. The various threads are picked up and worked into patterns as wool by needles. This is why the danger is equally one of eliminating too soon the digressions and contradictions. When Woolf criticizes D. H. Lawrence's style because his "thought plumps directly into his mind" (*CE*, I, 355), her conclusion is that his sentence lacks "architecture." More than "the mild curb of grammar and the occasional rigours of chapter divisions" (*CE*, II, 132), the novelist needs "the architecture of the sentence." Woolf's sentence cannot move in a straight line, against Russell's confessed inability to "ramble."[45] Her geometric scaffolding is created precisely by the veering attempt to follow all the non-sequiturs of sensible reality in one, ramifying itinerary. It is her conception of Fry's Principia Aesthetica: "As the process of pushing the theory proceeds, the argument is not only so subtle and so serpentine that it is fascinating to follow its windings, but it grazes so many solid objects in its passage that it acquires solidity; the theory becomes something we can see and touch" (*RF*, 258). Cézanne's style, in Fry's analysis, is similarly achieved by "incessant affirmations and contradictions" (*Cé*, 51). But if "[o]ther artists" can "shut themselves up for weeks alone with a dish of apples and a paint-box," emerging "to forget and distract themselves," "the novelist never forgets and is seldom distracted" (*CE*, II, 131). For the novelist's wandering, less like Mr. Ramsay's reading and writing, "pushing his way up and up a single narrow path" (*TL*, 283) and more like the London "perambulations" Leslie Stephen recommends for "compos[ing]" one's "writings" as a test of a "remarkable power of intellectual concentration" ("In

Praise of Walking," 281), never forgets the pencil-goal in the circuitous route to it. The movement inscribes the temporal series, "while the mind traced subtle winding paths" (*BP*, 15); "prose thus treated will show itself capable of rising high from the ground, not in one dart, but in sweeps and circles" (*CE*, II, 228) and, like Mr. Ramsay "with his pipe, of an evening, thinking up and down and in and out of the old familiar lanes" (*TL*, 68), will weave in and out in mental peregrinations a framework for them. The "cotton-wool" is transformed into fabric on a frame which gives it a rigid geometry; "the vagueness had to be expelled; the simmer had to be spun into a tough thread of argument that held the whole together" (*RF*, 265–6). The thread tying Lady Bruton to her departed guests and the string connecting the old lady to Big Ben striking (*MrsD*, 192) are caught in the web of time binding the private to a public. Alternatively, the writer "seethes" the stray voices in "a cauldron" (*BA*, 153), hardening the "amorphous" into the rigid.

The result is the structure of modern fiction. Like "the streets of any large town," it "is cut up into boxes, each of which is inhabited by a different human being who has put locks on his doors and bolts on his windows to ensure some privacy, yet is linked to his fellows by wires which pass overhead, by waves of sound which pour through the roof and speak aloud to him of battles and murders and strikes and revolutions all over the world" (*CE*, II, 222). It achieves the piecemeal unity Woolf describes in early notes she made on a Perugino fresco:

> I attain a different kind of beauty, achieve a symmetry by means of infinite discords, showing all the traces of the mind's passage through the world; achieve in the end, some kind of whole made of shivering fragments; to me this seems the natural process; the flight of the mind. (cited in *VW*, I, 138)

The work stands, like the unobserved table, like the empty house, poised between the worlds of subject and object, enclosing many possible perspectives, many alternatives closed to unreflective common sense. The movement is fixed; the pool gathering in sense-data, grave of the past, source of the future, becomes an impersonal mirror-perspective yielding its vision of time and change.

CHAPTER 8

The modern elegy

> Wordsworth expresses the familiar sentiment when he wishes that he could be "a pagan suckled in some creed outworn." . . . Now, as far as science is concerned, . . . Wordsworth is simply wrong. The Greek mythology gave an inaccurate representation of the facts. The more accurately we know them the better for us. A slight acquaintance with the law of storms is far more useful to the sailor than any guess about a mysterious being, capriciously raising from the waves . . . we are the better off the closer the correspondance between our beliefs and the external realities . . . Why should Wordsworth regret Proteus and Triton? Because the Greek derived from the sea the existence of beings the contemplation of whose power and beauty was a source of delight to him? But, in the first place, the facts are to Wordsworth what they were to the Greek. If the Greek thought the sea lovely in colour and form, the colour and form remain. The imaginary being in whom the phenomena were embodied could only be known through the phenomena. The beauty is beautiful still, though we no longer infer an imaginary cause. Nothing is lost but a dream, and a dream, which, by its nature, could only reflect the reality. Why not love the sea instead of loving Proteus, who is but the sea personified?
>
> (Stephen, *History of English Thought in the Eighteenth Century*, 14)

Acknowledging as does philosophy the altered landscape science reveals, Woolf's art situates itself with respect to it, for "it is an age clearly when we are not fast anchored where we are; things are moving round us; we are moving ourselves" (*CE*, II, 218). Art's role in the scientific age had been a major theme of nineteenth-century poetry, although not of the novel. In 1925 Whitehead would see Tennyson, Apostle of an earlier generation, as "the mouthpiece" of the century's attempt "to come to terms with science." But English poetry since Wordsworth bears "witness to the discord between the aesthetic intuitions of mankind and the mechanism of science" (*SMW*, 83). Tennyson's failure makes him also "the perfect example" of the "inconsistency in modern thought" (*SMW*, 74). Leslie Stephen had maintained that a new paradigm of thought means a "loss" not "of a mistaken theory about facts," but "of a system of symbols" (*HET*, 16) for "expressing our emotions" (*HET*, 15); "the imagination lags behind the reason" (*HET*, 14). The opening theme of Stephen's history is that a new system's "logical bearing" (*HET*, 13) did not guarantee its acceptance because "the ordinary mind . . . cares little for the ultimate logical consequences" (*HET*, 8). After all, religious belief lacks any "logical foundation" (*AAA*, 86). There must be "some channel for the emotions generated by the contemplation of the world and of ourselves" (*HET*, 13). "The new order, constructed by the reason, remains colourless and uninteresting" (*HET*, 14). A new art must supply a language for the emotions before the world of science. When Fry puts together "the disinterested study (science) and vision (art) of the universe" (*RF*, 271), he speaks then in Stephen's tradition. He too sees science and art replacing religion's two major functions. Religion, for Stephen, is "partly an attempt at a systematic statement of our knowledge, real or supposed" – "'religions,'" Woolf quotes Fry, "all pretend to do what science tries to do – namely discover the one universally valid construction" (*RF*, 271) – and "partly a more or less poetical embodiment of the feelings which have no direct relations to our actions" (*HET*, 13).

The Bloomsbury aesthetic is like other modernist aesthetics in its religious reference, although without reference to institutionalized belief, as with Joyce or Eliot. For Bloomsbury was agnostic, again Stephen's heir. There was no question of a return to belief (as for Eliot and even Wittgenstein). Religion as a system of knowledge had been superseded by science, Fry asserts. What remained of a religion emptied of belief was the emotion. It reentered in part under the heading "ethics," the legacy of earlier Cambridge thinkers. Setting the ethical apart, Woolf and Fry choose a more Russellian than Moorean emphasis.[1] Art for them connected feeling to knowledge.[2]

The word that stood most purely for the emotion was "mysticism." Russell's 1914 "Mysticism and Logic" is evidence of a contemporary debate which took in the aesthetic question during the period of Russell's interchange with Ottoline Morrell and Wittgenstein.

Although it "is not certain that Wittgenstein had read Russell's essay" in "compos[ing] the *Tractatus*," McGuinness writes in "The Mysticism of the *Tractatus*," "there is a considerable coincidence" between the two works (305). Russell's essay concentrates the ideas about mysticism circulating between Cambridge and Bloomsbury.

Russell's "mysticism" is like Stephen's "creed," divided between knowledge and "the mystical way of feeling": "mysticism is to be commended as an attitude towards life, not as a creed about the world" (*ML*, 11). In this conception, Russell includes art and literature. "The poet, the artist, and the lover" are mystics manqués: "the haunting beauty that they pursue is the faint reflection of its sun. But the mystic lives in the full light of the vision" (*ML*, 9). The mystic conception of time, for instance, he attributes to "poetic imagination, not science" (*ML*, 3). Fry operates in Russell's framework when he sees an "emotion" "colouring and informing all other thoughts and feelings" (*ML*, 11) as what distinguishes art from science. Art's "conclusion" can only be drawn from the "premises" of sensations "by one who is in an emotional state with regard to them" (*V&D*, 82). For Clive Bell also, "[r]eligion, like art, is concerned with the world of emotional reality, and with material things only, in so far as they are emotionally significant": "For the mystic, as for the artist, the physical universe is a means to ecstasy . . . Religion" he thinks "an expression of the individual's sense of the emotional significance of the universe," so it would not be surprising "that art was the expression of the same thing" (*Art*, 81–2).[3]

The discord between art and science "in the modern world" that Stephen and Whitehead hoped to see resolved received alternative accounts of which the *Tractatus* is currently the most familiar. Whitehead's is another. Russell's was "quite unable to combine into a harmonious total seventeenth-century knowledge, eighteenth-century beliefs and nineteenth-century enthusiasms" (*MyPhD*, 27). His art as mystical feeling remains at odds with logic. Fry's and Woolf's new aesthetic principles are enunciated in this broader arena. "The new mysticism which despised science and also Flaubert . . . was highly antipathetic to Roger Fry," Woolf writes (*RF*, 237). The new aesthetic, by contrast, will reconcile science and Flaubert "[w]hen the imaginative synthesis has overtaken the logical, when the bare framework of formulae has gathered round it the necessary associations" (*HET*, 15).[4]

ART AND SCIENCE MAKING STRANGE THE FAMILIAR

Isn't that why life's a perpetual – what shall I call it? – miracle? (Woolf, *The Years*, 383)

The new aesthetic does not reject mysticism; it adjusts mystical feeling to the world which science reveals as "extraordinary," "miraculous," "strange." The property provoking this mystical wonder is the world's contingency. In his theory of possible worlds, Leibniz, writes Russell, "argues that every particular thing in the world is 'contingent,' that is to say, it would be logically possible for it not to exist; and this is true, not only of each particular thing, but of the whole universe . . . there is nothing within the universe to show why it exists" (*HWP*, 587). As for "'blind fate,'" Stephen writes, "it is a mere word" and only "indicates that we cannot get into a region beyond knowledge which will explain to us why there should be a world at all, or why it should be such a world as we know" ("WM?," 144). This gratuitous reality both Whitehead and Russell call "givenness," the actualization of a logical possibility. Whitehead explains:

An eternal object is always a potentiality for actual entities; but in itself . . . it is neutral as to the fact of its physical ingression in any particular actual entity of the temporal world. "Potentiality" is the correlative of "givenness." The meaning of "givenness" is that what *is* "given" might not have been "given"; and that what *is not* "given" *might have been* "given." (*Process and Reality*, 70)

This is the "givenness" of Russell's particular. As Sainsbury puts it, "the logical independence of particulars . . . means that none of them is a necessary existent" (*Russell*, 51). Hence the mere fact that anything exists at all in no way follows from logic, whose "truth is independent of the existence of the universe" (*IMP*, 204). The existence of any individual is extraordinary. "The ontological proof of the existence of God, if it were valid, would establish the logical necessity of at least one individual. But it is generally recognized as invalid." Hence, "we seem driven to conclude that the existence of the world is an accident – *i.e.*, it is not logically necessary" (*IMP*, 203–4).

Whitehead's term "event," as "the emergence into actuality of something" (*SMW*, 89), explicitly denotes the actualization of a possible world. Its very actualness Whitehead calls "the element of value, of being valuable, of having value, of being an end in itself, of being something which is for its own sake" and connects to "the poetic rendering of concrete experience" (*SMW*, 89). Value is itself meaningless, being only the brute fact of something's existing rather than not: "'Value' is the word I use for the intrinsic reality of an event. Value is an element which permeates through and through the poetic view of nature" (*SMW*, 89). Value is only the achievement of existence: "Realisation therefore is in itself the attainment of value" (*SMW*, 89). It is via Whitehead's "value" that we understand Russell's assertion that the world of existence concerns "the value of life and the world" (*PP*, 100).

"Like Leibniz," Finch observes, Wittgenstein "wonders that anything exists at all, that there is something rather than nothing" (*Wittgenstein*, 174). "Not *how* the world is, is the mystical, but *that* it is," *Tractatus* 6.44 states, "mystical" designating the unpredictability of the world's existing. Black glosses 6.44 with a passage from Wittgenstein's *Ethics Lecture*, in which his wondering "*at the existence of the world*" makes him "inclined to use such phrases as 'how extraordinary that anything should exist' or 'how extraordinary that the world should exist'" (*Companion*, 374). The world's gratuitousness is miraculous.

So when Woolf recalls her first memory "of lying and hearing this splash and seeing this light, and feeling, it is almost impossible that I should be here" (*MB*, 65), when the protagonist of *The Voyage Out* is "overcome by the unspeakable queerness of the fact that she should be sitting in an arm-chair, in the morning, in the middle of the world" and "with awe that things should exist at all" (125), when "the strangeness of standing alone, alive, unknown, at half-past eleven in Trafalgar Square overcame" Peter Walsh (*MrsD*, 77–8) and Cam in the boat feels "the adventure (that she should be alive, that she should be there)" (*TL*, 280–1), they are feeling what Wittgenstein calls "*das künstlerische Wunder*" (*Notebooks 1914–1916*, 86, para. 5). Anscombe translates the passage as "Aesthetically, the miracle is that the world exists" (86e). McGuinness suggests that "'For an artist [or 'for art'] the miracle is . . .' would be better" ("The Mysticism of the *Tractatus*," 315, n. 18). Here we recognize Lily Briscoe's aim "to be on a level with ordinary experience," "at the same time," to feel "It's a miracle" (*TL*, 300). Art records that "the supreme mystery . . . was simply this: here was one room; there another. Did religion solve that, or love?" (*MrsD*, 193). Art is thus the expression of value, of Fry's "faith," an impulse prior to meaning inseparable from life itself, that "force working . . . not highly conscious" maintaining the house in existence (*TL*, 209): "'My faith in life is utterly unreasonable and groundless,'" Woolf quotes Fry, being "'the faith by which the animals live and move, perhaps the atoms themselves'" (*RF*, 278). "When science is considered contemplatively, not practically," Russell writes, "we find that what we believe we believe owing to animal faith, and it is only our disbeliefs that are due to science" (*SO*, 264).[5] The language of such faith is demonstrative, with the logical primitives' "givenness." "For there she was," *Mrs. Dalloway* concludes (296); "there she is; beautiful, emphatic," Woolf writes of her mother (*MB*, 40).

The eyeless world of logical forms in whose net the empirical is caught is no less extraordinary. The mystical impulse to discover "a Reality behind the world of appearance and utterly different from it" (*ML*, 9) shares something with logical analysis, which can, via "our familiar table," "show the strangeness and wonder lying just below the surface even in the commonest things of daily life" and suggest "that even the strangest hypotheses may not be true" (*PP*, 16). Strangeness is a by-product of science's method, whose aim is to make strange the familiar. Not an unfamiliar phantasy world but the real world becomes unreal. "The truth about physical objects *must* be strange" (*PP*, 38). The idea of a real table departing from appearances is as disturbing as there being nothing but a sensible table; Realism is perhaps stranger than Idealism. For Idealism is more familiar. "Mind," Russell says, has been regarded as the pattern after which the universe is to be conceived, for no better reason . . . than that such a universe would not seem strange, and would give us the cosy feeling that every place is like home" (*ML*, 42).

There is a connection between the defamiliarizing method and the resultant ontology, between the strangeness of "what there is" (*LK*, 269) and how the mind arrives at it. Both "the true objects of philosophy, and the habit of thought demanded for their apprehension, are strange, unusual, and remote" (*ML*, 17). Even the mind's coming to know indirectly what is never directly apprehensible is miraculous. "How could a soul know anything of matter except by a continuous miracle?" Leslie Stephen asks ("WM?," 134). The mind is "brought into connection" with matter "by a standing miracle" ("WM?," 147). So it is "extraordinary . . . strange, yes" that the old lady at the window is moved, puppet-like, by Big Ben striking (*MrsD*, 192): "Down, down, into the midst of ordinary things the finger fell making the moment solemn . . . Why creeds and prayers and mackintoshes? when, thought Clarissa, that's the miracle, that's the mystery" (*MrsD*, 193).

The mystical feeling lures the thinker out where things "lose their everyday banality" in "a mood of utter withdrawal from all the ordinary as well as all the poetic implications of things," as Fry says of Seurat (*Tr*, 191); there "the normal is abolished" (*W*, 101). It yields something like acquaintance with bare logical forms. The flash of insight comes to artist and scientist alike. Fry finds that "perhaps, the highest pleasure in art is identical with the highest pleasure in scientific theory" (*V&D*, 83). The artist exercises "the generalising intellect, or rather its analogue, in art," but "perhaps we ought to consider it as curiously akin to those cases of mathematical geniuses who have immediate intuition of mathematical relations which it is beyond their powers to prove" (*V&D*, 81). Feeling attends the apprehension of forms in both. "The emotion which accompanies the clear recognition of unity in a complex seems to be so similar in art and in science" (*V&D*, 83). Ecstatic contemplation has "a basis of purely physiological pleasure, as in seeing pure colours or hearing pure sounds," but "the specifically aesthetic emotion" is that "by means of which the necessity of relations is apprehended, and which corresponds in science to the purely logical process" (*V&D*, 83). "Whatever the world of aesthetic contemplation may be," Clive Bell likewise writes, "it is not the world of human business and passion; in it the chatter and tumult of material existence is unheard, or heard only as the echo of some more ultimate harmony" (*Art*, 70–1). "Art transports us from the world of man's activity to a world of aesthetic exaltation. For a moment we are shut off from human interests; our anticipations and memories are arrested; we are lifted above the stream of life" (*Art*, 25). The mathematician enjoys the closest equivalent to the artist's transport:

> The pure mathematician rapt in his studies knows a state of mind which I take to be similar, if not identical. He feels an emotion for his speculations which arises from no perceived relation between them and the lives of men, but springs, inhuman or super-human, from the heart of an abstract science. I wonder, sometimes, whether the appreciators of art and of mathematical solutions are not even more closely allied. Before we feel an aesthetic emotion for a combination of forms, do we not perceive intellectually the rightness and necessity of the combination? (*Art*, 25–6)

Impressionism and Post-Impressionism each has its specific wonder.

A FREE MAN'S WORSHIP: BRINGING THE EXTRAORDINARY TO THE LEVEL OF THE ORDINARY

[L]a science demande . . . une humilité à toute épreuve et une complète déintéressement. (Woolf, *Roger Fry*, 233)

Black calls Wittgenstein's "attitude towards the 'mystical'" "vacillating" and "equivocal" (*Companion*, 374). Bloomsbury shows a similar equivocation. Yet out of Lily Briscoe's equivocation over Mr. Ramsay's merits, the form of an aesthetic is built. To calibrate Stephen's "lag" and harmonize Whitehead's "discord" and "inconsistency" between feeling and scientific truth requires moving incessantly from one to the other. For the adjustment continually comes up against limits. The mystical feeling, like Freud's "oceanic feeling," is boundless. It desires to embrace and possess its object. – i.e., mysticism's sole model for knowledge is acquaintance. "English thought" had shown such knowledge to be narrowly private. Another knowledge, Russell came to see, was required for the physical world, one in which the object was separated from the knower by logical reasoning – "a chain of derivations from symbol to symbol," as Whitehead puts it (*Symbolism*, 83). Acquaintance was necessary – this is the principle of acquaintance – but the adjustment of feeling must accept the ultimate loss of the intimately known object. Like Russell's lover of nature embracing a skeletal, phantom "bride" (*SO*, 263), like Mr. Ramsay enfolding nothing or Lily wanting without having, the mystical impulse must accept ghostly formulae instead. The miraculous wonder must be redirected, via what Russell calls the "strange power" of "the austerer virtues" of which "love of truth is the chief" (*ML*, 69), to imaginatively grasp abstractions.

Hence those "moods" Russell invokes as the "negative side of the mystic's initiation" (*ML*, 8). Stephen's poetical emotions likewise "expressed horror as well as delight" (*HET*, 14). "Belief in a reality quite different from what appears to the senses" disturbs the usually direct relation between sensible object and sentient body, which suddenly finds itself at a distance from things: "the body alone listens to the passing bee, the wave breaking, the dog barking, far away, barking and barking" (*MrsD*, 59). The distant dog's bark, the distant breakers, recalling science's hypothetical waves, thus mark the intrusion of the problem of knowledge into Mr. Ramsay's "common man"'s everyday experience. As Whitehead sees it, "sometimes men are overstrained by their undivided attention to the causal elements in the nature of things. Then, in some tired moment there comes a sudden relaxation, and the mere presentational side of the world overwhelms with the sense of its emptiness" (*Symbolism*, 48). Russell describes it as "the strange feeling of unreality in common objects, the loss of contact with daily things, in which the solidity of the outer world is lost, and the soul seems, in utter loneliness, to bring forth, out of its own depths, the mad dance of fantastic phantoms which have hitherto appeared as independently real and living" (*ML*, 8). In such a moment in which the near recedes, Septimus Warren Smith hears his wife sobbing "far away," in reality next to him (*MrsD*, 136). Philosophy simulates "an inhibition of familiar sense-data" like those more everyday ones Whitehead discusses and "provokes the terrifying sense of vague presences." "Most living creatures," he comments, "of daytime habits, are more nervous in the dark, in the absence of the familiar visual sense-data" (*Symbolism*, 42–3).

Such moods arise also from the "arduous uncertainty" (*ML*, 1) which necessarily accompanies the search for truth, for truth, we saw, is for Russell by definition uncertain. Neither Realism nor Idealism is verifiable. The thinker must endure "blasts of doubt" like Lily Briscoe's about her art (*TL*, 237). "A flower turns to the light with much greater certainty than does a human being, and a stone conforms to the conditions set by its external environment with much greater certainty than does a flower" (Whitehead, *Symbolism*, 42). "Uncertainty" is only another name for the strangeness.

The prototype of such "moods" in the British tradition is that caused by Hume's "sceptical doubt" which, Hume says, "arises naturally from a profound and intense reflection on" world and self (*A Treatise*, 218). In Book I of the *Treatise*'s famous conclusion, which Leslie Stephen cites repeatedly, Hume confesses himself "first affrighted and confounded by that forlorn solitude, in which I am plac'd in my philosophy":

> When I turn my eye inward, I find nothing but doubt and ignorance . . . Where am I, or what? From what causes do I derive my existence, and to what condition shall I return? . . . I am confounded with all these questions, and begin to fancy myself in the most deplorable condition imaginable, inviron'd with the deepest darkness, and utterly depriv'd of the use of every member and faculty. (264–9)

Hume's doubt-inspired terror arises at the end of philosophical inquiry itself, like the giant figure luring the solitary traveller, at once philosophy's by-product and exorbitant to it: "This sceptical doubt, both with respect to reason and the senses," Hume writes, "is a malady," and "can never be radically cur'd" (218). For, Russell asserts, skepticism is "logically irrefutable" if "practically barren" (*OKnExW*, 74). "Skepticism is *not* irrefutable, but palpably senseless, if it would doubt where a question cannot be asked," is *Tractatus* 6.52's version. As the wonder's dark side, it includes the realization that "the world which Science presents" is "purposeless, . . . void of meaning" (*ML*, 45). "It is difficult to see what ground for cheerfulness modern physics provides. It tells us that the universe is running down," but "tells us practically nothing else" (*SO*, 93). It demonstrates "the irrelevance of human passions and of the whole subjective apparatus where scientific truth is concerned" (*ML*, 38). The philosopher finds no answers, no consolation, no reasons for his activity. The thinker must renounce mysticism's "theoretical desire for a comprehensive understanding of the Whole, the hope that the course of nature might be guided by some sympathy with our wishes" (*ML*, 95). "The search for an outside meaning that can *compel* an inner response must always be disappointed," Russell concludes, "all 'meaning' must be at bottom related to our primary desires, and when they are extinct no miracle can restore to the world the value which they reflected upon it" (*ML*, 36). "The sphere of values lies outside science," he explains, "except in so far as science consists in the pursuit of knowledge" (*SO*, 266). *Tractatus* 6.41 echoes this: "The sense of the world must lie outside the world. In the world everything is as it is and happens as it does happen. *In* it there is no value – and if there were, it would be of no value . . . For all happening and being-so is accidental."

Hume's questions Woolf raises. "Why is there not a discovery in life? Something one can lay hands on & say, 'This is it?' My depression is a harassed feeling – I'm looking; but that's not it . . . What is it? And shall I die before I find it?" (*Diary*, III, 62) Woolf acknowledges the unanswerability of the questions "it would be foolish to vex the moor with . . . – what? why?" (*JR*, 132), those "useless in such confusion to ask the night" (*TL*, 193), "those questions as to what, and why, and wherefore" "which tempt the sleeper from his bed to seek an answer" and convert the insomniac into "[t]he mystic, the visionary" (*TL*, 197). They are "[f]oolish questions, vain questions, questions one never asked if one were occupied. Is human life this? Is human life that? One never had time to think about it," Mr. Bankes muses (*TL*, 134–5). "For there are moments when one can neither think nor feel," Lily Briscoe reflects. "And if one can neither think nor feel, she thought, where is one?" (*TL*, 288). These questions show "the Russian influence," "the sense that there is no answer, that if honestly examined life presents question after question which must be left to sound on and on after the story is over in hopeless interrogation" and "despair" (*CE*, II, 109). Its is the "direct vision" shorn of dream Stephen hopes that "in time" we may be content with (*HET*, 16), Russell's "fearless acknowledgement of what is" (*ML*, 68).

Against "philosophical melancholy" (*A Treatise*, 269) Hume prescribes only temporary relief, for doubt should not destroy the impulse to know: "Carelessness and in-attention alone can afford us any remedy" and return "both an external world and an internal world" (218). Having "reached," Leslie Stephen comments, "the fullest expression of skepticism," we "are not surprised when Hume admits that his doubts disappear as he leaves his study" (*HET*, 44) for, Stephen adds, "the streets" (*HET*, 57). Or the antidote is the solitary traveller's return to "life" and "existence," to his housekeeper, "indoors among ordinary things"(*MrsD*, 87), amidst chatter and Hume's "lively impressions of the senses": "I dine, I play a game of back-gammon, I converse, and am merry with my friends; and when after three or four hours's amusement, I wou'd return to these speculations, they appear so cold, and strain'd and ridiculous, that I cannot find in my heart to enter into them any further" (*A Treatise*, 269). We almost see Hume at Mrs. Ramsay's dinner table with time passing outside. The table saves him from Septimus' leap. English fiction offers no answer to Russian despair save the celebration of "natural delight in humour and comedy, in the beauty of earth, in the activities of the intellect, and in the splendours of the body" (*CE*, II, 110).

The questions as to final causes are unanswerable. The seeker after knowledge must accede to "an abandonment of the great questions as insoluble" (*HET*, 43). For "it might be possible that the world itself is without meaning," as Septimus reflects (*MrsD*, 133). Hence "the mystical" is agnosticism positively conceived. It is Wittgenstein's "feeling of the world as a limited whole" (*Tractatus*, 6.45), "i.e. the feeling that there is something *beyond* the world" (Black, *Companion*, 373). It is nothing other than the acceptance of an ignorance of final causes. Russell's formulation of Leibniz's principle of sufficient reason makes apparent the connection to *Tractatus* 6.45: "everything has to have a sufficient reason, according to Leibniz's philosophy," Russell writes, "therefore the universe as a whole must have a sufficient reason, which must be outside the universe. This sufficient reason is God" (*HWP*, 587). Leibniz's God is only the guarantee that logic holds within the universe; logical economy dictates agnosticism as to why this is so.

While for Fry, the mysticism he wished he "hadn't got so hot about," as a too-powerful explanatory theory, names the refusal of limits, the position is the same. The "perfect description of mysticism," he thought, is "the attempt to get rid of mystery." It claims "there is no mystery"; it "can always explain every phenomenon." Science seeks to expand knowledge's boundaries, wants "a fresh vista into the world beyond," yet acknowledges that something will always escape it. "To have science one has both to accept mystery and to dislike it enough to try to clear it up which is so complicated a balance that there is no wonder it's rare" (*RF*, 271). So Fry "never believed that I knew what was the ultimate nature of art" (*V&D*, 284–5). Wittgenstein's position emphasizes that scientific "progress" presupposes its limits: "the notion that there are questions the answers to which will be discovered at some later date" is an "error" which "pervades my whole book," he said in December 1931; "even if all possible scientific questions be answered, the problems of life have still not been touched at all" (*Tractatus*, 6.52).

Wittgenstein's version of the acquiescence is "there is then no question left, and just this is the answer" (6.52). This is the burden of the statement he "wrote in the manuscript of my book, though it wasn't printed in the *Tractatus*, 'The solutions of philosophical questions must never come as a surprise. In philosophy nothing can be discovered.'"[6] The flatness of the adjustment to knowledge's limits brings the mystical wonder back to earth. What is extraordinary viewed from the private world turns out to be ordinary from other perspectives. Wonder is meaningless:

> It is nonsense to say that I wonder at the existence of the world, because I cannot imagine it not existing. I could of course wonder at the world round me being as it is. If for instance I had this experience while looking into the blue sky, I could wonder at the sky being blue as opposed to the case when it's clouded. But that's not what I mean. I am wondering at the sky being *what it is*. (*Tractatus*, 7, cited in Black, *Companion*, 374–5)

Whitehead's "Value is the outcome of limitation" (*SMW*, 89) aims at a comparable flattening; value stands simply for the fact – whether ordinary and extraordinary is irrelevant – that some thing is the way it is.

Russell's return to the ordinary is apparent in his insistence on the meaninglessness of positing existence of a particular. It also informs his project of making counter-intuitive conclusions "familiar to the imagination" (*ML*, 183). Science is only "extraordinary – from the point of view of tradition and common sense" (*ABCR*, 41). After logic leads the mind by stages to a surprising outcome, "it is necessary to cultivate logical imagination" in order "not to be a slave of" the hypothesis "which common sense has rendered easy to imagine" (*OKnExW*, 242). In the history of philosophy, he comments, "intelligible . . . seems to mean 'familiar to imagination' " (*ML*, 183). Logic's notion of intelligibility is, by contrast, unfamiliar. Whenever "an idea . . . familiar as an unanalysed whole" is analyzed, there is "almost always a feeling of unfamiliarity produced by the analysis" (*OKnExW*, 209). There then must be an imaginative attempt to become familiar with the unfamiliar. But "when once" the doctrine "is imaginatively realized, the difficulty is seen to disappear" (*OKnExW*, 180). This is Weierstrass' accomplishment:

> Weierstrass has been able, by embodying his views in mathematics, where familiarity with truth eliminates the vulgar prejudices of common sense, to invest Zeno's paradoxes with the respectable air of platitudes; and if the result is less delightful to the lover of reason than Zeno's bold defiance, it is at any rate more calculated to appease the mass of academic mankind. (*ML*, 76–7)

This is the adjustment between feeling and science Stephen and Whitehead have in mind. It perhaps motivates the early Russell's rejection of the distinction between necessary and contingent for the claim "that all propositions are necessary" (see Hylton, *Russell*, 153, 161). "Everything is in a sense a mere fact," he claimed, and "there seems to be no true proposition of which it makes sense to say that it might have been false . . . What is true, is true; what is false, is false; and concerning fundamentals, there is nothing more to be said" (*PofM*, 454). When feeling catches up with theory, the contingent's unexpectedness takes on the aspect of the necessary. Change seems "miraculous" in experienced time, discontinuous and jumpy, but when continuity is made "familiar and easy to the imagination as well as to deliberate thought" (*OKnExW*, 142), we see that at each instant the arrow is simply where it is. The "steady goers" moving through the alphabet "in order" must afterwards "miraculously, lump all the letters together in one flash" (*TL*, 55). Or the order is reversed. The mystic "way of wisdom, sudden, penetrating, coercive," may precede, to be followed by "the slow and fallible study of outward appearance by a science relying wholly on the senses" (*ML*, 8). Ultimately, science's world becomes imaginatively familiar when one accepts that it is all there is. Hence Cobden-Sanderson's effort "to 'overcome the ordinariness of ordinary life'" errs through mystic excess. Everything "was wonderful" and suffered "a curious magnification. Nothing exists in itself but only as a means to something else. The solid objects of daily life become . . . symbolical," Woolf comments. "The sense of reality grew fainter" (*CE*, IV, 95).

The limits appear also in the problem of transcription, of converting a private, incommunicable acquaintance into a transmittable knowledge by description:

> Most serious advances in philosophic thought result from some . . . direct contemplation of facts. But the outcome has to be expressed in words if it is to be communicable. Those who have a relatively direct vision of the facts are often incapable of translating their vision into words, while those who possess the words have usually lost the vision. It is partly for this reason that the highest philosophical capacity is so rare: it requires a combination of vision with abstract words which is hard to achieve, and too quickly lost in the few who have for a moment achieved it. (*Mind*, 212)

Lost in translation is the flash of insight; the limit is now one of language. Hence, the *Tractatus*' conclusion that the mystical is "the inexpressible" (6.522) and its injunction that "Whereof one cannot speak, thereof one must be silent" (6.54). Expression removes the wonder and replaces the demonstrative, which "shows" or "points," with a description: "To say nothing except what can be said, *i.e.* the propositions of natural science, *i.e.* something that has nothing to do with philosophy" (*Tractatus* 6.53). For language *is* description, and if answers cannot be formulated in it, the questions vanish as well. "The votary of common sense sometimes refuses to ask the ultimate questions at all," Stephen says of Hume (*HET*, 71). This is "the reason why men to whom after long doubting the sense of life became clear, could not then say wherein this sense consisted," Wittgenstein explains (*Tractatus*, 6.521). So when the sleepless in "Time Passes" "had suddenly an answer vouchsafed them," they observe the mystical silence, for "they could not say what it was" (*TL*, 198). Like Lily Briscoe's final vision, the answer can be shown but not said.

For Wittgenstein, however, Bloomsbury talk did not sufficiently observe language's limits, neither Fry's notorious loquaciousness in front of paintings nor Russell's "glibness," as witness "A Free Man's Worship." Julian Bell's satire turns Wittgenstein's pronouncements against him – "But Wittgenstein pontificates on Art"; "In every company he shouts us down,/And stops our sentence stuttering his own":

> For he talks nonsense, numerous statements makes,
> Forever his own vow of silence breaks:
> Ethics, aesthetics, talks of day and night.
> (Monk, *Wittgenstein*, 257)

Russell had said as much in his "Introduction" to the *Tractatus*, noting "after all, Mr Wittgenstein manages to say a good deal about what cannot be said, thus suggesting to the sceptical reader that possibly there may be some loophole through a hierarchy of languages" (22).[7] The "only strictly correct method" Wittgenstein invokes in *Tractatus* 6.53 requires demonstrating to anyone who "wished to say something metaphysical . . . that he had given no meaning to certain signs in his propositions" even though "he would not have the feeling we were teaching him philosophy." It thus dismisses the extension of knowledge represented by popular texts like *The Problems of Philosophy* that constituted the Bloomsbury project.

Woolf gives the mystical recognition of limits its structure of feeling in the "moment of being." In "daily miracles" (*TL*, 240), a sufficiency is conferred on their briefness and fragmentariness: "Only for a moment; but it was enough" (*MrsD*, 47). The self, shrunk to an instant, aware of its own ghostly strangeness, pronounces them enough: "Through the open window the voice of the beauty of the world came murmuring, too softly to hear exactly what it said – but what mattered if the meaning were plain?" (*TL*, 213); "why not accept this, be content with this, acquiesce and resign?" (*TL*, 214). Not themselves eternal, these moments hold within themselves eternity.

> Then (as I was walking through Russell Sqre last night) I see the mountains in the sky: the great clouds; & the moon which is risen over Persia; I have a

great & astonishing sense of something there, which is "it"[8] – It is not exactly beauty that I mean. It is that the thing is in itself enough: satisfactory; achieved. A sense of my own strangeness, walking on the earth is there too: of the infinite oddity of the human position . . . Who am I, & so on: these questions are always floating about in me; & then I bump against some exact fact etc. (*Diary*, III, 62)

In calibrating feeling to scientific knowledge, the mystic recognition of limits connects to the "unity-emotion" Fry's artist and mathematician share: it excludes all but the apprehension of "inevitable relations," "so that no need exists to make reference to what is outside the unity, and this becomes for the time being a universe" (*V&D*, 81). Modern art's formal principles add up the disparate perspectives, Russell Square and moonlit Persia, into a constellation strung out in abstract, meaningless order – "the so evident inevitability of all its correspondances and correlations" (*TR*, 191); the questions cease to be unanswered simply by the encounter with what there is – the bump against the fact. Fry's and Woolf's rejection of narrative thus follows from the rejection of an overarching meaning, the "elaborate logic, beginning with Parmenides, and culminating in Hegel and his followers," which "has been gradually developed, to prove that the universe is one indivisible Whole" (*ML*, 17). One should resist feeling "called upon to provide, some winter's night, a meaning for all my observations – a line that runs from one to another, a summing up that completes" (*W*, 115). The "imaginations" whose elements are "brought purposely together" (*TL*, 198) impose a meaning on that meaningless construction. The real order is only the continuity of relations. Like philosophy, content with "general forms" rather than "systems of the world," art supplies form but no meaning. It erects "completely self-consistent, self-supporting and self-contained . . . constructions which do not stand for something else, but appear to have ultimate value and in that sense to be real," constructions which, Fry adds, the "the man of science and the artist," alone in being "entirely opposed to symbolism," also "are alone in seeking" (*The Artist and Psychoanalysis*, 15). Art gives no all-embracing, cosmic answer. "Instead of manipulating reality so as to conform to the libido," Fry says, the novels that have endured "note the inexorable sequence in life of cause and effect, they mark the total indifference of fate to all human desires, and they endeavor to derive precisely from that inexorability of fate . . . the pleasure which consists in the recognition of inevitable sequences" (12). This is the property of the "great torrent" of life – "its complete indifference to the individuals, whom it swallowed up and rolled onwards" that fills Katharine Hilbery "with at least a temporary exaltation" (*ND*, 439).

Fry's formalism is the expression of the "enough." It transforms the mystic impulse to unity from the "denial of division" (*ML*, 10) to the "piecemeal" unity scientific philosophy yields (*ML*, 108), disburdened of unsupportable metaphysical claims. Fry emulates the scientific "process" Russell describes "of stripping away what is merely imagination, in order to reach the core of true scientific knowledge," one "nearer to bare structure, which is the mathematician's goal – not because it is the only thing in which he is interested as a human being, but because it is the only thing that he can express in mathematical formulae" (*ABCR*, 228–9). "To the non-mathematical mind," Russell comments, "the abstract character of our physical knowledge may seem unsatisfactory. From an artistic or imaginative point of view, it is perhaps regrettable" (*ABCR*, 230). "From the aesthetic point of view," he repeats elsewhere, "abstraction is likely to be wholly misleading" (*SO*, 82–3). Here is one of those places where the difference between Russell and Fry or Woolf will be not Russell's celebration of science but his characterization of art.

A modern art must then be cut to the dimensions of "the whole world that seems to be saying 'that is all'" (*MrsD*, 15, 58). The novels, "content," like Leslie Stephen's agnostic, "to trace the facts and their laws" ("WM?," 144), "content with this" (*TL*, 214), ultimately record "that is all" (*MrsD*, 15). Like Mrs. Ramsay watching the lighthouse's beam, the observer must accept the world's limits:

> she thought, watching it with fascination, hypnotised, as if it were stroking with its silver fingers some sealed vessel in her brain whose bursting would flood her with delight, she had known . . . intense happiness, and it silvered the rough waves . . . , as daylight faded, and the blue went out of the sea and it rolled in waves of pure lemon . . . and the ecstasy burst in her eyes and waves of pure delight raced over the floor of her mind and she felt, It is enough! It is enough! (*TL*, 99–100)

"Fear no more, says the heart in the body" (*MrsD*, 211) – the refrain from *Cymbeline* is reiterated by the waves surrounding the perspectives:

> So on a summer's day waves collect, overbalance, and fall; collect and fall; and the whole world seems to be saying 'that is all' more and more

ponderously, until even the heart in the body which lies in the sun on the beach says too, that is all . . . Fear no more says the heart, committing its burden to some sea, which sighs collectively for all sorrows and renews, begins, collects, lets fall. (*MrsD*, 58–9)

"That is all" is something less than all. Such propositions, like the lighthouse's "long steady stroke," permit Mrs. Ramsay to repeat "it will end, it will end . . . It will come" and to reject "that lie": "We are in the hands of the Lord" (*TL*, 97). Art answers "it is enough," adding nothing. The difference between the all and the enough Whitehead calls "[t]he contrast between the comparative emptiness of Presentational Immediacy and the deep significance disclosed by Causal Efficacy" which he pronounces "at the root of the pathos which haunts the world" (*Symbolism*, 47):

> "Pereunt et imputantur"
> is the inscription on old sundials in "religious" houses:
> "The hours perish and are laid to account."
> Here "Pereunt" refers to the world disclosed in immediate presentation, gay with a thousand tints, passing, and intrinsically meaningless. "Imputantur" refers to the world disclosed in its causal efficacy, where each event infects the ages to come, for good or for evil, with its own individuality. Almost all pathos includes a reference to lapse of time. (*Symbolism*, 47)

The contrast is of the colored realm of sense-data and the non-sensible domain of physics.

The limits are those set by the law of time, the sequence of seconds, moments, hours, days and years. For the subject in time, whose end is death, the first response is to its extraordinariness: "how unbelievable . . . that it must end; and no one in the whole world would know how she had loved it all" (*MrsD*, 185). That fact too is returned to the ordinary: "it was enough," as Clarissa Dalloway thinks, "that one day should follow another; Wednesday, Thursday, Friday, Saturday" (*MrsD*, 185). "Life is pleasant; life is good; after Monday comes Tuesday, and Wednesday follows Tuesday" (*W*, 27).

In this adjustment lies the restraint that defines Woolf's "modern" elegy. It brings the lament "Mrs. Ramsay!" and her death "on a level with . . . the table" (*TL*, 300). For "when we exclaim at the extravagant waste of such a life we are inclined no doubt to lose that view of the surrounding parts," Woolf writes, which "robs the single life of its arrow-like speed, and its tragic departure" (*MB*, 39). In this adjustment, "old Mr. Carmichael"'s valediction is completed; "looking like an old pagan god, shaggy, with weeds in his hair," he becomes Leslie Stephen's modern Proteus or Triton. The modern elegy's dimensions are not the lyric's, however, but the novel's, hence the substitution of the god's symbol – "the trident (it was only a French novel) in his hand" – desacralizing it, for what could be more secular than a French novel (*TL*, 309)?

The exaltation is something like the "agreement with that alien will on which I appear dependent" which Wittgenstein invokes (*Notebooks 1914–1916*, 75e). Yet the exaltation must be flattened; the modern elegy ends then with an anti-apotheosis. The elegiac mode reconnects with life, the ordinary, as Mrs. Ramsay's brown wool or Lady Bruton's spider's thread connects the external world to the private worlds, "these things with an inner life, with their own richness of content, these beings, with the destiny of the world hidden in their natures," which, as Whitehead says, are, "for all their vagueness," "what we want to know about. As we cross a road busy with traffic, we see the colours of their occupants" (*Symbolism*, 57). The impulse of science also contains this impulse to life, what Russell calls "the queen-impulse"; if it dies, "the death-dealing influence, though retarded a little by habit, spreads slowly through all the subsidiary impulses, and a whole tract of life becomes inexplicably colourless" (*ML*, 36).

The return to particulars, to traffic, to color, observes the principle of acquaintance. Woolf's fiction practices Hume's escape from the extraordinary world made strange by philosophy to the ordinary realm of gossip as a formal exercise bridging the gap between physics and sense. It rejects any larger meaning connecting the two realms. "Then the change must be so upsetting, Lily said. He comes in from his books and finds us all playing games and talking nonsense. Imagine what a change from the things he thinks about, she said" (*TL*, 71). Leslie Stephen's failure was the refusal to return to the lamplight, his tendency, after his wife's death, to engulf with meaning the fragile domain of the ordinary mind.

GRANITE AND RAINBOW: TRUTH AND FICTION

There must be truth; there must be a wall. ("The Lady in the Looking-Glass," Woolf, *Complete Shorter Fiction*, 216)

Hume's return to "drink and gossip" (*TL*, 198) is thus not an escape. The Post-Impressionist contemplation of forms must continuously reestablish contact with the objects of acquaintance. Fry's and Woolf's aesthetic, in its commitment to knowledge and realism, incorporates empirical truth. This is the natural progress of Orlando's reasoning: "So she went on to the nature of reality, which led her to truth, which in its turn, led . . ." (*O*, 145). Woolf shared with Russell and his generation, Leonard Woolf tells us, this "passion for what we called truth" alongside "a passion for literature and music" (*Sowing*, 159). The point of the surprising conjunction should not be missed. "Science as the pursuit of truth is the equal, but not the superior, of art," Russell asserts (*SO*, ix).

Fry's and Woolf's aesthetic is not then purely formal, purely aesthetic; it makes the further demand on its constructions that they, like Russell's logical fictions, correspond to fact. This is what art and science have in common. In "Art and Science," Fry disputes the claim that "the justification of the scientific theory" lies "in its aesthetic value," wondering whether "a theory that disregarded facts would have equal value for science with one which agreed with facts" and concluding: "The aesthetic value of a theory would surely depend solely on the perfection and complexity of the unity attained, and I imagine that many systems of scholastic theology, and . . . metaphysic, have only this aesthetic value" (*V&D*, 79). For "in a true scientific theory – the aesthetic value is reinforced by the curiosity value which comes in when we believe it to be true" (*V&D*, 80). This is that tension, "[s]o long as our knowledge is imperfect," between "a want of symmetry and a want of accuracy," Stephen notes (*HET*, 6).

This commitment to the truth of what there is also motivates Fry's and Woolf's conception of "modern" art. Its definitive separation from religion as "creed" or rival knowledge is its separation from Stephen's myths and symbols, from the concepts of "phantasy" and "wish-fulfilment" which James Strachey's Freud had given both Fry and Russell. For the "kernel of the scientific outlook is the refusal to regard our own desires, tastes, and interests as affording a key to the understanding of the world" (*ML*, 40). If, as Russell claims, "the scientific attitude is in some degree unnatural to man; the majority of our opinions are wish-fulfilments like dreams in the Freudian theory" (*SO*, 14), then one can expect a phantasy art. For the hopeful, "it was impossible to resist the strange intimation" in which every random element, every "gull, flower, tree, man and woman" (*TL*, 199) has a purpose, "that good triumphs, happiness prevails, order rules," because "dreams persisted" in "the minds of men" (*TL*, 198–9) which look for the "message," for "tokens of divine bounty" (*TL*, 201).[9] Philosophy itself is not immune – "Berkeley saved the universe and the permanence of bodies by regarding them as God's thoughts, but this was only a wish-fulfilment, not logical thinking" (*SO*, 80). "One of these groups into which I would divide artists," Fry explains, "is mainly preoccupied with creating a fantasy-world in which the fulfillment of wishes is realised." But, Fry insists, there is another "concerned with the contemplation of formal relations . . . detached from the instinctive life" and "in that respect on a par with science" (*The Artist and Psychoanalysis*, 4). Like that which Stephen hopes for, it is "content with direct vision, instead of mixing facts with dreams" (*HET*, 16):

> while there is an art which corresponds to the dream life, an art in which the phantasy-making power of the libido is at work to produce a wish-fulfilment, there is also an art which has withdrawn itself from the dream, which is concerned with reality, an art therefore which is pre-eminently objective and dis-interested. (*The Artist and Psychoanalysis*, 18)

This art has what Fry "call[s] the passion for pure beauty." Woolf would also see the novelist as freeing us "to take delight . . . in things in themselves," to "see the strangeness of them" when "habit" ceases "to immerse us in them, and we stand outside watching what has no power over us" (*CE*, II, 82).

Science's intellectual activity has two aspects, curiosity for facts and "the contemplation of inevitable relations" (*V&D*, 79), "the particularising and the generalising" (*V&D*, 80). So there is also "the literature of fact and the literature of opinion" (*TG*, 45). Art shows both an intellectual curiosity for the "data" and "[t]he other kind of intellectual activity," which like the scientist's search for formulae, "impels the artist to attempt the reduction of all forms, as it were, to some common denominator which will make them comparable with one another" (*V&D*, 80). The impulse to formalism is not surprisingly attached to the aesthetic. It is the insistence on the other impulse which is unexpected. As Fry says, "in so far as the artist's curiosity remains a purely intellectual curiosity it interferes with the perfection and purity of the work of art by introducing an alien and non-aesthetic element" (*V&D*, 80). There is "a valid objection to the intrusion of intellect, of however rudimentary a kind, into an aesthetic whole" (*V&D*, 81). Yet Fry's and Woolf's aesthetic will not banish such intrusions: they constitute the "jar on the nerves" which mars the perfected beauty of the whole, like Mrs. Ramsay's deer-stalker's hat (*TL*, 264) "For I am no mystic; something always plucks at me . . . interest in hairdressers and the like brings me to the surface" (*W*, 280) That jarring eruption of "something out of harmony with this jocundity and this serenity" (*TL*, 201) within the formal beauty of the whole guarantees against the phantasy that blinds itself complacently to interruptions of the real. It guarantees that the acceptance is of the inevitable and not the unavoidable, that coming to terms with this world is not its celebration as the best of all possible ones. Cobden-Sanderson's "unity of the whole" in which the antagonists in the trenches blowing one another's heads off were creating "the greater creation" (*CE*, IV, 94) is indeed a phantasized whole by contrast with the sea's refrain "it is enough." Likewise the "intrusion into a scene calculated to stir the most sublime reflections and lead to the most comfortable conclusions" of "Time Passes"'s ghostly ship, reminder of war in the midst of natural beauty, made it "difficult blandly to overlook" and "abolish" its "significance in the landscape; to continue, as one walked by the sea, to marvel how beauty outside mirrored beauty within" (*TL*, 201).

The "dream, of sharing, completing, of finding in solitude on the beach an answer, was then but a reflection in a mirror, and the mirror itself was but the surface glassiness which forms in quiescence when the nobler powers sleep beneath." With each shift "the mirror was broken" (*TL*, 202). The pieces can be put together again only in endless combinations according to principles which are solely formal. It is impossible to maintain the "aesthetic vision." Art must always allow the disruption of the real. To avoid the mystic phantasy that explains all, it is necessary to return periodically to the world of existence. Hence the need to ceaselessly rearrange the data. The pattern is only one of several possible hypothetical approximations to reality, "the many worlds which logic offers for our choice" (*PP*, 148). The danger remains the re-introduction of emphasis, value, supplied by the subject. Each levelling of the data reminds us that "this silence" is not divine bounty but "this indifference" (*TL*, 201). In its concern for reality, a modern art, as we saw with Cézanne, emulates less pure mathematics' formal perfection and more the physical sciences, seeking but not always finding the formal laws explaining empirical facts. Post-Impressionism presupposes Impressionism.

Modern "fiction" aims then to bring together "reality . . . figures, love and truth" (*ND*, 502). Fiction is normally an antonym of truth. Yet, just as the public object is constructed out of private sense-data and a still beauty out of changing moments, so truth is reached through fiction. The first person of *A Room of One's Own*, called upon to produce "a nugget of pure truth" (3) about "women and fiction," can only invent a fiction: "Lies will flow from my lips" (4). For the term "fiction" by which Woolf chooses to name her art has a history in British empiricism. "The belief that anything exists outside our mind, when not actually perceived, is a 'fiction.' The belief in a continuous subject which perceives the feelings is another fiction," Leslie Stephen summarizes Hume (*HET*, 44). "Fiction" is thus the name by which Hume dismisses physical objects and persons. "The subjective element implies unreality. All perceptions have a subjective element. Therefore, the supposed reality must be a 'fiction'" (*HET*, 47). For Hume, anything more than the shower of atoms is only an invention of custom:

> Thus reality is to be found only in the ever-varying stream of feelings, bound together by custom, regarded by a "fiction" or set of fictions as implying some permanent set of external or internal relations . . . Chance, instead of order, must, it would seem, be the ultimate objective fact, as custom, instead of reason, is the ultimate subjective fact. (*HET*, 44)

"Fiction" is the set of common-sense beliefs which analysis argues away. Physical reality and the subject are, in fact, the two lies Woolf's lecturer on fiction, "making use of all the liberties and licences of a novelist," invents: "what I am about to describe has no existence" and "'I'" stands "for somebody who has no real being" (*Room*, 4).

Russell, "who sometimes spoke of logical fictions instead of logical constructions" (Urmson, *Philosophical Analysis*, 38), borrows this negative term, as with Berkeley's unperceived perceptions, and makes it into something positive. He says explicitly of points as mathematical fictions, "[t]he word 'fiction' is used glibly in such connexions by many men who seem not to feel the necessity of explaining how it can come about that a fiction can be so useful in the study of the actual world" (*ML*, 112).[10] While it is nonsense to speak of the existence or non-existence of particulars, it makes sense to ask whether or not a given logical "fiction" corresponds to something real, we recall: "to say that something is a logical construction is not to say that it is in any way fictitious; the unicorn happens to be both a logical construction and fictitious, but the average man is a logical construction and not a fiction," Urmson comments (*Philosophical Analysis*, 38). Russell also rejects the idea that "the process of analysis is falsification, that when you analyse any given concrete whole you falsify it and that the results of analysis are not true" (*LK*, 178). Thus, when the narrator of *A Room of One's Own* says "Fiction here is likely to contain more truth than fact" (4), she is asserting in a similar fashion that the novelist's constructions have something to do with truth.[11]

Truth, meaningless when applied to the object of acquaintance, is, finally, by definition unembraceable, distant, "eyeless." To achieve that "disinterested contemplation which constitutes culture in the good sense of this much-misused word" (*ML*, 33), to achieve knowledge, which Russell calls "a form of union of Self and not-Self; like all union," one "impaired . . . by any attempt to force the universe into conformity with what we find in ourselves" (*PP*, 159), one cannot be "like the man who never leaves the domestic circle for fear his word might not be law" (*PP*, 160):

> The private world of instinctive interests is a small one, set in the midst of a great and powerful world which must, sooner or later, lay our private world in ruins. Unless we can so enlarge our interests as to include the whole outer world, we remain like a garrison in a beleagered fortress, knowing that the enemy prevents escape and that ultimate surrender is inevitable. (*PP*, 160)

One must abandon cozy privacy, which is "a prison to the intellect" (*PP*, 160) and "fetters contemplation to Self" (*PP*, 159), and follow Fry's impulse "'to go out into this tremendous unknown universe outside one,'" as Woolf quotes him (*RA*, 241). Science is the ideal of such knowledge. By contrast with the here-and-now-centeredness from which animals and human beings view the world,

> Science attempts to escape from this geographical and chronological prison. In physics the origin of co-ordinates in space-time is wholly arbitrary, and the physicist aims at saying things which have nothing to do with his point of view but would be equally true for an inhabitant of Sirius or of an extra-galactic nebula.
>
> Here again there are stages in emancipation. History and geology take us away from the now, astronomy takes us away from the here. The man

whose mind has been filled with these studies gets a feeling that there is something accidental, and almost trivial, about the fact that his ego occupies a very particular portion of the space-time stream. (Russell, *Portraits from Memory*, 179)

Amid "the world which Science presents . . . , if anywhere, our ideals henceforward must find a home" (*ML*, 45). There one becomes "a citizen of the universe, embracing distant countries, remote regions of space, and vast stretches of past and future within the circle of his interests" (*ML*, 37).

The first step is the externalization of sense-data: "in our sense-experience we know away from and beyond our own personality," Whitehead writes (*SMW*, 85). This is the step of Impressionism. The ultimate goal is to see the world "as far as possible as it is in itself, and not merely through the distorting medium of personal desire" (*ML*, 37–8). The importance of formalism becomes clear here: "the free intellect will value more the abstract and universal knowledge into which the accidents of private history do not enter, than the knowledge brought by the senses" (*PP*, 160). Truth is something that resides in the architectural framework, in the laws of the universe, which exist whether or not subjects can grasp them in their entirety. The novel, for Woolf, will be such a universe.

MYSTICISM AND IMPERSONAL KNOWLEDGE

The only truth which she could discover was the truth of what she herself felt – a frail beam when compared with the broad illumination shed by the eyes of all the people who are in agreement to see together. (Woolf, *Night and Day*, 313)

The mind is full of monstrous, hybrid, unmanageable emotions. That the age of the earth is 3,000,000,000 years; that human life lasts but a second; that the capacity of the human mind is nevertheless boundless; that life is infinitely beautiful yet repulsive; . . . that science and religion have between them destroyed belief; that all bonds of union seem broken, yet some control must exist – it is in this atmosphere of doubt and conflict that writers must now create, and the fine fabric of a lyric is no more fitted to contain this point of view than a rose leaf to envelop the rugged immensity of a rock. (Woolf, *Collected Essays*, II, 219)

For Russell the mystical way of knowing is bound up with "self-assertion" (*ML*, 17), in contrast to science's impersonal knowledge. Since Russell's mysticism includes art and literature, he retains a romantic aesthetic emphasizing expression of self. "The tendency of our perceptions is to emphasize increasingly the objective elements in an impression, unless we have some special reason, as artists have, for doing the opposite" (*OP,* 161). In his adolescence "[o]nly Shelley," Russell says, "was wholly congenial to me." Russell's impersonal ideal "it must be confessed," Warnock observes, was espoused not without "occasional flights of romantic rhetoric" (*English Philosophy*, 26) which did not pass with the likes of Wittgenstein or T. S. Eliot.[12] His "poetry" was not equal to his vision. Science permits us "to construct an impersonal metaphysic, independent of the accidents of our knowledge and ignorance," "impersonal" like physics, which "nominally pays no attention to sense-data" (*ML*, 143), again equating sense-data – color – with the personal and forgetting his hypothesis of impersonal although subjective "sense-data given to no one." He cannot imagine an art like his physics, beginning with impressions but not stopping with them, not because they are "any less 'real'" but "because they do not point to anything beyond themselves" (*OP,* 161). Art is personal. Both Woolf and Fry vehemently reject this relegation of art and literature to the personal: "the love of beauty," Fry wrote, "implies an almost complete detachment from personality and from the wishes made by our unsatisfied libido" (*The Artist and Psychoanalysis*, 19). In the Bloomsbury vocabulary, "impersonal" is in no sense pejorative. When Vanessa writes to Virginia of *The Waves*: "you have made one's human feelings into something less personal," these are words of praise (*Vanessa Bell*, 251). Woolf clearly sees art as sharing science's impersonality: "[t]he great poet and the lover [her conjunction of poet and lover recalling Russell's] are both representative – in some way anonymous" (*CE*, II, 276). The possibility of an impersonal aesthetic, the triumphantly recorded "point" of Woolf's 1921 dinner-table encounter with Russell she pronounced "one is old enough to cut the trimmings and get to," now stands clearly as a challenge to his assumptions about art. Fry's and Woolf's "modern" art demands the self's reduction. Clive Bell sees it in this characteristically Woolfean way: "Be they artists or lovers of art, mystics or mathematicians, those who achieve ecstasy are those who have freed themselves from the arrogance of humanity. He who would feel the significance of art must make himself humble before it" (*Art*, 70).

The opposition between impersonal and personal is a version of granite and rainbow – "personality" Woolf calls "rainbow-like" (*CE*, IV, 229). Literary Post-Impressionism requires "strain[ing] off what was personal and accidental in all these impressions" to reach a "pure," colorless "truth," she writes (*Room*, 25). The "life" of the great impersonal writers is "thin, modest, colourless, like blue skimmed milk" (*CE*, II, 276). In the 1921 exchange between Woolf and Russell, he contrasts his colorless world with her colors, which she pronounces "foolish" and he says she needs "for your writing." His subsequent question, "Do you never see things impersonally?," by its proximity, links the impersonal with the colorless, assuming colored writing is "personal." Woolf's answer, "Yes. I see literature like that; Milton, that is," rejects then Russell's assumption (*Diary*, II, 147). Woolf's aesthetic, while reserving a place for the personal, is itself impersonal.

There are "truths which transmit personality" (*CE*, IV, 223). Bloomsbury connected "personality" to biography. Personality shines with "the coloured light of biography" (*TG*, 45); "colourless" impersonality (*CE*, II, 276) emits "the white light of facts" (*TG*, 45). What is "coloured by its surroundings" and tinged by character must be combined with the "colourless" (*CE*, II, 277). Personality is designated by the ordinary proper name – hence, impersonality's anonymity. "The signature, the name, belongs to the surface-personality, and pertains to the world of information," Forster writes (*Anonymity*, 22). "Surface-personality" includes the recognizable face, "the envelope of personality" experience must penetrate. By constrast, "the impersonal life," "that impersonal condition" (*ND*, 271), is faceless. Personality dwells in social contact, "in the chatter of question and answer, in the torrents of gossip and examination papers" (*Anonymity*, 22) – Forster's terms echo Woolf's. Traces of the author's personality might be detected in a novel. So Forster allows "[t]he personality of a writer does become important after we have read his book and begin to study it." It can be recognized or reconstructed, but the process takes us outside the text:

> when the intelligible word is restored to the universe, when the co-partnership is over, then a book changes its nature, and we can ask ourselves questions about it such as "What is the author's name?" "Where did he live?" "Was he married?" and "Which was his favourite flower?" Then we are no longer reading the book, we are studying it and making it subserve our desire for information. (19)

"Study," Forster adds, "is only a serious form of gossip. It teaches us everything about the book but the central thing" (19).

The model of impersonality is painting. Vanessa Bell's paintings yield no clues as to their author:

> Is she dainty then, or austere? Does she like riding? Is she red haired or brown eyed? Was she ever at university? Does she prefer herrings or Brussels sprouts? Is she . . . not a woman at all, but a mixture of a Goddess and peasant . . . ? Any writer so ardently questioned would have yielded something to our curiosity. One defies a novelist to keep his life through twenty-seven volumes of fiction safe from scrutiny. But Mrs. Bell says nothing. Mrs. Bell is as silent as the grave. (Rosenbaum, *The Bloomsbury Group*, 171–2)

Woolf's fiction aspires to the grave silence and still life of Vanessa Bell's painting. In the "strange painters' world in which mortality does not enter and psychology is held at bay, and there are no words" (173), the little personalities take on their pathos, assuming a diminished place in the impersonal narrative. The "I," one among many and so less than the whole world, ceases to block the view. "He had found the house and so seeing it, he had also seen himself there; he had seen himself walking on the terrace, alone. He was walking up and down between the urns; and he seemed to himself very old and bowed" (*TL*, 247). Fiction is not the vehicle for the writer's personality but the language for something "very real, very big, very impersonal" (*VO*, 125). The novelist must not forget that "we are not entirely occupied in personal relations" (*CE*, II, 225). The modern novel must give "access to another world independent of personal affairs, a world of law, of philosophy, or more strangely a world such as he had had a glimpse of . . . when together they seemed to be sharing something, creating something . . . a vision flung out in advance of our actual circumstances" (*ND*, 487). It must represent, alongside the personal, "something impersonal," include "impersonal topics" (*ND*, 83), render an "impersonal life" (*ND*, 271) and the "impersonal condition" (*ND*, 271) and present the "impersonal outlook" (*ML*, 33), like "Greek . . . the impersonal literature" (*CE*, I, 1).

In characterizing *The Waves* as an "abstract mystical eyeless book" (*Diary*, III, 203), Woolf thereby equated logic's abstractness with mysticism, contra Russell. Its impersonal style is eyeless, faceless, selfless, sexless. In the early *Night and Day*, her female protagonist accepts the dichotomy between science and literature, choosing mathematics as a deliberate alternative to "helping her mother to produce a life of the great poet," her mother's father, a poet who would have been a contemporary of the Romantics, whose "Ode to

Winter" suggests Keats and who belonged to "the august circle of beings" that included "Wordsworth, Shelley" (39):

> in her mind mathematics were directly opposed to literature. She would not have cared to confess how infinitely she preferred the exactitude, the star-like impersonality, of figures to the confusion, agitation, and vagueness of the finest prose . . . seeing her own state mirrored in her mother's face, Katherine would shake herself awake with a sense of irritation. Her mother was the last person she wished to resemble. (*ND*, 46)

Katherine Hilbery has then Russell's position on poetry. Woolf, however, unlike her protagonist, did not choose "to study mathematics – to know about the stars" (*ND*, 195). Rather, between *Night and Day* and the 1921 exchange with Russell, she reconceived literature to make it, not the Romantic expression of personality, but an impersonal vision, to give to the prose which shows Mrs. Hilbery's vagueness a harder logic, to lift "ephemeral sounds through the misty sphere of anybody's language to the land where there is a perpetual marriage, a perpetual union" (*CE*, II, 50). That project is presented as the androgynous union of mysticism and logic. *Night and Day* had spoken of "the usual masculine impersonality" (17); *A Room of One's Own* labels this impersonality "androgyny," sexual identity relegated to personality. It is figured in *Night and Day* in the exchange Ralph Denham makes between "his own unfinished dissertation, with its mystical conclusion" and Katharine Hilbery's papers with mathematical figures (492).[13]

The new novel, Woolf writes, "will resemble poetry in this that it will give not only or mainly people's relations to each other and their activities together, as the novel has hitherto done, but it will give the relation of the mind to general ideas and its soliloquy in solitude" (*CE*, II, 225). This is the world whose limit is death, but within which life is captured. Personality does not disappear from modern fiction but shrinks to little islands of rainbow light, brightly lit private rooms, surrounded by colorless empty spaces. The prose function accomplishes this construction of multiple, personal perspectives. The poetic function gives "[t]he contemplation of what is non-human, the discovery that our minds are capable of dealing with material not created by them, above all, the realisation that beauty belongs to the outer world as to the inner" (*ML*, 65). Both require the elimination of the "I."

The model of impersonality is not a mystical merging of self and world. Cobden-Sanderson's "unity of the whole" presents the individual's engulfment in larger forces as the justification of war's horrors. This placid, retrospective death-wish is one Woolf makes the siren-song of the waves to which her art never yields. "A young man had killed himself" (*MrsD*, 280), nevertheless Mrs. Dalloway's party goes on. Yet the fact still intrudes: "And they talked of it at her party – the Bradshaws, talked of death" (*MrsD*, 280). It intrudes, protesting how men like Sir William Bradshaw made "life intolerable" (*MrsD*, 281), as Charlotte Brontë protests in *Jane Eyre*. The novel lets such protests in, as so many signs of the real, for the demands of truth meant its beauty

> was not beauty pure and simple – Bedford Place leading into Russell Square. It was straightness and emptiness of course; the symmetry of a corridor; but it was also windows lit up, a piano, a gramophone sounding; a sense of pleasure-making hidden, but now and again emerging when, through the uncurtained window, the window left open, one saw parties sitting over tables, young people slowly circling, conversations between men and women, maids idly looking out . . . , stockings drying on top ledges, a parrot, a few plants." (*MrsD*, 248)

There, once more, at the very center, the table is set, gathering around it the chatter of parties, the conversations between men and women, Hume, the Ramsays, the young Apostles and the Stephen sisters, Russell and Woolf, momentarily filling the emptiness. Again, it forms the center when "the lady at the table sat writing" (*W*, 268). And when those who occupy the room go out, it remains, with "the fixity of that woman writing" (*W*, 241). "Transfixed, stopped dead" (*W*, 240), it awaits the return of the traveller. "The kitchen table was something visionary" (*TL*, 232). Object of Russell's atomizing analysis and his subsequent hypothetical reconstruction, the table become kitchen table Fry makes fittingly the centerpiece of Cézanne's reconstruction of Impressionism. By turn, Woolf makes Fry's analysis of Cézanne's art of the table illustrate the principles of the new modernism. The table and the "solid objects" on it are "transformed" via "revelation and reconstruction" into things with the weight, the granite monumentality of mountains:

> Never was the development of a character or of a picture from the bare canvas to the infinite complexity of the finished work more closely followed or more subtly described . . . it is the bringing together from chaos and disorder of the parts that are necessary to the whole. When at last the apple, the kitchen table, and the bread-knife have come together, it is felt to be a victory for the human spirit over matter. The milk-jug and the ginger

jar are transformed. These common objects are invested with the majesty of mountains and the melody of music.

From the finished work the artist has vanished, like the critic in his commentary, leaving the eyeless vision of plastic color, the flower on the table immobilized on the circle of ground glass.

But in all this protracted and difficult business of revelation and reconstruction the critic's own identity has been consumed. Never does he draw attention by irrelevance or display to his own share in the work of reconstruction. The two gifts, the gift of analysis, the gift of sensibility, that so often conflict, here enhance each other – each contributes, neither dominates. "The concordance which we find in Cézanne between an intelligence rigorous, abstract and exacting to a degree, and a sensibility of extreme delicacy and quickness of response is here seen in masterly action." The words are true of Roger Fry himself. The flower has kept its colour and the microscope its clarity. (*RF*, 285)

What finally constitutes that "vision" which Woolf's artist "has had" and, once having it, disappears from, leaving as signature no single viewpoint, but a series of moments? It is a vision composed of fragments, yet ultimately achieving a strange, contingent unity – contingent on the very having occurredness of these moments, shaped by an uncompromising refusal to turn away from the consequences of this series of givens which constitute a life, a history, a novel. It transforms "O Death!" into the Post-Impressionist elegy, a free art's worship, a Tractatus of aesthetics, its goal a truth which records the world as it is and not as desire makes it. "Should this be the end of the story? a kind of sigh? a last ripple of the wave? . . . Let me touch the table – so – " (*W*, 267).

Notes

1 INTRODUCTION: TABLE TALK

1 In "Thoby's Room," Leon Edel says that "a feminine visitor" in this passage "lets her imagination wander into seats of masculinity," that "[t]he room was Cambridge, it was Trinity" (*Bloomsbury*, 65–6).

2 Since I began this study in 1975, treatments of Woolf and British philosophy by Avrom Fleishman, Graham Parkes, Patrick J. Whiteley and Gillian Beer have appeared besides Hintikka's and Rosenbaum's. Marianna Torgovnick acknowledges Woolf's "theory of perception and memory originating in visual images" of which she has "never come across a critical discussion" (*The Visual Arts*, 23). Earlier, Maxime Chastaing connected Woolf with British empiricism, while Floris Delattre argued Bergson's influence (*Le Roman Psychologique*, 136–42).

3 "When Leslie Stephen went up to Cambridge," Rosenbaum writes, "the only subjects" for the tripos were "classics and mathematics"; the natural and moral sciences were soon added (*Victorian Bloomsbury*, 111).

4 Stephen celebrates the "'patient and impartial enquiry'" which "Cambridge instilled . . . by honouring mathematics" (Annan, *Godless Victorian*, 189–90). See also Skidelsky, *John Maynard Keynes*, I, 39. Regretting "the unfortunate separation of different studies," Russell found psychologists "ignorant of mathematics and modern logic" and philosophers needing "some slight knowledge of logic, mathematics, and physics" (*OKnExW*, 100).

5 See Blackwell, "The Early Wittgenstein and the Middle Russell," and McGuinness, "The Mysticism of the *Tractatus*."

6 See also Black, *Companion*, 58. The parental taboo against philosophy Russell recounts equates philosophy with epistemology: whenever philosophy came up, his family repeated, "'What is mind? No matter. What is matter? Never mind'" (*Portraits from Memory*, 4). The questions parody Leslie Stephen's "What is the soul?" – "the opposite of matter . . . what is matter? – "the opposite of the soul" (*HET*, 25).

7 Skidelsky calls Bloomsbury "that London extension of Apostolic Cambridge" (*John Maynard Keynes*, I, 117). Leonard Woolf emphasizes

the Society's "immense . . . influence upon our minds" – "[o]f the ten men of Old Bloomsbury only Clive, Adrian and Duncan were not Apostles"; "Desmond [MacCarthy], Morgan [Forster], Lytton [Strachey], Saxon [Sydney-Turner], Maynard [Keynes] and I" were (*BeAg*, 21–6).

8 "Cambridge," Woolf says of Fry, "did not altogether escape his criticism." "Mon dieu," he wrote Marie Mauron in a French aiming beyond Cambridge, "quelle vie que celle des universitaires, des hommes charmants et intelligents, mais si bornés et fixés dans les ornières de cette vie provinciale" (*RF*, 287).

9 "I shall write no more mathematics. Perhaps I shall write philosophy," she quotes him. Russell's statement, "my intellect never quite recovered from the strain" (*AutoBR*, I, 202), recalls Woolf's comment about "the crippling effect of intensive brain work" on her father (*MB*, 126).

10 Lowe's two volumes of Whitehead's biography divide in 1910, as does Leonard Woolf's autobiography.

11 In *A Passage to India*, the term is insular *and* international: when the Englishman Fielding calls Miss Quested "'artistic'" and the Indian Aziz answers, "'a Post-Impressionist?,'" Fielding's "'Post Impressionism, indeed!'" offends Aziz: "he, an obscure Indian, had no right to have heard of Post-Impressionism – a privilege reserved for the Ruling Race" (70).

12 See Levy, *G. E. Moore*, 129 and *JR*, 39.

13 In *South From Granada*, Bloomsbury fellow-traveller Gerald Brenan, living "in such a remote spot," was "rebelling" against "English middle-class life" by substituting "more breathable atmospheres" for "stifling" ones to acquire "an education" (xii). Fresh air and broadened education justified "soaking myself in the ways of Mediterranean life" (1).

14 Instead of Bloomsbury being "elitist and narrowing," Zwerdling writes that "for a young woman . . . denied a university education," this "coterie" allowed "mental expansion," was "Woolf's private university" (*Virginia Woolf and the Real World*, 27).

15 McGuinness, *Wittgenstein*, 173. The Home University Library "volumes were sometimes called 'shilling shockers,'" Lowe explains (*Alfred North Whitehead*, II, 3).

16 Murray to Russell, in Lowe, *Alfred North Whitehead*, II, 19.

17 The "project" of University Extension, "always dear to individual Apostles," Levy writes (*G. E. Moore*, 86), was introduced at Cambridge by Apostle James Stuart. See Lowe, *Alfred North Whitehead*, I, 118; Levy, *G. E. Moore*, 85–6.

18 T. S. Eliot's mother's letter thanking Russell for "a copy of your book: *The Problems of Philosophy*" suggests the intended audience (Eliot, *The Letters of T. S. Eliot*, 130).

19 Ray Monk paints Russell in 1911 as "far from" a "strident rationalist."

He embraced "a kind of transcendental mysticism" (*Wittgenstein*, 38). Russell claimed Ottoline enabled him "to explain his philosophy to his popular audience" (Darroch, *Ottoline*, 122). See *CPBR* 12, 123–54.

20 Fry, his wife in a mental hospital, also discovered love c. 1910, briefly with Ottoline and then, in 1911, with Vanessa Bell. "Are you changing with the rest of the world?," Vanessa wrote Lytton in 1911 (Spalding, *Vanessa Bell*, 98). If love and war changed Russell, "love and colour," Spalding's title for 1910–12, changed Fry.

21 Russell, as Whitehead in his wish to teach women mathematics, thus differs from Wittgenstein, dissuading young men like Francis Skinner from academic careers (Monk, *Wittgenstein*, 359).

22 In London, "infinitely larger, more varied" than Cambridge, Lowe writes, Whitehead "would teach mathematics and mathematical physics" (*Alfred North Whitehead*, II, 2).

23 By contrast, T. S. Eliot, Russell's student at Harvard, wrote a dissertation on Bradley, Joyce studied Aquinas at University College, Dublin, and Proust had followed Bergson's lectures. On Eliot and philosophy, see Richard Wollheim, "Eliot and F. H. Bradley," Hugh Kenner, "Bradley," and Richard Shusterman's "long overdue recognition of Eliot's link" to "the analytical philosophical tradition," "primarily" to Russell but also to Wittgenstein and Moore, which "Eliot's obvious distaste for Russell's atheistic *Weltanschauung* and liberalist ethics has prevented previous scholars from appreciating" (*T. S. Eliot*, 2–3).

24 When "alone in her room," *Night and Day*'s Katharine Hilbery "rose early in the morning or sat up late at night to work . . . at mathematics [Woolf's ellipses]," hiding her paper in her father's Greek dictionary. "No force on earth would make her confess that" (45). Katharine's figures – "A plus B minus C equals *x y z*" – her mother finds "so dreadfully ugly" (*ND*, 483). Could Woolf have studied mathematics when "secure enough from surprise to concentrate her mind" (*ND*, 46)? Or philosophy? Had Leonard, shown her math scribblings like Ralph Denham, "followed her figures as far as his mathematics would let him" (*ND*, 492)?

25 But Forster, not "a Moore-ite," P. N. Furbank claims, "did not receive Moore's influence direct – I was not up to that and have never read *Principia Ethica*. It came to me at a remove, through those who knew the Master" (Rosenbaum, "*The Longest Journey*," 32–3), i.e., orally.

26 Andrew Ramsay, based on Thoby, "should have been a great mathematician" (*TL*, 289). The "great mathematician" Mr. Wolstenholme Woolf recalls at St. Ives (*MB*, 73) Quentin Bell thinks the model for Augustus Carmichael (*VW*, I, 32). His mathematics dies with Andrew to be transformed into Carmichael's poetry.

27 Her father's library must have contained "de longues rames de philosophie," as Charles Mauron translates ("Le Temps Passe," 125) "Time Passes" "long rows of books" (*TL*, 210). The catalogue of the

over 3,740 out of some 15,000 volumes the Woolfs' library contained now at Washington State University lists among philosophical works Berkeley's *A Treatise Concerning the Principles of Human Knowledge*, containing "The Three Dialogues between Hylas and Philonous" originally "from the Library of Leslie Stephen," Hume's *Essays and Treatises on Several Subjects* (containing *An Enquiry Concerning Human Understanding*) with "notes" in Leslie Stephen's hand (I, 51), one of two editions inscribed to "Laura Makepeace Stephen" (indicating a desire his daughters read philosophy) with notes by Stephen (I, 40), G. E. Moore's "The Refutation of Idealism," "belonging to or presented to Leonard Woolf," and ten works by Russell, two philosophical: *Philosophical Essays* of 1910 and *The Basic Writings*, postdating Virginia's death. There is a copy of Sir James Jeans' *The Mysterious Universe* (1930), recalling the Jeans in *Between the Acts*' Pointz Hall library alongside "Eddington, Darwin" (20), as well as Russell's *Icarus*. See Levy, *G. E. Moore*, 275.

28 Leonard told Levy: "Moore was the only philosopher who had any influence upon his wife's work" and "the only modern philosopher" she probably "read" (*G. E. Moore*, 275). Leonard "doubt[ed]" Delattre's claim she "read any Bergson" or "attended lectures in Manchester" (*LettersLW*, 485–6).

29 When Mrs. Flushing, echoing Ridley Ambrose, asks "'*Symposium*? . . . Latin or Greek?" and "'is there a good translation?'," he tells her "'to learn Greek'" (*VO*, 199). Woolf's Greek lessons with classicist Thomas Case's sister "covered some of Plato's dialogues" (Hintikka, "Virginia Woolf," fn. 43, 14). Woolf dates her acquaintance with Plato at least from age sixteen (*MB*, 104).

30 Woolf ends by saying Stephen "comes back now more as a contemporary. I must read him some day." Beer concludes that "Woolf disclaims having 'read' her father," despite "consonances between their written work" ("Hume, Stephen and Elegy," 92).

31 Woolf was "climbing Moore like some industrious insect" – a "sentence" makes her "head spin with the infinite meaning of words unadorned" (*Letters*, I, 340). Her "nightly 10 pages" reveals the "numbers of things in the world which I don't know – numbers I shall never understand" (347). Reading "the same page a number of times," she doubts she "can ask even an intelligible question" (352–3). "I split my head over [G. E.] Moore every night feeling ideas travelling to the remotest part of my brain, and setting up a feeble disturbance, hardly to be called a thought" (357). When she finished she was "not so dumb foundered as I was; but the more I understand, the more I admire" (364).

Rantavaara claims of "a certain black book" on Helen Ambrose's table in *The Voyage Out* that "[f]rom a quotation we deduce that book to be Prof. G. E. Moore's *Principia Ethica*" (*Virginia Woolf and Bloomsbury*, 7). Levy similarly identifies the "book" with "dark brown binding" in *The Voyage Out* (*G. E. Moore*, 233), recounting how when asked "if he had seen the reference to himself in the new novel," Moore wrote "Which novel?" in his diary, later discussing "Virginia's book" (276). See also Hussey, *The Singing of the Real World*, 98.

32 "To hear these young people talk," D. H. Lawrence writes after visiting Russell's rooms at Trinity, "really fills me with black fury: they talk endlessly, . . . each in a hard little shell of his own" (Rantavaara, *Virginia Woolf and Bloomsbury*, 102). Rosenbaum cites Woolf's statement that her knowledge of philosophy came "simply from listening to people talking" ("Philosophical Realism," 2).

33 See Levy, *G. E. Moore*, 113. Secrecy accompanied women's exclusion (xv), "leaks" were traceable to members confiding in women. While, Levy writes, Moore "never told his parents of his membership" (163), Fry "confided to his mother, 'I have just been elected to a secret society (not dynamitic though it sounds bad),' adding 'so you must not mention it much'" (*RF*, 49).

34 Leslie "Stephen's best essays" treat "the impact of one individual on another," writes Phyllis Grosskurth (*Leslie Stephen*, 30).

35 This passage disputes Hafley's claim that "[i]n this group Virginia Woolf was a 'silent partner'" and "hostess" (*The Glass Roof*, 5). Woolf presents Vanessa as "strong of brain," "quick to detect . . . fallacy of argument" (*MB*, 54).

36 Besides Moore's, Russell's lectures included: "On Scientific Method in Philosophy," delivered at Oxford in 1914; "The Ultimate Constituents of Matter," given to the Manchester Philosophical Society in 1915; "On the Notion of Cause," "On the Relations of Universals and Particulars," and "Knowledge by Acquaintance and Knowledge by Description," all read before the Aristotelian Society; *Our Knowledge of the External World*, the Harvard Lowell lectures of 1914 (with T. S. Eliot in the audience); *The Analysis of Mind*, given in Gordon Square in 1919; and "The Philosophy of Logical Atomism," delivered in London in 1918.

37 Leonard attended the previous week, finding Russell's lecture, Woolf reported, "interesting, though hard to follow. I hope to go next Tuesday, more to see the audience than to listen, I'm afraid" (*LettersVW*, II, 76). The series was "Principles of Social Reconstruction" (*CPBR*, 283), which she later read – "I've just finished Bertie upon Reconstruction" (*LettersVW*, II, 133). See Bishop, *Virginia Woolf Chronology*, 36.

38 Karin Costelloe's milieu "felt, far less than Lytton's generation, the influence of G. E. Moore," Quentin Bell writes (*VW*, I, 173). Of *The Misuse of Mind*, subtitled *A Study of Bergson's Attack on Intellectualism*, Leonard claimed "I happen to know that Mrs Woolf had not read that book" (*LettersLW*, 486). Neither Woolf nor Leonard liked Karin. See *LettersLW*, 220–1 and note, 581 and *LettersVW*, II, 76. Hers and Adrian's daughter Judith studied philosophy with Russell (*LettersLW*, 243).

39 Written to Apostle Henry Lamb, artist son of a mathematician. Russell recounts that "Karin read a paper in praise of Bergson to the

Aristotelian the other day – Moore and I attacked her with all imaginable ferocity, but she displayed undaunted courage" (*AutoBR*, 198).

40 Leonard Woolf claimed he "first met Whitehead" "through the Apostles." "Russell often used to come to Moore's room and discuss philosophical questions with him, but I do not remember ever seeing Whitehead there. My generation" respected him for *Principia Mathematica*, but "thought he went much too 'religious'" later (*LettersLW*, 540). Evelyn Whitbread, "ill again" (*MrsD*, 7), recalls Evelyn Whitehead, often a semi-invalid.

41 They "knew Wittgenstein," Leonard wrote, but not well, seeing "a certain amount of him" when he once stayed near them (*LettersLW*, 539). Woolf invokes in 1925 what Sydney-Turner "said to Wittgenstein . . . of the soul, and matter" (*LettersVW*, III, 212). In 1929, she reports Julian "says he tackled Maynard about Wittgenstein but was worsted," anticipating "the story tomorrow" (*LettersVW*, IV, 51). What Russell describes as "Clive Bell's son"'s "poems in heroic couplets against" Wittgenstein (*AutoBR*, I, 100–1) and Monk as his "Drydenesque satire," a "Bloomsbury riposte to . . . Wittgenstein's domineering, argumentative style," appeared in 1930 (*Wittgenstein*, 257). See von Wright, "Biographical Sketch," 12.

42 Perry Meisel operates with a conspiracy theory of the "matriarch of Bloomsbury"'s (*The Absent Father*, xii) refusal to "betray" her "silent borrowing" from her "intellectual paters," especially "bondage to Pater" (96). Woolf acknowledges her influences no less often than Russell, Wittgenstein or Meisel (for notions like "the anxiety of influence").

43 "Orlando" is, coincidentally, the pseudonym Russell chose for his "Self-Appreciation," published in 1897 (*CPBR*, I, 72).

44 Another example is Russell's reply "agnostic" to the warder's question about religion on arrival in prison (*Portraits from Memory*, 30). Stephen "made agnosticism a party name," Annan writes (*Godless Victorian*, 233), although it was Huxley's 1869 invention and still not current when Russell's warder "asked how to spell it, and remarked with a sigh: 'Well, there are many religions, but I suppose they all worship the same God'" (30). Moore too "remained 'a complete agnostic,'" Ayer writes (*Russell and Moore*, 138). *Why I am not a Christian* is Russell's agnostic's apology.

45 The *OED*'s first example is dated 1871; its second 1906. Stephen speaks (post-1882) of its being "contradictory to speak of sensations less than the *minima sensibilia* – the atomic ideas of which the sense world is constituted" ("Berkeley," 354). See also *CPBR*, IX, 264.

46 Russell's preparation for writing *The Problems of Philosophy* "may have taken him back to authors and issues which he had not thought about seriously since the 1890s," Hylton remarks (*Russell*, 362), and so to

A History of English Thought, for content and as a popular treatment of philosophy. Stephen's work, only minus Leibniz, resembles "the picture of the history of philosophy" Russell gives: "Descartes and Leibniz as Rationalists, Locke, Berkeley and Hume as Empiricists," along with Kant, "the canon of great modern philosophers that is still standard within the analytic tradition" (378, n. 63).

47 Although "the influence of his [Moore's] *Principia Ethica* on some of us was immense," Bell adds, it was "not on all" or "most." "I doubt whether either of the Miss Stephens gave much thought to the all important distinction between 'Good on the whole' and 'Good as a whole'" (*Old Friends*, 133). Adrian Stephen, "to be Virginia's chief companion" from 1907, declared Moore "a fraud," Quentin Bell writes (*VW*, I, 116). Clive Bell's comment about "the Greeks and Cretans" having "a poor reputation" for veracity (*Civilization*, 22) suggests a familiarity with Russell on the paradox of the liar (*IMT*, 62, fn).

Woolf mentions Russell twice in reconstructing "old Bloomsbury." In "the history of Bloomsbury," the chapter on Ottoline would include "Bertie Russell" (*MB*, 199). Queenie Leavis complains that the seriousness of Leslie Stephen et al. was "replaced by admiration for Russell's brittle intellect" (Bishop, *Virginia Woolf Chronology*, 38 fn.). "[T]he Bloomsbury set," Ayer more predictably thinks, "respected Russell as a philosopher but took Moore for their mentor" (*Russell and Moore*, 137).

48 To these two can be added Leonard Woolf's *Principia Politica*, postdating Woolf's death, evidence of the persisting emphasis on principles.

49 Writing from China to his aunt and mother that he was teaching Russell, Bell described it as "lecturing on all of you" (*Julian Bell*, 102).

50 McGuinness claims many of Wittgenstein's themes "were taken from the *Theory of Knowledge* manuscript" (*Wittgenstein*, 175). Blackwell likewise thinks "the Tractatus to be far more directed against Russell's philosophy than has been supposed" ("The Early Wittgenstein and the Middle Russell," 26–7).

51 Quentin Bell places Leonard among the "notable figures in the G. E. Moore *cénacle*" who "had received the gospel of *Principia Ethica* and regarded themselves as elect" (*VW*, I, 177). Russell and Leonard divide on Moore's nervous ticks. "'You,'" Russell told Woolf, "'said he had no complexes . . . Watch him putting his tongue round his mouth'" (*Diary*, II, 294). Leonard thought Moore "resembled Socrates," being "one of these divine 'sillies'" with "simple, unrestrained, passionate gestures . . . [A]t the crisis of an argument, . . . his tongue [would] shoot out of his mouth" (*Sowing*, 137).

52 Prescribing "Hume's Essays" as a "purge" for her images (*Diary*, II, 56), Woolf echoes Leonard's word "cathartic" of Moore's influence. But Leonard describes Moore's "mental constipation," qualifying each successive qualification to avoid falsity, making him "far from parsi-

monious" (*BeAg*, 25). Perhaps Woolf's statement "that only the most profound masters of style can tell the truth," but "a simple one-syllabled writer" is "without any doubt . . . lying" (*O*, 259) has Moore in mind. Feeling "shame at my own verbosity," she thought "[p]arsimony may be the end" of *Between the Acts* (*Diary* V, 352), making "the principle of parsimony" a stylistic imperative.

53 Russell is again like Stephen more than Moore in considering philosophy, as Passmore says, "continuous with social, psychological, physical, and mathematical investigation" (*Hundred Years*, 204). The Bloomsbury apolitical "attitude" Keynes traced to "Moore's own unworldliness" (Ayer, *Russell and Moore*, 137) was not Woolf's; she wrote essays on feminism, war and fascism, resembling in this her father and Russell.

54 Stephen also faults Berkeley, who "held slaves (Works, iv. 187)," for justifying his interests ("Berkeley," 351).

55 At their 1916 meeting, Woolf finds Moore "more human than his followers," notes "how they've copied him," but his greater "vigour" (*Letters VW*, II, 112). "He is a very great man, I think, so solid and direct: and not the least hard to talk to'" (*Letters VW*, II, 120). By 1920, she found "[a] lack of mass somewhere" and wondered "why he was the dominator and dictator of youth. Perhaps Cambridge is too much of a cave." She still admires his "innocency & shrewdness" without a "vestige of falsehood" (*Diary*, II, 49).

56 Ayer attributes to "the Bloomsbury circle" the "one time" Moore's "influence did extend to a wider circle" – it "did not divert him from the course of his quiet academic life." Passmore mentions his "influence on" Fry and Woolf (*Hundred Years*, 203, fn. 2).

57 Virginia Stephen probably first met "[t]he Bertram [sic] Russells" at lunch in 1905, finding it "amusing" (*A Passionate Apprentice*, 251; *MB*, 163). In 1908, she refused an invitation "to spend a week with the Russells," commenting to Vanessa, "[t]oo much elderly brilliance" and to Lytton "too elderly: I couldn't face it" (*Letters VW*, I, 351, 365). Later, "the Russells telegraphed on Monday to ask me to stay with them for four days, but as I had gone the telegram was returned" (*Letters VW*, I, 358). "Ought I to write to Mrs Russell?" she asks her sister. "I have never seen her." (Had she forgotten?) Woolf seemingly visited the Russells in January 1911 (*Letters VW*, I, 450). See also *Letters VW*, II, 115. We glimpse Virginia Stephen through Russell's eyes when he writes to Ottoline, anxious their liaison not become public, that Fry "'says the Stephens know,'" "'that Virginia is the dominant one among them, & that he impressed upon her . . . she must avoid even the slightest joke or gossip,'" and Russell through hers: "the argument" which Fry "'thought impressed her was that it might prevent my doing any work'" (Clark, *Life*, 143).

For Woolf, Russell was "Bertie" but Moore "Moore," following Bloomsbury's practice. Levy claims that in Moore's diaries, "only one other woman of his acquaintance . . . is referred to by Christian name" and that the two were "on more intimate terms than one would guess from the paucity of the mentions of each in the other's diaries." (*G. E. Moore*, 276).

58 This remark recalls Septimus' ravings about "the Toms and Berties in their starched shirt fronts oozing thick drops of vice," who "never saw him drawing pictures of them naked at their antics in his notebook" (*MrsD*, 135).

59 Lowe recounts how, "fearing that Russell would dance away with his ideas," Whitehead "refused to send Russell his notes for" *An Enquiry Concerning the Principles of Natural Knowledge.* Russell said this ended their collaboration (*Alfred North Whitehead*, I, 291). "Moore's and Russell's mutual influence" Levy pronounces "a vexed question" (*G. E. Moore*, 249), "[h]istorians of philosophy" being uncertain who had the greater influence on whom (132n).

60 "[A]gainst the solipsism of late-nineteenth-century idealism," Shusterman sees the "ally for [T. S.] Eliot's poetic cause" in the "external, definite, and independent reality . . . of Moore and Russell's successful modernist revolution in philosophy" (*T. S. Eliot*, 62–3). Eliot gives their agnostic Realism an alien certainty, however.

61 "Moore contends that God was right in maintaining" the newly created world "to be good," Russell teased at an Apostle's meeting – "it was already good in and for itself, and would have continued so even if God had not been looking" (Levy, *G. E. Moore*, 205).

62 Our project departs then from attempts like Hussey's to demonstrate that "[t]he Moorean universe, endorsed by such as Russell and Keynes, is continually questioned by the novels" (*Singing of the Real World*, 99) and to link Woolf to a philosophy outside her milieu.

63 Hintikka and Beer stress "the survival of the object without a perceiver" (Beer, "Hume, Stephen, and Elegy in *To the Lighthouse*," 78).

64 There is a sexual element in the "pleasure" Woolf describes in "this mind on springs" and the confidence inspired because "I wore my new black dress, & looked, I daresay, rather nice . . . So Bertie Russell was attentive" (*Diary*, I, 146–7).

65 Russell shared this assumption. "The generation of Keynes and Lytton" wanted, he wrote, "retirement among fine shades and nice feelings"; "the good" for them amounted to "the passionate mutual admirations of a clique of the elite," a doctrine "unfairly" "fathered" on Moore (*AutoBR*, I, 70–1).

66 Cf. Zwerdling's "perhaps the emphasis should fall on the word 'my'" (*Virginia Woolf*, 181).

2 THE GEOMETRY IN THE SENSIBLE WORLD: RUSSELL'S ANALYSIS OF MATTER

1 In "Apostolic jargon," Rosenbaum comments, an Apostle "is born into the Society and becomes real" and "people and things outside . . . are merely unreal"; "the code words 'real' and 'unreal' remained important for Bloomsbury" (*Victorian Bloomsbury*, 169).

2 Hintikka relates this passage to the unobserved ("Virginia Woolf," 6). A propos of the kitchen table, he adds, "The same problem [of the persistence of objects] reappears in *To the Lighthouse*" (13, n. 9).

3 Maxime Chastaing connects Woolf's philosopher to "[le] monisme neutre": "il ne croit pas plus . . . au matérialisme qu'à l'idéalisme, il se croit neutre," but finds that with "la formule . . . 'la table vue,'" he is "conduit aux thèses de Berkeley" and is led to "revivre l'odyssée de Russell" (*La Philosophie de Virginia Woolf*, 99).

4 Russell's "nominalisme méthodique," Vuillemin writes, never destroys "la réalité des relations" (*Leçons*, 265). Eames finds Russell's reduction of inferred entities had not "gone as far as nominalism" (*Bertrand Russell's Theory of Knowledge*, 193).

5 In "What is Materialism?" also, Stephen writes: "I know of this room and this table because I can see, touch, and grasp them" (140). John Bicknell points to it but wrongly claims that "unlike Ramsay's, Stephen's books are not about 'subject and object and the nature of reality'." See also Esch, "Think of a Kitchen Table."

6 Russell, *The Basic Writings of Bertrand Russell*, 35.

7 "If Woolf had opened Moore's book [*Philosophical Studies*, 1922] to the first page, she would have read, 'Chairs and tables and mountains seem to be very different from us,'" Erwin Steinberg claims ("G. E. Moore's Table and Chair," 164), quoting "The Refutation of Idealism," in Leonard's library.

8 Russell later writes that the distinction "to me historically was directed against idealism" (*Mind*, 142). See Fritz, *Bertrand Russell's Construction of the External World*, 115.

9 Is something like Moore's distinction in Stephen's "What Is Materialism?"? Materialists, he says, "find themselves logically bound to speak of a blue sensation instead of a sensation of blue," finding the "combination of words is without a meaning" (141–2). When the Idealist "thinks of 'yellow' and when he thinks of the 'sensation of yellow,'" Moore states, "he fails to see that there is anything whatever in the latter which is not in the former" (*Mind*, 442). Berkeley argues against some such distinction (*Three Dialogues*, 16). See Hirst, "Sensa," 407 and Ayer, *Bertrand Russell*, 69, on Moore's term "sense-datum."

10 Moore's lecture "Sense-Data" was delivered in London in December–January 1910–11, when Russell was writing *The Problems of Philosophy*. Woolf was then in London. On or before January 23, 1911, she went to

Russell's house from Oxford. See *Letters VW*, I, 450. She thus could either have heard the lectures or discussions of them.

11 Berkeley, *Three Dialogues Between Hylas and Philonous*, 35. Her father's copy of this text was in Woolf's library.

12 Hintikka insists that "sense-data were for Russell and Moore objectively existing entities" ("Virginia Woolf," 11). "In the light of the hindsight offered to us by the latest developments in epistemology and its logic," he goes on, "this objectivity of sense-data . . . appears fully justified." For, "sense-data are far too often dismissed . . . patronizingly by philosophers who could in reality learn a great deal from Russell and Moore" (11).

13 When Russell "counts sensibilia as physical," Mark Sainsbury concludes "they are not neutral" (*Russell*, 261). Yet they are already neutralized because also subjective. The issue is terminological for Sainsbury. See *BR*, 42, fn. 29, Ayer, *Bertrand Russell*, 114, Sainsbury, *Russell*, 268, Kilmister, *Russell*, 228–9 and Feigl, "Russell and Schlick," 325.

14 Terms of British philosophy, *private* and *privacy* conceivably originated with Russell. The *OED* Supplement records its earliest illustration of "private world" (without assigning it a philosophical meaning) from Aldous Huxley's *Crome Yellow* (126), whose Mr. Scogan caricatures Russell. Wittgenstein's "private language," which the *OED* Supplement first records in Anscombe's 1953 translation of *Philosophical Investigations*, doubtless derives from Russell. The phrase "private code" appears on *To the Lighthouse*'s first page.

15 Barry Gower has suggested to me the analogy between sensibilia and Mill's definition of matter as a "Permanent Possibility of sensation," an analogy Moore also makes. (Cf. "the Mill-Russell type" of view in Moore, *Philosophical Studies*, 224ff.) "The phrase became famous," Stephen comments (*The English Utilitarians*, III, 404). Stephen uses "potentialities of experience" (*HET*, 45). Hirst writes that "Hume himself toyed with the supposition that impressions might exist unobserved – that the gaps might be filled with unsensed sensa" ("Phenomenalism," 131).

16 Hintikka writes that "Virginia Woolf's emphasis on 'moments of being' has a neat counterpart in the importance of events in Whitehead's metaphysics" ("Virginia Woolf," 10).

17 Gilles Deleuze finds it "remarquable que l'analyse de Whitehead . . . semble tout à fait indépendente de celle de Leibniz" (Qu'est-ce qu'un Evénement?," *Le Pli*, 103–5). But Whitehead surely knew Leibniz, given Russell's 1900 dissertation.

18 Whitehead's "prehension," which Geach calls "the Cambridge philosophers' term of art" (*Truth, Love and Immortality*, 139), designates an "uncognitive apprehension," by analogy with Leibniz's perception and apperception. See Sherburne's glossary to *Process and Reality*, 235–6;

SMW, 67; Eames, *Bertrand Russell's Theory of Knowledge*, 59; *MyPhD*, 17; and Hintikka, "Virginia Woolf," 10.

19 Russell's metaphor recalls Fry's for the British public's exposure to African sculpture: "in the last sixty years, knowledge and perception have poured upon us so fast that the whole well-ordered system has been blown away, and we stand bare to the blast" (*V&D*, 99). Bloomsbury empiricism was exposure to raw uninterpreted reality.

20 Urmson insists on "the ease with which logical atomism seemed to fit in with the sense-datum theory" (*Philosophical Analysis*, 18).

21 In *The Voyage Out*, "Bennett . . . lived in an old windmill six miles out of Cambridge. He lived the perfect life, . . . caring only for the truth of things" (205). For about eight years beginning in 1899, Whitehead lived at the Mill House in Grantchester, "a place of gaiety to almost everyone except Bertie Russell," Lowe writes (*Alfred North Whitehead*, I, 207).

The name "Sandys" for the "barrister with a philosophic tendency" (*ND*, 64) who asks about Bennett's theory, is an anagram for (Arthur) Dakyns, a barrister who "was (so Russell said) the only person sympathetic to Russell's philosophy" (*LettersBR*, I, 434).

22 But see Ayer, *Russell and Moore*, 73.

23 "Moore's distinction between being and existence evolves" from "the Kantian distinction between noumena and phenomena which he advocates in his 1898 dissertation," Hylton observes (*Russell*, 131). See also Rosenbaum, *Victorian Bloomsbury*, 231. It is apparent in the Bradleyian title of *The Problems of Philosophy*'s first chapter, "Appearance and Reality." Clive Bell speaks of "what philosophers used to call 'the thing in itself'" (*Art*, 213); Orlando looks "at the thing itself" (*O*, 16–17).

24 See "On Denoting," *LK*, 41–56; *PP*, ch. 5; *ML*, 202–24; and *LK*, 127–74.

25 That Russell's argument was familiar in Bloomsbury is evidenced by Forster's observation à propos of the statement "the Emperor of Guatemala is dead" that "the Emperor cannot have died, because Guatemala is a Republic; and the Empress cannot be a widow, because she does not exist" (*Anonymity*, 20–1).

26 *Jacob's Room* associates naming with "Scott" and "Waverly": "'Waverly,' the villa on the road to Girton was called, not that Mr. Plummer admired Scott or would have chosen any name at all, but names are useful when you have to entertain undergraduates" (33).

27 "Facts are what we want," Woolf tells Russell (*Diary*, II, 294). In *The Novels of Virginia Woolf: Fact and Vision*, the one philosopher Alice van Buren Kelley mentions is the Moore of the ethics, finding it "a mistake to overemphasize the influence of philosophy" (2).

28 Pears thinks this "important but neglected passage" renders implausible "the commonly supposed" view that Russell "regarded all sense-data as simple particulars" ("Introduction," *The Philosophy of Logical Atomism*, 19). See also *TK*, 138, 161; and *PM*, 43. Hylton concludes Russell thinks "facts may be perceived" (348). But Russell distinguishes

"complex objects" from "complex facts," never saying the latter are perceived.

29 We can see Mrs. Ramsay's "the influence of something upon somebody" as a parody of Russell's skeletal form (*TL*, 22).

30 The term "scaffolding" occurs in *Tractatus* 6.124. Black comments: "*scaffolding* (Gerüst): this image also occurs at 3.42 (3), 4.023 (5). In both places W. talks of a 'logical scaffolding'" (*Companion*, 331).

31 See Black's discussion titled "The Impossibility of Representing Logical Form" (*Companion*, 188ff.).

32 The importance of "correlations" in Russell will emerge in the course of our exposition. Here T. S. Eliot's term "objective correlative" can be understood as a Russellian one.

33 Stephen, as Russell, no doubt found it in Berkeley's notion that "men combine together several ideas, apprehended by divers senses, or by the same sense at different times" but connected via "co-existence or succession" (*Three Dialogues*, 78). Hence, "this *cherry*" is "a congeries of sensible impressions . . . united in one thing (or have one name given them) by the mind" (81). An object approached from a distance is "a continued series of visible objects succeeding each other" (37).

3 THE WORLD SEEN WITHOUT THE SELF: WOOLF'S ANALYSIS OF MATTER

1 This pluralism could be seen in Woolf's "use of plurals" that Beer finds "recurrent" ("The Island and the Aeroplane," 281, 285).

2 Russell writes: "Leibniz held that monads do not interact, and that the fact of their continuing to mirror the same universe is to be explained by a pre-established harmony. This part of his doctrine is totally unacceptable. It is only through the causal action of the outer world upon us that we reflect the world in so far as we do reflect it" (*MyPhD*, 17).

3 The phrase "center of consciousness" comes from Henry James, acquaintance of the Stephens (*VW*, I, 32).

4 For DeSalvo, this conceptualization of childhood is a sign of pathology (*Virginia Woolf*, 125).

5 Hintikka writes that "Virginia Woolf's emphasis on 'moments of being' has a neat counterpart in the importance of events in Whitehead's metaphysics," connecting it to the "central role of space-time points" David Daiches discovers in Woolf. He sees "counterparts" also "in relativity theory," invoking Jean Guiguet's "apt phrase" – a Proustian one – "'Space and time regained'" ("Virginia Woolf," 9–10). See also Rosenbaum's observation that Woolf's moment was "static" and so unBergsonian ("Philosophical Realism," 19).

6 Among the sources from which the importance of the present in Russell's, Moore's and Whitehead's epistemology could have come to Woolf is

Leonard. In a letter of 1903, he describes going to see "the Yen," i.e., Moore; "about 11 Russell appeared," he writes, "& they tried to define 'the present' until 1. I was lost a thousand times" (*LettersLW*, 32).

7 Hafley is right to say that Moore's "states of mind" suggest Woolf's "moments of being," but too hasty in concluding that "the smallest amount of reflection makes evident a complete lack of correspondance between the two" (*The Glass Roof*, 5).

8 The connection was made by Yeats. "I listened," Spender recounts, "while Yeats" explained to Woolf "that her novel, *The Waves*?, expressed in fiction the idea of pulsations of energy throughout the universe" of "the modern theories of physicists" (*World Within World*, 164). Beer argues that in *The Waves* Woolf is "reappraising the world in the light of wave theory and the popular physics of Eddington and Jeans" ("The Island and the Aeroplane," 280). Pointz Hall's library in *Between the Acts* does, we saw, contain copies of their works. To them might be added Andrade's *The Structure of the Atom* (1923), reviewed by Russell in *The Nation and the Athenaeum* for Leonard Woolf (see *CPBR*, IX, 244), as well as Russell's *The ABC of Atoms.*

9 Beer claims "[w]ave theory disturbed the land-sea antinomies . . . Thresholds and boundaries lose definition" ("The Island and the Aeroplane," 279). But Russell comments that the "movement for making everything continuous" which culminated with Hertz, encountered "the discovery of the atomic structure of matter, and of the discrete structure of the atoms themselves" (*ABCR*, 74). Woolf will present the waves as obliterating appearances but maintaining the perspectives' boundaries.

10 Hence, English needs two verbs meaning "to know," one, like *connaître*, designating acquaintance and one, like *savoir*, knowledge by description (*PP*, 44).

11 Eames points to Russell's images of "the general view of the room which becomes specified," of "the object approaching through the fog" (*Bertrand Russell's Theory of Knowledge*, 58), all with a familiar Woolfian aura.

12 See Beer, "Hume, Stephen, and Elegy," 89.

13 See "The Lighthouse and the Searchlight" in Goldberg, *The Mirror and the Man.*

14 *Mrs. Dalloway*, on the analogy with *Ulysses*, confines the novel's action to a single June day on which is heard the tolling of clocks. Other possible influences of Joyce's novel on *Mrs. Dalloway* are the motor car with its unidentified passenger, recalling the viceregal carriage, and the "sirens" of the Solitary Traveller section.

15 Meisel finds this "a mixed metaphor," the fabric "woven together in an image 'irreconcilable' with the letter of 'welding'" (*The Absent Father*, 89). But Woolf imagines either a weaving frame, a canvas stretched on a

frame or the girders of a glass conservatory. The latter's source is Victorian architecture. Woolf recalls "the arch of glass burning at the end of Paddington Station" with "yellow and red" which "the iron girders made a pattern across" (*MB*, 93). A crystal palace with its "glass roof" (*W*, 72), it combines granite and rainbow.

16 Wittgenstein, in 1935, talks about an "entity which he then can't see, and it seems like a ghost," connecting it to "sense-data" or something "'intangible'" by contrast with "the chair or the table" (Monk, *Wittgenstein*, 355).

17 Woolf's image can be glossed by Moore's of consciousness as "extremely difficult to fix" (*PS*, 20), "transparent" (*PS*, 21), "diaphanous" (*PS*, 25) in "The Refutation of Idealism." Whiteley (*Knowledge and Experimental Realism*, 162) links Moore's statement to the passage in *Jacob's Room*, "We start transparent." Wittgenstein's "Thought is surrounded by a halo" could show the same influence (*Philosophical Investigations*, § 97). Tyndall had used the metaphor of the "vaporous envelope" of the photosphere and "the luminous envelope" which "[n]o human eye has ever seen" but theory had predicted (*Lectures on Light*, 157 and 166).

18 "Physical (she casts a shadow as no ghost can do), revenant, actual, unhaloed and unalloyed by symbol," Beer comments of Mrs. Ramsay in this passage ("Hume, Stephen, and Elegy, 86).

4 SOLUS IPSE, ALONE IN THE UNIVERSE

1 Clive Bell, *Proust*, 85. Perhaps Bloomsbury's preoccupation explains James Strachey's translation of Freud's "das Ich" by "ego," which Bruno Bettelheim criticized.

2 The question whether the cat was "born so, or had he lost his tail in an accident?" (*Room*, 13) resembles that Vanessa asks Virginia under the nursery table – "'Have black cats got tails?' she asked, and I said 'NO'" (*MB*, 78). Woolf comments that "'The others' were not brothers and sister, but beings possessed of knives, or enviable gifts for running or carving" (*MB*, 29).

"[A] cat without a tail" or "a Manx cat" illustrates the dangers of "'induction by simple enumeration'" which "[t]he man who argues that all cats he has seen have tails, therefore all cats have tails, is employing" (in Russell's *Scientific Outlook*, 68, a book cited in *Three Guineas*, 139, 186).

3 Seeing T. S. Eliot after working on *Jacob's Room* "cast shade upon" Woolf (*Diary*, II, 68).

4 The passage recalls Woolf finding Leonard's criticism of *Roger Fry* "like being pecked by a very hard strong beak" (*Diary*, V, 271). Hence her need to add to the passage in *A Room of One's Own* "[n]ot but what this

'I' was a most respectable 'I'; honest and logical," to claim to "respect and admire" it (*Room*, 103–4).

5 Quoted in Zwerdling, *Virginia Woolf*, 263. Zwerdling notes the passage's "suggestion of tumescence" (263). In Woolf's "Solid Objects," the male body is one such object: "nothing was so solid, so living, so hard, red, hirsute and virile as these two [men's] bodies" (*CSFVW*, 96). Objects in slanting light Woolf describes as "lengthened, swollen" (*W*, 208).

6 Stuart Hampshire uses the same vocabulary of Russell: he spoke "from within some hard and scaly carapace" ("Russell's Paradox," 10).

7 Writing to Clive Bell about reading Moore and "feeling ideas travelling to the remotest part of my brain, and setting up a feeble disturbance," Woolf's metaphor suggests philosophy's phallic foreignness: "It is almost a physical feeling, as though some little coil of my brain unvisited by any blood so far, and pale as wax, had got a little life into it at last; but had not a strength to keep it" (*Letters*, I, 357).

8 Herein lie the peculiar contradictions of Woolf's politics. She has no objections to revolutionary aims, but does to their means. Movements like suffragism involve "pleading for rights." Yet, until their ends are achieved, only a few "serene" minds can remain "unperturbed by scorn or censure." Woolf fears writing as Charles Tansley would. One can detect the fear that a woman of Woolf's class was reduced to the working-man's level – the dark side of Woolf's solidarity with "a working man, a negro" which her sex brought her to against her class.

9 A photograph Vanessa possessed showed her mother at a window (Spalding, *Vanessa Bell*, 153).

10 Woolf recalls never being with her mother without someone "always interrupting" (*MB*, 83).

11 Leslie Stephen "env[ied] men who can think consecutively under conditions distracting to others – in a crowded meeting or in the midst of their children" ("In Praise of Walking," 281).

12 Besides the St. Ives visitor botanist C. B. Clarke (*MB*, 74), Bankes before Lily Briscoe's canvas evokes Fry, botanist turned artist, before Vanessa's.

13 Leslie Stephen recalls the Cambridge mathematician "Wolstenholme, called 'the woolly' by you irreverent children" (*MBook*, 79). "The Woolly One," Woolf recalls also (*MB*, 73).

14 The name "Ramsay" was perhaps inspired by the philosopher Frank Ramsey, who Woolf met in 1923. She, like Quentin Bell in the biography, misspells his name "Ramsay," pronouncing him "a great mathematician" and "a true Apostle" (*Diary*, II, 231). See Moore's iterated "Mr Ramsey" in his 1927 Aristotelian Society paper "Facts and Propositions," on the proposition *p*, the relation *R*, etc. (*Philosophical Papers*, 60–88).

15 "Bertrand Russell has described the pleasure with which one used to watch Moore trying unsuccessfully to light his pipe when he was

arguing an important point," Leonard Woolf records (*Sowing*, 137). Edel claims as "evidence of Virginia Stephen's identification with her father" that "[s]he began to smoke a pipe a few weeks after his death," finding " 'it very soothing' " (*Bloomsbury*, 92).

16 The "two classes of men" echoes Leonard Woolf's "contrast between the two men and the two minds" of Moore and Russell. Russell's quickness of mind recalled a great chess player's: "he sees in a flash" in advance of others; "his conversation scintillates with wit" and "puckish humour." Their arguments were like "a race between the hare and the tortoise" where "often the tortoise won," which "was why Russell's thought had been so deeply influenced by Moore" (*Sowing*, 134).

17 Stephen's account is in "Hume," *DNB*, vol. 10; Strachey's in *Portraits in Miniature* and "Hume" (1928), reprinted in *The Shorter Strachey*, 79–85.

18 Russell had listed among the "doctrines of mysticism" "its belief that all evil is mere appearance" (*ML*, 10).

19 A common assumption is that Woolf thinks consciousness passive; see, e.g., Raymond Williams, *The English Novel*, 189.

20 Bazin argues Woolf's androgyny combines mania, a mystical state, with depression, its check (*Virginia Woolf*, 6). DeSalvo also sees Woolf alternating "periods of connection" and disconnection but denies the traumatic "moments of being" are "an expression of Woolf's philosophy about the nature of existence" (*Virginia Woolf*, 103).

21 Leslie Stephen also links thinking to city-walking, invoking "a distinguished person who composed his writings during such perambulations"; "the roar of the Strand" he considers "a more favourable environment than the quiet of my own study." Thoughts are "terribly hard to keep . . . in the track presented by logic. They jostle each other, and suddenly skip aside to make room for irrelevant and accidental neighbors." But "though a London street is full of distractions, they become so multitudinous that they neutralise each other" ("In Praise of Walking," 281–2). "Street Haunting" 's narrator is led to the Strand, like Katherine Hilbery, whose itinerary parallels her thinking: "should she walk on by the Strand or by the Embankment? It was not a simple question, for it concerned not different streets so much as different streams of thought" (*ND*, 270).

Another source for "Street Haunting" is Baudelaire's "The Painter of Modern Life," mentioned in Clive Bell's *An Account of French Painting* (183), which lists Woolf among Baudelaire's painter Constantin Guy's "benefactors" (185).

22 "Street Haunting," like *Mrs. Dalloway*, begins in the London streets and ends with a party in Mayfair on a June evening. See Daiches, "Le Londre de Virginia Woolf."

23 Clive Bell quotes Proust on the series of "I's" (*Proust*, 59–60).

24 Forster also believes "each mind has two personalities, one on the surface, one deeper down. The upper personality has a name" and "is

conscious and alert." The lower has "the force that makes for anonymity" (*Anonymity*, 16–17).

25 Spalding likens the photograph of the lost painting *Woman and Baby*, with "the faces hardly delineated," to the portraits of Virginia (*Vanessa Bell*, 125).

5 THE DUALISM OF DEATH

1 Russell gave Woolf an account of a brush with death: "The old poets were right. They made people think of death as going where they could not see the sun" (*Diary*, II, 293). The statement might gloss the lines from *A Winter's Tale*, "Fear no more the heat of the sun," which serve as a refrain in *Mrs. Dalloway*.

2 Cf. Abel, *Virginia Woolf*, 42.

3 "My father staggered from the bedroom," Woolf recounts of the morning of her mother's death, "I stretched out my arms to stop him, but he brushed past me, crying out something I could not catch; distraught" (*MB*, 91). So the arms that remained empty in life were Virginia Stephen's, and it was the father they tried to embrace. *In Memoriam*'s stanza 13, lines 1–4, reminiscent of Milton's Sonnet XXIII, is perhaps a source – "Tears of the widower, when he sees/A late-lost form that sleep reveals,/And moves his doubtful arms, and feels/Her place is empty."

4 Stephen recognizes the solipsism of sorrow: "the only real world is the world of intense gnawing pain" shutting out "brighter realities from outside" (*MBook*, 40).

6 FRY'S GRANITE AND RAINBOW: POST-IMPRESSIONISM AND IMPRESSIONISM

1 Added to 1929 edition of *OKnExW* (New York: New American Library), 90.

2 For Lawrence, Bertie's deficiency and, by extension, Cambridge philosophy's, is not the blindness Woolf and Fry criticize, but "visual consciousness" ("The Blind Man," 355).

3 Woolf "referred in her diary to her books as 'canvases,'" Torgovnick notes (*The Visual Arts*, 66).

4 See Rosenbaum on the term in Bloomsbury (*Victorian Bloomsbury*, 110).

5 See Antor, *The Bloomsbury Group*, 62. Fry found Mauron's "scientific work" marked his aesthetics (Introduction, *The Nature of Beauty in Art and Literature*, 6).

6 One is in the National Portrait Gallery, London (see figure 3). The other belongs to Philip Rieff. See Spalding, *Roger Fry*, 239.

7 Cf. also *ABCR*, 227 with *Tractatus* 4.0141.

8 So Woolf can enjoy fiction's formal properties "separately from any feeling of pity or pleasure aroused by the fortunes of the characters, as a blind man might enjoy the shape of a stone though unable to see its colour" (*CW*, 105). Mauron is the model. Blindness turned him to aesthetics, whose principles, as with science, did not require an "acquaintance" with paintings.
9 "'[E]verything is the proper stuff of fiction,'" Woolf echoes Fry (*CE*, II, 110)
10 Allen McLaurin finds "[i]n *To the Lighthouse*, 'white,' the absence of colour, symbolises" science. William Bankes seemed "clothed in a white scientific coat" (*Virginia Woolf*, 193).
11 Clive Bell distinguishes "[d]esign," "the organization of forms," from "drawing," their "shaping" (*Art*, 232), both translations of French *dessin*. For the quarrel's French history, see Lichtenstein, *La couleur eloquente*, 153–82.
12 Wittgenstein's remark c. 1946 that "Wisdom is grey" but "Life" is "full of colour" then uses Bloomsbury's language (*Culture and Value*, in Monk, (*Wittgenstein*, 490).
13 Woolf traces it to Leslie Stephen: "my natural love for beauty was checked by some ancestral dread," she says. "My father was spartan, ascetic, puritanical," with "no feeling for pictures; no ear for music; no sense of the sound of words" (*MB*, 68). Moore's *Principia* was Bloomsbury's revolt against this puritanism.
14 Moore's attack on "aesthetes" influenced Fry, Rosenbaum claims (*Victorian Bloomsbury*, 234). But Fry's anti-aestheticism could illustrate his anti-Moorism. *Principia Ethica*'s chapter "The Ideal," always cited as Bloomsbury's central philosophical influence, stresses "the cognition of really beautiful qualities" (194). Fry's "vision" is not of pre-existing beauty.
15 Woolf may have "The Waste Land" in mind.
16 At Constantinople, they "took art," Clive Bell writes, "in a rather too literary spirit" (*Art*, 134).
17 Elsewhere Woolf notes the effect of "the evening air which, already thinner, was taking the substance from leaves" (*TL*, 52); "the proportions of the landscape change" (*Diary*, III, 103).
18 Beer, "The Island and the Aeroplane," 272.
19 Fry's descriptions of Van Gogh's canvases – "all the forms appear to be quivering and rushing upward with a flame-like motion" (*TR*, 184) – recall Septimus' hallucinations: "leaves were alive; trees were alive" (*MrsD*, 32).
20 Hampshire pronounces Russell "not interested . . . in colors" ("Russell's Paradox," 10).
21 Fry's "plastic colour" resembles T. S. Eliot's Bradley-inspired formula of the "concrete" by contrast with the "abstract" universal.
22 Bradley, aiming to translate "this" and its "certainty of feeling" into

ideas, thought it impossible "*while still leaving that untransformed*" (*Essays*, 236).

23 Spalding, *Vanessa Bell*, 216. She adds: "'solidity' had become something of a catchword."

24 Spalding quotes Fry, that "Italian art is 'constructive,' modern and Dutch art is 'perceptive,'" commenting that for Fry "Italian naturalism" was not Impressionism's "passive, receptive approach," but showed "logical design" and "continuity" (*Roger Fry*, 70).

25 Fry, *Characteristics of French Art*, 145.

26 "Sonorous" here recalls Miss Marchmont's "philosophy that color is sound" (*JR*, 105).

27 See Twitchell, *Cézanne*, 15.

28 Fry, not Julia Stephen, provided the dish which transformed sense-data into art, writing to Woolf from St. Rémy: "I've made a boeuf en daube which is a dream" (*RF*, 283).

29 "Virtually all commentators," Matro writes, agree "that Lily's descriptions of her painting echo Roger Fry's formalist, postimpressionist aesthetic," citing Roberts, J. K. Johnstone, Sharon Wood Proudfit, McLaurin, Daiches, Bernard Blackstone, Glenn Pedersen, Ruby Cohn and Keith May ("Only Relations," 212).

30 Torgovnick connects "the Impressionists' fondness for series of paintings" to "the sequence of unfolding light" of *The Waves*' (*The Visual Arts*, 16).

31 The distinction between "the blue South or the grey North" (*CE*, II, 234) was a Bloomsbury one: "'There are two kinds of painting,'" Quentin Bell quotes Duncan Grant, "'the Northern and the Southern.'" "Foreword" to Collins, *The Omega Workshops*, vii. "[A] tradition which went back through Cézanne and Poussin, the High Renaissance, Piero della Francesca, Masaccio and Giotto to the walls of Byzantium," Bell claims, preserves "the old architectonic discipline" connected to geometry – Cézanne "assumed the existence of and still needs a cubic and rectilinear environment with vertical walls and horizontal floors . . . What I call 'Southern' art is, then, closely tied to architecture, whereas 'Northern' art, which grew up amidst coloured windows and darkened interiors, might find a congenial home within the pages of a book . . . in a volume with its own space and, it may be, its own world" (viii). Cézanne's landscapes have "the Mediterranean clarity" Forster invokes (*A Passage to India*, 295–6), the "sharp outlines . . . the landscapes of Greece afford," Russell associated with Greek philosophy (*Portraits from Memory*, 38). Flanked by India's lumpiness and England's muddle, by "life," stands "the beauty of form . . . without form, how can there be beauty? . . . it was part of the Mediterranean harmony" (313–14). "Mediterranean clarity" calmly contrasts with Indian life, logical form with sense-data. "The strong point of the English mind is its vigorous grasp of facts," Leslie Stephen wrote; "its

weakness is its comparative indifference to logical symmetry" (*HET*, 34). The English mind needed more sunshine.

Woolf too associates the Greek landscape with precision. To think of Sophocles in the English village, "we must annihilate the smoke and the damp and the thick wet mists. We must sharpen the lines of the hills. We must imagine a beauty of stone and earth rather than of woods and greenery" (*CE*, I, 2). Greece is the landscape of high noon. Woolf attributes the difference to "the climate." (Roland Barthes in *Sur Racine* conceives of Greek theatre similarly in terms of a stark landscape with intensity of sunlight.) The result contrasts the "out-of-doors manner" which is Greek to the "introspective melancholy of people accustomed to live more than half the year indoors," like the English (*CE*, I, 2). Northern art is the room of one's own, bathed in rainbow light, with, according to Bell, "the private quality of a great novel" (Collins, *The Omega Workshops*, viii). Woolf's espousal of Fry's aesthetic means her "modern fiction" includes more than the private room, has a grander architecture, containing both window and lighthouse, with the vast and vaulted spaces of "Time Passes" in between, an architecture based, like the Parthenon, on "a network of strokes" or "a mathematical diagram" (*JR*, 169). Woolf's description of a Vanessa Bell painting suggests this southern landscape: "The hill side is bare; the group of women is silent" (Rosenbaum, *The Bloomsbury Group*, 171). So does her description of the "sharp bare hills on the way to Olympia; and between them blue sea in triangular spaces" (*JR*, 141).

32 McLaurin comments of this passage, "Fry describes Seurat's landscapes in a way which could apply to Virginia Woolf's 'interludes'" (*Virginia Woolf*, 90; see also 92).

33 "To give so large a space to the consideration of the still-life paintings of this period may seem to demand apology – but it is hard to exaggerate their importance," Fry writes (*Cé*, 52). Torgovnick points to "[t]he window and the still life" as "motifs popular with artists like Vanessa Bell" which "also assume a special value in novels like *To the Lighthouse*" (*The Visual Arts*, 22). An example is Rose's bowl of fruit (*TL*, 146).

34 Wollheim emphasizes the philosophical implications of objects in T. S. Eliot ("Eliot and F. H. Bradley," 246).

35 Gillespie explores the analogy between V. Bell's landscapes and Woolf's descriptions (*The Sisters' Arts*, 268).

7 HOW DESCRIBE THE WORLD SEEN WITHOUT A SELF?

1 The argument is in *The Philosophical Investigations*. Russell wrote that "a logically perfect language" in "its vocabulary, would be very largely private to one speaker" (*LK*, 198). See Sainsbury, *Russell*, 40.

2 See Pears, "Introduction," 11.

3 See Urmson, *Philosophical Analysis*, 19 and Pears, *Bertrand Russell*, 46–7.

4 "Everything has a use, a meaning, is not an end in itself," Woolf complains of Lawrence (*CE*, I, 355).

5 Or an ordinary "proper name," John Searle writes, "refer[s] to the same object on different occasions" (*The Encyclopedia of Philosophy*, VI, 489).

6 See D'Aquila, *Bloomsbury and Modernism*, 225.

7 Torgovnick calls *The Waves*' "middle prologues" those "that correspond to the period of youth and personality development" (*The Visual Arts*, 132).

8 Russell, in the raptures of his romance with Ottoline, could speak of "the knowledge people believe themselves to possess of those with whom they are in love: the wall between different personalities seems to become transparent, and people think they see into another soul" (*PP*, 15).

9 Holroyd's questions echo philosopher Thomas Nagel's title "What Is It Like to be a Bat?," rather than describe Woolf's struggle to escape "the coiling meshes of her absorbed and tortured self-preoccupation" (*Lytton Strachey and the Bloomsbury Group*, 24) to achieve "resurrection through patricide by *felo de se*" (25). Holroyd reserves for Woolf his most purple prose, replacing biography with feuilleton, psychoanalysis with gothic soap-opera. She was "like an intelligent dog," "her nature was perpetually clogged with morbid self-obsession," etc. (23).

10 The distance between "Whittaker in his lodging-house" and "Lady Charles at the Manor" is also one of class.

11 For a complete account of the style, see my *Unspeakable Sentences*. Marguerite Lips' *Le Style Indirect Libre* (Paris: Payot) appeared in 1926. Woolf spoke of "oratio obliqua" in 1926; Bell in 1929.

12 See Banfield, *Unspeakable Sentences*, 94–5.

13 Russell composes such a sentence in a brief "story of adventure": " 'At this moment a blinding flash of lightning rent the air' " (*OKnExW*, 122).

14 See my "Describing the Unobserved: Events Grouped around an Empty Center."

15 Hintikka finds "a close analogue [of unperceived perspectives] in Virginia Woolf," who constructs . . . the world she is creating from the experiences of various characters" and in "passages which do not describe the impressions of any character," because there are "no fictional persons present who could have witnessed what is being described" ("Virginia Woolf," 10).

16 Chapter nine of Nicod's *La Géométrie dans le monde sensible*.

17 "All lives directly she [Julia Stephen] crossed them seemed to form themselves into a pattern," Woolf writes of her mother (*MB*, 35); she kept "that comprehensive view of the final proportions of things" (*MB*, 39).

18 See *TR*, 183, McLaurin, *Virginia Woolf*, 84 and Roberts, "Vision and Design," 842.

19 Fry's "états d'âme" link Moore's "states of mind," Russellian perspectives and novelistic point of view.
20 Rosenbaum, *The Bloomsbury Group*, 172.
21 Hintikka connects Russell's construction of "our common public world out of materials which included private worlds populated by sense-data," where "the true reality of a Russellian universe" might appear "immaterial and subjective," with "Virginia Woolf's emphasis on the inner world of consciousness" ("Virginia Woolf," 11).
22 "People, like Arnold Bennett, say I cant create, or didn't in *J's R*, characters that survive," Woolf writes. But "character is dissipated into shreds now" (*Diary*, II, 248).
23 "Russell did not remember . . . faces," Hampshire writes, saying "he remembered people by committing to memory a verbal description of them" ("Russell's Paradox," 10). The process resembles the analysis of names into descriptions.
24 Rantavaara calls *Jacob's Room* "an experimental attempt," reminiscent "of Bertrand Russell's theory that man is nothing but a series of distinct and separate events" (*Virginia Woolf*, 100–1).
25 In "No, it could not be a straw-bordered underwing" (*JR*, 23–4), the modal's shifted tense and the exclamation "no" indicate represented thought.
26 Patrick J. Whiteley calls Jacob "the Protagonist as Cipher" (*Knowledge and Experimental Realism*, 155). Torgovnick speaks of Woolf's "portrait of Mrs. Ramsay . . . through many different eyes" composing "the novel . . . around an absent center" (*The Visual Arts*, 120).
27 George Meredith's Vernon Whitford in *The Egoist* is the "other portrait" of Leslie Stephen beside Mr. Ramsay, according to Annan (*Godless Victorian*, 130).
28 "[I]f I were a solipsist, I should have to suppose that I had composed the works of Shakespeare and Newton and Einstein, since they have entered into my experience. Seeing how much better they are than my own books, and how much less labor they have cost me, I have been foolish to spend so much time composing with the pen rather than with the eye," Russell writes (*Matter*, 201).
29 Thus, the essay "Does History consist of the Biographies of Great Men?" on Jacob's table at Trinity combines Stephen and Russell (*JR*, 39).
30 There is another figure presenting form, alternatively, as a fusion: Fry's "crystallization." See my "Time Passes: Virginia Woolf, Post-Impressionism and Cambridge Time," forthcoming. Cf. also Matro, "Only Relations," 214 and Corner, "Mysticism and Atheism," 410–13.
31 After quoting Leonard Woolf in his *Proust*, Clive Bell writes: "A lady [Woolf?] once compared the individual as conceived by Proust with a cloud of midges" (63). A "passion" can "blow" the cloud "in all directions" to "re-form again in an entirely new shape." Proust's dependent clauses go "higgledy-piggledy like a flock of feeding starlings" (23).

32 See Matro, "Only Relations," 216 and Miller, "Mr. Carmichael," 188.

33 See Beer, "The Island and the Aeroplane," 285.

34 J. Hillis Miller's questions – "who is the narrator of *To the Lighthouse*? Where is she, he or it located?" – presuppose the concept to be justified. Its "extraordinary powers" are those of the author herself ("Mr. Carmichael," 172–3). Miller's narrator is explicitly "the Prime Mover" (180), all-present or "ubiquitous" (169), "truly omniscient, a fictional replacement of God" (180).

35 Hintikka, citing Auerbach's "Who is speaking," thinks Woolf's technique "to write, not from the viewpoint of any of her characters and yet not as an omniscient author-authority," uses " 'possible observers' not exemplified by any actual person in the story" and "is a writer's counterpart to Russell's use of possible perspectives" ("Virginia Woolf," 10).

36 "Newspapers are for the most part anonymous" as well, but Forster thought they ought not to be (*Anonymity*, 21).

37 Zwerdling finds Fry's statement betrays an unresolved conflict with his father (*Virginia Woolf*, 204).

38 "Most of her later novels are narrated by what she has called a 'nameless spirit,' " Naremore writes (*The World Without a Self*, 76). Torgovnick thus misinterprets Fry's phrase "nameless savages" as insidious, denying that "[t]he Western tradition" ever "confuse[s] the state of anonymity with that of being nameless" (*Gone Primitive*, 90).

39 The question is Miller's in "Mr. Carmichael and Lily Briscoe," 183. Miller reattaches the "impersonal mind for which the narrator speaks" ("Virginia Woolf's All Souls' Day," 107) to one named, sexed person. Against all evidence, "he" is male, "covertly embodied in the person of Augustus Carmichael" ("Mr. Carmichael," 177), to be collapsed androgynously with Mary Carmichael (184). Miller's evidence is the "fact that Mr. Carmichael, almost alone" of the novel's characters, is not "presented from the inside" via "indirect discourse" (171). But *Jacob's Room*, Woolf's novel with an explicit narrator, a woman, almost never represents Jacob's subjectivity (see note 25 above). "Here then was I, (call me Mary Beton, Mary Seton, Mary Carmichael or by any name you please – it is not a matter of any importance)" (*Room*, 5). Names from the Child ballad, they make "I" everywoman. (See Abel, *Virginia Woolf*, 88.) Miller reattaches "I" to the family tree, every Bloomsbury biography's obligatory first page, making Augustus Carmichael Mary Carmichael's father ("Mr. Carmichael," 184). Hence, "the characters" are "possessed," even "violated" by Miller's narrator ("Virginia Woolf's All Souls' Day," 102).

40 Zwerdling sees Woolf's espousal of anonymity exchanged in the thirties for "more directly expressive" forms like the diary or memoir (*Virginia Woolf*, 267–9). But the late *Three Guineas* is Woolf's strongest attack on (male) egotism. Its "society of outsiders" consists of nameless women. *Between the Acts*' author/playwright is the vanishing artist *par excellence.*

41 The phrase is Miller's in "Mr. Carmichael," 181.
42 Beer's formulation is close: "The material world is here sustained by . . . a kind of writing which deliberately obliterates any suggestion of a single perceiver" ("Hume, Stephen, and Elegy," 85).
43 See my "Tragic Time."
44 Her exaggeration is Mrs. Ramsay's, "looking for her spectacle case": " 'I lose thousands every summer.' " Mr. Tansley is "afraid to sanction such exaggeration" (*TL*, 293). But she corrects herself: "it did her husband good to be three thousand, or if she must be accurate, three hundred miles" away (*TL*, 43). *To the Lighthouse*'s Aunt Camilla (*TL*, 102) recalls Anny Thackery, as does *Between the Acts*'s Mrs. Swithin, who claims the sea was "a hundred miles away," "no, perhaps a hundred and fifty" (28). "Thirty-five only," Bart set things right, playing Leslie Stephen to her Anny, "as if he had whipped a tape measure from his pocket" (29).
45 Hampshire finds that Russell's "was a fully punctuated style and the firm full stops could always be heard in his talk: no Proustian channels and rivulets and no Jamesian coils were allowed" ("Russell's Paradox," 8–10).

8 THE MODERN ELEGY

1 "Fry once called such followers of Moore as Leonard Woolf mystics (VW/*RF* [Roger Fry], 270)," Rosenbaum writes. (*Victorian Bloomsbury*, 229–30). See also Fleishman, "Woolf and McTaggart," 167.
2 Feelings might include those "oceanic feelings" Freud attributes to the same Romain Rolland Fry mentions to Woolf (*LettersRF*, II, 525–6) and disavows in *Civilization and Its Discontents*, published with Hogarth in 1930, one year before *The Waves*.
3 See also Mauron, *Art and Literature*, 53.
4 Woolf has been made "into a mystic who denied empiricism and the reality of the everyday world" with perhaps some basis "in her works," Hintikka writes. But "one can raise similar questions about Russell the early epistemologist" ("Virginia Woolf," 11). "Whatever of prophecy or mysticism there may be in . . . Woolf" Ulysses L. D'Acquila finds "tempered and balanced by the analytic vigor and clear-eyed skepticism . . . of the Moore legacy" (*Bloomsbury and Modernism*, 220).
5 The phrase comes from Santayana's *Scepticism and Animal Faith*. See *SO*, 80 and Whitehead, *Symbolism*, 28.
6 In McGuinness, "The Mysticism of the *Tractatus*," 312–13.
7 "I had felt in his book a flavour of mysticism, but was astonished when I found that he had become a complete mystic," Russell writes to Ottoline (McGuinness, *Wittgenstein*, 279).
8 See Sherburne on Whitehead's "bare 'it' " (*Key*, 61).
9 Dreams persist in the unconscious of those once children, e.g., part three's Cam and James, put to bed by their mother in part one. *To the*

Lighthouse, operating for Woolf like psychoanalysis, reveals the parental figures internalized as personified repressive forces are an impersonal reality. Hence, Miller's claim that "Time Passes"' personifications show the narrative voice is not "so impersonal" ("Mr. Carmichael," 181) because "[w]herever there is language there will be personality" (182) accepts the phantasy Woolf exposes.

10 Russell's "logical fictions" do not imply "creations of the mind," Fritz writes (*Bertrand Russell's Construction*, 217) nor "that we only pretend that they exist," Pears says (*Bertrand Russell*, 38).

11 Beer derives Woolf's use of "fiction" from Jeans' *The Mysterious Universe* to the effect that "'the waves which form the universe, are in all probability fictitious . . . they exist in our minds'" ("The Island and the Aeroplane," 280). Russell's response is that "the physicist" is "like the Mad Hatter," claiming "the waves are in his formulae, and his formulae are in his head, from which, however, you must not infer that the waves are in his head" (*SO*, 95). See Russell's attack on Eddington and Jeans in this text, as well as Wittgenstein on Jeans' "worship" of science (Monk, *Wittgenstein*, 404, 416) and the idolatry of Jean's title *Mysterious Universe.* See also Jacques Bouveresse, *Wittgenstein*, 63.

12 Wittgenstein "loathed Russell's popular works," writes Monk: "*The Conquest of Happiness* was a 'vomative'" (*Wittgenstein*, 294). "A Free Man's Worship"'s "tone" Russell attributes to "the editor begg[ing] me to make the article 'as romantic as possible.'" Its Spinoza-inspired title (which *CPBR*, XII, 64 calls "conjectural") perhaps came from Russell's reading of Spinoza with Ottoline Morrell (see *HWP*, 581 and Rosenbaum, *Victorian Bloomsbury*, 285–6). Wittgenstein's reaction could betray a jealousy of the intellectual woman, rival for Russell's time. Monk cites Frances Partridge's contrast of Wittgenstein's inability "to discuss serious matters with members of the opposite sex" with the conversation of "the Bells, Stracheys and Stephens" (*Wittgenstein*, 256).

T. S. Eliot complains of "a modern emotional attitude" whose "most sentimental expression" is *A Free Man's Worship*" ("The Modern Mind," 134), criticizing Russell's "bad Prose" in "Style and Thought," his anonymous review of *Mysticism and Logic* (its "best review," Russell said [*CPBR*, XII, 62, Wood, *Bertrand Russell*, 94–5]). According to W. W. Robson, "Eliot's real target here is modern secularist religiosity" ("A Poet's Notebook," 156). For Fry's position, see *RF*, 118–19.

13 Rosenbaum invokes Leonard Woolf's "secular but not modernist" undergraduate paper on mysticism (*Victorian Bloomsbury*, 132). Fry's hostility to a mysticism Leonard defends to him and Leonard's critical "pecking" at Woolf's biography of Fry, her suspicion of Leonard's "persisting for some deep reason – disympathy with R?" (*Diary*, V, 271), suggest some rivalry Leonard felt toward Fry.

Bibliography

Abel, Elizabeth, *Virginia Woolf and the Fictions of Psychoanalysis* (Chicago: The University of Chicago Press, 1989).
Annan, Noel, *Leslie Stephen: The Godless Victorian* (London: Weidenfeld & Nicolson, 1984).
Leslie Stephen: His Thought and Character in Relation to his Time (London: MacGibbon & Kee, 1951).
Antor, Heinz, *The Bloomsbury Group: Its Philosophy, Aesthetics, and Literary Achievement* (Heidelberg: Carl Winter, Universitätsverlag, 1986).
Auerbach, Erich, *Mimesis: The Representation of Reality in Western Literature* (Princeton: Princeton University Press, 1953).
Ayer, A. J., *Bertrand Russell* (New York: The Viking Press, Inc., 1972).
Russell and Moore: The Analytical Heritage (London: Macmillan, 1971).
Banfield, Ann, "Describing the Unobserved: Events Grouped around an Empty Center," in *The Linguistics of Writing*, Nigel Fabb, Derek Attridge, Alan Durant and Colin MacCabe (eds.) (Manchester: Manchester University Press, 1987), 265–85.
"Tragic Time: the Problem of the Future in Cambridge philosophy and *To the Lighthouse*," *Modernism/Modernity*, 7 (Winter 2000), 43–75.
Unspeakable Sentences: Narration and Representation in the Language of Fiction (London: Routledge & Kegan Paul, 1982).
Barthes, Roland, *Sur Racine* (Paris: Seuil, 1963).
Baudelaire, Charles, "The Painter of Modern Life," in *Baudelaire: Selected Writings on Art & Artists*, P. E. Charvet (trans.) (Cambridge: Cambridge University Press, 1972), 390–435.
Bazin, Nancy Topping, *Virginia Woolf and the Androgynous Vision* (New Brunswick: Rutgers University Press, 1973).
Beckett, Samuel, *Three Novels* (New York: Grove Press, 1965).
Beer, Gillian, "Hume, Stephen, and Elegy in *To the Lighthouse*," in *Virginia Woolf's To the Lighthouse*, Harold Bloom (ed.) (New York: Chelsea House, 1988), 75–93.
"The Island and the Aeroplane: The Case of Virginia Woolf," in *Nation and Narration*, Homi K. Bhabha (ed.) (London: Routledge, 1990,) 265–90.
"The Victorians in Virginia Woolf: 1832–1941," *Arguing with the Past: Essays in Narrative from Woolf to Sidney* (London and New York, 1989), 138–58.

Bell, Clive, *An Account of French Painting* (London: Chatto & Windus, 1932).
Art (London: Chatto & Windus, 1914 [1931]).
Civilization: An Essay (London: Chatto & Windus, 1914 [1928]).
Old Friends: Personal Recollections (London: Chatto & Windus, 1956).
Proust (New York: Harcourt Brace and Company, 1929).
Bell, Julian, *Julian Bell: Essays, Poems and Letters*, Quentin Bell (ed.) (London: The Hogarth Press, 1938).
Bell, Quentin, *Bloomsbury* (London: Weidenfeld & Nicolson, 1966).
Virginia Woolf: A Biography, 2 vols. San Diego: Harcourt Brace Jovanovich, 1972).
Bergson, Henri, *Time and Free Will: An Essay on the Immediate Data of Consciousness* (New York: Harper & Row, 1960).
Berkeley, George, *Three Dialogues Between Hylas and Philonous*, (Robert Merrihew Adams (ed.) (Indianapolis: Hackett Publishing Company, 1979).
Bicknell, John W., "Mr Ramsay was Young Once," in *Virginia Woolf and Bloomsbury: A Centenary Celebration*, Jane Marcus (ed.) (Bloomington: Indiana University Press, 1987), 52–67.
Bishop, Edward, *A Virginia Woolf Chronology*, (Basingstoke: Macmillan, 1989).
Black, Max, *A Companion to Wittgenstein's "Tractatus"* (Ithaca: Cornell University Press, 1964).
Blackwell, Kenneth, "The Early Wittgenstein and the Middle Russell," in *Perspectives on the Philosophy of Wittgenstein*, Irving Block (ed.) (Oxford: Basil Blackwell, 1981), 1–30.
"Our Knowledge of *Our Knowledge*," in *Russell*, 12: 11–13.
Bouveresse, Jacques, *Wittgenstein: La Rime et la Raison: Science, Ethique et Esthétique* (Paris: Minuit, 1973).
Bradley, F. H., *Appearance and Reality: a Metaphysical Essay* (London: Oxford University Press, 1893 [1989]).
Essays on Truth and Reality (Oxford: Clarendon Press, 1914).
The Principles of Logic, vol. II (London: Oxford University Press, 1922).
Brenan, Gerald, *South From Grenada* (New York: Farrar, Straus and Cudahy, 1957).
Broad, C. D., *Scientific Thought* (London: K. Paul, Trench, Trubner & Co., 1923).
Catalogue of Books from The Library of Leonard and Virginia Woolf taken from Monks House, Rodmell, Sussex and 24 Victoria Square, London, and now in the possession of Washington State University, Pullman, U.S.A. (Brighton: Holleyman & Treacher Ltd., 1975).
Chastaing, Maxime, *La Philosophie de Virginia Woolf* (Paris: Presses Universitaires de France, 1951).
Clark, Ronald, *The Life of Bertrand Russell* (London: Jonathan Cape and Weidenfeld & Nicolson, 1975).
Collins, Judith, *The Omega Workshops* (Chicago: The University of Chicago Press, 1984).

Corner, Martin, "Mysticism and Atheism in *To the Lighthouse*," *Studies in the North*, 13:4 (Winter, 1981), 408–23.

Daiches, David, "Le Londre de Virginia Woolf," *Virginia Woolf et le Groupe de Bloomsbury*, Colloque de Cérisy, Union Générale des Editions, 1977), 83–112.

D'Aquila, Ulysses L., *Bloomsbury and Modernism* (New York: Peter Lang, 1989).

Darroch, Sandra Jobson, *Ottoline: The Life of Lady Ottoline Morrell* (New York: Coward, McCann & Geoghegan, Inc., 1975).

Davis, John B., *Keynes's Philosophical Development* (Cambridge: Cambridge University Press, 1994).

Delattre, Floris, *Le Roman Psychologique de Virginia Woolf* (Paris: Vrin, 1932).

Deleuze, Gilles, *Cinema 1: The Movement-Image* (Minneapolis: University of Minnesota Press, 1986).

Le Pli: Leibniz et le Baroque (Paris: Minuit, 1988).

DeSalvo, Louise, *Virginia Woolf: The Impact of Childhood Sexual Abuse on her Life and Work* (Boston: Beacon Press, 1989).

Dowling, David, *Bloomsbury Aesthetics and the Novels of Forster and Woolf* (London: Macmillan, 1985).

Dummett, Michael, *Les Origines de la Philosophie Analytique* (Paris: Gallimard, 1991).

Eames, Elizabeth Ramsden, *Bertrand Russell's Theory of Knowledge* (New York: George Braziller, 1969).

Edel, Leon, *Bloomsbury: A House of Lions* (Philadelphia: J. B. Lippincott Company, 1979).

Einstein, Albert, "Remarks on Bertrand Russell's Theory of Knowledge," *The Philosophy of Bertrand Russell*, Paul Schilpp (ed.) (New York: Harper, 1946), 277–91.

Eliot, T. S., *Knowledge and Experience in the Philosophy of F. H. Bradley* (New York: Columbia University Press, 1989).

The Letters of T. S. Eliot, Vol. 1, 1898–1922, Valerie Eliot (ed.) (London: Faber and Faber, 1988).

"The Modern Mind," in *The Use of Poetry and the Use of Criticism: Studies in the Relation of Criticism to Poetry in England* (London: Faber and Faber Limited, 1933, [1948]).

Selected Essays (London: Faber and Faber, 1932).

"Style and Thought," *Nation*, XXII: 25 (23 March 1918), 768–9.

Esch, Deborah, "'Think of a Kitchen Table': Hume, Woolf, and the Translation of Example," in *Literature as Philosophy/Philosophy as Literature*, Donald G. Marshall (ed.) (Iowa City: University of Iowa Press, 1987), 262–76.

Evans, Gareth, *The Varieties of Reference*, John McDowell (ed.) (Oxford: Clarendon Press, 1982).

Feigl, Herbert, "Russell and Schlick: A Remarkable Agreement on a Monistic Solution of the Mind-Body Problem," *Bertrand Russell*

Memorial Volume, George W. Roberts (ed.) (London: George Allen & Unwin; New York: Humanities Press, 1979).
Finch, Henry Leroy, *Wittgenstein – The Early Philosophy: An Exposition of the "Tractatus"* (New York: Humanities Press, 1971).
Fishman, Solomon, *The Interpretation of Art: Essays on the Art Criticism of John Ruskin, Walter Pater, Clive Bell, Roger Fry and Herbert Read* (Berkeley: University of California Press, 1963).
Fleishman, Avrom, "Woolf and McTaggart," in *Fiction and the Ways of Knowing* (Austin: University of Texas Press, 1978), 163–178.
Forster, E. M., *Anonymity: An Enquiry* (London: The Hogarth Press, 1925 [1954]).
Aspects of the Novel (New York: Harcourt, Brace and Company, 1927).
The Longest Journey (New York: Random House, 1922 [1962]).
A Passage to India (San Diego: Harcourt Brace Jovanovich, 1924 [1952]).
Where Angels Fear To Tread (New York: Random House, 1920).
Foucault, Michel, "How Much Does It Cost for Reason to Tell the Truth," *Foucault Live (Interviews, 1966–84)*, John Johnson (trans.), Sylvère Lotringer (ed.) (New York: Semiotext(e) Foreign Agents Series, 1989).
The Order of Things: An Archaeology of the Human Sciences (New York: Random House, 1970).
Freud, Sigmund, *Civilization and Its Discontents* (New York: W. W. Norton & Company, 1961).
Fritz, Charles A., Jr., *Bertrand Russell's Construction of the External World* (London: Routledge & Kegan Paul Ltd., 1952).
Fry, Roger, *The Artist and Psychoanalysis*, published by Leonard and Virginia Woolf (London: The Hogarth Press, 1924).
Cézanne: A Study of His Development (New York: Macmillan, 1927).
Characteristics of French Art (New York: Brentano's, 1933).
"The Courtauld Fund," *The Nation and the Athendeum* (30 January 1926), 613–14.
Henri-Matisse (New York: E. Weyhe, 1935).
Last Lectures (New York: The Macmillan Company, 1939).
"The Last Phase of Impressionism," *Post-Impressionists in England: The Critical Reception*, J. B. Bullen (ed.) (Routledge: London, 1988), 45–8.
Letters of Roger Fry, 2 vols., Denys Sutton (ed.) (London: Chatto & Windus, 1972).
Some Poems by Mallarmé (London: Chatto & Windus, 1936).
Transformations: Critical and Speculative Essays on Art (London: Chatto & Windus, 1926).
Vision and Design (London: Chatto & Windus, 1920).
Geach, Peter, *Truth, Love and Immortality: An Introduction to McTaggart's Philosophy* (Berkeley: University of California Press, 1979).
Gillespie, Diane Filby, *The Sisters' Arts: The Writing and Painting of Virginia Woolf and Vanessa Bell* (Syracuse: Syracuse University Press, 1988).

Goldberg, Benjamin, *The Mirror and Man* (Charlottesville: The University of Virginia Press, 1985).
Gouhier, Henri, "Introduction" to *Henri Bergson: Oeuvres* (Paris: Presses Universitaires de France, 1959).
Griffin, Nicholas, *Russell's Idealist Apprenticeship* (Oxford: Clarendon Press, 1991).
Grosskurth, Phyllis, *Leslie Stephen* (Harlow, Essex: Longmans, Green & Co., 1968).
Hafley, James, *The Glass Roof: Virginia Woolf as Novelist* (New York: Russell & Russell, Inc., 1963).
Hampshire, Stuart, "Russell's Paradox," in *The New York Review of Books*, 13 August 1992, 7–10.
Hawthorn, Jeremy, *Virginia Woolf's Mrs. Dalloway* (London, Sussex University Press, 1975).
Heidegger, Martin, "Language," *Poetry, Language, Thought* (New York: Harper & Row, 1971), 189–210.
Hintikka, Jaakko, "Virginia Woolf and Our Knowledge of the External World," *Journal of Aesthetics and Art Criticism*, 38 (Fall, 1979–80), 5–14.
Hirst, R. J., "Phenomenalism," in *The Encyclopedia of Philosophy*, vol. 6 (New York: Macmillan Publishing Co., Inc., 1967), 130–5.
"Sensa" in *The Encyclopedia of Philosophy*, vol. 7, 407–15).
Holroyd, Michael, *Lytton Strachey: A Biography* (Harmondsworth, Middlesex: Penguin, 1967).
Lytton Strachey and the Bloomsbury Group: His Work, Their Influence (Harmondsworth, Middlesex: Penguin, 1971).
Hume, David, "Of Suicide," in *Dialogues Concerning Natural Religion and the Posthumous Essays*, Richard Popkin (ed.) (Indianapolis: Hackett, 1980), 97–105.
A Treatise of Human Nature, L.A. Selby-Bigge (ed.) (Oxford: Clarendon Press, 1975).
Hussey, Mark, *The Singing of the Real World: The Philosophy of Virginia Woolf's Fiction* (Columbus: Ohio State University Press, 1986).
Hutcheon, Linda, *Formalism and the Freudian Aesthetic: The Example of Charles Mauron* (Cambridge: Cambridge University Press, 1984).
Huxley, Aldous, *Crome Yellow* (New York: Harper and Row, 1922).
Hylton, Peter, *Russell, Idealism and the Emergence of Analytic Philosophy* (Oxford: The Clarendon Press, 1990).
Jacob, Pierre (ed.), *De Vienne à Cambridge: l'héritage du positivisme logique* (Paris: Gallimard, 1980).
Jager, Ronald, *The Development of Bertrand Russell's Philosophy* (London: George Allen & Unwin Ltd.; New York: Humanities Press, 1972).
James, Henry, *What Maisie Knew* (London: Penguin, 1966).
Janik, Allan and Toulmin, Stephen, *Wittgenstein's Vienna* (New York: Simon and Schuster, 1973).

Jeans, James, *The Mysterious Universe* (Cambridge: Cambridge University Press, 1930).

Joyce, James, *Dubliners* (New York: Viking Press, 1967).

Joyce's Notes and Early Drafts for Ulysses: Selections from the Buffalo Collection, Philip F. Herring (ed.) (Charlottesville: University Press of Virginia, 1977).

Kelley, Alice van Buren, *The Novels of Virginia Woolf: Fact and Vision* (Chicago & London: Chicago University Press, 1973).

Kemp, Sandra, "'But How Describe a World Seen Without a Self?' Feminism, Fiction and Modernism," *Critical Quarterly*, 32:1 (Spring 1990), 99–118.

Kenner, Hugh, "Bradley," *The Invisible Poet: T. S. Eliot* (New York: Ivan Obolensky, 1959), 40–69.

Kenny, Anthony, *Wittgenstein* (Cambridge, MA: Harvard University Press, 1973).

Keynes, John Maynard, *Treatise on Probability* (1921), *The Collected Writings of John Maynard Keynes* vol. 8 (London: Macmillan, 1976).

Kilmister, C. W., *Russell* (New York: St. Martin's Press, 1984).

Lawrence, D. H., "The Blind Man," *The Complete Short Stories of D. H. Lawrence*, vol. 2 (New York: Viking Press, 1922 [1961]), 347–65.

Selected Letters (Harmondsworth, Middlesex: Penguin Books, 1950).

Leavis, Queenie, "Leslie Stephen – Cambridge Critic," *Scrutiny*, VII: 4 (March 1939), 404–15.

Leclerc, Ivor, *Whitehead's Metaphysics: An Introductory Exposition* (Bloomington: Indiana University Press, 1958).

Leibniz, *The Monadology and Other Philosophical Writings*, Robert Latta (trans.) (London: Oxford University Press, 1898).

Levy, Paul, *G. E. Moore and the Cambridge Apostles* (Oxford: Oxford University Press, 1981).

Lewis, Mary Tompkins, *Cézanne's Early Imagery* (Berkeley: University of California Press, 1989).

Lewis, Wyndham, *Time and Western Man*, Paul Edwards (ed.) (Santa Rosa: Black Sparrow Press, 1927 [1993]).

Lichtenstein, Jacqueline, *La Couleur Eloquente* (Paris: Flammarion, 1989).

Lowe, Victor, *Alfred North Whitehead: The Man and His Work*, vol. I, 1861–1910 (Baltimore: The Johns Hopkins University Press, 1985).

Lucas, F. L., *Tragedy in Relation to Aristotle's Poetics* (London: Hogarth Press, 1928).

Mach, Ernst, *Contributions to the Analysis of Sensations* (La Salle, IL: Open Court Publishing Company, 1890).

Maitland, F. W., *Life and Letters of Leslie Stephen* (London: Duckworth, 1906).

Matro, Thomas G., "Only Relations: Vision and Achievement in *To the Lighthouse*," *PMLA*, 99:2 (March 1984), 212–24.

Mauron, Charles, "A Propos de *The Longest Journey* 'The Cow is There': Le

Bien-et-le Mal," *CERVE* (*Cahiers des Etudes de Recherches Victoriennes et Edouardiennes*) (Montpellier: Université Paul Valery, 1977).

"The Cow," *The Criterion*, XII, XLVIII (1933), 454–67.

The Nature of Beauty in Art and Literature, Roger Fry (tr. and preface) (London: Hogarth Press, 1927).

"Le Temps Passe," translation of "Time Passes," *Commerce: Cahiers Trimestriels Publiés par les Soins de Paul Valéry, Léon–Paul Fargue, Valery Larbaud*, X (Hiver 1926) (Paris: Librairie Henri LeClerc, 1926), 89–133.

McGuinness, Brian, "The Mysticism of the *Tractatus*," *Philosophical Review*, 75 (1966), 305–28.

Wittgenstein: A Life, Young Ludwig 1889–1921 (Berkeley: The University of California Press, 1988).

McLaurin, Allen, *Virginia Woolf: The Echoes Enslaved* (Cambridge: Cambridge University Press, 1973).

McTaggart, J. McT. E., *The Nature of Existence*, vol. 2 (Cambridge: Cambridge University Press, 1927 [1988]).

Meisel, Perry, *The Absent Father: Virginia Woolf and Walter Pater* (New Haven: Yale University Press, 1980).

Mepham, John, "Mourning and Modernism," in Patricia Clements and Isobel Grundy, *Virginia Woolf: New Critical Essays* (London: Vision, 1983).

Miller, J. Hillis, "Mr. Carmichael and Lily Briscoe: The Rhythm of Creativity in *To the Lighthouse*," in *Modernism Reconsidered*, Robert Kiely (ed.), asst. by John Hildebidle (Cambridge, MA: Harvard University Press, 1983), 167–89.

"Virginia Woolf's All Souls' Day: The Omniscient Narrator in *Mrs. Dalloway*," in *The Shaken Realist: Essays in Modern Literature in Honor of Frederick J. Hoffman*, Melvin J. Friedman and John B. Vickery (eds.) (Baton Rouge: Louisiana State University Press, 1970), 100–27.

Monk, Ray, *Bertrand Russell: The Spirit of Solitude, 1872–1921* (New York and London: The Free Press, 1996).

Wittgenstein: The Duty of Genius (London: Penguin Books, 1991).

Moore, G. E., "An Autobiography," in *The Philosophy of G. E. Moore*, Paul Schilpp (ed.) (Chicago: Northwestern University Press, 1942), 3–39.

The Early Essays, Tom Regan (ed.) (Philadelphia: Temple University Press, 1986).

Philosophical Papers (London: George Allen & Unwin, 1959).

Philosophical Studies (London: Routledge & Kegan Paul Ltd, 1922).

Principia Ethica (Cambridge: Cambridge University Press, 1903).

"The Refutation of Idealism," *Mind*, XII: 48 (October 1903), 433–53.

"Some Judgments of Perception," *Proceedings of the Aristotelian Society*, XIX (1918–19), 1–29.

Some Main Problems of Philosophy (New York: Collier Books, 1962).

Naremore, James, *The World Without a Self: Virginia Woolf and the Novel* (New Haven: Yale University Press, 1973).

Nicod, Jean, *La Géométrie dans le Monde Sensible* (Paris: Presses Universitaires de France, 1923 [1962]).

Parkes, Graham, "Imagining Reality in *To the Lighthouse*," *Philosophy and Literature*, 6, nos. 1 & 2 (October 1982), 33–44.

Passmore, John, *A Hundred Years of Philosophy* (New York: Basic Books, 1966).

Pears, David, *Bertrand Russell and the British Tradition in Philosophy* (New York: Random House, 1967).

"Introduction" to Bertrand Russell *The Philosophy of Logical Atomism* (La Salle, IL: Open Court, 1985), 1–34.

Proust, Marcel, "A Propos du 'Style' de Flaubert," in *Contre Sainte-Beuve précédé de Pastiches et Mélanges et suivi de Essais et Articles* (Paris: Gallimard, 1971).

Rantavaara, Irma, *Virginia Woolf and Bloomsbury* (Helsinki: Suomalainen Tiedeakatemia, 1953).

Reichenbach, Hans, *The Rise of Scientific Philosophy* (New York: the Free Press, 1947).

Rhees, Rush (ed.), *Ludwig Wittgenstein: Personal Recollections* (Totowa, NJ: Rowman and Littlefield, 1981).

Ricoeur, Paul, *Time and Narrative*, vol. 2 (Chicago: University of Chicago Press, 1984).

Roberts, John Hawley, "Vision and Design in Virginia Woolf," *PMLA*, 61 (1946), 835–47.

Robson, W. W., "A Poet's Notebook: the Use of Poetry and the Use of Criticism," in *The Literary Criticism of T. S. Eliot: New Essays*, David Newton-De Molina (ed.) (London: The Athlone Press, 1977).

Rosenbaum, S. P. (ed.), *The Bloomsbury Group: A Collection of Memoirs, Commentary and Criticism* (Toronto: the University of Toronto Press, 1975).

"*The Longest Journey*: E. M. Forster's Refutation of Idealism," *E. M. Forster: A Human Exploration*, Centenary Essays, G. K. Das and John Beer (eds.) (New York: New York University Press, 1979), 32–54.

Victorian Bloomsbury: The Early Literary History of the Bloomsbury Group (New York: St. Martin's Press, 1987).

"Virginia Woolf's Philosophical Realism," in *English Literature and British Philosophy*, S. P. Rosenbaum (ed.) (Chicago: University of Chicago Press, 1971), 316–56.

Rosenman, Ellen, *The Invisible Presence: Virginia Woolf and the Mother-Daughter Relationship* (London: Louisiana State University Press, 1986).

Ruotolo, Lucio, *The Interrupted Moment: A View of Virginia Woolf's Novels* (Stanford: Stanford University Press, 1986).

Russell, Bertrand, *The ABC of Atoms* (London: Kegan Paul, Trench, Trubner & Co., Ltd.; New York: E. P. Dutton & Co., 1924).

The ABC of Relativity (New York: Harper & Brothers, 1925).

The ABC of Relativity, Felix Pirani (ed.), third revised edn. (New York: Mentor, 1969).

The Analysis of Matter (New York: Dover, 1927 [1954]).

The Analysis of Mind (London: George Allen & Unwin, 1921).

The Autobiography of Bertrand Russell, vol. 1, The Early Years: 1872 – World War I (London, George Allen & Unwin, 1967); *vol. 2, 1914–1944* (London: George Allen & Unwin, 1967–8).
The Basic Writings of Bertrand Russell: 1903–1959, Robert E. Egner and Lester E. Denonn (eds) (New York: Simon and Schuster, 1961).
The Collected Papers, 12 vols. (London: George Allen & Unwin, 1985–92).
A Critical Exposition of the Philosophy of Leibniz (London: George Allen and Unwin Ltd., 1900 [1937]).
History of Western Philosophy and its Connection with Political and Social Circumstances from the Earliest Times to the Present Day (London, George Allen & Unwin, 1961).
Human Knowledge: Its Scope and Limits (New York: Simon and Schuster, 1948).
An Inquiry into Meaning and Truth (Harmondsworth, Middlesex: Penguin, 1940 [1962]).
"The Interior of the Atom" *The Nation and the Athenaeum*, 33 (1 September 1923), 696–8.
Introduction to Mathematical Philosophy (New York: Simon and Schuster, [1919], n.d.).
Logic and Knowledge: Essays 1901–1950 (New York: Macmillan, 1956).
Mysticism and Logic (Garden City, New York: Doubleday, 1917 [1957]).
"On the Experience of Time," *The Monist*, XXV (Chicago: The Open Court Publishing Company, 1915) 212–33.
Our Knowledge of the External World: A Field for Scientific Method in Philosophy (London: George Allen & Unwin, 1914).
An Outline of Philosophy (Cleveland: The World Publishing Company, 1927 [1960]).
My Philosophical Development (London: Unwin, 1959).
Philosophical Essays (New York: Simon & Schuster, Inc., 1966).
The Philosophy of Bergson: With a Reply by Mr. H. Wildon Carr, Secretary of the Aristotelian Society, and a Rejoinder by Mr. Russell (Cambridge: For "The Heretics" by Bowes and Bowes, 1914).
Portraits from Memory and Other Essays (New York: Simon and Schuster, 1951).
(with Alfred North Whitehead) *Principia Mathematica* to *56 (Cambridge: Cambridge University Press, 1910 [1962]).
Principles of Mathematics (New York: W. W. Norton & Company, 1903 [n.d]).
The Problems of Philosophy (London: Oxford University Press, 1912 [1959]).
The Scientific Outlook (New York: W. W. Norton & Company, 1931).
The Selected Letters of Bertrand Russell, Volume 1, The Private Years, 1884–1914, Nicholas Griffin (ed.) (Boston: Houghton Mifflin, 1992).
Selected Papers of Bertrand Russell (New York: Random House, 1927).
Theory of Knowledge: The 1913 Manuscript, The Collected Papers of Bertrand Russell, Vol. 7, Elizabeth Ramsden Eames (ed.), in collaboration with Kenneth Blackwell (London: George Allen & Unwin, 1984).

Ryle, Gilbert, "Introduction," *The Revolution in Philosophy* (London: Macmillan, 1956), 1–11.

Sainsbury, Mark, *Russell* (London: Routledge & Kegan Paul, 1979).

Schneewind, J. B., "Leslie Stephen," in *The Encyclopedia of Philosophy*, vol. 8, Paul Edwards (editor in chief) (New York: Macmillan Publishing Co., Inc. & The Free Press, 1967), 14–15.

Searle, John, "Proper Names and Descriptions," *The Encyclopedia of Philosophy*, vol. 6, Paul Edwards (editor in chief) (New York: Macmillan Publishing Co., Inc. & The Free Press, 1967), 487–91.

Sherburne, Donald W., *A Key to Whitehead's Process and Reality* (New York: The Macmillan Company, 1966).

Shusterman, Richard, *T. S. Eliot and the Philosophy of Criticism* (New York: Columbia University Press, 1988).

Skidelsky, Robert, *John Maynard Keynes: Vol. I: Hopes Betrayed, 1883–1920*; *Vol. II: The Economist as Savior, 1920–1937* (London: The Penguin Press, 1994).

Spalding, Frances, *Roger Fry: Art and Life* (Berkeley: University of California Press, 1980).

Vanessa Bell (San Diego: Harcourt Brace Jovanovich, 1983).

Spender, Stephen, *World Within World: The Autobiography of Stephen Spender* (London: Hamish Hamilton, 1951).

Steinberg, Erwin R., "G. E. Moore's Table and Chair in *To the Lighthouse*," *Journal of Modern Literature*, XV: 1 (Summer, 1988), 161–8.

Stenius, Erik, *Wittgenstein's* Tractatus. *A Critical Exposition of Its Main Lines of Thought* (Oxford: Oxford University Press, 1960).

Stephen, Karin, "What Bergson Means by 'Interpenetration'," *Proceedings of the Aristotelian Society*, new series, Vol. XIII, 131–55.

The Misuse of Mind: A Study of Bergson's Attack on Intellectualism (New York: Harcourt, Brace & Company, Inc., 1922).

Stephen, Leslie, "A Bad Five Minutes in the Alps," *Men, Books, and Mountains: Essays*, S. O. A. Ullmann (ed.) (London: Hogarth Press, 1956).

"Berkeley," Vol. II; "Hume," Vol. X, *The Dictionary of National Biography*, Leslie Stephen and Sidney Lee (eds.) (Oxford: Oxford University Press, since 1917).

The English Utilitarians, vol. III (London, 1950).

History of English Thought in the Eighteenth Century, vol. I (London: Smith, Elder, & Co., 1876).

Hours in a Library, vol. II (London: Smith, Elder & Co., 1892).

"In Praise of Walking," *Studies of a Biographer*, vol. III (New York: G. P. Putnam's Sons; London: Duckworth & Co., 1902), 254–85.

The Mausoleum Book (Oxford: Clarendon Press, 1977).

"What is Materialism?," in *An Agnostic's Apology and Other Essays* (London: Smith, Elder, & Co., 1893, 2nd edn., 1903).

Strachey, Lytton, *Portraits in Miniature* (London: Chatto & Windus, 1931).

The Shorter Strachey, Michael Holroyd and Paul Levy (eds.) (Oxford: Oxford University Press, 1989).

Torgovnick, Marianna, *Gone Primitive: Savage Intellects, Modern Lives* (Chicago: University of Chicago Press, 1990).

The Visual Arts, Pictorialism, and the Novel: James, Lawrence, and Woolf (Princeton: Princeton University Press, 1985).

Twitchell, Beverly H., *Cézanne and Formalism in Bloomsbury* (Ann Arbor: UMI Research Press, 1987).

Tyndall, John, *Essays on the Use and Limit of the Imagination in Science* (London: Longmans, Green and Co., 1870).

Lectures on Light (New York: D. Appleton and Company, 1873).

On Radiation (New York: D. Appleton and Company, 1865).

Urmson, J. O., *Philosophical Analysis: Its Development Between the Two World Wars* (London: Oxford University Press, 1967).

Vesey, G. N. A., "Self-Acquaintance and the Meaning of 'I'," in *Bertrand Russell Memorial Volume*, George W. Roberts (ed.) (London: George Allen & Unwin; New York: Humanities Press, 1979).

von Wright, Georg Henrik, "Biographical Sketch," in Norman Malcolm, *Ludwig Wittgenstein: A Memoir* (London: Oxford University Press, 1977).

Vuillemin, J., *Leçons sur la Première Philosophie de Russell* (Paris: A. Colin, 1968).

Warnock, G. J., *English Philosophy Since 1900* (Oxford: Oxford University Press, 1969).

Whitehead, Alfred North, *Process and Reality: An Essay in Cosmology* (New York: Macmillan, 1929).

Science and the Modern World (New York: Mentor Books, 1925 [1948]).

Symbolism: Its Meaning and Effect (London: Macmillan; New York: G. P. Putnam's Sons, 1927).

"Technical Education and its Relation to Science and Literature," *The Aims of Education and Other Essays* (London: Collier Macmillan Publishers, 1929).

Whiteley, Patrick J., *Knowledge and Experimental Realism in Conrad, Lawrence, and Woolf* (Baton Rouge: Louisiana University Press, 1987).

Williams, Bernard, *Descartes: The Project of Pure Inquiry* (New Jersey: Humanities Press, 1978).

Williams, Raymond, *The English Novel* (New York: Oxford University Press, 1973).

Wittgenstein, Ludwig, *Notebooks 1914–1916*, 2nd edn., G. H. von Wright and G. E. M. Anscombe (eds.), G. E. M. Anscombe (trans.) (Chicago: University of Chicago Press, 1979).

Philosophical Investigations, G. E. M. Anscombe (trans.) (Oxford: Blackwell, 1963).

Tractatus Logico-Philosophicus, C. K. Ogden (trans.) (New York: Harcourt Brace & Company, Inc., 1922).

Wollheim, Richard, "Eliot and F. H. Bradley," in *On Art and the Mind: Lectures and Essays*) (Cambridge, MA: Harvard University Press, 1974).

F. H. Bradley (Harmondsworth, Middlesex: Penguin Books, 1959).

Wood, Alan, *Bertrand Russell: the Passionate Sceptic* (New York: Simon and Schuster, 1958).

Woolf, Leonard, *An Autobiography* (Oxford: Oxford University Press, 1980).

Beginning Again: An Autobiography of the Years 1911–1918 (London: The Hogarth Press, 1964).
Letters of Leonard Woolf, Frederic Spotts (ed.) (San Diego, New York, London: Harcourt Brace Jovanovich, 1989).
Principia Politica (London: Hogarth Press, 1953).
Sowing: An Autobiography of the Years 1880–1904 (New York: Harcourt Brace Jovanovich, 1960).
Woolf, Virginia, *Between the Acts* (New York: Harcourt Brace Jovanovich, 1941 [1969]).
Books and Portraits: Some Further Selections from the Literary and Biographical Writings of Virginia Woolf, Mary Lyon (ed.) (London: Hogarth, 1977).
Collected Essays, 4 cols. (London: The Hogarth Press, 1966–7).
The Complete Shorter Fiction of Virginia Woolf, Susan Dick (ed.) (San Diego: Harcourt Brace Jovanovich, 1985).
Contemporary Writers (New York: Harcourt, Brace & World, 1965).
The Diary of Virginia Woolf, Anne Olivier Bell (ed.), assisted by Andrew McNeillie, vol. 1, 1915–19; vol. 2, 1920–4; vol. 3, 1925–30; vol. 4, 1931–5 (New York: Harcourt Brace Jovanovich, 1977–80).
The Essays of Virginia Woolf vol. 1, 1904–1912, and vol. III, 1919–1924, Andrew McNeillic (ed.) (London: Hogarth Press, 1986).
Foreword to *Recent Painting by Vanessa Bell* (The London Artists' Association), February 4 to March 8, 1930, reprinted in Rosenbaum, *The Bloomsbury Group.*
Jacob's Room (New York: Harcourt Brace Jovanovich, 1922 [1950]).
The Letters of Virginia Woolf, vol. 1, 1882–1912; vol. 2, 1912–22; vol. 3, 1923–8; vol. 4, 1929–31; vol. 5, 1931–5, Nigel Nicolson and Joanne Trautmann (eds.) (New York and London: Harcourt Brace Jovanovich, 1975–80).
Moments of Being: Unpublished Autobiographical Writings, Jeanne Schulkind (ed.) (Sussex: The University Press, 1976).
Mrs. Dalloway (New York: Harcourt Brace Jovanovich, 1925 [1985]).
Night and Day (New York: Harcourt Brace Jovanovich, 1919 [1948]).
Orlando: A Biography (New York: Harcourt Brace Jovanovich, 1928).
A Passionate Apprentice: The Early Journals 1897–1909, Mitchell Leaska (ed.) (London: The Hogarth Press, 1990).
Roger Fry: A Biography (New York: Harcourt Brace Jovanovich, 1940 [1968]).
A Room of One's Own (New York: Harcourt, Brace & World, Inc., 1929 [1957]).
The Waves (New York: Harcourt Brace Jovanovich, 1931 [1959]).
The Years (New York: Harcourt Brace Jovanovich, 1937 [1965]).
Three Guineas (New York: Harcourt, Brace & World, 1938).
To the Lighthouse (New York: Harcourt Brace Jovanovich, 1927 [1955]).
A Writer's Diary (New York: Harcourt Brace Jovanovich, 1953).
Zwerdling, Alex, *Virginia Woolf and the Real World* (Berkeley: University of California Press, 1986).

Index

Abel, Elizabeth, xi, 406 n.2, 412 n.39
agnosticism, 47–51, 153–4, 344, 359, 368–9, 394 n.44
analysis, 1, 11–2, 50, 53, 62, 64–5, 67, 81, 85, 97, 107, 108, 156, 158, 162–3, 187–91, 194, 245–6, 250–1, 264, 269–70, 271, 294, 300, 306, 328–9, 363, 370, 380–1, 387–8
androgyny, 196–200, 201, 216, 276, 348, 354, 386, 405 n.20
Annan, Noel, 4, 37, 38, 45, 197, 312, 389 n.4, 394 n.44, 411 n.27
anonymity, 344, 346, 348
Antor, Heinz, 200, 406 n.5
atomism,
  logical, 79–82, 85, 194, 246–7, 250–1, 256–7, 269, 276, 296, 304–5, 400 n.20
  Platonic, 64, 83, 88, 251, 277
Auerbach, Erich, 311
Austen, Jane, 173, 304, 342
author, disappearance of, 342–51
Ayer, A. J., 42, 45, 60, 65, 67, 83, 84, 89, 394 n.44, 395 n.47, 396 n.53, 396 n.56, 398 n.9, 399 n.13, 400 n.22

Bally, Charles, 314
Banfield, Ann, 410 n.11, 410 n.12, 410 n.14, 411 n.30
Barthes, Roland, 236, 409 n.31
Bazin, Nancy Topping, 189, 405 n.20
Beer, Gillian, 28, 29–30, 238, 349, 389 n.2, 392 n.30, 397 n.63, 401 n.1, 402 n.8, 402 n.9, 402 n.12, 403 n.18, 407 n.18, 412 n.33, 413 n.42, 414 n.11
Bell, Clive, 11, 40, 41, 52, 101, 167, 239, 250, 252, 257, 260, 261, 272, 273, 276, 277, 278, 280, 282–3, 314–15, 318, 323, 360, 364, 383, 395 n.47, 400 n.23, 403 n.1, 405 n.23, 407 n.11, 407 n.16, 411 n.31
Bell, Julian, 41, 42, 372, 395 n.49
Bell, Quentin, 28, 42, 219, 235, 333, 393 n.38, 394 n.47, 395 n.51, 404 n.14, 408 n.31
Bell, Vanessa, 11, 12, 15, 17, 34, 171, 211, 248, 277, 298, 318, 321, 334, 383, 385, 391 n.20, 404 n.9, 409 n.31, 409 n.32, 409 n.35
Bennett, Arnold, 294, 324, 411 n.22
Bergson, Henri, 29, 35, 102–3, 137, 254, 307, 389 n.2, 391 n.23
Berkeley, George, 6, 36, 37, 39, 44, 48, 63, 64, 68–9, 70, 71, 74, 76, 77, 80, 98, 101, 122, 141, 149, 153, 173, 216, 247, 255, 272, 344, 378, 380, 396 n.54, 398 n.3, 398 n.9, 401 n.33
Bettelheim, Bruno, 403 n.1
biography, 99–101, 175, 198, 312–13, 321–36, 338, 384
Black, Max, 89, 90, 93, 254, 255, 276, 337, 362, 365, 368, 369, 389 n.6, 401 n.30, 401 n.31
Blackwell, Kenneth, 389 n.5, 395 n.50
blindness, see "eyelessness"
Bloomsbury, 8–9, 11, 12, 15–16, 17–18, 21, 33–4, 35, 40, 41, 45, 47, 51, 55, 171, 172, 247–8, 303, 319–20, 322, 334, 335, 344–5, 352, 359–60, 365, 372, 383, 384, 389 n.7, 390 n.14, 395 n.47, 396 n.53, 396 n.56, 398 n.1
Bradley, F. H., 6, 63, 80, 81, 92, 144, 152–3, 157, 164, 251, 302, 407 n.22
Brenan, Gerald, 390 n.13
Brontë, Emily, 173, 387

Cambridge University, 3–5, 8–10, 13, 21, 27, 31, 32, 38, 39, 41, 47, 74, 89, 92, 105, 133, 162–3, 188, 193, 194–5, 196, 213, 239, 247–50, 258, 290, 354, 360, 389 n.1, 389 n.3, 389 n.4, 390 n.8, 399 n.18
Cambridge Apostles, ix–x, 8, 11–12, 21–2, 30–6, 37, 42, 93, 157, 212, 236, 248–50, 358, 387, 389 n.7, 398 n.1
and women, 20–1, 31
causal theory of perception, 129

Cézanne, Paul, 50, 52, 247, 256–7, 258, 266, 267, 269–70, 272, 274, 276, 277, 278–81, 282, 283–5, 287, 288, 290, 292, 293, 299, 304, 311, 334, 337, 341, 343, 350, 356, 379, 387–8, 408 n.31
Chastaing, Maxime, 389 n.2, 398 n.3
Cobden-Sanderson, Thomas, 371, 379, 386
color, plastic, 251, 276–80, 283–4, 286, 319, 388, 407 n. 21
construction, logical, 48, 53, 74, 96–101, 107, 120, 138, 153, 156, 157, 166, 176, 255, 296, 316, 321, 329, 380–1
continuity, 73–4, 97–8, 102–5, 146–7, 179, 247, 254, 284, 307, 316, 323, 328, 336, 350, 370, 373, 402 n.9, 408 n.24
Corner, Martin, 344, 351, 411 n.30
correlation, 6, 97–9, 102, 104, 258, 285, 356, 373, 401 n.32
correlative, objective, 401 n.32
correspondance, 89–90, 288, 302, 329, 349, 373, 377, 381

Daiches, David, 401 n.5, 405 n.22
D'Aquila, Ulysses L., 410 n.6, 413 n.4
Darroch, Sandra Jobson, 195, 391 n.19
Delattre, Floris, 389 n.2
Deleuze, Gilles, 329, 399 n.17
demonstrative, 86, 164, 165, 166, 218, 296, 298–304, 307–11, 315, 317, 363
denoting, 87, 91, 297, 301, 302, 306, 308, 310
DeSalvo, Louise, 401 n.4, 405 n.20
Descartes, René 6, 7, 65, 162–3, 344
description, theory of, 87–8, 297
design, 13–14, 147, 249, 256, 258–63, 272, 274, 276, 277, 278, 279, 286, 288, 289, 291, 307, 320, 329, 336, 407 n.11
dualism, 13–14, 78–9, 148–54, 191–6, 216–17, 258–63, 297–8
Duckworth, George, 15, 16–17, 33
Duckworth, Stella, 33, 241
Dummett, Michael, 7

Eames, Elizabeth Ramsden, 13, 19, 35, 54, 107, 398 n.4, 400 n.18, 402 n.11
Edel, Leon, 235, 389 n.1, 405 n.15
Einstein, Albert, 6, 142, 148
elegy, 3, 146, 235–41, 375–6, 358–88
Eliot, George, 346
Eliot, T. S., 25, 250, 359, 383, 390 n.18, 391 n.23, 397 n.60, 401 n.32, 403 n.3, 407 n.15, 407 n.21, 409 n.34, 414 n.12
empiricism, 4, 6, 37, 39, 53, 63, 64, 65, 246, 248, 272, 274, 309, 355–6, 380, 389 n.2, 400 n.19
epistemology, see knowledge, theory of

Esch, Deborah, 398 n.5
Evans, Gareth, 307
events, 76–7, 101, 116, 267, 361–2, 399 n.16, 401 n.5
eyelessness and vision, 11–14, 21–2, 93, 157, 195, 198, 209–12, 217, 239, 247–58, 262, 278, 282, 337, 363, 381, 385, 388, 406 n.2

fact, 64, 77, 81, 89–90, 91, 92–4, 152, 166, 198, 253, 279, 302, 349, 377, 378
  atomic, 82, 253, 300, 302, 337
  complex, 90, 281, 286, 290, 400 n.28
Feigl, Herbert, 269, 319, 399 n.13
fiction, logical, 84, 148, 377, 380–1
Finch, Henry Leroy, 362
Flaubert, Gustave, 249, 314–15, 343, 350, 355, 360
form, logical, 91, 147, 157–8, 187, 190, 251–6, 265, 276, 279–81, 283, 287, 298, 306, 337, 363, 364
formalism, xi–xii, xiv–v, 149, 257, 266, 273, 277, 284, 296, 324, 373–4, 377, 378, 382
Forster, E. M., 391 n.25
  Anonymity: An Enquiry, 345, 348, 349, 350, 351, 384, 400 n.25, 405 n.24, 412 n.36
  Aspects of the Novel, 105, 296, 335
  Longest Journey, The, 3, 27, 216
  Passage to India, A, 271, 345, 390 n.11, 408 n.31
  Where Angels Fear to Tread, 27
Foucault, Michel, xi, xii, xv
Freud, Sigmund, xi, 137, 176, 237, 365, 377, 403 n.1, 413 n.2
Fritz, Charles A., Jr., 398 n.8, 414 n.10
Fry, Roger, 11–14, 15, 231, 239, 240
  Cézanne, 247, 258
  dissertation, 249
  Henri-Matisse, 252
  and McTaggart, 249
  and Russell, 250
  Transformations, 274
  Vision and Design, 256, 364

Geach, Peter, 14, 89, 399 n.18
geometry, 75, 102–6, 147, 179, 247, 256–7, 276–91, 318–21, 337, 357
Gillespie, Diane Filby, 409 n.35
Gower, Barry, 399 n.15
Grosskurth, Phyllis, 393 n.34

Hafley, James, 393 n.35, 402 n.7
Hampshire, Stuart, 351, 404 n.6, 407 n.20, 411 n.23, 413 n.44
Hegeliansim, 6, 39, 63, 66, 80, 101, 144
here-and-now, 75–8, 110, 115, 285, 302, 308, 317, 381

Hills, Jack, 33
Hintikka, Jaakko, x, 29, 36, 37, 42, 101, 116–17, 294, 392 n.29, 397 n.63, 398 n.2, 399 n.12, 399 n.16, 400 n.18, 401 n.5, 410 n.15, 411 n.21, 412 n.35, 413 n.4
Hirst, R. J., 398 n.9, 399 n.15
Holroyd, Michael, 312, 314, 410 n.9
Home University Library of Modern Knowledge, 18, 19, 23–4, 390 n.15
Hume, David, 29, 37, 38, 39, 44, 63, 66, 67, 68, 74, 164, 166, 168, 174, 193, 210, 233, 246, 272, 350, 366–7, 368, 376–7, 380
Hussey, Mark, 393 n.31, 397 n.62
Hutcheon, Linda, 303
Huxley, Aldous, 399 n.14
Hyde Park Gate, 8, 33
Hylton, Peter, 13, 18–19, 20, 38–9, 64, 65, 83, 84, 85, 88, 89, 90, 92, 248, 251, 253, 370, 394 n.46, 400 n.23, 400 n.28

Idealism, 4, 6, 36, 39, 47–8, 63–5, 79, 80–1, 84, 101, 116, 121, 133, 152–3, 163–4, 196, 198, 216, 247, 251, 259, 293, 302, 363, 366
impersonality, 78, 139–42, 147, 174, 178, 194, 206, 220, 347, 350, 357, 382–8
Impressionism, 13, 52, 117, 256–7, 271–4, 278, 281, 307, 313, 314, 319, 320, 324, 329, 337, 340–1, 342, 352, 355, 364, 380, 382, 387
interludes, 146–8

Jager, Ronald, 73
James, Henry, 168, 401 n.3
Janik, Allan, 14
Jarmin, Derek, xv
Jeans, Sir James, 414 n.11
Joyce, James, 315, 342, 359, 402 n.14
judgment, multiple relation theory of, 91

Kelley, Alice van Buren, 400 n.27
Kenny, Anthony, 253
Keynes, John Maynard, 23, 35, 38, 40, 41, 51, 149
Kilmister, C. W., 399 n.13
knowledge,
  by acquaintance, 14, 22, 82, 83, 85–6, 90, 92–3, 101, 115, 118, 136–7, 164–6, 167–8, 175–7, 183, 204, 217–18, 228, 253–5, 257, 266, 273, 277, 297, 299, 302, 331, 332, 344, 364, 365, 371, 376, 377, 402 n.10
  by description, 14, 22, 49, 85, 86–8, 94, 101, 137, 140–1, 147, 166, 175–81, 218, 228, 254–5, 257, 297, 301–2, 322, 332, 371, 402 n.10
  theory of, 4, 18–9, 20, 22, 37–8, 47–51, 60, 63, 64, 66, 70, 101, 106, 239, 260, 263, 297, 303, 314, 389 n.6
Knox, Ronald, 48–9

Lawrence, D. H., 326, 356, 393 n.32, 406 n.2, 410 n.4
Leavis, Queenie, 395 n.47
Leibniz, Gottfried Wilhelm von, 72, 74, 76, 99, 101, 110, 111, 143, 176, 321, 344, 361, 362, 369, 399 n.17, 399 n.18, 401 n.2
Levy, Paul, 17, 21, 25, 30, 33, 40–1, 42, 45, 352, 390 n.12, 390 n.17, 392 n.27, 392 n.31, 393 n.33, 397 n.57, 397 n.59, 397 n.61
Lichtenberg, Georg, 163, 298, 344, 407 n.11
logic, 10–11, 13, 24, 27, 48, 63, 64, 83, 85, 92–3, 95–6, 152–3, 181, 185, 193, 198–200, 296–7, 343, 354–5, 370, 386
lost objects, 134–6
Lowe, Victor, 10, 20, 21, 22, 23, 24, 25, 30, 105, 390 n.10, 390 n.15, 390 n.16, 390 n.17, 391 n.22, 397 n.59, 400 n.21
Lubbock, Percy, 252
Lucas, F. L., 344

MacCarthy, Desmond, 248
Mach, Ernst, 210
Mansfield, Katherine, 182
Matisse, Henri, 267, 275, 279, 280, 281, 283, 285, 288, 290, 307
Matro, Thomas, 286, 289, 408 n.29, 411 n.30, 412 n.32
Mauron, Charles, 36, 250, 256, 260, 277, 278, 303, 319–20, 391 n.27, 406 n.5, 407 n.8, 413 n.3
Mauron, Marie, 250, 390 n.8
McGuinness, Brian, 7, 20, 42, 65, 360, 362, 389 n.5, 390 n.15, 395 n.50, 413 n.6, 413 n.7
McLaurin, Allen, 269, 407 n.10, 409 n.32, 410 n.18
McTaggart, J. McT. E., 7, 44, 166, 222, 240, 328
Mediterranean clarity, 9–10, 290, 307, 354, 390 n.13, 408 n.31
Meinong, 84, 86
Meisel, Perry, 394 n.42, 402 n.15
memory, 239, 326–7, 389 n.2
  immediate, 82, 136–7, 183, 220–1
mental, 70, 166, 168
Mepham, John, 236
Meredith, George, 411 n.27
Miller, J. Hillis, 349, 412 n.32, 412 n.34, 412 n.39, 413 n.41, 414 n.9

Milton, John, 406 n.3
monadology, 1, 53, 81, 82, 98–9, 100–1, 109–10, 111, 113, 143, 176, 338, 401 n.2
Monet, Claude, 268, 270, 272
monism, 126, 163, 228, 338
  neutral, 63, 77, 78–9, 80, 81–2, 276, 318, 328, 398 n.3
Monk, Ray, 372, 390 n.19, 391 n.21, 403 n.16, 407 n.12, 414 n.12
Moore, G. E., 4, 7, 34, 35, 36, 42, 45, 55, 69, 191, 359, 392 n.28
  The Early Essays, 148–9
  "Nature of Judgment, The," 84
  Philosophical Papers, 163, 404 n.14
  Philosophical Studies, 399 n.15
  Principia Ethica, 9, 30, 36, 40–1, 45, 144, 250, 407 n.13, 407 n.14
  "Proof of an External World," 44
  "Refutation of Idealism, The," 7, 9, 40, 48, 63, 69, 84, 299, 403 n.17
  "Sense-Data," 398 n.10
  Some Main Problems of Philosophy, 7, 10, 17, 43, 46, 59, 84, 88–9, 133, 146
Moore, T. S., 46
Morrell, Ottoline, 15, 19–20, 21, 54, 195, 198, 359, 391 n.19, 391 n.20, 395 n.47, 396 n.57, 410 n.8, 414 n.12
mysticism, 194–6, 197–200, 228–9, 359–60, 361, 365–76, 382, 385, 386

Nagel, Thomas, 410 n.9
name,
  logically proper, 160, 164, 296, 299, 308, 310, 316, 324
  ordinary proper 324–6, 330–1
naming, 297, 301
Naremore, James, 297, 412 n.38
net, see logical scaffolding
neutral monism, see monism, neutral
neutrality, 67, 78–9, 98, 100, 101, 120, 156, 163, 168, 169–70, 174, 191, 298, 310, 318, 328, 334, 347, 348, 399 n.13
Nicod, Jean, 255, 410 n.16
nominalism, 63, 65, 84, 398 n.4
now, see here-and-now

Occam's razor, 49, 65, 94, 97, 154, 169, 349
Oxford University, 4–5, 10, 27

particulars, 10, 63, 79–82, 83, 97–8, 107, 156, 164, 187, 198, 296–7, 301, 306, 308, 310–11, 314, 315, 317–18, 324–5, 361, 370, 376, 380
  egocentric, 86, 265, 310–11, 349
  emphatic, 265, 329
Passmore, John, 42, 43, 45, 63, 102, 121, 259, 396 n.53, 396 n.56
Pater, Walter, 299
Pears, David, 30, 39, 60–1, 101, 167, 400 n.28, 409 n.2, 410 n.3, 414 n.10
perceptions, unperceived, see sensibilia
perspective, 1, 55, 73–9, 98–9, 109–22, 123–8, 129–34, 136, 146, 155, 169, 174, 176, 180, 202, 203, 204, 213, 217–8, 222, 263, 266, 277, 279, 290, 292, 307, 308, 310, 311–16, 320, 325, 328–9, 342–3, 349–50, 357, 373, 386
  occupied, 53, 72–5, 109, 134, 162, 167, 309, 336, see also private worlds
  unoccupied, 54, 73–5, 129, 134, 138, 142, 167, 183, 214, 220, 224, 238, 293, 309, 316–18, 327, 336, see also sensibilia
phallus, 169–74, 201
picture theory, 53, 93, 253–4, 337
Plato, 16, 29, 392 n.29
point of view, 114, 311–16
possible worlds, 24, 74, 113, 361
Post-Impressionism, 11, 13, 52, 256–7, 274–5, 276–93, 329, 330, 336, 337, 341, 356, 364, 377, 380, 383–4, 388, 390 n.11
  First Exhibition (1910), 11
Poussin, Nicolas, 287, 408 n.31
predicate, 63, 83, 87
prehension, 76–7, 399 n.18
presentation, 86, 300
principle of selection, 167, 203, 266–8, 328–9
privacy, 72–9, 112–16, 129, 163, 174, 175–81, 216, 217, 285, 293, 296–7, 312, 315, 342–3, 357, 380, 381, 399 n.14
private language, 296–8, 399 n.14
private world, 1, 109, 110–12, 113, 116, 119, 129, 130, 167, 168, 206, 237–8, 309, 321, 324, 326, 330, 332, 336, 342, 369, 376, 381
proposition, 53, 63–4, 83, 85, 86–96, 190, 253, 281, 286, 287, 296–7, 306, 316, 318, 337, 338, 348, 370, 372
  atomic, 253, 297–8, 300, 302–3, 309, 337
Proust, Marcel, 137, 202, 239, 288, 314–15, 318, 326, 391 n.23, 411 n.31
public world, 72, 96–101, 119–20, 129, 138, 145, 146, 148, 194, 285, 297, 316, 319, 324, 326, 334, 342, 357, 380

Ramsey, Frank, 404 n.14
Rantavaara, Irma, 3, 31, 392 n.31, 393 n.32, 411 n.24
realism, 4, 37, 39, 43, 47–8, 63–5, 85, 258–60, 273, 363, 366, 377
  literary, 59, 144–5, 247, 324, 335

relation, logical, 78, 83, 84–5, 90–2, 128, 142, 147, 150, 198, 240, 247, 252, 255, 256, 258, 262, 263, 266, 279, 281–2, 286–7, 289, 291, 300, 306, 321, 336–51, 364, 373, 378
internal, 82, 216, 253, 380
external, 81, 190, 380
relativity, theory of, 104, 142–3, 145
represented speech and thought (*style indirect libre/ oratio obliqua*), 314–16, 317, 320, 324, 336, 349, 410 n.11
Rhees, Rush, 31
Richardson, Dorothy, 342
Roberts, John Hawley, 248, 410 n.18
Robson, W. W., 414 n.12
Rosenbaum, S. P., x, 28, 60, 171, 318, 385, 389 n.3, 391 n.25, 393 n.32, 398 n.1, 400 n.23, 401 n.5, 406 n.4, 407 n.14, 409 n.31, 411 n.20, 414 n.12, 414 n.13
Russell, Bertrand, 178, 188–9
ABC of Relativity, The, 5, 13, 142–3, 253
Analysis of Mind, The, 34, 168, 188
Free Man's Worship, A 250, 414 n.12
interest in theory of knowledge, 6–7, 10, 18
Mysticism and Logic, 194, 224, 359, 414 n.12
"On Denoting," 88, 400 n.24
"On the Nature of Truth and Falsehood," 84
Our Knowledge of the External World, 7, 72
Outline of Philosophy, An, 39
Philosophy of Leibniz, 153, 281
"Place of Science in a Liberal Education, The," 25
Principia Mathematica, 7, 10, 30, 45, 55, 190, 250, 253, 351
Principles of Mathematics, The, 9, 83, 84–5, 103
"Prisons," 15, 19
Problems of Philosophy, The, 22, 43, 65, 72, 163, 269, 372, 394 n.46, 398 n.10, 400 n.23
"Relation of Sense-Data to Physics, The," 6, 7, 70, 72
Scientific Outlook, The, 30
Theory of Knowledge, 7, 35, 46, 48, 83, 165
Why I am not a Christian, 394 n.44
Ryle, Gilbert, 27, 38

Sainsbury, Mark, 77, 83, 85, 87, 100, 166–7, 321, 327–8, 361, 399 n.13, 409 n.1
Sand, George, 346
Santayana, George, 413 n.5
scaffolding, logical, 73, 92–4, 96, 104, 106–7, 108, 128, 155, 157, 195, 249, 259, 277–80, 282, 283, 293, 336–42, 401 n.29, 40 n.30
Schneewind, J. B., 39
Searle, John, 410 n.5
sense-data, 5, 14, 40, 67–8, 69–70, 71, 72, 75, 81, 108–10, 113, 129, 183–4, 220, 221–3, 231, 232, 238, 251, 260, 263, 264, 266, 267, 268, 269–70, 272, 273, 274, 275, 277, 279, 283, 286, 294–5, 297, 298–300, 307–11, 318–21, 324, 326, 328, 329, 330, 333, 341, 353, 355, 357, 366, 375, 380, 382, 383
sensibilia, 14, 39–40, 47, 48, 70–1, 73, 74, 75, 106–7, 220, 224, 259, 260, 273, 277, 290, 293, 297–8, 316–18, 327–8, 329, 334, 394 n.45, 399 n.13
Seurat, Georges, 274, 277, 281, 283, 285, 287, 289, 291, 292, 317, 320, 321, 356, 364, 409 n.32
Shakespeare, William, 201, 341, 348, 350
Shusterman, Richard, 391 n.23, 397 n.60
skeleton, see scaffolding
Skidelsky, Robert, 51, 149, 248, 389 n.4, 389 n.7
Smith, Alys Pearsall, 21
Spalding, Frances, 11, 248, 404 n.9, 406 n.6, 406 n.25 408 n.23, 408 n.24
Spender, Stephen, 41, 402 n.8
Steinberg, Erwin, 398 n.7
Stephen, Adrian, 33, 35, 37, 395 n.47
Stephen, Julia, 29, 32, 231, 235, 312, 319, 406 n.3, 408 n.28, 410 n.17
Stephen, Karin, 34–5, 46, 102, 144, 355, 393 n.38, 393 n.39
Stephen, Leslie, 6, 25, 28–9, 30, 37, 44, 45, 52, 64, 68–9, 79, 86, 93, 188–9, 191, 193, 194–5, 197, 222, 231, 355, 356, 360, 376, 389 n.3, 389 n.4, 393 n.34, 405 n.15, 406 n.3, 407 n.13
An Agnostic's Apology, 29, 37, 40, 236
"Berkeley," 396 n.54
Dictionary of National Biography, 335, 405 n.17
English Utilitarians, The, 29, 399 n.15
History of English Thought, 29, 37, 38, 39, 47, 66, 74, 98, 153, 174–5, 179, 245–6, 248, 250, 320, 349, 359, 360, 365, 368, 371, 377, 378, 380, 395 n.46, 399 n.15, 408 n.31
Hours in a Library, 52
"In Praise of Walking," 404 n.11, 405 n.21
Mausoleum Book, The, 334, 406 n.4
"What is Materialism?," 37, 39, 40, 48, 61, 83, 92, 98, 99, 111, 122, 126, 133, 140, 149, 150, 152–4, 157, 158, 159, 168, 175, 182, 194, 197, 212, 232, 276, 277, 283, 297–8, 300, 312, 361, 363, 398 n.5, 398 n.9

Stephen, Thoby, 28, 37, 235–6, 391 n.26
Sterne, Laurence, 304
Strachey, James, 32, 377, 403 n.1
Strachey, Lytton, 34–5, 40, 42, 171, 324, 405 n.17
subject, philosophical, 1, 48, 53, 62, 69, 73, 75, 159, 162–74, 183, 200–3, 310–11, 315, 322, 324, 333, 343
subjectivity, 68, 69, 70, 72, 75–6, 78, 349, see also privacy
suicide, 214, 233

Tennyson, Alfred Lord, 359
Thackery, William Makepiece, 343
"this," 92, 142
time, 75–8, 100, 102–6, 142–6, 285
Torgovnick, Marianna, 294, 389 n.2, 406 n.3, 408 n.30, 409 n.33, 410 n.7, 411 n.26, 412 n.38
Toulmin, Stephen, 14
tragedy, 233–4, 344
Tyndall, John, 29, 93, 150, 152, 208
  Essays, 195
  Lectures on Light, 124, 195, 212, 251, 254, 282, 288, 403 n.17
  On Radiation, 124–5, 189, 269

universals, 10, 63, 65, 78, 82–96, 164, 187, 193, 292, 306–7, 350
University College, London, 23
Urmson, J. O., 296–7, 302, 303, 380–1, 400 n.20, 410 n.3

vagueness, 186–8
van Gogh, Vincent, 269, 270, 275, 281, 407 n.19
Verral, Arthur, 25
Vesey, G. N. A., 166
vision, 13, 15, 263–71, 407 n.14
volume, psychological, 319–21, 325, 334
Vuillemin, J., 398 n.4

Warnock, G. J., 42, 43–4, 383
Weierstrass, Karl, 370
Whitehead, Alfred North, 4, 6, 7, 29, 35, 76, 118, 126, 360, 394 n.40
  Aims of Education and Other Essays, The, 5, 37
  Concerning the Principles of Natural Knowledge, 397 n.59
  departure from Cambridge, 10, 17, 21, 23
  Introduction to Mathematics, 24
  Principia Mathematica, 7, 10
  Process and Reality, 361
  Science and the Modern World, 189, 361–2, 370, 391 n.22
  Symbolism, 145, 246, 252, 265, 272, 273, 365, 366, 375, 376, 413 n.5
Whiteley, Patrick J., 389 n.2, 403 n.17, 411 n.26
Williams, Raymond, 405 n.19
A Winter's Tale, 406 n.1
Wittgenstein, Ludgwig, 7–8, 9, 30, 31, 34, 35, 41–2, 45, 53, 163, 297, 359–60, 365, 372, 383, 394 n.41, 403 n.16, 414 n.12
  Notebooks 1914–1916, 376
  Philosophical Investigations, 409 n.1
  Tractatus, 7, 9, 42, 89, 92–4, 128, 133, 190, 212, 253–4, 256, 259, 277, 287, 337, 360, 362, 367, 368–9, 371, 372, 406 n.7
Wollheim, Richard, 164, 391 n.23, 409 n.34
Women's War, the, 20
Woolf, Leonard, 7, 29, 35, 36, 40, 41, 42, 45, 54, 151, 323, 389 n.7, 390 n.10, 394 n.40, 394 n.41, 395 n.48, 395 n.51, 395 n.52, 402 n.6, 403 n.4, 405 n.15, 405 n.16, 414 n.13
Woolf, Virginia,
  Between the Acts, 139, 147, 207, 216, 287, 306, 338–40, 343, 347, 396 n.52, 402 n.8, 412 n.40, 413 n.43
  "Captain's Deathbed, The," 352
  "Cinema, The," 297
  "Death of the Moth, The," 217, 234
  Flush, 335
  and idealism, 247
  Jacob's Room, 3, 13, 18, 23, 30, 53, 123, 124, 133, 147, 207, 235–6, 238, 294, 313, 330–2, 342, 343, 354, 400 n.26, 403 n.17, 411 n.24, 412 n.39
  "Kew Gardens," 294
  "Leslie Stephen," 29
  madness, 199, 212, 226, 340, 352
  "Modern Fiction"/modern fiction, 26, 52, 53, 154, 158, 236, 247–8, 275, 293, 298, 304, 315, 319, 324, 329, 344, 357, 380, 385–6, 409 n.31
  "moment," 85, 105, 116–19, 286, 399 n.16, 401 n.5, 402 n.7
  Moths, The, 125
  Mrs. Dalloway, 5, 27, 62, 109, 124, 143–4, 157, 193, 204–5, 221–2, 236, 238, 239, 306, 310, 324, 325, 345, 363, 402 n.14, 406 n.1
  Night and Day, 24, 27, 96, 108, 143, 385, 386, 391 n.24
  "On Being Ill," 207, 223–4, 235
  Orlando, 202–3, 335, 338, 340
  Roger Fry, 335, 403 n.4
  Room of One's Own, A, 59, 84, 168, 210, 318, 331, 380, 381, 386, 403 n.4

and Russell, 36, 46, 54, 383–4, 396 n.57
"Street Haunting," 201, 204–5, 345, 352, 405 n.21, 405 n.22
Three Guineas, 17, 30, 31, 169, 194, 412 n.40
To the Lighthouse, 4, 25, 32, 37, 52, 55, 66, 111, 118, 119–20, 121, 123, 124, 127, 128, 132, 135, 137, 139, 140, 141, 142, 144, 147–8, 150, 151–2, 156, 157, 160, 176–8, 179–80, 187, 204, 205, 211, 213, 214, 222, 223, 235–6, 238, 247, 252, 258, 259, 277, 285–6, 288–9, 292, 304, 306, 315, 317, 319, 327, 336, 338, 344, 348, 351, 354, 371, 379, 409 n.31, 409 n.32, 413 n.43, 413 n.9
Voyage Out, The, 24–5, 31, 40, 50, 66, 123, 237, 362, 400 n.21
Waves, The, 27, 54, 67, 82, 114, 120, 124, 125, 126, 132, 141, 142, 143, 147, 155, 156, 160, 213, 214, 235–6, 238, 257, 270–1, 272, 277, 278, 281, 288, 289–90, 292, 297, 300, 308–9, 311, 315, 317, 319, 321, 323, 324–5, 338, 344, 383, 385, 402 n.8, 408 n.30, 410 n.7, 413 n.2
Years, The, 4, 142, 147, 156, 169, 209, 210, 218, 220, 292, 317, 347
Wordsworth, William, 358
World War I, 206, 208, 214, 227

Yeats, W. B., xi, 46, 402 n.8

Zeno, 103–5, 370
Zwerdling, Alex, xiv, 390 n.14, 397 n.66, 404 n.5, 412 n.37, 412 n.40